Brief Contents

P9-DUT-637

Contents

Features

Maps

Figures

Tables

Preface

In this ninth edition, *A People and A Nation, Brief,* has undergone significant revisions, while still retaining the narrative strength and focus that have made it so popular with students and teachers alike. Like other teachers and students, we are always re-creating our past, restructuring our memory, and rediscovering the personalities and events that have influenced us, injured us, and bedeviled us. This book represents our continuing rediscovery of America's history—its diverse people and the nation they created and have nurtured. As this book demonstrates, there are many different Americans and many different memories. We have sought to present as many of them as possible—in triumph and tragedy, in division and unity.

About *A People and A Nation, Brief*

A People and A Nation, first published in 1982, was the first major textbook in the United States to fully integrate social and political history. From the outset, the authors have been determined to tell the story of *all* the people of the United States. This book's hallmark has been its melding of social and political history—its movement beyond history's common focus on public figures and events to examine the daily life of America's people. All editions of the book have stressed the interaction of public policy and personal experience, the relationship between domestic concerns and foreign affairs, the various manifestations of popular culture, and the multiple origins of America and Americans. We have consistently built our narrative on a firm foundation in primary sources—on both well-known and obscure letters, diaries, public documents, oral histories, and artifacts of material culture. We have long challenged readers to think about the meaning of American history, not just to memorize facts. Both students and instructors have repeatedly told us how much they appreciate and enjoy our approach to the past.

This brief ninth edition, as with earlier brief editions, aims to preserve the integrity of the complete work—along with its unique approach—while condensing it. This edition reflects the scholarship, readability, and comprehensiveness of the full-length version. It also maintains the integration of social, cultural, political, economic, and foreign relations history that has been a hallmark of *A People and A Nation*.

Dr. Debra Michals has worked with us again, ensuring that the changes in content and organization incorporated in the full-length ninth edition were retained in the condensation. The authors attained reductions by paring down details rather than deleting entire sections. The brief ninth edition thus contains fewer statistics, fewer quotations, and fewer examples than the unabridged edition. The brief edition also includes more pedagogy than the unabridged edition: each main heading has a marginal question to give students a preview of the key topics covered. These questions are answered at the end of the chapter in the "Summary." Throughout the chapters, students get assistance from key terms that are boldfaced in the text and defined in the margins.

Themes in This Book

Several themes and questions stand out in our continuing effort to integrate political, social, and cultural history. We study the many ways Americans have defined themselves—gender, race, class, region, ethnicity, religion, sexual orientation—and the many subjects that have reflected their multidimensional experiences. We highlight the remarkably diverse everyday lives of the American people—in cities and on farms and ranches, in factories and in corporate headquarters, in neighborhoods and in legislatures, in love relationships and in hate groups, in recreation and in work, in the classroom and in military uniform, in secret national security conferences and in public foreign relations debates, in church and in voluntary associations, in polluted environments and in conservation areas. We pay particular attention to lifestyles, diet and dress, family life and structure, labor conditions, gender roles, migration and mobility, childbearing, and child rearing. We explore how Americans have entertained and informed themselves by discussing their music, sports, theater, print media, film, radio, television, graphic arts, and literature, in both "high" culture and popular culture. We study how technology has influenced Americans' lives, such as through the internal combustion engine and the computer.

Americans' personal lives have always interacted with the public realm of politics and government. To understand how Americans have sought to protect their different ways of life and to work out solutions to thorny problems, we emphasize their expectations of governments at the local, state, and federal levels; governments' role in providing answers; the lobbying of interest groups; the campaigns and outcomes of elections; and the hierarchy of power in any period. Because the United States has long been a major participant in world affairs, we explore America's participation in wars, interventions in other nations, empire-building, immigration patterns, images of foreign peoples, cross-national cultural ties, and international economic trends.

What's New in This Edition

This edition builds on its predecessors in continuing to enhance the global perspective on American history that has characterized the book since its first edition. From the "Atlantic world" context of European colonies in North and South America to the discussion of international terrorism, the authors have incorporated the most recent globally oriented scholarship throughout the volume. As in the eighth edition, we have worked to strengthen our treatment of the diversity of America's people by examining differences within the broad ethnic categories commonly employed and by paying attention to immigration, cultural and intellectual infusions from around the world, and America's growing religious diversity. We have also stressed the incorporation of different peoples into the United States through territorial acquisition as well as through immigration. At the same time, we have integrated the discussion of such diversity into our narrative so as not to artificially isolate any group from the mainstream. We have continued the practice of placing three probing questions at the end of each chapter's introduction to guide students' reading of the pages that follow.

Primary Sources

We believe students need lots of opportunities to engage in historical thinking around primary sources, and we have provided more opportunities for this type of work in the ninth edition. The new "Visualizing the Past" feature described below helps students engage with visual sources with guided captions and questions. In addition, the authors have identified for each chapter a set of primary sources that would add useful context for students; these are noted (with a feather icon) in the margins of the text. Students will be able to access each of these sources through links on the student CourseMate website. Instructors who want a fully integrated online primary source reader to use in conjunction with *A People and A Nation* will find it available as an "Editor's Choice" option inside the new CourseReader for U.S. History (described in the supplements section).

As always, the authors reexamined every sentence, interpretation, map, chart, illustration, and caption, refining the narrative, presenting new examples, and bringing to the text the latest findings of scholars in many areas of history, anthropology, sociology, and political science. Some chapter-opening vignettes are new to this edition. The maps have been completely redesigned and revised in this edition to be more dynamic, engaging, and relevant.

"Legacies," "Links to the World," and "Visualizing the Past"

Each chapter contains two brief feature essays: "Legacies for A People and A Nation" and "Links to the World." "Legacies" appears toward the end of each chapter and offers compelling and timely answers to students who question the relevance of historical study by exploring the historical roots of contemporary topics. New subjects of "Legacies" includes P.T. Barnum's publicity stunts, abstinence campaigns by moral reformers, Lincoln's second inaugural address, national parks, and mass-produced toys for children. Numerous other "Legacies" have been updated.

"Links to the World" examines both inward and outward ties between America (and Americans) and the rest of the world. "Links" appears at appropriate places in each chapter to explore specific topics at considerable length. Tightly constructed essays detail the often little-known connections between developments here and abroad. The topics range broadly over economic, political, social, technological, medical, and cultural history, vividly demonstrating that the geographical region that is now the United States has never lived in isolation from other peoples and countries. New to this edition are "Links" on turkeys, writing and stationery supplies, internal improvements, filibustering, the "back to Africa" movement, study abroad programs, Tokyo Rose, and swine flu. Each "Link" highlights global interconnections with unusual and lively examples that will both intrigue and inform students.

A brand new feature in this edition—"Visualizing the Past"—aims to give students the chance to examine primary source material and engage in critical thinking about them. For each chapter, the authors have selected one or two visual sources (including cartoons, photographic images, artwork, and magazine covers) that tell a story about the era with captions that help students understand how the careful examination of primary source content can reveal deeper insights into the period under discussion. We have chosen to focus on visual sources for this feature because these are often the hardest for instructors to find and prepare good pedagogy around—and because we have always given visual material a strong role in the text. An example from Chapter 25 includes a photograph of the women's "emergency brigade" demonstration during the 1937 sit-down strike by automobile workers in Flint, Michigan. The caption describes the scene and then asks questions that guide students in a deeper analysis of the image—and of its historical significance.

Section-by-Section Changes in This Edition

Mary Beth Norton, who had primary responsibility for Chapters 1 through 8 and served as coordinating author, augmented the treatment of early European explorations of the Americas (including the publicist Richard Hakluyt) and now explores the use of the calumet (the so-called peace pipe) by Indian nations and Europeans alike. She expanded the discussion of religious diversity in England and its colonies and the religious impulse for colonization and revised the section on the middle passage to give more attention to the experience of enslaved captives on shipboard. To clarify chronology, she moved some material on the French and Spanish colonies in North America from Chapter 3 to Chapter 4 and in the latter greatly increased coverage of the residents of the west in the eighteenth century—Native Americans, Spaniards, and French people alike. A new opening vignette is featured in Chapter 4 about Marie-Joseph Angélique, a slave convicted of starting a fire that destroyed the merchant quarter of Montreal. New scholarship on the Seven Years' War, the American Revolution, and the Constitutional Convention has been incorporated into Chapters 5 through 7. A table now conveniently summarizes state conventions' ratification votes. More information on women's political roles and aims has been added in conjunction with a considerably expanded treatment of partisanship in the early republic.

    Carol Sheriff, responsible for Chapters 9 and 11 through 13, enhanced coverage of the nationalistic culture of the early republic and early New Orleans and revised the discussion of the War of 1812 and Aaron Burr. She has added discussions of the penny press, Henry David Thoreau, science and engineering, women's activities, and penitentiaries. The treatment of politics in general has been reworked, with special attention to political violence, and a new chart detailing the era's presidents has been included. Chapter 13 now contains considerably more information on the southwestern borderlands, includes more quotations from residents of the American West, and deals with anti-expansionism and the abuse of Indians in Catholic missions.

    David W. Blight, who had primary responsibility for Chapter 10 and Chapters 14 through 16, has enhanced the discussion of the economic causes of secession and the Civil War and the economic history of the war itself, drawing on extensive new scholarship. Chapter 10 features a new chapter-opening vignette on the 1827 slave auction held at Monticello and Jefferson and Sally Hemings. He now considers the Union soldiers' ideology and has added material on the effects of the cultural impact of the large numbers of war dead in both North and South. Chapters 15 and 16 both include new treatments of judicial topics, and the latter also discusses scalawags and carpetbaggers at greater length than before.

Howard P. Chudacoff, responsible for Chapters 17 through 21 and Chapter 24, has extensively revised and updated the treatment of technological change in the late nineteenth century and of women's suffrage. He has added discussions of Native peoples in the Southwest, western folk heroes, government and water rights, labor violence in the West, female entertainers (and opposition to them from moralists like Anthony Comstock), Woodrow Wilson's racism, Marcus Garvey, and the Great Migration of African Americans to the North in the twenties. The new Chapter 20 opening vignette features the life of Frances Willard, the president of the Women's Christian Temperance Union. He has also consolidated the analysis of settlement houses in Chapter 21 to avoid repetition.

Fredrik Logevall, with primary responsibility for Chapters 22, 23, 26, and 28, updated the discussions of late nineteenth-century American imperialism and the origins of the Cold War and added new material on nurses and African American soldiers in WWI.

Beth Bailey, primarily responsible for Chapters 25, 27, and 29, incorporated new scholarship on popular culture, the institutional history of the New Deal, the ecological crisis of the thirties, the internment of Japanese citizens and Japanese Americans during WWII, the liberation of Europe, the GI Bill, and the return of veterans in the postwar period. She enhanced the discussion of wartime propaganda and censorship. The new Chapter 29 opening vignette on downwinders ties more closely to the cold war coverage through the chapter. Parts of Chapter 29 underwent extensive revision and reorganization as well.

Bailey and Logevall shared responsibility for Chapters 30 through 33. These chapters now include expanded consideration of the struggle for civil rights and social justice in the north and the opposition to that struggle in the form of protests against school busing. Chapter 31 has a new section on the freedom and responsibilities of youth and enhanced discussions of popular culture, women in the military, and religious cults. New material has been added on foreign policy and changes in American living patterns. As is always the case, Chapter 33, which covers the recent past, underwent thorough revision and reorganization. It covers the second term of George W. Bush, the election of Barack Obama, the Great Recession, and the Iraq and Afghanistan wars.

Teaching and Learning Aids

The supplements listed here accompany the ninth edition of *A People and A Nation*. They have been created with the diverse needs of today's students and instructors in mind.

For the Instructor

Aplia. Aplia™ is an online learning solution that helps students take responsibility for their learning by engaging them with course material, honing their critical thinking skills, and preparing them for class. Created by an instructor for other instructors, Aplia prompts history students to read carefully and think critically. For every chapter, text-specific exercises ask students to consider individual details that support larger historical concepts and draw conclusions rather than reciting historical facts. Every chapter includes at least one set of questions based on a map from the text. The assignments also give students experience reading and interpreting primary source documents, images, and other media. The automatically graded assignments include detailed, immediate explanations that ensure students put forth effort on a regular basis. Gradebook analytics help instructors monitor and address student performance on an individual or group basis. For more information, visit www.aplia.com/cengage.

Instructor Companion Site. Instructors will find here all the tools they need to teach a rich and successful U.S. History Survey course. The protected teaching materials include the *Instructor's Resource Manual* written by George C. Warren of Central Piedmont Community College, a set of customizable Microsoft® PowerPoint® lecture slides created by Barney Rickman of Valdosta State University, and a set of customizable Microsoft® PowerPoint® slides including all the images (photos, art, maps) from the text. The companion website also provides instructors with access to HistoryFinder and to the Wadsworth American History Resource Center (see descriptions below). Go to www.Cengage.com/history to access this site.

PowerLecture CD-ROM with ExamView® and JoinIn®. This dual-platform, all-in-one multimedia resource includes the *Instructor's Resource Manual*; Test Bank in Word® and PDF formats; customizable Microsoft® PowerPoint® slides of both lecture outlines and images from the text; and *JoinIn®* PowerPoint® slides with clicker content. Also included is ExamView®, an easy-to-use assessment and tutorial system that allows instructors to create, deliver, and customize tests in minutes. The test items, written by George C. Warren of Central Piedmont Community College, include multiple-choice, identification, geography, and essay questions.

HistoryFinder. This searchable online database allows instructors to quickly and easily search and download selections from among thousands of assets, including art, photographs, maps, primary sources, and audio/video clips. Each asset downloads directly into a Microsoft® PowerPoint® slide, allowing instructors to easily create exciting PowerPoint presentations for their classrooms.

eInstructor's Resource Manual. Written by George C. Warren of Central Piedmont Community College, this manual contains for each chapter a set of learning objectives, a comprehensive chapter outline, ideas for classroom activities, discussion questions, suggested paper topics, and a lecture supplement. It is available on the instructor's companion website and in the PowerLecture CD-Rom.

WebTutor™ on Blackboard® and WebCT®. With WebTutor's text-specific, pre-formatted content and total flexibility, instructors can easily create and manage their own custom course website. WebTutor's course management tool gives instructors the ability to provide virtual office hours, post syllabi, set up threaded discussions, track student progress with the quizzing material, and much more. For students, WebTutor offers real-time access to a full array of study tools, including audio chapter summaries, practice quizzes, glossary flashcards, and weblinks.

CourseMate. Cengage Learning's CourseMate brings course concepts to life with interactive learning, study, and exam preparation tools that support the printed textbook. Watch student comprehension soar as your class works with the printed textbook and the *A People and A Nation* CourseMate site, with interactive teaching and learning tools, and EngagementTracker, a first-of-its-kind tool that monitors student engagement in the course. Learn more at www.cengagebrain.com.

Student Resources

CourseMate. For students, CourseMate provides an online source of interactive learning, study, and exam preparation outside the classroom. Students will find outlines and objectives, focus questions, flashcards, quizzes, primary source links (including those noted in the text and marked with the feather icon), and video clips. CourseMate also includes an integrated **A People and A Nation eBook**. Students taking quizzes will be linked directly to relevant sections in the ebook for additional information. The ebook is fully searchable and students can even take notes and save them for later review. In addition, the ebook links to rich media assets such as video and MP3 chapter summaries, primary source documents with critical thinking questions, and interactive (zoomable) maps. Students can use the ebook as their primary text or as a companion multimedia support. It is available at www.cengagebrain.com.

Wadsworth American History Resource Center. Wadsworth's American History Resource Center gives your students access to a "virtual reader" with hundreds of primary sources, including speeches, letters, legal documents and transcripts, poems, maps, simulations, timelines, and additional images that bring history to life, along with interactive assignable exercises. A map feature, including Google Earth™ coordinates and exercises, will aid in student comprehension of geography and use of maps. Students can compare the traditional textbook map with an aerial view of the location today. It's an ideal resource for study, review, and research. In addition to this map feature, the resource center also provides blank maps for student review and testing. Ask your sales representative for more information on how to bundle access to the HRC with your text.

cengagebrain.com. Save your students time and money. Direct them to www.cengagebrain.com for choice in formats and savings and a better chance to succeed in class. Students have the freedom to purchase à la carte exactly what they need—when they need it. There, students can purchase a downloadable ebook or electronic access to the American History Resource Center, the premium study tools and interactive ebook in the *A People and A Nation* CourseMate, or eAudio modules from *The History Handbook.* Students can save 50 percent on the electronic textbook and can pay as little as $1.99 for an individual eChapter.

Reader Program. Cengage Learning publishes a number of readers, some containing exclusively primary sources, others a combination of primary and secondary sources, and many designed to guide students through the process of historical inquiry. Visit Cengage.com to browse the catalog of history offerings or ask your sales representative to recommend a reader that would work well for your specific needs.

Custom Options

Nobody knows your students like you, so why not give them a text tailored to their needs? Cengage Learning offers custom solutions for your course—whether it's making a small modification to *A People and A Nation* to match your syllabus or combining multiple sources to create something truly unique. You can pick and choose chapters, include your own material, and add supplementary map exercises along with the Rand McNally Atlas (including questions developed around the maps in the atlas) to create a text that fits the way you teach. Ensure that your students get the most out of their textbook dollar by giving them exactly what they need. Contact your Cengage Learning representative to explore custom solutions for your course.

Rand McNally Atlas of American History, 2e. This comprehensive atlas features more than 80 maps, with new content covering global perspectives, including events in the Middle East from 1945 to 2005, as well as population trends in the United States and around the world. Additional maps document voyages of discovery; the settling of the colonies; major U.S. military engagements, including the American Revolution and World Wars I and II; and sources of immigrations, ethnic populations, and patterns of economic change.

CourseReader. Cengage Learning's new CourseReader lets instructors create a customized electronic reader in minutes. Instructors can choose exactly what their students will be assigned by searching or browsing the extensive CourseReader database. Sources include hundreds of historical documents, images, and media, plus literary essays that can add interest and insight to a primary source assignment. Or instructors can start with the "Editor's Choice" collection created for *A People and A Nation* and then update it to suit their particular needs. Each source comes with all the pedagogical tools needed to provide a full learning experience—including headnotes and objective and essay questions, descriptive headnotes that put the reading into context, and both critical-thinking and multiple-choice questions designed to reinforce key points. Contact your local Cengage Learning sales representative for more information and packaging options.

Acknowledgments

The authors would like to thank the following persons for their assistance with the preparation of this edition: Philip Daileader, David Farber, Danyel Logevall, Jon Parmenter, Anna Daileader Sheriff, Benjamin Daileader Sheriff, and Selene Sheriff.

At each stage of this revision, a sizable panel of historian reviewers read drafts of our chapters. Their suggestions, corrections, and pleas helped guide us through this momentous revision. We could not include all of their recommendations, but the book is better for our having heeded most of their advice. We heartily thank:

Sara Alpern, Texas A&M University
Friederike Baer, Temple University
Troy Bickham, Texas A&M University
Robert Bionaz, Chicago State University
Victoria Bynum, Texas State University, San Marcos

Mario Fenyo, Bowie State University
Walter Hixson, University of Akron
Allison McNeese, Mount Mercy College
Steve O'Brien, Bridgewater State College
Paul O'Hara, Xavier University
John Putman, San Diego State University
Thomas Roy, University of Oklahoma
Manfred Silva, El Paso Community College
Michael Vollbach, Oakland Community College

The authors thank the helpful Cengage people who designed, edited, produced, and nourished this book. Many thanks to Ann West, senior sponsoring editor; Julia Giannotti, senior development editor; Jane Lee, content product manager; Debbie Meyer, project editor; Pembroke Herbert, photo researcher; and Charlotte Miller, art editor.

M. B. N.

C. S.

D. B.

H. C.

F. L.

B. B.

About the Authors

Mary Beth Norton

Born in Ann Arbor, Michigan, Mary Beth Norton received her B.A. from the University of Michigan (1964) and her Ph.D. from Harvard University (1969). She is the Mary Donlon Alger Professor of American History at Cornell University. Her dissertation won the Allan Nevins Prize. She has written *The British-Americans* (1972); *Liberty's Daughters* (1980, 1996); *Founding Mothers & Fathers* (1996), which was one of three finalists for the 1997 Pulitzer Prize in History; and *In the Devil's Snare* (2002), which was one of five finalists for the 2003 *LA Times* Book Prize in History and which won the English-Speaking Union's Ambassador Book Award in American Studies for 2003. She has co-edited three volumes on American women's history. She was also general editor of the *American Historical Association's Guide to Historical Literature* (1995). Her articles have appeared in such journals as the *American Historical Review, William and Mary Quarterly,* and *Journal of Women's History.* Mary Beth has served as president of the Berkshire Conference of Women Historians, as vice president for research of the American Historical Association, and as a presidential appointee to the National Council on the Humanities. She has appeared on Book TV, the History and Discovery Channels, PBS, and NBC and as a commentator on Early American history; and she lectures frequently to high school teachers through the Teaching American History program. She has received four honorary degrees and in 1999 was elected a fellow of the American Academy of Arts and Sciences. She has held fellowships from the National Endowment for the Humanities; the Guggenheim, Rockefeller, and Starr Foundations; and the Henry E. Huntington Library. In 2005–2006, she was the Pitt Professor of American History and Institutions at the University of Cambridge and Newnham College.

Carol Sheriff

Born in Washington, D.C., and raised in Bethesda, Maryland, Carol Sheriff received her B.A. from Wesleyan University (1985) and her Ph.D. from Yale University (1993). Since 1993, she has taught history at the College of William and Mary, where she has won the Thomas Jefferson Teaching Award, the Alumni Teaching Fellowship Award, and the University Professorship for Teaching Excellence. Her publications include *The Artificial River: The Erie Canal and the Paradox of Progress* (1996), which won the Dixon Ryan Fox Award from the New York State Historical Association and the Award for Excellence in Research from the New York State Archives, and *A People at War: Civilians and Soldiers in America's Civil War, 1854–1877* (with Scott Reynolds Nelson, 2007). Carol has written sections of a teaching manual for the New York State history curriculum, given presentations at Teaching American History grant projects, consulted on an exhibit for the Rochester Museum and Science Center, and appeared in the History Channel's *Modern Marvels* show on the Erie Canal, and she is engaged in several public-history projects marking the sesquicentennial of the Civil War. At William and Mary, she teaches the

U.S. history survey as well as upper-level classes on the Early Republic, the Civil War Era, and the American West. Most recently, Carol has been named Class of 2013 term distinguished professor in recognition of her teaching, scholarship, and service.

David W. Blight

Born in Flint, Michigan, David W. Blight received his B.A. from Michigan State University (1971) and his Ph.D. from the University of Wisconsin (1985). He is now Class of 1954 Professor of American History and director of the Gilder Lehrman Center for the Study of Slavery, Resistance, and Abolition at Yale University. For the first seven years of his career, David was a public high school teacher in Flint. He has written *Frederick Douglass's Civil War* (1989) and *Race and Reunion: The Civil War in American Memory, 1863–1915* (2001), which received eight awards, including the Bancroft Prize, the Frederick Douglass Prize, and the Abraham Lincoln Prize, as well as four prizes awarded by the Organization of American Historians. His most recent book is *A Slave No More: The Emancipation of John Washington and Wallace Turnage* (2007), which won three prizes. He has edited or co-edited six other books, including editions of W. E. B. DuBois, *The Souls of Black Folk* and *Narrative of the Life of Frederick Douglass*. David's essays have appeared in the *Journal of American History*, *Civil War History*, and Gabor Boritt, ed., *Why the Civil War Came* (1996), among others. In 1992–1993, he was senior Fulbright Professor in American Studies at the University of Munich, Germany; in 2006–2007, he held a fellowship at the Dorothy and Lewis B. Cullman Center, New York Public Library. A consultant to several documentary films, David appeared in the 1998 PBS series, *Africans in America*. He has served on the Council of the American Historical Association and teaches summer seminars for secondary school teachers as well as for park rangers and historians of the National Park Service.

Howard P. Chudacoff

Howard P. Chudacoff, the George L. Littlefield Professor of American History and Professor of Urban Studies at Brown University, was born in Omaha, Nebraska. He earned his A.B. (1965) and Ph.D. (1969) from the University of Chicago. He has written *Mobile Americans* (1972), *How Old Are You?* (1989), *The Age of the Bachelor* (1999), *The Evolution of American Urban Society* (with Judith Smith, 2004), and *Children at Play: An American History* (2007). He has also co-edited with Peter Baldwin *Major Problems in American Urban History* (2004). His articles have appeared in such journals as the *Journal of Family History*, *Reviews in American History*, and *Journal of American History*. At Brown University, Howard has co-chaired the American Civilization Program and chaired the Department of History, and serves as Brown's faculty representative to the NCAA. He has also served on the board of directors of the Urban History Association. The National Endowment for the Humanities, Ford Foundation, and Rockefeller Foundation have given him awards to advance his scholarship.

Fredrik Logevall

A native of Stockholm, Sweden, Fredrik Logevall is the John S. Knight Professor of International Studies and Professor of History at Cornell University, where he serves as director of the Mario Einaudi Center for International Studies. He received his B.A. from Simon Fraser University (1986) and his Ph.D. from Yale University (1993). His most recent book is *America's Cold War: The Politics of Insecurity* (with Campbell Craig, 2009). His other publications include *Choosing War* (1999), which won three prizes, including the Warren F. Kuehl Book Prize from the Society for Historians of American Foreign Relations (SHAFR); *The Origins of the Vietnam War* (2001); *Terrorism and 9/11: A Reader* (2002); as co-editor, *Encyclopedia of American Foreign Policy* (2002); and, as co-editor, *The First Vietnam War: Colonial Conflict and Cold War Crisis* (2007). Fred is a past recipient of the Stuart L. Bernath article, book, and lecture prizes from SHAFR and is a member of the SHAFR Council, the Cornell University Press faculty board, and the editorial advisory board of the Presidential Recordings Project at the Miller Center of Public Affairs at the University of Virginia. In 2006–2007, he was Leverhulme Visiting Professor at the University of Nottingham and Mellon Senior Fellow at the University of Cambridge.

Beth Bailey

Born in Atlanta, Georgia, Beth Bailey received her B.A. from Northwestern University (1979) and her Ph.D. from the University of Chicago (1986). She is now a professor of history at Temple University. Her research and teaching fields include war and society and the U.S. military, American cultural history (nineteenth and twentieth centuries), popular culture, and gender and sexuality. She is the author, most recently, of *America's Army: Making the All-Volunteer Force* (2009). Her other publications include *From Front Porch to Back Seat: Courtship in 20th Century America* (1988), *The First Strange Place: The Alchemy of Race and Sex in WWII Hawaii* (with David Farber, 1992), *Sex in the Heartland* (1999), and *The Columbia Companion to America in the 1960s* (with David Farber, 2001). She is co-editor of *A History of Our Time* (with William Chafe and Harvard Sitkoff, 7th ed., 2007). Beth has served as a consultant and/ or on-screen expert for numerous television documentaries developed for PBS and the History Channel. She has received grants or fellowships from the American Council of Learned Societies, the National Endowment for the Humanities, and the Woodrow Wilson International Center for Scholars; and she was named the Ann Whitney Olin scholar at Barnard College, Columbia University, where she was the director of the American Studies Program, and Regents Lecturer at the University of New Mexico. She has been a visiting scholar at Saitama University, Japan; at Trinity College at the University of Melbourne; and a senior Fulbright lecturer in Indonesia. She teaches courses on sexuality and gender and war and American culture.

A People & A Nation

Reconstruction: An Unfinished Revolution

1865–1877

The lower half of secession's seedbed, Charleston, South Carolina, lay in ruin when most of the white population evacuated on February 18, 1865. A bombardment by Union forces around Charleston harbor destroyed many of the low-country planters' homes. Fires broke out everywhere, ignited in bales of cotton stockpiled in public squares. To many observers, the flames were the funeral pyres of a dying civilization.

Among the first Union troops to enter Charleston, the Twenty-first U.S. Colored Regiment received the city's surrender from its mayor. For black Charlestonians, who were mostly former slaves, this was a time to celebrate their freedom. Charleston's freedpeople converted Confederate ruin into a vision of Reconstruction based on Union victory and black liberation.

During the war's last year, the Confederates transformed the planters' Race Course, a horseracing track, and its famed Jockey Club, into a prison. Kept outdoors in the middle of the track, 257 Union soldiers died there of exposure and disease and were buried in a mass grave behind the judges' stand. After the city fell, more than twenty black workmen reinterred the dead in marked graves. On the archway over the cemetery's entrance, they painted the inscription "Martyrs of the Race Course."

On the morning of May 1, 1865, a thousand people marched around the planters' Race Course, led by three thousand children carrying roses and singing "John Brown's Body." Black women with flowers and wreaths came next, followed by black men. The parade concluded with black and white Union regiments and white missionaries and teachers. At the gravesite, five black ministers read from Scripture, and a black children's choir sang "America," "The Star-Spangled Banner," and Negro spirituals. After the ceremony, the crowd retired to the Race Course for speeches, picnics, and military festivities.

African Americans founded this "Decoration Day"—now Memorial Day, to remember those lost in battle. In their vision, they were creating the Independence Day of a Second American Revolution.

The Civil War and its aftermath wrought unprecedented changes in American society, law, and politics, but economic power, racism, and judicial conservatism limited Reconstruction's revolutionary potential. The nation had to determine the nature of federal-state relations, whether confiscated land could be redistributed, and how to bring justice to freedpeople and aggrieved white southerners. Americans also had to heal psychologically from a bloody and fratricidal war. How they negotiated the relationship between healing and justice would determine the extent of change during Reconstruction.

The turmoil wrought by Reconstruction was most evident in national politics. Lincoln's successor, Andrew Johnson, fought with Congress over Reconstruction policies. Although a southerner, Johnson disliked the South's wealthy planters, and his initial actions suggested that he would be tough on "traitors." By late 1865, however, Johnson became the protector of southern interests.

Johnson imagined a lenient and rapid "restoration" of the South to the Union rather than the fundamental "reconstruction" that Republican congressmen favored. Between 1866 and 1868, the president and Republican leadership in Congress disagreed. Before it ended, Congress impeached the president, enfranchised freedmen, and gave them a role in reconstructing the South. The nation also adopted the Fourteenth and Fifteenth Amendments, ensuring equal protection of the law, citizenship, and universal manhood suffrage. But the cause of equal rights for African Americans fell almost as fast as it had risen.

By 1869, the Ku Klux Klan employed violence to thwart Reconstruction and undermine black freedom. As white Democrats in the South took over state governments, they encountered little opposition. Moreover, the wartime industrial boom created new opportunities and priorities. The West drew American resources like never before. Political corruption became a nationwide scandal, and bribery a part of business.

The white South's desire to reclaim control of its states and of race relations overwhelmed the national interest in stopping it. Thus, Reconstruction became a revolution eclipsed, leaving legacies with which the nation has struggled ever since.

As you read this chapter, keep the following questions in mind:

* Should the Reconstruction era be considered the Second American Revolution? By what criteria should we make such a judgment?

* What were the origins and meanings of the Fourteenth Amendment in the 1860s? What is its significance today?

* Reconstruction is judged to have "ended" in 1877. Over the course of the 1870s, what caused its end?

Retreat from Reconstruction
Political Implications of Klan Terrorism | *Industrial Expansion and Reconstruction in the North* | *Liberal Republican Revolt* | *General Amnesty* | *The West, Race, and Reconstruction* | *Foreign Expansion* | *Judicial Retreat from Reconstruction* | *Disputed Election of 1876 and Compromise of 1877*

LINKS TO THE WORLD *The "Back to Africa" Movement*

LEGACY FOR A PEOPLE AND A NATION *The Lost Cause*

SUMMARY

Chronology

1865	Johnson begins rapid and lenient Reconstruction	1871	Congress passes second Enforcement Act and Ku Klux Klan Act
	White southern governments pass restrictive black codes		Treaty with England settles Alabama claims
	Congress refuses to seat southern representatives	1872	Amnesty Act frees almost all remaining Confederates from restrictions on holding office
	Thirteenth Amendment ratified, abolishing slavery		Grant reelected
1866	Congress passes Civil Rights Act and renewal of Freedmen's Bureau over Johnson's veto	1873	*Slaughter-House* cases limit power of Fourteenth Amendment
	Congress approves Fourteenth Amendment		Panic of 1873 leads to widespread unemployment and labor strife
	In *Ex parte Milligan,* the Supreme Court reasserts its influence	1874	Democrats win majority in House of Representatives
1867	Congress passes First Reconstruction Act and Tenure of Office Act	1875	Several Grant appointees indicted for corruption
	Constitutional conventions called in southern states		Congress passes weak Civil Rights Act
1868	House impeaches and Senate acquits Johnson		Democratic Party increases control of southern states with white supremacy campaigns
	Most southern states readmitted to Union under Radical plan	1876	*U.S. v. Cruikshank* further weakens Fourteenth Amendment
	Fourteenth Amendment ratified		Presidential election disputed
	Grant elected president	1877	Congress elects Hayes president
1869	Congress approves Fifteenth Amendment (ratified in 1870)		

Wartime Reconstruction

Which two political acts recognized the centrality of slavery to the war?

How to best reconstruct the Union was an issue as early as 1863, well before the war ended. Specifically, four vexing problems compelled early thinking and would haunt the Reconstruction era. One, who would rule in the South once it was defeated? Two, who would rule in the federal government—Congress or the president? Three, what were the dimensions of black freedom, and what rights under law would the freedmen enjoy? And four, would Reconstruction be a preservation of the old republic or a second Revolution, inventing a new republic?

Lincoln's 10 Percent Plan

Abraham Lincoln had never been anti-southern. His fear was that the war would collapse into guerrilla warfare by surviving Confederates. Lincoln insisted on leniency for southern soldiers once they surrendered. In his Second Inaugural Address, delivered a month before his assassination, Lincoln promised "malice toward none; with charity for all."

Lincoln planned early for a swift and moderate Reconstruction. In his 1863 "Proclamation of Amnesty and Reconstruction," he proposed replacing majority rule with "loyal rule" to reconstruct southern state governments and pardoning ex-Confederates except the highest-ranking military and civilian officers. Once

10 percent of a given state's voting population in the 1860 general election had taken an oath to the United States and established a government, the new state would be recognized. Lincoln did not consult Congress in these plans, and "loyal" assemblies (known as "Lincoln governments") were created in Louisiana, Tennessee, and Arkansas in 1864, states largely occupied by Union troops on which they depended for survival.

Congress and the Wade-Davis Bill

Congress was hostile toward Lincoln's moves to readmit southern states prematurely. Radical Republicans, proponents of emancipation and of aggressively defeating the South, regarded the 10 percent plan a "mere mockery" of democracy. Led by Pennsylvania Congressman Thaddeus Stevens and Massachusetts Senator Charles Sumner, congressional Republicans proposed a harsher approach. Stevens advocated a "conquered provinces" theory, arguing that southerners organized as a foreign nation to war on the United States and, by secession, destroyed their statehood status. They therefore must be treated as "conquered foreign lands" and returned to the status of "unorganized territories" before applying for readmission.

In July 1864, the Wade-Davis bill, sponsored by Ohio Senator Benjamin Wade and Maryland Congressman Henry W. Davis, emerged from Congress with three specific conditions for southern readmission.

1. It demanded a "majority" of white male citizens participating in the creation of a new government.
2. To vote or be a delegate to constitutional conventions, men had to take an "ironclad" oath (declaring that they never aided the Confederate war effort).
3. All officers above the rank of lieutenant, and all civil officials in the Confederacy, would be disfranchised and deemed "not a citizen of the United States."

Lincoln pocket-vetoed the bill and issued a conciliatory proclamation that he would not commit to any "one plan" of Reconstruction.

This exchange occurred when the war's outcome and Lincoln's reelection were still in doubt. On August 5, Radical Republicans issued the "Wade-Davis Manifesto" to newspapers, accusing Lincoln of usurpation of presidential powers and disgraceful leniency toward an eventually conquered South. Lincoln saw Reconstruction as a means of weakening the Confederacy and winning the war; the Radicals saw it as a transformation of the nation's political and racial order.

Link to the Wade-Davis bill.

Thirteenth Amendment

In early 1865, Congress and Lincoln joined in two important measures that recognized slavery's centrality to the war. On January 31, Congress passed the **Thirteenth Amendment**, which abolished involuntary servitude and declared that Congress shall have the power to enforce this outcome by "appropriate legislation." When the measure passed by 119 to 56, just 2 votes more than the necessary two-thirds, Congress rejoiced.

But the Thirteenth Amendment had emerged from a congressional debate and considerable petitioning and public advocacy. One of the first and most remarkable petitions for a constitutional amendment abolishing slavery was submitted early in 1864 by Elizabeth Cady Stanton, Susan B. Anthony, and the Women's Loyal National League. Union women accumulated thousands of signatures. It was a long road from the Emancipation Proclamation to the Thirteenth Amendment—through

Thirteenth Amendment: The Constitutional amendment that abolished slavery; passed by Congress in 1865.

treacherous constitutional theory about individual "property rights," beliefs that the sacred document (the Constitution) ought never to be altered, and partisan politics.

Freedmen's Bureau

Freedmen's Bureau: Created by Congress in March 1865, this agency had responsibility for the relief, education, and employment of former slaves as well as white refugees

On March 3, 1865, Congress created the Bureau of Refugees, Freedmen, and Abandoned Lands—the **Freedmen's Bureau**, an unprecedented agency of social uplift. With thousands of refugees in the South, the government continued what private freedmen's aid societies started in 1862. In its four-year existence, the Freedmen's Bureau supplied food and medical services, built several thousand schools and some colleges, negotiated several hundred thousand employment contracts between freedmen and their former masters, and managed confiscated land.

The Bureau was a controversial aspect of Reconstruction. Southern whites hated it, and politicians divided over its constitutionality. Some bureau agents were devoted to freedmen's rights; others exploited the chaos of the postwar South. The war prompted an eternal question of republics: what are the social welfare obligations of the state toward its people, and what do people owe their governments in return? Apart from their conquest and displacement of the eastern Indians, Americans were inexperienced at the Freedmen's Bureau's task—social reform through military occupation.

Ruins and Enmity

In 1865, with the war's devastation, America was a land with ruins. Some cities lay in rubble, large stretches of the countryside were depopulated and defoliated, and thousands of people, white and black, were refugees. Many white refugees faced genuine starvation. Of the approximately 18,300,000 rations distributed across the South in the Freedmen's Bureau's first three years, 5,230,000 went to whites.

In October 1865, after a five-month imprisonment in Boston, former Confederate Vice President Alexander H. Stephens rode a train southward. When he reached northern Georgia, his native state, his expressed shock: "War has left a terrible impression.… Fences gone, fields all a-waste, houses burnt." Every northern traveler encountered hatred from white southerners. A North Carolina innkeeper told a journalist that Yankees killed his sons, burned his house, stole his slaves and left him "one inestimable privilege … to hate 'em."

The Meanings of Freedom

How did blacks exert their newfound freedom?

Black southerners entered life after slavery with hope and circumspection. A Texas man recalled his father's telling him, "Our forever was going to be spent living among the Southerners, after they got licked." Often the changes freed people valued most were personal—alterations in employer or living arrangements.

The Feel of Freedom

For former slaves, Reconstruction meant a chance to explore freedom. Former slaves remembered singing into the night after federal troops, who confirmed rumors of their emancipation, reached their plantations. A few people gave in to the desire to do what was formerly impossible. One angry grandmother dropped her hoe and confronted her mistress with, "I'm free! Ain't got to work for you no more!" Another man recalled that he and others "started on the move," either to search for family members or just to move on.

As slaves, they had learned to expect hostility from white people; they did not presume it would instantly disappear. Many freedpeople evaluated potential employers cautiously. After searching for better circumstances, a majority of blacks eventually settled as agricultural workers back on their former farms or plantations. But they relocated their houses and tried to control the conditions of their labor.

Reunion of African American Families

Throughout the South, former slaves focused on reuniting their families, separated during slavery by sale or hardship, and during the war by dislocation. By relying on the black community for help and by placing ads in black newspapers into the 1880s, some succeeded, while others searched in vain.

Husbands and wives who belonged to different masters established homes together to raise their children. When her old master claimed a right to whip her children, a mother replied, "he warn't goin' to brush none of her chilluns no more."

Blacks' Search for Independence

Many black people wanted to minimize contact with whites because, as Reverend Garrison Frazier told General Sherman in January 1865, "There is a prejudice against us … that will take years to get over." As such, blacks abandoned slave quarters and fanned out to distant corners of the land they worked. Some described moving "across the creek" or building a "saplin house … back in the woods." Other rural dwellers established small, all-black settlements that still exist along the South's back roads.

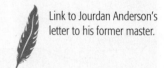

Link to Jourdan Anderson's letter to his former master.

Freedpeople's Desire for Land

In addition to a fair employer, freedpeople wanted to own land, which represented self-sufficiency and compensation for generations of bondage. General Sherman's special Field Order Number 15, issued in February 1865, set aside 400,000 acres of land in the Sea Islands for settlement of freedpeople. Hope swelled among ex-slaves as forty-acre plots and mules were promised to them. But President Johnson ordered them removed in October and the land returned to its original owners under army enforcement.

Most members of both political parties opposed land redistribution to the freedmen. Even northern reformers who administered the Sea Islands during the war showed little sympathy for black aspirations. The former Sea Island slaves wanted small, self-sufficient farms. Northern soldiers, officials, and missionaries brought education and aid to the freedmen but insisted that they grow cotton for competitive market. Ultimately, the U.S. government eventually sold thousands of acres in the Sea Islands, 90 percent of which went to wealthy northern investors.

Black Embrace of Education

Blacks hungered for education that previously belonged only to whites. With freedom, they started schools and filled dirt-floor classrooms, studying day and night. Children brought infants to school, and adults attended at night or after "the crops were laid by." Despite their poverty, many blacks paid tuition, typically $1 or $1.50

African Americans of all ages eagerly pursued the opportunity to gain an education in freedom. This young woman in Mt. Meigs, Alabama, is helping her mother learn to read.

Smithsonian Institution, photo by Rudolf Eickemeyer

a month, which constituted major portions of a person's agricultural wages and totaled more than $1 million by 1870.

In its brief life, the Freedmen's Bureau founded over four thousand schools, and northern reformers established others through private philanthropy. The Yankee schoolmarm—dedicated, selfless, and religious—became an agent of progress in many southern communities. By 1877, more than 600,000 African Americans were enrolled in elementary school.

Blacks and their white allies also established colleges and universities. The American Missionary Association founded seven colleges, including Fisk and Atlanta Universities, between 1866 and 1869. The Freedmen's Bureau helped establish Howard University in Washington, D.C., and northern religious groups, such as the Methodists, Baptists, and Congregationalists, supported seminaries and teachers' colleges.

During Reconstruction, African American leaders often were highly educated members of the prewar elite of free people of color. Francis Cardozo, who held various offices in South Carolina, attended universities in Scotland and England. P. B. S. Pinchback, who became lieutenant governor of Louisiana, was the son of a planter who sent him to school in Cincinnati.

Growth of Black Churches

Freed from slavery's restrictions, blacks could build their own institutions. The secret churches of slavery became public; in communities throughout the South, ex-slaves "started a brush arbor...shelter with leaves for a roof," where freed men and women worshiped.

Within a few years, branches of the Methodist and Baptist denominations attracted most southern black Christians. By 1877 in South Carolina, the African Methodist Episcopal (A.M.E.) Church had a thousand ministers, forty-four thousand members, and a school of theology, while the A.M.E. Zion Church had forty-five thousand members. In these churches, some of which became the wealthiest and most autonomous institutions in black life, freedpeople created enduring communities.

sharecropping: A system where landowners and former slaves managed a new arrangement, with laborers paying with a portion of their crops for the right to work their own land, thereby usually ending up in permanent debt.

Rise of the Sharecropping System

Since most former slaves lacked money to buy land, they preferred the next best thing: renting it. But the South had few sources of credit, and few whites would rent to blacks. Consequently, black farmers and white landowners turned to **sharecropping**, a system in which a landlord or a merchant "furnished" food and supplies, such as draft animals and seed, to farmers who worked the land and received payment from

Sharecropping: Enslaved to Debt

Sharecropping became an oppressive system in the postwar South. A new labor structure that began as a compromise between freedmen who wanted independence and landowners who wanted a stable work force, evolved into a method of working on "halves" and where tenants owed endless debts to the furnishing merchants, who owned plantation stores like this one, photographed in Mississippi in 1868. Merchants recorded in ledger books, like the one at right, the debts that few sharecroppers were able to repay. Why did both former slaves and former slaveowners initially find sharecropping an agreeable, if difficult, new labor arrangement? What were the short- and long-term consequences of the sharecropping system for the freedpeople and for the Southern economy?

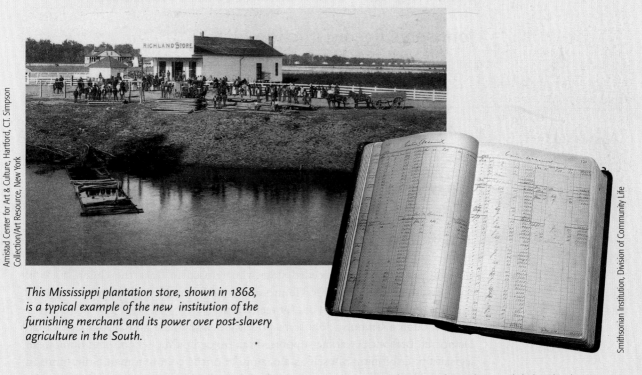

Amistad Center for Art & Culture, Hartford, CT. Simpson Collection/Art Resource, New York

This Mississippi plantation store, shown in 1868, is a typical example of the new institution of the furnishing merchant and its power over post-slavery agriculture in the South.

Smithsonian Institution, Division of Community Life

Furnishing merchants kept such ledger books for decades; they became the record of how sharecroppers fell deeper in debt from year to year, and "owed their soul" to the country store.

the crop. White landowners and black farmers bargained with one another; sharecroppers would hold out, or move from year to year. As the system matured during the 1870s and 1880s, most sharecroppers worked "on halves"—half for the owner and half for themselves.

The sharecropping system, which materialized as early as 1868, originated as a compromise between former slaves and landowners. It eased landowners' problems with cash and credit, and provided a permanent, dependent labor force; blacks accepted it because freed them from daily supervision. But share-cropping proved disastrous. Owners and merchants developed a monopoly of control over the agricultural economy, as sharecroppers faced ever-increasing debt (see page 411).

The fundamental problem was that southern farmers still concentrated on cotton. In freedom, black women often stayed away from cotton picking, favoring domestic chores, given the diminishing incentives of the cotton system. Even as the South recovered its prewar share of British cotton purchases, the rewards diminished. Cotton prices began a long decline, as world demand fell off.

Thus, southern agriculture slipped into depression. Black sharecroppers struggled under growing debt that bound them to landowners and to furnishing merchants almost as oppressively as slavery. Many white farmers gradually lost their land and became sharecroppers. By the end of Reconstruction, over one-third of southern farms were worked by sharecropping tenants, white and black.

Link to a sample sharecropping contract.

Johnson's Reconstruction Plan

What was Johnson's vision for Reconstruction?

Many people expected Reconstruction under President Andrew Johnson to be harsh. Throughout his career in Tennessee, he criticized wealthy planters and championed small farmers. When an assassin's bullet thrust Johnson into the presidency, former slaveowners feared Johnson would deal sternly with them. When northern Radicals suggested the exile or execution of ten or twelve leading rebels, Johnson replied, "How are you going to pick out so small a number?"

Andrew Johnson of Tennessee

Like Lincoln, Johnson moved from obscurity to power. With no education, he became a tailor's apprentice. But from 1829, while in his early twenties, he held nearly every office in Tennessee politics: alderman, state representative, congressman, two terms as governor, and U.S. senator by 1857. Although elected as a Democrat, Johnson was the only senator from a seceded state who refused to leave the Union. Lincoln appointed him war governor of Tennessee in 1862; hence his symbolic place on the ticket in the president's 1864 bid for reelection.

Although a Unionist, Johnson's political beliefs made him an old Jacksonian Democrat. Before the war, he supported tax-funded public schools and homestead legislation, fashioning himself as a champion of the common man. Still, Johnson advocated limited government. His philosophy toward Reconstruction: "The Constitution as it is, and the Union as it was."

Through 1865, Johnson alone controlled Reconstruction policy; Congress recessed before he became president and did not reconvene until December. Johnson formed new state governments in the South by using his power to grant pardons and offered easy terms to former Confederates.

Johnson's Racial Views

Johnson had owned house slaves, although he was never a planter. He accepted emancipation but did not believe that black suffrage could be imposed on a southern state by the federal government. This set him on a collision course with the Radicals. On race, Johnson was a white supremacist. He declared in his annual message of 1867 that blacks possessed less "capacity for government than any other race of people … wherever they have been left to their own devices they have shown a constant tendency to relapse into barbarism."

Such racial views affected Johnson's policies. Where whites were concerned, however, Johnson proposed rules that would keep the wealthy planter class at least temporarily out of power.

Johnson's Pardon Policy

White southerners were required to swear an oath of loyalty to gain amnesty, but Johnson barred from the oath former federal officials, high-ranking Confederate officers, and political leaders or graduates of West Point or Annapolis who joined the Confederacy. He also added ex-Confederates whose taxable property was worth more than $20,000. These individuals had to apply to the president for pardon. The president, it seemed, sought revenge on the old planter elite and to promote a new yeoman leadership.

Johnson appointed provisional governors, who began Reconstruction by calling state constitutional conventions. The delegates had to draft new constitutions that eliminated slavery and invalidated secession. After ratification, new governments could be elected, and the states restored to the Union. But only southerners who had taken the oath of amnesty and were eligible voters when the state seceded could participate. Thus, unpardoned whites and former slaves were ineligible.

Presidential Reconstruction

The old white leadership proved resilient; prominent Confederates won elections and turned up in appointive offices. Then Johnson started pardoning planters and leading rebels. By September 1865, hundreds of pardons were issued in one day. These pardons, plus the return of planters' abandoned lands, restored the old elite to power and made Johnson seem the South's champion.

Why did Johnson allow the planters to regain power? He may have enjoyed turning proud planters into pardon seekers. He also sought rapid Reconstruction to deny the Radicals any opportunity for thorough racial and political changes in the South. And Johnson needed southern support in the 1866 elections; hence, he declared Reconstruction complete only eight months after Appomattox. In December 1865, many Confederate congressmen claimed seats in the U.S. Congress, including former Confederate vice president Alexander Stephens, who was now Georgia's senator-elect.

Black Codes

Furthermore, to define the status of freed people and control their labor, some legislatures revised the slave codes by substituting the word *freedmen* for *slaves*. The new black codes compelled former slaves to carry passes, observe a curfew, and live in housing provided by a landowner. Vagrancy laws and restrictive labor contracts bound freedpeople to plantations, and "anti-enticement" laws punished anyone luring these workers to other employment. State-supported schools and orphanages excluded blacks.

It seemed to northerners that the South was intent on returning African Americans to servility and that Johnson's Reconstruction policy held no one responsible for the war. Thus, the Republican majority in Congress halted Johnson's plan. The House and Senate refused to admit newly elected southern representatives. Instead, they bluntly challenged the president's authority and established a joint committee to study a new direction for Reconstruction.

The Congressional Reconstruction Plan

What made Radical Reconstruction different from Johnson's plan?

The Constitution mentioned neither secession nor reunion, but it gave Congress the primary role in admitting states. Moreover, the Constitution declared that the United States shall guarantee to each state a "republican form of government." This provision, legislators believed, gave them the authority to devise Reconstruction policies.

The key question: What had rebellion done to the relationship between southern states and the Union? Congressmen who favored vigorous Reconstruction measures argued that the war had broken the Union and that the South was subject to the victor's will. Moderate congressmen held that the states forfeited their rights through rebellion and thus came under congressional supervision.

The Radicals

Link to Thaddeus Stevens's reconstruction speech.

Northern Democrats, weakened by their opposition to the war in its final year, denounced racial equality and supported Johnson's policies. Conservative Republicans, despite their party loyalty, favored a limited federal role in Reconstruction. Although a minority, Radical Republicans, led by Thaddeus Stevens, Charles Sumner, and George Julian, wanted to democratize the South, establish public education, and ensure freedpeople's rights. They favored black suffrage, supported some land confiscation and redistribution, and were willing to exclude the South from the Union to achieve their goals.

The Radicals brought a new civic vision; they wanted to create an activist federal government and the beginnings of racial equality. Many moderate Republicans, led by Lyman Trumbull, opposed Johnson's leniency but wanted to restrain the Radicals. They were, however, committed to federalizing the enforcement of civil, if not political, rights for the freedmen.

With the 1866 elections looming, Johnson and the Democrats sabotaged the possibility of a conservative coalition by refusing to cooperate with conservative or moderate Republicans. They insisted that Reconstruction was over, that the new state governments were legitimate, and that southern representatives should be admitted to Congress. The Radicals' influence grew with Johnson's intransigence.

Congress Versus Johnson

Link to the text of President Johnson's veto of the 1866 Civil Rights bill.

Republicans believed they reached a compromise with Johnson in spring 1866. Under its terms, Johnson would modify his program by extending the Freedmen's Bureau for another year and passing of a civil rights bill to counteract the black codes. This would force southern courts to practice equality under the scrutiny of the federal judiciary. Its provisions applied to public, not private, acts of discrimination. The Civil Rights Bill of 1866 was the first statutory definition of the rights of American citizens.

Johnson, however, vetoed both bills; they became law when Congress overrode his veto. Because the civil rights bill defined U.S. citizens as native-born persons who were taxed, Johnson claimed that it discriminated against "large numbers of intelligent, worthy, and patriotic foreigners…in favor of the negro." Hope of presidential-congressional cooperation was dead. In 1866, newspapers reported daily violations of blacks' rights in the South and carried alarming accounts of anti-Black violence. In Memphis, forty blacks were killed and twelve schools burned by white mobs, and in New Orleans, the toll was thirty-four African Americans dead and two hundred wounded. Violence convinced Republicans, and the northern public, that more needed to be done. A new Republican plan focused on the **Fourteenth Amendment** to the Constitution.

Fourteenth Amendment: Defined U.S. citizens as anyone born or naturalized in the United States, barred states from interfering with citizens' constitutional rights, and stated for first time that voters would be male.

Fourteenth Amendment

Of the five sections of the Fourteenth Amendment, the first would have the greatest legal significance. It conferred citizenship on "all persons born or naturalized in the United States" and prohibited states from abridging their constitutional "privileges and immunities" (see the Appendix for the Constitution and all amendments). It also barred states from taking a person's life, liberty, or property "without due process of law" and from denying "equal protection of the laws." These phrases have become powerful guarantees of African Americans' civil rights and the rights of all citizens, except for Indians, who were not granted citizenship rights until 1924.

Republicans almost universally agreed on the amendment's second and third sections. The fourth declared the Confederate debt null and void, and guaranteed the United States' war debt. Northerners rejected paying taxes to reimburse those who financed a rebellion, and business groups agreed on the necessity of upholding the U.S. government's credit. The second and third sections barred Confederate leaders from holding state and federal office. Only Congress, by a two-thirds vote of each house, could remove the penalty, thereby guaranteeing some punishment for Confederate leaders.

The second section of the amendment also dealt with representation and embodied the compromises that produced it. Northerners disagreed about whether blacks should have the right to vote. In truth, public will, North and South, lagged behind the egalitarianism of enactments that became constitutional cornerstones. Many northern states still maintained black disfranchisement laws during Reconstruction.

Emancipation ended the three-fifths clause for the purpose of counting blacks, which would increase southern representation. Thus, the postwar South stood to gain power in Congress, and if white southerners did not allow blacks to vote, former secessionists would derive the political benefit from emancipation. Consequently, Republicans determined that, if a southern state did not grant black men the vote, their representation would be reduced proportionally. The Fourteenth Amendment specified for the first time that voters were "male." As such, it provoked frustration in the women's rights movement. Advocates of women's equality worked with abolitionists for decades, often subordinating their cause to the slaves'. During the drafting of the Fourteenth Amendment, however, some leaders, such as Elizabeth Cady Stanton and Susan B. Anthony, ended their alliance with abolitionists and fought for women, infusing new life into the women's rights movement. Other female activists, however, argued that it was "the Negro's hour," causing strife among old allies. Many former male abolitionists, white and black, were willing to delay woman suffrage to secure freedmen the vote.

The South's and Johnson's Defiance

Johnson tried to block the Fourteenth Amendment. He urged state legislatures in the South to vote against ratification, and all but Tennessee rejected the amendment by a wide margin.

To present his case to northerners, Johnson organized a National Union Convention. He boarded a special train for a "swing around the circle" that carried his message into the Northeast, the Midwest, and back to Washington. Increasingly, audiences rejected his views, jeering at him. Johnson handed out American flags with thirty-six rather than twenty-five stars, declaring the Union already restored. And he labeled the Radicals "traitors" for attempting to take over Reconstruction.

MAP 16.1

The Reconstruction

This map shows the five military districts established when Congress passed the Reconstruction Act of 1867. As the dates within each state indicate, conservative Democratic forces quickly regained control of government in four southern states. So-called Radical Reconstruction was curtailed in most of the others, as factions within the weakened Republican Party began to cooperate with conservative Democrats.

Source: Copyright © Cengage Learning

In the 1866 elections, radicals and moderates whom Johnson denounced won reelection by large margins, and the Republican majority grew to two-thirds of both congressional houses. The North was clear: Johnson's policies of states' rights and white supremacy were giving the advantage to rebels and traitors. Thus Republican congressional leaders won a mandate to pursue their Reconstruction plan.

But nothing could be accomplished as long as the "Johnson governments" existed and the southern electorate remained exclusively white. Republicans resolved to form new state governments in the South and enfranchise the freedmen.

Reconstruction Acts of 1867–1868

After embittered debate, the First Reconstruction Act passed in March 1867. This plan, under which the southern states were readmitted to the Union, incorporated only a part of the Radical program. Union generals, commanding small garrisons and charged with supervising elections, assumed control in five military districts in the South (see Map 16.1). Confederate leaders designated in the Fourteenth Amendment were barred from voting until new state constitutions were ratified. The act guaranteed freedmen the right to vote and serve in state constitutional conventions. In addition, each southern state was required to ratify the Fourteenth Amendment and its new constitution by majority vote, then submit it to Congress for approval (see Table 16.1).

TABLE 16.1 Plans for Reconstruction Compared

	Johnson's Plan	Radicals' Plan	Fourteenth Amendment	Reconstruction Act of 1867
Voting	Whites only; high-ranking Confederate leaders must seek pardons	Give vote to black males	Southern whites may decide but can lose representation if they deny black suffrage	Black men gain vote; whites barred from office by Fourteenth Amendment cannot vote while new state governments are formed
Officeholding	Many prominent Confederates regain power	Only loyal white and black males eligible	Confederate leaders barred until Congress votes amnesty	Fourteenth Amendment in effect
Time out of Union	Brief	Several years; until South is thoroughly democratized	Brief	3–5 years after war
Other change in southern society	Little; gain of power by yeomen not realized; emancipation grudgingly accepted, but no black civil or political rights	Expand public education; confiscate land and provide farms for freedmen; expansion of activist federal government	Probably slight, depending on enforcement	Considerable, depending on action of new state governments

The Second, Third, and Fourth Reconstruction Acts, passed between March 1867 and March 1868, provided the details for voter registration boards, the adoption of constitutions, and the administration of "good faith" oaths by white southerners.

Failure of Land Redistribution

The Radicals blocked Johnson, but they had hoped Congress could do much more. Thaddeus Stevens, for example, argued that economic opportunity was essential to the freedmen. "He drew up a plan for extensive confiscation and redistribution of land, but it was never realized."

Racial fears and an American obsession with the sanctity of private property made land redistribution unpopular. Thus, black farmers were forced to seek work in a hostile environment in which landowners opposed their acquisition of land.

Constitutional Crisis

To restrict Johnson's influence and safeguard its plan, Congress passed several controversial laws. First, it limited Johnson's power over the army by requiring the president to issue military orders through the General of the Army, Ulysses S. Grant. Then Congress passed the Tenure of Office Act, which gave the Senate power to approve changes in the president's cabinet. Designed to protect Secretary of War Stanton, a Radical sympathizer, this law violated the tradition of presidents controlling cabinet appointments. These measures, along with the Reconstruction Acts, were passed by a two-thirds override of presidential vetoes. In response, Johnson limited the military's power in the South, increasing the powers of the civil governments he created in 1865. Then he removed military officers who were enforcing Congress's new law, preferring commanders who allowed disqualified Confederates to vote. Finally, he tried to remove Secretary of War Stanton, pushing the confrontation to its climax.

Impeachment of President Johnson

Impeachment: Process to remove a president from office; attempted but failed in case of Andrew Johnson.

Impeachment is a political procedure provided for in the Constitution as a remedy for crimes or serious abuses of power by presidents, federal judges, and other high government officials. Those who are impeached (judged or politically indicted) in the House are then tried in the Senate. Historically, this power was not used to investigate and judge the private lives of presidents, although more recently it was used this way against President Bill Clinton.

Twice in 1867, the House Judiciary Committee considered impeachment of Johnson, first rejecting it and then recommending it by a 5-to-4 vote, which was defeated by the House. After Johnson tried to remove Stanton, however, a third attempt to impeach him carried in early 1868. The indictment concentrated on his violation of the Tenure of Office Act, though modern scholars regard his efforts to obstruct enforcement of the Reconstruction Act of 1867 as a more serious offense.

Johnson's trial in the Senate lasted more than three months. The prosecution, led by Radicals, attempted to prove that Johnson was guilty of "high crimes and misdemeanors." But they also argued that the trial was a means to judge Johnson's performance. The Senate rejected such reasoning, which could have made removal from office a political weapon against any chief executive who disagreed with Congress. The prosecution fell one vote short of the necessary two-thirds majority. Johnson remained in office, politically weakened.

Election of 1868

congressional Reconstruction: The process by which the Republican-controlled Congress sought to make the Reconstruction of the ex-Confederate states longer, harsher, and under congressional control.

In the 1868 presidential election, Ulysses S. Grant, running as a Republican, defeated Horatio Seymour, a New York Democrat. Grant was not a Radical, but his platform supported **congressional Reconstruction** and endorsed black suffrage in the South. (Significantly, Republicans stopped short of endorsing black suffrage in the North.) Democrats, meanwhile, denounced Reconstruction and preached white supremacy, conducting the most openly racist campaign to that point in American history. Both sides waved the "bloody shirt," blaming each other for the war's sacrifices. By associating with rebellion and Johnson's repudiated program, Democrats were defeated in all but eight states, though the popular vote was close. Blacks voted en masse for General Grant.

In office, Grant vacillated in dealing with southern states, sometimes defending Republican regimes and sometimes currying favor with Democrats. Occasionally, Grant called out federal troops to stop violence or enforce congressional acts. But he never imposed a military occupation on the South. Rapid demobilization reduced a federal army of more than 1 million to 57,000 within a year of the Appomattox surrender. Thereafter, the number of troops in the South declined, until in 1874 there were only 4,000 in southern states outside Texas. The legend of "military rule," so important to southern claims of victimization during Reconstruction, was steeped in myth.

Fifteenth Amendment

Fifteenth Amendment: Prohibited states from denying the vote to any citizen on account of "race, color, or previous condition of servitude."

In 1869, the Radicals pushed through the **Fifteenth Amendment**, the final major measure in Reconstruction's constitutional revolution. It forbade states to deny the vote "on account of race, color, or previous condition of servitude." Such wording did not guarantee the right to vote. It left states free to restrict suffrage on other grounds so that northern states could continue to deny suffrage to women and certain men—Chinese immigrants, illiterates, and those too poor to pay poll taxes.

The Fifteenth Amendment became law in 1870. Although African Americans rejoiced, it left open the possibility for states to create countless qualification tests to obstruct voting.

Politics and Reconstruction in the South

How did black voters in the early days of Reconstruction transform the South?

From the start, white southerners resisted Reconstruction and opposed emancipation, as evident in the black codes. The former planter class proved especially unbending because of their tremendous financial loss in slaves. For many poor whites who never owned slaves and yet sacrificed in the war, destitution, plummeting agricultural prices, disease, and the uncertainties of a growing urban industrialization drove them off land toward cities and into hatred of black equality.

White Resistance Some planters attempted to postpone freeing slaves by denying or misrepresenting events. Former slaves reported that their owners "didn't tell them it was freedom" or "wouldn't let [them] go." To retain workers, some landowners claimed control over black children and used guardianship and apprentice laws to bind black families to the plantation.

Adamant resistance by whites soon manifested itself in other ways, including violence. A local North Carolina magistrate clubbed a black man on a public street, and in several states bands of "Regulators" terrorized blacks who displayed independence. And after President Johnson encouraged the South to resist congressional Reconstruction, many white conservatives captured the new state governments, while others boycotted the polls to defeat Congress's plans.

Black Voters and the Southern Republican Party Enthusiastically, blacks went to the polls, voting Republican, as one man said, to "stick to the end with the party that freed me." Illiteracy did not prohibit blacks (or uneducated whites) from making intelligent choices. Mississippi's William Henry could read only "a little," but he said, "We saw D. Sledge vote; he owned half the county. We knowed he voted Democratic so we voted the other ticket so it would be Republican." Women, who could not vote, encouraged their husbands and sons, and preachers exhorted their congregations to use the franchise.

Thomas Waterman Wood, who had painted portraits of society figures in Nashville before the war, sensed the importance of Congress's decision in 1867 to enfranchise the freedmen. This oil painting, one in a series on suffrage, emphasizes the significance of the ballot for the black voter.

Cheekwood Museum of Art, Nashville, Tennessee

Thanks to a large black turnout and the restrictions on prominent Confederates, a new southern Republican Party came to power in the 1868–1870 constitutional conventions. Republican delegates consisted of a sizable black contingent (265 out of the more than 1,000 delegates throughout the South), northerners who had moved to the South, and native southern whites seeking change. The new constitutions they drafted were more democratic than anything previously adopted in the South. They eliminated property qualifications for voting and holding office, turned many appointed offices into elective posts, and provided for public schools and institutions to care for the mentally ill, the blind, the deaf, the destitute, and the orphaned.

The conventions broadened women's rights in property holding and divorce. Usually the goal was not equality but providing relief to thousands of suffering debtors. Since husbands typically contracted the debts, giving women legal control over their own property provided some protection for families.

Triumph of Republican Governments

Under these new constitutions, southern states elected Republican-controlled governments. For the first time, state legislators in 1868 included black southerners. Contrary to what white southerners later claimed, Republican state governments did not disfranchise ex-Confederates as a group. James Lynch, a leading black politician from Mississippi, saw disfranchising whites as foolish. Landless former slaves "must be in friendly relations with the great body of the whites in the state," he explained. "Otherwise…peace can be maintained only by a standing army." Despised and lacking power, southern Republicans strove for safe ways to gain a foothold in a depressed economy.

Far from vindictive toward the race that enslaved them, most southern blacks appealed to white southerners to be fair. Hence, the South's Republican Party condemned itself to defeat if white voters would not cooperate. Within a few years, most fledgling Republican parties in southern states would be struggling for survival against violent white hostility.

Industrialization and Mill Towns

Reconstruction governments promoted industry via loans, subsidies, and short-term exemptions from taxation. The southern railroad system was rebuilt and expanded, and coal and iron mining made possible Birmingham's steel plants. Between 1860 and 1880, the number of manufacturing establishments in the South nearly doubled.

This emphasis on big business, however, produced higher state debts and taxes, drew money from schools and other programs, and multiplied possibilities for corruption. The alliance between business and government often operated at the expense of farmers and laborers. It also doomed Republicans to failure in building support among poorer whites.

Poverty remained the lot of many southern whites. The war caused a massive loss of income-producing wealth, such as livestock, and a steep decline in land values. From 1860 to 1880, the South's share of per capita income fell to 51 percent of the national average. In many regions, the old planter class still ruled the best land and access to credit or markets.

As poor whites and blacks found farming less tenable, they moved to cities and mill towns. Industrialization did not sweep the South as it did the North, but it laid deep roots. Attracting textile mills to southern towns became a competitive crusade.

In 1860, the South counted some 10,000 mill workers; by 1880, the number grew to 16,741 and by century's end to 97,559. Many poor southerners moved from farmer to mill worker and other low-income wage work.

Republicans and Racial Equality

Whites who controlled the southern Republican Party were reluctant to allow blacks a share of offices proportionate to their electoral strength. Aware of their weakness, black leaders did not push hard for revolutionary change. Instead, they led efforts to establish public schools, although without pressing for integrated facilities. In 1870, South Carolina passed the first comprehensive school law in the South. By 1875, 50 percent of that state's black school-age children were enrolled in school, and approximately one-third of the three thousand teachers were black.

Those African American politicians who did fight for civil rights and integration were typically from cities such as New Orleans or Mobile, where large populations of light-skinned free blacks existed before the war. Their experience made them sensitive to issues of status. Laws requiring equal accommodations won passage but often went unenforced.

Economic progress, particularly land ownership, was a major concern for most freedpeople. Land reform failed because in most states whites were the majority, and former slaveowners controlled the best land and financial resources. Much land did fall into state hands for nonpayment of taxes. Such land was sold in small lots. But most freedmen had too little cash to bid against investors or speculators. Any widespread land redistribution had to arise from Congress, which never supported such action.

Myth of "Negro Rule"

Within a few years, white hostility to congressional Reconstruction increasingly prevailed. Conservatives had always wanted to fight Reconstruction through pressure and racist propaganda began to do so. Charging that the South had been turned over to ignorant blacks, conservatives used "black domination," as a rallying cry for a return to white supremacy.

Such attacks were part of the growing myth of "Negro rule," which would become a central theme in battles over the memory of Reconstruction. African Americans participated in politics but hardly dominated. They were a majority in only two of ten state constitutional conventions. In state legislatures, only in South Carolina's lower house did blacks constitute a majority. Sixteen blacks won seats in Congress before Reconstruction was over. Only eighteen served in a high state office, such as lieutenant governor, treasurer, superintendent of education, or secretary of state.

Some four hundred blacks served in political office during Reconstruction, an enormous achievement. Elected officials, such as Robert Smalls in South Carolina, labored for cheaper land prices, better healthcare, access to schools, and the enforcement of civil rights. For too long, the black politicians of Reconstruction were forgotten heroes of this seedtime of America's long civil rights movement.

Carpetbaggers and Scalawags

Conservative propaganda denounced northern whites as "**carpetbaggers**," greedy crooks planning to pour stolen tax revenues into their luggage made of carpet material. In fact, most northerners who settled in the South came seeking business opportunities, as schoolteachers, or to find a warmer climate; most never entered politics. Those who entered politics generally wanted to democratize the South and to introduce northern ways such as industry and public education.

carpetbaggers: Derogatory nickname southerners gave to northerners who moved south after the Civil War, perceiving them as greedy opportunists who hoped to cash in on the South's plight.

scalawags: Term used by conservative southerners to describe other white southerners who were perceived as aiding or benefiting from Reconstruction.

Conservatives also invented the term **scalawag** to discredit white southerners cooperating with Republicans, as many wealthy men did. Most scalawags were yeoman farmers from mountain areas and nonslaveholding districts who were Unionists under the Confederacy. They hoped to benefit from the education and opportunities Republicans promoted. Sometimes banding with freedmen, they pursued common class interests to make headway against long-dominant planters. Over time, however, most black-white coalitions floundered due to racism.

Tax Policy and Corruption as Political Wedges

Republicans wanted to repair the war's destruction, stimulate industry, and support such new ventures as public schools—all of which required tax money. But the Civil War damaged the South's tax base. One category of valuable property—slaves—had disappeared entirely. Hundreds of thousands of citizens lost much their property—money, livestock, and buildings—to the war. Tax increases (sales, excise, and property) was necessary for even traditional services. Inevitably, Republican tax policies aroused strong opposition, especially among yeomen.

Corruption charges also plagued Republicans. Many carpetbaggers and black politicians engaged in fraudulent schemes or sold their votes, participating in what scholars recognize was a nationwide surge of corruption in an age ruled by "spoilsmen" (see pages 516). Corruption crossed party lines, but Democrats pinned the blame on unqualified blacks and greedy carpetbaggers among southern Republicans.

Ku Klux Klan: A terrorist organization established by six Confederate war veterans that sought to reestablish white supremacy in the South, suppress black voting, and topple Reconstruction governments.

Ku Klux Klan

Republican leaders also allowed factionalism along racial and class lines to undermine party unity. At the same time, the **Ku Klux Klan**, a secret veterans' club that began in Tennessee in 1866, spread through the South, rapidly becoming a terrorist organization. Klansmen sought to frustrate Reconstruction and keep the freedmen in subjection with nighttime harassment, whippings, rapes, and murders.

Although the Klan tormented blacks, its main purpose was political. Lawless nightriders targeted active Republicans, killing leading whites and blacks in several states. After freedmen who worked for a South Carolina scalawag started voting, terrorists visited the plantation and, as one victim noted, "whipped every … [black] man they could lay their hands on." Klansmen also attacked Union League clubs—Republican organizations that mobilized the black vote—and schoolteachers who aided freedmen.

Specific social forces shaped and directed Klan violence, with Alamance and Caswell Counties in North Carolina receiving the worst Klan violence. Slim Republican majorities there rested on cooperation between black voters and white yeomen. Together, these black and white Republicans ousted long-entrenched officials. The wealthy and powerful men who lost their accustomed political control were the Klan's county officers and local chieftains. By intimidation and murder, the Klan weakened the Republican coalition and restored a Democratic majority.

The Granger Collection, New York

Cartoon, depicting a freedman, John Campbell, vainly begging for mercy in Moore County, North Carolina, August 10, 1871. The image evokes the power, fear, and mystery of the Klan without actually showing its bloody deeds.

Klan violence injured Republicans across the South. One of every ten black delegates to the 1867–1868 state constitutional conventions was attacked, seven fatally. In one judicial district of North Carolina, the Ku Klux Klan was responsible for twelve murders, over seven hundred beatings, along with many cases of rape and arson. A single attack on Republicans in Eutaw, Alabama, left four blacks dead and fifty-four wounded. According to historian Eric Foner, the Klan "made it virtually impossible for Republicans to campaign or vote in large parts of Georgia."

Thus Republican mistakes, racial hostility, and terror brought down the Republican regimes. In most states, Radical Reconstruction lasted only a few years (see Map 16.1). The most enduring failure of Reconstruction, however, was that it failed to alter the South's social structure or its distribution of wealth and power.

Retreat from Reconstruction

What led the North to lose interest in reconstructing the South?

During the 1870s, northerners lost the will to sustain Reconstruction, as they confronted economic and social transformations in their regions and the West. Radical Republicans like Albion Tourgée, a former Union soldier who moved to North Carolina and was elected a judge, condemned Congress's timidity. He and many African Americans believed that, during Reconstruction, the North "threw all the Negroes on the world without any way of getting along." As the North lost interest in the South, Reconstruction collapsed.

Political Implications of Klan Terrorism

Whites in the old Confederacy referred to this decline of Reconstruction as "southern redemption." During the 1870s, "redeemer" Democrats claimed to be the South's saviors from alleged "black domination" and "carpetbag rule." Violence and terror emerged as a tactic in politics.

In 1870 and 1871, the Ku Klux Klan's violent campaigns forced Congress to pass two **Enforcement Acts** and an anti-Klan law. These laws made actions by individuals against the civil and political rights of others a federal criminal offense. They also provided for election supervisors and permitted martial law and suspension of the writ of habeas corpus to combat murders, beatings, and Klan threats. In 1872 and 1873, Mississippi and the Carolinas saw many prosecutions; but in other states, the laws were ignored. Southern juries sometimes refused to convict Klansmen; less than half of the 3,310 cases ended in convictions. Although many Klansmen fled their state to avoid prosecution, and the Klan officially disbanded, paramilitary organizations known as Rifle Clubs and Red Shirts often took the Klan's place.

Still, there were ominous signs that the North's commitment to racial justice was fading, as some influential Republicans opposed the anti-Klan laws. Rejecting other Republicans' arguments that the Thirteenth, Fourteenth, and Fifteenth Amendments made the federal government the protector of citizens' rights, dissenters charged that Congress was infringing on states' rights. This foreshadowed a general revolt within Republican ranks in 1872.

Enforcement Acts: Laws that sought to protect black voters and made violations of civil and political rights a federal offense and sought to end Ku Klux Klan violence.

Industrial Expansion and Reconstruction in the North

Immigration and industrialization surged in the North. Between 1865 and 1873, 3 million immigrants entered the country, most settling in the industrial cities of the North and West. Within only eight years, industrial production increased by 75 percent. For the first time, nonagricultural workers outnumbered farmers, and wage earners outnumbered independent craftsmen. Government policies encouraged this rapid growth. Low taxes on investment and high tariffs on manufactured goods helped create a new class of powerful industrialists, especially railroad entrepreneurs.

From 1865 to 1873, 35,000 miles of new track were laid, this fueled the banking industry and made Wall Street the center of American capitalism. Eastern railroad magnates, such as Thomas Scott of the Pennsylvania Railroad, created economic empires with the assistance of huge government subsidies of cash and land. Railroad corporations also bought up mining operations, granaries, and lumber companies. Big business now employed lobbyists to curry favor with government. Corruption ran rampant, with some congressmen and legislators paid retainers by major companies.

As captains of industry amassed unprecedented fortunes, gross economic inequality polarized American society. The work force, worried a Massachusetts business leader, was in a "transition state … living in boarding houses" and becoming a "permanent factory population." In New York or Philadelphia, workers increasingly lived in unhealthy tenement housing. Thousands would list themselves on the census as "common laborer" or "general jobber." Concerned, in 1868 Republicans passed an eight-hour workday bill that applied to federal workers. The "labor question" (see Chapter 18) now preoccupied northerners far more than the "southern" or "freedmen" question.

Then the Panic of 1873 ushered in more than five years of economic contraction. Three million people lost their jobs, especially in large cities. Debtors and the unemployed sought easy-money policies to spur expansion (workers and farmers desperately needed cash). Businessmen, disturbed by the strikes and industrial violence that accompanied the panic, defended property rights and demanded "sound money" policies. The chasm between farmers and workers and wealthy industrialists widened.

Liberal Republican Revolt

Disenchanted with Reconstruction, a largely northern group calling itself the Liberal Republicans bolted the party in 1872 and nominated Horace Greeley, editor of the *New York Tribune,* for president. A varied group, Liberal Republicans included foes of corruption and advocates of a lower tariff. Two popular attitudes united them: distaste for federal intervention in the South and an elitist desire to let market forces and the "best men" determine policy.

Democrats also nominated Greeley in 1872, but it was not enough to keep Grant from reelection. Greeley's campaign for North-South reunion was a harbinger of the future in American politics. Organized Blue-Gray fraternalism (gatherings of Union and Confederate veterans) began as early as 1874. Grant continued to use military force sparingly and in 1875 refused a desperate request from Mississippi's governor for troops to quell racial and political terrorism there.

Grant made a series of poor appointments that fueled public dissatisfaction with his administration. His secretary of war, his private secretary, and officials in the Treasury and Navy Departments were involved in bribery or tax-cheating scandals. Instead of exposing the corruption, Grant defended the culprits. In 1874,

Democrats recaptured the House of Representatives, signaling the end of the Radical Republican vision of Reconstruction.

General Amnesty

Democratic gains in Congress weakened legislative resolve on southern issues. Congress already lifted the political disabilities of the Fourteenth Amendment from many former Confederates. In 1872, it adopted an Amnesty Act, which pardoned most of the remaining rebels. In 1875, Congress passed a **Civil Rights Act**, partly in tribute to the recently deceased Charles Sumner, purporting to guarantee black people equal accommodations in public places, such as inns and theaters, but the bill was watered down and contained no enforcement provisions. (The Supreme Court later struck down this law; see page 523.)

Civil Rights Act of 1875: Designed to desegregate public places but lacked enforcement provisions.

Democrats regained control of four state governments before 1872 and eight by the late January 1876 (see Map 16.1). In the North, Democrats successfully stressed the failure and scandals of Reconstruction governments. Sectional reconciliation now seemed crucial for commerce. The nation was expanding westward, and the South was a new investment frontier.

The West, Race, and Reconstruction

As the Fourteenth Amendment and other enactments granted blacks the beginnings of citizenship, other non-whites faced continued persecution. Across the West, the federal government pursued a containment policy against Native Americans. In California, where white farmers and ranchers often forced Indians into captive labor, some civilians practiced "Indian hunting." By 1880, thirty years of violence left an estimated forty-five hundred California Indians dead at the hands of white settlers.

In Texas and the Southwest, expansionists still deemed Mexicans and other mixed-race Hispanics to be "lazy" and incapable of self-government. In California and the Far West, initially few whites objected to the Chinese who did the dangerous work of building railroads through the Rocky Mountains. But when the Chinese competed for urban, industrial jobs, conflict emerged. Anti-coolie clubs appeared in California in the 1870s, seeking laws against Chinese labor, inciting racism, and organizing vigilante attacks on Chinese workers and the factories that employed them. Western politicians sought white votes by pandering to prejudice, and in 1879 the new California constitution denied Chinese the vote.

Viewing America from coast to coast, the Civil War and Reconstruction years dismantled racial slavery and fostered a volatile new racial complexity, especially in the West. Some African Americans asserted that they were more like whites than "uncivilized" Indians, while others, like the Creek freedmen of Indian Territory, sought an Indian identity. In Texas, whites, Indians, blacks, and Hispanics had mixed for decades, and by the 1870s forced reconsideration in law and custom of exactly who was white.

America was undergoing what one historian has called a reconstruction of the concept of race itself. The turbulence of the expanding West reinforced the new nationalism and the reconciliation of North and South based on a resurgent white supremacy.

Foreign Expansion

In 1867, new expansion pressures led Secretary of State William H. Seward to purchase Alaska from Russia (see Chapter 22). Opponents ridiculed Seward's $7.2 million venture, but Seward convinced congressmen of Alaska's economic potential, and other lawmakers favored the dawning of friendship with Russia.

The "Back to Africa" Movement

In the wake of the Civil War, and especially after the despairing end of Reconstruction, some African Americans sought to leave the South for the American West or North, but also to relocate to Africa. Liberia had been founded in the 1820s by the white-led American Colonization Society (ACS), an organization dedicated to relocating blacks "back" in Africa. Some eleven thousand African Americans had emigrated voluntarily to Liberia by 1860, with largely disastrous results. Many died of disease, and others felt disoriented in the strange new land and ultimately returned to the United States.

Reconstruction reinvigorated the emigration impulse, especially in cotton-growing districts where blacks had achieved political power before 1870 but were crushed by violence and intimidation in the following decade. When blacks felt confident in their future, the idea of leaving America fell quiet; but when threatened or under assault, whole black communities dreamed of a place where they could become an independent "race," a "people," or a "nation" as their appeals often announced. Often that dream, more imagined than realized, lay in West Africa.

Before the Civil War, most blacks had denounced the ACS for its racism and its hostility to their sense of American birthright. But letters of inquiry flooded into the organization's headquarters after 1875. Wherever blacks felt the reversal of the promise of emancipation the keenest, they formed local groups such as the Liberia Exodus Association of Pinesville, Florida, or the Liberian Exodus Arkansas Colony, and many others.

At emigration conventions, and especially in churches, blacks penned letters to the ACS asking for maps or any information about a new African homeland. Some local organizers would announce 80 or 100 recruits "widawake for Liberia," although such enthusiasm rarely converted into an Atlantic voyage. The impulse was genuine, however. "We wants to be a People," wrote the leader of a Mississippi emigration committee; "we can't be it heare and find that we ar compel to leve this Cuntry." Henry Adams, a former Louisiana slave, Union soldier, and itinerant emigration organizer, advocated Liberia, but also supported "Kansas fever" with both Biblical and natural rights arguments. "God ... has a place and a land for all his people," he wrote in 1879. "It is not that we think the soil climate or temperature" elsewhere is "more congenial to us—but it is the idea that pervades our breast 'that at last we will be free,' free from oppression, free from tyranny, free from bulldozing, murderous southern whites."

By the 1890s, Henry McNeal Turner, a freeborn former Georgia Reconstruction politician, and now Bishop of the African Methodist Episcopal Church, made three trips to Africa and vigorously campaigned through press and pulpit for blacks to "Christianize" and "civilize" Africa. Two shiploads of African Americans did sail to Liberia, although most returned disillusioned or ill. Turner's plan of "Africa for the Africans" was as much a religious vision as an emigration system, but like all such efforts then and since, it reflected the despair of racial conditions in America more than realities in Africa. The numbers do not tell the tale of the depth of the impulse in this link to the world: in 1879–1880, approximately twenty-five thousand southern blacks moved to Kansas, whereas from 1865 to 1900, just under four thousand emigrated to West Africa.

Departure of African American emigrants to Liberia aboard the Laurada, *Savannah, Georgia, March 1896. The large crowd bidding farewell to the much smaller group aboard the ship may indicate both the fascination and the ambivalence for this issue among blacks in the South. (Illustrated American Magazine, March 21, 1896).*

© Bettmann/Corbis

Also in 1867 the United States took control of the Midway Islands, a thousand miles northwest of Hawai'i. Through diplomacy, Seward and his successor, Hamilton Fish, resolved wartime grievances with Great Britain by arranging a financial settlement for damage done by the *Alabama* and other cruisers built in England and sold to the Confederacy. Sectional reconciliation in Reconstruction America would serve new ambitions for world commerce and expansion.

Judicial Retreat from Reconstruction

Meanwhile, the Supreme Court played its part in the northern retreat from Reconstruction. During the Civil War, the Court was cautious and inactive. Reaction to the *Dred Scott* decision (1857) was so vehement, and the Union's wartime emergency so great, that the Court had avoided interference with government actions. But that changed in 1866 when *Ex parte Milligan* reached the Court.

Lambdin P. Milligan of Indiana had plotted to free Confederate prisoners of war and overthrow state governments. Consequently, a military court sentenced Milligan, a civilian, to death. Milligan challenged the military tribunal's authority, claiming he was entitled to a civil trial. The Supreme Court declared that military trials were illegal when civil courts were open and functioning.

In the 1870s, the Court renewed its challenge to Congress's actions when it narrowed the meaning of the Fourteenth Amendment. The *Slaughter-House* cases (1873) began in 1869, when the Louisiana legislature granted one company a monopoly on livestock slaughtering in New Orleans. Rival butchers sued, and their attorney, former Supreme Court justice John A. Campbell, argued that Louisiana had violated the rights of some citizens in favor of others. The Fourteenth Amendment, Campbell contended, had brought individual rights under federal protection.

But in the *Slaughter-House* decision, the Supreme Court dealt a blow to the scope of the Fourteenth Amendment. It declared state citizenship and national citizenship separate. National citizenship involved only matters such as the right to travel freely from state to state, and only such narrow rights, held the Court, were protected by the Fourteenth Amendment.

Shrinking from a role as "perpetual censor" for civil rights, the Court's majority declared that the framers of the recent amendments had not intended to "destroy" the federal system, in which the states exercised "powers for domestic and local government, including the regulation of civil rights." Thus, the justices severely limited the amendment's potential for protecting the rights of black citizens—its original intent.

The next day, the Court decided *Bradwell v. Illinois,* a case in which Myra Bradwell, a female attorney, was denied the right to practice law in Illinois because she was a married woman, and hence not a free agent. Using the Fourteenth Amendment, Bradwell's attorneys contended that the state had unconstitutionally abridged her "privileges and immunities" as a citizen. The Supreme Court disagreed, declaring a woman's "paramount destiny … to fulfill the noble and benign offices of wife and mother."

In 1876, the Court further weakened the Reconstruction era amendments. In *U.S. v. Cruikshank,* the Court overruled the conviction under the 1870 Enforcement Act of Louisiana whites who had attacked a meeting of blacks and conspired to deprive them of their rights. The justices ruled that the Fourteenth Amendment did not give the federal government power to act against these whites. The duty of protecting citizens' equal rights, the Court said, "rests alone with the States." Such judicial conservatism blunted the revolutionary potential of the Civil War amendments.

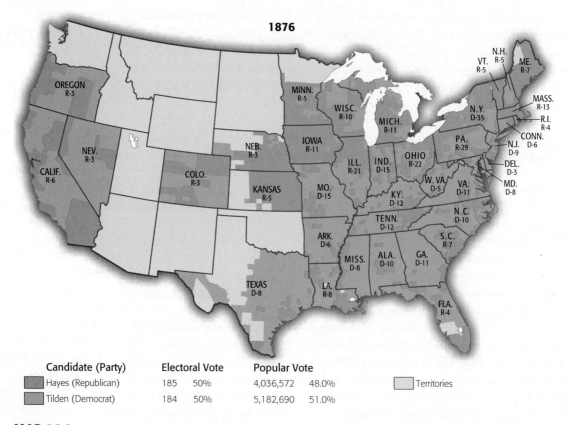

1876

Candidate (Party)	Electoral Vote		Popular Vote	
Hayes (Republican)	185	50%	4,036,572	48.0%
Tilden (Democrat)	184	50%	5,182,690	51.0%

Territories

MAP 16.2

Presidential Election of 1876 and the Compromise of 1877

In 1876, a combination of solid southern support and Democratic gains in the North gave Samuel Tilden the majority of popular votes, but Rutherford B. Hayes won the disputed election in the electoral college, after a deal satisfied Democratic wishes for an end to Reconstruction.
Source: Copyright © Cengage Learning

Disputed Election of 1876 and Compromise of 1877

As the 1876 presidential election approached, the nation was focused on economic issues, and the North lost interest in Reconstruction. Samuel J. Tilden, the Democratic governor of New York, ran strongly in the South and needed one electoral vote to beat Rutherford B. Hayes, the Republican nominee. Nineteen electoral votes from Louisiana, South Carolina, and Florida (the only southern states not yet under Democratic rule) were disputed; both Democrats and Republicans claimed to have won those states despite fraud committed by their opponents (see Map 16.2).

To resolve this unprecedented situation, Congress established a fifteen-member electoral commission, balanced between Democrats and Republicans. Because the Republicans held the majority in Congress, they prevailed, 8 to 7, on every attempt to count the returns, with commission members voting along strict party lines. Hayes would become president if Congress accepted the commission's findings.

But Democrats controlled the House and could filibuster to block action on the vote. Many citizens feared another civil war, as some southerners vowed, "Tilden or Fight!" The crisis ended when Democrats acquiesced in the election of Hayes

The Lost Cause

All major wars compel a struggle over their histori-cal memory. After the Civil War, white southerners and their northern allies constructed a "Lost Cause" tradition, a racially exclusive version of the war and Reconstruction which persists today.

For ex-Confederates, the Lost Cause served as a psy-chological response to the trauma of defeat. Over time, it also included reinterpretations of the war's causes, southern resistance to Reconstruction, doctrines of white supremacy, and a mythic popular culture in the North and South. Lost Cause advocates—from officers to soldiers to women leading memorial associations—argued that the war was never about slavery, that the Confederates lost due to Yankee numbers and resources, and that southern and northern sacrifice should be equally honored. In the industrial, multiethnic America of the emerging twentieth century, an Old South of benevolent masters and faithful slaves, of Robert E. Lee as America's truest Christian soldier, provided a sentimentalized road to reunion.

By the 1890s, elite southern white women—among them the United Daughters of the Confederacy—built monuments, lobbied congressmen, delivered lectures, ran contests for schoolchildren, and strove to control the content of history textbooks, to exalt the South. Above all, Lost Causers advocated what one historian has called a "victory narrative" of the nation's triumph over Reconstruction's racial revolution and constitutional transformations. In his 1881 memoir, Jefferson Davis declared: "Well may we rejoice in the regained possession of self-government.... This is the great victory... a total non-interference by the Federal government in the domestic affairs of the States."

These stories endure in Civil War memorabilia, such as the epic *Gone with the Wind*, the 2003 film *Gods and Generals*, and uses of the Confederate flag to oppose civil rights. And the Confederate state rights tradition is employed today by states and advocacy groups to resist federal stimulus money and national healthcare reform.

based on a "deal" between Hayes's supporters and southerners who wanted fed-eral aid to railroads, internal improvements, and removal of troops from southern states. Northern and southern Democrats decided not to contest the election of a Republican who would not continue Reconstruction.

Southern Democrats rejoiced, but African Americans grieved over the betrayal of their hopes for equality. In a Fourth of July speech in Washington, D.C., in 1875, Frederick Douglass reflected on fifteen years of unparalleled change for his people and worried about the hold of white supremacy on America's historical memory: "If war among the whites brought peace and liberty to the blacks, what will peace among the whites bring?"

Summary

Reconstruction left a contradictory record. It was an era of tragic aspirations and failures but also of unprecedented legal, political, and social change. The Union victory brought increased federal power, stronger nationalism, sweeping federal intervention in the southern states, and landmark Constitutional amendments. But northern commitment to make lasting changes eroded, leaving the revolution unfin-ished. The promise for new lives and liberties among the freedpeople had eroded if not died.

The North embraced emancipation, black suffrage, and constitutional alterations strengthening the central government primarily to defeat the rebellion. As wartime pressures declined, Americans, especially northerners, retreated from Reconstruction. The people and the courts maintained a preference for state authority and distrusted federal power. Free labor ideology stressed respect for property and individual self-reliance. Racism transformed into Klan terror and theories of black degeneration.

New challenges gradually overwhelmed the aims of Reconstruction. Industrialization promised prosperity but also wrought increased exploitation of labor. Moreover, industry increased the nation's power and laid the foundation for an enlarged American role in international affairs. In the wake of the Civil War, Americans faced two profound tasks—healing and dispensing justice. Making sectional reunion compatible with black freedom and equality overwhelmed American politics, and the nation faced this ongoing dilemma more than a century later.

Chapter Review

Wartime Reconstruction

Which two political acts recognized the centrality of slavery to the war?

Passage of the Thirteenth Amendment and establishment of the Freedmen's Bureau in early 1865 sent a clear signal that slavery was a major cause for the Civil War. The Thirteenth Amendment first abolished slavery ("involuntary servitude") and second gave Congress the power to enforce it. Then, a few months later in March, Congress established the Bureau of Refugees, Freedmen and Abandoned Lands, known as the Freedmen's Bureau, to help former slaves. During its four years as a federal agency, it supplied food and medical services, built thousands of schools and colleges, negotiated job contracts between former slaves and masters, and managed confiscated lands.

The Meanings of Freedom

How did blacks exert their newfound freedom?

With emancipation, former slaves sought to reunite families broken apart through slave sales. Community also became important, as they built their own churches that ultimately served to unify racial ties. Seeking greater control over their work lives, African Americans wanted fairer employers and hoped to own land; when that was not possible, they rented land from former masters under the sharecropping system, in which they paid for supplies and rent by giving owners' half their crops on average. Former slaves also embraced the education that had been denied them under slavery and started schools, colleges, and universities throughout the South or attended those launched by the Freedmen's Bureau.

Johnson's Reconstruction Plan

What was Johnson's vision for Reconstruction?

Johnson's approach to Reconstruction could be summed up in a single quote: "The Constitution as it is, and the Union as it was." As president, he controlled Reconstruction policy through 1865, pardoning former Confederates and reestablishing state governments in the South. Despising the planter class, he initially insisted that ex-Confederates with property worth more than $20,000 apply directly to him for pardons. Gradually, Johnson pardoned planters, too, which restored the former elite to power, possibly because he wanted to block Radical Republicans from implementing extensive and racial political changes in the South. Deeply racist, Johnson remained silent when southern states implemented black codes to restrict former slaves' freedom by requiring them to carry passes, obey curfew laws, and live in housing provided by a landowner. Nonetheless, after just eight months, Johnson declared Reconstruction was completed.

The Congressional Reconstruction Plan

What made Radical Reconstruction different from Johnson's plan?

Radical Republicans in Congress were upset at Johnson's moderate approach, which seemed to hold no one responsible for the war and reestablished racial hierarchies and the southern elite. Initially a minority, the Radicals' popularity grew as Johnson increasingly dug in his heels. Radicals wanted to democratize the South through black suffrage, civil rights, and land confiscation and redistribution. They secured passage of the Fourteenth Amendment, which conferred citizenship on "all persons born or naturalized in the United States," and granted voting rights to males. They also passed four strident Reconstruction acts with strict and detailed plans for readmitting southern states to the Union. They barred ex-Confederates from voting until freedmen could and outlined the rules for voter registration boards and the adoption of state constitutions. Unpopular, land redistribution never materialized, but in 1869, Radicals pushed through their final measure, the Fifteenth Amendment, which prohibited states from denying the vote based on "race, color, or previous condition of servitude."

Reconstruction Politics and Economy in the South

How did black voters in the early days of Reconstruction transform the South?

With a large black voter turnout and prominent confederates barred from the polls and political positions, a new southern variant on the Republican Party came to power during the 1868 to 1870 state constitutional conventions. Their constitutions were highly democratic, eliminating property qualifications for voting and political office, shifting some appointed offices to elected ones, and establishing public schools. They also gave women greater rights in terms of property-holding and divorce. Blacks became state legislators for the first time in 1868. Angry whites charged they were being ruled by Negroes, and some resorted to violent resistance. In truth, while blacks did play a greater role in government, they remained a minority.

Retreat from Reconstruction

What led the North to lose interest in reconstructing the South?

During the 1870s, northerners faced economic and social transformations at home and became increasingly disillusioned with Reconstruction. Some northerners thought federal expansion had cut too far into states' rights. Second, while immigration and industrialization made northern economies boom from 1865 to 1873, it also widened the gap between the richest and the poorest and created a powerful new class of industrialists. When the Panic of 1873 brought hard times and job losses, interest in Reconstruction faded beside regional economic concerns. The Supreme Court also played a role, challenging congressional Reconstruction in several decisions. The Court ultimately narrowed the meaning of the Fourteenth Amendment by declaring state and national citizenship as separate issues and limited the amendment's ability to safeguard black citizens, as it was intended to do.

Suggestions for Further Reading

David W. Blight, *Race and Reunion: The Civil War in American Memory* (2001)

W. E. B. Du Bois, *Black Reconstruction in America* (1935)

Eric Foner, *Reconstruction: America's Unfinished Revolution, 1863–1877* (1988)

William Gillette, *Retreat from Reconstruction, 1869–1879* (1980)

Moon-Ho Jung, *Coolies and Cane: Race, Labor, and Sugar in the Age of Emancipation* (2006)

Gerald Jaynes, *Branches Without Roots: The Genesis of the Black Working Class in the American South, 1862–1882* (1986)

Michael Perman, *The Road to Redemption* (1984)

George Rable, *But There Was No Peace* (1984)

Heather Richardson, *West from Appomattox: The Reconstruction of America after the Civil War* (2007)

Elliot West, "Reconstructing Race," *Western Historical Quarterly* (Spring 2003)

Go to the CourseMate website for primary source links, study tools, and review materials for this chapter.
www.cengagebrain.com

17

The Development of the West

In 1893, historian Frederick Jackson Turner delivered a stunning lecture at the World's Columbian Exposition in Chicago that shaped views of the American West for generations. Titled "The Significance of the Frontier in American History," the paper argued that "free land, its continuous recession, and the advancement of American settlement westward" created a distinctive spirit of democracy and egalitarianism. The settlement of several frontier Wests from colonial times onward explained American progress and character.

Across the street, the folk character Buffalo Bill Cody dramatized the conquest of frontiers and the creation of an American identity in a staged extravaganza called "The Wild West." Whereas Turner described a peaceful settlement of empty western land, Cody portrayed violent conquest of territory occupied by savage Indians. Turner's heroes were farmers who tamed the wilderness with plows. Buffalo Bill's heroes were scouts who braved danger and vanquished Indians with firepower. Turner used log cabins, wagon trains, and wheat fields to argue that the frontier fashioned a new, progressive people. Cody depicted the West as a place of brutal aggression and heroic victory.

The American West inspired material progress, and it witnessed the domination of one group over another and over the environment. Turner and Cody believed that by the 1890s, the frontier era had ended. Over time, Turner's theory was abandoned (even by Turner himself) as simplistic, and Buffalo Bill was relegated to the gallery of rogues and showmen. Yet both Wests persisted in the romance of American history, even while they obscured the complex story of western development in the late nineteenth century.

Much of the West was not empty, and its inhabitants utilized resources differently. On the Plains, for example, the Pawnees planted crops in the spring, left their fields in summer to hunt buffalo, then returned for harvesting. They sometimes battled with Cheyennes and Arapahos over access to hunting grounds and crops. In what now is the American Southwest, natives shared the land and sometimes integrated with Hispanic people,

Chapter Outline

who were descendants of Spanish colonists. As white immigrants built communities in the West in the late nineteenth century, they exploited the environment for profit more extensively than did Indians. They excavated the earth for minerals, felled forests for construction, built railroads, dammed rivers, and plowed soil with machines. Their goal included buying and selling in regional, national, and international markets. As they transformed the landscape, their market economies transformed the nation.

The West by 1870 spanned from the Mississippi River to the Pacific Ocean and consisted of several regions of varied economic potential. Abundant rainfall along the northern Pacific coast fed forests. Farther south, California's woodlands and grasslands provided fertile valleys for vegetables and oranges. Eastward, from the Cascades and the Sierra Nevada to the Rocky Mountains, gold, silver, and other minerals lay buried. East of the Rockies, the Great Plains divided into a semiarid western side of few trees and buffalo grass and an eastern sector of ample rainfall and tall grasses that could support grain crops and livestock.

Before contact with whites, Indian peoples moved around the region, warring, trading, and negotiating as they searched for food and shelter. In the Southwest, Hispanics moved between Mexican and American territory, establishing towns, farms, and ranches. After the Civil War, white Americans overwhelmed the native and Hispanic peoples, swelling from 7 million to nearly 17 million whites between 1870 and 1890.

The West's abundance of exploitable land and raw materials made white Americans believe that anyone persistent enough could succeed. This confidence rested on a belief that white people were superior and asserted itself at the expense of native people and the environment.

By 1890 farms, ranches, mines, towns, and cities existed throughout present-day continental United States, but vast stretches remained unsettled. Although symbolically important to Turner, the fading frontier had little impact on behavior. Pioneers who failed in one locale tried again elsewhere. A surplus of seemingly uninhabited land gave Americans a feeling that second chances abounded. This belief, more than Turner's theory of frontier democracy or Cody's heroic reenactments left a deep imprint on the American character.

As you read this chapter, keep the following questions in mind:

* **How did the interaction between people and the environment shape the physical landscape of the West and the lives of the region's inhabitants?**

* **How did the U.S. government's relations with Native Americans change over time throughout the late nineteenth century?**

* **Describe the societal and technological changes that revolutionized the lives of farmers and ranchers on the Great Plains.**

The Ranching Frontier
The Open Range | Barbed Wire | Ranching as Big Business

LEGACY FOR A PEOPLE AND A NATION *National Parks*

SUMMARY

Chronology

1862	Homestead Act grants free land to citizens who live on and improve the land
	Morrill Land Grant Act gives states public land to sell in order to finance agricultural and industrial colleges
1864	Chivington's militia massacres Black Kettle's Cheyennes at Sand Creek
1869	First transcontinental railroad completed
1872	Yellowstone becomes first national park
1876	Lakotas and Cheyennes ambush Custer's federal troops at Little Big Horn, Montana
1877	Nez Percé Indians under Young Joseph surrender to U.S. troops
1878	Timber and Stone Act allows citizens to buy timberland cheaply but also enables large companies to acquire huge tracts of forest land
1879	Carlisle School for Indians established in Pennsylvania

1881–82	Chinese Exclusion Acts prohibit Chinese immigration to the United States
1883	National time zones established
1884	U.S. Supreme Court first denies Indians as wards under government protection
1887	Dawes Severalty Act ends communal ownership of Indian lands and grants land allotments to individual native families
1887–88	Devastating winter on Plains destroys countless livestock and forces farmers into economic hardship
1890	Final suppression of Plains Indians by U.S. Army at Wounded Knee
	Census Bureau announces closing of the frontier
	Yosemite National Park established
1892	Muir helps found Sierra Club
1902	Newlands Reclamation Act passed

The Economic Activities of Native Peoples

Native Americans settled the West long before other Americans migrated there; Indians shaped the environment for centuries. Nevertheless, several factors weakened almost all native economic systems in the late nineteenth century.

What factors undermined Native Americans' subsistence in the late nineteenth century?

Subsistence Cultures

Western Indian communities varied. Some natives inhabited permanent settlements; others, temporary camps. Most Indians were participants and recipients in a flow of goods, culture, language, and disease carried by migrating bands. Indian economies were based in differing degrees on four activities: crop growing; livestock raising; hunting, fishing, and gathering; and trading and raiding. Corn was the most common crop; sheep and horses, acquired from Spanish colonizers and other Indians, were the livestock; and buffalo (American bison) were the primary prey of hunts. Indians raided one another for food, tools, and horses. When a buffalo hunt failed, they subsisted on crops and hunted buffalo, or stole food and horses when crops failed.

For Indians on the Great Plains, life focused on the buffalo. They cooked and preserved buffalo meat; fashioned hides into clothing, moccasins, and blankets; used sinew for thread and bowstrings; and carved tools from bones and horns. Buffalo were so valuable that Pawnees and Lakotas fought over access to herds. **Plains Indians** periodically set fire to tall-grass prairies, which burned away dead plants, facilitating growth of new grass so horses could feed all summer.

Plains Indians: Diverse Native American societies inhabiting the region from the Dakotas to Texas.

In the Southwest, Indians led varying lifestyles, depending on the environment. For example, in southeastern Arizona and northwestern Mexico, some of the O'odham (in English, "The People") grew irrigated crops in the few river valleys while those who inhabited the mountainous and desert regions followed a hunter-gatherer existence. The Navaho (or Dine', also meaning "The People") were herders, whose sheep, goats, and horses provided status and security.

What buffalo were to Plains Indians and sheep were to southwestern Indians, salmon were to northwestern Indians. Before the mid-nineteenth century, the Columbia River and its tributaries supported the densest Indian population To harvest fish, the Clatsops, Klamath, and S'Klallams developed technologies of stream diversion, platform construction, and special baskets. Like other natives, they traded for horses, buffalo robes, beads, cloth, and knives.

Slaughter of Buffalo   On the Plains and parts of the Southwest, native worlds gradually dissolved after 1850, when whites competed with Indians for natural resources. Perceiving buffalo and Indians as hindrances, whites endeavored to eliminate both. The U.S. Army refused to enforce treaties that reserved hunting grounds for exclusive Indian use, so railroads sponsored hunts in which eastern sportsmen shot at buffalo from slow-moving trains. Unbeknownst to Indians and whites, however, a combination of circumstances doomed the buffalo before the slaughter of the late 1800s. Natives depleted herds by increasing their kills to trade hides with whites and other Indians. Also, in the dry years of the 1840s and 1850s, Indians relocated to river basins, pushing buffalo out of nourishing grazing territory to face starvation. Whites, too, settled in basin areas, further forcing buffalo away. At the same time, lethal animal diseases, such as anthrax and brucellosis, brought by white-owned livestock, decimated buffalo already weakened by malnutrition and drought. Increasing numbers of horses, oxen, and sheep, owned by white newcomers and some Indians, devoured grasses that buffalo needed. The mass killing only struck the final blow. By the 1880s, a few hundred of the 25 million buffalo estimated on the Plains in 1820 remained.

Decline of Salmon   In the Northwest, salmon suffered a similar fate. White commercial fishermen and canneries moved into the Columbia and Willamette River valleys during the 1860s and 1870s, and by the 1880s they had greatly diminished salmon runs. By the early 1900s, construction of dams on the river and its tributaries further impeded salmon's reproduction. The U.S. government protected Indian fishing rights, and hatcheries restored some salmon supplies, but dams built to provide power, combined with overfishing and pollution, diminished salmon stocks.

Denver Art Museum

Using buffalo hides to fashion garments, Indians often exhibited artistic skills in decorating their apparel. This Ute Indian hide dress shows symbolic as well as aesthetic representations.

The Transformation of Native Cultures

Buffalo slaughter and salmon reduction undermined Indian subsistence, but demographic changes also contributed. Throughout the nineteenth century, white migrants were overwhelmingly young, single males in their twenties and thirties, the age when they were most prone to violent behavior. In 1870, white men outnumbered white women by three

How did the U.S. government's reservation policy make way for the market economy in the West?

to two in California, two to one in Colorado, and two to one in Dakota Territory. By 1900, preponderances of men remained throughout these places. Indians were most likely to come into contact first with white traders, trappers, soldiers, prospectors, and cowboys—almost all of whom owned guns and would use them on animals and humans who got in their way.

Western Men   Moreover, these men subscribed to prevailing attitudes that Indians were primitive, lazy, and devious. Such contempt made exploiting and killing natives easier, further justified by claims of threats to life and property. When Indians raided white settlements, they sometimes mutilated bodies, burned buildings, and kidnapped women, acts that were embellished in campfire stories and popular fiction to portray Indians as savages. In saloons and cabins, men boasted about fighting Indians and showed off scalps and other body parts from victims.

Indian warriors, too, were young, armed, and prone to violence. Valuing bravery, they boasted of fighting white interlopers. But Indian communities contained excesses of women, the elderly, and children, making native bands less mobile and more vulnerable. They also were susceptible to bad habits of bachelor white society, copying their binges on cheap whiskey and prostitution. The syphilis and gonorrhea that Indian men contracted from Indian women infected by white men killed many and hindered reproduction, which their populations, already declining from smallpox and other white diseases, could not afford. Thus, the age and gender structure of the white frontier population, combined with racist contempt, further threatened western Indians' existence.

Government Policy and Treaties   Government policy reinforced efforts to remove Indians. North American natives were organized not into tribes, as whites believed, but into bands, confederacies, and villages. Two hundred languages and dialects separated these groups, making it difficult for Indians to unite against white invaders. Although a language group could be defined as a tribe, separate bands and clans had different leaders, and seldom did a chief hold widespread power. Moreover, bands often spent more time battling among themselves than with white settlers.

Nevertheless, the U.S. government needed some way of categorizing Indians. After 1795, American officials considered Indian tribes as nations with which they could make treaties ensuring peace and land boundaries. This was a faulty assumption because chiefs who agreed to a treaty did not always speak for the whole band and the group might not abide by it. Moreover, whites seldom accepted treaties as guarantees of Indians' land rights. On the Plains, whites settled wherever they wished, often commandeering choice farmland. In the Northwest, whites considered treaties protecting Indians' fishing rights on the Columbia River to be nuisances and ousted Indians from the best locations.

Reservation Policy   Prior to the 1880s, the federal government tried to force western Indians onto reservations, where they might be "civilized." Reservations usually consisted of areas in a group's previous territory that were least desirable to whites. The government promised protection from white encroachment, along with food, clothing, and other necessities.

Reservation policy helped make way for the market economy. In the early years, trade had benefited Indians and whites equally. Indians acquired clothing, guns, and horses in return for furs, jewelry, and, sometimes, military assistance against other Indians. Over time, Indians became more dependent, and whites increasingly dictated trade. For example, white traders persuaded Navajo weavers in the Southwest to produce heavy rugs for eastern customers and to change designs and colors to boost sales. Meanwhile, Navajos raised fewer crops and were forced to buy food. Soon they were selling land and labor to whites, and their dependency made it easier to force them onto reservations.

Indians had no say over their affairs on reservations. Supreme Court decisions in 1884 and 1886 defined them as wards (like helpless children under government protection) and denied them U.S. citizenship. Thus, they were unprotected by the Fourteenth and Fifteenth Amendments, which extended citizenship to African Americans. Second, pressure from white farmers, miners, and herders who sought Indian lands made it difficult for the government to preserve reservations intact. Third, the government ignored native history, even combining on one reservation enemy bands. Rather than serving as civilizing communities, reservations weakened Indian culture.

Native Resistance

Not all Indians succumbed to market forces and reservation restrictions. Apaches in the Southwest battled whites even after being forced onto reservations. Pawnees in the Midwest resisted disadvantageous deals from white traders. In the Northwest, Nez Percé Indians escaped reservations by fleeing to Canada in 1877. They eluded U.S. troops until, 1,800 miles later in Montana, their leader, Young Joseph, recognized they could not succeed and ended the flight. Sent to a reservation, Joseph unsuccessfully petitioned the government to return his peoples' ancestral lands.

Link to an explanation of the Pima Indian's calendar sticks.

Whites responded to western Indian defiance militarily. In 1860, Navajos reacted by raiding Fort Defiance in Arizona Territory. The army then attacked and starved the Navajo into submission, and in 1863–1864 forced them on a "Long Walk" from their homelands to a reservation at Bosque Redondo in New Mexico. In the Sand Creek region of Colorado in 1864, a militia commanded by Methodist minister John Chivington attacked Cheyennes led by Black Kettle, killing almost every Indian. In 1879, four thousand U.S. soldiers forced surrender from Utes who were resisting further land concessions.

The most publicized battle occurred in June 1876, when 2,500 Lakotas and Cheyennes led by Chiefs Rain-in-the-Face, Sitting Bull, and Crazy Horse annihilated 256 government troops led by the rash Colonel George A. Custer near the Little Big Horn River in southern Montana. Although Indians demonstrated military skill, supply shortages and relentless pursuit by U.S. soldiers eventually overwhelmed armed Indian resistance. Native Americans were not so much conquered as they were harassed and starved into submission.

Reform of Indian Policy

In the 1870s and 1880s, reformers and government officials sought more purposely to "civilize" natives through landholding and education. This meant outlawing customs deemed "savage and pressuring natives to adopt American values of ambition, thrift, and materialism." In doing so, the United States copied other nation's imperialist policies, such as France, which banned native religious ceremonies in its Pacific island colonies.

Others argued for sympathetic—and sometimes patronizing—treatment. Reform treatises, such as George Manypenny's *Our Indian Wards* (1880) and Helen Hunt Jackson's *A Century of Dishonor* (1881), aroused the American conscience.

In the United States, the most active Indian reform organizations were the Women's National Indian Association (WNIA) and the Indian Rights Association (IRA). The WNIA sought to use women's domestic skills and compassion to help the needy and urged gradual assimilation of Indians. The more influential IRA, which had few Native American members, advocated citizenship and landholding by individual Indians. Most white reformers believed Indians were culturally inferior and could succeed economically only by embracing middle-class values of diligence and education.

Reformers deplored Indians' sexual division of labor. Native women seemed to do all the work—tending crops, raising children, cooking, curing hides, making tools and clothes—while being servile to men, who hunted but were otherwise idle. WNIA and IRA wanted Indian men to bear more responsibilities, treat Indian women more respectfully, and resemble male heads of white middle-class households. But when Indian men and women adopted this model of white society, Indian women lost the economic independence and power over daily life they once had.

Zitkala-Sa

Indians like Zitkala-Sa (Red Bird) used white-controlled education to their advantage. Born on South Dakota's Pine Ridge reservation in 1876, at age twelve this Yankton Sioux girl attended an Indiana boarding school and later Earlham College and the Boston Conservatory of Music. An accomplished orator and violinist, her major contribution was her writing on behalf of her people's needs and advocating cultural preservation. In 1901, Zitkala-Sa published *Old Indian Legends,* translating Sioux oral tradition into stories. Zitkala-Sa married a mixed-race army captain who had taken the name Ray Bonnin and became known as Gertrude Bonnin. Subsequently, she was elected the first full-blooded Indian secretary of the Society of American Indians (see page 553).

Dawes Severalty Act

Dawes Severalty Act: U.S. law designed to "civilize" Indians by dividing up and distributing communal tribal lands to individuals.

In 1887, Congress reversed its reservation policy and passed the **Dawes Severalty Act**. It authorized dissolution of community-owned Indian property and granted land to individual Indian families. The government held that land in trust for twenty-five years, so families could not sell their allotments. The law awarded citizenship to those accepting allotments (an act of Congress in 1906 delayed citizenship for those Indians who had not yet taken their allotment). It also entitled the government to sell unallocated land to whites.

Indian policy, under the Interior Department, now embraced two main tactics for assimilating Indians into white American culture. First, under the Dawes Act, the government distributed reservation land to individual families believing that private property would integrate Indians into the larger society as productive citizens. Second, officials believed that Indians would abandon their "barbaric" habits faster if their children were educated in boarding schools.

The Dawes Act represented a Euro-American and Christian worldview that a society of families headed by men was ideal. Government agents, reformers, and educators used schools to create a patriotic, industrious citizenry. Following Virginia's Hampton Institute, founded in 1869 to educate newly freed slaves,

Attempts to Make Indians Look and Act Like "Americans"

Government officials believed that they could "civilize" Indian children in boarding schools by not only educating them to act like white people but also to make them look like white people. Thus the boys in the photograph on the left were given baseball uniforms and the girl on the right was made to wear a dress and carry a purse and umbrella, all of which were foreign to native people. These images convey information about how Indians were treated, but they also suggest attitudes of the photographer and the artist who made the images. What messages about "civilizing" natives did the person who photographed the baseball team and the artist who drew the picture of the girl reuniting with her people want the viewer to receive?

In an attempt to inculcate "American" customs into its native students, the Fort Spokane Indian School in Spokane, Washington, created a baseball team for the young men who boarded there.

In an 1884 edition, Frank Leslie's Weekly, one of the most popular illustrated news and fiction publications of the late nineteenth century and early twentieth, depicted an "Americanized" Indian girl dressed as a proper young lady returning from the Carlisle boarding to school to visit her home on Pine Ridge Agency in South Dakota.

teachers established the Carlisle School in Pennsylvania in 1879 as the flagship of the government's Indian school system. Boarding schools imposed white-defined sex roles: boys learned farming and carpentry, and girls learned sewing, cleaning, and cooking.

Ghost Dance

With resistance suppressed, Lakotas and others turned to the **Ghost Dance** as a spiritual means of preserving native culture. The Ghost Dance involved movement in a circle until dancers reached a trancelike state and envisioned a day when buffalo would return and all elements of white society would disappear.

Ghost Dancers forswore violence, but as the religion spread government agents worried about possible of renewed Indian uprisings. Charging that the cult was anti-Christian, they arrested Ghost Dancers. Late in 1890, the government sent Custer's old regiment, the Seventh Cavalry, to detain Lakotas moving toward Pine Ridge, South Dakota. Although the Indians were starving, the army assumed they were armed for revolt. Overtaking them at a creek called **Wounded Knee**, the troops massacred about three hundred men, women, and children.

The Losing of the West

Indian wars and the Dawes Act effectively accomplished what whites wanted and Indians feared: it reduced native control over land. Between 1887 and the 1930s, native landholdings dwindled from 138 million acres to 52 million. Land-grabbing whites were particularly cruel to the Ojibwas of the northern plains. In 1906, Senator Moses E. Clapp of Minnesota attached to an Indian appropriations bill a rider declaring that mixed-blood adults on the White Earth reservation were "competent" (meaning educated in white ways) enough to sell their land without the Dawes Act's twenty-five-year waiting period. When the bill became law, speculators duped many Ojibwas into signing away their land for counterfeit money and worthless merchandise. The Ojibwas lost more than half their original holdings, and economic ruin overtook them.

Ultimately, political and ecological crises overwhelmed most western Indian groups. Buffalo extinction, enemy raids, and disease, along with military campaigns, hobbled subsistence culture until Native Americans could only yield their lands to market-oriented whites. Believing themselves superior, whites determined to transform Indians by teaching about private property and American ideals, and eradicating their "backward" languages, lifestyles, and religions. Indians tried to retain their culture but by century's end, they lost control of their land and faced increasing pressure to shed their group identity.

Life on the Natural Resource Frontier

Unlike Indians, who used natural resources for subsistence needs and small-scale trading, whites who migrated to the West and Great Plains saw the vast territory as untapped sources of wealth (see Map 17.1). Extracting its resources advanced settlement, created new markets at home and abroad, and fueled revolutions in transportation, agriculture, and industry across the United States in the late nineteenth century. This same extraction of nature's wealth led to environmental wastefulness and fed racial and sexual oppression.

Ghost Dance: Ritual where Sioux dancers moved in a circle, accelerating until they reached a trancelike state and experienced visions of the future where white society would vanish from Indian lands.

Wounded Knee: South Dakota site of a bloody clash between Sioux Indians and whites. Within minutes, white troops—mistakenly assuming the starving Indians were armed for revolt—slaughtered three hundred Indians including seven infants.

What sparked the rise of the conservation movement?

Mining and Lumbering In the mid-1800s, the mining frontier drew thousands of people to Nevada, Idaho, Montana, Utah, and Colorado. California's gold rush helped populate a thriving state by 1850 and furnished many of the miners traveling to nearby states. Others followed traditional routes from the East to the West.

Prospectors climbed mountains and trekked across deserts seeking precious metals. They shot game for food and financed their explorations by convincing merchants to advance credit for equipment in return for a share of the as-yet-undiscovered lode. Unlucky prospectors whose credit ran out took jobs and saved up for another search.

MAP 17.1

The Development and Natural Resources of the West

By 1890, mining, lumbering, and cattle ranching had penetrated many areas west of the Mississippi River, and railroad construction had linked together the western economy. These activities, along with the spread of mechanized agriculture, altered both the economy and the people who were involved in them.

Source: Copyright © Cengage Learning

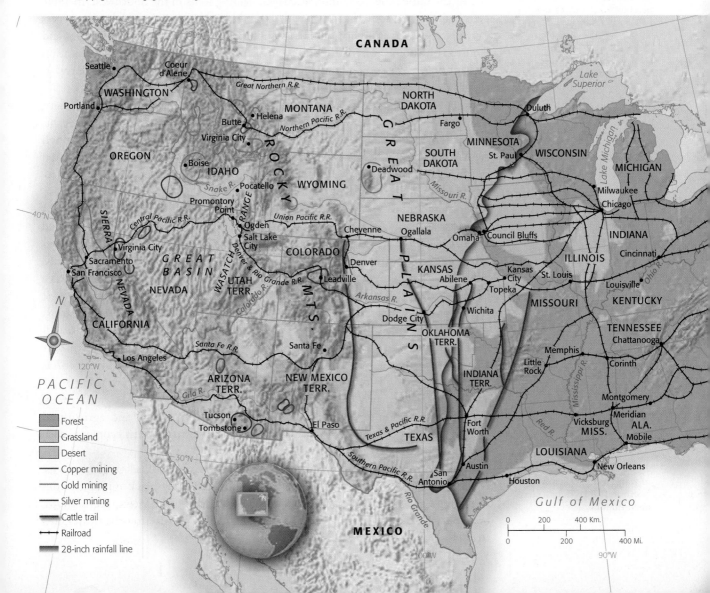

Digging up and transporting minerals was expensive, so prospectors who made discoveries sold their claims to large mining syndicates, such as the Anaconda Copper Company. Financed by eastern capital, these companies brought in engineers, heavy machinery, railroad lines, and work crews, making western mining as corporate as eastern manufacturing. Although discoveries of gold and silver sparked national publicity, mining companies usually exploited equally lucrative lead, zinc, tin, quartz, and copper.

Unlike mining, cutting trees for lumber for construction and heating materials required vast tracts of forest land to be profitable. Because tree supplies in the upper Midwest and South were depleted, lumber corporations moved into northwestern forests. The 1878 Timber and Stone Act sought to stimulate settlement in California, Nevada, Oregon, and Washington by allowing private citizens to buy inexpensive 160-acre plots. Lumber companies grabbed millions of acres by hiring seamen from waterfront boarding houses to register claims to timberland and then transfer them to the companies. By 1900, private citizens had bought over 3.5 million acres, but most of it belonged to corporations.

At the same time, oil companies began drilling wells in the Southwest. In 1900, petroleum came from the Appalachians and the Midwest, but rich oil reserves were discovered in southern California and eastern Texas, turning Los Angeles and Houston into boom cities. Although oil and kerosene were used mostly for lubrication and lighting, oil discovered in the Southwest later became a vital new fuel source.

Complex Communities

As the West developed, it became a multiracial society, including Native Americans, white migrants, Mexicans, African Americans, and Asians. A crescent of territory from western Texas through New Mexico and Arizona to northern California (including Mexico), supported ranchers and sheepherders, descendants of early Spanish settlers. In New Mexico, Spaniards mixed with Indians to form a *mestizo* population. Across the Southwest, Mexican immigrants moved into American territory to find work. Some returned to Mexico seasonally. Although the Treaty of Guadalupe Hidalgo (1848) guaranteed property rights to Hispanics, "Anglo" (the Mexican name for a white American) miners, speculators, and railroads used fraud to steal Hispanic landholdings. Consequently, many Mexicanos moved to cities such as San Antonio and Tucson and became wage laborers.

Before the Chinese Exclusion Act of 1882 prohibited them from immigrating, some 200,000 Chinese—mostly young, single males—entered the United States, building communities in California, Oregon, and Washington. Many came with five-year labor contracts for railroad construction; others labored in the fields. By the 1870s, Chinese composed half of California's agricultural work force, often working in citrus groves. In cities such as San Francisco, they labored in textile and cigar factories.

Japanese and European immigrants also worked in mining and agricultural communities. The region consequently developed its own migrant economy, with workers relocating to take short-term jobs.

exodusters: Freedmen who migrated from the South to the North and Midwest for better opportunities.

Many African Americans were "**exodusters**" who built all-black western towns. Nicodemus, Kansas, for example, was founded in 1877 by black migrants from Lexington, Kentucky. Despite challenges, the town developed newspapers, shops, churches, a hotel, and a bank. It declined when businesses left after the town failed to obtain railroad connections.

The major exodus occurred in 1879, when some six thousand blacks, including former slaves, moved from the South to Kansas, aided by the Kansas Freedmen's Relief Association. Other migrants, encouraged by editors and land speculators, went to Oklahoma Territory, where they founded thirty-two all-black communities in the 1890s and early 1900s.

Western Women

Link to *Letters of a Woman Homesteader* by Elinore Stewart.

Although unmarried men dominated the frontier, many white women similarly headed west to find fortune. In mining areas, they usually accompanied a husband or father, however. Using their labor as a resource, women earned money by cooking and laundering, and sometimes as sex workers in houses of prostitution. In the Northwest, they worked in canneries, cleaning and salting fish.

White women helped bolster family and community life as members of the home mission movement. They broke from traditional male-dominated Protestant missions. Using the slogan "Woman's work for women," they established missionary societies aiding women—unmarried mothers, Mormons, Indians, and Chinese—who they believed had fallen prey to men or who had not yet adopted Christian virtue.

Significance of Race

For white settlers, race became an important means to control labor and social relations. They classified people into five races: Caucasians (themselves), Indians, Mexicans (both Mexican Americans, who had originally inhabited western lands, and Mexican immigrants), "Mongolians" (a term applied to Chinese), and "Negroes." With these categories, whites imposed racial distinctions on people who, with the possible exception of African Americans, never before considered themselves a "race," and then judged them permanently inferior. In 1878, for example, a federal judge in California ruled that Chinese could not become U.S. citizens because they were not "white persons."

Racial minorities occupied the bottom of a two-tiered labor system and experienced prejudice as whites tried to reserve for themselves the West's riches. Whites dominated the top tier of managerial and skilled positions, while Irish, Chinese, Mexican, and African American laborers held unskilled positions. Anti-Chinese violence erupted during hard times. When the Union Pacific Railroad tried to replace white workers with lower-waged Chinese in Rock Springs, Wyoming, in 1885, whites burned down the Chinese part of town, killing twenty-eight. Mexicans, many of whom were the original landowners in California and elsewhere, saw their property claims ignored or stolen by whites.

Because so many white male migrants were single, intermarriage with Mexican and Indian women was common. Such unions were acceptable for white men, but not for white women, especially with Asian immigrants. Most miscegenation laws passed by western legislatures sought to prevent Chinese and Japanese men from marrying white women.

Conservation Movement

Questions about natural resources caught Americans between desire for progress and fear of spoiling nature. After the Civil War, people eager to protect the natural landscape organized a conservation movement. Sports hunters, concerned about loss of wildlife, opposed commercial hunting and lobbied state legislatures to pass hunting regulations. Artists and tourists in 1864 persuaded Congress to preserve

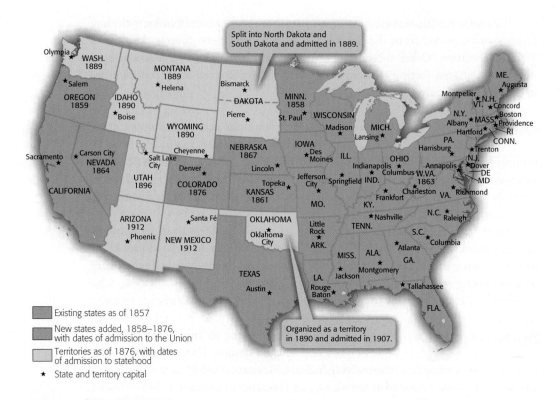

MAP 17.2

The United States, 1876–1912

A wave of admissions between 1889 and 1912 brought remaining territories to statehood and marked the final creation of new states until Alaska and Hawai'i were admitted in the 1950s.

Source: Copyright © Cengage Learning

the Yosemite Valley by granting it to California for public use. In 1872, Congress designated the Yellowstone River region in Wyoming as the first national park. And in 1891 conservationists, led by naturalist John Muir, pressured Congress to authorize President Benjamin Harrison to create forest reserves—public lands protected from private timber companies.

Link to "The Approach to the Valley," from John Muir's, *The Yosemite*.

Despite Muir's activism and efforts by the Sierra Club (which Muir helped found in 1892) and corporations supporting rational resource development, opposition was loudest in the West, where people remained eager to exploit nature. By prohibiting trespass in areas such as Yosemite and Yellowstone, conservation policy deprived Indians and white settlers of wildlife, water, and firewood previously available on federal lands.

Admission of New States

Development of mining and forest regions, along with farms and cities, brought western territories to the threshold of statehood (see Map 17.2). In 1889, Republicans seeking to solidify control of Congress passed an omnibus bill granting statehood to North Dakota, South Dakota, Washington, and Montana. Wyoming and Idaho, which allowed women to vote, were admitted the following year. Congress denied statehood to Utah until 1896, wanting assurances from the Mormons, a majority of the territory's population, that they would prohibit polygamy.

Western states' varied communities flavored American folk culture and fostered a "go-getter" optimism that distinguished the American spirit. The lawlessness of places such as Deadwood, in Dakota Territory, and Tombstone, in Arizona Territory, gave their region notoriety and romance. Legends arose about characters whose lives magnified the western experience, and promoters such as Buffalo Bill enhanced western folklore's appeal.

Western Folk Heroes   Arizona's mining towns, with their free-flowing cash and loose law enforcement, attracted gamblers, thieves, and opportunists who came symbolize the Wild West. Near Tombstone, the infamous Clanton family and their partner John Ringgold (Johnny Ringo) were smugglers and cattle rustlers. The Earp brothers—Wyatt, Jim, Morgan, Virgil, and Warren—and their friends William ("Bat") Masterson and John Henry ("Doc") Holliday operated on both sides of the law as gunmen, gamblers, and politicians. A feud between the Clantons and Earps climaxed on October 26, 1881, in a shootout at the OK Corral, where three Clantons were killed and Holliday and Morgan Earp were wounded.

Writers Mark Twain, Bret Harte, and others captured the flavor of western life, and characters such as Buffalo Bill, Annie Oakley, and Wild Bill Hickok became western folk heroes. But violence and eccentricity were uncommon. Most miners and lumbermen worked long hours, often for corporations, and had little time or money for gambling, carousing, or gunfights. Women worked as teachers, laundresses, storekeepers, and housewives. Only a few were sharpshooters or dance-hall queens. For most, western life was a struggle for survival.

Irrigation and Transportation

How did government policies aid the development of the West?

Western economic development is the story of how public and private interests used technology and organization to utilize the region's sometimes scarce water resources to make the arid land agriculturally productive.

For centuries, Indians irrigated southwestern fields for subsistence farming. When the Spanish arrived, they tapped the Rio Grande River to irrigate farms. Later, they channeled water to San Diego and Los Angeles. The Mormons were the first Americans of northern European ancestry to practice extensive irrigation. Arriving in Utah in 1847, they diverted streams and rivers into canals, enabling them to farm the hard-baked soil. By 1890, Utah boasted over 263,000 irrigated acres supporting more than 200,000 people.

Rights to Water   Efforts at land reclamation through irrigation in Colorado and California sparked conflict over rights to the precious streams that flowed through the West. Americans inherited the English common-law principle of riparian rights, which held that the stream belonged to God; those who lived nearby could take water as needed but should not diminish the river. Intended to protect nature, this principle discouraged economic development by prohibiting property owners from damming or diverting water at the expense of others who lived downstream.

Western settlers rejected riparianism and embraced prior appropriation, which awarded a river's water to the first person claiming it. Westerners, taking cues from eastern Americans who diverted waterways to power mills, asserted that water existed to serve human needs and advance profits. Anyone intending a "reasonable" (economically productive) use of river water should have the right to appropriation. The courts generally agreed.

Government Supervision of Water Rights

Under appropriation, those who dammed and diverted water often reduced its flow downstream. People disadvantaged by such action could either sue or establish a public authority to regulate water usage. Thus in 1879, Colorado created several divisions to regulate water rights. In 1890, Wyoming added a constitutional provision declaring that the state's rivers were public property subject to supervision.

Destined to become the most productive agricultural state, California maintained a mixed legal system that upheld riparianism while allowing for some appropriation. This system disadvantaged irrigators, who sought to change state law. In 1887, the legislature passed a bill permitting farmers to organize into districts that would construct and operate irrigation projects. An irrigation district could purchase water rights, seize private property for irrigation canals, and finance projects through taxation or by issuing bonds. As a result, California became the nation's leader in irrigated acreage, with more than 1 million irrigated acres by 1890, making the state's fruit and vegetable agriculture the most profitable nationwide.

Newlands Reclamation Act

Even so, the federal government owned most western land in the 1890s. Prodded by land-hungry developers, states wanted the federal government to turn over part of public domain lands, claiming they could make them profitable through reclamation—and irrigation. Congress generally refused such transfers because of potential controversies. Who would regulate waterways that flowed through more than one state? If, for example, California controlled the Truckee River, which flowed westward out of Lake Tahoe on the California-Nevada border, how would Nevadans ensure that California would give them sufficient water? Only the federal government had the power to regulate regional water development.

Newlands Reclamation Act: Authorized the U.S. government to sell western public lands to finance dams and irrigation projects in the West.

In 1902, after years of debates, Congress passed the **Newlands Reclamation Act**. It allowed the federal government to sell western public lands to individuals in parcels not to exceed 160 acres and to use proceeds to finance irrigation. The Newlands Act provided for control but not conservation of water, and instead fell within the tradition of development of nature for human profit. It represented a decision by the federal government to aid the agricultural and general economic development of the West.

Railroad Construction

Between 1865 and 1890, railroad expansion boomed, as tracks grew from 35,000 to 200,000 miles, mostly west of the Mississippi River (see Map 17.1). By 1900, the United States contained one-third of all railroad track in the world. The Central Pacific employed thousands of Chinese; the Union Pacific used mainly Irish. Workers lived in shacks and tents that were dismantled, loaded on flatcars, and relocated each day.

After 1880, when steel rails began replacing iron rails, railroads helped to boost the nation's steel industry to international leadership. Railroad expansion also spawned related industries: coal, rail-car manufacturing, and depot construction. Railroads also fueled western urbanization. Transporting people and freight, railroads accelerated the growth of hubs such as Chicago, Omaha, Kansas City, Cheyenne, Los Angeles, Portland, and Seattle.

The Australian Frontier

Australia, founded like the United States as a European colony, had a frontier society that resembled the American West in its mining development, folk society, and treatment of indigenous people. Australia experienced a gold rush in 1851, two years after the United States did, and large-scale mining companies moved into its western regions to extract lucrative mineral deposits.

Promise of mineral wealth lured thousands of mostly male immigrants to Australia in the late nineteenth century. As in the United States, anti-Chinese riots erupted, and beginning in 1854, Australia passed laws restricting Chinese immigration. When the country became an independent British federation in 1901, it implemented a literacy test that terminated Chinese immigration for over fifty years.

Although Australians immortalized folk heroes symbolizing white masculinity and a spirit of personal liberty and opportunism, they considered indigenous peoples, whom they called "Aborigines," as savages. Christian missionaries viewed aborigines as pagan and tried to convert them. In 1869, the government of Victoria Province passed an Aborigine Protection Act that, like American policy toward Indians, encouraging removal of native children from their families to learn European customs in white schools. Aborigines adapted. They formed cricket teams, and those with light skin sometimes told census takers they were white. In the end, Australians resorted to reservations to "protect" Aborigines, much as Americans isolated native peoples on reserved land. Like the Americans, white Australians could not find a place for indigenous people in their land of opportunity.

Much like the American counterpart, the Australian frontier was populated by natives before Anglo colonists arrived. The Aborigines, as the Australian natives were called, lived in villages and utilized their own culture to adapt to the environment. This photo shows a native camp in the Maloga Reserve.

National Library of Australia

Railroad Subsidies   Railroads received some of the largest government subsidies in American history. Promoters argued that because railroads were a public benefit, the government should give them land from the public domain, which they could then sell to finance construction. During the Civil War, Congress, dominated by business-minded Republicans granted railroad corporations over 180 million acres, mostly for interstate routes. Railroads funded construction by using the land as security for bonds or by selling it. State legislators, who often had financial interests in a railroad's, granted some 50 million acres. Cities and towns also assisted, usually via loans or by purchasing railroad bonds or stocks.

Without public help, few railroads could have prospered sufficiently to attract private investment. Although capitalists often opposed government involvement in corporate business, railroads accepted aid and pressured governments for assistance. The Southern Pacific, for example, threatened to bypass Los Angeles unless the city paid a bonus and built a depot. Some laborers and farmers fought subsidies, arguing that companies would become too powerful. Many communities boomed, however, as railroads attracted investment into the West and drew farmers into the market economy.

Standard Gauge, Standard Time   Railroad construction triggered important technological and organizational reforms. By the late 1880s, almost all lines had adopted standard-gauge rails so their tracks could connect. Air brakes, automatic car couplers, and other devices made rail transportation safer and more efficient. The need for gradings, tunnels, and bridges spurred the growth of the American engineering profession. Organizational advances included systems for coordinating passenger and freight schedules, and the adoption of uniform freight-classification systems. However, railroads also reinforced racism by segregating black and white passengers on cars and in stations.

Railroads altered conceptions of time and space. First, instead of expressing the distance between places in miles, people referred to the time it took to travel from place to place. Second, railroad scheduling required the nationwide standardization of time. Before railroads, local clocks struck noon when the sun was overhead, and people set clocks accordingly. But because the sun was not overhead at the same moment everywhere, time varied from place to place. Boston's clocks differed from New York's by almost twelve minutes. In 1883, without authority from Congress, the nation's railroads established four standard time zones for the country. Railroad time became national time.

Farming the Plains

What helped ease farmers' hardships as settlers in the West?

While California led the nation agriculturally, the Great Plains developed rapidly. There, farming in the late 1800s exemplified two important achievements: the transformation of arid prairies into crop-producing land and the transformation of agriculture into big business via mechanization, long-distance transportation, and scientific cultivation. Irrigation and the mechanized agriculture enabled farmers to feed the nation's burgeoning population and turned the United States into the world's breadbasket.

Settlement of the Plains

The number of farms tripled between 1860 and 1910, as hundreds of thousands of hopeful farmers headed to the Plains. The Homestead Act of 1862 and other measures to encourage western settlement offered cheap or free plots to people who would reside on and improve them. Land-rich railroads advertised affordable land, arranging credit terms, and offering reduced fares. Railroad agents—often former immigrants—traveled to Denmark, Sweden, Germany, and other European nations to recruit settlers.

To most families, the West seemed to promise a second chance, a better life. Railroad expansion enabled remote farmers to ship produce to market, and construction of grain elevators eased storage problems. Worldwide and national population growth sparked demand for farm products, and the prospects for commercial agriculture became increasingly favorable.

Hardship on the Plains

Farm life, however, was harder than advertisements and railroad agents insinuated. Migrants often encountered scarcities of essentials they had once enjoyed. Barren prairies contained insufficient lumber so pioneer families built houses of sod and burned buffalo dung for heat. Water was sometimes scarce also. Machinery for drilling wells was expensive, as were windmills for drawing water to the surface.

Weather posed formidable challenges. The climate between the Missouri River and the Rocky Mountains divides along a line running from Minnesota southwest through Oklahoma, then south, bisecting Texas. West of this line, annual rainfall averages less than twenty-eight inches, not enough for most crops or trees (see Map 17.3).

Weather was unpredictable. Weeks of torrid summer heat and parching winds suddenly gave way to violent storms that washed away crops and property. Winter blizzards piled up snowdrifts that halted outdoor movement. Melting snow swelled streams, and floods threatened millions of acres. In fall, a rainless week turned dry grasslands into tinder, and the slightest spark could ignite a prairie fire. Severe drought in Texas between 1884 and 1886 drove many farmers off the land.

Nature could be cruel even under good conditions. Weather favorable for crops also bred insects. In the 1870s and 1880s, grasshopper swarms devoured everything: plants, tree bark, and clothing. One farmer lamented, the "hoppers left behind nothing but the mortgage."

Social Isolation

Settlers also faced social isolation. New England and European farmers lived in villages, traveling daily to nearby fields. In the Plains, the Far West and South, peculiarities of land division compelled rural dwellers to live far apart. Because most plots were rectangular—usually encompassing 160 acres—at most four families could live nearby, but only if they congregated around their shared four-corner intersection. In practice, farm families lived away from boundary lines with a half-mile separating farmhouses. Men might find escape by occasionally traveling to sell crops or buy supplies. Women were more isolated, confined by domestic chores to the household with sporadic trips to exchange food and services with neighbors.

Letters that Ed Donnell, a young Nebraska homesteader, wrote to his family in Missouri reveal how circumstances could dull optimism. In fall 1885, Donnell rejoiced to his mother, "I like Nebr first rate....I have saw a pretty tuff time a part

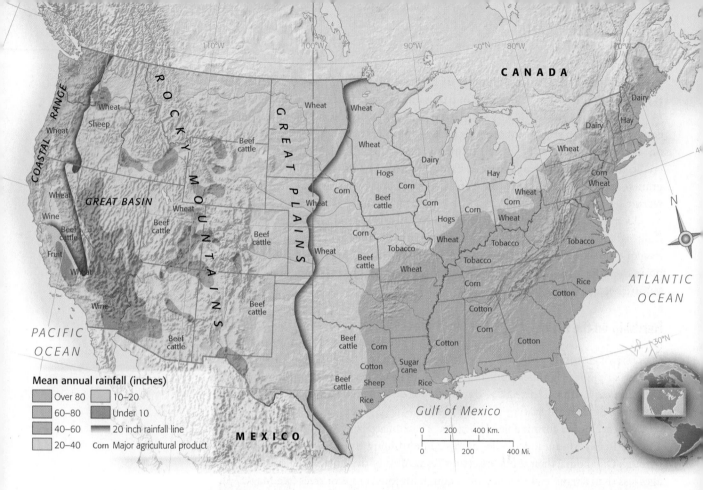

Mean annual rainfall (inches)

- Over 80
- 60–80
- 40–60
- 20–40
- 10–20
- Under 10
- 20 inch rainfall line
- Corn Major agricultural product

MAP 17.3

Agricultural Regions of the United States, 1890

In the Pacific Northwest and east of the twenty-eight-inch-rainfall line, farmers could grow a greater variety of crops. Territory west of the line was either too mountainous or too arid to support agriculture without irrigation. The grasslands that once fed buffalo herds could now feed beef cattle.

Source: Copyright © Cengage Learning

of the time since I have been out here, but I started out to get a home and I was determined to win or die in the attempt.... Have got a good crop of corn, a floor in my house and got it ceiled overhead." But Donnell was lonely. "You wanted to know when I was going to get married. Just as quick as I can get money ahead to get a cow."

A year and a half later, Donnell's dreams were dissolving and, still a bachelor, he was beginning to look elsewhere. By fall, Donnell lamented, "We have been having wet weather for 3 weeks.... My health has been so poor this summer and the wind and the sun hurts my head...if I can sell I will...move to town for I can get $40 a month working in a grist mill." Thousands shared Donnell's hardships, and their cityward migration fueled late-nineteenth-century urban growth (see Chapter 19).

Mail-Order Companies and Rural Free Delivery Farm families organized churches and clubs to ease isolation. By 1900, two developments brought rural settlers into closer contact with modern consumer society. First, mail-order companies, such as Montgomery Ward and Sears Roebuck, made new products attainable. Ward and Sears received letters that reported family news and

Evelyn Cameron was a British-born Montana settler whose diaries and photographs portrayed the hardship and beauty of the frontier in the 1890s and early 1900s. Here, she depicted two homesteaders and their simple dwelling with its dirt floor, wood stove, and boxes serving as furniture.

sought advice on needs from gifts to childcare. A Washington man wrote, "As you advertise everything for sale that a person wants, I thought I would write you, as I am in need of a wife, and see what you could do for me."

Second, after farmers petitioned Congress for extension of the postal service, in 1896 the government made Rural Free Delivery (RFD) widely available. Farmers who previously picked up mail in town could now receive letters and catalogs in a roadside mailbox almost daily. In 1913, the postal service inaugurated parcel post, which made shipping costs much cheaper.

Mechanization of Agriculture

Machinery drove the agricultural revolution. When the Civil War took men off farms in the upper Mississippi River valley, women and older men who remained behind began using reapers and other mechanical implements. After the war, demand encouraged farmers to utilize machines, and inventors developed new implements. Seeders, combines, binders, mowers, and rotary plows, improved grain growing on the Plains and in California, while the centrifugal cream separator, patented in 1879, sped the skimming of cream from milk.

TABLE 17.1   Summary: Government Land Policy

Railroad land grants (1850–1871)	Granted 181 million acres to railroads to encourage construction and development
Homestead Act (1862)	Gave 80 million acres to settlers to encourage settlement
Morrill Act (1862)	Granted 11 million acres to states to sell to fund public agricultural colleges
Other grants	Granted 129 million acres to states to sell for other educational and related purposes
Dawes Act (1887)	Allotted some reservation lands to individual Indians to promote private property and weaken tribal values among Indians and offered remaining reservation lands for sale to whites (by 1906, some 75 million acres had been acquired by whites)
Various laws	Permitted direct sales of 100 million acres by the Land Office

Source: Goldfield, David; Abbott, Carl E., Anderson, Virginia Dejohn; Argersinger, Jo Ann E.; Argersinger, Peter H.; Barney, William; Weir, Robert M., *American Journey, The*, Volume II, 3rd ed., © 2004. Printed and electronically reproduced by permission of Pearson Education, Inc., Upper Saddle River, New Jersey.

For centuries, farmers planted only what they could harvest by hand. Machines—driven first by animals, then by steam—significantly increased productivity and reduced costs. For example, before mechanization, a farmer working alone could harvest about 7.5 acres of wheat. Using an automatic binder that cut and bundled the grain, he could harvest 135 acres. Machines dramatically reduced the time and cost of farming other crops as well. (See Table 17.1)

Legislative and Scientific Aids

Congress and scientists worked to improve existing crops and develop new ones. The 1862 Morrill Land Grant Act gave states federal lands to sell to finance agricultural research. Consequently new public universities were established in Wisconsin, Illinois, Minnesota, California, and other states. A second Morrill Act in 1890 aided more schools, including several all-black colleges. The Hatch Act of 1887 provided for agricultural experiment stations in every state, further advancing farming science and technology.

Science enabled farmers to use the soil more efficiently. Researchers developed dry farming, a plowing and harrowing technique that minimized evaporation. Botanists perfected varieties of "hard" wheat whose seeds could withstand northern winters. Agriculturists adapted new varieties of alfalfa from Mongolia, corn from North Africa, and rice from Asia. George Washington Carver, a son of slaves who became a chemist and taught at Alabama's Tuskegee Institute, created hundreds of products from peanuts, soybeans, and sweet potatoes. Other scientists combated plant and animal diseases. Technology helped American farmers expand productivity in the market economy.

The Ranching Frontier

How did ranching shift from small, individual-owned endeavors to big business?

Western commercial farming ran headlong into one of the region's most romantic industries—ranching. Beginning in the sixteenth century, Spanish landholders raised cattle in Mexico and what would become the American Southwest. They employed Indian and Mexican cowboys, called *vaqueros*, who tended herds and rounded up cattle.

Anglo ranchers moving into Texas and California in the early nineteenth century hired *vaqueros* to teach them roping, branding, horse training, and saddle making.

By the 1860s, cattle-raising became increasingly profitable, as population growth boosted the demand for beef and railroads simplified food transportation. By 1870, drovers were herding thousands of Texas cattle northward to Kansas, Missouri, and Wyoming (see Map 17.1). At the northern terminus, the cattle were sold or loaded onto trains bound for Chicago and St. Louis slaughterhouses and international markets.

The long drive gave rise to romantic lore of bellowing cattle, buckskin-clad cowboys, and smoky campfires. Trekking 1,000 miles or more for months made cattle sinewy and tough. Herds traveling through Indian territory and farmers' fields were sometimes shot at. When ranchers discovered that crossing Texas longhorns with heavier Hereford and Angus breeds produced sturdier and more profitable animals, cattle raising expanded northward. Herds in Kansas, Nebraska, Colorado, Wyoming, Montana, and Dakota crowded out already declining buffalo.

The Open Range

Cattle raisers minimized expenses by purchasing a few acres bordering a stream and turning their herds loose on adjacent public domain that no one wanted because it lacked water access. By using open-range ranching, cattle raisers could utilize thousands of acres by owning a hundred. Neighboring ranchers often formed associations and allowed herds to graze together, burning an identifying brand into each animal's hide. But as ranchers flowed into the Plains, cattle overran the range, and other groups challenged ranchers over use of the land.

Sheepherders from California and New Mexico were also using the public domain, sparking territorial clashes. Ranchers complained that sheep ruined grassland by eating to the roots and that cattle refused to graze where sheep had been. Occasionally, ranchers and sheepherders resorted to violence rather than settle disagreements in court, where a judge might discover that both were using public land illegally.

More important, the farming frontier generated new land demands. Lacking sufficient timber and stone for traditional fencing, western settlers could not easily define their property. Tensions flared when farmers accused cattle raisers of allowing herds to trespass on cropland and when herders charged that farmers should fence their property.

Barbed Wire

The solution was barbed wire. Invented in 1873 by Joseph F. Glidden, a DeKalb, Illinois, farmer, this inexpensive and mass-produced fencing consisted of wires held in place by sharp spurs. It enabled Plains homesteaders to protect their farms from grazing cattle. It also ended open-range ranching and made roundups unnecessary, as large-scale ranchers enclosed their herds within private property. Similarly, the development of the round silo for storing and making fodder enabled cattle raisers to feed their herds without grazing.

Ranching as Big Business

By 1890, big businesses were taking over the cattle industry and applying scientific methods of breeding and feeding. Corporations also used technology to squeeze larger returns from meatpacking. Every part of a cow had uses: half was meat, but larger profits came from hides for leather, blood for fertilizer, hooves for glue, fat for candles and soap, and the rest for sausages. Cattle processing harmed the environment, as meatpackers and leather tanners dumped unsold goods into waterways. By the late nineteenth century, the Chicago River created a powerful stench that made nearby residents sick.

Open-range ranching made beef a staple of the American diet and created a few fortunes, but it could not survive the rush of history. Overgrazing destroyed Plains grass supplies, and the brutal winter of 1886–1887 destroyed 90 percent of some herds and drove small ranchers out of business. By 1890, large-scale ranchers owned or leased the land they used. Cowboys formed labor organizations and struck for higher pay. The myth of the cowboy's freedom and individualism lived on, but ranching became a corporate business.

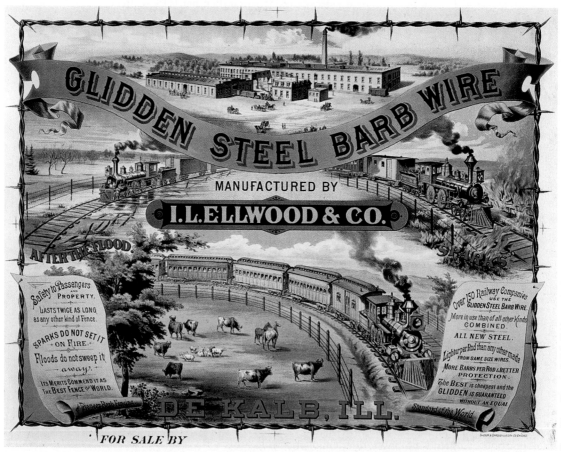

Bordered by the product it was promoting, this advertisement conveyed the message that railroads and farmers could protect their property from each other by utilizing a new type of fencing.

Elwood House Museum, DeKalb, Illinois

National Parks

Embodying greatness in the majesty of national parks is a uniquely American contribution to world culture. Initially, however, Congress did not recognize this possibility: in 1872, it created Yellowstone National Park but appropriated no funds to protect it. In 1886, however, the secretary of the interior was granted cavalry soldiers to supervise the park; meant to be temporary, they stayed until 1922.

Slowly, Congress created other parks, including Yosemite and Sequoia in California in 1890 and sites in Oregon, Utah, Arizona, Montana, and Colorado between 1902 and 1915. But conflicts arose between those who, like naturalist John Muir and the Sierra Club, wished to preserve parks in pristine quality and those, such as Senator William A. Clark of Montana, who wanted to lease the land for logging, mining, railroads, and tourism. Congress in 1916 created the National Park Service (NPS) to conserve natural and historic territory for their enjoyment by Americans. Stephen Mather, head of the service, took preservation seriously but also allowed hotel construction in parks for visitors.

Initially, national parks were in the West, but after 1920 the Park Service established eastern sites, beginning with the Great Smokies in Tennessee and North Carolina and Shenandoah in Virginia. In 1933, President Franklin Roosevelt transferred supervision of all national monuments and historic sites to the NPS, including the Statue of Liberty and Civil War battlefields. A few years later, NPS began adding seashores to its sphere, and from the 1960s onward urban sites such as Golden Gate National Recreation Area near San Francisco were incorporated.

By 1950, 30 million people visited national parks annually. Roads fell into disrepair, campgrounds were dilapidated, and litter was piling up. Moreover, those eager for the economic development of park lands lobbied for permission to dam rivers; expand roads; and build hotels, gas stations, and restaurants. In 1964, Congress passed a bill providing funds for future park land acquisition, but balancing preservation and public use remains controversial. Today, there are almost 400 national park units, encompassing more than 84 million acres. They stand a legacy from the past that poses challenges for the future.

Summary

History revealed that Frederick Jackson Turner's image of the West as the home of democratic spirit and Buffalo Bill's depiction of it as the battlefield of white man's victory were incomplete.

The American West exerted lasting influence on the complex mix of people there. Living mostly in small groups, Indians—the original inhabitants—hunted, farmed, and depended on delicate resources such as buffalo herds and salmon runs. When they came into contact with commerce-minded European-Americans, their resistance to the market economy, diseases, and violence that whites brought into the West failed.

Mexicans, Chinese, African Americans, and Anglos discovered a reciprocal relationship between human activities and the environment. Miners, timber cutters, farmers, and builders extracted raw minerals for eastern factories, used irrigation and machines to yield agricultural abundance, filled pastures with cattle and sheep to expand food sources, and constructed railroads to tie the nation together. But the environment exerted power through climate, insects and parasites, and other hazards.

The West's settlers employed violence and greed that sustained discrimination within a multiracial society, left many farmers feeling cheated, provoked contests over water and pastures, and sacrificed environmental balance for market profits. The region's raw materials and agricultural products raised living standards and hastened industrial progress, but not without costs.

Chapter Review

The Economic Activities of Native Peoples

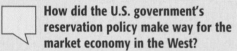

What factors undermined Native Americans' subsistence in the late nineteenth century?

The Native American economic system was increasingly eroded after 1850 by a number of factors, some natural and some resulting from increasing interaction with, and encroachment by, whites. Southwestern and Plains Indian economies were devastated by the declining buffalo herd due to drought, diseases brought by white-owned livestock, excessive Native American hunting and trade, white settlement on Indian lands used for grazing, and whites' efforts to eliminate the buffalo to make way for railroads. Northwestern Indian economies, which relied on salmon fishing, similarly suffered when white commercial fisheries diminished salmon supplies and dammed up rivers and tributaries that were vital for fishing stocks.

The Transformation of Native Cultures

How did the U.S. government's reservation policy make way for the market economy in the West?

U.S. reservation policy before the 1880s forced Indians onto western reservations, promising to protect this territory from white encroachment. Once on reservations, Indians' dependency on whites for trade goods such as clothing, guns, horses, and food made it easier for whites to control Indian affairs. The 1887 Dawes Severalty Act dissolved community-owned Indian land, granting it instead to qualifying individual Indian families. The land was held in trust for twenty-five years and allowed the U.S. government to sell unassigned allotments (typically to whites). The goal of this was to "civilize" Indians and assimilate them into white culture via private property, but in truth it reduced their land holdings by more than half and made way for land sales and further white settlement of the West.

Life on the Natural Resources frontier

What sparked the rise of the conservation movement?

Mining for precious metals, cutting trees for lumber, and drilling for oil drew thousands of people to the West seeking fortune and a better life. It also transformed the natural landscape, contributed to environmental wastefulness and sparked a debate over the desire for progress and the need to preserve nature. This gave rise to a conservation movement after the Civil War.

Recreational hunters and families that depended on wild game for meat lobbied legislatures; artists and tourists pressured Congress to protect Yosemite Valley by granting it to California for public use; and in 1862, the Yellowstone River region in Wyoming became the first national park. Congress also authorized President Benjamin Harrison to create forest reserves, at the urging of a group led by activist John Muir, who founded the environmental group the Sierra Club in 1892.

Irrigation and Transportation

How did government policies aid the development of the West?

Two ways: first, during the Civil War era, government subsidies for railroad construction—among the largest in U.S. history—included massive land grants, which companies could use for interstate routes or sell to finance construction. Federal land grants topped 180 million acres, while states handed over another 50 million acres, and cities and towns helped by offering loans or buying railroad stocks. Second, through the Newlands Reclamation Act (1902), Congress supported the sale of western lands in parcels smaller than 160 acres to individuals, with the funds being used to finance irrigation projects in the region. That, in turn, facilitated the agricultural and economic development.

Farming the Plains

What helped ease farmers' hardships as settlers in the West?

Migrants hoped to find a better life in the West, but often experienced loneliness, isolation, the lack of essential products and services they previously knew, and even shortages of lumber needed to build homes. But the arrival of the railroad, the extension of the postal service into the West, and the advent of the mail-order business ended some of their problems by bringing products and people to the region. New technology and mechanization also made farming easier, and the creation of social clubs, churches and other organizations helped ease social isolation.

The Ranching Frontier

How did ranching shift from small, individual-owned endeavors to big business?

With the increasing demand for beef and expansion of herds, ranchers overgrazed the land, which destroyed grass supplies that fed Plains herds. A brutal winter in 1886 to 1887 killed off 90 percent of some ranchers' herds and drove many out of business. By 1890, big business took over the cattle industry and used scientific methods for breeding and feeding to eliminate dependency on grass and grazing lands.

Suggestions for Further Reading

William Cronon, *Nature's Metropolis: Chicago and the Great West* (1991)

Karl Jacoby, *Crimes Against Nature: Squatters, Poachers, Thieves and the Hidden History of American Conservation* (2001)

Karl Jacoby, *Shadows at Dawn: A Borderlands Massacre and the Violence of History* (2009)

Patricia Nelson Limerick, *The Legacy of Conquest: The Unbroken Past of the American West* (1987)

Eugene P. Moehring, *Urbanism and Empire in the Far West, 1840–1890* (2004)

Robert M. Utley, *The Indian Frontier of the American West, 1846–1890* (1984)

Richard White, *"It's Your Misfortune and None of My Own": A New History of the American* (1991)

Donald Worster, *A Passion for Nature: The Life of John Muir* (2008)

Go to the CourseMate website for primary source links, study tools, and review materials for this chapter.
www.cengagebrain.com

The Machine Age

18

1877–1920

In 1911, iron molders at the Watertown Arsenal, a government weapons factory near Boston, went on strike after a coworker, Joseph Cooney, was fired for objecting when an efficiency expert timed his work with a stopwatch. Other molders, fearing that the time study was the first step in management's imposition of new labor standards, defended Cooney. Iron molders' union president John Frey explained, "The workman believes when he goes on strike that he is defending his job."

The army officers who ran the factory thought that they owned the molders' labor and that the output was "one-half what it should be." To increase production, they hired Dwight Merrick, an expert in a new field called "scientific management," to time workers and speed performance.

The day Merrick began his study, a molder named Perkins secretly timed the same task. Merrick reported that the job should take twenty-four minutes and that workers were wasting time and materials; Perkins found that the job required fifty minutes and there was no waste. That evening, the molders discussed how to respond to the discrepancy between Merrick's report and theirs. Cooney argued for resisting scientific management; the workers drew up a petition and the next day walked out.

Eventually, Watertown molders and their bosses compromised, but this incident reveals a significant consequence of industrialization. Four themes characterized the era. First, manufacturers harnessed technology to increase production. Second, they divided work routines into repetitive tasks organized by the clock. Workers who previously felt valued for their skills now struggled to avoid becoming slaves to machines. Third, a new consumer society emerged as new goods such as canned foods and machine-made clothing became common by the late 1800s. Fourth, in their quest for growth and profits, corporation owners amassed power through new forms of organization. Defenders of the new system justified it, while laborers tried to combat what they thought were abuses of power.

In the mid-nineteenth century, an industrial revolution swept through parts of the United States, and its mechanization powered a second round in the late 1800s and early 1900s. Four technological developments propelled this process: electricity, steel production, the internal-combustion engine, and new applications in the use of chemicals. Electricity provided a needed alternative to less efficient steam engines. Steel provided the material for new machines. The demand for transportation beyond railroads spurred progress in automobile manufacture. The textile industry's experiments with dyes, bleaches, and cleaning agents advanced chemical research.

In 1860, only one-fourth of the American labor force worked in manufacturing and transportation; by 1900, over half did. As the twentieth century dawned, the United States was the world's largest producer of raw materials and food, and the most productive industrial nation (see Map 18.1). Between 1877 and 1920, labor-saving machines (see Chapter 19) boosted productivity. Innovations in business organization and marketing also fueled the drive for profits.

Industrialization paralleled and was furthered by extraction of natural resources and agricultural expansion (see Chapter 17). Together, these developments dramatically altered living standards and everyday life. These processes combined people, the environment, and technology in ways that were both constructive and destructive.

As you read this chapter, keep the following questions in mind:

* How did mechanization affect the lives of average workers and the makeup of the labor force?

* In what ways did technological innovation alter the American standard of living?

* What ideas did some Americans use to justify industrialization, and how did others criticize it?

Technology and the Triumph of Industrialization

How did technological innovations transform American industry?

In 1876, **Thomas Edison** and his associates opened an "invention factory" in Menlo Park, New Jersey, where they intended to turn out "a minor invention every ten days and a big thing every six months or so." Activity at the U.S. Patent Office, created by the Constitution to "promote the Progress of science and useful Arts," reveals how innovative Americans were becoming. Between 1790 and 1860, the government granted 36,000 patents and registered another 1.5 million from 1860 to 1930. Inventions in areas such as electricity, internal combustion, and industrial chemistry often sprang from a marriage between technology and business organization.

Thomas A. Edison: Inventor, founder of the first industrial research laboratory.

Chronology

1869	Knights of Labor founded		1893–97	Economic depression causes high unemployment and business failures
1873–78	Economy declines		1894	Workers of Pullman Palace Car Company strike
1877	Widespread railroad strikes protest wage cuts		1895	*U.S. v. E. C. Knight Co.* limits Congress's power to regulate manufacturing
1878	Edison Electric Light Company founded		1896	*Holden v. Harcy* upholds law regulating miners' working hours
1879	George's *Poverty and Progress* argues for taxing unearned wealth		1903	Women's Trade Union League (WTUL) founded
1881	First federal trademark law begins spread of brand names		1905	*Lochner v. New York* overturns law limiting bakery workers' working hours
1882	Standard Oil Trust founded			Industrial Workers of the World (IWW) founded
1884–85	Economy declines		1908	*Muller v. Oregon* upholds law limiting women to ten-hour workday
1886	Haymarket riot in Chicago protests police brutality against labor demonstrations			First Ford Model T built
	American Federation of Labor (AFL) founded		1911	Triangle Shirtwaist Company fire in New York City leaves 146 workers dead
1890	Sherman Anti-Trust Act outlaws "combinations in restraint of trade"		1913	Ford begins moving assembly-line production
1892	Homestead (Pennsylvania) steelworkers strike against Carnegie Steel Company		1919	Telephone operators strike in New England

Birth of the Electrical Industry

Most of Edison's one thousand inventions used electricity to transmit light, sound, and images. In 1878, he embarked on a search for an efficient means of indoor lighting. After tedious experiments, Edison perfected the incandescent bulb. His Edison Electric Light Company also devised a system of power generation and distribution to widely provide electricity.

Link to the diary of Thomas Edison.

Edison's system of direct current could transmit electricity only a mile or two, losing voltage the farther it traveled. George Westinghouse, an inventor from Schenectady, New York, solved the problem. Westinghouse purchased European patent rights to generators that used alternating current and to transformers that reduced high-voltage power, thus making long-distance transmission efficient.

Other entrepreneurs created new practices to market Edison's and Westinghouse's breakthroughs. Samuel Insull, formerly Edison's private secretary, organized Edison power plants nationwide, amassing an electric utility empire. In the late 1880s and early 1890s, financiers Henry Villard and J. P. Morgan bought up patents in electric lighting and merged small equipment-manufacturing companies into the General Electric Company. General Electric and Westinghouse Electric established research laboratories to create electrical products for everyday use.

Meanwhile, inventors continued to work independently and sell their handiwork and patents to corporations. Granville T. Woods, an engineer sometimes called "the black Edison," patented thirty-five devices vital to electronics and communications. Most were sold to companies such as General Electric, including an automatic

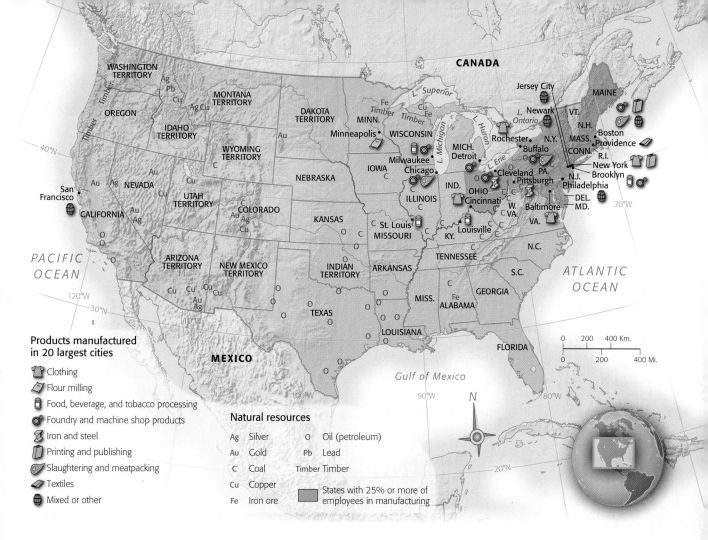

MAP 18.1

Industrial Production, 1919

By the early twentieth century, each state could boast at least one kind of industrial production. Although the value of goods produced was still highest in the Northeast, states such as Minnesota and California had impressive dollar values of outputs. *Source:* Data from U.S. Bureau of the Census, *Fourteenth Census of the United States, 1920, Vol. IX, Manufacturing* (Washington, D.C.: U.S. Government Printing Office, 1921).

circuit breaker, an electromagnetic brake, and instruments aiding communications between railroad trains.

Henry Ford and the Automobile Industry

In 1885, a German engineer, Gottlieb Daimler, built a lightweight internal combustion motor driven by vaporized gasoline. In the 1890s, **Henry Ford**, an electrical engineer in Detroit's Edison Company, experimented with Daimler's engine to power a vehicle. Applying organizational genius to this invention, Ford spawned a massive industry.

Ford had a scheme as well as a product, declaring in 1909, "I am going to democratize the automobile. When I'm through, everybody will be able to afford one." Ford proposed to mass-produce thousands of identical cars, and engineers set up assembly lines that drastically reduced time and production costs. Instead of performing numerous tasks, each worker did just one, repeatedly, assembling the entire car along a conveyor belt.

Henry Ford: Founder of the Ford Motor Company and pioneer of modern assembly lines used in mass production.

Links to the World

The Atlantic Cable

During the late nineteenth century, as American manufacturers expanded their markets overseas, their ability to communicate with customers and investors improved immeasurably because of telegraph cable beneath the Atlantic Ocean. Cyrus Field, who pioneered the idea of laying undersea cable, was an American. Yet most of the engineers and capitalists involved were British. In 1851, a British company laid the first successful undersea telegraph cable from Dover, England, to Calais, France, proving that an insulated wire could carry signals underwater. This venture inspired British and American businessmen to attempt a larger project across the Atlantic.

The first attempts failed, but in 1866 a British ship, funded by British investors, successfully laid a telegraph wire that operated without interruption. Thereafter, England and the United States grew more closely linked in diplomatic relations, and citizens developed greater concern for each other. When American president James Garfield was assassinated in 1881, the news traveled almost instantly to Great Britain, and Britons mourned the death profusely.

Some people lamented the stresses that near-instant international communications created. But financially savvy individuals welcomed the benefits. Rapid availability of stock quotes helped the New York and London stock exchanges boom. Newspaper readers enjoyed reading about events overseas the next day, instead of a week later. By 1902, underwater cables circled the globe. The age of global telecommunications had begun.

Library of Congress

Laid by British ships across the ocean in 1866, the Atlantic cable linked the United States with England and continental Europe so that telegraph communications could be sent and received much more swiftly than ever before. Now Europeans and Americans could exchange news about politics, business, and military movements almost instantly, whereas previously such information could take a week or more to travel from one country to another.

In 1913, the Ford Motor Company's first assembly line opened in Highland Park outside Detroit, and the next year, Ford sold 248,000 cars. Soon, other manufacturers entered the field. Rising automobile output created jobs, higher earnings, and greater profits for related industries, too, such as steel, oil, paint, rubber, and glass. Moreover, assembly-line production required new companies to fabricate precision machine tools for making standardized parts.

By 1914, a Ford car cost $490, about one-fourth of its price a decade earlier. Yet that was too expensive for many workers, who earned at best $2 a day. That year, Ford tried to spur productivity, prevent labor turnover, head off unionization, and better enable his workers to buy the cars they produced through his Five-Dollar-Day plan—a combination of wages and profit sharing.

Carnegie and Steel

Many new products required strong, hard metal. Though in use for centuries, steel production was inefficient until British engineer Henry Bessemer developed a process that enabled mass production of inexpensive, high-quality steel from molten iron. American industrialist Andrew Carnegie, who observed the process while in England in 1872, immediately recognized the benefits of the Bessemer process. Carnegie built his Edgar Thompson steel plant near Pittsburgh. Using funds from investors, Carnegie purchased other steel mills, notably the Homestead Steel Company in 1888, and sold steel, initially used to manufacture rails and bridge girders for railroads, to companies using new technologies for plating and pressing steel to make barbed wire, tubing, and other products. In 1892, he formed the Carnegie Steel Company and by 1900 controlled about 60 percent of the steel business. In 1901, Carnegie sold his holdings to a group organized by J. P. Morgan, who formed the huge U.S. Steel Corporation.

The Du Ponts and the Chemical Industry

The du Pont family similarly transformed the chemical industry. In 1902, fearing antitrust prosecution for the company's near monopoly of the explosives industry, three cousins, Alfred, Coleman, and Pierre, took over E. I. du Pont de Nemours and Company and broadened production into fertilizers, dyes, and other chemical products. In 1911, du Pont scientists in the nation's first corporate research laboratory adapted cellulose to produce such consumer goods as photographic film, textile fibers, and plastics. The du Pont company also pioneered methods of management, accounting, and reinvestment of earnings, which contributed to efficient production, better recordkeeping, and higher profits.

Technology and Southern Industry

The South's major staple crops, tobacco and cotton, drew industry to the region after the Civil War. Americans used tobacco mainly for snuff, cigars, and chewing. But in 1876, James Bonsack, an eighteen-year-old Virginian, invented a cigarette-rolling machine. Sales soared after 1885 when North Carolina tobacco magnate James B. Duke mass-produced cigarettes with Bonsack's machine and enticed consumers with free samples, trading cards, and billboard ads. By 1900, his American Tobacco Company was a global business, employing black and white workers (including women), though in separate workrooms.

New technology helped relocate the textile industry to the South. Factories with electric looms were more efficient than New England's water-powered mills, required fewer workers, and provided lighting that expanded production hours.

Investors built new plants in southern communities, where a cheap labor was available. By 1900, the South had more than four hundred textile mills. Women and children earned 50 cents a day for twelve or more hours—about half the wages of northern millworkers. Most mills only hired black workers as janitors. Companies built villages around their mills, where they controlled housing, stores, schools, and churches and banned company criticism and union organization.

Northern and European investors joined southerners in financing other southern industries. During the 1880s, northern capitalists developed southern iron and steel manufacturing, much of it in Birmingham, Alabama. Between 1890 and 1900, northern lumber syndicates moved into the pine forests of the Gulf states, boosting production 500 percent. Southern wood production advanced the construction industry and relocated furniture and paper production from the North to the South. Challenging the power of the planter elite, a business class of manufacturers, merchants, and financiers heralded the emergence of a New South and made southern cities nerve centers of a new economic order.

Consequences of Technology

Machines broadly altered everyday life. Telephones and typewriters made face-to-face communication less important and facilitated correspondence and recordkeeping in growing insurance, banking, and industrial firms. Electric sewing machines made mass-produced clothing. Refrigeration enabled the preservation and shipment of meat, fruit, vegetables, and dairy products. Cash registers and adding machines revamped accounting and created new clerical jobs. At the same time, American universities established programs in engineering.

Technological advances often originated abroad. Europeans made early discoveries in electricity and internal combustion engines. The Bessemer process for producing steel was developed in England, and the du Ponts imported capital and machinery from France for their gunpowder operation. But Americans adapted and advanced these developments, which enabled the United States to surpass other industrializing nations in output by the turn of the century.

Profits resulted from higher production at lower costs. As technological innovations made large-scale production more economical, owners replaced small workshops with large factories. Between 1850 and 1900, average capital investment in a manufacturing firm increased by 250 percent. Only large companies could afford to buy complex machines. And large companies received discounts for buying raw materials and shipping in bulk—advantages economists call economies of scale.

Profitability depended as much on how production was organized. Where once workers such as the Watertown molders controlled the methods of production, by the 1890s engineers and managers with "expert" knowledge planned every task to increase output. Through standardization, they reduced the need for human skills, boosting profits at the expense of worker independence.

Frederick W. Taylor and Efficiency

The most influential advocate of efficient production was Frederick W. Taylor. As foreman and engineer for the Midvale Steel Company in the 1880s, Taylor concluded companies could best reduce costs and increase profits by applying studies of "how quickly the various kinds of work...ought to be done." This meant producing more for lower cost per unit, usually by eliminating unnecessary workers.

In 1898, Taylor took his stopwatch to the Bethlehem Steel Company to illustrate his principles of scientific management. His experiments required studying workers and devising "a series of motions which can be made quickest and best." For shoveling ore, Taylor designed fifteen kinds of shovels and prescribed proper motions for each, thereby reducing a crew of 600 men to 140. Soon other companies, including the Watertown Arsenal, applied Taylor's theories.

Consequently, time, as much as quality, became the measure of acceptable work, and management dictated how things were done. As elements of the assembly line, which divided work into specific time-determined tasks, employees feared they were becoming another interchangeable part.

Mechanization and the Changing Status of Labor

By 1900, the status of labor shifted dramatically. Technological innovation and assembly-line production created new jobs, but because most machines were labor saving, fewer workers could produce more in less time. Instead of producers, the working class now consisted mainly of employees who

> How did mechanization and new systems of management change the nature and status of work?

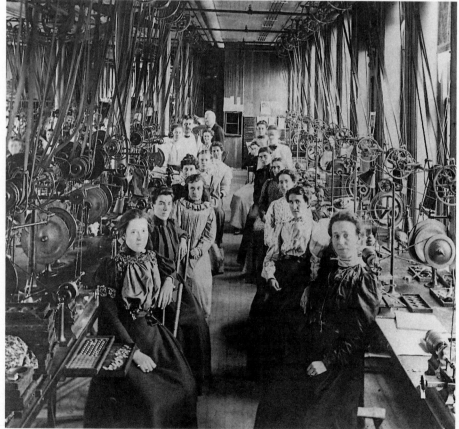

Chicago Historical Society

The combination of machines and workers still required meticulous handwork in some industries. Often women with nimble fingers could find jobs in industries such as jewelry and watchmaking where, as at this room at the Elgin National Watch Company, they could swiftly manipulate tiny production processes.

worked for hire. Producers were paid based on the quality of what they produced; employees received wages for time spent on the job.

Mass Production   With manufacturing subdivided into small tasks, mass production required workers to repeat the same standardized operation all day every day. One investigator found that a worker became "a mere machine." Workers no longer decided when to begin and end the workday or what tools and techniques to use. The clock regulated them. As a Massachusetts factory laborer testified in 1879, "During working hours the men are not allowed to speak to each other...on pain of instant discharge. Men are hired to watch and patrol the shop."

Workers such as the Watertown iron molders struggled to retain autonomy. Artisans—glass workers and coopers (barrel makers)—caught in the transition from hand labor to machine production, fought to preserve their work customs, say, by appointing a fellow worker to read a newspaper aloud while they worked. Immigrant factory workers tried to persuade foremen to hire their relatives and friends. After hours, workers enjoyed drinking and holiday celebrations, ignoring employers' attempts to control their social lives.

Employers, concerned with efficiency, wanted behavior standards upheld. Ford Motor Company required workers to satisfy the company's behavior code before becoming eligible for a part of the Five-Dollar-Day plan. To increase worker incentives, some employers established piecework rates, paying per item produced rather than an hourly wage. Employers eager to increase productivity tried to make workers perform like machines.

Restructuring of the Work Force   As machines reduced the need for skilled workers, employers cut labor costs by hiring women and children, and paying them low wages. Between 1880 and 1900, the numbers of employed women soared from 2.6 million to 8.6 million (see Figure 18.1). The proportion of women in domestic service (maids, cooks, laundresses)—the most common and lowest-paid female employment—dropped as jobs opened in other sectors. In manufacturing, women usually held menial positions in textile mills and food-processing plants that paid $1.56 for seventy hours week. (Unskilled men received $7 to $10.) Although the number of female factory hands tripled between 1880 and 1900, the proportion of women workers remained constant.

Expansion of the clerical and retail sectors boosted the numbers and percentages of women who were typists, bookkeepers, and sales clerks—previously male jobs. Inventions, such as the typewriter, cash register, and adding machine, simplified these tasks, and employers replaced males with lower-paid females. By 1920, women filled nearly half of all clerical jobs; in 1880, only 4 percent were women. Although poorly paid, women were attracted to sales jobs because of the respectability, pleasant surroundings, and contact with affluent customers. Nevertheless, sex discrimination persisted. In department stores, only male cashiers handled cash transactions. Women held some low-level supervisory positions, but males dominated managerial ranks.

Meanwhile, the number in nonagricultural occupations tripled between 1870 and 1900. In 1890, over 18 percent of children ages ten to fifteen were employed, particularly in textile and shoe factories (see Figure 18.2). Mechanization created

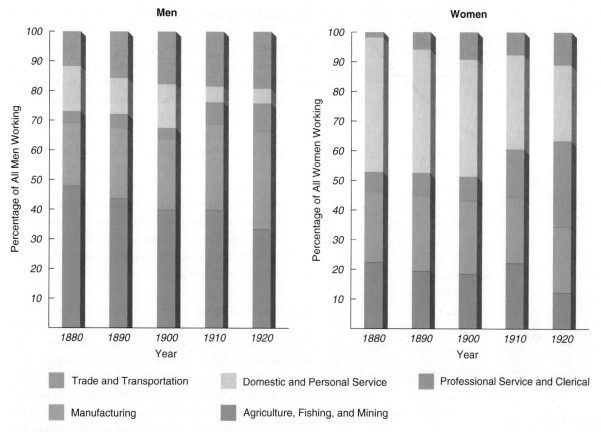

FIGURE 18.1

Distribution of Occupational Categories Among Employed Men and Women, 1880–1920

The changing lengths of the bar segments of each part of this graph represent trends in male and female employment. Over the forty years covered by this graph, the agriculture, fishing, and mining segment for men and the domestic service segment for women declined the most, whereas notable increases occurred in manufacturing for men and professional services (especially store clerks and teachers) for women.

Source: U.S. Bureau of the Census, *Census of the United States, 1880, 1890, 1900, 1910, 1920* (Washington, D.C.: U.S. Government Printing Office).

numerous light tasks, such as running errands, which children could handle cheaply. Conditions were especially hard for child laborers in the South, where mill owners induced desperate white sharecroppers and tenant farmers to bind their children to factories at miserably low wages.

Several states, especially in the Northeast, passed laws specifying minimum ages and maximum hours for child labor. But statutes regulated only firms operating within state borders, not those engaged in interstate commerce. Enforcing age requirements proved difficult because many parents, needing income, lied about their children's ages. After 1900, state laws and automation, along with compulsory school attendance laws, reduced the number of children employed in manufacturing, and Progressive era reformers sought federal legislation restricting child labor (see Chapter 21). Still, many children continued to work at street trades—shining shoes and peddling—while poor children scavenged city streets for coal and wood, discarded clothing, and furniture.

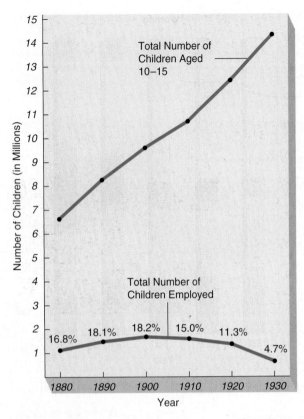

FIGURE 18.2
Children in the Labor Force, 1880–1930
The percentage of children in the labor force peaked around the turn of the century. Thereafter, the passage of state laws requiring children to attend school until age fourteen and limiting the ages at which children could be employed caused child labor to decline.
Source: Data from *The Statistical History of the United States from Colonial Times to the Present* (Stamford, CT.: Fairfield Publishers, 1965).

Industrial Accidents

Repetitive tasks using high-speed machinery dulled concentration, and the slightest mistake could cause serious injury. Industrial accidents rose steadily before 1920, killing or maiming hundreds of thousands of people each year. In 1913, after factory owners installed safety devices, 25,000 people died in industrial mishaps, and 1 million were injured. There was no disability insurance to replace lost income, and families suffered acutely.

The most notorious tragedy was a fire at New York City's Triangle Shirtwaist Company in 1911, which killed 146 workers, mostly teenage immigrant women trapped in locked workrooms. Despite public clamor, prevailing free-market views hampered passage of legislation regulating working conditions, and employers denied responsibility for employees' well-being.

Freedom of Contract

To justify their treatment of workers, employers asserted the principle of "freedom of contract," claiming wages and working conditions resulted from supply and demand. Employers asserted that since workers entered into a contract with bosses, workers could seek another job if they did not like the wages and hours. Actually, employers used supply and demand to set wages as low as laborers would accept. Employees felt trapped. A factory worker told Congress in 1879, "The market is glutted, and…the pay is cut down; our tasks are increased, and if we remonstrate, we are told our places can be filled."

Court Rulings on Labor Reform

Reformers and union leaders lobbied for laws to improve working conditions, but the Supreme Court limited such legislation by narrowly defining which jobs were dangerous and which workers needed protection. In *Holden v. Hardy* (1896), the Court upheld a law regulating miners' working hours, concluding that overly long workdays increase potential injuries. In *Lochner v. New York* (1905), however, the Court voided a law limiting bakery workers to a sixty-hour week and ten-hour day. It ruled that baking was not a dangerous enough occupation to justify restricting workers' right to sell their labor freely. Such restriction, according to the Court, violated the Fourteenth Amendment's guarantee that no state could "deprive any person of life, liberty, or property without due process of law."

In *Muller v. Oregon* (1908), the Court used a different rationale to uphold limiting women in laundries to a ten-hour workday. It set aside its *Lochner* argument to assert that women's well-being as potential childbearers "becomes an object of public interest and care in order to preserve the strength and vigor of the race." The

Impact of the 1911 Triangle Shirtwaist Fire

On March 25, 1911, the worst factory fire in U.S. history occurred at the Triangle Shirtwaist Company, which occupied the top three floors of a building in New York City. Fed by piles of fabric, the fire spread quickly, killing 146 of the 500 young women, mostly Jewish immigrants, employed in the factory. Many of the victims were burned to death because they were locked inside workrooms by their employer; others plunged from windows. These three images show how the public received news of the tragedy, one through friends and relatives who came to identify and claim the bodies of victims, one through a critical cartoon, and the other through the front page of a newspaper. Which of these images seems most powerful and likely to inspire reform? How do mass tragedies get communicated to the public today? What limitations in communications existed in 1911?

Many of the victims of the Triangle Shirtwaist fire of 1911 were lined up in coffins, and their bodies were identified by relatives arriving at a make-shift morgue.

John French Sloan, an artist with radical leanings, drew this cartoon in the wake of the Triangle fire. Eager to assert that profit-minded capitalists were responsible for unnecessary deaths, Sloan used stark images to convey his message.

Using a large-print headline and grisly photograph, the New York Tribune, one of New York City's and the nation's oldest and most-respected newspapers, filled much of its front page with news of the event.

469

case represented a victory for reformers seeking government regulation of women's hours and working conditions. As a result of the *Muller* decision, labor laws barred women from occupations, such as in printing and transportation, that required heavy lifting, long hours, or night work, further confining women to low-paying, dead-end jobs.

Labor Violence and the Union Movement

How did employers and others respond to increasing strikes and labor unrest in the late nineteenth century?

Workers adjusted to mechanization as best they could, but anxiety over lost independence and desire for better wages, hours, and working conditions drew disgruntled workers into unions. Trade unions for skilled workers in crafts such as printing and iron molding dated from the early 1800s, but their influence was limited. But by the 1870s, the spread of companies with large labor forces and the tightening of management control spurred a unionization response.

Railroad Strikes of 1877

In the economic slump that followed the Panic of 1873, railroad managers cut wages, increased workloads, and laid off workers, especially union members. Workers responded with strikes and riots. The year 1877 marked a crisis. In July, unionized railroad men organized strikes to oppose wage cuts. Violence spread from Pennsylvania and West Virginia to the Midwest, Texas, and California, derailing trains and burning rail yards. State militias, organized and commanded by employers, broke up picket lines and fired into threatening crowds. Factory workers, wives, and merchants aided the strikers, while railroads enlisted strikebreakers to replace union men.

Pittsburgh experienced the worst violence. On July 21, state troops bayoneted and fired on rock-throwing demonstrators, killing ten and wounding many more. Infuriated, the mob drove the troops into a roundhouse and set fires that destroyed 39 buildings, 104 engines, and 1,245 freight and passenger cars. The next day, the troops shot their way out and killed twenty more citizens before fleeing. After a month, President Rutherford B. Hayes sent in federal soldiers—the first significant use of the army to quell labor unrest.

Knights of Labor

About the same time, the Knights of Labor tried to attract a broad base of laborers. Founded in 1869 by Philadelphia garment cutters, the Knights recruited other workers in the 1870s. In 1879, Terence V. Powderly, a machinist and mayor of Scranton, Pennsylvania, was elected grand master. Under his guidance, Knights membership grew, peaking at 730,000 in 1886. In contrast to most craft unions, Knights welcomed unskilled and semiskilled workers, including women, immigrants, and African Americans (but not Chinese).

The Knights sought a workers' alliance offering an alternative to profit-oriented industrial capitalism. They intended to eliminate conflict between labor and management by establishing a cooperative society in which workers, not capitalists, owned factories, mines, and railroads. The goal, argued Powderly, was to "eventually make every man his own master—every man his own employer." The cooperative idea, attractive in the abstract, was unattainable because employers could outcompete laborers who might try to establish businesses. Strikes might achieve immediate goals, but Powderly and other Knights leaders argued that strikes diverted attention from the long-term goal of a cooperative society and that workers lost more by striking.

Some Knights, however, supported militant action. In 1886, railroad magnate **Jay Gould** refused to negotiate when Knights demanded higher wages and union recognition from Southwest Railroad. A strike began in Texas, then spread to Kansas, Missouri, and Arkansas. Powderly met with Gould and called off the strike, hoping for a settlement. But Gould rejected concessions, and the Knights gave in. Militant craft unions deserted the Knights, upset by Powderly's compromise.

After the Haymarket riot (see next section), Knights membership dwindled, although the union made a brief attempt to unite with Populists in the 1890s (see Chapter 20). Craft unions replaced the Knights' broad-based but often vague appeal, and labor unity faded.

Jay Gould: Captain of industry and owner of the Union Pacific Railroad.

Haymarket Riot

While the Knights were striking, other groups calling for an eight-hour workday generated the largest labor demonstration in the country's history. On May 1, 1886, in Chicago, some 100,000 such workers turned out, including anarchists who believed in using violence. Chicago police, fearing that European radicals were transplanting a tradition of violence to the United States, mobilized. The day passed calmly, but two days later, police stormed an area near the McCormick reaper plant and broke up a battle between striking unionists and nonunion strikebreakers, killing two unionists and wounding others.

The next evening, laborers protested police brutality at Haymarket Square near downtown Chicago. As police approached, a bomb exploded, killing seven and injuring sixty-seven. Authorities made mass arrests, and a court convicted eight anarchists of the bombing, despite questionable evidence. Four were executed, and one committed suicide in prison. The remaining three received pardons in 1893 from Illinois governor John P. Altgeld.

The Haymarket bombing, like the 1877 railroad strikes, heightened fears of labor discontent and of radicalism. The participation of anarchists and socialists, many of them foreign-born, created a feeling that civic leaders act swiftly to prevent social turmoil. Private Chicago donors helped establish a military base near the city. Elsewhere, governments strengthened police forces and armories. Employer associations countered labor militancy by circulating blacklists of union activists whom they would not employ and by hiring private detectives to suppress strikes.

American Federation of Labor

The **American Federation of Labor** (AFL) emerged from the 1886 upheavals as the major workers' organization. An alliance of national craft unions, the AFL had about 140,000 members, mostly skilled workers. Led by **Samuel Gompers**, former head of the Cigar Makers' Union, the AFL pressed for higher wages, shorter hours, and the right to bargain collectively. Unlike the Knights, the AFL accepted capitalism and worked to improve conditions within it.

The AFL avoided party politics, adhering instead to Gompers's dictum of supporting labor's friends and opposing its enemies, regardless of party.

American Federation of Labor (AFL): Skilled craft unions united under leadership of Samuel Gompers.

Samuel Gompers: AFL leader who focused on practical goals like improved wages, hours, and working conditions.

Link to the debate on May 18, 1920, between Samuel Gompers and Henry Justin Allen, the Republican Governor of Kansas.

No woman

AFL membership grew to 1 million by 1901 and 2.5 million by 1917, when it consisted of 111 national unions and 27,000 locals. Member unions organized by craft had little interest in recruiting unskilled workers or women. Of 6.3 million employed women in 1910, fewer than 2 percent belonged to unions. Male unionists rationalized women's exclusion by insisting that women should not be employed. According to one labor leader, "The mental and physical makeup of woman is in revolt against wage service. She is competing with the man who is her father or husband or is to become her husband." Mostly, unionists worried that, because women were paid less, men's wages would be lowered or their jobs given to cheaper female workers.

Influenced by nativism and racism, organized labor excluded most immigrants and African Americans, fearing they, too, would depress wages. A few trade unions welcomed immigrants. Blacks were prominent in the coal miners' union and were partially unionized in such trades as construction, barbering, and dock work, which employed numerous African American workers. But they could belong only to segregated unions in the South, and most northern AFL unions had exclusion policies. Long-held prejudices were reinforced when blacks and immigrants, eager for work, replaced striking whites.

Homestead and Pullman Strikes

The AFL and the labor movement suffered setbacks in the early 1890s, when labor violence stirred public fears. In July 1892, the AFL-affiliated Amalgamated Association of Iron and Steelworkers went on strike against pay cuts in Homestead, Pennsylvania. In response to the **Homestead Strike**, Henry C. Frick, president of Carnegie Steel Company, closed the plant. Shortly thereafter, Frick hired three hundred guards from the Pinkerton Detective Agency to protect the factory and floated them in by barge at night. Lying in wait, angry workers attacked and routed the Pinkertons. State troops intervened, and after five months the strikers gave in. By then, public opinion turned against the union.

In 1894, workers at the Pullman Palace (railroad passenger) Car Company walked out over exploitative policies at the company town near Chicago. The paternalistic owner, George Pullman, provided everything for the twelve thousand residents of the so-called model town named after him. His company controlled all land and buildings, the school, the bank, and the water and gas systems. It paid wages, fixed rents, and spied on disgruntled employees.

One thing Pullman would not do was negotiate with workers. When hard times hit in 1893, Pullman protected profits by cutting wages 25 to 40 percent while holding firm on rents and prices. Hard-pressed workers sent a committee to Pullman to protest. He reacted by firing three committee members. Enraged workers, most of them from the American railway union, called a strike; Pullman closed the factory. The union, led by **Eugene V. Debs**, refused to handle Pullman cars attached to any trains. Pullman rejected arbitration. The railroad owners' association enlisted aid from U.S. Attorney General Richard Olney, a former railroad lawyer, who obtained a court injunction to prevent the union from "obstructing the railways and holding up the mails." President Grover Cleveland ordered federal troops to Chicago. Within a month strikers gave in, and Debs was imprisoned for defying the injunction. The Supreme Court upheld Debs's six-month sentence, arguing that the federal government could legally remove obstacles to interstate commerce.

Homestead Strike: Workers walk out after wage cuts at a Carnegie Steel plant in 1892; officials responded to the strike by shutting down the plant.

Eugene V. Debs: Indiana labor leader who organized workers in the Pullman Strike of 1893; would be the Socialist Party of America's presidential candidate five times between 1900 and 1920.

Labor Violence in the West

In the West, unionized miners, led by the Western Federation of Miners (WFM), engaged in highly violent strikes during the 1890s. Membership in the WFM rose, as did antiunion sentiment among employers.

In Idaho, federal troops were called out three times to combat striking miners and protect company property during the 1890s. In 1899, after strikers blew up Bunker Hill Mining Company buildings, soldiers arrested every male in the town, and Governor Frank Steunenberg declared martial law. In 1905, Steunenberg, no longer in office, was assassinated; speculation arose that the WFM had killed him. Investigation by Pinkerton Detective James McParland resulted in the arrest of WFM Secretary-Treasurer William "Big Bill" Haywood and two other WFM officials. Tried for murder in 1907, Haywood was acquitted after his attorney, the famed Clarence Darrow, subverted testimony of a key witness.

In 1905, rebel unionists formed a new, radical labor organization, the **Industrial Workers of the World (IWW)**. Like the Knights, it strove to unite all laborers of all. Its motto was "An injury to one is an injury to all." But the "Wobblies," as IWW members were known, espoused violence and sabotage. Embracing socialism and the rhetoric of class conflict, Wobblies believed workers should seize and run the nation's industries. Leaders such as Haywood; Mary "Mother" Jones, an Illinois coalfield union organizer; Elizabeth Gurley Flynn, a fiery orator known as the "Joan of Arc of the labor movement"; Italian radical Carlo Tresca; and Swedish-born organizer and songwriter Joe Hill headed a series of strikes. Although the Wobblies' anticapitalist goals and aggressive tactics attracted publicity, the organization collapsed during World War I when federal prosecution sent many of its leaders to jail and local police violently harassed IWW members.

Industrial Workers of the World (IWW): Radical labor organization that sought to unionize all workers; nicknamed Wobblies, the IWW embraced Socialism and led mass strikes of mine workers in Nevada and Minnesota and timber workers in Louisiana, Texas, and the Northwest.

Women Unionists

Despite exclusion from unions, some women organized and fought employers as strenuously as men. The "Uprising of the 20,000" in New York City, a 1909 strike by male and female immigrant members of the International Ladies' Garment Workers' Union (ILGWU), was one of the country's largest strikes. Female trade-union membership grew during the 1910s, but men monopolized national leadership.

Women did dominate one union: the Telephone Operators' Department of the International Brotherhood of Electrical Workers. Organized in Boston in 1912, the union spread throughout the Bell system, the nation's monopolistic telephone company and single largest employer of women. To promote solidarity among their mostly young female members, union leaders organized dances, excursions, bazaars, and educational programs. The union resisted scientific management techniques and rigid supervision. In 1919, several militant union branches paralyzed the phone service of five New England states, but the union collapsed after a failed strike in 1923.

A key organization promoting laboring women's interests was the Women's Trade Union League (WTUL), founded in 1903 and patterned after a similar organization in England. The WTUL sought legislation to improve conditions and reduce hours, sponsored educational activities, and campaigned for woman suffrage.

It helped telephone operators organize, and in 1909 it supported the ILGWU's massive strike against New York City sweatshops. Initially, the WTUL's highest officers were middle-class women, but control shifted in the 1910s to forceful working-class leaders, notably Agnes Nestor, a glove maker, and Rose Schneiderman, a cap maker. The WTUL advocated opening apprenticeship programs to women and training female workers for leadership. It served as a vital link between the labor and women's movements into the 1920s.

The Experience of Wage Work

Dramatic strikes aside, only a small fraction of American wage workers belonged to unions. In 1900, about 1 million of 27.6 million total workers were unionized. By 1920, union membership had grown to 5 million, only 13 percent of the work force. Unionization was strong in construction trades, transportation, communications, and, to a lesser extent, manufacturing. For many workers, getting and keeping a job took priority over higher wages and shorter hours. Job instability and the seasonal nature of work seriously hindered union-organizing. Few companies employed workers year-round; most hired during peak seasons and laid workers off during slack periods. The millions of men, women, and children who were not unionized tried to cope with machine age pressures. Many native-born and immigrant workers joined fraternal societies, such as the Polish Roman Catholic Union, the African American Colored Brotherhood and Sisterhood of Honor, and the Jewish B'nai B'rith. For small contributions these organizations provided life insurance, sickness benefits, and burial costs.

During the machine age, industrial wages rose between 1877 and 1914, boosting purchasing power and creating a mass market for standardized goods. Yet in 1900 most employees worked sixty hours a week at wages averaging 20 cents an hour for skilled work and 10 cents an hour for unskilled. Even as wages rose, living costs increased even faster.

Standards of Living

What was the impact of the new consumer culture on people's lives?

The industrial system improved everyday life. American ingenuity combined with mass production and mass marketing to make available myriad goods that previously had not existed or had been the province of the wealthy. The new material well-being, symbolized by canned foods, ready-made clothing, and home appliances, absorbed Americans into consumer communities and accentuated differences between those who could afford goods and services and those who could not.

Commonplace Luxuries   If a society's affluence is measured by how it converts luxuries into commonplace articles, the United States was becoming affluent between 1880 and 1920. By 1899, manufactured goods and perishable foodstuffs had become increasingly available. That year, Americans consumed 100 crates of oranges for every 1,000 people, bought 2 billion machine-produced cigarettes, and spent about 63 cents per person on soap. By 1921, Americans smoked 43 billion cigarettes (403 per person), ate 248 crates of oranges per 1,000 people, and spent $1.40 on soap.

Data for the period show that incomes rose broadly. By 1920, the richest 5 percent of the population received almost one-fourth of all earned income. Incomes also rose among the middle class. Average pay for clerical workers rose 36 percent between 1890 and 1910 (see Table 18.1). In 1900, federal employees averaged $1,072 a year (around $30,000 in modern dollars). The middle class could afford comfortable housing. A six- or seven-room house cost around $3,000 to buy (about $70,000 in current dollars) and from $15 to $20 per month ($400 to $500 in current dollars) to rent.

Although hourly wages for industrial employees increased, workers spent a disproportionate amount on necessities. Average annual wages of factory laborers rose about 30 percent, from $486 in 1890 (about $12,000 in modern dollars) to $630 in 1910 (about $15,500 in current dollars). In industries with large female work forces, hourly pay rates remained lower than in male-dominated industries. Nevertheless, as Table 18.1 shows, most wages moved upward.

Cost of Living

Wage increases mean little, however, if living costs rise as fast or faster. The weekly cost of living for a typical family of four rose over 47 percent between 1889 and 1913. Goods that cost $68 in 1889 increased, after a slight dip in the mid-1890s, to $100 by 1913.

How, then, could working-class Americans afford goods and services? Many could not. The daughter of a textile worker, recalling her school days, described how "some of the kids would bring bars of chocolate, others an orange.... I suppose they

TABLE 18.1   American Living Standards, 1890–1910

	1890	1910
Income and Earnings		
Annual income		
Clerical worker	$848	$1,156
Public school teacher	256	492
Industrial worker	486	630
Farm laborer	233	336
Hourly wage		
Soft-coal miner	0.18[a]	0.21
Iron worker	0.17[a]	0.23
Shoe worker	0.14[a]	0.19
Paper worker	0.12[a]	0.17
Labor Statistics		
Number of people in labor force	28.5 mil.	41.7 mil.[b]
Average workweek in manufacturing	60 hrs.	51 hrs.

[a]1892

[b]1920

were richer than a family like ours. My father used to buy a bag of candy and a bag of peanuts every payday.... And that's all we'd have until the next payday."

Supplements to Family Income

Still, a family could raise its income and partake modestly in consumer society by sending children and women into the labor market (see pages 466-468). Where a father alone made $600 a year, wages of other family members might lift total family income to $800 or $900. Many families also rented rooms to boarders and lodgers, yielding up to $200 annually. Between 1889 and 1901, working-class families markedly increased expenditures for life insurance and new leisure activities (see Chapter 19), improving their living standard.

More than ever, working Americans lived within a money economy and living in which wages and living standards were closely linked. Between 1890 and 1920, the labor force increased by 50 percent, from 28 million workers to 42 million. These figures represent a change in the nature of work as much as increases in available jobs. In rural households of the nineteenth century, women and children performed crucial tasks of cooking, cleaning, planting, and harvesting—labor absent from employment figures because they earned no wages. As the nation industrialized and the agricultural sector declined, paid employment became more common. The proportion of Americans who worked probably did not increase markedly. What was new was the increase in paid employment, making consumer goods and services more affordable.

Higher Life Expectancy

Medical advances, better diets, and improved housing sharply reduced death rates and extended life. Between 1900 and 1920, life expectancy rose by six years, and the death rate dropped by 24 percent. Notable declines occurred in deaths from typhoid, diphtheria, influenza (except for a harsh pandemic in 1918 and 1919), tuberculosis, and intestinal ailments. There were, however, significantly more deaths from cancer, diabetes, and heart disease, afflictions of an aging population and of new environmental factors, such as smoke and chemical pollution. Homicides and automobile-related deaths also increased dramatically.

Not only were amenities and luxuries more available but upward mobility seemed more accessible, too. Public education, aided by construction of new schools and laws requiring children to stay in school to age fourteen, equipped young people to achieve a living standard higher than their parents'. The creation of managerial and sales jobs helped counter downward mobility when mechanization pushed skilled workers from their crafts. And mass production added greater convenience to workers' lives.

Flush Toilets and Other Innovations

At the vanguard of a revolution in lifestyles stood the toilet. The chain-pull, washdown water closet, invented in England around 1870, reached the United States in the 1880s. Shortly after 1900, the flush toilet appeared. Before 1880, only luxury hotels and wealthy families had private indoor bathrooms. By the 1890s, the germ theory of disease was raising fears about carelessly disposed human waste as a source of infection and water contamination. Middle-class Americans installed modern toilets in urban houses. By the 1920s, toilets were prevalent in working-class homes, too. Edward and Clarence Scott, who manufactured white tissue in perforated rolls, provided Americans a more convenient form of toilet tissue than the rough paper they previously used. Bodily functions took on an unpleasant image, and the home bathroom became a place of utmost privacy.

Before the mid-nineteenth century, Americans typically ate only foods in season. Drying, smoking, and salting could preserve meat for a short time, but the availability of fresh meat and milk was limited due to spoilage. A French inventor developed the cooking-and-sealing process of canning around 1810, and in the 1850s an American man named Gail Borden devised a means of condensing and preserving milk. Sales of canned goods and condensed milk increased during the 1860s, but there were production problems. In the 1880s, inventors fashioned machines to peel fruits and vegetables, and mass-produce cans from tin plate. Now, people everywhere could consume tomatoes, milk, oysters, and other alternatives to previously monotonous diets.

Other inventions broadened Americans' diets. Growing urban populations created demands for more produce. Railroad refrigerator cars enabled growers and meatpackers to ship perishables farther and preserve them longer. By the 1890s, northern city dwellers could enjoy southern and western strawberries, grapes, and tomatoes for several months. Home iceboxes enabled middle-class families to store perishables, and by 1900 the nation had two thousand ice plants, many making home deliveries.

Dietary Reform

Availability of new foods also inspired health advocates to reform American diets. In the 1870s, John H. Kellogg, nutritionist at the Western Health Reform Institute in Battle Creek, Michigan, began serving patients health foods, including peanut butter and wheat flakes. Years later, his brother, William K. Kellogg, invented corn flakes, and another nutritionist, Charles W. Post, introduced Grape-Nuts, replacing eggs, potatoes, and meat with supposedly healthier cereal. Before World War I, scientists discovered the dietetic value of vitamins A and B. Cookbooks and cooking schools increasingly reflected heightened interest in food's possibilities for health and enjoyment.

As in the past, the poorest people still consumed cheap foods, heavy in starches and carbohydrates and little meat. Workers spent almost half of a breadwinner's wages on food, but they never suffered the malnutrition that plagued other developing nations.

Ready-Made Clothing

The sewing machine and standardized sizes sparked a revolution in clothing. Invented in Europe but refined in the mid-nineteenth century by Americans Elias Howe Jr. and Isaac M. Singer, the sewing machine facilitated clothing and shoe manufacture. Demand for uniforms during the Civil War boosted the ready-made clothing industry, and by 1890 annual retail sales reached $1.5 billion. Mass production enabled manufacturers to turn out quality apparel at low cost and to standardize sizes. By 1900, only the poorest families could not afford "ready-to-wear" clothes. Tailors and seamstresses were relegated to repair work. Many women continued to make clothing at home, but commercial dress patterns simplified home production and injected another form of standardization into everyday life.

Mass-produced garments altered clothing styles and tastes. As women's participation in work and leisure activities increased, dress designers shifted from burdensome Victorian designs to more comfortable styles. In the 1890s, hemlines receded, and high-boned collars disappeared. By the 1920s, a dress required three yards of material instead of ten.

Men's clothes, too, became lightweight. Before 1900, men in the middle and well-off working classes would have owned two suits: one for Sundays and special occasions, and one for everyday. After 1900, however, manufacturers produced inexpensive garments from seasonal fabrics. Men replaced derbies with felt hats, and stiff collars and cuffs with soft ones; somber, dark-blue serge gave way to lighter shades and more intricate weaves.

Department and Chain Stores

Department stores and chain stores helped create and serve this new consumerism. Between 1865 and 1900, Macy's Department Store in New York, Wanamaker's in Philadelphia, Marshall Field in Chicago, and the Emporium in San Francisco became urban landmarks. Previously, working classes bought goods in stores with limited inventories, and wealthier people patronized fancy shops; prices, quality of goods, and social custom discouraged each from shopping at the other's establishments. Now, department stores with open displays caused a merchandising revolution, offering home deliveries, exchange policies, and charge accounts.

Meanwhile, the Great Atlantic Tea Company, founded in 1859, became the first grocery chain. Renamed the Great Atlantic & Pacific Tea Company in 1869 (known as A&P), the firm bought in volume and sold to the public at low prices. By 1915, there were eighteen hundred A&P stores, and twelve thousand more over the next ten years.

Advertising

In the late nineteenth century, companies that mass-produced consumer goods hired advertisers to create "consumption communities" of brand-loyal consumers. In 1881, Congress passed a trademark law enabling producers to register brand names. Thousands of companies registered products as varied as Hires Root Beer, Uneeda Biscuits, and Carter's Little Liver Pills. Advertising agencies—a service pioneered by N. W. Ayer & Son of Philadelphia—offered expert advice on cultivating brand loyalty. In 1865, retailers spent about $9.5 million on advertising; $95 million by 1900 and nearly $500 million by 1919. Newspapers served as the prime instrument for advertising, as people read them to find out what was for sale as well as what was happening.

Outdoor billboards and electrical signs were also important selling devices. Billboards on city buildings, in railroad stations, and alongside roads promoted such products as Gillette razors, Wrigley chewing gum, and Budweiser beer. In the mid-1890s, electric lights made billboards exciting. The flashing electrical signs on New York City's Broadway gave the street its label "the Great White Way."

The Corporate Consolidation Movement

What led corporations to increasingly consolidate in the late nineteenth century?

Neither new products nor marketing techniques could mask unsettling economic factors. The huge capital investment for new technology required that factories operate near capacity to recover costs. But the more manufacturers produced, the more they had to sell, which meant spending more on advertising and reducing prices. To compensate, they further expanded production and often reduced wages. To expand, they sold stocks and borrowed money. And to repay loans, they had to produce and sell even more. This spiraling process strangled small firms and thrust workers into constant uncertainty.

In this environment, optimism could dissolve at the hint that debtors could not meet their obligations. Economic downturns occurred regularly—1873, 1884, 1893. Some business leaders blamed overproduction; others, underconsumption; still others blamed lax credit and investment practices. To combat uncertainty, many adopted tighter and larger forms of centralized organization.

Rise of Corporations

Industrialists never questioned the capitalist system. They sought new ways to enlarge the state laws of the early 1800s, which encouraged commerce and industry. Under such laws, anyone could start a company and raise money by selling stock. Stockholders shared in profits without personal risk, because laws limited their liability for company debts to the amount of their investment. Responsibility for company administration rested with its managers.

By 1900, two-thirds of all U.S. manufactured goods were produced by corporations such as General Electric and the American Tobacco Company. In the 1880s and 1890s, the Supreme Court ruled that corporations, like individuals, are protected by the Fourteenth Amendment. States could not deny corporations equal protection nor deprive them of property rights without due process of law. Such rulings insulated corporations from government interference.

Pools and Trusts

Between the late 1880s and early 1900s, business consolidation produced massive conglomerates that have since dominated the nation's economy. At first, such alliances were informal, consisting of cooperative agreements among firms manufacturing the same product or offering the same service. Through these arrangements, called *pools,* competing companies tried to control the market by agreeing how much each should produce and sharing profits. During slow periods, however, pool members secretly reduced prices or sold more than the agreed quota to boost profits.

In 1879, one of **John D. Rockefeller's** lawyers, Samuel Dodd, devised a more reliable means of dominating a market. Dodd suggested adapting a legal device called a *trust,* in which one company could control an industry by luring or forcing stockholders of smaller companies in that industry to yield control of their stock "in trust" to the larger company's board of trustees. This allowed Rockefeller to achieve *horizontal integration*—the control of similar companies—of the profitable petroleum industry in 1882 by combining his corporation with other refineries.

John D. Rockefeller: Creator of Standard Oil and master of the use of pools and trusts to monopolize an industry.

Holding Companies

In 1888, New Jersey adopted laws allowing corporations chartered there to own property in other corporations in other states. This facilitated creation of the *holding company,* which owned a partial or complete interest in other companies and merged assets (buildings, equipment, inventory, and cash) under single management. Rockefeller's Standard Oil combined forty independents. By 1898, Standard Oil refined 84 percent of all oil produced in the nation, controlled most pipelines, and engaged in natural-gas production and ownership of oil-producing properties.

Believing that Rockefeller's Standard Oil monopoly was exercising dangerous power, this political cartoonist depicts the trust as a greedy octopus whose sprawling tentacles already ensnare Congress, state legislatures, and the taxpayer, and are reaching for the White House.

vertical integration: Business strategy in which a holding company would seek to control all aspects of the industry in which it functioned, fusing related businesses together under one management.

To dominate their markets, many holding companies sought control over all aspects of the industry, including raw-materials, manufacturing, and distribution. A model of such **vertical integration**, which fused related businesses under unified management, was Gustavus Swift's Chicago meat-processing operation. During the 1880s, Swift invested in livestock, slaughterhouses, refrigerator cars, and marketing to ensure profits from meat sales at prices he could control.

Mergers provided orderly profits. Between 1889 and 1903, three hundred combinations were formed, mostly trusts and holding companies. Other mammoth combinations included Amalgamated Copper Company, American Sugar Refining Company, and U.S. Rubber Company. These huge companies ruthlessly put thousands of small firms out of business.

Financiers

The merger movement created a new species of businessman, whose vocation was financial organizing. Shrewd investors sought opportunities for combination, formed a holding company, raised money by selling stock and borrowing from banks, then persuaded producers to sell their firms to the new company. Investment bankers such as J. P. Morgan and Jacob Schiff piloted the merger movement, inspiring awe with their financial power.

Corporate growth turned stock and bond exchanges into hubs of activity. In 1886, trading on the New York Stock Exchange passed 1 million shares daily. By 1914, the number of industrial stocks traded reached 511, compared with 145 in

1869. Between 1870 and 1900, foreign investment in American companies rose from $1.5 billion to $3.5 billion. Assets of savings banks, concentrated in the Northeast and the West Coast, rose by 700 percent between 1875 and 1897. These institutions, along with commercial banks and insurance companies, invested heavily in railroads and industrial enterprises.

The Gospel of Wealth and Its Critics

How did business leaders use Social Darwinism to justify their mergers and consolidations?

Business leaders used corporate consolidation to minimize competition and justified their tactics with the doctrine of **Social Darwinism**. This ideology loosely grafted Charles Darwin's theory of survival of the fittest onto laissez faire, the doctrine that government should not interfere in private economic matters. Social Darwinists reasoned that, in a free-market economy, wealth would flow naturally to those most capable of handling it. In this view, large corporations represented the natural accumulation of economic power by those best suited for it.

Social Darwinists reasoned, too, that wealth carried moral responsibilities. Steel baron **Andrew Carnegie** asserted "the Gospel of Wealth"—that as guardians of society's wealth, he and other industrialists had a duty to serve society. Carnegie donated more than $350 million to libraries, schools, peace initiatives, and the arts. Such philanthropy, however, also enabled benefactors such as Carnegie to define what was good and necessary for society; it did not translate into paying workers decent wages.

Social Darwinism: Extended Charles Darwin's theory of "survival of the fittest" to the free market system, arguing that competition would weed out weaker firms and allow stronger, fitter firms to thrive.

Andrew Carnegie: Scottish immigrant who built an enormous steel company and became a renowned philanthropist.

Government Assistance to Business

Leaders in the corporate consolidation movement extolled initiative while requesting government assistance. Denouncing efforts to legislate maximum working hours or factory conditions as interference, they nonetheless lobbied for public subsidies and tax relief to encourage business growth. Grants to railroads (see Chapter 17) were one form of such assistance. Tariffs, which benefited American products by placing taxes on imported products, were another. Industrialists argued that tariff protection encouraged the development of new products and enterprises. But tariffs also forced consumers to pay artificially high prices (see page 518).

Dissenting Voices

Critics charged that these methods stifled opportunity and originated from greed. Such charges from farmers, workers, and intellectuals, reflected a fear of monopoly—the domination of an economic activity (such as oil refining) by one powerful company (such as Standard Oil). Those who feared monopoly believed that large corporations fixed prices, exploited workers, destroyed opportunity by crushing small businesses, and threatened democracy by corrupting politicians.

By the mid-1880s, some intellectuals challenged Social Darwinism and laissez-faire economics. Philosopher and psychologist William James led this trend, arguing that human will, independent of the environment, could alter existence.

Sociologist Lester Ward, in his book *Dynamic Sociology* (1883), proffered that a system that guaranteed survival only to the fittest was wasteful and brutal. Instead, Ward reasoned, cooperative activity fostered by government intervention

Link to the preface of George M. Beard's *American Nervousness: Its Causes and Consequences.*

was fairer. Economists Richard Ely, John R. Commons, and Edward Bemis denounced laissez-faire and praised the assistance that government could offer to ordinary people.

Visionaries such as Henry George and Edward Bellamy questioned why the United States had so many poor people while a few became wealthy. George, a printer with a seventh-grade education, was an avid reader of economic theory. He believed that inequality stemmed from the ability of a few to profit from rising land values, which made landowners rich from high rents. To prevent profiteering, George proposed replacing all taxes with a "single tax" on the "unearned increment"—the rise in property values caused by increased market demand. Argued in *Progress and Poverty* (1879), George's popular plan almost won him the mayoralty of New York City in 1886.

Novelist Edward Bellamy proposed that government own the means of production. In his popular novel, *Looking Backward* (1888), Bellamy depicted Boston in the year 2000 as a peaceful community run by benevolent elders managing the economy so everyone had a job. Bellamy hoped that a "principle of fraternal cooperation" would replace vicious competition and wasteful monopoly. Dubbed "Nationalism," his vision sparked new Nationalist clubs nationwide and kindled appeals for political reform, social welfare measures, and government ownership of railroads and utilities.

Antitrust Legislation

Several states took steps to prohibit monopolies and regulate business. By 1900, twenty-seven states banned pools, and fifteen had constitutional provisions outlawing trusts (see Chapter 20). But state governments lacked the staff and judicial support for an effective attack on big business, and corporations found ways to evade restrictions. Congress moved hesitantly toward legislation but in 1890 passed the Sherman Anti-Trust Act. Introduced by Ohio Senator John Sherman, the law made illegal "every contract, combination in the form of trust or otherwise, or conspiracy in the restraint of trade." Those found guilty of violating the law faced fines and jail terms, and those wronged by illegal combinations could sue for triple damages. However, the law was watered down when rewritten by pro-business eastern senators. It did not clearly define "restraint of trade" and consigned interpretation of its provisions to the often business-allied courts.

Judges used the law's vagueness to blur distinctions between reasonable and unreasonable restraints of trade. When in 1895 the federal government prosecuted the Sugar Trust for owning 98 percent of the nation's sugar-refining capacity, eight of nine Supreme Court justices ruled in *U.S. v. E. C. Knight Co.* that control of manufacturing did not necessarily mean control of trade. According to the Court, the Constitution empowered Congress to regulate interstate commerce, but not manufacturing.

Between 1890 and 1900, the federal government prosecuted only eighteen cases under the Sherman Anti-Trust Act. The most successful involved railroads involved in interstate commerce. Ironically, the act equipped the government to break up labor unions: courts that did not consider monopolistic production a restraint on trade willingly applied antitrust provisions to boycotts by striking unions.

Technology of Recorded Sound

Today's digital recorders and downloadable music derive from technology, chemistry, and human resourcefulness that came together in the late nineteenth century. In 1877, Thomas A. Edison devised a way to preserve and reproduce his voice by storing it on indentations made in tin foil. Edison intended his "speaking machine" to help businesses store dictation. But in 1878, a rivalry with telephone inventor Alexander Graham Bell, who was working on a similar device, drew Edison to invent a phonograph for recorded music. By the 1890s, audiences paid to hear recorded sounds from these machines.

By 1901, companies such as the Columbia Phonograph Company produced machines that played music recorded on cylinders molded from a durable wax compound. Over the next ten years, inventors improved the phonograph so sound played back from a stylus (needle) vibrating in grooves of a shellac disc. Records' playing time increased from two minutes to four.

Phonograph records replaced sheet music as the most popular medium, but soon radio emerged and boosted record sales. Radio's popularity was only possible via another electronic technology: the microphone. This device improved sound quality over megaphones. As phonograph prices declined and sound quality improved, more records became available.

The 1938 invention of the idler wheel, which enabled a phonograph turntable to spin a disk at speeds necessary for the stylus to pick up sound accurately, brought an important advance. Shortly thereafter, significant inventions in sound recording, such as the magnetic tape recorder, allowed for more manipulation of sound in the recording studio. In 1963 Philips, a Dutch electronics firm, introduced the compact audio cassette. Two decades later, Philips joined with the Japanese corporation Sony to adapt digital laser discs, invented by an American for video storage, to hold music The compact disc (CD) was born, and from there it was a short step for the Apple Computer Company to create the iPod, storing CD-quality music on an internal hard drive.

Summary

Mechanization and inventions thrust the United States into the vanguard of industrial nations and altered daily life. By the early twentieth century, American industrial output surpassed that of Great Britain, France, and Germany combined. By 1900, factories, stores, and banks converted America from a debtor, agricultural nation into an industrial, financial, and exporting power.

But aggressive industrial consolidation changed the nature of work from individual activity by skilled producers to mass production by wage earners. Laborers fought to retain control of their work and organized unions. The outpouring of products created a mass society based on consumerism and dominated by technology and the communications media.

The enforcement problems with the Sherman Anti-Trust Act reflected the uneven distribution of power. Corporations consolidated to control resources, production, and politics. Laborers and reformers benefited from material gains that technology and mass production provided, but they accused businesses of acquiring influence and profits at their expense. Some people celebrated the economic transformation. Others struggled with the dilemma of industrialism: whether new accumulations of wealth would undermine the republican ideal of democracy and equality.

Industrial expansion proved unstoppable because so many people were benefiting from it. Moreover, the waves of newcomers pouring into the nation's cities were increasingly furnishing workers and consumers for America's expanding productive capacity.

Chapter Review

Technology and the Triumph of Industrialization

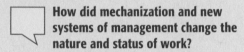

How did technological innovations transform American industry?

New inventions and technological advances made production of goods and services faster and cheaper, which in turn fueled the rise of mass production and consumption. Big factories replaced small workshops as large-scale production became increasingly economical. Thomas Edison's system for inexpensively distributing electricity facilitated the emergence of countless other inventions in the late nineteenth and early twentieth centuries. Henry Ford built on a European invention for engines to create his assembly-line process that would mass produce thousands of identical—ultimately affordable—cars in the early twentieth century. The du Pont family similarly revolutionized the chemical industry; electric looms advanced textile production and relocated it from North to South; while North Carolinian James B. Duke mass-produced cigarettes and remade the tobacco industry.

Mechanization and the Changing Status of Labor

How did mechanization and new systems of management change the nature and status of work?

Innovation created new jobs, but labor-saving machines also meant that fewer workers could produce more in less time. Instead of doing many different tasks, workers now did only one task repeatedly. As workers rather than producers, they lost control over their work days and techniques and instead were regulated by the time clock and the production mandates of bosses. Skill became less important, and as the need for skilled workers declined, manufacturers saw a way to cut labor costs by hiring women and children, whom they could pay much less. The advent of typewriters and other office machines opened clerical and white collar jobs to women, as well. But in manufacturing, long days and harsh and often hazardous working conditions led to increasing number of accidents as well as labor unrest.

Labor Violence and the Union Movement

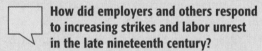

How did employers and others respond to increasing strikes and labor unrest in the late nineteenth century?

Labor activism against long hours, pay cuts, and difficult working conditions became increasingly violent beginning with the Railroad Strike of 1877. After the Haymarket riot of 1886 and other strikes, labor violence and the participation of socialists and anarchists in the labor movement, heightened fears of radicalism. Governments strengthened police forces and armories; employer associations circulated blacklists of union activists, whom they agreed not to employ and they hired private detectives to suppress strikes. State and federal governments also sent in troops, as in the case of the Homestead and Pullman strikes, to break the strikes.

Standards of Living

What was the impact of the new consumer culture on people's lives?

On the one hand, mass production made goods previously deemed luxuries affordable to mainstream Americans, improving everyday life—among them flush toilets, railroad car refrigeration, ready-made clothing, and retail stores. On the other hand, however, workers' wages did not always keep pace with the cost of goods.

Most industrial workers spent a large proportion of their income on necessities. To afford the basics, working families often began to rely on additional sources of income from wives and children, either via factory work or taking in boarders. Advances in nutrition and medical science helped Americans to live longer and healthier lives, although those at the lowest rungs of society still ate diets high in carbohydrates and starches with little meat, and often spent half of the breadwinner's wages even on this meager diet.

The Corporate Consolidation Movement

What led corporations to increasingly consolidate in the late nineteenth century?

Big companies saw consolidation as a way to guarantee profits and control downward economic cycles. They believed the more they pooled resources to set prices and influence profits by determining how much to supply the market, the more they could manage a downturn. Until the 1880s, however, laws made it illegal for companies to own stock in another firm. Instead, businessmen such as John D. Rockefeller turned to trusts, luring stockholders of smaller companies to yield control of their stock "in trust" to the larger company's board of trustees. Once states allowed companies within their borders to own stock in corporations in other states, holding companies emerged, where one firm would own partial or complete interest in another and merge their assets and resources. Holding companies also found it easier to dominate their markets by controlling all aspects of an industry from raw materials to manufacturing to distribution.

The Gospel of Wealth and Its Critics

How did business leaders use Social Darwinism to justify their mergers and consolidations?

Social Darwinism applied Charles Darwin's theory of survival of the fittest to laissez-faire economics, which stressed that government should let the economy manage itself. Social Darwinists argued that in a free-market economy, wealth would flow to those most capable of handling it, and that corporations represented that accumulation of power in the best hands. On the flip side, many believed those with wealth had a moral obligation to use it to improve society; hence, some business leaders such as Andrew Carnegie donated millions to the arts, education, and other worthy causes. Such largesse did not, however, translate into better wages or working conditions for their employees.

Suggestions for Further Reading

Edward L. Ayers, *The Promise of the New South: Life After Reconstruction* (1992)

Ileen A. DeVault, *United Apart: Gender and the Rise of Craft Unionism* (2004)

Steven J. Diner, *A Very Different Age: Americans of the Progressive Era* (1998)

John F. Kasson, *Civilizing the Machine: Technology and Republican Values in America, 1776–1900* (1976)

Alice Kessler-Harris, *Out to Work: A History of Wage-Earning Women in the United States* (2003)

T. J. Jackson Lears and Richard W. Fox, eds., *The Culture of Consumption: Critical Essays in American History, 1880–1980* (1983)

David Montgomery, *The Fall of the House of Labor: The Workplace, the State and American Labor Activism, 1865–1925* (1987)

Jeffrey Sklansky, *The Soul's Economy: Market Society and Selfhood in American Thought, 1820–1920* (2002)

Go to the CourseMate website for primary source links, study tools, and review materials for this chapter.
www.cengagebrain.com

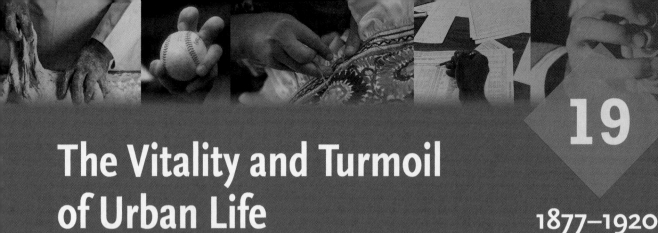

19

The Vitality and Turmoil of Urban Life

1877–1920

Crowds on the street gasped as they looked upward. A man, bound in a straitjacket was hanging by his heels high above New York's Times Square. Suddenly, he wriggled wildly. In seconds Harry Houdini, the early twentieth century's most celebrated showman, was free. As he had done many times, Houdini fed the public's taste for suspense, courage, and entertainment with a death-defying feat.

Born as Erich Weiss in Hungary in 1874, Houdini and his family emigrated to Wisconsin in 1878. After Erich's father lost his job as a rabbi, the family moved to New York City, where father and son worked in a necktie factory. When Erich's father died in 1892, the young man became an entertainer. After a few lackluster years as a magician, Erich discovered his talent as an illusionist and escape artist. He changed his name to Harry Houdini and became one of America's most enthralling performers.

By the early 1900s, "The Great Houdini" was a feature in vaudeville, a new form of urban entertainment. His specialty was escaping from elaborate and dangerous confinements: ropes, manacles, and padlocked containers. Houdini was also a skillful self-publicist, advertising his act with posters and leaflets. Around 1913, Houdini introduced his famous "Chinese water torture cell" escape, in which he extracted himself from being bound and suspended upside down in a water-filled, locked glass-and-steel cabinet. Houdini escaped by manipulating his five-foot-five frame in unusual ways but also by concealing picks and keys, which he sometimes regurgitated. Although he constantly defied death in his act, Houdini could not escape the abdominal infection that took his life in 1926.

Like many people in the late nineteenth and early twentieth centuries, the Weiss family were immigrants who fled poverty and tried to remake themselves in a burgeoning American city. They faced challenges of where to live and work, how to deal with a cash-based economy, how to preserve their ethnic consciousness amid bigotry, how to achieve independence and respectability.

Such challenges made cities places of hope, frustration, achievement, and conflict.

Not until the 1880s did the United States begin to become an urban nation. The technological innovations and industrialization of the late nineteenth century sparked economic and geographical expansion, funneling millions of people cityward. By 1920, the census showed that, for the first time, a majority of Americans (51.4 percent) lived in cities (settlements with more than 2,500 people). Cities were filled with new kinds of consumerism as urban dwellers patronized dance halls, theatrical performances, vaudeville, movies, and sporting events in record numbers. By idolizing Houdini, sports heroes, and movie celebrities, or by benefiting from the largesse of a political boss, ordinary working- and middle-class people could believe in the potential of individuals to free themselves from the uncertainties of an emerging technological and urban society. At the same time, poverty and discrimination haunted the lives of countless urban dwellers, combining the era's opportunities with persistent of inequality and prejudice. Whatever people's personal experiences, cities had become central to American life. How people built cities and adjusted to their environments shaped modern American society.

As you read this chapter, keep the following questions in mind:

* **What were the most important factors contributing to the urban growth of the period 1877–1920?**

* **How did immigrants adjust to and reshape their adopted homeland?**

* **How did industrialization and urbanization affect patterns of family life and leisure time?**

Growth of the Modern City

> What fueled urban growth in the late nineteenth century?

Initially, commercial centers cities became the main arenas for industrial development in the late nineteenth century. As labor, transportation, and communication hubs, cities supplied everything factories needed. The further industrialization advanced, the more opportunities it created for jobs and investment, which, in turn drew more people to cities. As workers and consumers, they fueled yet more industrialization.

Industrial Development While manufacturing enterprises varied, cities increasingly specialized. Mass production of clothing concentrated in New York City, the shoe industry in Philadelphia, and textiles in New England cities. Other cities created goods derived from surrounding agricultural regions: flour in Minneapolis, cottonseed oil in Memphis, beef and pork in Chicago. Still others

Chronology

1867	First law regulating tenements passes in New York State	1893	Columbian Exposition opens in Chicago
1870	One-fourth of Americans live in cities	1895	Hearst buys *New York Journal,* which becomes another popular yellow-journalism newspaper
1876	National League of Professional Baseball Clubs founded	1898	Race riot erupts in Wilmington, North Carolina
1880s	"New" immigrants from eastern and southern Europe begin to arrive in large numbers	1900–10	Immigration reaches peak
		1903	Boston beats Pittsburgh in baseball's first World Series
1883	Brooklyn Bridge completed Pulitzer buys *New York World,* creating major publication for yellow journalism	1905	Intercollegiate Athletic Association, forerunner of National Intercollegiate Athletic Association (NCAA) is formed, restructuring rules of football
1885	Safety bicycle invented	1915	Griffith directs *Birth of a Nation,* one of first major technically sophisticated movies
1886	First settlement house opens in New York City		
1889	Edison invents motion picture and viewing device	1919	Race riot erupts in East St. Louis, Illinois
1890s	Electric trolleys replace horse-drawn mass transit	1920	Majority (51.4 percent) of Americans live in cities

processed natural resources: gold and copper in Denver, fish and lumber in Seattle, iron in Pittsburgh and Birmingham, oil in Houston and Los Angeles. Such activities increased cities' attraction for people seeking steady employment.

The compact city of the early nineteenth century, where residences mingled among shops, factories, and warehouses, sprawled miles beyond the original settlement. No longer did walking distance determine a city's size. Instead, cities separated into working- and middle-class neighborhoods, commercial strips, downtown, and a ring of suburbs. Two forces were responsible for this: mass transportation, which propelled people and enterprises outward, and economic change, which drew human and material resources inward.

Mechanization of Mass Transportation

By the 1870s, horse-drawn vehicles shared city streets with faster motor-driven conveyances. In the 1880s, cable cars started operating in Chicago, San Francisco, and other cities. In the 1890s, electric-powered streetcars began replacing horse cars and cable cars. In a few cities, companies raised track onto trestles, enabling "elevated" vehicles to travel above jammed downtown streets. In Boston, New York, and Philadelphia, transit firms solved traffic problems by digging underground subway tunnels. Because "els" were expensive to construct, they appeared only in cities with enough riders to ensure profits.

Urban Sprawl

Mass transit launched urban dwellers into remote neighborhoods and created a commuting public. Streetcar lines serviced districts that promised the most riders and increase company revenues. Working-class families, who needed every cent, found streetcars unaffordable. But the growing middle class who could afford the fare—usually 5 cents a ride—could escape to quiet, tree-lined neighborhoods on the outskirts and commute to the inner city for work, shopping, and entertainment.

Electric trolley cars and other forms of mass transit enabled middle-class people such as these women and men to reside on the urban outskirts and ride into the city center for work, shopping, and entertainment.

When consumers moved outward, businesses followed, locating near mass transit. Department stores and banks joined groceries, theaters, taverns, and shops to create neighborhood shopping centers. Meanwhile, the urban core became a work zone, where tall buildings loomed over streets clogged with people, horses, and vehicles.

Population Growth

Between 1870 and 1920, the number of Americans living in cities increased from 10 million to 54 million. During this period, the number of cities with more than 100,000 people swelled from 15 to 68; those with more than 500,000 rose from two to twelve (see Map 19.1).

American urban growth derived from the annexation of bordering land and people and net migration (excess of in-migrants over out-migrants). For example, in 1898, New York City, previously consisting of Manhattan and the Bronx, merged with Brooklyn, Staten Island, and part of Queens and doubled to 3 million people. Suburbs desired annexation for the schools, water, fire protection, and sewer systems that cities provided.

Link to the 1910 Federal Census Data Information search tool.

Urban In-Migration

In-migration from the countryside and immigration from abroad made the greatest contribution to urban population growth. Urban newcomers arrived from two major sources: the American countryside and Europe. Asia, Canada, and Latin America also supplied smaller numbers of immigrants.

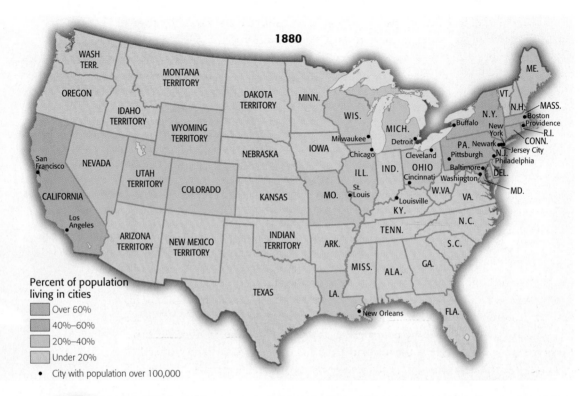

MAP 19.1

Urbanization, 1880 and 1920

In 1880, the vast majority of states were still heavily rural. By 1920, only a few had less than 20 percent of their population living in cities.

Source: Copyright © Cengage Learning

Rural populations declined as urban populations burgeoned. Low crop prices and high debts drove white farmers toward opportunities that cities seemingly offered. Migrants filled major cities, such as Detroit, Chicago, and San Francisco, but also secondary cities, such as Indianapolis, Salt Lake City, Nashville, and San Diego. The thrill of city life beckoned especially to young people. For every four men who migrated cityward, five women did the same, often to escape unhappy homes and enjoy the independence that urban employment offered.

Thousands of rural African Americans also moved cityward, seeking better employment and fleeing crop liens, ravages of the boll weevil on cotton crops, racial violence, and political oppression. Black migration accelerated after 1915, but thirty-two cities already had more than ten thousand black residents by 1900. Because few factories would employ African Americans, most found jobs in the service sector—cleaning, cooking, and driving. Since these were traditionally female jobs, black women outnumbered black men in most cities. In the South, rural black migrants became an important source of unskilled labor in growing cities. By 1900, almost 40 percent of the population of Atlanta, Georgia, and Charlotte, North Carolina, was black.

In the West, Hispanics also moved into cities such as Los Angeles, San Diego, and San Antonio. They took unskilled construction jobs previously held by Chinese laborers driven from Southern California cities by racism. In some Texas cities, native Mexicans (called *Tejanos*) held the majority of unskilled jobs. Mexican men often left home to take temporary jobs in cities, leaving behind female heads of household.

New Foreign Immigration

Most newcomers were foreign immigrants fleeing villages and cities in Europe, Asia, Canada, and Latin America for the United States. Many wanted only to make enough money to return home and live in greater comfort. For every hundred foreigners who entered the country, thirty ultimately left. Still, like Houdini's family, most of the 26 million immigrants arriving between 1870 and 1920 remained, settling largely in cities.

New U.S. immigration was part of a worldwide movement, triggered by population pressures, land redistribution, industrialization, and religious persecution in Europe, Asia, Canada, and Latin America.

Immigrants from northern and western Europe had long made the United States their destination, but after 1880 economic and demographic changes propelled immigrants from other regions. Increased numbers came from eastern and southern Europe, plus smaller groups from Canada, Mexico, and Japan. Between 1900 and 1909, two-thirds of immigrants came from Italy, Austria-Hungary, and Russia. By 1910, arrivals from Mexico outnumbered arrivals from Ireland, and numerous Japanese moved to the West Coast and Hawai'i. Foreign-born blacks, chiefly from the West Indies, also came. (See the Cengage web site for the nationalities of immigrants.)

Many long-settled Americans feared these "**new immigrants**," whose customs, Catholic and Jewish faiths, and poverty made them seem particularly alien. Unlike immigrants from Great Britain and Ireland, new immigrants did not speak English, and often worked in low-skill occupations. Yet old and new immigrants like the Weisses made family the focus of all undertakings. New arrivals usually knew where to go and how to get there from relatives who already immigrated. Workers helped kin obtain jobs, and family members pooled resources to improve their standard of living.

new immigrants: Wave of immigrants after 1880 coming from mainly southern and eastern Europe.

Geographic and Social Mobility

Once they arrived, in-migrants and immigrants rarely stayed put. Each year, millions of families went elsewhere. The Weiss family stayed in Appleton, Wisconsin, only a few years before leaving for New York City. More than half the families residing in a city were gone ten years later. Even within a city, it was common for a family to live at three or more different addresses over a ten- or fifteen-year period. One in every three or four families moved each year (today the rate is one in five). Migration offered one escape to opportunity.

Advancement up the social scale through better jobs was available mostly to white males. Thousands of businesses were needed to supply goods and services to burgeoning urban populations, and as corporations grew and centralized operations, they required new personnel. An aspiring merchant could open a saloon for a few hundred dollars. Knowledge of accounting could qualify workers for white-collar jobs with higher incomes than manual labor.

Such advancement occurred often, but few could accumulate large fortunes. Most of the era's wealthiest businessmen began their careers with advantages: American birth, Protestant religion, education, and affluent parents. Yet considerable movement occurred along the road from poverty to moderate success, from manual to nonmanual work.

Rates of upward occupational mobility were slow but steady between 1870 and 1920. In fast-growing cities such as Atlanta and Los Angeles, approximately one in five white manual workers rose to white-collar or owner's positions within ten years. In older cities such as Boston and Philadelphia, upward mobility averaged closer to one in six workers in ten years. Some men slipped from a higher to a lower rung, but rates of upward movement usually doubled downward rates. Immigrants generally experienced less upward and more downward mobility than the native-born, yet the chances for a white male rising to a higher-status job than his father were good.

The definition of a better job varied. Many immigrant artisans considered an accountant's job unmanly. People who took pride in working with their hands neither desired nonmanual jobs nor encouraged their children to seek them. As one Italian tailor explained, "I want that my oldest boy learn my trade because I tell him that you could always make at least enough for the family."

Failure rates were high among small proprietors in working-class neighborhoods,

Fresh off the boat and wearing homeland clothing, immigrants pose for a photograph outside the federal immigration station at Ellis Island, offshore from New York City. Situated in the shadow of the Statue of Liberty, Ellis Island immigration officials processed millions of newcomers such as these, asking them questions about their background and examining them for health problems.

Records of the Public Health Service. (90-G-125-29)/US GOV National Archives

because customers' low incomes made profits uncertain. Many manual workers sought security rather than mobility, preferring a steady wage to risks of ownership.

Many women held paying jobs but since their standing was defined by the men in their lives, their chief means of mobility came from marrying men with wealth or potential. Laws limited what women could inherit; educational institutions blocked their training in such professions as medicine and law; and prevailing assumptions attributed higher aptitude for manual skills and business to men. Assigned to the lowest-paying occupations by prejudice, African Americans, American Indians, Mexican Americans, and Asian Americans made even fewer gains.

A person might achieve social mobility by acquiring property, which was not easily accomplished. Banks and savings-and-loan institutions had strict lending practices, and mortgage loans carried high interest rates and short repayment periods. Nevertheless, some families succeeded in amassing down payments on property. Ownership rates varied regionally—higher in western cities, lower in eastern cities—but 36 percent of all urban American families owned their homes in 1900, the highest homeownership rate of any western nation except for Denmark, Norway, and Sweden.

Many, particularly unskilled workers, did not improve their status; they simply floated from one low-paying job to another. Others found greener pastures. The possibilities for upward mobility tempered people's dissatisfaction with the stresses of city life. For every story of rags to riches, there were myriad small triumphs. Although the gap between rich and poor widened, for those in between, the expanding economies of American cities created room.

Urban Neighborhoods

American cities were characterized by collections of subcommunities where people, most of whom had migrated from somewhere else, coped with daily challenges to their cultures. Rather than yield completely to assimilation, migrants and immigrants interacted with the urban environment to retain their identity while altering their outlook and the social structure of cities.

How did immigrants adapt to their new lives in U.S. cities?

Cultural Retention and Change

In new surroundings, immigrants first anchored their lives to what they knew: their culture. Old World customs persisted in immigrant districts of Italians from the same province, Japanese from the same island district, and Russian Jews from the same *shtetl*. Newcomers re-created mutual aid societies from their homeland. For example, the Japanese recreated *ken* societies, which organized social celebrations and relief services. The Chinese reproduced loan associations, called *whey,* which raised money to help members acquire businesses, and village associations called *fongs,* which rented apartments to members. Southern Italians transplanted the system whereby a *padrone* (boss) found jobs for unskilled workers by negotiating with—and receiving payoffs from—an employer. All newcomers practiced religion as they always had, held traditional feasts and pageants, and married within their group.

Urban Borderlands

In large cities, such as Chicago, Philadelphia, and Detroit, European immigrants initially clustered in inner neighborhoods where low-skill jobs and cheap housing were most available. These districts often were multi-ethnic, "urban borderlands," where diverse people coexisted. Even within districts identified with a certain group, such as Little Italy, Jewtown, Polonia, or Greektown, rapid mobility undermined homogeneity, as newcomers moved and older inhabitants left. Neighborhoods often housed several ethnic groups, but businesses and institutions, such as bakeries, butcher shops, churches, and club headquarters— operated by and for one ethnic group—gave a neighborhood its identity.

For first- and second-generation immigrants, their neighborhoods acted as havens until individuals were ready to cross from the borderland into the majority society—sometimes within just a few years. The expansion of mass transportation and outward movement of factories enabled people to move to areas where they interspersed with families of their socioeconomic class but not necessarily their ethnicity. European immigrants encountered prejudice, such as the exclusion of Jews from certain neighborhoods, professions, and clubs, but discrimination rarely was systematic. For people of color, however—African Americans, Asians, and Mexicans— discrimination kept them from becoming multiethnic.

Racial Segregation and Violence

Although small numbers of African Americans may have lived near or interspersed with whites in the eighteenth and early nineteenth centuries, by the late nineteenth century rigid racial discrimination forced them into highly segregated ghettos. By 1920, in Chicago, Detroit, Cleveland, and other cities, two-thirds or more of the total black population inhabited only 10 percent of the residential area. Within their neighborhoods, African Americans nurtured institutions to cope with city life: shops, clubs, theaters, dance halls, newspapers, and saloons. Churches, particularly branches of Baptist and African Methodist Episcopal (AME) Protestantism, were especially influential. Pittsburgh blacks boasted twenty-eight such churches in the early 1900s. Membership in Cincinnati's black Baptist churches doubled between 1870 and 1900. In Louisville, blacks built their own theological institute. Black religious activity dominated urban life and represented cooperation across class lines.

The only way blacks could relieve overcrowding from increased migration was to expand residential borders into surrounding, previously white neighborhoods, a process that resulted in harassment and attacks by white residents who feared that blacks would reduce property values. African Americans' increased presence in cities, as well as their competition with whites for housing, jobs, and political influence, sparked race riots. In 1898, white residents of Wilmington, North Carolina, resenting African Americans' involvement in local government and incensed by an African American newspaper editorial accusing white women of loose sexual behavior, rioted and killed dozens of blacks. White supremacists overthrew the city government, expelling black and white officeholders, and instituted restrictions to prevent blacks from voting. An influx of unskilled black strikebreakers into East St. Louis, Illinois, heightened racial tensions in 1917, triggering a riot in which nine whites and thirty-nine blacks were killed and three hundred buildings were destroyed.

Asians also encountered discrimination and segregation. Although Chinese immigrants often preferred to live apart from Anglos in Chinatowns of San Francisco, Seattle, Los Angeles, and New York City, creating their own business, government, and social institutions, Anglos also tried to keep them separated. Using the slogan "The Chinese must go," Irish immigrant Denis Kearney and his followers intimidated employers into refusing to hire Chinese, and drove hundreds of Asians out of the city. San Francisco's government prohibited Chinese laundries from white neighborhoods and banned the wearing of queues, the traditional Chinese hair braid. In 1882, Congress passed the Chinese Exclusion Act, which suspended Chinese immigration and prohibited naturalization of Chinese already residing in the United States. And in 1892, Congress approved the Geary Act, which extended immigration restriction and required Chinese Americans to carry certificates of residence issued by the Treasury Department. The U.S. Supreme Court upheld the Geary Act in 1893 in *Fong Yue Ting v. United States*. Similarly prevented from becoming American citizens, Japanese immigrants, called Issei, also developed communities.

Mexican Barrios

Mexicans in southwestern cities experienced complex residential patterns. In places such as Los Angeles, Santa Barbara, and Tucson, Mexicans had been the original inhabitants; Anglos were newcomers who pushed Mexicans into increasingly isolated districts on the outskirts called *barrios*. Frequently, real-estate covenants, by which property owners pledged not to sell homes to Mexicans (or to African Americans or Jews), kept Mexican families confined in barrios. These areas were outside central-city multiethnic borderlands housing European immigrants. As such, racial bias hindered African Americans', Asians', and Mexicans' opportunities to remake their lives.

Cultural Adaptation

Virtually everywhere immigrants lived, Old World culture mingled with New World realities. Although many foreigners identified themselves by their village or region of birth, native-born Americans categorized them by nationality. People from County Cork and County Limerick, for example, were merged into Irish; those from Calabria and Campobasso into Italians. Immigrant institutions, such as newspapers and churches, had to appeal to the entire nationality to survive.

Moreover, the diversity of American cities prompted foreigners to modify their habits and previous ways of life. Although many immigrants tried to preserve their language, English, taught in schools and needed at work, soon penetrated most communities. Foreigners fashioned homeland styles garments but used American rather than traditional fabrics. Italians went to American doctors but still carried amulets to ward off evil spirits. Polka bands blended American and Polish folk music. Mexican ballads now described border crossing and hardships in the United States.

The influx of so many immigrants between 1870 and 1920 transformed the United States from a basically Protestant nation into a diverse collection of Protestants, Catholics, Orthodox Christians, Jews, Buddhists, and Muslims. Newcomers from Italy, Hungary, Polish lands, and Slovakia joined Irish and Germans to boost the proportion of Catholics in many cities. German and Russian immigrants gave New York City one of the largest Jewish populations in the world.

Many Catholics and Jews tried to accommodate their faiths to the new environment. Catholic and Jewish leaders from earlier immigrant groups supported liberalizing trends—use of English in services, the phasing out of such Old World rituals as saints' feasts, and a preference for public over religious schools. As new immigrants continued to arrive, however, these trends met stiff resistance. Newcomers usually held onto familiar religious practices, whether the folk Catholicism of southern Italy or the Orthodox Judaism of eastern Europe. Despite church attempts to make American Catholicism more uniform, bishops acceded to pressures from predominantly Polish congregations for Polish priests. Eastern

European Jews, convinced that Reform Judaism sacrificed too much to American ways, established the Conservative branch, which retained traditional ritual but abolished the segregation of women in synagogues and allowed English prayers. But, second-generation Catholics and Jews marrying coreligionists of other ethnic groups—an Italian Catholic marrying a Polish Catholic—kept religious identity strong while undercutting ethnic identity.

The cities nurtured rich cultural variety: American folk music and literature, Italian and Mexican cuisine, Irish comedy, Yiddish theater, African American jazz and dance, and much more. Newcomers changed their environment as much as they were changed by it.

Living Conditions in the Inner City

What made cities seem particularly dangerous?

The central sections of American cities were plagued by poverty, disease, crime, and the tensions that occur when manifold people live close together. City dwellers coped, and technology, private enterprise, and public authority achieved some remarkable successes.

Inner-City Housing

In spite of massive construction, population growth outpaced housing supplies. Lack of inexpensive living quarters especially distressed working-class families who, because of low wages, had to rent homes. Landlords exploited housing shortages by splitting up existing buildings to house more people, constructing multiple-unit tenements, and hiking rents. Low-income families adapted to high costs and short supply by sharing space and expenses. A one-family apartment was typically occupied by two or three families, or by one family plus several boarders.

The result was unprecedented crowding. In 1890, New York City's immigrant-packed Lower East Side averaged 702 people per acre, one of the highest population densities in the world.

Conditions were harsh. The largest rooms were barely ten feet wide, and interior rooms either lacked windows or opened onto narrow shafts that bred vermin and rotten odors. Few buildings had indoor plumbing; residents used privies (outdoor toilets) in the back yard or basement. Often, the only source of heat was dangerous, polluting coal-burning stoves.

Housing Reform

Housing problems sparked widespread reform campaigns. New York State led with laws in 1867, 1879, and 1901 that established light, ventilation, and safety codes for new tenement buildings. Reformers, such as journalist Jacob Riis and humanitarian Lawrence Veiller, advocated "model tenements," with spacious rooms and better facilities for low-income families. Model tenements meant lower profits, however—a sacrifice few landlords would make. Reformers and public officials opposed government financing of better housing, fearing it would undermine private enterprise. Still, housing codes and regulatory commissions strengthened local government's power to oversee construction.

New Home Technology

Technology ultimately revolutionized home life. Advanced systems of central heating (furnaces), electric lighting, and indoor plumbing created more comfort, first for middle-class households and

Inner-city dwellers used not only indoor space as efficiently as possible, but also what little outdoor space was available to them. Scores of families living in this cramped block of six-story tenements in New York strung clotheslines behind the buildings. Notice that there is virtually no space between buildings—only rooms at the front and back received daylight and fresh air.

later for most others. Whereas formerly families bought coal or chopped wood for cooking and heating, made candles for light, and hauled bath water, their homes increasingly connected to outside pipes and wires for gas, water, and electricity. Moreover, these utilities helped create new attitudes about privacy. Middle-class bedrooms and bathrooms became private retreats. Scientific and technological advances eventually enabled city dwellers and the nation to live healthier. By the 1880s, doctors began to accept the theory that microorganisms (germs) cause disease. Cities established more efficient water purification and sewage disposal, which control such dread diseases as cholera, typhoid fever, and diphtheria.

Meanwhile, street paving, modernized firefighting equipment, and electric street lighting spread rapidly across urban America. Steel-frame construction, which uses a metal skeleton rather than with masonry walls for building support, enabled the erection of skyscrapers—and thus more efficient vertical use of scarce land. Steel-cable suspension bridges, developed by John A. Roebling and epitomized by his Brooklyn Bridge (completed in 1883), linked metropolitan sections more closely.

Poverty Relief   None of these improvements, however, lightened the burden of poverty. Since colonial days, Americans have disagreed about public responsibility for poor relief. According to traditional beliefs, still widespread in the early twentieth century, anyone could escape poverty through hard work and clean living; moral weakness caused indigence. Such reasoning bred fear that aiding the poor encouraged them to rely on public support rather than their own efforts. As business cycles fluctuated and poverty increased, this attitude hardened, and city governments discontinued direct grants of food, fuel, and clothing to needy families. Instead, cities provided relief in return for work on public projects and sent special cases to state-run almshouses, orphanages, and homes for the blind, deaf, and mentally ill.

Between 1877 and 1892, philanthropists in ninety-two cities formed Charity Organization Societies to make social welfare (like business) more efficient by merging disparate charities into coordinated units. Believing poverty to be caused by personal defects, such as alcoholism and laziness, these organizations visited poor families to identify the "deserving" poor and encourage them to be thriftier and more virtuous. Close observation of the poor, however, prompted some humanitarians to conclude that people's environments, not personal shortcomings, caused poverty and that society should help improve conditions. They believed they could reduce poverty through better housing, education, sanitation, and job opportunities. This fueled campaigns for building codes, factory regulations, and public health measures in the Progressive era of the early twentieth century (see Chapter 21). Still, most middle- and upper-class Americans embraced the creed that only the unfit were poor and that poverty relief should be tolerated but never encouraged.

Crime and Violence

Crime and disorder, as much as crowding and poverty, nurtured fears that cities, especially their slums, threatened the nation. While homicide rates declined in industrialized nations, America's rose alarmingly: 25 murders per million people in 1881; 107 per million in 1898. Domestic violence, muggings, and gang fights made cities turbulent as did pickpockets, swindlers, and burglars. Urban outlaws, such as Rufus Minor, acquired as much notoriety as western desperadoes. Short and bald, Minor resembled a shy clerk, but one police chief labeled him "one of the smartest bank sneaks in America." Minor was implicated in bank heists in New York City, Cleveland, Detroit, Providence, Philadelphia, Albany, Boston, and Baltimore between 1878 and 1882.

Urban crime may have become more conspicuous rather than more prevalent. Undeniably, concentrations of wealth and the mingling of different peoples provided opportunities for larceny, vice, and assault. But urban lawlessness and brutality probably did not exceed that of backwoods mining camps and southern plantations. Nativists were quick to blame immigrants for crime, but the law-breaking population included native-born Americans and foreigners.

Managing the City

What facilitated the rise of political machines in cities?

Burgeoning populations and physical expansion created urgent needs for sewers, police and fire protection, schools, parks, and other services. Such needs strained municipal resources and city governments. In addition to a mayor and a city council, various governmental boards administered health regulations, public works, poverty relief, and other functions. Philadelphia at one time had thirty such boards. State governments also interfered in local matters, appointing board members and limiting cities' abilities to levy taxes and borrow money.

Water Supply and Sewage Disposal

Finding sources of clean water and a way to dispose of waste became increasingly pressing challenges. In the early 1800s, urban households used privies to dispose of human excrement, and factories dumped untreated sewage into rivers, lakes, and bays. By the late nineteenth century, sewer systems and flush toilets, plus use of water as a coolant in factories, overwhelmed waterways, contaminating drinking-water sources. The stench of rivers was often unbearable, and pollution bred disease. In 1878, nineteen thousand people fled a yellow fever epidemic in Memphis. Acceptance in the 1880s of the germ theory of disease prompted cities to reduce chances that human waste and other pollutants would endanger water supplies. Some states legally prohibited discharging raw sewage into rivers and streams, and a few cities began the expensive process of chemically treating sewage. Gradually, water managers installed mechanical filters, and cities, led by Jersey City, began purifying water supplies by adding chlorine. These efforts dramatically reduced deaths from typhoid fever.

But waste disposal remained a thorny problem. Experts in 1900 estimated that every New Yorker generated annually some 160 pounds of garbage (food and bones); 1,200 pounds of ashes (from stoves and furnaces); and 100 pounds of rubbish. Solid waste from factories and businesses included tons of scrap metal and wood. Each of the estimated 3.5 million horses in American cities in 1900 daily dropped about 20 pounds of manure and a gallon of urine that rain washed into nearby water sources. By the twentieth century, this refuse was a health and safety hazard.

Urban Engineers

Citizens' groups, led by women's organizations, began discussing these dilemmas in the 1880s, and by 1900 urban governments began to hire sanitary engineers, to design garbage collection systems, disposing of it in incinerators and landfills. American engineers developed systems and standards of worldwide significance that made cities more livable, such as street lighting, bridge and street construction and fire protection. Elected officials depended on engineers' expertise in aiding urban expansion. Insulated within bureaucratic agencies from tumultuous party politics, engineers made lasting contributions to urban management.

Law Enforcement

After the mid-nineteenth century, urban dwellers increasingly depended on professional police to protect life and property, but law enforcement became complicated and controversial, as various groups differed about how laws should be enforced. Ethnic and racial minorities were more likely to be arrested and police officers applied the law less harshly to members of their own ethnic groups and to people offering bribes.

Often poorly trained and prone to corruption, police were squeezed between demands for swift and severe action on the one hand and for leniency on the other. Some people clamored for police crackdowns on saloons, gambling halls, and houses of prostitution, while those who profited from and patronized such customer-oriented criminal establishments favored loose law enforcement. Achieving balance between criminal law and personal freedom grew increasingly difficult.

Political Machines

Out of the apparent confusion surrounding urban management arose **political machines**, organizations whose main goals were the rewards—money, influence, and prestige—of getting and keeping power. Machine politicians routinely used fraud and bribery to further their ends. But they also provided relief, security, and services to voters.

Machines bred leaders, called **bosses**, who built power bases among working classes, especially immigrants. Most bosses had immigrant backgrounds and grew

political machines: Organizations that emerged in urban, often working-class and immigrant neighborhoods; they solicited votes for particular candidates and promised jobs and other services to supporters; putting their candidates in office gave them power over local government.

bosses: Headed political machines; often of similar background to constituents; popular local figures who exchanged votes for money, support and other favors.

Street Cleaning and Urban Reform

As street cleaning became an ever-increasing necessity in burgeoning cities, the numbers of employees of sanitation departments multiplied and the tools they used on their job became more elaborate. As early as 1896, inventors were designing machines and vehicles with brushes to replace the brooms used by past street-cleaning crews and scrapers for clearing snow. One such inventor, Charles Brooks of Newark, New Jersey, not only patented a street-cleaning and snow-removal truck but also designed a receptacles for storing trash and other litter picked up by his machine. But to the minds of engineers and sanitarians, improving the technology of street cleaning was not enough. The process needed to be organized and controlled in what to their minds was a logical way, giving workers a sense of value and professionalism. These two images reveal an important change in the appearance of the New York City street-cleaning force between 1868 and 1920. What reform attitudes do the contrasting images represent? Given the contrasting dress of the two crews, how would the general public have reacted to each?

Beginning of New York's Street Cleaning Department. Calling the roll, 1868

This shows the great improvements made by Colonel Waring as Street Commissioner. Calling the roll in 1920

Miriam and Ira D. Wallach Division of Art, Prints and Photographs, The New York Public Library, Astor, Lenox and Tilden Foundations

By the early 1900s, the profession of sanitary engineer became an important one to the urban environment. As the human and horse populations of cities grew, garbage, litter, and manure became nagging inconveniences and health hazards. In 1868, street sweepers hired to clean the streets, often consisted of crews hired by political bosses and were required to report to a supervisor for morning roll call.

up in the inner city. They knew their constituents' needs firsthand and gained power by dealing with problems of everyday life. In return for votes, bosses provided jobs, built parks and bathhouses, distributed food and clothing to the needy, and helped when someone ran afoul of the law. New York's "Big Tim" Sullivan, for example, gave out shoes and sponsored annual picnics. Bosses, moreover, made politics a full-time profession. They attended weddings and wakes, joined clubs, and held open houses in saloons where neighborhood folk could speak to them personally. According to George Washington Plunkitt, a neighborhood boss in New York City, "As a rule [the boss]…plays politics every day and night in the year and his headquarters bears the inscription, Never closed."

Link to the *New York Times* article about Tim Sullivan's annual picnic.

To finance their activities and election campaigns, bosses exchanged favors for votes and money. Power over local government enabled machines to control who received public contracts, utility and streetcar franchises, and city jobs. Recipients were expected to repay the machine with a portion of their profits or salaries and to cast supporting votes. Critics called this process graft; bosses called it gratitude.

Bosses such as Philadelphia's "Duke" Vare, Kansas City's Tom Pendergast, and New York's Richard Croker lived like kings, though their official incomes were slim. Yet machines were rarely as dictatorial or corrupt as critics charged. Rather, several machines evolved into tightly structured operations, such as New York's Tammany Hall organization (named after a society that began as a patriotic fraternal club), which blended public accomplishments with personal gain. The system rested on a popular base held together by loyalty and service. Most machines were coalitions of smaller organizations that derived power directly from inner-city neighborhoods. Machine-led governments constructed the urban infrastructure—public buildings, sewer systems, schools, bridges, and mass-transit lines—and expanded urban services—police, firefighting, and health departments.

Machine politics, however, was rarely neutral. Racial minorities and new immigrant groups, such as Italians and Poles, received only token jobs and nominal favors, if any. And bribes and kickbacks made machine projects and services costly to taxpayers. Cities could not ordinarily raise enough revenue for construction projects from taxes and fees, so they financed expansion with loans from the public in the form of municipal bonds, which caused public debts, and then taxes, to soar. And payoffs from gambling, prostitution, and illicit liquor traffic became important sources of machine revenue. But bosses were no guiltier of discrimination and self-interest than were business leaders who exploited workers, spoiled the environment, and manipulated government in pursuit of profits.

Civic Reform

Many middle- and upper-class Americans feared that immigrant-based political machines menaced democracy and wasted municipal finances. Anxious over the poverty and disorder that accompanied city growth, civic reformers organized to install more responsible leaders who would run government efficiently, like a business.

To implement business principles in government, civic reformers supported structural changes, such as city-manager and commission forms of government, which would place administration in the hands of experts rather than politicians, and nonpartisan citywide rather than neighborhood-based election of officials. Reformers believed they could cleanse city government of party politics and weaken bosses' power bases.

A few reform mayors also addressed social problems. Hazen S. Pingree of Detroit, Samuel "Golden Rule" Jones of Toledo, and Tom Johnson of Cleveland worked to provide jobs to poor people, reduce charges by streetcar and utility companies, and promote governmental responsibility for citizens' welfare. They also supported public ownership of gas, electric, and telephone companies, quasi-socialist reforms that alienated their business allies. But Pingree, Jones, and Johnson were exceptions. Civic reformers achieved some successes but rarely held office for long.

Social Reform

Social reformers—mostly young and middle class—also wanted to solve urban problems. Housing reformers pressed local governments for building codes ensuring safety in tenements. Educational reformers sought to use public schools to prepare immigrant children for citizenship by teaching them American values. Health reformers tried to improve medical care for those who could not afford it. And residents of settlement-houses, located in inner-city neighborhoods to bridge the gulf between classes offered vocational classes, lessons in English, and childcare, and they sponsored programs to improve nutrition and housing. Settlement-house workers such as **Jane Addams** and **Florence Kelley** of Chicago and Lillian Wald of New York broadened their scope to fight for school nurses, factory safety codes, and public playgrounds, they became reform leaders in cities and in the nation (see pages 543–544).

Jane Addams: Social worker, pioneer of the settlement house movement and founder of Chicago's Hull House, which provided education, training, and social activities for immigrants and the poor.

Florence Kelley: Settlement-house worker who later became the chief factory inspector for Illinois in 1893.

The City Beautiful Movement

Male reformers similarly worked to improve cities by organizing the City Beautiful movement. Inspired by the 1893 Columbian Exposition, a dazzling world's fair built in Chicago, architects and planners urged the construction of civic centers, parks, and boulevards that would make cities economically efficient and attractive. Projects were underway in Chicago, San Francisco, and Washington, D.C., in the early 1900s. Yet neither government nor private businesses could finance large-scale projects, and planners disagreed among themselves and with social reformers over whether beautification would solve urban problems.

Urban reformers wanted to save cities, but they often failed to realize cities' diverse populations and people's varying visions of reform. To civic reformers, appointing government workers on the basis of civil service exams rather than party loyalty meant progress, but to working-class men, civil service signified reduced employment opportunities. Moral reformers believed that restricting alcoholic beverage sales would prevent breadwinners from squandering wages, but immigrants saw it as interference. Planners saw new streets and buildings as modern necessities, but such structures often displaced the poor. Well-meaning humanitarians criticized immigrant mothers for the way they dressed, did housework, and raised children, without regard for their financial situation. Thus urban reform merged idealism with naiveté and insensitivity.

Family Life

What factors led to declining birth rates in the late nineteenth-century United States?

Urbanization and industrialization strained family life. New institutions—schools, social clubs, political organizations, unions—increasingly competed with the family to provide nurture and education. Clergy and journalists warned that the growing separation between home and work, rising divorce rates, entrance of women into the work force, and loss of parental control over children spelled peril for home and family. Yet the family remained a cushion in an uncertain world.

Family and Household Structures

Until recently, most American households (75 to 80 percent) consisted of nuclear families—usually a married couple, with or without children. Only a few households consisted of extended families—usually a married couple, their children, and one or more relatives. Not many people lived alone.

Several factors explain this pattern. Because immigrants tended to be young, the American population as a whole was young. In 1880, the median age was under twenty-one; by 1920, it was still only twenty-five. (Median age at present is thirty-five.) Moreover, in 1900, the death rate among people aged forty-five to sixty-four was double what it is today. Only 4 percent of the population was sixty-five or older, versus 12 percent today. Thus, few families could form extended three-generation households, and fewer children than today had living grandparents.

Declining Birth Rates

Most of Europe and North America experienced falling birth rates in the nineteenth century. In 1880, the birth rate was 40 live births per 1,000 people; by 1900, it dropped to 32; by 1920, to 28. Although fertility was higher among black, immigrant, and rural women, birth rates of all groups fell.

In part, this decline occurred because, as the United States became more urbanized, the economic value of children lessened. On farms, each child born represented an addition to the family labor force. In the wage-based urban economy, children could not contribute significantly to the family income for many years, and a new child represented a draw on family income. Second, infant mortality fell as diet and medical care improved, and families did not have to bear many children to ensure that some would survive.

Perhaps most importantly, as American society industrialized and urbanized, the idea of a child as an innocent being who needed shelter from society's corruptions spread, first among the middle class and gradually to the working class. A mother's care could be more effective if she had fewer children. That seems to have stimulated decisions to limit family size—either by abstaining from sex or using contraception. Families with six or eight children became rare; three or four became more usual. Birth-control technology—diaphragms and condoms—had been utilized for centuries, but in this era, new materials made devices more convenient and dependable.

Stages of Life

Before the late nineteenth century, stages of life were less distinct than they are today. Childhood, for instance, was regarded as a period during which young people prepared for adulthood by gradually assuming more responsibilities. Subdivisions of youth—toddlers, schoolchildren, teenagers, and the like—were not recognized. Because married couples had more children over a longer time span, parenthood occupied most of adult life. And because few people lived to advanced age, older people were not isolated from other age groups. By the late nineteenth century, however, decreasing birth rates shortened the period of parental responsibility, so more middle-aged couples experienced an "empty nest" when children grew up and left home. Longer life expectancy and a tendency by employers to force aged workers to retire separated the old from the young.

New patterns of childhood also emerged. To be sure, youngsters in working-class families still helped out—working in factories, scavenging streets for scraps of wood and coal, and peddling newspapers. But as states passed compulsory school attendance laws in the 1870s and 1880s, education occupied more of children's daily time than ever, filling nine months of the year until they were teenagers. Schools strengthened peer rather than family influence over behavior. Researchers such as G. Stanley Hall and Luther H. Gulick advocated that teachers and parents match education and play activities to children's changing developmental stages. "Child-saving" advocates asserted that adult-supervised playgrounds would protect children from dangerous activities.

The Unmarried

Although marriage rates were high, large numbers of city dwellers were unmarried. In 1890, almost 42 percent of adult American men and 37 percent of women were single, almost twice as high as in 1960 but slightly lower than today. About half still lived with parents, but others inhabited boarding houses. Mostly young, these men and women constituted a separate subculture that supported institutions such as dance halls, saloons, cafés, and the Young Men's Christian Association (YMCA) and Young Women's Christian Association (YWCA).

Some unmarried people were part of the homosexual populations that thrived in large cities such as New York, San Francisco, and Boston. Although difficult to estimate numerically, gay men had their own subculture of clubs, restaurants, coffeehouses, theaters, and support networks. A number of same-sex couples, especially women, formed lasting marital-type relationships, sometimes called "Boston marriages." People in this subculture were categorized more by how they acted—men acting like women, women acting like men—than by who their sexual partners were. The term *homosexual* was not used. Men who dressed and acted like women were called "fairies." Gay women remained more hidden, and a lesbian subculture did not develop until the 1920s.

Boarding and Lodging

In every city, boarding houses and lodging hotels were common, but families also took in boarders to occupy rooms vacated by grown children and for additional income. By 1900, as many as 50 percent of city residents, including Erich Weiss's family, had lived either as, or with, boarders at some point. Housing reformers charged that boarding and lodging caused overcrowding and loss of privacy. For people on the move, boarding was a transitional stage, providing a quasi-family environment until they set up their own households. Especially in communities where housing was expensive or scarce, newlyweds sometimes lived temporarily with one spouse's parents. Families also took in widowed parents or unmarried siblings.

Functions of Kinship

At a time when welfare agencies were scarce, the family was the institution to which people turned when in need. Relatives often resided nearby and helped with childcare, meals, advice, and consolation. They also obtained jobs for relatives. According to one new arrival, "After two days my brother took me to the shop he was working in and his boss saw me and he gave me the job."

But kinship obligations were not always welcome. Immigrant families pressured last-born daughters to stay home to care for aging parents, a practice that stifled opportunities for education, marriage, and independence. Generational tensions also developed when immigrant parents and American-born children clashed over the abandonment of Old World ways or the amount of wages that employed children should contribute. Nevertheless, kinship helped people cope with stresses of urban-industrial society.

Thus, family life and functions were both changing and holding firm. New institutions were assuming tasks formerly performed by the family. Schools made education a community responsibility. Employment agencies, personnel offices, and labor unions took responsibility for employee recruitment and job security. Age-based peer groups exerted greater influence over people's values and activities. Migration seemed to be splitting families apart. Yet, kinship remained a dependable though not always appreciated institution.

Holiday Celebrations   Family togetherness became especially visible at holiday celebrations. Thanksgiving, Christmas, and Easter were special times for family reunion and child-centered activities. Birthdays, too, became increasingly festive, and served as a milestone for measuring what an individual had experienced and accomplished relative to others of the same age. In 1914, President Woodrow Wilson signed a proclamation designating the second Sunday in May as Mother's Day, capping a six-year campaign by schoolteacher Anna Jarvis, who believed grown children neglected their mothers. Ethnic and racial groups adapted national celebrations to their cultures, preparing special ethnic foods and engaging in special ceremonies.

The New Leisure and Mass Culture

What fueled the rise of commercial leisure?

On December 2, 1889, as workers paraded through Worcester, Massachusetts, seeking shorter working hours, carpenters hoisted a banner proclaiming "Eight Hours for Work, Eight Hours for Rest, Eight Hours for What We Will." That last phrase laid claim to a segment of daily life belonging to the individual. Increasingly, leisure activities filled this time.

Increase in Leisure Time   Mechanization and assembly-line production cut the average manufacturing workweek from sixty-six hours in 1860 to sixty in 1890 and forty-seven in 1920. This meant shorter workdays and freer weekends. White-collar employees spent eight to ten hours a day on the job and often worked only half a day or not at all on weekends. Laborers in steel mills and sweatshops endured twelve- or fourteen-hour shifts with little leisure time. As the economy shifted from production to consumption, more Americans engaged in recreation, and a substantial segment of the economy provided for—and profited from—leisure.

Amusement became a commercial activity, as home entertainment expanded. Mass-produced pianos and sheet music for middle-class families made singing of popular songs a common form of home entertainment. The vanguard of new leisure pursuits, however, was sports. Formerly a fashionable indulgence of elites, organized sports became a favored pastime of all classes.

Baseball

The most popular sport was baseball. Derived from older bat, ball, and base-circling games, in 1845 the Knickerbocker Club of New York standardized the rules of play. By 1860, at least fifty baseball clubs existed, and youths played informal games on city lots and fields nationwide. The National League of Professional Baseball Clubs, founded in 1876, gave the sport a businesslike structure. But as early as 1867, a "color line" excluded black players from professional teams. Still, by the 1880s, professional baseball was big business. In 1903, the National League and competing American League (formed in 1901) began a World Series between their championship teams. The Boston Red Sox beat the Pittsburgh Pirates in that first series.

Croquet and Cycling

Baseball appealed mostly to men. But croquet, also popular, attracted both sexes. Middle- and upper-class people held croquet parties and night contests. Consequently, croquet increased opportunities for social contact between the sexes.

Meanwhile, cycling achieved popularity rivaling baseball, especially after 1885, when the cumbersome velocipede, with its huge front wheel and tall seat, gave way to safety bicycles with pneumatic tires and identical-size wheels. By 1900, Americans owned 10 million bicycles, and clubs petitioned state governments to build more paved roads. African American cyclists were allowed to compete professionally, and one rider, Major Taylor, achieved success in Europe and the United States between 1892 and 1910. Moreover, the bicycle freed women from the constraints of Victorian fashions. To ride the dropped-frame female models, women had to wear divided skirts and simple undergarments. As the 1900 census declared, "Few articles…have created so great a revolution in social conditions as the bicycle."

Football

American football, as an intercollegiate competition, attracted mostly spectators wealthy enough to have access to higher education. By the late nineteenth century, however, the game appealed to a broader audience. The 1893 Princeton-Yale game drew fifty thousand spectators, and informal games were played throughout the country. Soon, however, football became a national scandal because of its violence and use of "tramp athletes," nonstudents hired to help teams win. Critics accused football of mirroring undesirable features of American society. An editor of *The Nation* charged in 1890 that "the lack of moral scruple which pervades the struggles of the business world meets with temptations equally irresistible in the miniature contests of the football field."

The scandals climaxed in 1905, when 18 players died from game-related injuries and 159 were seriously injured. President Theodore Roosevelt, an advocate of athletics, convened a White House conference to discuss ways to eliminate brutality. The gathering founded the Intercollegiate Athletic Association (renamed the National College Athletic Association—NCAA—in 1910) to police college sports. In 1906, the association altered the game to make it less violent and more open.

As more women enrolled in college, they participated in such sports as rowing, track, and swimming. Invented in 1891 as a winter sport for men, basketball—soon women's most popular sport—received women's rules (which limited dribbling and running, and encouraged passing) from Senda Berenson of Smith College.

Links to the World

Japanese Baseball

Baseball, the "national pastime," was one new leisure-time pursuit that Americans took into different parts of the world. The Shanghai Base Ball Club was founded by Americans in China in 1863, but was denounced by the Imperial Court as spiritually corrupting. However, when Horace Wilson, an American teacher, taught baseball rules to his Japanese students around 1870, the game received an enthusiastic reception as a reinforcement of traditional virtues and became a part of Japanese culture.

During the 1870s, scores of Japanese high schools and colleges sponsored organized baseball, and in 1883 Hiroshi Hiraoka, a railroad engineer educated in Boston, founded the first official local team, the Shimbashi Athletic Club Athletics.

Before baseball, the Japanese had no team sports or recreational athletics. Once they learned about baseball, they found the idea of a team sport fit their culture well. But for them, baseball was serious business, involving often brutal training. Practices at Ichiko, one of Japan's two great high school baseball teams

in the late nineteenth century, were dubbed "Bloody Urine" because many players passed blood after a day of drilling. There was a spiritual quality as well, linked to Buddhist values. According to one Japanese coach, "Student baseball must be the baseball of self-discipline, or trying to attain the truth, just as in Zen Buddhism." This attitude prompted the Japanese to consider baseball a new method for pursuing the spirit of Bushido, the way of the samurai.

When Americans played baseball in Japan, the Japanese admired their talent but found them lacking discipline and respect. Americans insulted the Japanese by refusing to remove their hats and bow when they stepped up to bat. An international dispute occurred in Tokyo in 1891 when an American professor, late for a game, climbed over a sacred fence and was attacked by Japanese fans. The American embassy lodged a formal complaint. Americans assumed their game would encourage Japanese to become like westerners, but the Japanese transformed baseball into a uniquely Japanese expression of team spirit, discipline, and nationalism.

Replete with bats, gloves, and uniforms, this Japanese baseball team of 1890 very much resembles its American counterpart of that era. The Japanese adopted baseball soon after Americans became involved in their country but also added their cultural qualities to the game.

Japanese Baseball Hall of Fame

Show Business

Three branches of American show business—popular drama, musical comedy, and vaudeville—matured and became popular commercial entertainment. Theatrical performances offered audiences escape into melodrama, adventure, and comedy. For urban people unfamiliar with the frontier, plays made the mythical Wild West and Old South come alive through stories of Davy Crockett, Buffalo Bill, and the Civil War. Virtue and honor always triumphed in melodramas such as *Uncle Tom's Cabin* and *The Old Homestead,* reinforcing faith that, in an uncertain world, goodness would prevail.

George M. Cohan: Singer, dancer, and songwriter who drew on patriotic and traditional values in songs.

The American musical derived from Europe's lavishly costumed operettas. **George M. Cohan**, a singer, dancer, and songwriter born into an Irish family of entertainers, became master of American musical comedy in the early twentieth century. Drawing on patriotism and traditional values in songs such as "Yankee Doodle Boy" and "You're a Grand Old Flag," Cohan boosted morale during the First World War. Initially, American comic operas imitated European musicals, but by the early 1900s composers such as Victor Herbert were writing for American audiences.

Probably the most popular mass entertainment in early-twentieth-century America, vaudeville offered something for everyone. Shows included jugglers, magicians, acrobats, comedians, singers, dancers, and specialty acts like Houdini's escapes. Around 1900, the number of vaudeville theaters and troupes skyrocketed, and operators such as Tony Pastor and the partnership of Benjamin Keith and Edward Albee consolidated theaters and acts under their management. Producer Florenz Ziegfeld brilliantly packaged stylish shows—the Ziegfeld Follies—and gave the nation a new model of femininity, the Ziegfeld Girl, whose graceful dancing and alluring costumes suggested a haunting sensuality.

Link to video and audio of Eva Tanguay singing her theme song "I Don't Care."

Opportunities for Women and Minorities

Show business provided social mobility to female, African American, and immigrant performers, but also encouraged stereotyping and exploitation. Comic opera diva Lillian Russell, vaudeville singer-comedienne Fanny Brice, and burlesque queen Eva Tanguay attracted loyal fans and handsome fees. In contrast to the demure Victorian female, they conveyed pluck and independence. There was something shocking and confident about Eva Tanguay singing, "It's All Been Done Before but Not the Way I Do It." But lesser female performers and showgirls (called "soubrettes") were often exploited by male promoters and theater owners who wanted to profit by titillating the public with scantily clad women.

minstrel shows: Early stage shows in which white men wore blackface makeup and played to the prejudices of white audiences by offering demeaning and caricatured portrayals of African Americans in songs, dances, and skits.

Before the 1890s, the chief form of commercial entertainment employing African Americans was the **minstrel show**, but vaudeville opened new opportunities. Pandering to prejudices of white audiences, composers ridiculed blacks, and black performers were forced to portray demeaning characters. In songs such as "He's Just a Little Nigger, But He's Mine All Mine," blacks were degraded on stage as they were in society. Burt Williams, an educated black comedian and dancer, achieved success by wearing blackface makeup and playing stereotypical roles of a smiling fool and dandy, but the humiliation tormented him.

Like Houdini, many performers were immigrants, and their acts reflected their experiences and daily difficulties. Vaudeville utilized ethnic humor and exaggerated dialects. Skits and songs were fast-paced, replicating the tempo of factories, offices, and the streets. Performances reinforced ethnic stereotypes, but such distortions were more sympathetic than those directed at blacks. A typical scene involving Italians, for example, highlighted a character's uncertain grasp of English, which caused him to confuse *diploma* with *the plumber* and *pallbearer* with *polar bear*. Such scenes allowed audiences to laugh with, rather than at, foibles of the human condition.

Movies

Shortly after 1900, live entertainment yielded to the more accessible motion pictures. Perfected by Thomas Edison in the 1880s, movies began as slot-machine peepshows in arcades and billiard parlors. Eventually, images were projected onto a screen for large audiences. Producers, many of them from Jewish immigrant backgrounds, discovered that a film could tell a story in exciting ways. Using themes of patriotism and working-class experience, early filmmakers helped shift American culture away from its straitlaced Victorian values to a cosmopolitan outlook.

Movies presented controversial social messages as well as innovative technology and styles of expression. *Birth of a Nation* (1915), by director D. W. Griffith, was a stunning but viciously racist epic film about the Civil War and Reconstruction that fanned racial prejudice by depicting African Americans as threats to white moral values. The National Association for the Advancement of Colored People (NAACP), formed in 1909, led organized protests against it. But the film's groundbreaking techniques—close-ups, fade-outs, and battle scenes—heightened its drama.

Technology and entrepreneurship also made news a mass consumer product. Using high-speed printing presses, cheaply produced paper, and profits from growing advertisement revenues, shrewd publishers created an in-demand medium. Increased leisure time seemed to nurture a fascination with the sensational, and from the 1880s onward popular urban newspapers increasingly whetted that appetite.

Yellow Journalism

Joseph Pulitzer, a Hungarian immigrant who bought the *New York World* in 1883, made news a mass commodity. Pulitzer filled the *World* with stories of disasters, crimes, and scandals and featured screaming headlines, set in large, bold type. Pulitzer's journalists sought out news and created it. Reporter Nellie Bly (real name, Elizabeth Cochrane) faked her way into a mental asylum and wrote a brazen exposé of the sordid conditions she found. Other reporters staged stunts and wrote heart-rending human-interest stories. Pulitzer also popularized comics, and the yellow ink in which they were printed gave rise to the term *yellow journalism* as a synonym for sensationalism.

In one year, the *World*'s circulation increased from 20,000 to 100,000, and by the late 1890s it reached 1 million. Other publishers, such as William Randolph Hearst, who bought the *New York Journal* in 1895 and started a newspaper empire, adopted Pulitzer's techniques. Pulitzer, Hearst, and their rivals boosted circulation by featuring sports and women's news. Newspapers previously reported sporting events, but yellow-journalism papers gave such stories greater prominence with separate, expanded sports pages. For women, newspapers added special sections devoted to household tips, fashion, etiquette, and club news.

Other Mass-Market Publications

By the early twentieth century, mass-circulation magazines overshadowed the expensive elitist journals of earlier eras. Publications such as *McClure's, Saturday Evening Post,* and *Ladies' Home Journal* offered human-interest stories, muckraking exposés (see page 542), fiction, photographs, colorful covers, and eye-catching ads. Meanwhile, the number of published books more than quadrupled between 1880 and 1917, reflecting the growing literacy. Between 1870 and 1920, the proportion of Americans over age ten who could not read fell from 20 percent to 6 percent.

Other forms of communication also expanded. In 1891, there was less than 1 telephone for every 100 people in the United States; by 1901, the number reached 2.1, and by 1921, it swelled to 12.6. In 1900, Americans used 4 billion postage stamps; in 1922, they bought 14.3 billion. More than ever before, people in different parts of the country knew about and discussed the same news event. America was becoming a mass society where the same products, technology, and information dominated everyday life.

Anthony Comstock

Anthony Comstock: Leader of the moral purity crusade against what he saw as vice and corruption; known for his efforts to censor sexually explicit material, including, as postal inspector, seeking to ban birth control literature from the mail.

The new leisure and amusements did not go unopposed. Most prominent among reactionary moralists was **Anthony Comstock**, who made a career of efforts to censor sexually explicit and suggestive literature and entertainment. In 1873, Comstock created the Society for the Supression of Vice and convinced Congress to outlaw the distribution of "lewd and lascivious" material. He secured appointment as a postal inspector and worked to ban marriage manuals and birth control literature from the mails. Between the 1870s and his death in 1915, Comstock constantly campaigned against what he considered indecent performances, especially in New York City. His targets also included paintings of nude women, an exhibition of physical culture, and a play by noted British author George Bernard Shaw that had prostitution among its themes.

But crusaders such as Comstock could not alter cultural change. Mass culture represented democracy because influences flowed upward from the experiences and desires of ordinary people as much as, if not more than, from the rich. The popularity of sports, the themes in movies and on stage, and the content of publications reveal that savvy entrepreneurs understood the need to cater to the new consumers. And producers helped people adapt by providing information about new social and economic conditions and by making some of the disruptive factors more tolerable through drama and humor. The major exception was the portrayal and treatment of African Americans with an unrelenting viciousness.

To some extent, cities' new amusements and media had a homogenizing influence, allowing different social groups to share common experiences. Yet different consumer groups adapted parks, ball fields, vaudeville shows, movies, and feature sections of newspapers to their own cultural needs. To the dismay of reformers who hoped that public recreation and holidays would assimilate newcomers, immigrants used parks for ethnic gatherings and converted picnics and Fourth of July celebrations into occasions for boisterous drinking and sometimes violent behavior. Young working-class men and women resisted parents' and moralists' warnings, and frequented urban dance halls, where they explored forms of courtship and sexual behavior. Thus, leisure—like work and politics—was shaped by the pluralistic forces that thrived in urban life.

Children and Mass-Produced Toys

For children, the new form of mass-produced amusement came from commercial toys. Many of the toys and games that remain popular today were created in this era. In the 1880s, George S. Parker, founder of what became Parker Brothers game company, began fashioning board games with entertaining themes to replace previous games with mostly moral lessons.

Many new mass-marketed toys reinforced gender roles. Tinkertoys, erector sets, and model trains anticipated boys' manhood by introducing them to building and mechanics. Baby dolls with more realistic features encouraged girls to practice motherhood tasks of feeding and caring, while paper dolls introduced them to fashion and consumerism. Some dolls, such as Raggedy Ann and Andy and the Campbell Soup Kids, were derived from stories and product advertising.

Most toys reflected a prevailing belief that childhood was a special time in which children should engage in what one educator called "joyous play." But these notions also inspired efforts to provide kids with toys aiding intellectual development, too. Milton Bradley's early games often had educational themes, and Parker Brothers marketed four games on the Spanish-American War.

In the 1920s, 1930s, and 1940s, the toy industry began an interrelationship with mass media such as comics (Katzenjammer Kids and Superman toys), movies (Shirley Temple dolls and Buck Rogers ray guns), and Disney items. In the 1950s, television intensified the links between toys and programming and created an explosion of toy advertising. In the 1970s, the modern electronic toy industry arose, with games such as Pong and Pac-Man. These and other items of children's amusement are legacies of the rise of leisure and child-centeredness from more than a century ago.

Summary

People and technology made the late nineteenth and early twentieth centuries the "age of the city." Flocking cityward, migrants already in America and those from foreign parts remade themselves, like Houdini, and remade the urban environment, too. They brought cultures that in turn enriched American culture. They found escape in new forms of mass leisure and entertainment.

American cities experienced an "unheralded triumph" by the early 1900s. Amid corruption and political conflict, engineers modernized sewer, water, and lighting services, and urban governments made cities safer by expanding professional police and fire departments. When native inventiveness met the traditions of European, African, and Asian cultures, a new society emerged. The jumble of social classes, ethnic and racial groups, and political and professional organizations sometimes lived in harmony, sometimes not.

Optimists envisioned the American nation as a melting pot, where various nationalities would fuse into a unified people. Instead, many ethnic groups proved unmeltable, and racial minorities got burned on the bottom of the pot. Instead, the United States became a pluralistic society in which cultural influences moved in both directions: imposed from above by people with power and influence and adopted from below through the traditions brought to cities by disparate peoples.

By 1920, immigrants and their offspring outnumbered the native-born in many cities, and the national economy depended on these new workers and consumers. Migrants and immigrants transformed the United States into an urban nation. They gave American culture its varied texture and, like Harry Houdini, helped change the course of entertainment and consumerism. Together, they laid the foundations for the liberalism that would characterize American politics in the twentieth century.

Chapter Review

Growth of the Modern City

What fueled urban growth in the late nineteenth century?

Cities grew two ways: by annexing areas that bordered them, as New York City did when it merged with Brooklyn, Staten Island, and parts of Queens, doubling its population to 3 million. Cities also expanded via in-migration from rural areas and immigration from abroad. Within the United States, low crop prices and heavy debts pushed some white farmers from the country to the city; in other cases, young men sought to escape economic hardship for the excitement of cities while young women left unhappy homes for greater independence. Similarly, African Americans headed to cities for better jobs and to escape crop liens and racial violence. Population pressures, land redistribution, industrialization, and religious persecution pushed many immigrants to leave Europe, Asia, Canada, and Latin America for the United States.

Urban Neighborhoods

How did immigrants adapt to their new lives in U.S. cities?

While most immigrants sought to retain old world traditions, once in the United States, those former folkways were changed by, and also helped change, American cities. Traditions held on longer in neighborhoods with immigrants from the same region or district. Immigrants recreated the mutual aid societies, newspapers, and churches that existed in their homelands. While immigrants tried to hold fast to their native languages, English—which children learned in schools—soon dominated ethnic neighborhoods. Foreigners adapted their traditional garments to American fabrics, and their music evolved as well to include American influences or tales of

their adjustment to life here. Catholics and Jews sought to merge their faiths with their new surroundings by liberalizing or eliminating some old world rituals.

Living Conditions in the Inner City

What made cities seem particularly dangerous?

Overcrowding and housing shortages in inner cities, along with poverty and crime, led to fears that cities were dangerous places filled with violence, muggings, gang fights, and even murder. While murder rates did increase fourfold from 1881 to 1898, crime in cities was not greater than that in backwoods mining camps or southern plantations. The high concentrations of people, particularly those of different classes and ethnic/racial backgrounds, mingling in cities simply made urban crime more visible, which in turn made cities seem scarier from the outside looking in.

Managing the City

What facilitated the rise of political machines in cities?

Political machines emerged in typically working class and immigrant neighborhoods to provide relief, security, and services to voters in exchange for votes, money, influence, and prestige. Each machine had a leader, or boss, who helped his constituents obtain jobs, clothing, or legal assistance. Bosses also attended weddings and wakes and had enormous personal appeal with their constituencies. The power they exerted over local government meant machines could control which firms or individuals got public contracts and city jobs and insist that those receiving these awards repay the machine with a share of their profits or salaries. Machine-led governments did build sewer systems, schools, bridges, and transportation lines and expand police and fire, but the bribes and kickbacks they commanded made their projects expensive to taxpayers.

Family Life

> **What factors led to declining birth rates in the late nineteenth-century United States?**

On farms, children were seen as part of the family's much-needed labor. But as more people left farms for city life, children's economic value lessened. Instead of being need to help with farm work, in cities, they were idle and a drain on family's income. Improvements in health, medicine, and diet lowered the infant mortality rate, which meant families no longer needed to bear more children in the hopes that some might survive. And as the United States became increasingly urbanized, the notion of children needing protection from the city's harsh realities meant that mothers could be more effective caregivers if they had fewer children to raise. Meanwhile, new technology led to better materials for condoms, diaphragms, and other birth control devices, which made them more convenient and reliable.

The New Leisure and Mass Culture

> **What fueled the rise of commercial leisure?**

Mechanization and new, more efficient means of production, along with labor activism, led to shorter work weeks and hours—which, in turn, gave workers more time to use as they saw fit. New mass entertainment rose to fill this need, and included baseball and football leagues, bicycling, and other outdoor activities, as well as theater, vaudeville, and later film. Vaudeville was among the most popular entertainment because its shows tried to appeal to the broadest audiences with jugglers, magicians, comedians, singers, and dancers. Vaudeville, like other forms of show business, also provided new work opportunities for blacks, immigrants, and women, even while reinforcing negative stereotypes of ethnic and racial performers.

Suggestions for Further Reading

John Bodnar, *The Transplanted: A History of Immigrants in Urban America* (1985)

Howard P. Chudacoff and Judith E. Smith, *The Evolution of American Urban Society*, 6th ed. (2005)

John D'Emilio and Estelle Freedman, *Intimate Matters: A History of Sexuality in America* (1988)

Nancy Foner and George M. Frederickson, eds., *Not Just Black and White: Historical and Contemporary Perspectives on Immigration, Race, and Ethnicity in the United States* (2004)

Kenneth T. Jackson, *The Crabgrass Frontier: The Suburbanization of the United States* (1985)

Matthew Frye Jacobson, *Whiteness of a Different Color: European Immigrants and the Alchemy of Race* (1998)

Erika Lee, *At America's Gates: Chinese Immigration During the Exclusion Era, 1882–1943* (2003)

Martin V. Melosi, *The Sanitary City: Urban Infrastructure in America from Colonial Times to the Present* (2000)

Robyn Muncy, *Creating a Female Dominion in American Reform, 1890–1935* (1991)

Kathy Peiss, *Cheap Amusements: Working Women and Leisure in Turn-of-the-Century New York* (1986)

Go to the CourseMate website for primary source links, study tools, and review materials for this chapter. www.cengagebrain.com

Gilded Age Politics

20

1877–1900

Growing up in rural Wisconsin with no toys except those she made herself, young Frances Willard climbed fences, chopped trees, and once tried to ride a cow. When she turned sixteen in 1855, Frances suddenly had to act and dress like a woman. As she later wrote, "the hampering long skirts were brought, with their hampering corset and high heels… and "[f]rom that time on I always realized and was obedient to the limitations thus imposed." That included living in a supposedly democratic society that refused women the right to vote.

Willard never accepted those limitations. Instead, she advocated combining women's traditional roles with improving society. From 1879 until her death in 1898, Willard served as president of the Women's Christian Temperance Union (WCTU), the nation's largest female organization, making thousands of speeches against alcohol and for women's suffrage.

Not an extremist, Willard believed that giving women voting rights would enable them to use their domestic talents to improve society, especially by removing harmful alcohol. After her sixteenth birthday, she saw the Civil War and its aftermath plus the rise of large corporations big business between 1877 and 1900 influence politics and government. It was an era characterized by greed, special interest, and political exclusion.

The obsession with riches seemed so widespread that, when Mark Twain and Charles Dudley Warner satirized America as a land of money grubbers in their novel *The Gilded Age* (1874), the name stuck and is still used by historians to describe the era.

But economic and political accomplishments occurred at national and state levels. Despite partisan and regional rivalries, Congress achieved legislative landmarks in railroad regulation, tariff and currency reform, civil service, and other important issues. Meanwhile, the judiciary countered reform by supporting big business and defending property rights against state and federal regulation. Exclusion prevented most Americans—including women, southern blacks, Indians, uneducated whites, and unnaturalized immigrants—from voting. This concerned Willard and many others, though they were not always willing to create opportunity for all, especially people of color.

Until the 1890s, a stable party system and sectional balance held the political equilibrium. Then, in the 1890s, rural discontent rumbled through the West and South, and a deep economic depression bared the industrial system's flaws. The 1896 presidential campaign stirred Americans, as a new party arose, old parties split, and sectional unity dissolved. The nation emerged from the turbulent 1890s with new economic and political configurations.

As you read this chapter, keep the following questions in mind:

* What were the functions of government in the Gilded Age, and how did they change?

* How did policies of exclusion and discrimination make their mark on the political culture of the age?

* How did the economic climate give rise to the Populist movement?

The Nature of Party Politics

Public interest in elections reached an all-time high between 1870 and 1896. Around 80 percent of eligible voters (white and black males in the North, somewhat lower rates among mostly white males in the South) consistently voted. Featuring parades, picnics, and speeches, politics served as recreation, more popular than baseball or circuses.

> How did factional disputes complicate party politics in the Gilded Age?

Cultural-Political Alignments

In the Gilded Age, party loyalty was fierce. With some exceptions, people who opposed government interference in personal liberty identified with the Democratic Party; those who believed government could be an agent of reform identified with the Republicans. Democrats included foreign-born and second-generation Catholics and Jews. Republicans consisted mostly of native-born Protestants, who believed in the power of legislation for social improvement.

 Link to a cartoon that shows the political fallout from the Civil War and Reconstruction.

There was also a geographic dimension to these divisions. Northern Republicans capitalized on bitter memories of the Civil War by "waving the bloody shirt" at Democrats. Northern Democrats focused more on urban and economic issues, but southern Democratic candidates waved a different bloody shirt, calling Republicans traitors to white supremacy and states' rights.

Partisan politicians battled over how much government should control people's lives. The most contentious issues were leisure time and celebration of Sunday, the Lord's day. Protestant Republicans tried to keep the Sabbath holy through legislation that closed bars, stores, and commercial amusements on Sundays. Immigrant Democrats, accustomed to feasting after church, fought saloon closings and other restrictions.

Allegiances to national parties were so evenly divided that no faction gained control for long. Between 1877 and 1897, Republicans held the presidency for three terms, Democrats for two. Rarely did one party control the presidency and Congress simultaneously. From 1876 through 1892, presidential elections were close. The outcome often hinged on a few populous northern states—Connecticut, New York, New

Chronology

1873	Congress ends coinage of silver dollars			"Mississippi Plan" uses poll taxes and literacy tests to prevent African Americans from voting
1873–78	Economic hard times hit			National Woman Suffrage Association formed
1877	Georgia passes poll tax, disfranchising most African Americans		1890s	Jim Crow laws, discriminating against African Americans in legal treatment and public accommodations, passed by southern states
1878	Bland-Allison Act requires Treasury to buy between $2 and $4 million in silver each month		1892	Populist convention in Omaha draws up reform platform
1881	Garfield assassinated; Arthur assumes presidency		1893	Sherman Silver Purchase Act repealed
1883	Pendleton Civil Service Act introduces merit system		1893–97	Major economic depression hits United States
	Supreme Court strikes down 1883 Civil Rights Act		1894	Wilson-Gorman Tariff passes
				Coxey's Army marches on Washington, D.C.
1886	*Wabash* case declares that only Congress can limit interstate commerce rates		1896	*Plessy v. Ferguson* establishes separate-but-equal doctrine
1887	Farmers' Alliances form		1898	Louisiana implements "grandfather clause," restricting voting by African Americans
	Interstate Commerce Commission begins regulating rates and practices of interstate shipping		1899	*Cummings v. County Board of Education* applies separate-but-equal doctrine to schools
1890	McKinley Tariff raises tariff rates			
	Sherman Silver Purchase Act commits Treasury to buying 4.5 million ounces of silver each month			

Jersey, Ohio, Indiana, and Illinois. Both parties tried to gain advantages by nominating presidential candidates from these states (and by committing vote fraud).

Party Factions

Factional quarrels split both the Republican and the Democratic Parties. Among Republicans, New York's senator Roscoe Conkling led one faction, known as "Stalwarts" and worked the spoils system to win government jobs for supporters. Stalwarts' rivals were the "Half Breeds," led by Maine Congressman James G. Blaine, who also blatantly pursued influence. On the sidelines stood more idealistic Republicans, or "**Mugwumps**" (supposedly an Indian term meaning "mug on one side of the fence, wump on the other"). Mugwumps, such as Missouri Senator Carl Schurz, believed that only righteous, educated men should govern. Republican allies of big business supported gold as the standard for currency, whereas those from mining regions favored silver. Democrats subdivided into white-supremacist southerners, working-class, immigrant-stock supporters of urban political machines, business-oriented advocates of low tariffs and the gold standard, and debtor-oriented advocates of free silver.

Mugwumps: Term used for idealistic Republican reformers.

In each state, one party usually dominated, and often the state "boss" was a senator who doled out jobs and parlayed his clout into national influence. (Until ratification of the Seventeenth Amendment to the Constitution in 1913, state legislatures elected U.S. senators.) These men exercised their power brazenly.

Issues of Legislation

What was at issue in the debate over the gold standard versus free silver?

In Congress, sectional controversies, patronage abuses, railroad regulation, tariffs, and currency provoked heated debates and partisanship. From the end of the Civil War into the 1880s, Congress debated soldiers' pensions. The **Grand Army of the Republic**, an organization of 400,000 Union Army veterans, allied with the Republican Party and cajoled Congress into providing generous pensions for former Union soldiers and their widows. Many were deserved: Union troops were poorly paid. The Union Army spent $2 billion fighting the Civil War, but veterans' pensions cost $8 billion, one of the largest welfare commitments the federal government ever made. By 1900, soldiers' pensions accounted for roughly 40 percent of the federal budget. Confederate veterans were excluded, though some southern states funded small pensions and built old-age homes for ex-soldiers.

Grand Army of the Republic (GAR): A social and political lobbying organization of northern Civil War veterans that convinced Congress to provide $8 billion in pensions for former Union soldiers and widows.

Civil Service Reform

Few politicians dared oppose pensions, but some attempted to dismantle the spoils system, the practice of awarding government jobs to the party faithful regardless of their qualifications. During the Civil War, the federal government expanded considerably, and the spoils system increasingly flourished. As the postal service, diplomatic corps, and other government agencies grew, the number of federal jobs tripled from 53,000 in 1865 to 166,000 in 1891. Elected officials scrambled to control these jobs to benefit their party. In return for short hours and high pay, appointees to federal positions pledged votes and part of their earnings to patrons.

Shocked by corruption, especially after the scandals in the Grant administration, some reformers began advocating appointments based on merit—civil service. Support for change accelerated in 1881 with formation of the National Civil Service Reform League. That year, the assassination of President James Garfield by a distraught job seeker hastened the drive for reform. The **Pendleton Civil Service Act**, passed by Congress in 1882, created the Civil Service Commission to oversee competitive examinations for government positions. The act gave the commission jurisdiction over 10 percent of federal jobs, though the president could expand the list. Because the Constitution barred Congress from interfering in state affairs, civil service at state and local levels developed more haphazardly.

Pendleton Civil Service Act: Attempt to end the spoils system; created the Civil Service Commission to oversee competitive exams for government jobs.

Economic policy was the Gilded Age's main issue. Railroads particularly provoked controversy. In their quest for customers, railroads launched rate wars and angered shippers with inconsistent freight charges. On noncompetitive routes, railroads often boosted charges to compensate for unprofitably low rates on competitive routes. Railroads also played favorites, reducing rates to large shippers and offering free passes to preferred customers and politicians.

Railroad Regulation

Such favoritism stirred farmers, small merchants, and reform politicians to demand rate regulation. By 1880, fourteen states established commissions to limit freight and storage charges of state-chartered lines. Railroads fought back, arguing that the Fourteenth Amendment to the Constitution guaranteed them freedom to acquire and use property without government restraint. But in 1877, in *Munn v. Illinois,* the Supreme Court upheld state regulation, declaring that grain warehouses owned by railroads acted in the public interest and therefore must submit to regulation for "the common good."

Only the federal government could regulate interstate lines, as affirmed by the Supreme Court in the *Wabash* case of 1886. To expand federal regulation, Congress passed the **Interstate Commerce Act** in 1887, which prohibited rebates and rate discrimination, and created the Interstate Commerce Commission (ICC), the nation's first regulatory agency, to investigate railroad rate-making and issue cease-and-desist orders against illegal practices. The legislation's weak enforcement provisions, however, left railroads room for evasion, and judges minimized ICC powers. In the *Maximum Freight Rate* case (1897), the Supreme Court ruled that the ICC lacked power to set rates, and in the *Alabama Midlands* case (1897), it overturned prohibitions against long-haul/short-haul discrimination. Still, regulation, though weakened, remained in force.

Interstate Commerce Act:
1887 law that established the Interstate Commerce Commission, the nation's first regulatory agency, to investigate railroad rate-making and discriminatory rate practices.

Tariff Policy

From 1789 onward, Congress created tariffs, which levied duties (taxes) on imported goods, to protect American products from European competition. But tariffs quickly became a tool special interests used tp enhance profits. By the 1880s, these interests succeeded in obtaining tariffs on more than four thousand items. A few economists and farmers argued for free trade, but most politicians insisted that tariffs were necessary to support industry and preserve jobs.

The Republican Party put protective tariffs at the core of its agenda. Democrats complained that tariffs made prices artificially high by keeping out less expensive foreign goods, thereby benefiting domestic manufacturers while hurting consumers and farmers whose crops were not protected.

During the Gilded Age, revenues from tariffs and other levies created a federal budget surplus. Most Republicans liked that government was earning more than it spent and hoped to keep the surplus as a reserve or use it for projects that would aid commerce. Democrats acknowledged a need for protection of some manufactured goods and raw materials, but they favored lower tariff duties to encourage foreign trade and reduce the Treasury surplus.

Manufacturers and their congressional allies controlled tariff policy. The McKinley Tariff of 1890 boosted already-high rates by 4 percent. When House Democrats passed a bill to trim tariffs in 1894, Senate Republicans, aided by southern Democrats, added six hundred amendments restoring most cuts (the Wilson-Gorman Tariff). In 1897, the Dingley Tariff raised rates further. Attacks on duties made tariffs a symbol of privileged business in the public mind.

Monetary Policy

When increased industrial and agricultural production caused prices to fall after the Civil War, debtors (have-nots) and creditors (haves) had opposing reactions. Farmers suffered because crop prices dropped and because demand for a limited supply of available money raised interest rates on loans, making it costly to borrow funds to pay mortgages and debts. They favored coinage of silver to increase the amount of currency in circulation which in turn would reduce interest rates. Small businessmen, also in need of loans, agreed. Large businesses and bankers favored a stable, limited money supply backed only by gold, fearing currency fluctuations that would threaten investors' confidence in the U.S. economy. The money debate also reflected sectional cleavages: western silver-mining areas and agricultural regions of the South and West against the industrial Northeast.

Before the 1870s, the federal government bought gold and silver to back its paper money (dollars), setting a ratio that made a gold dollar worth sixteen times more than a silver dollar. Discovery and mining of gold in the West, however, increased gold supplies and lowered market prices relative to silver. Consequently, silver dollars disappeared from circulation as owners hoarded them. In 1873, Congress officially halted silver coinage. The United States unofficially adopted the gold standard.

Within a few years, new mines in the West began flooding the market with silver, and its price dropped. Gold now became relatively less plentiful, worth more than sixteen times the value of silver. Silver producers wanted the government to resume buying silver at the old sixteen-to-one ratio. Debtors, hurt by the economic hard times of 1873–1878, saw silver as a means of expanding the currency supply, so they pressed for resumption of silver coinage at the old sixteen-to-one ratio.

With parties split into silver and gold factions, Congress tried to compromise. The Bland-Allison Act (1878) authorized the Treasury to buy $2 million to $4 million worth of silver monthly, and the **Sherman Silver Purchase Act** (1890) increased the government's silver purchase by specifying weight (4.5 million ounces) rather than dollars. Neither measure satisfied various interest groups. Creditors wanted the government to stop buying silver, whereas for debtors, the legislation failed to expand the money supply satisfactorily. The issue would intensify during the 1896 presidential election (see pages 534–535).

Sherman Silver Purchase Act: Law that instructed the treasury to buy, at current market prices, 4.5 million ounces of silver monthly.

Legislative Accomplishments

Members of Congress addressed thorny issues under difficult conditions. They earned small salaries yet had to maintain two residences: in their home district and in Washington. Most Congressmen had no private offices, worked long hours, wrote their own speeches, and paid for staff themselves. Yet, they managed to pass significant legislation.

Tentative Presidents

Operating under the cloud of Andrew Johnson's impeachment, Grant's scandals, and doubts about the legitimacy of the 1876 election (see Chapter 16), American presidents between 1877 and 1900 moved to restore authority to their office. Proper and honest, Presidents Rutherford Hayes (1877–1881), James Garfield (1881), Chester Arthur (1881–1885), Grover Cleveland (1885–1889 and 1893–1897), Benjamin Harrison (1889–1893), and William McKinley (1897–1901) tried to act as legislative leaders. Each president cautiously initiated legislation and used vetoes to guide national policy.

What actions did American presidents between 1877 and 1900 take to restore authority to their office?

Hayes, Garfield, and Arthur

Rutherford B. Hayes had been a Union general and Ohio congressman and governor before his disputed presidential election, which prompted opponents to label him "Rutherfraud." Hayes served as conciliator, emphasizing national harmony over sectional rivalry and opposing racial violence. He tried to overhaul the spoils system by appointing civil service reformer Carl Schurz to his cabinet and battling New York's patronage king, Senator Conkling.

When Hayes declined to run for reelection in 1880, Republicans nominated another Ohio congressman and Civil War hero, James A. Garfield, who won by 40,000 votes out of 9 million cast. By winning the pivotal states of New York and Indiana, Garfield carried the electoral college by 214 to 155. Garfield hoped to reduce the tariff and develop economic relations with Latin America, and he rebuffed Conkling's patronage demands. But in July 1881, Charles Guiteau shot him in a Washington railroad station. Garfield lingered for seventy-nine days before dying on September 19.

Garfield's successor was Vice President Chester A. Arthur, the New York Stalwart whom Hayes had fired. Arthur became a temperate executive. He signed the Pendleton Civil Service Act, urged Congress to modify outdated tariff rates, and supported federal railroad regulation. He wielded the veto aggressively, killing bills that excessively benefited railroads and corporations. Arthur wanted to run for president in 1884 but Republicans nominated James G. Blaine instead.

Democrats picked New York's governor, Grover Cleveland, a bachelor who admitted during the campaign that he had fathered an out-of-wedlock son. Cleveland beat Blaine by only 29,000 popular votes; his tiny margin of 1,149 votes in New York secured that state's 36 electoral votes, enough for a 219-to-182 victory in the electoral college. Cleveland may have won New York thanks to remarks of a Protestant minister, who equated Democrats with "rum, Romanism, and rebellion." Democrats publicized the slur among New York's large Irish-Catholic population, urging voters to support Cleveland.

Cleveland and Harrison

Cleveland, the first Democratic president since James Buchanan (1857–1861), expanded civil service, vetoed private pension bills, and urged Congress to cut tariff duties. When advisers worried about his chances for reelection, the president retorted, "What is the use of being elected or reelected, unless you stand for something?" Senate protectionists killed tariff reform, and when Democrats renominated Cleveland in 1888, businessmen convinced him to moderate his attacks on tariffs.

Republicans in 1888 nominated Benjamin Harrison, former Indiana senator and grandson of President William Henry Harrison (1841). Bribery and multiple voting helped him win Indiana by 2,300 votes and New York by 14,000. (Democrats also indulged in frauds, but Republicans proved more successful at them.) Although Cleveland outpolled Harrison by 90,000 popular votes, Harrison carried the electoral college by 233 to 168.

The first president since 1875 whose party had majorities in both Congressional houses, Harrison influenced legislation with everything from threats of vetoes to informal dinners and consultations with politicians. Partly in response, the Congress of 1889–1891 passed 517 bills, 200 more than the average passed by Congresses between 1875 and 1889. Harrison showed support for civil service by appointing reformer Theodore Roosevelt as civil service commissioner. But pressured by special interests, Harrison signed the Dependents' Pension Act, which provided pensions for Union veterans and widows and children, doubling the number of welfare recipients from 490,000 to 966,000.

The Pension Act and other appropriations in 1890 pushed the federal budget past $1 billion for the first time. Democrats blamed the "Billion-Dollar Congress" on spendthrift Republicans and in 1890 voters unseated seventy-eight Republican congressmen. Capitalizing on voter unrest, Democrats nominated Grover Cleveland

The Spectacle of Gilded Age Politics

During the Gilded Age, political events, especially presidential elections, provided opportunity for elaborate spectacle, and politicians occupied the limelight as major celebrities. A presidential campaign functioned as a public festival at a time when mass entertainments such as movies and sports did not exist to offer people outlets for their emotions by attending parades, cheering, watching fireworks, and listening to marching bands. These two images, one an artist's rendering and the other a means for displaying one's preference for a particular candidate, present evidence of how people of the era might have expressed themselves politically. What similarities to modern-day campaign events and symbols do the images represent? In what ways are they different? Did politics and campaigning in the Gilded Age play a different role in the nation's culture than they do at present?

© Bettmann/Corbis

Collection of Janice L. and David J. Frent

The presidential campaign of Rutherford B. Hayes excited strong emotions. The inset image is that of a campaign brooch reminding voters of Hayes's Civil War record, and the drawing illustrates the gala of Haye's inauguration in 1876.

to run against Harrison in 1892. With large business contributions, Cleveland beat Harrison by 370,000 popular votes (3 percent of the total), easily winning the electoral vote.

In office again, Cleveland addressed currency, tariffs, and labor unrest, but his actions reflected political weakness. Cleveland promised sweeping tariff reform, but Senate protectionists undercut his efforts. And he bowed to requests from railroads, sending federal troops to put down the Pullman strike of 1894. In spite of Cleveland's efforts, major events—particularly economic downturn and agrarian ferment—pushed the country in another direction.

Discrimination, Disfranchisement, and Responses

How did southerners find legal means to discriminate against newly enfranchised African Americans in the decades following the Civil War?

Despite speeches about freedom and opportunity during the Gilded Age, policies of discrimination haunted more than half the nation's population. Racial issues long shaped politics in the South, home to the majority of African Americans. Southern white farmers and workers feared that newly enfranchised African American men would challenge their political and social superiority (real and imagined). Wealthy landowners and merchants fanned these fears, keeping blacks and whites from uniting to protest their own economic subjugation.

In the North, discrimination in housing, employment, and access to facilities such as parks, hotels, department stores kept African Americans separate and "in their place." Whether via lower wages or lower crop returns, African Americans felt their imposed inferiority.

Violence Against African Americans

In 1880, 90 percent of southern blacks farmed or worked in personal and domestic service—just as they had as slaves. Between 1889 and 1909, more than seventeen hundred African Americans were lynched in the South, often in sparsely populated districts where whites felt threatened by an influx of migrant blacks. Most **lynching** victims were accused of assault—rarely proved—on a white woman.

lynching: Vigilante hanging of those accused of crimes; used primarily against blacks.

Ida B. Wells: African American journalist and activist who mounted a national anti-lynching campaign.

Blacks did not suffer violence silently. Their most notable activist was **Ida B. Wells**, a Memphis schoolteacher, who was forcibly removed from a railroad car in 1884 when she refused to surrender her seat to a white man. In 1889, Wells became partner of a Memphis newspaper, the *Free Speech and Headlight*, in which she published attacks against white injustice, particularly the case of three black grocers lynched in 1892 after defending themselves against whites. She subsequently toured Europe, drumming up opposition to lynching and discrimination. Unable to return to hostile Memphis, she moved to Chicago and became a powerful advocate for racial justice.

Link to a document from an African American mass protest meeting about mistreatment.

Disfranchisement

Southern white leaders, eager to reassert racial superiority, instituted measures to prevent blacks from voting. Despite threats and intimidation post-Reconstruction, blacks formed the backbone of the southern Republican Party and won numerous elective positions. In North Carolina, for example, eleven African Americans served in the state Senate and forty-three in the House between 1877 and 1890. Unacceptable to racist whites, beginning with Tennessee in 1889 and Arkansas in 1892, southern states levied taxes of $1 to $2 on all voters—prohibitive to most blacks, who were poor and in debt. Other schemes disfranchised—or deprived voting rights to—blacks who could not read.

Furthering disfranchisement, the Supreme Court determined in *U.S. v. Reese* (1876) that Congress had no control over local and state elections other than upholding the Fifteenth Amendment, which prohibits states from denying the vote "on account of race, color, or previous condition of servitude." State legislatures found ways to exclude black voters, however. An 1890 state constitutional convention established the "Mississippi Plan," requiring voters to pay a poll tax eight months before each election, present the tax receipt at election time, and prove they could read and interpret the state constitution. Registration officials applied stiffer standards to blacks than to whites, even declaring black college graduates ineligible due to illiteracy.

Such restrictions proved effective. In South Carolina, 70 percent of eligible blacks voted in the 1880 election; by 1896, the rate dropped to 11 percent. By the 1900s, African Americans effectively lost political rights in the South. Disfranchisement also affected poor whites, few of whom could meet poll tax, property, and literacy requirements. Consequently, total number of eligible voters in Mississippi shrank from 257,000 in 1876 to 77,000 in 1892.

Legal Segregation

Existing customs of racial separation also expanded. In a series of cases during the 1870s, the Supreme Court opened the door to racial discrimination by ruling that the Fourteenth Amendment protected citizens' rights only against infringement by state governments—but not from individuals, businesses, or local governments. These rulings climaxed in 1883 when, in the *Civil Rights* cases, the Court struck down the 1875 Civil Rights Act, which prohibited segregation in facilities, such as streetcars, theaters, and parks. Thus railroads, such as the Chesapeake & Ohio Railroad, could maintain discriminatory policies.

The Supreme Court also upheld legal segregation on a "separate-but-equal" basis in **Plessy v. Ferguson** (1896). This case began in 1892 when a New Orleans organization of African Americans chose Homer Plessy, a dark-skinned creole who was only one-eighth black (but considered black by Louisiana law), to sit in a whites-only railroad car. Plessy was arrested, and the appeal of his conviction reached the U.S. Supreme Court in 1896. The Court affirmed that a state law providing for separate facilities for the two races was reasonable because it preserved "public peace and good order." To the Court, a law separating the races did not necessarily "destroy the legal equality of the races." Although the ruling did not specify the phrase "separate but equal," it legalized separate facilities for black and white people as long as they were equal. In 1899, the Court legitimated school segregation in *Cummins v. County Board of Education*, until it was overturned by *Brown v. Board of Education* in 1954.

Segregation laws—known as Jim Crow laws—multiplied throughout the South, reminding African Americans of inferior status. State and local statutes passed in the 1890 restricted blacks to the rear of streetcars, to separate public drinking fountains and toilets, and to separate sections of hospitals and cemeteries.

Plessy v. Ferguson: Supreme Court ruling validating legal segregation; legalized separate facilities for blacks and whites as long as they were equal.

African American Activism

African American women and men challenged injustice. Some boycotted discriminatory businesses; others promoted "Negro enterprise." In 1898, Atlanta University professor John Hope urged blacks to become their own employers and support Negro Business Men's Leagues. Some blacks used higher education to elevate their status. In all-black teachers' colleges, men and women sought opportunities for themselves and their race.

While disfranchisement pushed African American men from public life, African American women used domestic roles as mothers, educators, and moral guardians to uplift the race and seek improvements. Along with seeking the vote, they successfully lobbied southern governments for cleaner city streets, expanded charity services, and vocational education. Black women and white women sometimes united to achieve their goals, white women often sympathized with white men in supporting racial exclusion.

Women Suffrage

Some women challenged male power structures by seeking the right to vote. An intensely religious woman, Frances Willard believed that (Chrstian) faith would empower women to uplift society, urging women who joined the Women's Christian Temperance Union to sign a pledge to abstain from alcohol to protect families from the evils of drink. But Willard also believed that the WCTU could best do the Lord's work if women could vote. Thus, at its 1884 convention, the WCTU passed a resolution deploring the "disenfranchisement of 12 million people who are citizens." Giving speeches nationwide, Willard became the best-known woman in America.

Courtesy of Heritage Hall, Livingstone College, Salisbury, North Carolina

Livingstone College in North Carolina was one of several institutions of higher learning established by and for African Americans in the late nineteenth century. With a curriculum that emphasized training for educational and religious work in the South and in Africa, these colleges were coeducational, operating on the belief that both men and women could have public roles.

The suffrage crusade was spearheaded by two organizations, the National Woman Suffrage Association (NWSA) and the American Woman Suffrage Association (AWSA). The NWSA, led by Elizabeth Cady Stanton and Susan B. Anthony, advocated women's rights in courts and workplaces as well as at the ballot box.

The AWSA, led by former abolitionists Lucy Stone, focused narrowly on suffrage, particularly at the state level. The two groups merged in 1890 to form the National American Woman Suffrage Association with Stanton as president.

Anthony's effort for a constitutional woman suffrage amendment received little support, with senators claiming suffrage would interfere with women's family obligations. Moreover, the women's suffrage campaign was tainted by racial intolerance, as many movement leaders espoused white superiority and accommodated racial prejudices to retain support. AWSA and NWSA membership was white and mostly middle class. Blacks who joined the WCTU had a separate Department of Colored Temperance. Also, leaders, such as Anthony and Stanton felt humiliated that the Fifteenth Amendment had enfranchised black men but not women. Many believed that "educated" white women should vote and that "illiterate" blacks should not.

The Beautiful Life of Frances E. Willard by Anna A. Gordon, 1898/Picture Research Consultants & Archives

Frances Willard became the second and best-known president of the National Women's Christian Temperance Union (WCTU), founded in 1874. Beyond promoting abstinence from drinking alcohol, Willard and the WCTU also were involved in other reforms, including women's suffrage. In 1893, Willard took her crusade worldwide and became the first president of the International Council of Women. Here Willard's status is symbolized by her seat amid major American and British suffrage leaders, all officers of the World's WCTU.

Women did win partial victories. Between 1870 and 1910, eleven states (mostly in the West) legalized limited woman suffrage. By 1890, nineteen states allowed women to vote on school issues, and three granted suffrage on tax and bond issues. The right to vote in national elections awaited a later generation, but leaders such as Ida B. Wells, Susan B. Anthony, and Lucy Stone proved that women could be politically active even without the vote.

Agrarian Unrest and Populism

How did farmers' discontent crystallize in the Grange movement and Farmers' Alliances?

Economic inequity also sparked a mass movement. Despite rapid industrialization and urbanization in the Gilded Age, the United States remained an agrarian society with 64 percent of the population living in rural areas in 1890. The expression of farmers' discontent with economic hardship—a mixture of strident rhetoric, nostalgic dreams, and hard-headed egalitarianism—began in Grange organizations in the early 1870s. It accelerated when Farmers' Alliances formed in Texas in the late 1870s and spread across the South and Great Plains in the 1880s. The movement flourished where debt, weather, and insects demoralized struggling farmers and inspired visions of a cooperative, democratic society.

Sharecropping and Tenant Farming in the South

Southern agriculture did not benefit much from mechanization. Tobacco and cotton, principal southern crops, required hoeing and weeding by hand. Tobacco leaves matured at different rates and stems were too fragile for machines. Also, mechanical devices were not precise enough to pick cotton. Thus, after the Civil War, southern agriculture remained labor-intensive, and labor lords replaced slaves with sharecroppers and tenant farmers.

Sharecropping and tenant farming—where farmers rented rather than owned their land—entangled millions of black and white southerners in debt and humiliation, weighed down by crop liens. Too poor to have ready cash, most farmers borrowed to buy necessities, offering future crops as collateral. To get supplies, a farmer dealt with a "furnishing merchant," who would exchange provisions for a "lien," or legal claim, on the farmer's forthcoming crop. After the crop was harvested and brought to market, the merchant collected the portion of the crop that would repay the loan. Often, however, the debt exceeded the crop's value. The farmer could pay off only part of the debt but borrowed more for food and supplies for the coming year, sinking deeper into debt.

Merchants frequently took advantage by inflating prices and charging excessive interest on the advances farmers received. Suppose, for example, that a farmer needed a 20-cent bag of seed. The furnishing merchant would sell it to him on credit but for 28 cents. At year's end, that loan would have accumulated interest of 50 percent or more. The farmer, pledging more than his crop's worth against such debts, fell behind and never recovered, risking eviction.

In the southern backcountry, after the Civil War, farmers shifted from diversified and subsistence agriculture to commercial farming, namely cotton. Consequently, yeoman began purchasing supplies such as flour, potatoes, peas, meat, corn, and syrup from merchants. This specialized farming came about for two reasons: constant debt forced farmers to grow crops that would net cash, and railroads enabled them to easily transport cotton to market. As backcountry yeomen devoted more acres to cotton, they raised less of what they needed and were frequently at the mercy of merchants.

Hardship in the Midwest and West

In the Midwest, as growers cultivated more land, as mechanization boosted productivity, and as foreign competition increased, supplies of agricultural products exceeded

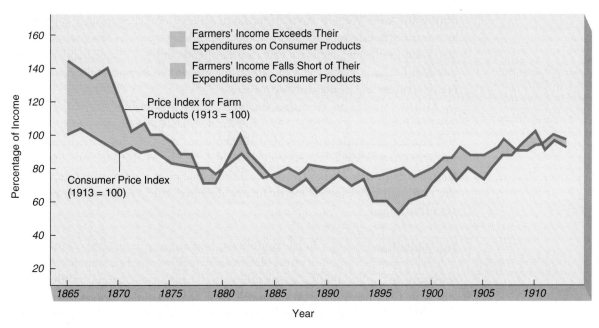

FIGURE 20.1
Consumer Prices and Farm Product Prices, 1865–1913
Until the late 1870s, in spite of falling farm prices, farmers were able to receive from their crops more income than they spent on consumer goods. But beginning in the mid-1880s, consumer prices leveled off and then rose, while prices for farm products continued to drop. As a result, farmers found it increasingly difficult to afford consumer goods, a problem that plagued them well into the twentieth century.

national and worldwide demand. Prices for staple crops dropped steadily. A bushel of wheat that sold for $1.45 in 1866 brought only 80 cents in the mid-1880s and 49 cents by the mid-1890s. Meanwhile, transportation and storage fees remained high. To buy necessities and pay bills, farmers had to produce more. But the more they produced, the lower crop prices dropped (see Figure 20.1).

The West suffered special hardships. In Colorado, absentee capitalists seized control of transportation and water, and concentration of technology by large mining companies pushed out small firms. Charges of monopolistic behavior by railroads echoed among farmers, miners, and ranchers in Wyoming and Montana. In California, Washington, and Oregon, wheat and fruit growers found opportunities blocked by railroads' control of transportation and storage rates.

Grange Movement   With aid from Oliver H. Kelley, a clerk in the Bureau of Agriculture, farmers in almost every state during the 1860s and 1870s founded the Patrons of Husbandry, or the Grange, dedicated to improving economic and social conditions. By 1875, the Grange had twenty thousand branches and a million members. Strongest in the Midwest and South, Granges sponsored meetings and educational events to relieve the loneliness of farm life. Family-oriented local Granges welcomed women's participation.

As membership flourished, Granges turned to economic and political action. Many joined the **Greenback Labor Party**, formed in 1876 to advocate expanding the money supply by keeping "greenbacks"— paper money created by the government

Greenback Labor Party:
Advocated expanding the money supply through the government printing of money not backed by gold.

during the Civil War—in circulation. Local Grange branches formed cooperative associations to buy supplies and market crops and livestock. A few Grangers operated farm-implement factories and insurance companies. Most enterprises failed, however, because farmers lacked capital for large-scale buying and because large manufacturers and dealers undercut them.

In the late 1870s, Granges convinced states to establish agricultural colleges and pressed state legislatures for Granger laws to regulate transportation and storage rates. But in the 1886 *Wabash* case, the U.S. Supreme Court overturned Granger laws by denying states the power to regulate railroad rates. Disavowing party politics, Grangers did not challenge business interests within the two major parties. Their influence declined, and Granges became social organizations.

The White Hats

In the Southwest, migration of English-speaking ranchers into Mexican pastureland sparked sometimes violent resistance. In the late 1880s, a group calling itself Las Gorras Blancas, or White Hats, struggled to control formerly ancestral lands. They burned buildings, destroyed fences that Anglos had erected, and threatened the town of Las Vegas in New Mexico territory. However, they could not halt Anglos from legally buying and using public land. By 1900, many Hispanics had given up farming to work as agricultural laborers or migrate to cities.

Farmers' Alliances

By 1890, two networks of Farmers' Alliances—one in the Great Plains, one in the South—constituted a new mass movement. The first Alliances arose in Texas, where hard-pressed farmers rallied against crop liens, merchants, railroads, and money power. Using traveling lecturers to recruit members, Alliance leaders expanded the movement into other southern states, boasting two million members by 1889. A separate Colored Farmers' National Alliance claimed one million black members. In the late 1880s, the Plains movement organized two million members in Kansas, Nebraska, and the Dakotas. Women participated actively in Alliance activities.

To bypass corporate power and control markets, Alliances, like the Grange, proposed that farmers form cooperatives, joining together to sell crops and livestock and buy supplies. By pooling resources, Alliances reasoned, farmers could exert greater economic pressure and share the benefits of their hard work rather than competing against each other.

To relieve shortages of cash and credit, Alliances proposed a government aid system called a subtreasury. The plan first called for the federal government to construct warehouses where farmers could store nonperishable crops while awaiting higher market prices; the government would then loan farmers Treasury notes amounting to 80 percent of the market price of stored crops. Farmers could use these notes for debts and purchases. Once the crops were sold, farmers would repay the loans plus small interest and storage fees, thereby avoiding the exploitative crop lien system.

The subtreasury plan's second part would provide low-interest government loans to farmers to buy land. These loans, along with the Treasury notes for stored crops, would inject cash into the economy and encourage the kind of inflation that advocates hoped would raise crop prices without raising other prices.

Problems in Achieving Alliance Unity

Had Farmers' Alliances been able to unite politically, they could have wielded formidable power; but racial and sectional differences thwarted merger efforts. Racial voting restrictions weakened Alliance voter strength, and racism blocked acceptance of blacks by white Alliances. Some southern leaders, such as Georgia's Senator Tom Watson, tried to unite distressed black and white farmers, but poor whites held fast to prejudices. Many considered African Americans inferior and took comfort that there always would be people worse off than they were. Regional differences also prevented unity. Northern Alliances favored protective tariffs to keep out foreign grain, whereas white southerners wanted low tariffs to curb costs of imports. However, both favored railroad regulation, equitable taxation, currency reform, an end to alleged election frauds, and prohibition of landownership by foreign investors.

Rise of Populism

By 1890, farmers had elected several sympathetic office-holders, especially in the South, where Alliances controlled four governorships, eight state legislatures, forty-four seats in the House of Representatives, and three in the Senate. In the Midwest, Alliance candidates running on third-party tickets, such as the Greenback Labor Party, won some victories in Kansas, Nebraska, and the Dakotas. Leaders crisscrossed the country to recruit support for a new party. In summer 1890, the Kansas Alliance held a "convention of the people" and nominated candidates who swept the state's fall elections. Formation of this People's Party, or **Populist Party**, gave a title to Alliance political activism. (Populism is the political doctrine that asserts the rights and powers of common people versus elites.) By 1892, southern Alliance members joined northern counterparts in summoning a People's Party convention in Omaha, Nebraska, on July 4 to draft a platform and nominate a presidential candidate.

Charging that inequality (between white classes) threatened to splinter society, the new party's platform declared, "The fruits of the toil of millions are boldly stolen to build up colossal fortunes for a few," and that "wealth belongs to him that creates it." It addressed three central sources of rural unrest: transportation, land, and money. Frustrated with weak regulation, Populists demanded government ownership of railroad and telegraph lines. The monetary plank called on the government to make more money available for farm loans and to restore unlimited coinage of silver. Other planks advocated a graduated income tax, postal savings banks, direct election of U.S. senators, and a shorter workday. As its presidential candidate, the party nominated James B. Weaver of Iowa, a former Union general and supporter of an expanded money supply.

Populist Party: "People's Party;" agrarian-based, third-party challenge to the Republicans and Democrats; advocated for the rights of the common man.

Link to Hamlin Garland's short story, "Under the Lion's Paw," which was read before the audience at the Populist Convention in 1892.

Populist Spokespeople

The Populist campaign featured dynamic personalities such as Mary Lease and "Sockless Jerry" Simpson, an unschooled rural reformer so nicknamed after he ridiculed silk-stockinged wealthy people, causing a reporter to muse that Simpson probably wore no stockings. The South produced leaders, such as Georgia's Tom Watson and North Carolina's Leonidas Polk. Colorado's governor, Davis "Bloody Bridles" Waite, attacked mine owners, and Minnesota's Ignatius Donnelly, pseudoscientist and writer of apocalyptic novels, became chief visionary of the northern plains, penning the Omaha platform's thunderous language.

Links to the World

Russian Populism

Before American Populism, a different form of populism emerged in another largely rural country: Russia. Whereas American Populism came from the Alliance farm organizations, Russian populism was created by intellectuals seeking to educate peasants to agitate for social and economic freedom.

Russian society began to modernize in the mid-nineteenth century. Town governments were given control of local taxation, and education became more widespread. Perhaps most importantly, in 1861 Czar Alexander II signed an Edict of Emancipation, freeing Russian serfs (slaves attached to specific lands) and granting them compensation to buy land. Reforms progressed slowly, prompting some educated Russians, called nihilists, to press for radical reforms, including socialism. The reformers became known as *narodniki*, or populists, from *narod*, the Russian term for "peasant."

Narodniki envisioned a society of self-governing village communes, somewhat like the cooperatives proposed by American Farmers' Alliances. One leader, Peter Lavrov, believed intellectuals must get closer to the people and help them improve their lives. Russian populists believed only an uprising against the czar could realize their goals. When Alexander instituted repressive policies against the *narodniki* in the late 1870s, many turned to terrorism, culminating in Alexander II's assassination in 1881.

Russian peasants remained tied to tradition and could not abandon loyalty to the czar. Arrests and imprisonments after Alexander's assassination discouraged populists' efforts, and the movement declined. Nevertheless, populist ideas became the cornerstone of the 1917 Russian Revolution and of subsequent Soviet social and political ideology.

Bettmann/Corbis

Russian peasants, like American tenant farmers and owners of small landholdings, suffered from poverty and pressures of the expanded market economy. The plight of struggling Russian farm families stirred up empathy from young populist intellectuals, who adopted radical solutions that did not capture as much political fervor among farmers as American populism did.

In the 1892 presidential election, Populist candidate James Weaver garnered 8 percent of the popular vote, majorities in four states, and twenty-two electoral votes. Not since 1856 had a third party done so well in its first national effort. Populists were only successful in the West. The vote-rich Northeast ignored Weaver, and Alabama was the only southern state that gave Populists as much as one-third of its votes.

Still, Populism gave southern and western rural dwellers faith in a future of cooperation and democracy, as they looked toward the 1896 presidential election. Amid hardship and desperation, millions came to believe that a cooperative democracy in which government would ensure equal opportunity could overcome corporate power.

The Depression and Protests of the 1890s

Why did socialism fail to take hold in the United States amid the labor activism of the late nineteenth century?

In 1893, shortly before Grover Cleveland's second presidency began, the Philadelphia & Reading Railroad, once a thriving and profitable line, went bankrupt. Like other railroads, it had borrowed heavily to lay track and build stations and bridges. Overexpansion cut into profits, and ultimately the company could not pay its debts.

The same problem beset manufacturers. Output at McCormick farm machinery factories was nine times greater in 1893 than in 1879, but revenues had only tripled. The company bought more equipment and squeezed more work from fewer laborers, but it only increased debt and unemployment. Jobless workers could not pay their bills. Banks suffered when customers defaulted. The failure of the National Cordage Company in May 1893 sparked a chain reaction of business and bank closings. By year's end, five hundred banks and sixteen hundred businesses failed. Between 1893 and 1897, the nation suffered a devastating economic depression.

Nearly 20 percent of the labor force was jobless during the depression. Falling demand caused prices to drop between 1892 and 1895, but layoffs and wage cuts more than offset declining living costs. Many people could not afford necessities. The New York police estimated that twenty thousand homeless and jobless people roamed city streets.

Continuing Currency Problems

As the depression deepened, the currency dilemma reached a crisis. The Sherman Silver Purchase Act of 1890 had committed the government to use Treasury notes (silver certificates) to buy 4.5 million ounces of silver monthly. Recipients could redeem these certificates for gold, at the ratio of one ounce of gold for every sixteen ounces' of silver. But a western mining boom increased silver supplies, causing its market value to fall and prompting holders of silver certificates and Civil War greenbacks to exchange their notes for more valuable gold. As a result, the nation's gold reserve dwindled, falling below $100 million in early 1893.

If investors believed the country's gold reserve was disappearing, they would lose confidence in America's economic stability and refrain from investing. British capitalists, for example, owned $4 billion in American stocks and bonds and were likely to stop investing if dollars depreciated. The lower the gold reserve dropped, the more people rushed to redeem their money. Panic spread, causing more bankruptcies and unemployment.

To protect the gold reserve, President Cleveland called a special session of Congress to repeal the Sherman Silver Purchase Act. Repeal passed in late 1893, but the run on gold continued. In early 1895, reserves fell to $41 million, and, desperate, Cleveland accepted an offer of 3.5 million ounces of gold for $65 million worth of federal bonds from a banking syndicate led by financier J. P. Morgan. When the bankers resold the bonds, they made a $2 million profit. Cleveland claimed that he had saved the reserves, but discontented farmers, workers, silver miners, and some of Cleveland's Democratic allies saw only humiliation in the president's deal with big businessmen.

The deal between Cleveland and Morgan did not end the depression. After improving slightly in 1895, the economy plunged again. Farm income, declining since 1887, slid further; factories closed; banks restricted withdrawals. The tight money supply depressed housing construction, drying up. Cities like Detroit encouraged citizens to cultivate "potato patches" on vacant land to alleviate food shortages. Urban police stations filled up nightly with homeless people.

Consequences of Depression

In the late 1890s, gold discoveries in Alaska, good harvests, and industrial growth brought relief. But the downturn hastened the crumbling of the old economic system and emergence of a new one. The American economy expanded beyond sectional bases; when western farmers fell into debt, their depressed condition weakened railroads, farm-implement manufacturers, and banks in other regions. Moreover, the corporate consolidation that characterized the new business system tempted many companies to expand too rapidly. When contraction occurred, their reckless debts dragged them down, and they pulled other industries with them.

A new global marketplace was emerging, forcing American farmers to contend with discriminatory transportation rates and falling crop prices at home, along with Canadian and Russian wheat growers, Argentine cattle ranchers, Indian and Egyptian cotton manufacturers, and Australian wool producers. Consequently, one country's economy affected that of other countries. With the glutted domestic market, American businessmen sought new markets abroad (see Chapter 22).

Depression-Era Protests

The depression exposed fundamental tensions in the industrial system. Technological and organizational changes had been widening the gap between employees and employers for half a century. Labor protest began with the railroad strikes of 1877. Their vehemence and support from working-class people raised fears that the United States would experience a popular uprising like the one in France in 1871, which briefly overturned the government and introduced communist principles. The 1886 Haymarket riot, prolonged 1892 strike at the Carnegie Homestead Steel plant, and labor violence among miners in the West heightened anxieties (see Chapter 18). In 1894, there were over thirteen hundred strikes and countless riots. Contrary to accusations of business leaders, few protesters were immigrant anarchists or communists. Rather, they were Americans who believed that in a democracy their voices should be heard.

Socialists

Small numbers of socialists participated in these confrontations. Some socialists believed workers should control factories and businesses; others supported government ownership. All, however, opposed the private enterprise of capitalism. Their ideas derived from Karl Marx (1818–1883), the German philosopher and father of communism, who contended that whoever controls the means of production determines how well people live. Marx wrote that industrial capitalism profits by paying workers less than the value of their labor and that mechanization and mass production alienated workers from their labor. According to Marx, only by abolishing the return on capital—profits— could labor receive its true value, possible only if workers owned the means of production. Marx predicted that workers worldwide would revolt and seize factories, farms, banks, and transportation lines. This revolution would establish a socialist order of justice and equality. Marx's vision appealed to some workers because it promised independence and to some intellectuals because it promised to end class conflict and crass materialism.

In America, socialists disagreed over how to achieve Marx's vision. Much of the movement was influenced by immigrants—first Germans, later Russian Jews, Italians, Hungarians, and Poles. It splintered into small groups, such as the Socialist Labor Party, which failed to attract the mass of laborers because it often focused on doctrine rather than workers' everyday needs. Workers hoped they would benefit through education and acquisition of property; most American workers sought individual advancement rather than the betterment of all.

Eugene V. Debs

In 1894, a new and inspiring Socialist leader emerged. The Indiana-born Eugene V. Debs headed the newly formed American Railway Union, which had carried out that year's strike against the Pullman Company. Jailed for defying the injunction against the strike, Debs read Karl Marx's works in prison. Once released, he became the leading spokesman for American socialism, combining visionary Marxism with Jeffersonian and Populist antimonopolism. Debs captivated audiences with attacks on the free-enterprise system. "Many of you think you are competing," he would lecture. "Against whom? Against Rockefeller?" By 1900, the group soon to be called the Socialist Party of America was uniting around Debs.

Coxey's Army

In 1894, however, a quiet businessman named Jacob Coxey from Massillon, Ohio, captured public attention. Coxey had believed that, to aid debtors, the government should issue $500 million of "legal tender" paper money and make low-interest loans to local governments, which would use the funds to pay unemployed men to build roads and other public works. He planned to publicize his scheme by leading a march from Massillon to Washington, D.C., gathering unemployed workers en route. Coxey's army of about 200 left in March 1894. Hiking across Ohio into Pennsylvania, the marchers received food and housing in depressed industrial towns and rural villages and attracted additional recruits. A dozen similar processions from places such as Seattle, San Francisco, and Los Angeles also trekked eastward. Sore feet prompted some marchers to commandeer trains, but most marches were law-abiding.

Coxey's band of 500 entered Washington on April 30. The next day (May Day, the anniversary of the Haymarket violence), the group, armed with "war clubs of peace," advanced to the Capitol. When Coxey and a few others vaulted a wall surrounding the grounds, mounted police routed the demonstrators. Police dragged Coxey away. As arrests and clubbings continued, Coxey's dream of a demonstration of 400,000 jobless workers dissolved. Unlike socialists, who wished to replace the capitalist system, Coxey's troops merely wanted more jobs and better living standards. The brutal reactions of officials, however, reveal how threatening dissenters like Coxey and Debs seemed to the existing social order.

The Silver Crusade and the Election of 1896

How did Bryan's focus on free silver undermine his presidential campaign and the Populist Party?

Social protest and economic depression made the 1896 presidential election seem pivotal. Debates over money and power were climaxing, Democrats and Republicans battled to control Congress and the presidency. The key question, however, was whether voters would abandon old party loyalties for the Populist party.

Free Silver

The Populist crusade against "money power" settled on the issue of silver, which many believed would solve the nation's complex ills. To them, coinage of silver symbolized an end to special privileges for the rich and the return of government to the people by lifting common people out of debt, increasing the cash in circulation, and reducing interest rates.

As the 1896 election approached, Populists had to decide whether to join with sympathetic factions of the major parties, thus risking a loss of identity, or remain an independent third party. Except in mining areas of Rocky Mountain states, where free coinage of silver had strong support, Republicans were unlikely allies because their support for the gold standard and big-business represented what Populists opposed.

Alliance with northern and western Democrats was more plausible since the party there retained vestiges of antimonopoly ideology and sympathy for a looser currency system, despite the influence of "gold Democrats," such as President Cleveland and Senator David Hill of New York. Linking with Southern Democrats seemed less viable since candidates' failure to carry out their promises left southern farmers feeling betrayed. Whichever option they chose, Populists ensured that the 1896 election would be the most issue oriented since 1860.

Nomination of McKinley

Both major parties were divided. For a year, Ohio industrialist Marcus A. Hanna maneuvered to win the Republican nomination for Ohio's governor, William McKinley, and corralled enough delegates to succeed. The Republicans' only distress occurred when they adopted a platform supporting the gold standard, rejecting a prosilver stance proposed by Colorado senator Henry M. Teller. Teller, a party founder forty years earlier, left the convention in tears, taking a small group of silver Republicans with him.

During the Democratic convention, prosilver delegates wearing silver badges and waving silver banners paraded through the Chicago Amphitheatre. A *New York*

World reporter remarked that "all the silverites need is a Moses." They found one in **William Jennings Bryan**.

William Jennings Bryan

Bryan arrived at the Democratic convention as a member of a contested Nebraska delegation. A former congressman whose support for coinage of silver annoyed President Cleveland, Bryan found the depression's impact on midwestern farmers distressing. Shortly after the convention seated Bryan, he joined the resolutions committee and helped write a platform calling for unlimited coinage of silver. Bryan's now-famous closing words ignited the delegates.

> Having behind us the producing masses of this nation and the world, supported by the commercial interests, the laboring interests, and the toilers everywhere, we will answer [the wealthy classes'] demand for a gold standard by saying to them: You shall not press down upon the brow of labor this crown of thorns, you shall not crucify mankind upon a cross of gold.

After that speech, it took five ballots to win Bryan the nomination, but the magnetic "Boy Orator" proved irresistible. In accepting the silverite goals of southerners and westerners, and repudiating Cleveland's policies, the Democratic Party became more attractive to discontented farmers. But, it alienated a minority wing, who withdrew and nominated their own candidate.

Bryan's nomination presented the Populist party convention with a dilemma. Should Populists join Democrats in support of Bryan or nominate their own candidate? Some reasoned that supporting a separate candidate would split the anti-McKinley vote and guarantee a Republican victory. The convention compromised, first naming Tom Watson as its vice-presidential nominee to preserve party identity (Democrats had nominated Maine shipping magnate Arthur Sewall) and then nominating Bryan for president.

The campaign, as Kansas journalist William Allen White observed, "took the form of religious frenzy." Bryan preached that "every great economic question is in reality a great moral question." Republicans countered Bryan's attacks on privilege by predicting chaos if he won. Hanna invited thousands of people to McKinley's home in Canton, Ohio, where the candidate plied them with homilies on moderation and prosperity, promising something for everyone. In an appeal to working-class voters, Republicans stressed the new jobs that a protective tariff would create.

Election Results

The election revealed that the political standoff had ended. McKinley, symbol of urban and corporate ascendancy, beat Bryan by 600,000 popular votes and won in the electoral college by 271 to 176 (see Map 20.1). Bryan worked hard to rally the nation, but obsession with silver prevented Populists from building the urban-rural coalition that would have expanded their appeal. Urban workers, who might have benefited from Populist goals, feared that silver coinage would shrink the value of their wages. Labor leaders, such as the AFL's Samuel Gompers, though partly sympathetic, would not commit fully because they viewed farmers as businessmen, not workers. And socialists denounced Populists as "retrograde" because they believed in free enterprise. Thus, the Populist crusade collapsed. Although Populists and fusion candidates won a few state and congressional elections, the Bryan-Watson ticket of the Populist party polled only 222,600 votes nationwide.

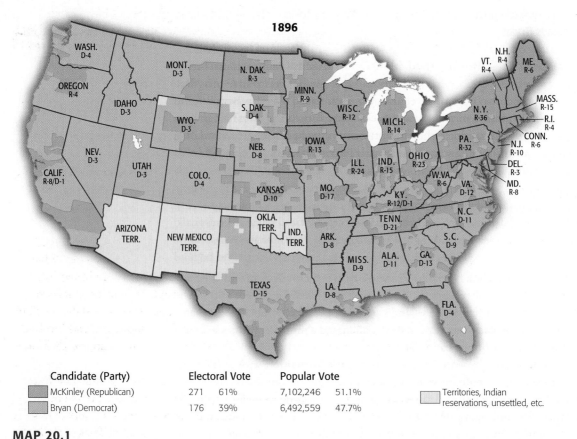

1896

Candidate (Party)	Electoral Vote		Popular Vote	
McKinley (Republican)	271	61%	7,102,246	51.1%
Bryan (Democrat)	176	39%	6,492,559	47.7%

Territories, Indian reservations, unsettled, etc.

MAP 20.1

Presidential Election, 1896

William Jennings Bryan had strong voter support in the South and West, but the numerically superior industrial states, plus California, created majorities for William McKinley.

Source: Copyright © Cengage Learning

The McKinley Presidency

As president, McKinley reinforced his support of business by signing the Gold Standard Act (1900), requiring that all paper money be backed by gold. A seasoned politician, McKinley guided passage of record-high tariff rates as congressman in 1890. He accordingly supported the Dingley Tariff of 1897, which raised duties even higher. A believer in opening new markets abroad to sustain profits at home, McKinley encouraged imperialistic ventures in Latin America and the Pacific. Better times and victory in the Spanish-American War helped him beat Bryan again in 1900.

Summary

Though buffeted by special interests, Gilded Age politicians prepared the nation for the twentieth century. Laws encouraging economic growth with some principles of regulation, measures expanding government agencies while reducing crass patronage, and federal intervention in trade and currency issues evolved during the 1870s and 1880s.

Nevertheless, the United States remained a nation of inconsistencies. Those who supported disfranchisement of African Americans and continued discrimination against blacks and women still polluted politics. People in power could not tolerate

Interpreting a Fairy Tale

The Wizard of Oz, (1939) one of the all-time most popular movies, began as a work of juvenile literature penned by journalist L. Frank Baum in 1900. Originally titled *The Wonderful Wizard of Oz*, the story used memorable characters to create an adventurous quest.

Adults have searched the story for hidden meanings. In 1964, scholar Henry M. Littlefield asserted that Baum intended to write a Populist parable illustrating the conditions of overburdened farmers and laborers. Dorothy, he theorized, symbolized the well-intentioned common person; the Scarecrow, the struggling farmer; the Tin Man, the industrial worker. Hoping for a better life, these friends, along with the Cowardly Lion (William Jennings Bryan), followed a yellow brick road (the gold standard) that led nowhere. The Emerald City was presided over by a wizard, who tried to be all things to all people, but Dorothy revealed him as a fraud. Dorothy was able to leave this muddled society and return to her simple Kansas farm family of Aunt Em and Uncle Henry by using her magical silver slippers (representing coinage of silver, though the movie made them red).

Subsequent theorists identified additional symbols, such as Oz being the abbreviation for ounces (oz.), the chief measurement of gold. The Wicked Witch of the East—who, Baum wrote, kept the little people (Munchkins) "in bondage"—could represent industrial capitalism.

But in 1983, historian William R. Leach asserted that Baum's tale actually was a celebration of urban consumer culture. Its language exalted the opulence of Emerald City, which to Leach resembled the "White City" of the 1893 Chicago World's Fair and Dorothy's optimism symbolized the optimism of industrialism. Baum's career supported this new interpretation. Before writing, he designed display windows and was involved in theater—activities that gave him an appreciation of modern urban life.

The real legacy of *The Wonderful Wizard of Oz* has been its ability to provoke differing interpretations. Baum's fairy tale, the first truly American work of this sort, has bequeathed many fascinating images about the diversity and contradictions of American culture.

radical views like socialism or Populism, but many of those ideas continued to find supporters in the new century.

The 1896 election realigned national politics. The Republican Party, founded in the 1850s amid a crusade against slavery, became the majority party by emphasizing government aid to business, drawing the urban middle class, and playing down moralism. The Democratic Party miscalculated on the silver issue but held its support in the South and in urban political machines. At the national level, however, loyalties lacked their former potency. Suspicion of party politics increased, and voter participation declined. The Populists tried to energize a third-party movement, but their success was fleeting. Still, as the twentieth century progressed, many Populist goals were incorporated by the major parties, including regulation of railroads, banks, and utilities; shorter workdays; a variant of the subtreasury plan; a graduated income tax; and direct election of senators. These reforms succeeded because various groups united behind them. Immigration, urbanization, and industrialization had transformed the United States into a pluralistic society in which compromise had become a political fact of life. As the Gilded Age ended, business was still ascendant, and large segments of the population remained excluded from political and economic opportunity. But the winds of dissent and reform had begun to blow more strongly.

Chapter Review

The Nature of Party Politics

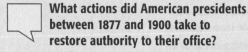

How did factional disputes complicate party politics in the Gilded Age?

Most Democrats sought to restrict government power and included immigrants and Catholics, while most Republicans were native-born Protestants who believed government should play a bigger role in reforming society. Both parties were ultimately divided by factional rifts that kept them from simultaneously controlling the presidency and Congress or holding power in either for very long. Republican factions included Stalwarts and Half Breeds, who each sought to wield influence and jobs toward supporters, and Mugwumps who, thought only the most upstanding men should be allowed in government. Democrats split into white-supremacist southerners, immigrant and working-class advocates of urban political machines, businessmen who sought lower tariffs and the gold standard, and those who embraced free silver. Such divisions within parties made unity difficult.

Issues of Legislation

What was at issue in the debate over the gold standard versus free silver?

The debate over gold versus free silver was in many ways a struggle between debtors and creditors in the late nineteenth century. Farmers and small businessmen (debtors) pushed for silver coinage, which they believed would put more money in circulation and lower interest rates, thereby making it easier for them to repay mortgages and other debts. Large businesses (creditors) preferred money backed by gold, because they considered it more stable, and therefore likely to maintain foreign investors' confidence in the U.S. economy. In effect, the debate became a class struggle, as well as a sectional one: those in the West and South where mining and agriculture dominated, favored silver; those in the industrial Northeast, gold.

Tentative Presidents

What actions did American presidents between 1877 and 1900 take to restore authority to their office?

After Andrew Johnson's impeachment and the scandals plaguing both the Grant administration and the 1876 election, the presidency was tarnished. Presidents Rutherford Hayes (1877–1881), James Garfield (1881), Chester Arthur (1881–1885), Grover Cleveland (1885–1889 and 1893–1897), Benjamin Harrison (1889–1893), and William McKinley (1897–1901) sought to bring integrity back to federal government through various legislative initiatives. They all supported civil service (and its expansion) as a means to end the corruption of the spoils system. With varying success, they addressed currency, tariffs, railroad regulation, and labor unrest.

Discrimination, Disfranchisement, and Responses

How did southerners find legal means to discriminate against newly enfranchised African Americans in the decades following the Civil War?

To keep blacks from voting, southern leaders instituted measures such as poll taxes, which most blacks could not afford, and literacy tests. These measures were upheld in the Supreme Court, which noted that the Fifteenth Amendment could only prohibit states from denying the vote based on "race, color, or previous condition of servitude," but could not control the local election process. Similarly, Jim Crow, or segregation laws, confined African Americans to separate areas in public places such as streetcars, hospitals, and parks, thereby deliberately reminding them of their inferior status. These laws were upheld by the Supreme Court in *Plessy v. Ferguson*, which allowed that states could legally segregate on a "separate-but-equal" basis. Violence against African Americans—particularly lynching—provided a reminder of the extremes of white racism and hostility.

Agrarian Unrest and Populism

How did farmers' discontent crystallize in the Grange movement and Farmers' Alliances?

As farm prices dropped, farmers found it increasingly difficult to earn a living from their land. Those conditions were made worse by the fact that as smallholders, most could not compete with large firms, which could negotiate lower costs for transportation and supplies by virtue of their size. In response, farmers founded local organizations called Granges in the 1860s and 1870s partly as social clubs and partly to enable them to join forces in cooperatives where they could get the same competitive advantage as larger firms. Granges declined in the late 1870s, replaced a decade later by Farmers' Alliances, which rallied against crop liens, merchants, railroads, and money power. Along with cooperatives, Alliances sought a government aid system called a subtreasury that they hoped would provide low-interest loans to farmers seeking to buy land and would assist farmers in warehousing crops until market prices increased.

The Depression and Protests of the 1890s

Why did socialism fail to take hold in the United States amid the labor activism of the late nineteenth century?

The depression and thousands of strikes beginning with the 1877 railroad strike revealed general worker dissatisfaction that certainly created the conditions ripe for socialism to flourish, particularly once its charismatic leader Eugene V. Debs came to the fore in the 1890s. But American socialists could not agree on how best to implement Marxist strategies for worker control of the means of production and the end of capitalism's inequities. Socialism was also thwarted by that distinctly American celebration of social mobility and individual achievement. While workers found some aspects of socialism attractive, their ultimate aim was individual advancement, which they were unwilling to sacrifice for the greater good of all workers.

The Silver Crusade and the Election of 1896

How did Bryan's focus on free silver undermine his presidential campaign and the Populist Party?

Populists embraced the issue of silver because they believed it would end special privileges for the rich by lifting mainstream Americans from debt, increasing the money in circulation and lowering interest rates. Populists fused these ideas to the Democratic Party by joining forces with them behind William Jennings Bryan for president in 1896. Bryan was singularly focused on silver, but this cost him votes from urban workers, who feared silver coinage would cut their wages. Labor leaders equated farmers with businessmen, and as such, could not join forces with Populists on this issue. Bryan received only 222,600 votes nationwide, and while Populists continued to influence elections, the party itself collapsed.

Suggestions For Further Reading

Edward L. Ayers, *The Promise of the New South: Life After Reconstruction* (1992)

Jean Baker, *Sisters: The Lives of America's Suffragists* (2005)

Glenda Elizabeth Gilmore, *Gender and Jim Crow: Women and the Politics of White Supremacy in North Carolina, 1896–1920* (1996)

Steven Hahn, *A Nation Under Our Feet: Black Political Struggles in the Rural South, from Slavery to the Great Migration* (2003)

Michael Kazin, *The Populist Persuasion: An American History* (1995)

Jean V. Matthews, *The Rise of the New Woman: The Women's Movement in America, 1875–1930* (2003)

Nick Salvatore, *Eugene V. Debs: Citizen and Socialist* (1992)

Go to the CourseMate website for primary source links, study tools, and review materials for this chapter. www.cengagebrain.com

The Progressive Era

21

1895–1920

What Ben Lindsey saw made him furious. As a young Colorado lawyer in the 1890s, a judge asked him to defend two boys, about twelve years old, accused of burglary. The boys had been imprisoned for sixty days without a trial and did not understand what *burglary* meant or how the justice system worked. Visiting them in jail, Lindsay found the youngsters playing poker with two older cellmates—a safecracker and a horse thief. Outraged that children were housed with hardened criminals, Lindsey later wrote, "Here were two boys, neither of them serious enemies of society, who were about to be convicted of burglary and have felony records. . . . I had made up my mind to smash the system that meant so much injustice to youth."

In 1901, Lindsey ran for county judge and began fighting for juvenile protection from criminal prosecution, exploitative labor practices, and burdens of poverty. He and his wife, Henrietta, promoted a separate juvenile court system and aid to families with children at risk of becoming criminals. They wrote reform laws adopted by many states and countries. The Lindseys' efforts showed compassion and middle-class bias as part of a broader movement seeking solutions to modern America's social and economic problems.

During the 1890s, economic depression, labor violence, political upheaval, and foreign entanglements shook the nation. Numerous Americans continued to suffer from poverty and injustice. Some critics regarded industrialists as monsters who controlled markets and prices to maximize profits at the expense of laborers. Others believed government was corroded by bosses who enriched themselves by abusing power. Tensions created by urbanization and industrialization fragmented society into conflicting interest groups.

By 1900, the previous decade's political tumult had calmed, and economic depression subsided. The nation emerged victorious from a war against Spain (see Chapter 22), and a new era of political leaders, including Theodore Roosevelt and Woodrow Wilson, was dawning. A sense of renewal both intensified anxiety over continuing problems and raised hopes that democracy could be reconciled with capitalism.

Between 1895 and 1920, a complex reform campaign emerged to renovate or restore American society, values, and institutions. By the 1910s, reformers from Republican and Democratic Parties were calling themselves Progressives; in 1912, Progressives formed their own party. Historians have used the term *Progressivism* to refer to the era's spirit, while disagreeing over its meaning and over who actually was Progressive.

The reform impulse had many sources. Industrial capitalism created awesome technology, unprecedented productivity, and copious consumer goods. But it also brought harmful overproduction, domineering monopolies, labor strife, and destruction of natural resources. Burgeoning cities facilitated the distribution of goods and services but also bred poverty, disease, and crime. Rising immigration and a new professional class reconfigured the social order. And the depression of the 1890s forced leading citizens to realize what working people already knew: America's central promise of, equality of opportunity, was elusive.

Middle-class reformers organized around three goals. First, they sought to end abuses of power by making trustbusting, consumers' rights, and good government compelling political issues. Second, Progressives like Ben Lindsey wished to supplant corrupt power with humane institutions, such as schools, courts, and medical clinics. They asserted that society had responsibility and power to improve individual lives and that government must protect the common good and elevate public interest above self-interest. They challenged entrenched views on women's roles, race relations, education, legal and scientific thought, and morality. Third, Progressives wanted to entrust experts who would end wasteful competition and promote social and economic order. Just as corporations applied scientific management to achieve economic efficiency, Progressives advocated expertise and planning to achieve social and political efficiency.

Progressives had faith in humankind's ability to create a better world. Rising incomes, new educational opportunities, and increased availability of goods and services inspired confidence that social improvement would follow. Judge Lindsey expressed the Progressive creed when he wrote, "In the end the people are bound to do the right thing, no matter how much they fail at times."

As you read this chapter, keep the following questions in mind:

* What were the major characteristics of Progressivism?

* In what ways did Progressive reform succeed, and in what ways did it fail?

* How did women and racial minorities challenge previous ways of thinking about American society?

Theodore Roosevelt and Revival of the Presidency

Theodore Roosevelt | Regulation of Trusts | Pure Food and Drug Laws | Race Relations | Conservation | Gifford Pinchot | Panic of 1907 | Taft Administration | Candidates in 1912 | New Nationalism Versus New Freedom

Woodrow Wilson and Extension of Progressive Reform

Woodrow Wilson | Wilson's Policy on Business Regulation | Tariff and Tax Reform | Election of 1916

LEGACY FOR A PEOPLE AND A NATION *Margaret Sanger, Planned Parenthood, and the Birth-Control Controversy*

SUMMARY

Chronology

1895	Booker T. Washington gives Atlanta Compromise speech		White Slave Traffic Act (Mann Act) prohibits transportation of women for "immoral purposes"
	National Association of Colored Women founded		Taft fires Pinchot
1898	*Holden v. Hardy* upholds limits on miners' working hours	1911	Society of American Indians founded
		1913	Sixteenth Amendment ratified, legalizing income tax
1901	McKinley assassinated; T. Roosevelt assumes presidency		Seventeenth Amendment ratified, providing for direct election of senators
1904	*Northern Securities* case dissolves railroad trust		Underwood Tariff institutes income tax
1905	*Lochner v. New York* removes limits on bakers' working hours		Federal Reserve Act establishes central banking system
1906	Hepburn Act tightens ICC control over railroads	1914	Federal Trade Commission created to investigate unfair trade practices
	Meat Inspection Act passed		Clayton Anti-Trust Act outlaws monopolistic business practices
	Pure Food and Drug Act Passed		
1908	*Muller v. Oregon* upholds limits on women's working hours	1919	Eighteenth Amendment ratified, establishing prohibition of alcoholic beverages
1909	NAACP founded	1920	Nineteenth Amendment ratified, giving women the vote in federal elections
1910	Mann-Elkins Act reinforces ICC powers		

The Varied Progressive Impulse

How did Progressive reform cut across class lines?

After the heated election of 1896, party loyalties eroded and voter turnout declined. In northern states, voter participation in presidential elections dropped from the 1880s' levels of 80 percent to under 60 percent. In southern states, where poll taxes and literacy tests prevented most African American and many poor white males from voting, it fell below 30 percent. At the same time, new interest groups championing their own causes gained influence.

National Associations and Foreign Influences Many formerly local organizations became nationwide after 1890. These included professional associations, such as the American Bar Association; women's organizations, such as the National American Woman Suffrage Association; issue-oriented groups, such as the National Consumers League; civic-minded clubs, such as the National Municipal League; and minority-group associations, such as the National Negro Business League and the Society of American Indians. Because they usually acted outside of parties, such groups made politics more fragmented and issue-focused than in earlier eras.

Reformers also adopted foreign models. Some were introduced by Americans who encountered them while studying in England, France, and Germany; others, by foreigners visiting the United States. Americans copied from England the settlement house, in which reformers lived among and aided the urban poor, and workers' compensation for victims of industrial accidents. Other reforms, such as old-age insurance, subsidized workers' housing, city planning, and rural reconstruction, were modified in America.

Although Populist rural-based goals of moral regeneration, political democracy, and antimonopolism continued after the movement faded, the Progressive quest for social justice, educational and legal reform, and government streamlining had a largely urban quality.

The New Middle Class and Muckrakers

Progressive goals—ending abuse of power, protecting the welfare of all classes, reforming institutions, and promoting social efficiency—existed across society. But a new middle class—men and women in law, medicine, engineering, social service, religion, teaching, and business—formed the reform vanguard. Offended by corruption and immorality in business, government, and human relations, they determined to apply the rational techniques of their professions to social problems. They also believed that they could create a unified nation by "Americanizing" immigrants and Indians through education stressing middle-class customs.

Progressive views were voiced by journalists whom Theodore Roosevelt dubbed **muckrakers** (after a character in the Puritan allegory *Pilgrim's Progress,* who, rather than looking heavenward at beauty, looked downward and raked the muck). Muckrakers fed public tastes for scandal by exposing social, economic, and political wrongs. Investigative articles in popular magazines attacked adulterated foods, fraudulent insurance, prostitution, and political corruption. Lincoln Steffens hoped his exposés of bosses' misrule in *McClure's* would inspire outrage and reform. Other celebrated muckraking works included Upton Sinclair's *The Jungle* (1906), exposing outrages of the meatpacking industry; and Ida M. Tarbell's disparaging history of Standard Oil (first published in *McClure's,* 1902–1904).

muckrakers: Journalists who wrote articles exposing urban political corruption and corporate wrongdoing.

Progressives advocated nonpartisan elections to prevent fraud and bribery bred by party loyalties. To make officeholders more responsible, they urged adoption of the initiative, which permitted voters to propose new laws; the referendum, which enabled voters to accept or reject a law; and the recall, which allowed voters to remove offending officials and judges from office.

Upper-Class Reformers

The Progressive spirit also stirred some businessmen and wealthy women. Executives like Alexander Cassatt of the Pennsylvania Railroad supported some government regulation and political restructuring to protect their interests from more radical reformers. Others, like E.A. Filene, founder of a Boston department store, were humanitarians who worked for social justice. Business-dominated organizations like the U.S. Chamber of Commerce thought that running schools, hospitals, and local government like businesses would stabilize society. Elite women financed settlement houses and organizations like the Young Women's Christian Association (YWCA), which aided unmarried working women.

Settlement Houses

Young, educated middle-class women and men worked to bridge the gap between social classes by living in inner-city settlement houses. Residents envisioned them as places where people could mitigate modern problems through education, art, and reform. Between

1886 and 1910, over 400 settlements were established, mostly in big cities, sponsoring activities such as English-language classes, kindergartens and nurseries, health clinics, vocational training, playgrounds, and art exhibits. The vanguard of progressivism, settlement house workers backed housing and labor reform, offered meeting space to unions, and served as school nurses, juvenile probation officers, and teachers.

Though men helped initiate the settlement movement, women were its most influential participants. Jane Addams of Chicago's Hull House settlement, Lillian Wald of New York's Henry Street settlement, Vida Scudder of Boston's Denison House, and Florence Kelley of Hull House not only broadened traditional female roles as settlement house leaders but used their work a springboard to larger reform roles. Kelley's investigations into the exploitation of child labor prompted Illinois governor John Altgeld to appoint her state factory inspector; she later founded the National Consumers League. Wald helped make nursing a respected profession and co-founded the NAACP. And Addams's efforts toward world peace garnered her the Nobel Peace Prize in 1931.

Working-Class Reformers

Vital elements of what became modern American liberalism derived from working-class urban experiences. By 1900, many urban workers were pressing "bread-and-butter reforms" such as safe factories, shorter workdays, workers' compensation, protection of child and women laborers, better housing, and a more equitable tax structure. Politicians trained in machine politics, and their constituents supported political bosses. Yet bossism was not necessarily incompatible with humanitarianism. "Big Tim" Sullivan, an influential boss in New York's Tammany Hall political machine, said he supported shorter workdays for women because "I had seen me sister go out to work when she was only fourteen and I know we ought to help these gals by giving 'em a law which will prevent 'em from being broken down while they're still young." Working-class advocates opposed prohibition, Sunday closing laws, civil service, and nonpartisan elections, but joined with other reformers to pass laws aiding labor and promoting social welfare.

The Social Gospel

Much of Progressive reform rested on religious values. A movement known as the **Social Gospel**, led by Protestant ministers Walter Rauschenbusch, Washington Gladden, and Charles Sheldon, countered competitive capitalism by interjecting Christian churches into worldly matters, such as arbitrating industrial harmony and improving the conditions of the poor. Believing that helping others provided the way to individual salvation and creating God's kingdom on earth, Social Gospelers governed their lives by asking, "What would Jesus do?"

Others tried to "Americanize" immigrants and Indians by expanding educational, economic, and cultural opportunities. But imposing their values on people of different cultures undermined their efforts. Working-class Catholic and Jewish immigrants, for example, sometimes rejected the Americanization efforts of Social Gospelers and resented middle-class reformers' interference in their child-rearing.

Socialists

Disillusioned immigrant intellectuals, industrial workers, former Populists, and women's rights activists turned to socialism. They wanted the United States to follow the example of Germany,

Social Gospel: Movement launched in the 1870s that stressed that true Christianity commits men and women to fight social injustice wherever it exists.

England, and France, where the government sponsored such socialist goals as low-cost housing, workers' compensation, old-age pensions, public ownership of municipal services, and labor reform. By 1912, the Socialist Party of America claimed 150,000 members, and 700,000 subscribers to its newspaper *Appeal to Reason*.

Politically, socialists united behind Eugene V. Debs, the American Railway Union organizer who drew nearly 100,000 votes as Socialist Party candidate in 1900. A spellbinding orator who appealed to urban immigrants and western farmers alike, Debs won 400,000 votes in 1904 and 900,000 in 1912, at the pinnacle of his and his party's career. Although Debs and other Socialist leaders did not always agree on tactics, they made compelling overtures to reformers.

While some Progressives joined the Socialist Party, most reformers favored capitalism too much to want to overthrow it. Municipal ownership of public utilities represented their limit of drastic change. Some AFL unions supported socialist goals and candidates, but many unions opposed reforms like unemployment insurance because it would increase taxes. Moreover, private real-estate interests opposed government intervention in housing, and manufacturers fought socialism by blacklisting militant laborers.

Southern and Western Progressivism   Progressive reform in the South included the same goals as in the North—railroad and utility regulation, factory safety, pure food and drug legislation, and moral reform. The South pioneered some political reforms; the direct primary originated in North Carolina; the city-commission plan arose in Galveston, Texas; and the city-manager plan began in Staunton, Virginia.

In the West, several politicians championed humanitarianism, putting the region at the forefront of efforts to expand federal and state government functions.

Library of Congress

Although their objectives sometimes differed from those of middle-class Progressive reformers, socialists also became a more active force in the early twentieth century. Socialist parades on May Day, like this one in 1910, were meant to express the solidarity of all working people.

Links to the World

Foreign Universities and Study Abroad

The university as a degree-granting institution originated during Medieval times in Islamic Morocco and Egypt. Shortly thereafter, universities arose in Italy, France, England, and Spain. By the end of the nineteenth century, the chief models for the modern university existed in German cities and in British institutions at Oxford and Cambridge. Their academic freedom and dynamic faculty attracted young Americans. German universities were especially inexpensive; with travel costs, they were only a third as much as comparable American institutions.

Their time at British and European universities inspired many Americans with ideas about improving society. The muckraking journalist Lincoln Steffens, for example, received an undergraduate degree from the University of California, then studied at German universities to learn from the great minds that his California professors "quoted and looked up to as their

high priests." Scholar and civil rights activist W.E.B. Du Bois pursued graduate work at the University of Berlin. Progressive historian Charles Beard was moved by his studies at Oxford University, and Edith Abbott, who pioneered social work in America, studied welfare policy at the London School of Economics.

Some American students were exposed to the European ideology of social democracy, a movement related to socialism but that emphasized reform through politics rather than revolution. Social democrats aligned with the working class and often called themselves "socialists." But they stressed moral issues rather than pitting one class against another. When these Americans returned home, they brought an opposition to the every-man-for-himself implications of laissez faire and an impetus for using the government for the betterment of all—important underpinnings of Progressive reform.

Lincoln Steffens, born in 1866 in Sacramento, California, graduated from the University of California at Berkeley in 1889, then went abroad to "learn culture" by studying at universities in Germany and France. Upon his return to the United States, he became a police reporter in New York City, then wrote articles for the muckraking magazine McClure's, including pieces on corruption in American cities. He compiled the articles into a book, The Shame of the Cities, that became one of the most famous publications of the Progressive Era.

Edith Abbott grew up in Grand Island, Nebraska, and taught high school before receiving an undergraduate degree from the University of Nebraska and a Ph.D. in economics from the University of Chicago. In 1906, at the age of thirty, she received a fellowship to study in England at the London School of Economics, where she learned new theories about dealing with poverty. After a few years, she joined Jane Addams at Hull House and became a pioneer in progressive reform.

546

Nevada's Progressive Senator Francis Newlands advocated national planning and federal control of water resources. California Governor Hiram Johnson fought for direct primaries, regulation of child and women's labor, workers' compensation, a pure food and drug act, and educational reform. Southern and western women, white and black, contributed to Progressive causes. In western states, women could vote on state and local matters, but often their reform efforts occurred outside of politics, in racially distinct projects. White women crusaded against child labor, founded social service organizations, and challenged unfair wages. African American women, as homemakers and religious leaders—which whites found more acceptable than political activism—advocated for cleaner streets, better education, and health reforms.

Opponents of Progressivism

It would be incorrect to assume that a Progressive spirit captivated all of America between 1895 and 1920. Defenders of free enterprise opposed regulatory measures believing government programs undermined the initiative and competition basic to a free-market system. "Old-guard" Republicans, such as Senator Nelson W. Aldrich of Rhode Island and House Speaker Joseph Cannon of Illinois, championed this ideology.

Moreover, prominent Progressives were not always "progressive." Their attempts to Americanize immigrants reflected prejudice as well as naiveté. Governor Hiram Johnson promoted discrimination against Japanese Americans, and most southern governors rested their power on appeals to white supremacy. In the South, the disfranchisement of blacks meant that electoral reforms affected only whites. Settlement houses in northern cities kept blacks and whites in separate programs and buildings.

Progressive reformers generally occupied the center of the ideological spectrum, believing on one hand that laissez faire was obsolete and on the other that a radical departure from free enterprise was dangerous. Like Thomas Jefferson, they expressed faith in the will of the people; like Alexander Hamilton, they desired strong central government to act in the interest of conscience.

Government and Legislative Reform

According to Progressives, what was the government's role in improving society?

Mistrust of tyranny traditionally prompted Americans to believe that democratic government should be small, interfere in private affairs only in unique circumstances, and withdraw quickly. In the late 1800s, this viewpoint weakened when economic problems led corporations to pursue government aid and protection. Discontented farmers sought government regulation of railroads and other monopolistic businesses. City dwellers, accustomed to favors from political machines, expected government to act on their behalf. Before 1900, state governments had been concerned largely with railroads and economic growth; the federal government had focused primarily on tariffs and the currency. After 1900, public opinion, roused by muckraking media, influenced change.

Restructuring Government

Middle-class Progressive reformers rejected laissez-faire principles of government, reasoning that in a complex industrial age public authority needed to counteract inefficiency and exploitation. But to tap this power, activists would have to reclaim government from politicians whose greed they believed soiled the democratic system.

Prior to the Progressive era, reformers attacked corruption in city governments through such structural reforms as civil service, nonpartisan elections, and scrutiny of public expenditures. After 1900, campaigns to make cities more efficient resulted in city-manager and commission forms of government, in which urban officials were chosen for professional expertise rather than for political connections. At the state level, Progressives supported several skillful governors. Wisconsin's Robert M. La Follette was one of the most dynamic Progressive governors. A small-town lawyer, La Follette rose through the state Republican Party to become governor in 1900. There, he initiated direct primaries, more equitable taxes, and railroad regulation. After three terms as governor, La Follette became a U.S. senator. "Battling Bob" displayed a rare ability to approach reform scientifically proclaiming that his goal was "not to smash corporations, but to drive them out of politics."

Crusades against corrupt politics made the system more democratic. Political reformers achieved a major goal in 1913 with adoption of the Seventeenth Amendment to the Constitution, which provided for direct election of U.S. senators, replacing election by state legislatures. But party bosses were still able to control elections, and special-interest groups spent large sums to influence voting.

Labor Reform

At the instigation of middle-class/working-class coalitions, many states enacted factory inspection laws, and by 1916 nearly two-thirds of states required compensation for victims of industrial accidents. Some legislatures granted aid to mothers with dependent children. Under pressure from the National Child Labor Committee, nearly every state set a minimum age for employment (varying from twelve to sixteen) and limited hours that children could work. Labor laws were imperfect, however. They seldom provided for the close inspection of factories that enforcement required. And families needing extra income falsified their children's ages to employers.

Several groups also united to achieve restricted working hours for women and aided retirees. After the Supreme Court, in *Muller v. Oregon*, upheld Oregon's ten-hour limit in 1908, more states passed laws protecting female workers. In 1914, the American Association for Old Age Security secured old-age pensions in Arizona. Judges struck down the law, but demand for pensions continued, and in the 1920s many states enacted such laws.

Prohibition

Reformers did not always agree about whether laws should regulate behavior such as drinking habits and sexual conduct. The **Anti-Saloon League**, formed in 1893, allied with the Woman's Christian Temperance Union (founded in 1874) to publicize alcoholism's role in health problems and family distress. The League successfully shifted attention from the immorality of drunkenness to the alleged link between the drinking and accidents, poverty, and poor productivity.

The war on saloons prompted many states and localities to restrict liquor consumption. By 1900, one-fourth of the nation's population lived in "dry" communities, prohibiting liquor sales. But alcohol consumption increased with the influx of immigrants whose cultures included social drinking, convincing prohibitionists that a nationwide ban was needed. In 1918, Congress passed the **Eighteenth Amendment** (ratified in 1919 and implemented in 1920), outlawing the manufacture, sale, and transportation of intoxicating liquors. Not all prohibitionists were Progressive

Anti-Saloon League: Advocacy group founded in 1893 that sought to ban alcohol by publicizing its harmful effects on families and individuals and its link to accidents and health problems.

Eighteenth Amendment: Amendment to the Constitution that established national prohibition of alcohol.

reformers, and vice versa. Nevertheless, the Eighteenth Amendment embodied the Progressive goal to protect family and workplace through reform legislation.

Controlling Prostitution Moral outrage erupted when muckraking journalists charged that international gangs were kidnapping women and forcing them into prostitution, a practice called white slavery. Accusations were exaggerated, but they alarmed moralists who falsely perceived a link between immigration and prostitution, and who feared that prostitutes were producing genetically inferior children. Reformers prodded governments to investigate and pass corrective legislation. The Chicago Vice Commission undertook a "scientific" survey of dance halls and illicit sex and published its findings as *The Social Evil in Chicago* in 1911. The report concluded that poverty, gullibility, and desperation drove women into prostitution. Such investigations publicized rising numbers of prostitutes but failed to prove that criminal organizations lured women into "the trade."

Reformers nonetheless believed they could attack prostitution by punishing those who promoted and practiced it. In 1910, Congress passed the White Slave Traffic Act (Mann Act), prohibiting interstate and international transportation of a woman for immoral purposes. By 1915, nearly every state outlawed brothels and solicitation of sex.

Like prohibition, the Mann Act reflected sentiment that government could improve behavior by restricting it. Middle-class reformers believed the source of evil was not human nature but the social environment. Intervention via laws could help create a heaven on earth, although working classes resented such attempts to control them. Thus, when Chicagoans voted on a referendum to make their city dry before the Eighteenth Amendment was passed, three-fourths of the city's immigrant voters opposed it, and the measure was defeated.

Link to *Hoke v. United States, 227 U.S. 308*, a case that tested the Mann Act.

New Ideas in Social Institutions

What was the impact of Progressive education reforms?

Preoccupation with efficiency and scientific management infiltrated education, law, religion, and social science. Darwin's theory of evolution challenged beliefs in a God-created world; immigration created complex social diversity; and technology made old production habits obsolete. Professionals grappled with how to embrace progress yet preserve the best from the past.

John Dewey and Progressive Education As late as 1870, when families needed children to do farm work, Americans attended school only a few months a year for four years. By 1900, however, the urban-industrial economy and its expanding middle class advanced childhood as a special life stage, sheltering youngsters from society's dangers and promoting their physical and emotional growth. That meant ensuring that youngsters were exposed to age-appropriate educational materials and activities.

Educators argued that expanded schooling produced better adult citizens and workers. In the 1870s and 1880s, laws required children to attend school to age fourteen. The number of public high schools grew from five hundred in 1870 to ten thousand in 1910. By 1900, educational reformers, such as philosopher John Dewey, asserted that schools needed to prepare children for a modern world by making personal development the focus of the curriculum.

Progressive education, based on Dewey's *The School and Society* (1899) and *Democracy and Education* (1916), stressed that learning should involve real-life problems and that children needed to learn from experience, not by rote memorization. Dewey and his wife, Alice, tested these ideas in their Laboratory School at the University of Chicago.

Growth of Colleges and Universities

A more practical curriculum also drove higher education reform. Previously, American colleges resembled their European counterparts: in training a select few for careers in law, medicine, and religion. But in the late 1800s, institutions of higher learning multiplied via state and federal grants. Between 1870 and 1910, American colleges and universities grew from 563 to nearly 1,000. Curricula broadened to make learning more appealing and keep pace with technological and social changes. Harvard University, under President Charles W. Eliot, pioneered new teaching methods and substituted electives for required courses. Many schools considered athletics vital to a student's growth, and men's intercollegiate sports became a permanent feature.

Southern states created segregated colleges for blacks and whites. Although African Americans continued to suffer from inferior educational opportunities, they found intellectual stimulation in all-black colleges and used education to help uplift their race.

Between 1890 and 1910, the number of women attending colleges swelled from 56,000 to 140,000. Roughly 106,000 attended coeducational institutions (mostly state universities); the rest enrolled in women's colleges. By 1920, 283,000 women attended college, accounting for 47 percent of total enrollment. But women were encouraged (and usually sought) to take home education courses, and most medical schools refused to admit women. Separate women's medical schools, such as the Women's Medical College of Philadelphia, trained female physicians, but most of these schools were absorbed or put out of business by larger, male-dominated institutions.

By 1920, 78 percent of children ages five and seventeen were enrolled in public schools; another 8 percent attended private and parochial schools. There were 600,000 college and graduate students in 1920, compared with only 52,000 in 1870. Yet critical analysis seldom tested the faith that schools could promote equality as well as personal growth and responsible citizenship.

Progressive Legal Thought

Harvard law professor Roscoe Pound and Oliver Wendell Holmes Jr., associate justice of the Supreme Court (1902–1932) led an attack on the traditional view of law as universal and unchanging. Their opinion that law should reflect society's needs challenged the practice of invoking inflexible legal precedents. Louis D. Brandeis, a lawyer who later joined Holmes on the Supreme Court, insisted that judges' opinions be based on scientifically gathered information about social realities. Brandeis collected data on harmful effects of long working hours to convince the Supreme Court, in *Muller v. Oregon* (1908), to uphold Oregon's ten-hour limit on women's workday.

Judges raised on laissez-faire economics and strict interpretation of the Constitution overturned laws that Progressives thought necessary. Thus in

1905, the Supreme Court, in *Lochner v. New York,* revoked a state law limiting bakers' working hours. The Court's majority argued that the Fourteenth Amendment protected an individual's right to make contracts without government interference.

Several decisions, beginning with *Holden v. Hardy* (1898), in which the Supreme Court sustained a Utah law regulating miners' working hours, confirmed the use of state police power to protect health, safety, and morals. Judges also affirmed federal police power and Congress's authority over interstate commerce by upholding legislation, such as the Pure Food and Drug Act, the Meat Inspection Act, and the Mann Act.

But even if one agreed that laws should address society's needs, whose needs should prevail? In many localities, a native-born Protestant majority imposed Bible reading in public schools (offending Catholics and Jews), required businesses to close on Sundays, limited women's rights, restricted religious practices of Mormons and others, prohibited interracial marriage, and enforced racial segregation. Justice Holmes asserted that laws should be made for "people of fundamentally differing views," but how to accomplish that continues to spark debates today.

Social Science

Social science—the study of society and its institutions— also changed. Economics scholars used statistics to argue that laws governing economic relationships were not timeless but should reflect prevailing social conditions. A new breed of sociologists led by Lester Ward, Albion Small, and Edward A. Ross agreed, adding that citizens should work to cure social ills.

Meanwhile, historians Frederick Jackson Turner, Charles A. Beard, and Vernon L. Parrington examined the past to explain the present. Beard, like other Progressives, believed that the Constitution was a flexible document. His *Economic Interpretation of the Constitution* (1913) argued that a group of merchants and business-oriented lawyers created the Constitution to defend private property. If the Constitution served special interests in one age, he argued, it could be changed to serve broader interests in another.

In public health, organizations such as the National Consumers League (NCL), founded by Florence Kelley in 1899, joined physicians and social scientists to secure far-reaching Progressive reforms. NCL pursued protection of female and child laborers and elimination of potential health hazards. Local branches united with women's clubs to advance consumer protection measures, such as the licensing of food vendors and inspection of dairies. They urged city governments to fund neighborhood clinics providing medical care to the poor.

Eugenics

The Social Gospel was a response to Social Darwinism, the application of biological natural selection and survival of the fittest to human interactions. But another movement, eugenics, sought to apply Darwinian principles more intrusively. The brainchild of Francis Galton, an English statistician and cousin of Charles Darwin, eugenics rested on the belief that human character and habits could be inherited, including unwanted traits, such as criminality and mental illness. Eugenicists believed society had an obligation to prevent the reproduction of the so-called mentally defective and criminally inclined by preventing them from marrying and, in extreme cases, sterilizing them. Such ideas targeted immigrants and people of color. Supported by such American notables as

Alexander Graham Bell, Margaret Sanger, and W. E. B. Du Bois, eugenics was discredited, especially after it became a linchpin of Nazi racial policies.

Some reformers endorsed eugenics; others embraced immigration restriction to control the composition of American society. Madison Grant's *The Passing of the Great Race* (1916) bolstered theories that immigrants from southern and eastern Europe threatened to weaken American society because they were inferior mentally and morally to earlier Nordic immigrants. Thus many people, including some Progressives, sought to curtail the influx of Poles, Italians, Jews, and other eastern and southern Europeans, and Asians. In the 1920s, restrictive legislation closed the door to "new" immigrants.

Challenges to Racial and Sexual Discrimination

What strategies did women use in their quest for equality in the early twentieth century?

White male reformers of the Progressive era dealt primarily with politics and institutions and ignored issues affecting former slaves, nonwhite immigrants, Indians, and women. Yet these groups caught the Progressive spirit and made strides toward their own advancement. Their efforts, however, posed a dilemma. Should women and nonwhites aim to imitate white men's values and gain their rights? Or was there something unique about racial and sexual cultures worth preserving at the risk of broader gains?

Continued Discrimination for African Americans

In 1900, nine-tenths of African Americans lived in the South, where repressive Jim Crow laws multiplied in the 1880s and 1890s (see page 523). In 1910, only 8,000 out of 970,000 high-school-age blacks were enrolled in southern high schools. Many African Americans moved northward in the 1880s, accelerating their migration after 1900. Although conditions in places like Chicago, Cleveland, and Detroit represented improvement, job discrimination, inferior schools, and segregated housing prevailed.

African American leaders differed over how—and whether—to assimilate. After emancipation, ex-slave Frederick Douglass urged "ultimate assimilation through self-assertion." Others supported emigration to Africa or the establishment of all-black communities in Oklahoma Territory and Kansas. Still others advocated militancy.

Booker T. Washington and Self-Help

Booker T. Washington:
Leading black activist of the late nineteenth century who advocated education and accommodation with white society as the best strategy for racial advancement.

Most blacks could neither escape nor conquer white society. Self-help, a strategy articulated by educator **Booker T. Washington**, offered one popular alternative. Born into slavery in Virginia in 1856, Washington obtained an education and in 1881 founded Tuskegee Institute, an all-black vocational school, in Alabama. There he developed a philosophy that blacks' best hopes lay in at least temporarily accommodating whites. Rather than fighting for political rights, Washington counseled African Americans to work hard, acquire property, and prove they were worthy of respect. "Dignify and glorify common labor," he urged in an 1895 speech that became known as the Atlanta Compromise. Washington observed that "in all things that are purely social we can be as separate as the fingers, yet one as the hand in all matters essential to mutual progress."

Because he said what they wanted to hear, white businesspeople, reformers, and politicians regarded Washington as representing all African Americans. Washington endorsed a separate-but-equal policy and never argued that blacks were inferior; rather, he asserted that they could enhance their dignity through self-improvement.

Some blacks, however, concluded that Washington endorsed second-class citizenship. In 1905, a group of "anti-Bookerites" convened near Niagara Falls and pledged militant pursuit of unrestricted voting, economic opportunity, integration, and equality before the law. Representing the Niagara movement was **W. E. B. Du Bois**, an outspoken critic of the Atlanta Compromise.

W. E. B. Du Bois: African American educator and activist who demanded full racial equality, including the same educational opportunities open to whites, and called on blacks to resist all forms of racism.

W. E. B. Du Bois and the "Talented Tenth"

A New Englander and the first black to receive a Ph.D. from Harvard, Du Bois was a Progressive and member of the black elite. While a faculty member at Atlanta University, Du Bois compiled sociological studies of black urban life and wrote in support of civil rights. He treated Washington politely but could not accept accommodation. Du Bois believed an intellectual vanguard of cultured, educated blacks, the "Talented Tenth," should lead in pursuing racial equality. In 1909, he joined white liberals similarly discontented with Washington's accommodationism to form the **National Association for the Advancement of Colored People (NAACP)**. The organization aimed to end racial discrimination, eradicate lynching, and obtain voting rights through legal redress in the courts. By 1914, the NAACP had fifty branch offices and six thousand members.

National Association for the Advancement of Colored People (NAACP): Organization that called for sustained activism, including legal challenges, to achieve political equality for blacks and full integration into American life.

African Americans struggled with questions about their place in white society. Du Bois voiced this dilemma, observing that "one ever feels his twoness—an American, a Negro, two souls, two thoughts, two unreconciled strivings, two warring ideals in one dark body." As Du Bois wrote in 1903, a black "would not bleach his Negro soul in a flood of white Americanism, for he knows that Negro blood has a message for the world. He simply wishes to make it possible for a man to be both a Negro and an American."

Link to the chapter "Of Booker T. Washington and Others" in W. E. B Dubois's *The Souls of Black Folk*.

Society of American Indians

In 1911, middle-class Indians formed their own association, the Society of American Indians (SAI), to work for better education, civil rights, and healthcare. It also sponsored "American Indian Days" to cultivate pride and offset the images of savage peoples promulgated in Wild West shows.

SAI's emphasis on racial pride, however, was squeezed between pressures for assimilation and tribal allegiance. Its small membership did not fully represent the diverse and unconnected Indian nations. Individual hard work was not enough to overcome prejudice, and attempts to redress grievances legally faltered for lack of funds. Ultimately, SAI had little effect on poverty-stricken Indians who seldom knew that the organization even existed. Torn by internal disputes, the association folded in the early 1920s.

"The Woman Movement"

Women's groups faced similar struggles about the tactics they should use to achieve rights. Should they try to achieve equality within a male-dominated society? Or use female qualities to create new roles for themselves within society?

Heavyweight Boxing Champion Jack Johnson as Race Hero

It is probable that more African Americans in the 1910s paid attention to Jack Johnson than they did to either Booker T. Washington or W. E. B. Du Bois. In 1908, Jackson became the first black heavyweight champion of the world by knocking out Tommy Burns. Immediately, white boxing fans began searching for a "Great White Hope" to recapture the title, and in 1910, former champion James J. Jeffries came out of retirement to fight Johnson, boasting that he would "demonstrate that a white man is king of them all." But after fifteen rounds of pummeling from Johnson, Jeffries gave up. African Americans around the nation celebrated their hero's victory, and in some places race riots erupted as angry whites attacked jubilant revelers. Racist reaction was particularly strong because Johnson refused to accept white standards for the way a black man should behave. He courted and married white women, flaunted his consumer tastes, and dealt with opponents and reporters with a pompous attitude. In 1915, Johnson, then thirty-seven years old, lost his title to Jess Willard in Cuba. The fight took place outside the country because in 1913 Johnson had been convicted of violating the Mann Act in transporting Belle Schreiber, a white prostitute, across state lines for "immoral purposes." Sentenced to a year in jail, Johnson fled the country but returned in 1920 to serve a one-year jail sentence. How do these three images reveal racial attitudes, both black and white toward Jack Johnson? What messages do they convey to someone viewing them?

© Bettmann/Corbis

Jack Johnson's first white wife was Etta Terry Duryea, a socialite and former wife of an automobile manufacturer. Their turbulent marriage ended in 1912 when Duryea committed suicide.

Library of Congress

UNCLE TOM'S CABIN — AS IT WILL HAVE TO BE PLAYED IF JOHNSON WINS.

Puck, America's first successful humor magazine, caricatured how "Uncle Tom's Cabin" would have to be performed if Jack Johnson were to beat James Jeffries in 1910. The magazine cover shows Johnson as a large, wealthy man knocking down the slaveholder Simon Legree.

© Stefano Bianchetti/CORBIS

The Italian poster artist Achille Beltrame depicted Jack Johnson's reception by jubilant African Americans in his hometown of Chicago after his triumph over Jim Jeffries in 1910. As a result of that victory, Johnson acquired an international as well as national reputation.

The answers that women found involved a subtle but important shift in their politics. Before 1910, women's rights activists called themselves "the woman movement." Often middle-class, these women strove to move beyond the household into higher education and paid professions. They claimed that women's special, even superior, traits as guardians of family and morality would humanize all of society. Settlement-house founder Jane Addams, for example, endorsed woman suffrage by asking, "If women have in any sense been responsible for the gentler side of life which softens and blurs some of its harsher conditions, may not they have a duty to perform in our American cities?"

Women's Clubs

Originating as literary and educational organizations, women's clubs began taking stands on public affairs in the late nineteenth century. They asserted traditional female responsibilities for home and family as the rationale for reforming society through an enterprise that historians have called social housekeeping. These female reformers worked for factory inspection, regulation of children's and women's labor, improved housing, and consumer protection.

African American women had their own club movement, including the Colored Women's Federation, which sought to establish a training school for "colored girls." Founded in 1895, the National Association of Colored Women was the nation's first African American social service organization; it concentrated on establishing nurseries, kindergartens, and retirement homes. Black women also developed reform organizations within Black Baptist and African Methodist Episcopal churches.

Feminism

Around 1910, some people concerned with women's place in society began using the term *feminism*. Whereas the woman movement spoke of moral purity, feminists emphasized rights and self-development. Charlotte Perkins Gilman, a major figure in the movement, declared in her book *Women and Economics* (1898) that domesticity was obsolete and attacked men's monopoly on economic opportunity. Arguing that paid employees should handle domestic chores, Gilman asserted that modern women must have access to jobs to be independent.

Margaret Sanger's Crusade

Several feminists joined the birth-control movement led by Margaret Sanger. A former visiting nurse who believed in women's rights to sexual pleasure and determining when to have a child, Sanger helped reverse state and federal laws banning publication and distribution of information about sex and contraception. Opposition came from those who saw birth control as a threat to family and morality. Sanger also was a eugenicist who perceived birth control as a means of limiting the numbers of children born to "inferior" immigrant and nonwhite mothers. In 1921, she formed the American Birth Control League, enlisting physicians and social workers to convince judges to allow distribution of birth-control information. Most states still prohibited the sale of contraceptives, but Sanger provoked public debate.

Woman Suffrage

A new generation of Progressive feminists, represented by Harriot Stanton Blatch, daughter of nineteenth-century suffragist Elizabeth Cady Stanton, carried on women's battle for the vote. Blatch linked voting rights to the improvement of women's working conditions. She joined the Women's Trade Union League and founded the Equality League of Self Supporting Women in 1907. Declaring that every woman worked, for wages or unpaid housework, Blatch believed all women's efforts contributed to society's betterment. Thus, women should exercise the vote to promote and protect women's economic roles.

Nine states, all in the West, allowed women to vote in state and local elections by 1912 (see Map 21.1). Suffragists' tactics ranged from persistent letter-writing and publications of the National American Woman Suffrage Association, led by **Carrie Chapman Catt**, to meetings and militant marches of the National Woman's Party, led by Alice Paul and Harriot Stanton Blatch. More decisive, however, was women's service during World War I as factory laborers, medical volunteers, and municipal workers. By convincing legislators that women could shoulder public responsibilities, women's wartime contributions facilitated passage of the national suffrage amendment (the Nineteenth) in 1920.

During the Progressive era, leaders like Blatch, Paul, and Catt helped clarify issues that concerned women and but winning the vote was only a first step. Discrimination in employment, education, and law continued to shadow women for decades. As feminist Crystal Eastman observed after: "women, if I know them, are saying, Now at last we can begin.'. . . Now they can say what they are really after, in common with all the rest of the struggling world, is freedom."

Carrie Chapman Catt: President of the National American Woman Suffrage Association in the early twentieth century.

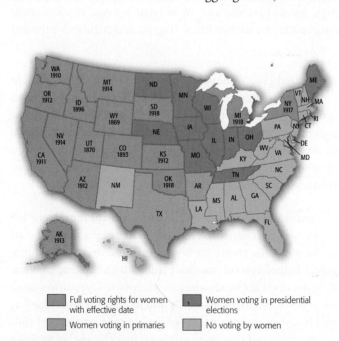

Full voting rights for women with effective date

Women voting in presidential elections

Women voting in primaries

No voting by women

MAP 21.1

Woman Suffrage Before 1920

Before Congress passed and the states ratified the Nineteenth Amendment, woman suffrage already existed, but mainly in the West. Several midwestern states allowed women to vote only in presidential elections, but legislatures in the South and Northeast generally refused such rights until forced to do so by constitutional amendment.

Source: Copyright © Cengage Learning

Theodore Roosevelt and Revival of the Presidency

The Progressive era' reform focused on the federal government as the foremost agent of change. Although the federal government had notable accomplishments during the Gilded Age, its role was mainly to support rather than control economic expansion. Then, in September 1901, the assassination of President William McKinley by anarchist Leon Czolgosz vaulted **Theodore Roosevelt**, the young vice president, into the White House. As governor of New York, Roosevelt angered state Republican bosses by showing sympathy for regulatory legislation. He would become the nation's most forceful president since Lincoln, one who bestowed the office with much of its twentieth-century character.

> Theodore Roosevelt was known as a trustbuster, but was he?

Theodore Roosevelt: Youthful successor to slain president William McKinley in 1901; U.S. president, 1901–1909; promoted an agenda of progressive reform.

Theodore Roosevelt

Driven by a lifelong obsession to overcome his physical limitations, Roosevelt exerted what he called "manliness"— a zest for action and display of courage. In his teens, he became a marksman and horseman and later competed on Harvard's boxing and wrestling teams. In the 1880s, he lived on a Dakota ranch, roping cattle and brawling with cowboys. Descended from a Dutch aristocratic family, Roosevelt had wealth, but he also inherited a sense of civic responsibility that guided him into public service. He served three terms in the New York legislature, sat on the federal Civil Service Commission, served as New York City's police commissioner, was assistant secretary of the navy, and earned a reputation as a combative, crafty leader. In 1898, he thrust himself into the Spanish-American War by organizing a volunteer cavalry brigade, called the Rough Riders, to fight in Cuba. Although his dramatic act had little impact on the war's outcome, it made him a media hero.

Roosevelt carried his youthful exuberance into the White House. A Progressive, he concurred with allies that a small, uninvolved government would not suffice in the industrial era. Instead, economic progress necessitated a government powerful enough to guide national affairs. Especially in economic matters, Roosevelt wanted government to decide when big business was good and when it was bad.

Regulation of Trusts

The federal regulation of business that characterized twentieth-century America began with Roosevelt's presidency. Although labeled a trust-buster, Roosevelt actually considered

Theodore Roosevelt (1858–1919) liked to think of himself as a great outdoorsman. He loved most the rugged countryside and believed that he and his country should serve as examples of "manliness."

California Museum of Photography, University of California

business consolidation an efficient means to material progress. He believed in distinguishing between good and bad trusts and preventing bad ones from manipulating markets. Thus, he instructed the Justice Department to use antitrust laws to prosecute railroad, meatpacking, and oil trusts, which he believed unscrupulously exploited the public. Roosevelt's policy triumphed in 1904 when the Supreme Court ordered the breakup of Northern Securities Company, the huge railroad combination created by J. P. Morgan. Roosevelt did not attack other trusts, such as U.S. Steel, another of Morgan's creations.

When prosecution of Northern Securities began, Morgan reportedly asked Roosevelt, "If we have done anything wrong, send your man to my man and they can fix it up." The president refused but was more sympathetic to cooperation between business and government than might seem. He urged the Bureau of Corporations (part of the newly created Department of Labor and Commerce) to assist companies in merging and expanding. Through investigation and consultation, the administration cajoled businesses to regulate themselves.

Hepburn Act: Legislation that strengthened regulatory powers of the Interstate Commerce Commission, particularly over railroads, and later other businesses and industries.

Roosevelt also supported regulatory legislation. After a year of wrangling, Roosevelt persuaded Congress to pass the **Hepburn Act** (1906), which gave the Interstate Commerce Commission (ICC) greater authority set railroad freight rates and extend that authority over ferries, express companies, storage facilities, and oil pipelines. The Hepburn Act still allowed courts to overturn ICC decisions, but it now required shippers to prove they had not violated regulations, rather than making the government demonstrate violations.

Pure Food and Drug Laws

Roosevelt showed willingness to compromise to ensure pure food and drug legislation. For decades, reformers urged government regulation of processed meat and patent medicines. Public outrage at fraud flared in 1906 when Upton Sinclair published *The Jungle*, a fictionalized exposé of Chicago meatpacking plants. Sinclair, a socialist who sought to improve working conditions, shocked public sensibilities with vivid descriptions.

> There would be meat stored in great piles; water from leaky roofs would drip over it, and thousands of rats would race about on it … a man could run his hand over these piles of meat and sweep off handfuls of dried dung of rats. These rats were a nuisance, and the packers would put poisoned bread out for them; they would die, and then rats, bread, and meat would go into the hoppers together.

Roosevelt ordered an investigation, and finding Sinclair's descriptions accurate, supported the Meat Inspection Act (1906). This law required government agents monitor the quality of processed meat. But as part of a compromise with meatpackers and their congressional allies, the government had to finance inspections, and meatpackers could appeal adverse decisions. Nor were companies required to provide date-of-processing information on canned meats. Most large meatpackers welcomed legislation because it restored foreign confidence in American meat products.

The Pure Food and Drug Act (1906) also addressed abuses in the patent medicine industry. Makers of tonics and pills had long been making undue claims about their products' effects and used alcohol and narcotics as ingredients. The law required that labels list the ingredients—a goal consistent with Progressive confidence that with information, people would make wiser purchases.

Roosevelt's approach to labor resembled his compromises with business. When the United Mine Workers struck against Pennsylvania coal-mine owners in 1902 over an eight-hour workday and higher pay, the president urged arbitration. Owners refused to recognize the union or arbitrate grievances. As winter approached and fuel shortages loomed, Roosevelt threatened to use federal troops to reopen the mines, thus forcing management to accept. The arbitration commission decided in favor of higher wages and reduced hours and required management to deal with miners' grievance committees. But, it did not mandate recognition of the union. The decision, according to Roosevelt, provided a "square deal" for all. The settlement embodied Roosevelt's belief that the president or his representatives should determine which labor demands were legitimate and which were not.

Race Relations

Although he invited Booker T. Washington to the White House to discuss racial matters, Roosevelt believed in white superiority and was neutral toward blacks only when it helped him politically. Case in point: in 1906 the army transferred African American soldiers from Nebraska to Brownsville, Texas. Anglo and Mexican residents resented their presence and banned them from parks and businesses. On August 14, a battle between blacks and whites broke out, and a white man was killed. Brownsville residents blamed soldiers, but soldiers refused to help investigators identify participants. Consequently, Roosevelt discharged 167 black soldiers without a hearing and prevented them from receiving their pay and pensions. Black leaders were outraged. To preserve black support for Republican candidates in the 1906 elections, Roosevelt waited until after the elections to sign discharge papers.

Conservation

Roosevelt's Progressive impulse for efficiency and love for the outdoors inspired lasting contributions to resource conservation. Government establishment of national parks began in the late nineteenth century. Roosevelt advanced the movement by favoring *conservation* over *preservation*. Thus, he not only exercised presidential power to protect such natural wonders as the Grand Canyon in Arizona by declaring them national monuments, but also backed a policy of "wise use" of forests, waterways, and other resources. Previously, the government transferred ownership of natural resources on federal land to the states and private interests. Roosevelt, however, believed efficient resource conservation demanded federal management over lands in the public domain.

Bettmann/Corbis

Makers of unregulated patent medicines advertised their products' exorbitant abilities to cure almost any ailment and remedy any unwanted physical condition. Loring's Fat-Ten-U tablets and Loring's Corpula were two such products. The Pure Food and Drug Act of 1906 did not ban these items but tried to prevent manufacturers from making unsubstantiated claims.

Roosevelt used federal authority over resources by protecting waterpower sites from sale to private interests and charging permit fees for users who wanted to produce hydroelectricity. He also supported the Newlands Reclamation Act of 1902, which controlled sale of irrigated federal land in the West (see page 446). Roosevelt tripled the number of national forests and backed conservationist Gifford Pinchot in creating the U.S. Forest Service.

Gifford Pinchot

As principal advocate of "wise use" policy, Pinchot promoted scientific management of the nation's woodlands. He obtained Roosevelt's support for transferring management of the national forests from the Interior Department to his bureau in the Agriculture Department. The Forest Service charged fees for grazing livestock within the national forests, supervised bidding for the cutting of timber, and hired university-trained foresters as federal employees.

Pinchot and Roosevelt did not seek to preserve resources permanently; rather, they wanted to conserve their efficient use and make companies profiting from using public lands pay the government. Many involved in natural-resource exploitation welcomed such a policy because it enabled them to better control products, such as when Roosevelt and Pinchot encouraged lumber companies to engage in reforestation.

Panic of 1907

In 1907, a financial panic caused by reckless speculation forced some New York banks to close to prevent frightened depositors from withdrawing money. J. P. Morgan helped stem the panic by persuading financiers to stop dumping stocks. In return for Morgan's aid, Roosevelt approved a deal allowing U.S. Steel to absorb the Tennessee Iron and Coal Company—a deal at odds with Roosevelt's trustbusting aims.

During his last year in office, Roosevelt retreated from the Republican Party's friendliness to big business. He supported stronger business regulation and heavier taxation of the rich. Promising that he would not seek reelection, Roosevelt backed Secretary of War **William Howard Taft** in 1908. Taft easily defeated three-time Democratic nominee William Jennings Bryan by 1.25 million popular votes and a 2-to-1 margin in the electoral college.

William Howard Taft: Roosevelt's hand-picked successor for president (1909–1913); later served as Supreme Court Justice.

Taft Administration

Taft faced political problems that Roosevelt had postponed, foremost, extremely high tariffs. Honoring Taft's pledge to cut tariffs, the House passed a bill providing numerous reductions. Protectionists in the Senate prepared to amend the bill and revise rates upward. But Senate Progressives attacked the tariff for benefiting special interests, trapping Taft between reformers who claimed to be preserving Roosevelt's antitrust campaign and protectionists who dominated the Republican Party. In the end, Rhode Island Senator Nelson Aldrich restored most cuts, and Taft signed what became known as the Payne-Aldrich Tariff (1909). To Progressives, Taft had failed to fill Roosevelt's shoes.

In reality, Taft was as sympathetic to reform as Roosevelt was. He prosecuted more trusts than Roosevelt, expanded national forest reserves, signed the Mann-Elkins Act (1910), which bolstered regulatory powers of the ICC, and supported such labor reforms as shorter work hours and mine safety legislation. The Sixteenth Amendment, which legalized the federal income tax and the Seventeenth Amendment, which provided for direct election of U.S. senators, were initiated during Taft's presidency (and ratified in 1913). Like Roosevelt, Taft compromised with big business, but unlike Roosevelt, he was unable to manipulate the public with spirited rhetoric. Roosevelt expanded presidential power. Taft believed in the strict restraint of law. He had been a successful lawyer and judge and returned to the bench as chief justice of the United States between 1921 and 1930.

Candidates in 1912

In 1910, when Roosevelt returned from Africa, he found his party torn and tormented. Reformers formed the National Progressive Republican League and rallied behind Robert La Follette for president in 1912, though many hoped Roosevelt would run. Another wing of the party remained loyal to Taft. Disappointed by Taft, Roosevelt spoke out for "the welfare of the people" and stronger business regulation. When La Follette became ill early in 1912, Roosevelt, proclaiming himself fit as a "bull moose," sought the Republican presidential nomination.

Taft's supporters controlled the Republican convention and nominated him for a second term. In protest, Roosevelt's supporters formed a third party—the Progressive, or Bull Moose, Party—and nominated the former president. Meanwhile, Democrats took forty-six ballots to select their candidate, New Jersey's Progressive governor **Woodrow Wilson**. Socialists, by now a growing party, again nominated Eugene V. Debs.

Woodrow Wilson: Democratic president whose election in 1912 ushered in a second wave of progressive reforms on the national level; served as president until 1921.

New Nationalism Versus New Freedom

Central to Theodore Roosevelt's campaign was a scheme called the New Nationalism, which envisioned an era of national unity in which government would coordinate and regulate economic activity. Roosevelt asserted that he would establish regulatory commissions to protect citizens' interests and ensure wise use of economic power. Wilson offered a more idealistic proposal, the "New Freedom." He argued that concentrated economic power threatened individual liberty and that monopolies should be broken up to ensure a free marketplace. But he would not restore laissez faire. Like Roosevelt, Wilson would enhance government authority to protect and regulate. "Without the watchful ... resolute interference of the government, there can be no fair play between individuals and such powerful institutions as the trust," he declared. Wilson stopped short, however, of advocating the cooperation between business and government inherent in Roosevelt's New Nationalism.

Link to Theodore Roosevelt's New Nationalism speech from 1910.

Roosevelt and Wilson stood closer together than their rhetoric implied. Both believed in individual freedom. Both supported equality of opportunity (chiefly for white males), conservation of natural resources, fair wages, and social betterment. Neither would hesitate to expand government intervention through strong leadership and bureaucratic reform.

In the election, the popular vote was inconclusive. The victorious Wilson won just 42 percent, though he did capture 435 out of 531 electoral votes. Roosevelt received 27 percent of the popular vote. Taft polled 23 percent of the popular vote and only 8 electoral votes. Debs won 6 percent but no electoral votes.

Three-quarters of the electorate supported alternatives to Taft's view of restrained government.

Woodrow Wilson and Extension of Progressive Reform

Woodrow Wilson
How did participation in World War I alter Wilson's position on business?

Born in Virginia in 1856 and raised in the South, Wilson was the son of a Presbyterian minister. He earned a B.A. degree at Princeton University, studied law at the University of Virginia, received a Ph.D. degree from Johns Hopkins University, and became a professor of history, jurisprudence, and political economy at Princeton. Between 1885 and 1908, he published several respected books on American history and government.

Wilson was a superb orator who could inspire loyalty with religious imagery and eloquent expressions of American ideals. But he harbored disdain for African Americans, had no misgivings about Jim Crow laws, and opposed admitting blacks to Princeton. At Princeton, he battled against aristocratic elements and earned a reputation as a reformer so that in 1910 New Jersey's Democrats nominated Wilson for governor. Once elected, Wilson repudiated the party bosses and promoted Progressive legislation. A poor administrator, he often lost his temper and refused to compromise. His accomplishments nevertheless won him the 1912 Democratic presidential nomination.

Wilson's Policy on Business Regulation

As president, Wilson blended New Freedom competition with New Nationalism regulation, setting the direction of federal economic policy. Corporate consolidation made restoration of open competition impossible. Wilson sought to prevent abuses by expanding government regulation. He supported congressional passage in 1914 of the Clayton Anti-Trust Act and a bill creating the **Federal Trade Commission** (FTC). The Clayton Act corrected deficiencies of the Sherman Anti-Trust Act of 1890 by outlawing such practices as price discrimination (lowering prices in some regions but not others) and interlocking directorates (management of two or more competing companies by the same executives). The act also aided labor by exempting unions from its anticombination provision, thereby making peaceful strikes, boycotts, and picketing less vulnerable to government interference. The FTC could investigate companies and issue cease-and-desist orders against unfair practices to protect consumers.

Federal Trade Commission:
Agency formed in 1914 to ensure fair trade and practices.

Under Wilson, the Federal Reserve Act (1913), established the nation's first central banking system since 1836. To break the power that syndicates like that of J. P. Morgan held over the money supply, the act created twelve district banks to hold reserves of member banks nationwide. District banks, supervised by the Federal Reserve Board, would lend money to member banks at a low interest rate called the discount rate. By adjusting this rate (and thus the amount a bank could afford to borrow), district banks could increase or decrease the amount of money in circulation, enabling the Federal Reserve Board to loosen or tighten credit, thereby making interest rates fairer.

Tariff and Tax Reform   Wilson and Congress attempted to restore competition with the Underwood Tariff of 1913. By reducing or eliminating certain tariffs, the Underwood Tariff encouraged importation of cheaper foreign goods. To replace revenues lost because of tariff reductions, the act levied a graduated income tax on U.S. residents. Incomes under $4,000 were exempt; thus, almost all factory workers and farmers escaped taxation. Individuals and corporations earning between $4,000 and $20,000 had to pay a 1 percent tax; thereafter rates rose to a maximum of 6 percent on earnings over $500,000.

The outbreak of World War I (see Chapter 23) and the approaching 1916 presidential election prompted Wilson to support stronger reforms. He backed the Federal Farm Loan Act, which created twelve federally supported banks that could lend money at moderate interest to farmers who belonged to credit institutions—a diluted version of the Populists' subtreasury plan proposed a generation earlier (see page 528). To forestall railroad strikes, Wilson in 1916 pushed passage of the Adamson Act, which mandated eight-hour workdays and time-and-a-half overtime pay for railroad laborers. He pleased Progressives by appointing Brandeis, the "people's advocate," to the Supreme Court, though an anti-Semitic backlash almost blocked Senate approval of the Court's first Jewish justice. Wilson also backed laws regulating child labor and providing workers' compensation for federal employees who suffered work-related injuries or illness.

But Wilson never overcame his racism. He fired several black federal officials, and his administration preserved racial separation in restrooms, restaurants, and government office buildings. When the pathbreaking but inflammatory film about the Civil War and Reconstruction, *The Birth of a Nation,* was released in 1915, Wilson allowed a showing at the White House, though he prohibited it during World War I.

Election of 1916   Republicans snubbed Theodore Roosevelt as their candidate in 1916, choosing Charles Evans Hughes, Supreme Court justice and former reform governor of New York. Aware of public anxiety over the world war in Europe since 1914, Wilson ran on neutrality and Progressivism, using the slogan "He Kept Us Out of War." The election was close. Wilson received 9.1 million votes to Hughes's 8.5 million and barely won in the electoral college, 277 to 254. The Socialist candidate drew only 600,000 votes, largely because Wilson's reforms won over some Socialists and because the ailing Eugene Debs was no longer the party's standard-bearer.

During Wilson's second term, U.S. involvement in World War I increased government regulation of the economy. Mobilization and war, he believed, required greater coordination of production and cooperation between the public and private sectors. The War Industries Board exemplified this: private businesses submitted to the board's control on condition that their profit motives would be satisfied. After the war, Wilson's administration dropped such measures, including farm price supports, guarantees of collective bargaining, and high taxes. This retreat from regulation, prompted partly by the election of a Republican Congress in 1918, stimulated a new era of business ascendancy in the 1920s.

Margaret Sanger, Planned Parenthood, and the Birth-Control Controversy

Some Progressive era reforms illustrate how earnest intentions can become tangled in divisive moral issues. Such is the legacy of birth-control advocate Margaret Sanger. In 1912, Sanger produced a column on sex education in the *New York Call* entitled "What Every Girl Should Know." Moralists accused her of writing obscene literature because she publicly discussed venereal disease and contraception. She counseled poor women on New York's Lower East Side about how to avoid frequent childbirth, miscarriage, and bungled abortion. In 1914, Sanger launched *The Woman Rebel*, a monthly newspaper advocating a woman's right to practice birth control. Indicted for distributing obscenity through the mails, she fled to England, where she gave speeches promoting family planning and enjoying sexuality without fear of pregnancy.

Returning to the United States, Sanger opened the country's first birth-control clinic in Brooklyn in 1916. She was arrested, but when a court exempted physicians from a law prohibiting dissemination of contraceptive information, she set up a doctor-run clinic in 1923. Staffed by female doctors and social workers, the Birth Control Clinical Research Bureau became a model for other clinics. Sanger organized the American Birth Control League (1921) and sought support from medical and social reformers, even from the eugenics movement, for legalized birth control. After falling out with some allies, she resigned from the American Birth Control League in 1928.

The movement continued, and in 1938 the American Birth Control League and the Birth Control Clinical Research Bureau merged to form the Birth Control Federation of America, renamed the Planned Parenthood Federation of America (PPFA) in 1942. The organization's mission was to strengthen the family and stabilize society with governmental support, rather than focus on the right to voluntary motherhood. Throughout the 1940s, the PPFA emphasized family planning through making contraceptives more accessible. In 1970, it began receiving federal funds.

In the 1960s, new feminist agitation for women's rights and rising concerns about overpopulation made birth control and abortion controversial. Although PPFA initially dissociated from abortion, the debate between a woman's "choice" and a fetus's "right to life" drew the organization into the fray, especially after 1973, when the Supreme Court validated women's right to an abortion in *Roe v. Wade*. PPFA fought legislative and court attempts to make abortions illegal, and in 1989 it helped organize a women's march on Washington. Some Latino and African American groups attacked the PPFA's stance, charging that abortion was a eugenics program meant to reduce births among nonwhites.

PPFA's involvement in abortion politics resulted in several clinics becoming targets of picketing and violence by those who believe abortion is immoral. PPFA operates nearly nine hundred health centers providing medical services and education. But birth control's legacy to a people and a nation includes disagreement over whose rights and whose morality should prevail.

Summary

By 1920, a quarter-century of reform had wrought momentous changes. Progressives established the principle of public intervention to ensure fairness, health, and safety. Concern over poverty and injustice reached new heights. But reformers could not sustain their efforts indefinitely. Although Progressive values lingered after World War I, a mass-consumer society refocused people's attention from reform to materialism.

Multiple and sometimes contradictory goals characterized the era because there was no single Progressive movement. National programs ranged from Roosevelt's faith in big government as a coordinator of big business to Wilson's promise to dissolve economic concentrations and legislate open competition. At state and local levels, reformers pursued causes as varied as neighborhood improvement, government reorganization, public ownership of utilities, and better working conditions. Women and African Americans developed new consciousness about identify, and although women made some inroads into public life, both groups still found themselves in confined social positions.

Successes aside, the failure of many Progressive initiatives indicates the strength of the opposition, as well as weaknesses within the reform movements. As issues such as Americanization, eugenics, prohibition, education, and moral uplift illustrate, social reform often merged into social control—attempts to impose white, middle-class values on all of society. Courts asserted constitutional and liberty-of-contract doctrines in striking down key Progressive legislation, notably the federal law prohibiting child labor. Federal regulatory agencies rarely had enough resources for thorough investigations; they had to depend on information from the very companies they policed. In 1920, as in 1900, government remained under the influence of business.

Yet Progressive era reforms reshaped the national outlook. Trustbusting, however faulty, made industrialists more sensitive to public opinion. Progressive legislation equipped government with tools to protect consumers against price fixing and dangerous products. Social reformers relieved some ills of urban and industrial life. Although the questions they raised about American life remained unresolved, Progressives made the nation acutely aware of its principles and promises.

Chapter Review

The Varied Progressive Impulse

How did Progressive reform cut across class lines?

The impulse to improve society at the turn of the twentieth century had variants in the working, middle, and wealthier classes. An emerging class of educated male and female professionals stood at the vanguard of Progressivism and sought to apply the techniques of professions such as law, engineering, medicine, social service, and teaching to end the abuse of power and inefficiency in business and government, and to protect the welfare of all classes. They also believed they could unify society through education and Americanization programs for new immigrants and Native Americans. Muckraking journalists exposed corruption and social wrongs, including fraudulent insurance, prostitution, and political corruption, as well as industrial outrages such as Upton Sinclair's exposé of the meatpacking industry. Workers, too, pressed for reforms to improve safety and housing and to include workers' compensation for injuries on the job. There was even a religious component as Protestant ministers sought to counter the negative impact of competitive capitalism and industrialization with a message of Christian salvation known as the "Social Gospel."

Government and Legislative Reform

According to Progressives, what was the government's role in improving society?

Unlike earlier generations of Americans who believed in a limited role for government, Progressives felt the government not only had an obligation to improve society but could protect people and families by restricting behavior. Progressives pushed officials to adopt regulations that would end labor abuses (notably, factory inspection laws), compensation for injured workers, minimum age and wage laws, child labor laws, and protective legislation regulating the hours women could work. Many also supported women's suffrage. Next, Progressives focused on ending vice, pushing for the passage of state laws and later a constitutional amendment (the Eighteenth Amendment, implemented in 1920) banning the manufacture and sale of alcohol—which they believed contributed to accidents, poverty, and poor productivity. Inspired by muckraking articles about gangs forcing white women into prostitution (dubbed "white slavery"), Progressives called for government investigations and new laws. Congress passed the Mann Act in 1910, prohibiting the interstate and international transportation of women for immoral purposes. By 1915 nearly every state outlawed brothels and solicitation of sex.

New Ideas in Social Institutions

What was the impact of Progressive education reforms?

Increasing concerns about the social impact of industrialization, along with a penchant for scientific management and efficiency, drove Progressive approaches to education. Reformers such as John Dewey not only wanted to ensure that children were exposed to age-appropriate materials, but they also focused on preparing children for the modern world by teaching them to use their ingenuity to solve real-life problems. College curricula shifted from their previous nearly exclusive focus on preparing primarily white men for a few professions such as medicine, religion, and law, to a focus on learning that kept pace with technological and social changes. Regarded as vital to a student's growth, athletics became a permanent feature. The number of colleges expanded, including all-black land grant colleges and women's colleges.

Challenges to Racial and Sexual Discrimination

What strategies did women use in their quest for equality in the early twentieth century?

Women's organizations had long struggled over whether to focus on their shared humanity with men or accentuate their unique female qualities in pursuit of equality and new social roles for women. Calling themselves "the woman movement" before 1910, they played up women's special, even superior, traits as guardians of the family and morality. After that date, activists adopted the term *feminism*, emphasizing women's right to citizenship and self-development. Activist styles ranged from moderate to radical, but all saw the vote as a first and vital step to influencing the laws affecting them, be it improving

women's working conditions or assuring their economic roles. Women's participation in the war effort also showed their ability and willingness to serve their country and made it impossible for legislators to continue to justify denying them the vote (which women finally received in 1920).

Theodore Roosevelt and the Revival of the Presidency

Theodore Roosevelt was known as a trustbuster, but was he?

Yes and no. As a Progressive, Roosevelt believed government should guide national affairs and economic development and determine when business was a positive or negative force. But he also thought there were times when business consolidation and mergers could aid economic progress and urged the Bureau of Consolidation to assist them in these efforts. At the same time, he was willing to step in when business consolidation led to corruption and market manipulation, as he did when he had the Justice Department use antitrust laws to prosecute railroad, meatpacking, and oil trusts, which he believed exploited the public. Roosevelt similarly supported regulatory legislation over interstate commerce and the quality of food and drugs. While Roosevelt supported the breakup of J. P. Morgan's Northern Securities Company, he did not break up the huge U.S. Steel Corp and actually allowed it to acquire additional companies during the economic panic of 1907.

Woodrow Wilson and the Extension of Progressive Reform

How did participation in World War I alter Wilson's position on business?

In his first term as president, Wilson was disheartened by the corporate merger movement that seemed to weaken the prospects of fair business competition. To restore that, he increased government regulation of the business sector, supporting the Clayton Antitrust Act and the establishment of the Federal Trade Commission to ensure fair business practices and protect labor. He also established banking regulation with the Federal Reserve Act of 1913 and similarly supported tariff reform and farm loans. With war mobilization a priority in his second term, Wilson sought greater cooperation between the private and public sector. Businesses agreed to submit to the federal War Industry Board's directives in exchange for the promise of profits. After the war, Wilson retreated from the regulation that had been his prewar policy, dropping farm supports, collective bargaining guarantees for labor, and high taxes, thereby inaugurating a new era of big business in the 1920s.

Suggestions for Further Reading

Francis L. Broderick, *Progressivism at Risk: Electing a President in 1912* (1989)

Nancy F. Cott, *The Grounding of Modern Feminism* (1987)

Steven J. Diner, *A Very Different Age: Americans of the Progressive Era* (1998)

Glenda Gilmore, *Who Were the Progressives?* (2002)

Hugh D. Hindman, *Child Labor: An American History* (2002)

Alice Kessler-Harris, *Out to Work: A History of Wage-Earning Women in the United States*, 20th anniversary ed. (2003)

Michael McGerr, *A Fierce Discontent: The Rise and Fall of the Progressive Movement in America, 1870–1920* (2003)

Patricia A. Schecter, *Ida B. Wells and American Reform, 1880–1930* (2001)

David Tyack, *Seeking Common Ground: Public Schools in a Diverse Society* (2003)

The Quest for Empire

22

1865–1914

"oreign devil!" they shouted at Lottie Moon. The Southern Baptist missionary, half a world away from home, braced herself against the cries of the Chinese "rabble" whom she sought to convert to Christianity in the 1880s. She walked "steadily and persistently" through the hecklers, silently vowing to win their acceptance and their souls.

Born in 1840 in Virginia and educated at what is now Hollins College, Charlotte Diggs Moon volunteered in 1873 for "woman's work" in northern China. There she taught and proselytized, largely among women and children, until her death in 1912.

In the 1870s and 1880s, Lottie Moon (Mu Ladi, or 幕拉第) made sometimes dangerous evangelizing trips to isolated Chinese hamlets. Curious peasant women pinched her, pulled on her skirts, purring, "How white her hand is!" They asked: "How old are you?" "Where do you get money to live on?" Speaking in Chinese, Lottie held a picture book about Jesus Christ, drawing attention to the "foreign doctrine" she hoped would displace Confucianism, Buddhism, and Taoism.

In the 1890s, a "storm of persecution" against foreigners swept China, and missionaries upending traditional ways and authority became hated targets. One missionary conceded that, in "believing Jesus," girls and women alarmed men who worried that "disobedient wives and daughters" would no longer "worship the idols when told." In the Shaling village in early 1890, Lottie Moon's Christian converts were beaten. Fearing for her life, she left China for several months in 1900 during the violent Boxer Rebellion.

Lottie Moon and thousands of missionaries converted only a small minority of Chinese people to Christianity. Although she, like other missionaries, probably never shed the western view that she represented a superior religion and culture, she felt affection for the Chinese. In letters and articles for U.S. audiences, she lobbied to recruit Christian women to stir up "a mighty wave of enthusiasm for Woman's Work for Woman." To this day, the

Lottie Moon Christmas Offering in Southern Baptist churches raises millions of dollars for missions abroad.

Like so many Americans who went overseas in the late nineteenth and early twentieth centuries, Lottie Moon helped spread American culture and influence abroad. Other peoples sometimes adopted and sometimes rejected American ways. American participants likewise were transformed. Lottie Moon, for example, strove to understand the Chinese and learn their language. She assumed their dress and abandoned such derogatory phrases as "heathen Chinese." She reminded less sensitive missionaries that the Chinese rightfully took pride in their ancient history.

Lottie Moon also changed—in her own words—from "a timid self-distrustful girl into a brave self-reliant woman." As she questioned the Chinese confinement of women, most conspicuous in arranged marriages, foot binding, and sexual segregation, she advanced women's rights. She understood that she could not convert Chinese women unless they had the freedom to listen to her appeals. She also challenged male domination of America's religious missions. When the Southern Baptist Foreign Mission Board denied woman missionaries the right to vote in meetings, she resigned. The board soon reversed itself.

Decades later, critics labeled missionaries' activities as "cultural imperialism," accusing them of subverting indigenous traditions and sparking destructive cultural clashes. Defenders of missionary work have celebrated their efforts to break down cultural barriers. Either way, Lottie Moon's story illustrates how Americans in the late nineteenth century interacted with the world; how the categories domestic and foreign intersected; and how Americans expanded abroad not only to seek land, trade, investments, and strategic bases but also to promote American culture.

Between the Civil War and the First World War, an expansionist United States joined the great world powers. Before the Civil War, Americans repeatedly extended the frontier: they bought Louisiana; annexed Florida, Oregon, and Texas; pushed Indians out of the path of white migration westward; seized California and other western areas from Mexico; and acquired southern parts of present-day Arizona and New Mexico from Mexico (the Gadsden Purchase). Americans also developed a lucrative foreign trade with most of the world and promoted American culture everywhere.

By the 1870s, most of Europe's powers were carving up Africa and large parts of Asia and Oceania for themselves. By 1900, they had conquered more than 10 million square miles and 150 million people. As the century turned, France, Russia, and Germany were spending heavily on modern steel navies, challenging an overextended Great Britain. In Asia, a rapidly modernizing Japan was expanding at the expense of China and Russia.

Engineering advances altered the world's political geography through the Suez Canal (1869), the British Trans-Indian railroad (1870), and the Russian Trans-Siberian Railway (1904), while steamships, machine guns, telegraphs, and malaria drugs facilitated the imperialists' task. Simultaneously, European leaders' general optimism in the 1850s and 1860s gave way to a pessimistic sense of impending warfare informed by notions of racial conflict and survival of the fittest.

Observant Americans argued that the United States risked being left behind if it failed to join the scramble for territory and markets. Republican senator Henry Cabot Lodge of Massachusetts argued that "civilization and the advancement of the [Anglo-Saxon] race" were at stake. Such thinking enticed Americans to reach beyond the continental United States for land, markets, cultural penetration, and power.

By 1900, the United States emerged as a great power with particular clout in Latin America, especially as Spain declined and Britain disengaged from the Western Hemisphere. In the Pacific, the new U.S. empire included Hawai'i, American Samoa, and the Philippines. In the decade that followed, President Theodore Roosevelt would seek to consolidate this power.

Most Americans applauded expansionism—the outward movement of goods, ships, dollars, people, and ideas. But many became uneasy whenever expansionism gave way to imperialism—the imposition of control over other peoples, undermining their sovereignty. Abroad, native nationalists, commercial competitors, and other imperial nations tried to block the spread of U.S. influence.

As you read this chapter, keep the following questions in mind:

* **What accounts for the increased importance of foreign policy concerns in American politics in the closing years of the nineteenth century?**

* **What key arguments were made by American anti-imperialists?**

* **How did late-nineteenth-century imperialism transform the United States?**

Imperial Dreams

What drove U.S. expansion overseas in the late nineteenth century?

Foreign policy assumed a new importance for Americans at the end of the nineteenth century. Internal matters such as industrialization, the construction of the railroads, and the settlement of the West still preoccupied many, but political and business leaders now began to advocate an activist approach to world affairs. Their motives were complex, but all emphasized the supposed benefits to the country's domestic health.

These leaders who guided America's expansionist foreign relations also guided the economic development of the machine age, forged the transcontinental railroad, built America's bustling cities and giant corporations, and shaped a mass culture. They unabashedly believed that the United States was an exceptional nation, different from and superior to others because of its Anglo-Saxon heritage and its God-favored and prosperous history.

Along with exceptionalism, American leaders were influenced by nationalism, capitalism, Social Darwinism, and a paternalistic attitude toward foreigners. "They are children and we are men in these deep matters of government," future president Woodrow Wilson announced in 1898. His words reveal the gender and age bias of American attitudes. Where these attitudes intersected with foreign cultures, the result was a mix of adoption, imitation, and rejection.

Chronology

1861–69	Seward sets expansionist course
1867	United States acquires Alaska and Midway
1876	Pro-U.S. Daíz begins thirty-four-year rule in Mexico
1878	United States gains naval rights in Samoa
1885	Strong's Our Country celebrates Anglo-Saxon destiny of dominance
1887	United States gains naval rights to Pearl Harbor, Hawai`i
	McKinley Tariff hurts Hawaiian sugar exports
1893	Economic crisis leads to business failures and mass unemployment
	Pro-U.S. interests stage successful coup against Queen Lili'uokalani of Hawai`i
1895	Cuban revolution against Spain begins
	Japan defeats China in war, annexes Korea and Formosa (Taiwan)
1898	United States formally annexes Hawai`i
	U.S. battleship Maine blows up in Havana harbor
	United States defeats Spain in Spanish-American War
1899	Treaty of Paris enlarges U.S. empire
	United Fruit Company forms and becomes influential in Central America
	Philippine insurrection breaks out, led by Emilio Aguinaldo
1901	McKinley assassinated; Theodore Roosevelt becomes president
1903	Panama grants canal rights to United States
	Platt Amendment subjugates Cuba
1904	Roosevelt Corollary declares United States a hemispheric "police power"
1905	Portsmouth Conference ends Russo-Japanese War
1906	San Francisco School Board segregates Asian schoolchildren
	United States invades Cuba to quell revolt
1907	"Great White Fleet" makes world tour
1910	Mexican revolution threatens U.S. interests
1914	U.S. troops invade Mexico
	First World War begins
	Panama Canal opens

Foreign Policy Elite It would take time for most Americans to grasp the changes under way. Foreign policy is usually dominated by what scholars have labeled the foreign policy elite—opinion leaders in politics, journalism, business, agriculture, religion, education, and the military. Better read and traveled than most Americans and more politically active in the post-Civil War era, they believed that U.S. prosperity and security depended on the nation's influence abroad. Increasingly in the late nineteenth century, the expansionist-minded elite urged imperialism. They talked about building a bigger navy and digging a canal across Panama, Central America, or Mexico; establishing colonies; and selling surpluses abroad. Among them was Theodore Roosevelt, appointed assistant secretary of the navy in 1897; Senator Henry Cabot Lodge, who joined the Foreign Relations Committee in 1896; and the corporate lawyer Elihu Root, who later served as secretary of war and secretary of state.

These American leaders believed that selling, buying, and investing in foreign marketplaces were important to the United States. One reason was profits from foreign sales. Another was the belief that foreign commerce might serve as a safety valve to relieve overproduction, unemployment, and economic depression since the nation's farms and factories produced more than Americans could consume especially during the 1890s' depression. Economic ties also permitted political influence to be exerted abroad and helped spread the American way of life, especially capitalism.

Messages in Advertising

The American march toward empire was also reflected in advertising. On the front and back covers of this 1901 promotional booklet, the Singer Sewing Machine Company is marketing not only its product but the idea that a sewing machine can unite nations. The image that emerges of the United States is that

of peacemaker and unifier. In the 1892 Singer sewing machine advertisement card, the Zulu natives are sewing American-style clothes. What message is being sent here, do you think? How does it compare to the recent advertising campaigns by firms such as Starbucks, Nike, and Subaru that push the product in question only indirectly and instead show people around the world connecting despite their differences?

Sewing machines and therefore world peace?

Rare Book, Manuscript & Special Collections, Duke University Library

Singer sewing machine advertisement card, showing six people from Zululand (South Africa) with Singer sewing machine.

Library of Congress

Foreign Trade Expansion

Foreign trade figured prominently in the United States' economic growth after the Civil War. Foreign commerce stimulated the building of a larger protective navy, the professionalization of the foreign service, calls for more colonies, and an interventionist foreign policy. In 1865, U.S. exports totaled $234 million; by 1900, they climbed to $1.5 billion. By 1914, exports hit $2.5 billion. In 1874, the United States reversed its historically unfavorable balance of trade (importing more than it exported) and began to enjoy a long-term favorable balance. Most of America's products went to Britain, continental Europe, and Canada, but increasing amounts flowed to new markets in Latin America and Asia. Meanwhile, American investments abroad reached $3.5 billion by 1914, placing the United States among the top four investor countries.

Agricultural goods accounted for about three-fourths of total exports in 1870 and about two-thirds in 1900, with grain, cotton, meat, and dairy products topping the list. Farmers' livelihoods thus became tied to world-market conditions and foreign wars. Wisconsin cheesemakers shipped to Britain; the Swift and Armour meat companies exported refrigerated beef to Europe.

In 1913, manufactured goods led U.S. exports for the first time (see Figure 22.1). Substantial proportions of America's steel, copper, and petroleum were sold abroad, making many workers in those industries dependent on American exports.

Race Thinking and the Male Ethos

In expanding U.S. influence overseas, many officials championed a nationalism based on notions of American supremacy. Some found justification for expansionism in racist theories then permeating western thought. For decades, the western scientific establishment classified humankind by race, and students of physical anthropology drew on phrenology and physiognomy—the analysis of skull size and facial features—to produce a hierarchy of superior and inferior races. One French researcher claimed

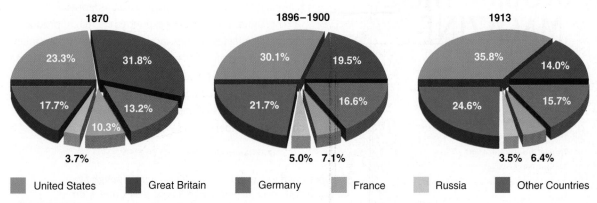

FIGURE 22.1
The Rise of U.S. Economic Power in the World
These pie charts showing percentage shares of world manufacturing production for the major nations of the world demonstrate that the United States came to surpass Great Britain in this significant economic measurement of power.
Source: Friedberg, Aaron L., *The Weary Titan.* © 1988 Princeton University Press, 1989 paperback edition. Reprinted by permission of Princeton University Press.

Links to the World

National Geographic

In early 1888, thirty-three members of Washington, D.C.'s elite Cosmos Club considered "organizing a society for the increase and diffusion of geographical knowledge." The result was the National Geographic Society, the world's largest nonprofit scientific and educational institution.

At the heart of the enterprise was *National Geographic Magazine*, which debuted in October 1888. Early issues were brief and bland, and sales lagged. When Alexander Graham Bell became the society's president in 1898, he shifted emphasis from newsstand sales to society membership, reasoning correctly that belonging to a distinguished fellowship would draw members. He also appointed a talented editor, Gilbert H. Grosvenor, age twenty-three, who commissioned articles and filled eleven pages with photographs.

Early photos showed people posed in their native costumes, displayed as anthropological specimens. By 1908, pictures occupied half of the magazine. In 1910, the first color photographs appeared in a twenty-four-page spread on Korea and China—then the largest collection of color photographs published in a single issue of any magazine. *National Geographic's* other photographic firsts included the first natural-color photos of Arctic life and the undersea world.

The society also sponsored expeditions, such as Robert Peary's and Matthew Henson's 1909 journey to the North Pole and, later, Jacques Cousteau's oceanic explorations and Jane Goodall's observations of wild chimpanzees. These adventures then appeared in the magazine's pages. By the end of Grosvenor's tenure as editor, in 1954, circulation topped 2 million.

Less admirably, Grosvenor's editors pressured photographers for pictures of pretty girls. One photographer recalled, "Hundreds of bare-breasted women, all from poorer countries, were published at a time of booming subscription rates." Editors developed a well-earned reputation for presenting a rosy world-view. An article about Berlin published before the start of World War II, for example, contained no criticism of the Nazi regime and no mention of its persecution of Jews. Recently, the magazine has featured more newsworthy topics—AIDS, stem cell research, Hurricane Katrina, global warming—but in measured tones.

Throughout, the society expanded its reach, producing books, atlases, globes, and television documentaries. Targeting overseas readers, the society in 1995 launched a Japanese-language edition and subsequently twenty-five other foreign editions. *National Geographic*, after a century of linking Americans to faraway places, now connected readers worldwide to the United States.

VOLUME XXI   NUMBER TWO

THE NATIONAL GEOGRAPHIC MAGAZINE

FEBRUARY, 1910

CONTENTS

A Traveler's Notes on Java . . . . . HENRY G. BRYANT
With 17 Illustrations

An Ancient Capital . . . . ISABEL F. DODD
With 11 Illustrations

The International Millionth Map of the World
With Diagram   BAILEY WILLIS

The Land of the Crossbow . . . GEORGE FORREST
With 15 Illustrations

The Great Natural Bridges of Utah . . BYRON CUMMINGS
With 7 Illustrations

The South Polar Expedition
With Map

Wilkes and d'Urville's Discoveries in Wilkes Land
REAR ADMIRAL JOHN E. PILLSBURY, U. S. N.

The Barrage of the Nile . . . . DAY ALLEN WILLEY
With 14 Illustrations

PUBLISHED BY THE
NATIONAL GEOGRAPHIC SOCIETY
HUBBARD MEMORIAL HALL
WASHINGTON, D.C.

$2.50 A YEAR   25 CTS. A COPY

National Geographic Society Image Collection

National Geographic *had already gone through five different cover formats when Robert Weir Crouch, an English-born Canadian decorative artist, came up with a design that cemented the magazine's visual identity. Singular and immediately recognizable, the oak-and-laurel frame on the cover of the February 1910 issue would remain largely unchanged for nearly half a century, though the buff-colored border would be replaced with a golden one.*

that blacks represented a female race and "like the woman, the black is deprived of political and scientific intelligence."

The language of U.S. leaders was also weighted with words like *manliness* and *weakling*. The warrior and president Theodore Roosevelt viewed people of color (or "darkeys," as he called them) as effeminate weaklings who were unable to govern themselves and could not cope with world politics. Americans debased Latin Americans as half-breeds needing supervision or distressed damsels begging for manly rescue. The gendered imagery in U.S. foreign relations joined race thinking to place women, people of color, and nations weaker than the United States low in the hierarchy of power and, hence, in a dependent status justifying U.S. dominance.

Link to Josiah Strong's *Expansion Under New World Conditions.*

Race thinking—popularized in magazine photos and cartoons, world's fairs, postcards, textbooks, museums, and political orations—reinforced notions of American greatness, influenced the way U.S. leaders dealt with other peoples, and obviated the need to think about the subtle textures of other societies. *National Geographic,* which began publication in 1888, photographically chronicled America's new overseas involvements in Asia and the Pacific, regularly featuring images of exotic, premodern peoples who had not become "Western." Fairs also put so-called uncivilized people of color on display in the "freak" or "midway" section. Dog-eating Filipinos aroused comment at the 1904 St. Louis World's Fair. Such racism downgraded diplomacy and justified domination and war.

Similar thinking permeated attitudes toward immigrants, whose entry into the United States was first restricted in these years. Although the Burlingame Treaty (1868) provided for free immigration between the United States and China, riots against Chinese immigrants continuously erupted in the American West. An 1880 treaty permitted Congress to suspend Chinese immigration to the United States. Tensions continued: in 1885, white coal miners and railway workers in Rock Springs, Wyoming, massacred at least twenty-five Chinese.

In 1906, the San Francisco School Board ordered Chinese, Koreans, and Japanese segregated in special schools. Tokyo protested such discrimination, and President Roosevelt quieted the crisis by striking a "gentleman's agreement" with Tokyo restricting Japanese immigration. San Francisco rescinded its segregation order. Relations with Tokyo worsened again in 1913 when the California legislature denied Japanese residents the right to own property.

The "Civilizing" Impulse

Expansionists believed that empire benefited Americans and those who came under their control. When the United States intervened in weaker states, Americans claimed they were extending liberty and prosperity to less fortunate people. William Howard Taft, as civil governor of the Philippines (1901–1904), described the United States' mission in its new colony as lifting Filipinos up "to a point of civilization" that will make them "call the name of the United States blessed." Later, Taft said about the Chinese that "the more civilized they become ... the wealthier they become, and the better market they become for us."

Missionaries dispatched to Africa and Asia, like Lottie Moon, helped spur the transfer of American culture and power abroad—"the peaceful conquest of the world," as Reverend Frederick Gates put it. In 1915, ten thousand American missionaries worked overseas. In China by 1915, more than twenty-five hundred mostly female American Protestant missionaries taught, preached the gospel, and administered medical care.

Ambitions and Strategies

What happened to Seward's vision
of an American empire?

The U.S. empire grew gradually, as American leaders defined guiding principles and built institutions to support overseas ambitions. William H. Seward, one of its chief architects, argued for extension of the American frontier as a senator from New York (1849–1861) and secretary of state (1861–1869). Seward envisioned a large U.S. empire encompassing Canada, the Caribbean, Cuba, Central America, Mexico, Hawai'i, Iceland, Greenland, and the Pacific islands. This empire would result from a natural process of gravitation toward the United States. Commerce would hurry the process, as would a canal across Central America, a transcontinental American railroad, and a telegraph system to speed communications.

Seward's Quest for Empire

Most of Seward's grandiose plans did not reach fruition in his lifetime. In 1867, his efforts for a treaty with Denmark to buy the Danish West Indies (Virgin Islands), was scuttled by Senate foes and a hurricane that wrecked St. Thomas. The Virgin Islanders, who voted for annexation, would wait until 1917 for official U.S. status. Seward's scheme with unscrupulous Dominican Republic leaders to gain a Caribbean naval base at Samaná Bay also failed. The corruption surrounding this deal foiled President Ulysses S. Grant's initiative in 1870 to buy the island nation.

Anti-imperialism, not just politics, blocked Seward. Opponents of empire argued that creating a showcase of democracy and prosperity on unsettled land at home would best persuade other peoples to adopt American principles. Some anti-imperialists, sharing the era's racism, opposed the annexation of territory populated by dark-skinned people.

Seward enjoyed some successes. In 1866, citing the Monroe Doctrine, he sent troops to the Mexico border and demanded that France abandon its puppet regime there. Also facing angry Mexican nationalists, Napoleon III abandoned the Maximilian monarchy that he forcibly installed three years earlier. In 1867, Seward paid Russia $7.2 million for the 591,000 square miles of Alaska—land twice the size of Texas. That same year, Seward claimed the Midway Islands (two small islands and a coral atoll northwest of Hawai'i).

International Communications

In 1866, through the efforts of financier Cyrus Field, an underwater transatlantic cable linked European and American telegraph networks. Backed by J. P. Morgan, communications pioneer James A. Scrymser strung telegraph lines to Latin America, entering Chile in 1890. In 1903, a submarine cable spanned the Pacific to the Philippines; three years later, it reached Japan and China. Information about markets, crises, and war flowed steadily and quickly. Drawn closer to one another through improved communications and transportation, nations found that faraway events had greater impact on them. Increasingly, American diplomats negotiated with their European counterparts as equals—signaling the United States' arrival on the international stage. Washington officials, for example, successfully confronted European powers over Samoa, islands in the South Pacific located 4,000 miles from San Francisco on the trade route to Australia. In 1878, the United States gained exclusive right to a coaling station at Samoa's coveted port of Pago Pago. Eyeing the same prize, Britain and Germany began cultivating ties with Samoan leaders. Tensions grew, and war seemed possible. At the eleventh hour, however, Britain, Germany, and the United States met in Berlin in 1889 and, without consulting the Samoans, devised a three-part protectorate that limited Samoa's independence. Ten years later, the three powers partitioned Samoa: the United States received Pago Pago through annexation of part of the islands (now called American Samoa); Germany took what is today independent Western Samoa; and Britain obtained the Gilbert Islands and Solomon Islands.

Alfred T. Mahan and Navalism

Calling attention to the naval buildup by European powers, notably Germany, U.S. expansionists argued for a bigger, modernized navy, adding the "blue water" command of the seas to its traditional role of "brown water" coastline defense. **Captain Alfred Thayer Mahan**, a popularizer of this New Navy, argued that because foreign trade was essential, the nation required an efficient navy to protect its shipping; and a navy required colonies for bases. Mahan's ideas were published as *The Influence of Sea Power upon History* (1890). Theodore Roosevelt and Henry Cabot Lodge consulted Mahan, sharing his belief in the links between trade, navy, and colonies and his alarm over Germany's aggressive military spirit.

Captain Alfred T. Mahan: Author of *The Influence of Sea Power upon History* (1890) and an advocate of a stronger navy and imperialism.

Moving toward naval modernization, Congress in 1883 authorized construction of the first steel-hulled warships. American factories produced steam engines, high-velocity shells, powerful guns, and precision instruments. The navy shifted from sail power to steam and from wood construction to steel. New Navy ships, such as the *Maine, Oregon,* and *Boston,* thrust the United States into naval prominence.

Crises in the 1890s: Hawai'i, Venezuela, and Cuba

What typically imperialist actions did the United States take in its dealings with Hawai'i and Venezuela?

In the depression-plagued 1890s, crises in Hawai'i and Cuba—and the belief that the frontier at home had closed—reinforced the expansionist argument. In 1893, historian Frederick Jackson Turner postulated that the ever-expanding continental frontier, which shaped the American character, was gone. He did not say a new frontier had to be found overseas, but he did claim that "American energy will continually demand a wider field for its exercise."

Annexation of Hawai'i

Hawai'i, the Pacific Ocean archipelago of eight major islands located 2,000 miles from the West Coast of the United States, emerged as America's new frontier. The Hawaiian Islands had long commanded American attention—commercial, missionary religious, naval, and diplomatic. By 1881, Secretary of State James Blaine already declared the Hawaiian Islands "essentially a part of the American system." By 1890, Americans owned about three-quarters of Hawai'i's wealth and subordinated its economy to that of the United States through sugar exports that entered the U.S. marketplace duty-free.

Hawai'i: Island nation in the Pacific that became an American territory in 1898. It was significant from a military and economic standpoint.

In Hawai'i's multiracial society, Chinese and Japanese nationals far outnumbered Americans, who represented just 2.1 percent of the population. Prominent Americans on the islands organized secret clubs and military units to contest the royal government. In 1887, they forced the king to accept a constitution that granted foreigners the vote and shifted decision making from the monarchy to the legislature. That year, Hawai'i granted the United States naval rights to Pearl Harbor. Many native Hawaiians believed that the *haole* (foreigners)—especially Americans—were stealing their country.

The native government was further undermined when the 1890 McKinley Tariff eliminated the duty-free status of Hawaiian sugar exports in the United States. Suffering declining sugar prices and profits, the American island elite pressed for annexation by the United States, thereby classifying their sugar as domestic. When Princess Lili'uokalani assumed the throne in 1891, she sought to roll back the political power of the *haole*. The next year, the white oligarchy formed the subversive Annexation Club.

The annexationists struck in January 1893 in collusion with John L. Stevens, America's chief American diplomat in Hawai'i, who dispatched troops from the USS *Boston* to occupy Honolulu. The queen, arrested and confined, surrendered. Rather than yield to the new provisional regime, headed by Sanford B. Dole, son of missionaries and a prominent attorney, she relinquished authority to the U.S. government. President Benjamin Harrison hurriedly sent an annexation treaty to the Senate.

Sensing foul play, incoming president Grover Cleveland ordered an investigation, which confirmed a conspiracy that most Hawaiians opposed annexation. But when Hawai'i proved a strategic and commercial way station to Asia and the Philippines during the Spanish-American War, President William McKinley maneuvered annexation through Congress on July 7, 1898. Under the Organic Act of June 1900, the people of Hawai'i became U.S. citizens. Statehood came in 1959.

Venezuelan Boundary Dispute

The Venezuelan crisis of 1895 also saw the United States in an expansive mood. For decades, Venezuela and Great Britain quarreled over the border between Venezuela and British Guiana, a territory containing rich gold deposits and a commercial gateway to northern South America via the Orinoco River. Venezuela sought U.S. help, and in July 1895, Secretary of State Richard Olney brashly lectured the British that the Monroe Doctrine prohibited European powers from denying self-government to nations in the Western Hemisphere. With almost no Venezuelan input, in 1896 an Anglo-American arbitration board divided the disputed territory between Britain and Venezuela. Thus, the United States displayed a typical imperialist trait: disregard for the rights of small nations.

In 1895, Cuba was the site of another crisis. From 1868 to 1878, the Cubans battled Spain for their independence, winning only the end of slavery. While the Cuban economy suffered, repressive Spanish rule continued. Insurgents committed to *Cuba libre* waited for another chance, and José Martí, one of the heroes of Cuban history, collected money, arms, and men in the United States.

Revolution in Cuba

Cuban and American culture intersected in many ways, notably in Baltimore, New York, Boston, and Philadelphia, where many Cubans settled or sent their children to school. When these expatriates returned home, many spoke English, had American names, played baseball, and jettisoned Catholicism for Protestant denominations.

The Cuban and U.S. economies were also intertwined. American investments of $50 million, mostly in sugar plantations, dominated the island. More than 90 percent of Cuba's sugar was exported to the United States, and most island imports came from the United States. Havana's famed cigar factories relocated to Key West and Tampa to evade U.S. tariffs. Martí, however, feared that "economic union means political union," for "the nation that buys, commands" and "the nation that sells, serves."

Martí's fears of a conquering U.S. policy were prophetic. In 1894, the Wilson-Gorman Tariff imposed a duty on Cuban sugar. The Cuban economy, highly dependent on exports, plunged into crisis, hastening the island's revolution against Spain and its further incorporation into the American system. Incorporation into "the American system."

In 1895, from American soil, Martí launched a revolution against Spain. Rebels burned sugar-cane fields and razed mills. U.S. investments were incinerated, and Cuban-American trade dwindled. To separate insurgents from their supporters, Spanish general Valeriano Weyler instituted a policy of "reconcentration." Some 300,000 Cubans were herded into fortified towns and camps, where starvation and disease caused tens of thousands of deaths. As reports of atrocity became headline news in the United States, Americans sympathized with the insurrectionists. In late 1897, a new government in Madrid modified reconcentration and promised some autonomy for Cuba, but the insurgents gained ground.

Sinking of the *Maine*

President William McKinley took office as an imperialist who advocated foreign bases for the New Navy, the export of surplus production, and U.S. supremacy in the Western Hemisphere. Vexed by Cuba's turmoil, he explored purchasing Cuba from Spain for $300 million. In January 1898, when antireform pro-Spanish loyalists and army rioted in Havana, Washington ordered the battleship *Maine* to Havana harbor to demonstrate U.S. concern and to protect American citizens.

On February 15, an explosion ripped the *Maine*, killing 266 of 354 American officers and crew. A week earlier, William Randolph Hearst's inflammatory *New York Journal* published a stolen private letter written by the Spanish minister in Washington, Enrique Dupuy de Lôme, belittling McKinley and suggesting that Spain would fight on. Congress complied unanimously with McKinley's request for $50 million for defense. Vengeful Americans blamed Spain. (Later, official and unofficial studies attributed the sinking to an accidental internal explosion.)

McKinley's Ultimatum and War Decision

Though reluctant to go to war, McKinley sent Spain an ultimatum: accept an armistice, end reconcentration, and designate McKinley as arbiter. Madrid made concessions. It abolished reconcentration and rejected, then accepted, an armistice. The president would no longer tolerate chronic disorder 90 miles off the U.S. coast. On April 11, McKinley asked Congress for authorization to use force "to secure a full and final termination of hostilities between ... Spain and ... Cuba, and to secure in the island the establishment of a stable government, capable of maintaining order." McKinley listed the reasons for war: the "cause of humanity"; the protection of American life and property; the "very serious injury to the commerce, trade, and business of our people"; and, referring to the destruction of the *Maine*, the "constant menace to our peace." On April 19, Congress declared Cuba free and independent and directed the president to use force to remove Spanish authority. The legislators also passed the Teller Amendment, which disclaimed U.S. intention to annex Cuba or control the island except to ensure its "pacification." McKinley blocked a congressional amendment to recognize the rebel government, arguing they were not ready for self-government.

The Spanish-American War and the Debate over Empire

What were the anti-imperialist arguments against U.S. annexation of the Philippines after the Spanish-American War?

By the time the Spanish concessions were on the table, prospects for compromise appeared dim. Cuban insurgents wanted full independence, and no Spanish government could have given up and remained in office. Nor did the United States welcome a truly independent Cuban government that might attempt to reduce U.S. interests.

Motives for War

Mixed motives drove those Americans who favored war. McKinley's April message expressed a humanitarian impulse to stop the bloodletting, a concern for commerce and property. Republicans wanted the Cuba question solved to secure their party's victory in the upcoming congressional elections. Many businesspeople and farmers believed that ejecting Spain from Cuba would open new markets for surplus production. Imperialists,

The Spanish fleet in the Caribbean was commanded by Admiral Pascual Cervera y Topete. His squadron entered Santiago Bay, Cuba, May 19, 1898, where it was immediately blockaded by Admiral William T. Sampson's fleet. On July 3, Cervera—following orders from Madrid—tried a heroic but unsuccessful escape from the U.S. blockade. This painting by Henry Reuterdahl depicts the destruction of the squadron. Cervera survived and became a prisoner of war.

The Story of the Spanish-American War of 1898 as told by W. Newphew King, Lieutenant U.S.N./Picture Research Consultants & Archives

meanwhile, saw the war as an opportunity to fulfill expansionist dreams, while conservatives, alarmed by Populism and labor strikes, welcomed war as a national unifier. One senator commented that "internal discord" was disappearing in the "fervent heat of patriotism." Theodore Roosevelt and others too young to remember the bloody Civil War looked on war as adventure.

More than 263,000 regulars and volunteers served in the army, and another 25,000 in the navy during the war. Most, however, never left the United States. The typical volunteer was young (early twenties), white, unmarried, native-born, and working class. Deaths numbered 5,462, mostly from a typhoid epidemic in Tennessee, Virginia, and Florida. Only 379 died in combat. About 10,000 African American troops in segregated regiments found no relief from racism, even though black troops were central to the victorious battle for Santiago de Cuba. For all, food, sanitary conditions, and medical care were bad. Still, Roosevelt could hardly contain himself. Although his Rough Riders, a motley unit of Ivy Leaguers and cowboys, proved undisciplined and ineffective, Roosevelt's self-serving publicity efforts ensured they received good press.

Dewey in the Philippines

The first war news came from faraway Asia, from the Spanish colony of the Philippine Islands, where Filipinos were also seeking independence. On May 1, 1898, Commodore George Dewey's New Navy ship *Olympia* led an American squadron into Manila Bay and wrecked the Spanish fleet. Dewey received orders from Washington to attack the islands if war broke out. Manila was a choice harbor, and the Philippines sat en route to China's potentially huge market.

Facing Americans and rebels in Cuba and the Philippines, Spanish resistance collapsed rapidly. U.S. ships blockaded Cuban ports and insurgents cut off supplies from the countryside, causing starvation and illness for Spanish soldiers. American troops landed near Santiago de Cuba on June 22 and laid siege to the city. On July 3, U.S. warships sank the Spanish Caribbean squadron in Santiago harbor. American forces assaulted the Spanish colony of Puerto Rico, gaining another Caribbean base for the navy and pushing Madrid to sue for peace.

Treaty of Paris

On August 12, Spain and the United States signed an armistice ending the war. In Paris, in December 1898, they agreed on the peace terms: independence for Cuba from Spain; cession of the Philippines, Puerto Rico, and the Pacific island of Guam to the United States for $20 million. The U.S. empire now stretched deep into Asia, and the annexation of Wake Island (1898), Hawai'i (1898), and Samoa (1899) gave American traders, missionaries, and naval promoters other steppingstones to China.

During the war, the *Washington Post* detected that "The taste of empire is in the mouth of the people." But anti-imperialists such as the author Mark Twain, Nebraska politician William Jennings Bryan, reformer Jane Addams, and industrialist Andrew Carnegie argued against annexation of the Philippines. Their concern that a war to free Cuba had led to empire stimulated debate over American foreign policy.

Link to William Graham Sumner's essay, "The Fallacy of Territorial Expansion" from 1911.

Anti-Imperialist Arguments

Imperial control could be imposed either formally (by military occupation, annexation, or colonialism) or informally (by economic domination, political manipulation, or the threat of intervention). Anti-imperialist ire focused mostly on formal imperial control. Some critics cited the Declaration of Independence and the Constitution, arguing that the conquest of people against their will violated the right of self-determination.

Other anti-imperialists feared that the American character was being corrupted by imperialist zeal. Jane Addams, seeing children play war games on Chicago streets, noted that they were not freeing Cubans but rather slaying Spaniards. Hoping to build a distinct foreign policy constituency from prominent women like Addams championed peace and an end to imperial conquest.

Some anti-imperialists protested that the United States was practicing a double standard—"offering liberty to the Cubans with one hand, cramming liberty down the throats of the Filipinos with the other, but with both feet planted upon the neck of the negro," as an African American politician from Massachusetts put it. Still others warned that annexing people of color would undermine Anglo-Saxon purity and supremacy at home.

For Samuel Gompers and other anti-imperialist labor leaders, the issue was jobs. Might not the new colonials be imported as cheap contract labor to drive down American wages? Would not exploitation of the weak abroad become contagious and lead to further exploitation of the weak at home? The anti-imperialists, however, never launched an effective campaign. Although they organized the Anti-Imperialist League in November 1898, they differed so profoundly on domestic issues that they found it difficult to speak with one voice on a foreign question.

Imperialist Arguments   The imperialists, for their part, appealed to patriotism, destiny, and commerce. They envisioned American merchant ships plying the waters to boundless Asian markets, naval vessels protecting America's Pacific interests, and missionaries uplifting inferior peoples. It was America's duty, they insisted, quoting a then-popular Rudyard Kipling poem, to "take up the white man's burden." Furthermore, Filipino insurgents were beginning to resist U.S. rule, and it seemed cowardly to pull out under fire, especially with Germany and Japan ready to seize the islands.

In February 1899, by a 57-to-27 vote, the Senate passed the Treaty of Paris, ending the war with Spain. Most Republicans voted yes and most Democrats no. An amendment promising independence once the Filipinos formed a stable government lost by only the tie-breaking ballot of the vice president.

Asian Encounters: War in the Philippines, Diplomacy in China

Why was the Open Door policy such a key component of U.S. diplomacy?

Emilio Aguinaldo: Nationalist leader of Filipino war against American occupation.

The Philippine crisis was far from over. **Emilio Aguinaldo**, the Philippine nationalist leader who battled the Spanish for years, believed that American officials promised independence for his country. But after the victory, U.S. officers ordered Aguinaldo out of Manila. In early 1899, he proclaimed an independent Philippine Republic and took up arms.

Philippine Insurrection and Pacification   Both sides fought viciously; American soldiers burned villages and tortured captives, while Filipino forces staged brutal hit-and-run guerilla ambushes. U.S. troops introduced a variant of the Spanish reconcentration policy; in the province of Batangas, for instance, U.S. troops forced residents to live in designated zones to separate insurgents from supporters. Poor sanitation, starvation, and malaria and cholera killed thousands. Outside secure areas, Americans destroyed food supplies to starve out the rebels. At least one-quarter of the population of Batangas died or fled.

Before the Philippine insurrection was suppressed in 1902, some 20,000 Filipinos died in combat, and 600,000 succumbed to starvation and disease. More than 4,000 Americans lay dead. Resistance to U.S. rule, however, continued. When the fiercely independent, often violent Muslim Filipinos of Moro Province refused to knuckle under, the U.S. military threatened extermination. In 1906, 600 Moros, including women and children, were slaughtered at the Battle of Bud Dajo.

U.S. officials soon tried to Americanize the Philippines, instituting a new education system with English as the main language. The architect Daniel Burnham, leader of the City Beautiful movement, planned modern Manila. The Philippine economy grew as an American satellite, and a sedition act sent U.S. critics to prison. In 1916, the Jones Act vaguely promised independence once the Philippines established a "stable government." But the United States did not end its rule until 1946.

China and the Open Door Policy

In China, McKinley successfully focused on a policy emphasizing negotiation. Outsiders had pecked away at China since the 1840s. Taking advantage of the Qing (Manchu) dynasty's weakness, the major imperial powers carved out spheres of influence (regions over which they claimed political control and exclusive commercial privileges): Germany in Shandong, Russia in Manchuria, France in Yunnan and Hainan, and Britain in Kowloon and Hong Kong. Then, in 1895, Japan claimed victory over China in a short war and assumed control of Formosa and Korea and parts of China proper (see Map 22.1). American religious and business leaders petitioned Washington to halt the dismemberment of China before they were closed out.

Secretary of State John Hay knew that missionaries like Lottie Moon had become targets of Chinese nationalist anger and that American oil and textile companies had been disappointed with their investments there. Thus, in September 1899, Hay sent nations with spheres of influence in China a note seeking their respect for the principle of equal trade opportunity—an Open Door. The recipients sent evasive replies, privately complaining that the United States was seeking, for free, the trade rights in China that they had gained at considerable cost.

The next year, the Boxers, a Chinese secret society (so named in the western press because some members were martial artists), sought to expel foreigners. They rioted, killing many outsiders and laying siege to the foreign legations in Beijing in what is known as the **Boxer Rebellion**. The United States joined the other imperial powers in sending troops. Hay also sent a second Open Door note instructing other nations to preserve China's territorial integrity and honor "equal and impartial trade." China continued for years to be fertile soil for foreign exploitation, especially by the Japanese.

The **Open Door policy** became a cornerstone of U.S. diplomacy. While the United States had long opposed barriers to international commerce, after 1900, when the U.S. emerged emerge as the premier world trader, the Open Door policy became an instrument first to pry open markets and then to dominate them. The Open Door also developed as an ideology with several tenets: first, that America's domestic

Boxer Rebellion: Chinese insurgency against Christians and foreigners, defeated by an international force.

Open Door policy: Foreign policy proposed by U.S. Secretary of State John Hay, in which he asked the major European powers to assure trading rights in China by opening the ports in their spheres of influence to all countries.

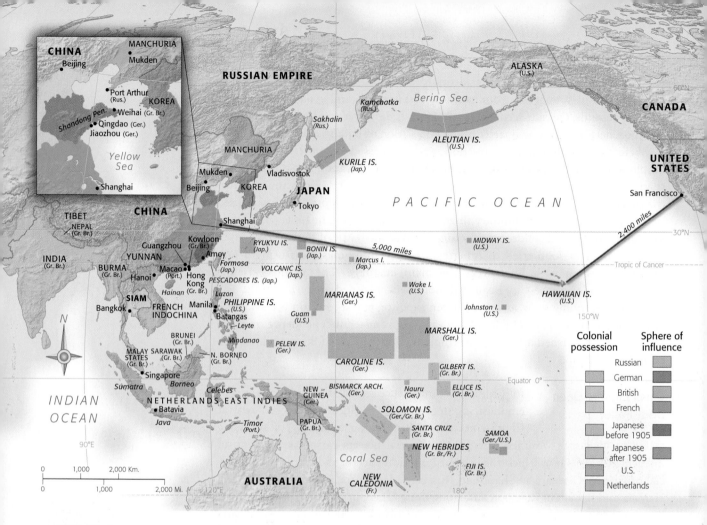

MAP 22.1

Imperialism in Asia: Turn of the Century

China and the Pacific region had become imperialist hunting grounds by the turn of the century. The European powers and Japan controlled more areas than the United States, which nonetheless participated in the imperial race by annexing the Philippines, Wake, Guam, Hawai'i, and Samoa; announcing the Open Door policy; and expanding trade. As the spheres of influence in China demonstrate, that besieged nation succumbed to outsiders despite the Open Door policy.

Source: Copyright © Cengage Learning

well-being required exports; second, that foreign trade would suffer interruption unless the United States intervened abroad; and third, that the closing of any area to American products, citizens, or ideas threatened the survival of the United States.

TR's World

What solidified U.S.–British ties heading into World War I?

Theodore Roosevelt played an important role in shaping U.S. foreign policy in the McKinley administration. As assistant secretary of the navy (1897–1898), as a Spanish-American War hero, and then as vice president in McKinley's second term, Roosevelt worked to make the United States a great power. Long fascinated by power, he also relished hunting and killing. After an argument with a girlfriend in his youth, he vented his anger by shooting a neighbor's dog. Roosevelt justified the slaughtering of American Indians, if necessary, and took his Rough Riders to Cuba, desperate to get in on the fighting.

Like Americans of his day, Roosevelt took for granted the superiority of Protestant Anglo-American culture and believed in using American power to shape world affairs. In TR's world there were "civilized" and "uncivilized" nations; the former, primarily white and Anglo-Saxon or Teutonic, had a right and a duty to intervene in the affairs of the latter (generally nonwhite, Latin, or Slavic, and therefore "backward") to preserve order and stability, even if that meant using violence.

Presidential Authority Roosevelt's love of the good fight caused many to rue his ascension to the presidency after McKinley's assassination in September 1901. But the cowboy was also an astute analyst of foreign policy. Roosevelt understood that American power, though growing, remained limited and that in many parts of the world the United States would have to rely on diplomacy to achieve satisfactory outcomes.

Roosevelt's first efforts were focused on Latin America, where U.S. economic and power towered (see Map 22.2). He also focused on Europe, where repeated disputes

MAP 22.2

U.S. Hegemony in the Caribbean and Latin America

Through many interventions, territorial acquisitions, and robust economic expansion, the United States became the predominant power in Latin America in the early twentieth century. The United States often backed up the Roosevelt Corollary's declaration of a "police power" by dispatching troops to Caribbean nations, where they met nationalist opposition.

Source: Copyright © Cengage Learning

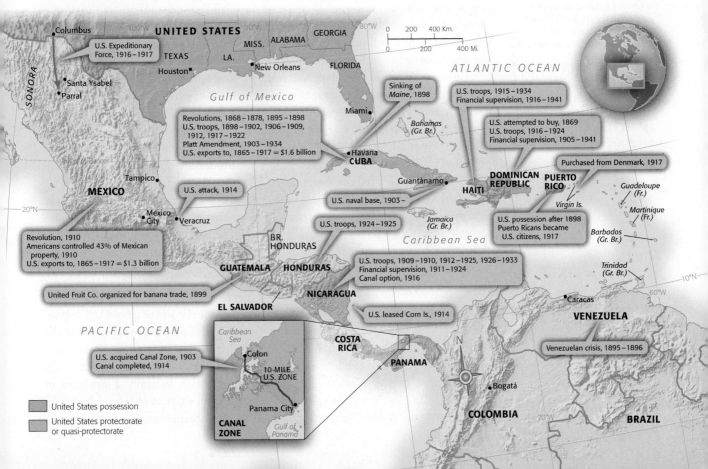

persuaded Americans to develop friendlier relations with Great Britain while avoiding the continent's troubles, which Americans blamed on Germany.

As U.S. economic interests expanded in Latin America, so did U.S. political influence. Exports to Latin America rose from $50 million in the 1870s to more than $120 million in 1901 and $300 million in 1914. Investments by U.S. citizens in Latin America climbed to $1.26 billion in 1914. In 1899, two large banana importers merged to form the United Fruit Company. United Fruit, owning much of the land in Central America (more than a million acres in 1913), and the railroad and steamship lines. The company worked to eradicate yellow fever and malaria while bankrolling favored officeholders.

Cuba and the Platt Amendment

After the destructive war in Cuba, U.S. citizens and corporations dominated the island's economy, controlling the sugar, mining, tobacco, and utilities industries, and most of the rural lands. Private U.S. investments grew from $50 million before the revolution to $220 million by 1913, and U.S. exports to the island rose from $26 million in 1900 to $196 million in 1917. The Teller Amendment outlawed the annexation of Cuba, but Washington officials used its call for "pacification" to justify U.S. control. American troops remained there until 1902.

U.S. authorities restricted voting rights to propertied Cuban males, excluding two-thirds of adult men and all women. American officials also forced Cubans to add the **Platt Amendment** to their constitution. This prohibited Cuba from making treaties that might impair its independence; in practice, this meant all treaties required U.S. approval. Most important, the Platt Amendment granted the United States "the right to intervene" to preserve the island's independence and maintain domestic order. Finally, it required Cuba to lease a naval base to the United States (at Guantánamo Bay, still under U.S. jurisdiction today). Formalized in a 1903 treaty, the amendment governed Cuban-American relations until 1934.

Platt Amendment: Added to Cuba's constitution of 1903 under American pressure, it gave the United States the right to intervene if Cuban independence or internal order were threatened, and granted a naval base to the United States at Guantánamo Bay.

Link to the Platt Amendment.

Cubans protested the Platt Amendment, and a rebellion in 1906 prompted another U.S. invasion. The marines stayed until 1909, returned briefly in 1912 and again from 1917 to 1922. U.S. officials helped develop a transportation system, expand the public school system, found a national army, and increase sugar production. When Dr. Walter Reed's experiments, based on the theory of the Cuban physician Carlos Juan Finlay, proved that mosquitoes transmitted yellow fever, sanitary engineers eradicated the disease.

Puerto Rico, the Caribbean island taken as a spoil of war in the Treaty of Paris, first welcomed the United States as an improvement over Spain. But the U.S. military governor, General Guy V. Henry, regarded Puerto Ricans as children who needed "kindergarten instruction in controlling themselves without allowing them too much liberty." Some residents warned against the "Yankee peril"; others applauded the "Yankee model" and futilely anticipated statehood.

Panama Canal

Panama, meanwhile, became the site of a bold U.S. expansionist venture. In 1869, the world marveled when the newly completed Suez Canal facilitated travel between the Indian Ocean and Mediterranean Sea and enhanced the British Empire's power. Surely that feat could be duplicated in the Western Hemisphere, possibly in Panama, a province of Colombia. Business interests joined politicians, diplomats, and navy officers in insisting that the United States control such an interoceanic canal.

But the Clayton-Bulwer Treaty with Britain (1850) provided for joint control of a canal. The British, recognizing their diminishing influence in the region and cultivating friendship with the United States as a counterweight to Germany, permitted a solely U.S.-run canal in the Hay-Pauncefote Treaty (1901). When Colombia resisted Washington's terms, Roosevelt encouraged Panamanian rebels to declare independence and ordered American warships to back them.

In 1903, the new Panama awarded the United States a canal zone and long-term rights to its control. The treaty also guaranteed Panama its independence. (In 1922, the United States paid Colombia $25 million in "conscience money" but did not apologize.) A technological achievement, the **Panama Canal** was completed in 1914.

Panama Canal: Major waterway built by the United States for $352 million that traverses the Isthmus of Panama in Central America, connecting the Atlantic and Pacific Oceans. Construction began in 1906 and was completed in 1914.

Link to the Roosevelt Corollary to the Monroe Doctrine, in President Roosevelt's fourth annual message to Congress in 1904.

Roosevelt Corollary

Elsewhere in the Caribbean, Roosevelt affirmed U.S. hegemony. Worried that Latin American nations' defaults on debts owed to European banks were provoking European intervention, the president in 1904 issued the Roosevelt Corollary to the Monroe Doctrine. He warned Latin Americans to stabilize their politics and finances or risk "intervention by some civilized nation." Roosevelt's declaration provided the rationale for frequent U.S. interventions in Latin America.

From 1900 to 1917, U.S. presidents ordered American troops to Cuba, Panama, Nicaragua, the Dominican Republic, Mexico, and Haiti to quell civil wars, thwart challenges to U.S. influence, gain ports and bases, and forestall European meddling (see Map 22.2). U.S. authorities ran elections, trained nationals, and shifted foreign debts to U.S. banks. They also controlled tariff revenues and government budgets (as in the Dominican Republic, from 1905 to 1941).

U.S.-Mexican Relations

U.S. officials focused particular attention on Mexico, where long-time dictator Porfirio Díaz (1876–1910) aggressively recruited foreign investors through tax incentives and land grants. American capitalists came to own Mexico's railroads and mines and invested heavily in petroleum and banking, thereby dominating Mexico's foreign trade in the early 1890s. By 1910, Americans controlled 43 percent of Mexican property and produced more than half of the country's oil. The Mexican revolutionaries who ousted Díaz in 1910 wanted to end their economic dependence on the United States.

In a suit and hat, President Theodore Roosevelt occupies the controls of a ninety-five-ton power shovel at a Panama Canal worksite. Roosevelt's November 1906 trip to inspect the massive project was the first time a sitting president left the United States.

AP/Wide World

The revolution descended into a bloody civil war with strong anti-Yankee overtones, and the Mexican government intended to nationalize American-owned properties. President Woodrow Wilson twice ordered troops onto Mexican soil: once in 1914, at Veracruz, to overthrow President Victoriano Huerta, and again in 1916, in northern Mexico, where General John J. "Black Jack" Pershing spent months pursuing Mexican rebel Pancho Villa for raiding an American border town. Failing to capture Villa and facing another nationalistic government, U.S. forces departed in January 1917.

As the United States reaffirmed the Monroe Doctrine, European nations reluctantly honored U.S. hegemony in Latin America. In turn, the United States continued to stand outside European embroilments. Theodore Roosevelt did help settle a Franco-German clash over Morocco by mediating a settlement at Algeciras, Spain (1906), but he drew American criticism this involvement. Americans endorsed the Hague peace conferences (1899 and 1907) and negotiated arbitration treaties, but generally stayed outside the European arena, except for trade.

Peacemaking in East Asia

In East Asia, though, both Roosevelt and his successor, William Howard Taft, sought to preserve the Open Door and to contain Japan's rising power. Many race-minded Japanese interpreted the U.S. advance into the Pacific as an attempt by whites to gain ascendancy over Asians. The United States gradually made concessions to Japan to protect the Philippines and sustain the Open Door policy. Japan continued to plant interests in China and then smashed the Russians in the Russo-Japanese War (1904–1905). President Roosevelt mediated the negotiations at the Portsmouth Conference in New Hampshire and won the Nobel Peace Prize for helping to preserve a balance of power in Asia.

Link to excerpts of notes between the U.S. Secretary of State Elihu Root and Japanese Ambassador Kogoro Takahira.

In 1905, in the Taft-Katsura Agreement, the United States conceded Japanese hegemony over Korea in return for Japan's respect for the U.S. position in the Philippines. Three years later, in the Root-Takahira Agreement, Washington recognized Japan's interests in Manchuria, and Japan again pledged the security of U.S. Pacific possessions and endorsed the Open Door in China. Roosevelt deterred the Japanese with reinforced naval power; in late 1907, he sent the navy's Great White Fleet on a world tour. Impressed, the Japanese expanded their navy.

Dollar Diplomacy

President Taft hoped to counter Japanese advances in Asia through dollar diplomacy—the use of private funds to serve American diplomatic goals while garnering profits for American financiers and bringing reform to developing countries. Taft induced American bankers to join an international consortium to build a railway in China. But it seemed only to embolden Japan to solidify its holdings in China.

In 1914, when World War I broke out in Europe, Japan seized Shandong and some Pacific islands from the Germans. In 1915, Japan issued its Twenty-One Demands, insisting on hegemony over China. The United States lacked power in Asia to block Japan's imperialisms. A new president, Woodrow Wilson, worried about how the "white race" could blunt the rise of "the yellow race."

Guantánamo Bay

Four hundred miles from Miami, near the southeastern corner of Cuba, sits U.S. Naval Base Guantánamo Bay. The oldest American base outside the United States, it is the only one located in a country with which Washington does not have an open political relationship. The United States has occupied Guantánamo since the aftermath of the Spanish-American War, leasing it from Cuba for $4,085 per year (originally $2,000 in gold coins).

Cuban leaders were dissatisfied with the deal early on, and after Fidel Castro's communist takeover in 1959, Guantánamo fueled tensions between the two countries. Castro called it "a dagger pointed at Cuba's heart" and refused to cash the rent checks. That he cashed the very first check, however, enabled Washington to argue that Castro's government accepts the lease.

Since late 2001, "Gitmo" has contained a detainment camp for alleged combatants captured in Afghanistan and, later, Iraq and elsewhere. By 2005, there were more than five hundred detainees from forty countries. The George W. Bush administration called the detainees "unlawful enemy combatants" but promised to follow the Geneva accords governing prisoners of war. Soon, there were allegations of abuse and complaints that holding detainees without trial, charges, or any prospect of release was unlawful. Some detainees committed suicide. For critics, the camp became an international symbol of American heavy-handedness that hurt America's image abroad.

In June 2006, the U.S. Supreme Court ruled that President Bush overstepped his power in establishing procedures for the Guantánamo detainees without congressional authority—and that the procedures violated the Uniform Code of Military Justice and the Geneva accords. Bush said he would like to close the Guantánamo camp but some prisoners were too "darned dangerous" to release or deport. The question for a people and a nation remained: how would the United States balance security with due process and the rule of law?

Anglo-American Rapprochement

British officials shared this concern, though their attention was focused on rising tensions in Europe. Anglo-American cooperation blossomed during the Roosevelt-Taft years. The intense German-British rivalry and the rise of the United States to world power furthered London's quest for friendship with Washington. The two nations shared a common language and respect for private property rights, and Americans appreciated British support in the 1898 war and the Hay-Pauncefote Treaty, London's virtual endorsement of the Roosevelt Corollary, and the withdrawal of British warships from the Caribbean.

British-American trade and U.S. investment in Britain also secured ties. By 1914, more than 140 American companies operated in Britain, including H. J. Heinz's processed foods and F. W. Woolworth's "penny markets." Many decried an Americanization of British culture. Such exaggerated fears, however, gave way to cooperation, especially in 1917 when the United States entered World War I supporting Britain against Germany.

Summary

By 1914, Americans held extensive economic, strategic, and political interests world-wide. The outward reach of U.S. foreign policy from Seward to Wilson sparked opposition from domestic critics, other imperialist nations, and foreign nationalists, but expansionists prevailed, and the trend toward empire endured.

Economic and strategic needs motivated and justified expansion. The belief that the United States needed foreign markets to absorb surplus production joined missionary zeal in reforming other societies through American products and culture. Notions of racial and male supremacy and appeals to national greatness also fed the appetite for foreign adventure. The greatly augmented navy became a primary means for satisfying America's expansionist desires.

Revealing the diversity of America's intersection with the world, missionaries like Moon, generals, companies, and politicians carried American ideas, guns, and goods abroad to a mixed reception. When world war broke out in August 1914, the United States' self-proclaimed greatness and political isolation from Europe were tested.

Chapter Review

Imperial Dreams

What drove U.S. expansion overseas in the late nineteenth century?

American leaders increasingly believed in the decades after the Civil War that the nation's future prosperity and security depended on greater U.S. investment in and influence over other parts of the world. They believed foreign trade could prevent future economic downturns in the U.S.—an increasing concern with the depression of the 1890s—by shipping surplus products made here overseas. Economic ties also permitted political influence to be exerted abroad and helped spread the American way of life, especially capitalism, which fueled dramatic growth of U.S. exports. Leaders also embraced the notion of American "exceptionalism"—that the United States was unique and superior to other regions because of its heritage and God-favored prosperity. Nationalism, capitalism, Social Darwinism, and a paternalistic racism provided rationales for U.S. expansion and imperialism; hence, expansionists argued that when they intervened and sometimes colonized these regions, they were helping to bring prosperity and liberty to weaker, less fortunate peoples.

Ambitions and Strategies

What happened to Seward's vision of an American empire?

Secretary of State William Seward longed for a U.S. empire that would extend the frontier to include Canada, the Caribbean, Cuba, Central America, Mexico, Hawai'i, Iceland, Greenland, and the Pacific islands. He anticipated these areas would naturally gravitate to—and easily become enveloped by—the United States, and that foreign trade and certain infrastructure developments—such as a transcontinental U.S. railroad, a canal across Central America, and a telegraph system—would speed things along. Most of his vision never came to pass, blocked by anti-imperialists, political foes, and failed schemes. He had a few successes, however, including chasing the French puppet government from Mexico in 1866, purchasing Alaska from the Russians in 1867, and claiming the Midway Islands for the United States that year.

Crises in the 1890s: Hawai'i, Venezuela, and Cuba

What typically imperialist actions did the United States take in its dealings with Hawai`i and Venezuela?

In both cases, the United States showed disregard for the rights of foreign peoples. Hawai'i was annexed despite the objections of its queen and most Hawaiians because it proved strategically and commercially important to the United States—particularly during the Spanish-American War, when it served as a way station to Asia and the Philippines. Venezuela, meanwhile, sought U.S. assistance in its border dispute with Great Britain over where its boundary with British Guiana should lie. The Anglo-American arbitration board divided up the territory, which was rich with gold and provided a commercial gateway to South America, between Britain and Venezuela, with almost no input from the latter.

The Spanish-American War and the Debate over Empire

What were the anti-imperialist arguments against U.S. annexation of the Philippines after the Spanish-American War?

Anti-imperialists expressed a wide range of concerns about the potential annexation of the Philippines. For many, it seemed hypocritical for Americans to fight a war for Cuban liberation, only to acquire another small nation in the process. Some argued that it violated the fundamental right of a people to self-determination that Americans themselves embraced in the Declaration of Independence and Constitution. Prominent women such as Jane Addams felt imperialist zeal corrupted the American character, and cited children's playing war games as evidence of this. Racists saw the annexation of nonwhite nation as a potential threat to Anglo-Saxon purity and supremacy, while labor leaders feared the new colonists might become a cheap labor force to drive down American wages.

Asian Encounters: War in the Philippines, Diplomacy in China

Why was the Open Door policy such a key component of U.S. diplomacy?

The Open Door Policy originated in the late nineteenth century as a solution to U.S. trade difficulties in China. The concept called for nations with spheres of influence in turbulent China to respect the principle of equal trade opportunity in the region. After 1900, when the United States became the world's preeminent trader, the Open Door became the tool by which it could first pry open new markets and then dominate them. As it developed, the Open Door included the following tenets: that America's economy required exports to remain strong; that trade abroad could be interrupted unless the United States intervened; and that any effort to keep U.S. citizens, products, or ideas from other regions threatened U.S. survival.

TR's World

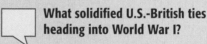

What solidified U.S.-British ties heading into World War I?

Aside from their shared language and respect for private property rights, England and the United States were united by several other factors. Both were concerned about growing Japanese influence in Asia. U.S. investment in Britain, along with increased trade, further strengthened their bonds. British support for the Roosevelt Corollary to Monroe doctrine (granting the United States hegemony in the Western Hemisphere) and the withdrawal of British ships from the Caribbean made relations easier, as did England's respect for the United States' growing status as a world power. Increased tensions between Germany and England, along with British support for the 1898 war, increased cooperation between the two countries and ensured that many Americans would take England's side in the impending global conflict.

Suggestions for Further Reading

Gail Bederman, *Manliness and Civilization: A Cultural History of Gender and Race in the United States, 1880–1917* (1995)

Kristin L. Hoganson, *Fighting for American Manhood: How Gender Politics Provoked the Spanish-American and Philippine-American Wars* (1998)

Michael H. Hunt, *Ideology and U.S. Foreign Policy* (1987)

Paul A. Kramer, *The Blood of Government: Race, Empire, the United States, and the Philippines* (2006)

Walter LaFeber, *The American Search for Opportunity, 1865–1913* (1993)

Brian M. Linn, *The Philippine War, 1899–1902* (2000)

Eric T. Love, *Race over Empire: Racism and U.S. Imperialism, 1865–1900* (2004)

Stuart Creighton Miller, *"Benevolent Assimilation": The American Conquest of the Philippines, 1899–1903* (1982)

John Offner, *An Unwanted War: The Diplomacy of the United States and Spain over Cuba, 1895–1898* (1992)

Louis A. Perez Jr., *The War of 1898: The United States and Cuba in History and Historiography* (1998)

Americans in the Great War

23

1914–1920

On May 7, 1915, Secretary of State William Jennings Bryan was lunching with cabinet members in Washington when he received a bulletin: the luxurious British ocean liner *Lusitania* had been sunk, apparently by a German submarine. He rushed to his office, and at 3:06 p.m. received confirmation from London: "THE LUSITANIA WAS TORPEDOED OFF THE IRISH COAST AND SANK IN HALF AN HOUR." The giant vessel sank in eighteen minutes; 1,198 people perished, including 128 Americans. With Europe at war, Bryan feared such a calamity. Britain had imposed a naval blockade on Germany, and the Germans had responded with submarine warfare against Allied shipping, proclaiming the North Atlantic a danger zone, then sinking British and Allied ships. As a passenger liner, the *Lusitania* was supposed to be spared, but German officials warned Americans in newspaper notices that they traveled on British or Allied ships at their own risk; passenger liners suspected of carrying munitions or contraband were subject to attack. For weeks, Bryan urged President Woodrow Wilson to stop Americans from booking passage on British ships; Wilson refused.

The *Lusitania*, it soon emerged, *was* carrying munitions. Desperate to keep the United States out of the war, Bryan urged Wilson to condemn Germany and Britain's blockade and to ban Americans from traveling on belligerent ships. Others, including former president Theodore Roosevelt, called the sinking "an act of piracy" and pressed for war. Wilson did not want war, but disagreed with Bryan about treating British and German violations the same. He sent a strong note to Berlin, insisting Germany end its submarine warfare.

As Bryan pressed his case, he became increasingly isolated within the administration. When in early June Wilson refused to ban Americans from travel on belligerent ships and sent a second protest note to Germany, Bryan resigned.

The division between the president and his secretary of state reflected divisions within the American populace over Europe's war. Eastern newspapers charged Bryan with betraying

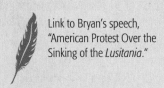

Link to Bryan's speech, "American Protest Over the Sinking of the *Lusitania*."

the country. But in the Midwest and South, Bryan won praise from pacifists and German American groups. Weeks later, speaking to fifteen thousand people at Madison Square Garden, Bryan was applauded when he warned against "war with any of the belligerent nations." Although many Americans agreed with Wilson that honor ranked above peace, others shared Bryan's position that some sacrifice of neutral rights was reasonable to keep the country out of war.

To many, full-scale war seemed unthinkable. The new machine guns, howitzers, submarines, and dreadnoughts were awesome death engines; one social reformer lamented that using them would mean "civilization is all gone, and barbarism come."

For almost three years, President Wilson kept America out of the war, while protecting U.S. trade interests and improving the nation's military posture. But American property, lives, and neutrality fell victim to British and German naval warfare. When, two years after the *Lusitania* went down, the president asked Congress for a declaration of war, he insisted America would not just win but "make the world safe for democracy."

A year and a half later, the Great War would be over. Some 10 million soldiers perished. Europeans experienced the destruction of ideals, confidence, and goodwill, and immense economic damage. The Great War toppled four empires of the Old World—the German, Austro-Hungarian, Russian, and Ottoman Turkish—and left two others, the British and French, drastically weakened.

Losses for the United States were comparatively small, yet American involvement tipped the scales in favor of the Allies by contributing troops, supplies, and loans. The war years also witnessed a massive international transfer of wealth from Europe across the Atlantic, as the United States went from the world's largest debtor nation to its largest creditor. The conflict marked the United States as a world power.

At home, World War I intensified social divisions. Racial tensions accompanied the northward migration of southern blacks, and pacifists and German Americans were harassed. The federal government trampled on civil liberties to silence critics. After Russia's communist revolution, a Red Scare in America repressed radicals and tarnished America's democratic image. Although reformers continued to address issues like prohibition and woman suffrage, the war splintered the Progressive movement.

Abroad, Americans who marched to battle grew disillusioned with the peace process. They recoiled from victors squabbling over the spoils, and they chided Wilson for failing to deliver his promised "peace without victory." After negotiating the Treaty of Versailles at Paris following World War I, the president urged U.S. membership in the new League of Nations, which he believed would reform world politics. The Senate rejected his appeal (the League nonetheless organized without U.S. membership), because many Americans feared the League might threaten the U.S. empire and entangle Americans in Europe's problems.

As you read this chapter, keep the following questions in mind:

* **Why did the United States try to remain neutral and then enter the European war in 1917?**

* **How was American society changed by the war?**

* **What were the main elements of Woodrow Wilson's postwar vision, and why did he fail to realize them?**

Chronology

1914	First World War begins in Europe
1915	Germans sink *Lusitania* off coast of Ireland
1916	After torpedoing the *Sussex*, Germany pledges not to attack merchant ships without warning
	National Defense Act expands military
1917	Germany declares unrestricted submarine warfare
	Russian Revolution ousts the czar; Bolsheviks later take power
	United States enters First World War
	Selective Service Act creates draft
	Espionage Act limits First Amendment rights
	Race riot breaks out in East St. Louis, Illinois
1918	Wilson announces Fourteen Points for new world order
	Sedition Act further limits free speech

	U.S. troops at Château-Thierry help blunt German offensive
	U.S. troops intervene in Russia against Bolsheviks
	Spanish flu pandemic kills 20 million worldwide
	Armistice ends First World War
1919	Paris Peace Conference punishes Germany and launches League of Nations
	May Day bombings help instigate Red Scare
	American Legion organizes for veterans' benefits and antiradicalism
	Wilson suffers stroke after speaking tour
	Senate rejects Treaty of Versailles and U.S. membership in League of Nations
	Schenck v. U.S. upholds Espionage Act
1920	Palmer Raids round up suspected radicals

Precarious Neutrality

> How viable was U.S. neutrality during World War I?

The war that erupted in August 1914 grew from years of European competition over trade, colonies, allies, and armaments. Two powerful alliance systems had formed: the Triple Alliance of Germany, Austria-Hungary, and Italy, and the Triple Entente of Britain, France, and Russia. All had imperial holdings and wanted more. As Germany challenged Great Britain for world leadership, many Americans saw Germany as an excessively militaristic nation that threatened U.S. interests in the Western Hemisphere.

Outbreak of the First World War Crises in the Balkans triggered events that shattered Europe's delicate balance of power. Slavic nationalists sought to enlarge independent Serbia by annexing regions such as Bosnia, then a province of the Austro-Hungarian Empire. On June 28, 1914, Archduke Franz Ferdinand, heir to the Austro-Hungarian throne, was assassinated by a Serbian nationalist while visiting Sarajevo, the capital of Bosnia. Austria-Hungary consulted its Triple Alliance partner Germany, which urged toughness. When Serbia called on its Slavic friend Russia for help, Russia enlisted France and began mobilizing its armies.

Germany struck first, declaring war against Russia on August 1 and against France two days later. Britain hesitated, but when German forces slashed into neutral Belgium to get at France, London declared war against Germany on August 4. Eventually, Turkey (the Ottoman Empire) joined Germany and Austria-Hungary as the Central Powers, and Italy (switching sides) and Japan teamed up with Britain, France, and Russia as the Allies. Japan seized Shandong, Germany's area of influence in China.

Link to Wilson's Appeal for Neutrality.

President Wilson initially distanced America by proclaiming neutrality—the traditional U.S. policy toward European wars. Privately, he worried that without neutrality, "our mixed populations would wage war on each other."

Taking Sides

Despite Wilson's appeal for unity at home, ethnic groups took opposing sides. Many German Americans and anti-British Irish Americans (Ireland was then trying to break free from British rule) cheered for the Central Powers. Americans with roots in Allied nations championed the Allied cause. Germany's attack on Belgium confirmed for many that Germany was the archetype of unbridled militarism.

The pro-Allied sympathies of Wilson's administration also weakened the U.S. neutrality proclamation. Wilson shared the conviction with British leaders that a German victory would destroy free enterprise and government by law. If Germany won the war, he prophesied, "it would change the course of our civilization and make the United States a military nation."

U.S. economic links with the Allies also rendered neutrality difficult, if not impossible. England, a long-time customer, flooded America with new orders, especially for arms. Sales to the Allies helped end an American recession. Between 1914 and 1916, American exports to England and France grew 365 percent, from $753 million to $2.75 billion. Largely because of Britain's naval blockade, exports to Germany dropped by more than 90 percent, from $345 million to only $29 million. Loans to Britain and France from private American banks—totaling $2.3 billion during neutrality—financed much of U.S. trade with the Allies. Germany received only $27 million in the same period.

To Germans, the links between the American economy and the Allies meant that the United States had become the Allied arsenal and bank. Americans, however, worried that cutting economic ties with Britain would constitute a nonneutral act in favor of Germany. Under international law, Britain—which controlled the seas—could buy both contraband (war-related goods) and noncontraband from neutrals. It was Germany's responsibility, not America's, to stop such trade as international law prescribed by blockading the enemy's territory, seizing contraband from neutral (American) ships, or by confiscating goods from belligerent (British) ships.

Wilsonianism

"Wilsonianism," the cluster of ideas that Wilson espoused, consisted of traditional American principles (such as democracy and the Open Door) and a vision of the United States as a beacon of freedom. Only the United States could lead the convulsed world into a peaceful era of unobstructed commerce, free-market capitalism, democratic politics, and open diplomacy. "America had the infinite privilege of fulfilling her destiny and saving the world," Wilson claimed. Empires had to be dismantled to honor the principle of self-determination. Critics charged that Wilson often violated his own credos while forcing them on others—as his military interventions in Mexico in 1914, Haiti in 1915, and the Dominican Republic in 1916 testified. Nonetheless, his ideals served American commercial purposes.

To say that U.S. neutrality was never a possibility given ethnic loyalties, economic ties, and Wilsonian preferences is not to say that Wilson sought to enter the war. In early 1917, the president remarked that "we are the only one of the great white nations that is free from war today, and it would be a crime against civilization for us to go in." But go in the United States finally did. Why?

Violations of Neutral Rights The short answer is that Americans got caught in the Allied–Central Power crossfire. The British sought to cripple the German economy by severing neutral trade. They declared a blockade of water entrances to Germany. They seized cargoes and defined a broad list of contraband (including foodstuffs) that they prohibited neutrals from shipping to Germany. Furthermore, to counter German submarines, the British flouted international law by arming their merchant ships and flying neutral (sometimes U.S.) flags. Wilson protested British violations of neutral rights, but London deflected Washington's criticism by paying for confiscated cargoes, while German provocations made British behavior appear less offensive in comparison.

Germany looked for victory at sea by using submarines. In February 1915, Berlin declared a war zone around the British Isles, warned neutral vessels to stay out so as not to be mistakenly attacked, and advised passengers to stay off Allied ships. Wilson informed Germany that it would be held accountable for any losses of American life and property.

Wilson interpreted international law strictly and expected Germans to warn passenger or merchant ships before attacking, so that passengers and crew could disembark safely into lifeboats. The Germans thought that surfacing its slender and sluggish *Unterseebooten* (U-boats) would leave them vulnerable to attack. Berlin protested that Wilson was denying it the one weapon that could break the British economic stranglehold, disrupt the Allies' substantial connection with U.S. producers and bankers, and win the war. To British, Germans, and Americans, naval warfare became a matter of life and death.

The Decision for War

Ultimately, it was the war at sea that doomed the prospects for U.S. neutrality. In early 1915, German U-boats sank ship after ship, notably the *Lusitania* on May 7. Germany's subsequent promise to refrain from attacking passenger liners ended in August when another British vessel, the *Arabic,* was sunk off Ireland. Three Americans died. Germany quickly pledged that an unarmed passenger ship would never again be attacked without warning. But the *Arabic* incident led critics to ask: why not require Americans to sail on American craft? From August 1914 to March 1917, after all, only 3 Americans died on an American ship (the tanker *Gulflight,* sunk by a German U-boat in May 1915), whereas about 190 were killed on belligerent ships.

> How did the Zimmermann telegram finally push Americans to abandon neutrality?

Peace Advocates In March 1916, a U-boat attack on the *Sussex,* a French vessel crossing the English Channel, injured four Americans and brought the United States close to war. Wilson warned Berlin that the United States would sever diplomatic relations if the attacks continued. Again, the Germans retreated. At the same time, U.S.-British relations soured after Britain's crushing of the Easter Rebellion in Ireland and further British restriction of U.S. trade with the Central Powers.

As the United States became more entangled in the Great War, many Americans urged Wilson to keep the nation out. In early 1915, Jane Addams, Carrie Chapman Catt, and other suffragists helped found the Woman's Peace Party, the U.S. section of the Women's International League for Peace and Freedom. Later that year, pacifist Progressives organized an antiwar coalition, the American Union Against Militarism. The businessmen Andrew Carnegie and Henry Ford financed peace efforts, standing with socialist Eugene Debs.

Antiwar advocates emphasized that war drained a nation of its youth, resources, and reform impulse; that it fostered repression at home; that it violated Christian morality; and that wartime business barons reaped huge profits at the expense of the people. Militarism and conscription, Addams pointed out, were what millions of immigrants left behind in Europe. Although the peace movement was splintered, it articulated several ideas that Wilson, who campaigned on a peace platform in the 1916 election, shared. Wilson futilely labored to bring the belligerents to the conference table, urging them in early 1917 to temper their acquisitive war aims and embrace "peace without victory."

Unrestricted Submarine Warfare

In Germany, Wilson's overture went unheeded. Since August 1916, German leaders debated whether to resume the unrestricted U-boat campaign. Opponents feared a break with the United States, but proponents claimed that only through an all-out attack on Britain's supply shipping could Germany win the war. True, the United States might enter the war, but victory might be achieved before U.S. troops crossed the Atlantic. Consequently, in early February 1917, Germany launched unrestricted submarine warfare, attacking all warships and merchant vessels—belligerent or neutral—in the declared war zone. Wilson quickly broke diplomatic relations with Berlin.

In late February, British intelligence intercepted and passed to U.S. officials a telegram addressed to the German minister in Mexico from German foreign secretary Arthur Zimmermann. Its message: If Mexico joined a military alliance against the United States, Germany would help Mexico recover the territories it lost in 1848. Zimmermann hoped to "set new enemies on America's neck—enemies which give them plenty to take care of over there." Although Mexico City rejected Germany's offer, Wilson judged Zimmermann's telegram "a conspiracy against this country." The prospect of a German-Mexican collaboration turned the tide of opinion in the American Southwest, where antiwar sentiment had been strong.

Soon afterward, Wilson asked Congress for "armed neutrality" to defend American lives and commerce, seeking authority to arm American merchant ships, for example. During the debate, Wilson released Zimmermann's telegram to the press. Americans were outraged. Still, antiwar senators Robert M. La Follette and George Norris, among others, saw the armed-ship bill as a blank check for the president to move the country to war, and they filibustered it to death. Wilson armed America's commercial vessels anyway but acted too late to prevent the sinking of several American ships. War cries escalated.

Link to Wilson's War Message to Congress.

War Message and War Declaration

On April 2, 1917, the president stepped before a hushed Congress and enumerated U.S. grievances: Germany's violation of freedom of the seas, disruption of commerce, interference with Mexico, and breach of human rights by killing innocent Americans.

Congress declared war against Germany on April 6 by a vote of 373 to 50 in the House and 82 to 6 in the Senate. (This vote was for war against Germany only; a declaration of war against Austria-Hungary came months later, on December 7.) Montana's Jeannette Rankin, the first woman to sit in Congress, cast a ringing no vote.

For principle, morality, honor, commerce, security, reform—for these reasons, Wilson took the United States into the Great War. The submarine was certainly the culprit that drew a reluctant president and nation into the maelstrom. Critics blamed Wilson's rigid definition of international law and his contention that Americans should be entitled to travel anywhere, even on a belligerent ship loaded with contraband. Most Americans accepted Wilson's view that the Germans had to be checked to ensure an open, orderly world in which U.S. principles and interests would be safe.

The United States went to war to reform world politics, not to destroy Germany. By early 1917, the president concluded that the United States would not be able to claim a seat at the postwar peace conference unless it became a combatant. At the peace conference, Wilson intended to promote the principles he thought essential to a stable world order, to advance democracy and the Open Door, and to outlaw revolution and aggression. In designating the United States an "Associated" rather than an Allied nation, Wilson tried to preserve part of his country's neutrality, but to no avail.

Winning the War

What was the impact of modern, trench warfare on soldiers?

Even before the U.S. declaration of war, the Wilson administration strengthened the military under the banner of "preparedness." The National Defense Act of 1916 provided for increases in the army and National Guard, and for summer training camps modeled on the one in Plattsburgh, New York, where some of America's elite trained in 1915 as "citizen-soldiers." The Navy Act of 1916 started the largest naval expansion in American history.

The Draft and the Soldier

To raise an army, Congress in May 1917 passed the **Selective Service Act**, requiring males between age twenty-one and thirty (later changed to eighteen and forty-five) to register. National service, proponents believed, would prepare the nation for battle and instill patriotism and respect for order, democracy, and personal sacrifice. Critics feared it would lead to the militarization of American life.

Selective Service Act: Law that required all men between twenty-one and thirty (later expanded to eighteen through forty-five) to register with local draft boards.

On June 5, 1917, more than 9.5 million men signed up for the "great national lottery." By war's end, 24 million men were registered by local draft boards. Millions received deferments from military duty because they worked in war industries or had dependents.

The typical soldier was in his early to mid-twenties, white, single, American-born, and poorly educated (most had not attended high school, and perhaps 30 percent could not read or write). Tens of thousands of women enlisted in the army Nurse Corps, served as "hello girls" (volunteer bilingual telephone operators) in the army Signal Corps, and became clerks in the navy and Marine Corps. Some 400,000 African Americans also served in the military. Many southern politicians feared arming blacks, but the army drafted them into segregated units and assigned them to menial labor. They endured abuse and miserable conditions. Ultimately more than 40,000 African Americans would see combat in Europe, and several black units served with distinction in the French army. The all-black 369th Infantry Regiment spent more time in the trenches—191 days—and received more medals than any other American outfit.

Although French officers had their share of racial prejudice and often treated the soldiers from their own African colonies poorly, black Americans serving with the French reported a degree of respect lacking in the American army. The irony was not lost on African American leaders, such as W. E. B. Du Bois, who endorsed the National Association for the Advancement of Colored People's (NAACP) support for the war and urged blacks to volunteer.

Approximately 3 million men evaded draft registration. Some were arrested, others fled to Mexico or Canada, but most stayed home and were never discovered. Another 338,000 men who registered never showed up for induction. According to arrest records, most of these "deserters" and the more numerous "evaders" were lower-income agricultural and industrial laborers. Nearly 65,000 draftees applied for conscientious-objector (CO) status (refusing to bear arms for religious or pacifist reasons), but some changed their minds or failed preinduction examinations. Quakers and Mennonites were numerous among the 4,000 inductees classified as COs. COs who refused noncombat service, such as in the medical corps, faced imprisonment.

John J. Pershing: Commander of American Expeditionary Force that fought in Europe.

American Expeditionary Forces: U.S. soldiers who fought in Europe during World War I.

Trench Warfare

U.S. general **John J. Pershing**, head of the **American Expeditionary Forces** (AEF), insisted that his "sturdy rookies" remain a separate army. He refused to turn over his "soldiers" to Allied commanders, who favored deadly trench warfare. Since fall 1914, zigzag trenches fronted by barbed wire and mines stretched across France. Between the muddy, stinking trenches lay "no man's land," denuded by artillery fire. When ordered out, soldiers would charge enemy trenches only to face machine gun fire and poison gas.

First used by the Germans in April 1915, chlorine gas stimulated overproduction of fluid in the lungs, leading to death by drowning. Gas in a variety of forms (mustard and phosgene, in addition to chlorine) would be used throughout the war, sometimes blistering, sometimes incapacitating, often killing.

The death toll in trench warfare was overwhelming. At the Battle of the Somme in 1916, the British and French suffered 600,000 dead or wounded to earn only 125 square miles; the Germans lost 400,000 men. At Verdun that year, 336,000 Germans perished, and at Passchendaele in 1917 more than 370,000 British men died to gain about 40 miles of mud and barbed wire.

Shell Shock

Not long after arriving on the French front, U.S. units faced the horrors caused by advanced weaponry. Some suffered shell shock, a mental illness also known as war psychosis. Symptoms included a fixed, empty stare; violent tremors; paralyzed limbs; listlessness; jabbering; screaming; and haunting dreams. The illness could strike anyone; even soldiers who appeared courageous cracked after days of incessant shelling and inescapable human carnage. Red Cross canteens, staffed by women volunteers, provided relief and offered haircuts, food, and recreation.

National Archives

A U.S. soldier of Company K, 110th Infantry Regiment, receives aid during fighting at Verennes, France.

In Paris, where forty large houses of prostitution thrived, venereal disease became such a problem that French prime minister Georges Clemenceau offered licensed, inspected prostitutes to the U.S. army. Still, by war's end, about 15 percent of America's soldiers contracted venereal disease, costing the army $50 million and 7 million days of active duty. Periodic inspections, chemical prophylactic treatments, and the threat of court-martial for infected soldiers kept the problem from being greater.

American Units in France

Soldiers filled their diaries and letters with descriptions of local customs and "ancient" architecture, and noted how the grimy and war-torn French countryside bore little resemblance to the groomed landscapes in paintings. "Life in France for the American soldier meant marching in the dirt and mud, living in cellars in filth, being wet and cold and fighting," the chief of staff of the Fourth Division remarked. "He had come to help...but these French people did not seem to appreciate him at all."

With both sides exhausted, the Americans tipped the balance toward the Allies. But not right away. Initially, the U.S. Navy battled submarines and escorted troop carriers and pilots in the U.S. Air Service, flying mostly British and French aircraft, saw limited action. American flying "aces" like Eddie Rickenbacker defeated their German counterparts in aerial "dogfights" and became heroes in France and their own country. But only ground troops could make a decisive difference, and American units did not engage in much combat until after the harsh winter of 1917–1918.

The Bolshevik Revolution

The military and diplomatic situation changed dramatically as a result of the Bolshevik Revolution in Russia. In November 1917, the liberal-democratic government of Aleksander Kerensky, which led the country since the czar's abdication early in the year, was overthrown by by V. I. Lenin's radical socialists. Lenin vowed to change world politics and end imperial rivalries on terms that challenged Wilson's. To Lenin, the war signaled the impending end of capitalism and the rise of a global revolution of workers. For western leaders, the prospect of Bolshevik-style revolutions worldwide was too frightening to contemplate.

In the weeks following their takeover, the Bolsheviks attempted to embarrass the capitalist governments and incite world revolution. They published Allied secret agreements for dividing up the colonies and other territories of the Central Powers if Allies were victorious. Wilson confided to Colonel House that he wanted to tell the Bolsheviks to "go to hell," but he accepted the colonel's argument that he would have to address Lenin's claims that there was little to distinguish the two warring sides and that socialism represented the future.

Fourteen Points: President Wilson's program for world peace; presented to Congress in a 1918 speech, in the midst of World War I.

Link to Wilson's Fourteen Points delivered to the Joint Session of Congress.

Fourteen Points

In the **Fourteen Points**, unveiled in January 1918, Wilson reaffirmed America's commitment to an international system governed by laws and renounced territorial gains as a legitimate war aim. The first five points called for diplomacy "in the public view," freedom of the seas, lower tariffs, armament reductions, and the decolonization of empires. The next eight points specified the evacuation of foreign troops from Russia, Belgium, and France and appealed for self-determination for nationalities in Europe, such as the Poles. For Wilson, the fourteenth point was the mechanism for achieving the others: "a general association of nations," or League of Nations.

Lenin was unimpressed and called for an immediate end to the fighting, the eradication of colonialism, and self-determination for all peoples. Lenin also made a separate peace with Germany—the Treaty of Brest-Litovsk, signed on March 3, 1918. The deal erased centuries of Russian expansion, as Poland, Finland, and the Baltic states were taken from Russia and Ukraine was granted independence. One of Lenin's motives was to allow Russian troops loyal to the Bolsheviks to return home to fight anti-Bolshevik forces attempting to oust his government.

Americans in Battle

In March 1918, the Germans launched a major offensive. By May, they were within 50 miles of Paris. U.S. First Division troops helped blunt the German advance at Cantigny (see Map 23.1). In June the Third Division and French forces held positions along the Marne River at Château-Thierry, and the Second Division attacked the Germans in the Belleau Wood. American soldiers won the battle after three weeks of fighting, but thousands died or were wounded in sacrificial frontal assaults against German machine guns.

Allied victory in the Second Battle of the Marne in July 1918 stemmed German advances. In September, French and American forces took St. Mihiel

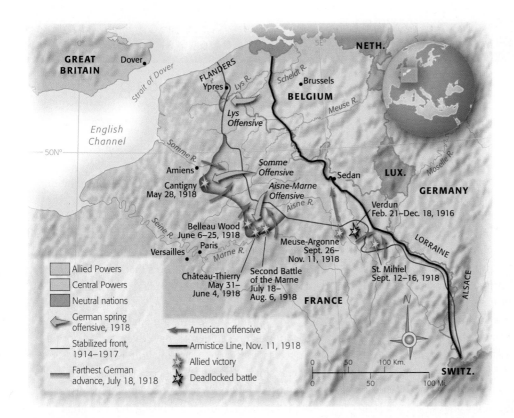

MAP 23.1

American Troops at the Western Front, 1918

America's 2 million troops in France met German forces head-on, ensuring the defeat of the Central Powers in 1918.

Source: Copyright © Cengage Learning

in a ferocious battle. Then, in the Meuse-Argonne offensive, over 1 million Americans joined British and French troops in weeks of combat; some twenty-six thousand Americans died before the Allies claimed the Argonne Forest on October 10. For Germany—its ground and submarine war stymied, its troops and cities mutinous, its allies Turkey and Austria dropping out, its Kaiser abdicating—peace became imperative. The Germans accepted a punishing armistice effective November 11, 1918.

Casualties

The cost of the war is impossible to compute: the belligerents counted 10 million soldiers and 6.6 million civilians dead and 21.3 million people wounded. Fifty-three thousand American soldiers died in battle, and another 62,000 died from disease, mainly a virulent strain of influenza that ravaged the world in late 1918. Economic damage was colossal and output dwindled, contributing to widespread starvation in Europe in the winter of 1918–1919.

The German, Austro-Hungarian, Ottoman, and Russian empires were gone. For a time, it appeared the Bolshevik Revolution might spread westward, as communist

Links to the World

The Influenza Pandemic of 1918

In summer and fall 1918, a terrible plague swept the earth. It claimed more than twice as many lives as the Great War itself—between 25 and 40 million people. In the United States, 675,000 people died.

The first cases were identified in Midwestern military camps in early March. At Fort Riley, Kansas, forty-eight men died. Soldiers shipped out to Europe in large numbers (eighty-four thousand in March), some unknowingly carrying the virus. The illness appeared on the western front in April. By June, an estimated 8 million Spaniards were infected, giving the disease its name, the Spanish flu.

In August, a second, deadlier form of the influenza erupted simultaneously in three cities on three continents: Freetown, Sierra Leone, in Africa; Brest, France, and Boston, Massachusetts. In September, the disease swept down the East Coast, killing twelve thousand Americans.

People could be healthy at the start of the weekend and dead by the end of it. Some experienced rapid accumulation of fluid in the lungs and literally drowned.

Others died slowly. Mortality rates were highest for twenty- to twenty-nine-year-olds—the same group dying in the trenches.

In October, the epidemic hit full force, spreading to Japan, India, Africa, and Latin America. In the United States, 200,000 perished. There was a nationwide short-age of caskets and gravediggers, and funerals were limited to fifteen minutes. Bodies were left in gutters or on front porches, to be picked up by trucks that drove the streets.

Suddenly, in November, for reasons still unclear, the epidemic eased, though the dying continued into 1919. In England and Wales, the final toll was 200,000, while in India the epidemic may have claimed 20 million. It was, in the historian Roy Porter's words, "the greatest single demographic shock mankind has ever experienced." World War I helped spread the disease. Americans, accustomed to thinking that two great oceans isolated them, were reminded that they were immutably linked to the rest of humankind.

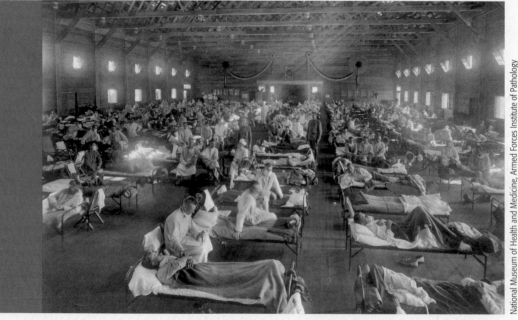

National Museum of Health and Medicine, Armed Forces Institute of Pathology

The influenza pandemic of 1918 perhaps started in earnest here, at Camp Funston, Kansas, in the spring of that year. Soldiers were struck with a debilitating illness they called "knock me down fever."

uprisings shook Germany and parts of central Europe. Before the armistice, revolutionaries temporarily took power in the German cities of Bremen, Hamburg, and Lübeck. In Moscow, the new Soviet state sought to consolidate its power.

Mobilizing the Home Front

How did wartime labor shortages create new opportunities for American workers?

Though the United States was belligerent for only nineteen months, the war had a tremendous impact on America. The federal government expanded its power over the economy to meet war needs and intervened in American life as never before. The enlarged Washington bureaucracy managed the economy, labor force, military, and public opinion. The government spent more than $760 million a month from April 1917 to August 1919. As tax revenues lagged, the administration resorted to deficit spending (see Figure 23.1). To Progressives of the New Nationalist persuasion, the wartime expansion and centralization of government power were welcome, but others worried about the dangers of concentrated federal power.

Business-Government Cooperation The federal government and private business became partners during the war. Early on, the government relied on industrial committees for advice on purchases and prices. But evidence of businesspeople cashing in on the national interest aroused public protest. The head of the aluminum advisory committee, for example, was also president of the largest aluminum company. Consequently, committees were

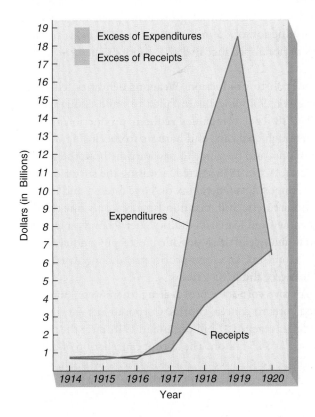

FIGURE 23.1
The Federal Budget, 1914–1920

During the First World War, the federal government spent more money than it received from increased taxes. It borrowed from banks or sold bonds through Liberty Loan drives. To meet the mounting costs of the war, in other words, the federal government had to resort to deficit spending. Expenditures topped receipts by more than $13 billion in 1919. Given this wartime fiscal pattern, moreover, the U.S. federal debt rose from $1 billion in 1914 to $25 billion in 1919.

Source: U.S. Department of Commerce, *Historical Statistics of the United States: Colonial Times to 1957* (Washington, D.C.: Bureau of the Census, 1960), p. 711.

War Industries Board:
Government agency established to coordinate military purchasing, ensure production efficiency, and provide weapons and supplies to the military.

Link to "Recipe for Victory: Food and Cooking in Wartime," a collection of books and government publications documenting the national effort to promote and implement a plan to make food the key to winning World War I.

replaced in July 1917 with a single manager, the **War Industries Board**. The government also suspended antitrust laws and signed cost-plus contracts, guaranteeing companies healthy profits and a means to head off labor strikes with higher wages. Competitive bidding was virtually abandoned, and big business grew bigger.

Hundreds of new government agencies, staffed primarily by businesspeople, used economic controls to shift the nation's resources to the Allies, the AEF, and war-related production. The Food Administration, led by engineer and investor Herbert Hoover, urged Americans to grow "victory gardens" and eat meatless and wheatless meals—but it also set prices and regulated distribution. The Railroad Administration took over the railway industry. The Fuel Administration controlled coal supplies and rationed gasoline. When strikes threatened the telephone and telegraph companies, the federal government seized and ran them.

The largest of the superagencies was the War Industries Board (WIB), headed by the financier Bernard Baruch. This Wall Streeter told Henry Ford that he would dispatch the military to seize his plants unless the automaker accepted WIB limits on car production. Designed to coordinate the national economy, the WIB made purchases, allocated supplies, and fixed prices at levels that business requested. The WIB also ordered the standardization of goods to streamline production. The varieties of automobile tires, for example, were reduced from 287 to 3.

Economic Performance

About one-quarter of American production was diverted to war needs. As farmers enjoyed boom years, they put more acreage into production and mechanized. Gross farm income from 1914 to 1919 increased more than 230 percent. Although manufacturing output leveled off in 1918, wartime demand fueled substantial growth for such industries as steel, which reached a peak production of 45 million tons in 1917, twice the prewar figure. Overall, the gross national product in 1920 stood 237 percent higher than in 1914.

Mistakes happened in the rush to production. Weapons deliveries fell short; the bloated bureaucracy of the War Shipping Board failed to build enough ships. In the severe winter of 1917–1918, coal companies reduced production to raise prices; railroads did not have enough coal cars; and harbors froze, closing out coal barges. People died from pneumonia and freezing. To pay wartime bills, the government increased taxes. The Revenue Act in 1916 started by raising the surtax on high incomes and corporate profits, imposing a federal tax on large estates, and increasing the tax on munitions manufacturers. Still, taxation financed only one-third of the war. The other two-thirds came from loans, including Liberty bonds sold to the American people. The War Revenue Act of 1917 provided a steeply graduated personal income tax, a corporate income tax, an excess-profits tax, and increased excise taxes on alcoholic beverages, tobacco, and luxury items.

Although taxes curbed excessive corporate profiteering, there were loopholes. Sometimes companies inflated costs to conceal profits. Corporate net earnings for 1913 totaled $4 billion; in 1917 they reached $7 billion; and in 1918, after the tax bite and the war's end, they still stood at $4.5 billion. The abrupt cancellation of billions of dollars' worth of contracts at war's end, however, caused a brief downturn, a short boom, and then an intense decline (see Chapter 24).

Visualizing the Past

Eating to Win

The war effort mobilized Americans as never before and also demanded that they make sacrifices. Hebert Hoover's Food Administration used colorful posters to persuade Americans to change their eating habits. The poster below uses bold type and a man standing over a fallen German soldier to send a patriotic message to eat less and save food for the troops. The poster at right has a 1940s Uncle Sam as teacher with a book promoting City and Farm Gardens and asking folks to learn more. The poster below and to the right uses religion (and guilt) to motivate the public. Which poster do you find most effective, and why? How are Americans persuaded today to change their eating habits?

In this colorful 1917 poster, Uncle Sam, posing as a teacher, says, "Garden to cut food costs." The poster offers a free Department of Agriculture "bulletin on gardening—it's food for thought."

Hispanic artist Francis Luis Mora used strong graphics for his 1918 poster showing a man standing over a fallen German soldier.

This 1917 poster showing a bounty of fall harvest fruits and vegetables—"This is what God gives us"—uses richly detailed illustration and colorful red type to get attention and ask the question, "What are you giving so that others may live?"

607

Picture Research Consultants & Archives

Stella Young (1896–1989), a Canadian-born woman from Chelsea, Massachusetts, became widely known as the "Doughnut Girl" because of her service during the First World War with the American branch of the Salvation Army, an international organization devoted to social work. She arrived in France in March 1918 and worked in emergency canteens near the battle front, providing U.S. troops with coffee, cocoa, sandwiches, doughnuts, pie, and fruit. Stella Young became famous when this picture of her wearing a khaki uniform and a "doughboy" steel helmet was widely circulated as a postcard. A piece of sheet music was even written about her. She served again in World War II. Chelsea named a city square in her honor in 1968.

Labor Shortage

For American workers, the full-employment wartime economy increased earnings. With the higher cost of living, however, workers saw minimal improvement. Turnover rates escalated as workers switched jobs for better pay and conditions. Some employers sought to overcome labor shortages by expanding social programs and by establishing personnel departments.

To meet the labor crisis, the Department of Labor's U.S. Employment Service matched laborers with job vacancies, attracting workers from the South and Midwest to war industries in the East. The department also temporarily relaxed the literacy-test and head-tax provisions of immigration law to attract farm labor, miners, and railroad workers from Mexico. As workers crammed into cities, the U.S. Housing Corporation and Emergency Fleet Corporation built row houses in Newport News, Virginia, and Eddystone, Pennsylvania.

The tight wartime labor market meant new job opportunities for women. In Connecticut, a special motion picture, *Mr. and Mrs. Hines of Stamford Do Their Bit*, appealed to housewives' patriotism, urging them to take factory jobs. Although the number of women in the work force increased slightly, many women moved into formerly male jobs, trading domestic service or textile jobs for those in factories, offices or firearms plants. At least 20 percent of employees in the wartime electrical-machinery, airplane, and food industries were women. For the first time, department stores employed African American women as elevator operators and cafeteria waitresses. But most working women were single and remained in the sex-segregated occupations of typists, nurses, teachers, and domestic servants.

Women also participated in the war effort as volunteers, making clothing for refugees and soldiers, serving at Red Cross facilities, and teaching French to nurses assigned to the war zone. Many worked for the Women's Committee of the Council of National Defense, a network of state and local organizations publicizing government mobilization programs, encouraging home gardens, sponsoring drives to sell Liberty bonds, and promoting social welfare reforms. This patriotic work improved prospects for passing the Nineteenth Amendment granting woman suffrage. "We have made partners of women in this war," Wilson said as he endorsed woman suffrage in 1918. "Shall we admit them only to a partnership of suffering and sacrifice . . . and not to a partnership of privilege and right?"

War mobilization encouraged a great migration of southern African Americans to northern cities to work in railroad yards, packing houses, steel mills, shipyards, and coal mines. Between 1910 and 1920, Cleveland's black population swelled by more than 300 percent, Detroit's by more than 600 percent, and Chicago's by 150 percent. All told, about a half-million African Americans moved to the North, with families pooling savings or selling household goods to fund the journey. Most migrants were unmarried and skilled or semiskilled males in their early twenties. Northern wartime jobs provided an escape from low wages, sharecropping, tenancy, crop liens, debt peonage, lynchings, and political disfranchisement. One African American wrote to a friend in Mississippi, "I just begin to feel like a man.... I don't have to humble to no one ... Will vote the next election."

National War Labor Board   To keep factories running smoothly, Wilson instituted the National War Labor Board (NWLB) in early 1918. The NWLB discouraged strikes and lockouts and urged management to negotiate with unions. In July, after the Western Union Company fired eight hundred union members for trying to organize the firm's workers, the president nationalized the telegraph lines and put the laborers back to work. But in September the NWLB ordered striking Bridgeport, Connecticut, machinists back to munitions factories, threatening to revoke the draft exemptions they received for working in an essential industry.

Labor leaders hoped the war would offer opportunities for recognition and better pay through partnership with government. Samuel Gompers threw the AFL's loyalty to Wilson, promising to deter strikes. He and other moderate labor leaders accepted appointments to federal agencies. The antiwar Socialist Party blasted the AFL for becoming a "fifth wheel on [the] capitalist war chariot," but union membership climbed from roughly 2.5 million in 1916 to more than 4 million in 1919.

The AFL, however, could not curb strikes by the radical Industrial Workers of the World (IWW, also known as Wobblies) or rebellious AFL locals, especially those controlled by socialists. In the nineteen war months, more than six thousand strikes expressed workers' demands for a living wage and improved working conditions. Unions sought to create industrial democracy, a more representative workplace with labor helping to determine job categories and content. Defying the AFL, labor parties sprung up in twenty-three states by 1920.

Civil Liberties Under Challenge

> How did free speech come under fire during World War I?

Wilson and his advisers enjoyed the support of newspapers, religious leaders, and public officials. They were less certain, however, about ordinary Americans. An official and unofficial campaign soon began to silence dissenters who questioned Wilson's decision for war or who protested the draft. The Wilson administration compiled one of the worst civil liberties records in American history.

Targets of governmental and quasi-vigilante repression included hundreds of thousands of Americans and aliens: pacifists, conscientious objectors, socialists, radical labor groups, the debt-ridden Oklahoma tenant farmers who staged the Green Corn Rebellion against the draft, the Non-Partisan League, reformers like Robert La Follette and Jane Addams, and others. In the wartime debate over democratic free speech, the concept of "civil liberties" emerged for the first time as a major public policy issue (see "Legacy for a People and a Nation," page 616)

Committee on Public Information: Wartime propaganda agency, headed by journalist George Creel. While claiming merely to combat rumors with facts, the Creel committee in reality publicized the government's version of events and discredited all who questioned that version.

The Committee on Public Information

Spearheading the administration's war campaign war was the **Committee on Public Information** (CPI), formed in April 1917 and headed by Progressive journalist George Creel. Employing talented writers and scholars, the CPI used propaganda to mobilize public opinion. Pamphlets and films demonized the Germans, and CPI "Four-Minute Men" spoke at movie theaters, schools, and churches to pump up patriotism. Encouraged by the CPI, film companies and the National Association of the Motion Picture Industry produced documentaries, newsreels, and anti-German movies, such as *The Kaiser, the Beast of Berlin* (1918).

The committee also urged the press to practice self-censorship and encouraged people to spy on neighbors. Ultrapatriotic groups, such as the Sedition Slammers and the American Defense Society, used vigilantism. In Hilger, Montana, citizens burned history texts mentioning Germany. To avoid trouble, the Kaiser-Kuhn grocery in St. Louis changed its name to Pioneer Grocery. Townspeople in Berlin, Iowa, henceforth hailed from Lincoln. The German shepherd became the Alsatian shepherd.

With Liberty Loan quotas to fill, towns sometimes bullied "slackers" into purchasing bonds. Nativist advocates of "100% Americanism" exploited the atmosphere to exhort immigrants to throw off their Old World cultures. Companies offered English language and naturalization classes and refused jobs and promotions to those who did not learn English. Even labor's drive for compulsory health insurance, which before the war gained advocates in several states, became victimized by the poisoned atmosphere. Many physicians and insurance companies previously denounced health insurance as "socialistic"; after the United States entered the war, they discredited it as "Made in Germany."

Espionage Act: Law that set fines and prison sentences for a variety of loosely defined antiwar activities.

Even institutions that had prided themselves on tolerance became contaminated. Wellesley College economics professor Emily Greene Balch was fired for her pacifist views (she won the Nobel Peace Prize in 1946). Three Columbia University students were apprehended in mid-1917 for circulating an antiwar petition. Columbia fired Professor J. M. Cattell, a distinguished psychologist, for his antiwar stand. His colleague Charles Beard, a historian with a prowar perspective, resigned in protest. Local school boards also dismissed teachers who questioned the war.

Espionage and Sedition Acts

The Wilson administration guided through an obliging Congress the **Espionage Act** (1917) and the Sedition Act (1918), giving the government wide latitude to crack down on critics. The first statute forbade "false statements" designed to impede the draft or promote military insubordination, and it banned from the mails materials considered treasonous. The Sedition Act made it unlawful to obstruct the sale of war

Chicago History Museum

A member of the Eighth Regiment of the Illinois National Guard with his family, circa 1918. Originally organized as a volunteer regiment during the Spanish-American War in 1898, the Eighth Regiment achieved its greatest fame during World War I. The only regiment to be entirely commanded by blacks and headquartered at the only black armory in the U.S., the "Fighting 8th" served with distinction in France, with 143 of its members losing their lives.

bonds and to use "disloyal, profane, scurrilous, or abusive" language to describe the government, the Constitution, the flag, or the military uniform. More than two thousand people were prosecuted under the acts, with many others intimidated into silence.

Progressives and conservatives used the war emergency to throttle the Industrial Workers of the World and the Socialist Party. Government agents raided IWW meetings, and the army put down IWW strikes. By war's end, most of the union's leaders were in jail. In summer 1918, the Socialist Party leader Eugene V. Debs was arrested by federal agents for an oration extolling socialism and freedom of speech—including the freedom to criticize Wilson on the war. Debs told the court what many thought of the Espionage Act: it was "a despotic enactment in flagrant conflict with democratic principles and with the spirit of free institutions." Handed a ten-year sentence, Debs remained in prison until he was pardoned in late 1921.

The Supreme Court endorsed such convictions. In *Schenck v. U.S.* (1919), the Court upheld the conviction of a Socialist Party member who mailed pamphlets urging draft resistance. In wartime, Justice Oliver Wendell Holmes wrote, the First Amendment could be restricted when words "are of such a nature as to create a clear and present danger that they will bring about the substantial evils that Congress has a right to prevent."

Red Scare, Red Summer

How did the Red Scare that took place after World War I dash hopes for a more egalitarian postwar America?

The line between wartime suppression of dissent and the postwar Red Scare is not easily drawn. Together they stabbed at the Bill of Rights and wounded radicalism in America. While wartime fears focused on subversion, after the armistice it was revolution; and while the prewar target was often German Americans, in 1919 it was frequently organized labor. Alarmed by the Russian Revolution and the communist uprisings in Europe, American fears grew in 1919 when the Soviet leadership formed the Communist International (or Comintern) to export revolution worldwide. Terrified conservatives sought out pro-Bolshevik sympathizers (or "Reds," from the red flag used by communists) in the United States, especially in immigrant groups and labor unions.

Labor Strikes   Labor union leaders emerged from the war determined to secure higher wages and retain wartime bargaining rights. Employers instead rescinded benefits they were forced to grant to labor during the war, including recognition of unions. The result more than 3,300 strikes involving 4 million laborers in 1919. On May 1, a day of celebration for workers worldwide, bombs were sent to prominent Americans, though most were intercepted and dismantled. Police never captured the conspirators, but many blamed anarchists and others bent on destroying the American way of life. When the Boston police went on strike in September, some claimed a Bolshevik conspiracy, but others thought it ridiculous to label Boston's Irish American, Catholic cops "radicals."

Unrest in the steel industry in September stirred more ominous fears. Many steelworkers worked twelve hours a day, seven days a week, and lived in squalid housing, counting on the National Committee for Organizing Iron and Steel Workers to improve their lives. When postwar unemployment in the industry climbed and the U.S. Steel Corporation refused to meet with committee representatives, 350,000 workers walked off the job, demanding the right to collective bargaining, a shorter workday, and a living wage. The steel barons hired strikebreakers and sent agents to club strikers. The strike collapsed in early 1920.

Political and business leaders dismissed the steel strike as a foreign threat orchestrated by American radicals. There was no conspiracy, and the American left was splintered. Two defectors from the Socialist Party, John Reed and Benjamin Gitlow, founded the Communist Labor Party in 1919. The rival Communist Party of the United States of America, composed largely of aliens, was launched the same year. But their combined membership did not exceed 70,000—and in 1919 the harassed Socialist Party could muster barely 30,000 members.

American Legion   Although divisiveness signified radicals' weakness, Progressives and conservatives interpreted the advent of new parties as strengthening the radical menace. Organized in May 1919 to lobby for veterans' benefits, the American Legion soon preached an antiradicalism that fueled the Red Scare. By 1920, 843,000 Legion members, mostly middle- and upper-class, embraced an impassioned Americanism demanding conformity.

Wilson's attorney general, A. Mitchell Palmer, also insisted that Americans think alike. A Progressive reformer, Quaker, and ambitious politician, Palmer appointed J. Edgar Hoover to head the Radical Division of the Department of Justice. Hoover compiled index cards naming allegedly radical individuals and organizations. During 1919, agents jailed IWW members; Palmer made sure that 249 alien radicals, including anarchist Emma Goldman, were deported to Russia.

States passed peacetime sedition acts and arrested hundreds of people. Vigilante groups and mobs flourished once again, their numbers swelled by returning veterans. In November 1919, in Centralia, Washington, American Legionnaires broke from a parade to storm the IWW hall. Several were wounded, others arrested, and one ex-soldier was taken from jail by a mob, then beaten, castrated, and shot. The New York State legislature expelled five elected Socialist Party members in early 1920.

Palmer Raids   The Red Scare reached a climax in January 1920 in the Palmer Raids. Planned and directed by J. Edgar Hoover, government agents in thirty-three cities broke into meeting halls and homes without search warrants, jailing four thousand people without counsel. In Boston, four hundred people were detained on bitterly cold Deer Island; two died of pneumonia, one leaped to his death, and another went insane. Because of court rulings and the courageous efforts of Assistant Secretary of Labor Louis Post, most of the arrestees were released, although in 1920–1921 nearly six hundred aliens were deported.

Palmer's disregard for elementary civil liberties drew criticism, with many charging that his tactics violated the Constitution. When Palmer called for a peacetime sedition act, he alarmed liberal and conservative leaders. His prediction that pro-Soviet radicals would incite violence on May Day 1920 proved mistaken—no disturbances occurred anywhere. Palmer, who called himself the "Fighting Quaker," was jeered as the "Quaking Fighter."

Racial Unrest   Palmer also blamed communists for the racial violence that gripped the nation, though the charge was baseless. African Americans realized well before the war ended that their participation did little to change discriminatory white attitudes. The Ku Klux Klan was reviving, and racist films like D. W. Griffith's *The Birth of a Nation* (1915) fed prejudice with its celebration of the Klan and demeaning depiction of blacks. Despite wartime declarations of humanity, between 1914 and 1920, 382 blacks were lynched, some of them in military uniform.

Northern whites who resented "the Negro invasion" rioted, as in East St. Louis, Illinois, in July 1917 and a month later in Houston. During the bloody Red Summer of 1919 (so named by African American author James Weldon Johnson for the blood that was spilled), race riots rocked two dozen cities and towns. The worst violence occurred in Chicago, a favorite destination for migrating African Americans. In the hot days of July 1919, an African American youth swimming at a segregated white beach was hit by a thrown rock and drowned. Soon African Americans and whites were battling each other. Stabbings, burnings, and shootings continued for days until state police restored some calm. Thirty-eight people died, twenty-three African Americans and fifteen whites.

A disillusioned W. E. B. Du Bois vowed a struggle: "We return. We return from fighting. We return fighting." Or, as poet Claude McKay put it after the Chicago riot in a poem he titled "If We Must Die,"

> Like men we'll face the murderous cowardly pack.
> Pressed to the wall, dying, but fighting back.

Black Militancy   Du Bois and McKay reflected a newfound militancy among African American veterans and northern African American communities. Editorials in African American newspapers subjected white politicians to increasingly harsh criticism and implored readers to embrace their prowess and beauty. The NAACP stepped up its campaign for civil rights and equality, vowing in 1919 to publicize the terrors of lynching and seek legislation against it. Other blacks, doubting the potential for equality, turned to the charismatic Jamaican immigrant Marcus Garvey, who called on African Americans to seek a separate black nation.

The crackdown on laborers and radicals, and the resurgence of racism in 1919, dashed wartime hopes. Although the passage of the **Nineteenth Amendment** in 1920, guaranteeing women the right to vote, showed that reform could happen, it was the exception. Unemployment, inflation, racial conflict, labor upheaval, a campaign against free speech inspired disillusionment in the immediate postwar years.

Nineteenth Amendment: Amendment to the Constitution that granted women the right to vote.

The Defeat of Peace

What kept the United States out of the League of Nations?

President Wilson seemed focused on confronting the threat of radicalism more abroad than at home. He revealed his ardent anti-Bolshevism when he ordered five thousand American troops to northern Russia and ten thousand more to Siberia, where they joined other Allied contingents in fighting what was now a Russian civil war. Wilson did not consult Congress. He said the military expeditions would guard Allied supplies and Russian railroads from German seizure and would also rescue Czechs who wished to fight the Germans.

Seeking to smash the infant Bolshevik government, Wilson backed an economic blockade of Russia, sent arms to anti-Bolshevik forces, and refused to recognize Lenin's government. The United States also secretly passed military information to anti-Bolshevik forces and used food relief to shore up Soviet opponents in the Baltic region. Later, at the Paris Peace Conference, Soviets were denied a seat. U.S. troops did not leave Russia until spring 1920, after the Bolsheviks demonstrated their staying power. Wilson faced a monumental task in securing a postwar settlement, though some critics said his own actions did not help. During the 1918 congressional elections, Wilson misstepped in suggesting that patriotism required the election of a Democratic Congress; Republicans blasted the president for questioning their love of country. The GOP gained control of both houses, and Wilson aggravated his political problems by not naming a senator to his advisory American Peace Commission. He also refused to take any prominent Republicans to Paris or to consult with the Senate Foreign Relations Committee before the conference.

Wilson was greeted by adoring crowds in Paris, London, and Rome, but their leaders—Georges Clemenceau of France, David Lloyd George of Britain, and Vittorio Orlando of Italy (with Wilson, the Big Four)—became formidable adversaries. After four years of war, the Allies were not going to be cheated out of the fruits of victory. The late-arriving Americans had not suffered as France and Great Britain had. Germany would have to pay big for the calamity it caused.

Paris Peace Conference   The Big Four tried to work out an agreement, mostly behind closed doors. The victors demanded that Germany (which had been excluded from the proceedings) pay a huge reparations bill. Wilson instead called for a small indemnity, fearing that an economically hobbled Germany might turn to Bolshevism. Unable to moderate the Allied position, the president reluctantly agreed to a clause blaming the war on Germany and to the creation of a commission to determine reparations (later set at $33 billion). Wilson acknowledged that the peace terms were hard, but he also believed that "the German people must be made to hate war."

As for dismantling empires and the principle of self-determination, Wilson could only deliver some of his goals. The conferees created a League-administered "mandate" system that placed former German and Turkish colonies under the control of other imperial nations. Japan gained authority over Germany's Pacific colonies, while France obtained what became Lebanon and Syria, while the British received the three former Ottoman provinces that became Iraq. Britain also secured Palestine, on the condition that it promote "the establishment in Palestine of a national home for the Jewish people" without prejudice to "the civil and religious rights of existing non-Jewish communities"—the so-called Balfour Declaration of 1917.

Elsewhere in Europe, Wilson's prescriptions fared better. Out of Austria-Hungary and Russia came the newly independent states of Austria, Hungary, Yugoslavia, Czechoslovakia, and Poland. Wilson and his colleagues also built a *cordon sanitaire* (buffer zone) of new westward-looking nations (Finland, Estonia, Latvia, and Lithuania) around Russia, to quarantine the Bolshevik contagion.

League of Nations: Wilson's plan for an international deliberative body, viewed as necessary to keep the peace; rejected by the U.S Senate; the U.S. never joined.

League of Nations and Article 10   Wilson worked hardest on the charter for the **League of Nations**, the centerpiece of his plans for the postwar world. He envisioned the League as having power over disputes among states; as such, it could transform international relations. Even so, the great powers would have preponderant say: the organization would have an influential council of five permanent members and elected delegates from smaller states, an assembly of all members, and a World Court.

Wilson identified Article 10 as the "kingpin" of the League covenant: "The Members of the League undertake to respect and preserve as against external aggression the territorial integrity and existing political independence of all Members of the League." Wilson insisted that there could be no future peace with Germany without a league to oversee it.

German representatives initially refused to sign the punitive treaty but submitted in June 1919. They gave up 13 percent of Germany's territory, 10 percent of its population, all of its colonies, and a huge portion of its national wealth. Many people wondered how the League could function in the poisoned postwar atmosphere of humiliation and revenge.

Critics of the Treaty

Critics in the United States were not so sure. In March 1919, thirty-nine senators (enough to deny the treaty the necessary two-thirds vote) signed a petition stating that the League's structure did not adequately protect U.S. interests. Wilson denounced his critics as "pygmy" minds, but he persuaded the peace conference to exempt the Monroe Doctrine and domestic matters from League jurisdiction. Wilson would budge no more. Could his critics not see that membership in the League would give the United States "leadership in the world"?

By summer, criticism intensified: Wilson had bastardized his own principles. He conceded Shandong to Japan and killed a provision affirming the racial equality of all peoples. The treaty ignored freedom of the seas, and tariffs were not reduced. Reparations promised to be punishing on Germany. Critics on the left protested that the League would perpetuate empire. Conservative critics feared that the League would limit American freedom of action in world affairs, stymie U.S. expansion, and intrude on domestic questions. And Article 10 raised serious questions: Would the United States be obligated to use armed force to ensure collective security? And would the League feel compelled to crush colonial rebellions, such as in Ireland or India?

Henry Cabot Lodge of Massachusetts led the Senate opposition to the League. A Harvard-educated Ph.D. and partisan Republican who disliked Wilson, Lodge packed the Foreign Relations Committee with critics and introduced several reservations to the treaty, most importantly that Congress had to approve any obligation under Article 10.

In September 1919, Wilson embarked on a speaking tour of the United States. Growing more exhausted, he dismissed antagonists as "contemptible quitters." While doubts about Article 10 multiplied, Wilson highlighted neglected features of the League charter—such as the arbitration of disputes and an international conference to abolish child labor. In Colorado, the president awoke to nausea and uncontrollable facial twitching. Days later, he suffered a massive stroke that paralyzed his left side. He became peevish and more stubborn, increasingly unable to conduct presidential business. Advised to placate Lodge and other "Reservationist" senatorial critics so the Versailles treaty might receive Congressional approval, Wilson rejected "dishonorable compromise."

Link to Henry Cabot Lodge's reservations regarding the Treaty of Versailles.

Freedom of Speech and the ACLU

Before World War I, those with radical views often received harsh treatment for exercising their freedom of speech. During the war, however, the Wilson administration's suppression of dissidents led some Americans to reformulate the traditional definition of allowable speech. Roger Baldwin, a conscientious objector, and Crystal Eastman, a woman suffrage activist, were among the first to advance the idea that the content of political speech could be separated from the identity of the speaker and that patriotic Americans could—indeed should—defend the right of others to express political beliefs abhorrent to their own. After defending conscientious objectors, Baldwin and Eastman—joined by activists such as Jane Addams, Helen Keller, and Norman Thomas—formed the American Civil Liberties Union (ACLU).

Since 1920, the ACLU, which today has some 300,000 members, has aimed to protect the basic civil liberties of all Americans. It has been involved in almost every major civil liberties case in U.S. courts, among them the landmark *Brown v. Board of Education* case (1954), which ended federal tolerance of racial segregation. More recently, the ACLU was involved in the 1997 Supreme Court case, ruling that the 1996 Communications Act banning "indecent speech" violated First Amendment rights.

Conservatives have long criticized the ACLU for its opposition to official prayers in public schools and its support of legal abortion, as well as its decisions on whose freedom of speech to defend. ACLU proponents counter that it has also defended those on the right, such as Oliver North, a key figure in the 1980s Iran-contra scandal.

Either way, the principle of free speech is today broadly accepted by Americans. Membership in the ACLU skyrocketed since the September 11, 2001, terrorist attacks, due to concern about government policies eroding privacy and legal protections, not only for Americans and foreign detainees at the Guantánamo Bay. Ironically, the Wilson administration's crackdown on dissent produced an expanded commitment to freedom of speech for a people and a nation.

Senate Rejection of the Treaty and League

Twice in November the Senate rejected the Treaty of Versailles and thus U.S. membership in the League. In March 1920, the Senate again voted; this time, a majority (49 for and 35 against) favored the treaty with reservations, but the tally fell short of the two-thirds needed. Had Wilson permitted Democrats to compromise—to accept reservations—he could have achieved his goal of membership in the League, which, despite the U.S. absence, came into being.

At the core of the debate lay a basic foreign policy issue: whether the United States would endorse collective security or continue the more solitary path articulated in George Washington's Farewell Address and the Monroe Doctrine. In a world dominated by imperialist states unwilling to subordinate their strategic ambitions to an international organization, Americans preferred their traditional nonalignment and freedom of choice over binding commitments to collective action. Wilson countered that the League promised something better than the status quo for the United States and the world; collective security in place of the frail protection of alliances and the instability of a balance of power.

An Unsafe World Ultimately, World War I did not make the world safe for democracy, but it did make the United States a greater world power. By 1920, the United States was the world's leading economic power, producing 40 percent of its coal, 70 percent of its petroleum, and half of its pig iron. It also ranked first in world trade. American companies used the war to nudge Germans and British out of foreign markets, especially in Latin America. Meanwhile, the United States shifted from a debtor to a creditor nation, becoming the world's leading banker.

After the disappointment of Versailles, the peace movement revitalized, and the military became more professional. The Reserve Officers Training Corps (ROTC) became permanent; military colleges provided upper-echelon training; and the Army Industrial College, founded in 1924, pursued business-military cooperation in logistics and planning. The National Research Council, created in 1916 with government money and Carnegie and Rockefeller funds, continued a defense research alliance. Tanks, quick-firing guns, armor-piercing explosives, and oxygen masks for high-altitude-flying pilots were among the technological advances emerging from World War I.

The international system born in these years was fragmented. Nationalist leaders active during World War I, such as Ho Chi Minh of Indochina and Mohandas K. Gandhi of India, vowed independence for their peoples. Communism became a disruptive force in world politics, and the Soviets bore a grudge against those who tried to thwart their revolution. The new states in central and eastern Europe proved weak. Germans bitterly resented the harsh peace settlement, and German war debts and reparations problems dogged international order for may years.

Summary

The war years marked the emergence of the United States as a world power, and Americans could take justifiable pride in their contribution to the Allied victory. But the war exposed deep divisions among Americans: white versus black, nativist versus immigrant, capital versus labor, men versus women, radical versus Progressive and conservative, pacifist versus interventionist, nationalist versus internationalist.

During the war, the federal government intervened in the economy and influenced people's everyday lives as never before. Although the Wilson administration shunned reconversion plans (war housing projects, for example, were sold to private investors) and quickly dismantled the many government agencies, the World War I experience of the activist state served as guidance for 1930s reformers battling the Great Depression (see Chapter 25). The partnership of government and business in managing the wartime economy advanced the development of a mass society through the standardization of products and the promotion of efficiency. Wilsonian wartime policies also nourished the concentration of corporate ownership by suspending anti-trust laws. Business power dominated the next decade, while labor entered lean years.

Although the disillusionment evident after Versailles did not cause the United States to adopt isolationism (see Chapter 26), skepticism about America's ability to right wrongs abroad marked the postwar American mood. People recoiled from photographs of shell-shocked faces and of bodies dangling from barbed wire. American soldiers, tired of idealism, craved regular jobs. Many Progressives lost their enthusiasm for crusades, disgusted by the bickering of the victors. By 1920, idealism faded. Americans were sure what their country's newfound status as a leading world power meant for the nation. With uneasiness and a mixed legacy from the Great War, the country entered the 1920s.

Chapter Review

Precarious Neutrality

How viable was U.S. neutrality during World War I?

President Woodrow Wilson, like most Americans, not only embraced neutrality, he took pride in being one of the few western nations to be free from the war for its first three years. Still, U.S. economic links with Allied nations and Wilson's shared belief with the British that a German victory would spell the end of free enterprise and the rule of law made pure neutrality less believable to the outside world and less possible in the long run. The United States relied on sales to Allied nations to end its recession. It was also difficult to claim U.S. neutrality while American banks made extensive loans to Britain and France and sold arms to the Allies. Indirectly, or at least via commerce, the United States was engaged in the war even before officially entering the battlefields.

The Decision for War

How did the Zimmerman telegram finally push Americans to abandon neutrality?

For months in early 1917, Germany had launched a submarine attack on both warships and commercial vessels regardless of stated neutrality or whether the ships were commercial or warships. Americans were already outraged by this when British intelligence passed on to the United States an intercepted telegram in which the German minister in Mexico, Arthur Zimmerman, promised to help Mexico regain the territories it lost to the United States in 1848 if it united with Germany against the United States. The idea was to bring an enemy into America's back yard, but Mexico refused. Wilson released the telegram to the press, and anti-German sentiment skyrocketed. When several American ships were sunk shortly thereafter, war cries heightened, and Wilson asked Congress to declare war against Germany.

Winning the War

What was the impact of modern, trench warfare on soldiers?

Aside from an increased risk of casualty or fatality, trench warfare was mentally debilitating. Battles would be fought in zigzag, muddy, vile-smelling trenches fronted by barbed wire and mines across France. Soldiers would charge enemy trenches, often facing machine gun fire or poison gas. Many surviving soldiers suffered a mental illness dubbed "shell shock." Though not labeled as such at the time, its victims faced a kind of post-traumatic stress disorder, with symptoms including a fixed stare, violent tremors, paralyzed limbs, listlessness, jabbering, screaming, and nightmares. Trench warfare also produced extraordinarily high casualty rates.

Mobilizing the Home Front

How did wartime labor shortages create new opportunities for American workers?

A full employment economy during the war not only meant that workers saw salaries increase (albeit sometimes only slightly ahead of inflation), but they also could easily leave jobs with low salaries or harsh conditions for something better. Worker shortages enabled women to move into higher-paying, formerly male jobs, trading domestic service for factories, shifting from clerking in department stores to stenography and typing, or leaving textile mills for firearms plants. Blacks made gains, too, as war mobilization pushed a half million African Americans to migrate to northern cities, leaving behind low-paid sharecropping and tenant farming for better wages in railroad yards, packing houses, steel mills, shipyards, and coal mines.

Civil Liberties Under Challenge

How did free speech come under fire during World War I?

Passage of the Espionage Act (1917) and the Sedition Act (1918) empowered the federal government to legally prosecute its critics (nearly 20,000 were prosecuted), while others were intimidated into silence. Federal agents arrested Socialist Party leader Eugene V. Debs when he spoke out about socialism and freedom of speech, including the freedom to criticize Wilson's move to war. Professors who articulated pacifist views found themselves fired or forced to resign. Labor unions were similarly quashed. Outside government, ultrapatriotic groups employed vigilantism, burning textbooks that mentioned Germany or bullying people to buy war bonds.

Red Scare, Red Summer

How did the Red Scare that took place after World War I dash hopes for a more egalitarian postwar America?

Fears of a communist invasion began shortly after the Bolshevik Revolution and heightened when the Communist Party promised to spread its message worldwide. As membership in both the Socialist and Communist Parties in the United States grew, nationwide crackdowns began against radicals, with labor a particular target. The passage of the Nineteenth Amendment granting women the right to vote in 1920 provided a glimmer of hope for postwar social improvement, but it was the rare exception. Instead, violations of the Bill of Rights and freedom of speech combined with unemployment, inflation, resurgent racism, and a revitalized Ku Klux Klan to dampen hopes for a more promising, egalitarian postwar America.

The Defeat of Peace

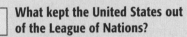

What kept the United States out of the League of Nations?

While the League of Nations was Wilson's brainchild, the United States never joined. To Wilson, the League promised a more stable world based on collective security. But this notion of collectivity was problematic for a people used to operating independently in world affairs. Critics on the left feared that the League would perpetuate empire. Conservative critics worried that it might limit America's freedom to act as it saw fit in world affairs, block U.S. expansion, and intrude on domestic concerns. Worse, critics at home worried about being compelled to participate in collective action deemed necessary by the League.

Suggestions for Further Reading

John Milton Cooper Jr., *Breaking the Heart of the World: Woodrow Wilson and the Fight for the League of Nations* (2001)

Alan Dawley, *Changing the World: American Progressives in War and Revolution, 1914–1924* (2003)

David S. Foglesong, *America's Secret War Against Bolshevism* (1995)

James B. Grossman, *Land of Hope: Chicago, Black Southerners, and the Great Migration* (1989)

Michael Kazin, *A Godly Hero: The Life of William Jennings Bryan* (2006)

Jennifer D. Keene, *Doughboys, the Great War, and the Remaking of America* (2001)

David M. Kennedy, *Over Here: The Home Front in the First World War* (1980)

Thomas J. Knock, *To End All Wars: Woodrow Wilson and the Quest for a New World Order* (1992)

Margaret MacMillan, *Paris 1919: Six Months That Changed the World* (2002)

Robert H. Zieger, *America's Great War: World War I and the American Experience* (2000)

 Go to the CourseMate website for primary source links, study tools, and review materials for this chapter. www.cengagebrain.com

The New Era

24

1920–1929

Beth and Robert Gordon were incompatible marriage partners. Beth was frumpy and demanding; Robert liked to party. One evening at a nightclub, he met Sally Clark, who liked to party, too. When Robert came home smelling of perfume, the couple argued, and then subsequently divorced. Soon, however, he missed Beth's intellect. Meanwhile, Beth bought new clothes and makeup, turning herself into a glamorous beauty. Beth and Robert coincidentally visited the same summer resort and rekindled their romance. When Robert was injured in an accident, Beth nursed him back to health, much to Sally's disappointment. In the end, Beth and Robert remarried.

This story is the plot of the 1920 motion picture *Why Change Your Wife?*—one of dozens of films directed by Cecil B. DeMille. DeMille gave audiences what they fantasized about doing. Beth, Robert, and Sally dressed stylishly, went out dancing, listened to phonograph records and visited resorts. Although DeMille's films and others of the 1920s usually ended by reinforcing marriage, ruling out premarital sex, and supporting the work ethic, they also exuded a new morality. Male and female characters shed old-style values for the pursuit of luxury, fun, and sexual freedom, just as actors such as Gloria Swanson and Thomas Meighan, stars of *Why Change Your Wife?* did in their off-screen lives. In this way, the film was a harbinger of a new era.

During the 1920s, consumerism flourished. Although poverty beset small farmers, workers in declining industries, and non-whites in inner cities, most other people enjoyed a high standard of living relative to previous generations. Spurred by advertising and installment buying, Americans acquired radios, automobiles, real estate, and stocks. As in the Gilded Age, the federal government nurtured a favorable climate for business. In contrast to the Progressive era, few people worried about abuses of power. Yet state and local governments undertook important reforms.

It was an era in which people embraced new technology while trying to preserve long-held values. New forms of amusement coincided with creativity in the arts and advances in science and technology. Changes in work habits, family responsibilities, and healthcare fostered new uses of time and new attitudes about behavior, including encouragements to "think young." While many people experienced material bounty, others continued to endure hardship. The decade's modernism and materialism were appealing to many but unsettling to those who clung to tradition.

The glitter of consumer culture that dominated DeMille's films blinded Americans to rising debt and uneven prosperity. A devastating depression would bring the era to a brutal close.

As you read this chapter, keep the following questions in mind:

* How did developments in technology and the workplace stimulate social change during the 1920s?

* What were the benefits and costs of consumerism, and how did people deal with challenges to old-time values?

* What caused the stock market crash and the ensuing deep depression that signaled the end of the era?

The Age of Play
Movies and Sports | Sports Heroes | Movie Stars and Public Heroes | Prohibition

Cultural Currents
Literature of Alienation | Harlem Renaissance | Jazz

The Election of 1928 and the End of the New Era
Herbert Hoover | Al Smith | Hoover's Administration | Stock Market Crash | Declining Demand | Corporate Debt and Stock Market Speculation | Economic Troubles Abroad; Federal Failures at Home

LEGACY FOR A PEOPLE AND A NATION
Intercollegiate Athletics

SUMMARY

Big Business Triumphant

The 1920s began with economic decline. After World War I, industrial output dropped as wartime orders evaporated. In the West, railroads and the mining industry suffered, and layoffs spread through New England as textile companies abandoned outdated factories for the South's convenient raw materials and cheap labor. When demobilized soldiers flooded the work force, unemployment, around 2 percent in 1919, passed 12 percent in 1921. Consumer spending dwindled, causing more contraction and joblessness.

What helped turn the economy around in the 1920s?

New Economic Expansion

Electric energy prompted a recovery in 1922 that continued unevenly until 1929. Electric motors replaced steam engines, producing goods more cheaply and efficiently. Most urban households now had electric service, enabling them to utilize new appliances, such as refrigerators and vacuum cleaners. The growing economy gave Americans more spending money for new services, too, such as restaurants, beauty salons, and movie theaters. Installment, or time-payment, plans drove the new consumerism. Of 3.5 million automobiles sold in 1923, 80 percent were bought on credit.

Although Progressive era trust-busting had reined in big business, it had not eliminated oligopoly, the control of an entire industry by one or a few large firms. By the 1920s, a few sprawling companies, such as U.S. Steel and General Electric, dominated basic industries, and oligopolies controlled marketing, distribution, and finance.

Chronology

1920	Volstead Act implements prohibition (Eighteenth Amendment)
	Nineteenth Amendment ratified, legalizing vote for women in federal elections
	Harding elected president
	KDKA transmits first commercial radio broadcast
1920–21	Postwar deflation and depression
1921	Federal Highway Act funds national highway system
	Emergency Quota Act establishes immigration quotas
	Sacco and Vanzetti convicted
	Sheppard-Towner Act allots funds to states to set up maternity and pediatric clinics
1922	Economic recovery raises standards of living
	Coronado Coal Company v. United Mine Workers rules that strikes may be illegal actions in restraint of trade
	Bailey v. Drexel Furniture Company voids restrictions on child labor

	Federal government ends strikes by railroad shop workers and miners
	Fordney-McCumber Tariff raises rates on imports
1923	Harding dies; Coolidge assumes presidency
	Adkins v. Children's Hospital overturns a minimum wage law affecting women
1923–24	Government scandals (Teapot Dome) exposed
1924	Snyder Act grants citizenship to all Indians not previously citizens
	National Origins Act revises immigration quotas
	Coolidge elected president
1925	Scopes trial highlights battle between religious fundamentalists and modernists
1927	Lindbergh pilots solo transatlantic flight
	The Jazz Singer, first movie with sound, released
1928	Stock market soars
	Hoover elected president
1929	Stock market crashes; Great Depression begins

Associations and "New Lobbying"

Business and professional organizations also expanded in the 1920s. Retailers and manufacturers formed trade associations to swap information, and professionals expanded their organizations. Farm bureaus promoted scientific agriculture and tried to stabilize markets. These special-interest groups participated in what is called the "new lobbying." With government playing an increasingly influential role, hundreds of organizations sought to convince legislators to support their interests.

Government policies helped business thrive, and legislators depended on lobbyists' expertise. Prodded by lobbyists, Congress cut taxes on corporations and wealthy individuals in 1921 and passed the Fordney-McCumber Tariff Act in 1922. Presidents Warren G. Harding, Calvin Coolidge, and Herbert Hoover appointed cabinet officers who were favorable toward business. Regulatory agencies, such as the Federal Trade Commission and the Interstate Commerce Commission, cooperated with corporations more than they regulated them. Key Supreme Court decisions sheltered business from government regulation and hindered organized labor. In *Coronado Coal Company v. United Mine Workers* (1922), Chief Justice and former president William Howard Taft ruled that a striking union, like a trust, could be prosecuted for illegal restraint of trade, yet in *Maple Floor Association v. U.S.* (1929), the Court decided that trade associations that distributed anti-union information were not acting in restraint of trade. The Court also voided restrictions on child labor (*Bailey v. Drexel Furniture Company,* 1922), and overturned a minimum wage law affecting women because it infringed on liberty of contract (*Adkins v. Children's Hospital,* 1923).

Setbacks for Organized Labor

Public opinion turned against organized labor in the 1920s, linking it with communism brought to America by radical immigrants. Using Red Scare tactics, the Harding administration in 1922 obtained a sweeping court injunction to quash a strike by 400,000 railroad workers. State and federal courts issued injunctions to prevent other strikes and permitted businesses to sue unions for damages suffered from labor actions.

Some companies imposed yellow dog contracts, which made refusal to join a union a condition of employment. Companies also countered the appeal of unions by offering pensions, profit sharing, and company-sponsored picnics and sporting events—a policy known as welfare capitalism. State legislators aided employers by prohibiting closed shops (workplaces where union membership was mandatory) and permitting open shops (where employers could hire nonunion employees). As a result of court action, welfare capitalism, and ineffective leadership, union membership fell from 5.1 million in 1920 to 3.6 million in 1929.

Languishing Agriculture

Agriculture languished during the 1920s, as farmers faced international competition and went into debt when they tried to increase productivity by investing in machines, such as harvesters and tractors. Irrigation and mechanization made large-scale farming so efficient that fewer farmers could produce more crops than ever before. As a result, crop prices plunged, big agribusinesses took over, and small landholders and tenants struggled, especially as incomes plummeted and debts rose.

Politics and Government

A series of Republican presidents extended Theodore Roosevelt's government-business cooperation, but they made government a compliant coordinator rather than the active manager Roosevelt advocated. President **Warren G. Harding**, elected in 1920, was a symbol of government's good will toward business. He captured 16 million popular votes to 9 million for the Democratic nominee, Ohio governor James M. Cox. (The total vote in the 1920 presidential election was 36 percent higher than in 1916, reflecting the first-time participation of women voters.)

What happened to Progressive reform in the 1920s?

Warren G. Harding: 29th President of the United States in office from 1921 to 1923.

Scandals of the Harding Administration

A small-town newspaperman and senator from Ohio, Harding appointed assistants who promoted business growth, notably Secretary of State Charles Evans Hughes, Secretary of Commerce Herbert Hoover, Secretary of the Treasury Andrew Mellon, and Secretary of Agriculture Henry C. Wallace. Harding also backed reforms. But he had personal weaknesses, notably, his extramarital affairs and poor judgment in appointments. In 1917, he began a relationship with Nan Britton, thirty-one years his junior, that resulted in a daughter in 1919. Britton revealed the secret in a book, *The President's Daughter* (1927), although Harding never acknowledged his illegitimate offspring.

Of greater consequence, Harding appointed cronies who used office holding for personal gain. Charles Forbes, head of the Veterans Bureau, went to federal prison, convicted of fraud and bribery in government contracts. Notoriously, a

Teapot Dome: Scandal that rocked the Harding administration after Harding's Secretary of the Interior was found guilty of secretly leasing government oil reserves to two oilmen in exchange for a bribe.

congressional inquiry in 1923 and 1924 revealed that Secretary of the Interior Albert Fall accepted bribes to lease government property to oil companies. Fall was fined $100,000 and spent a year in jail for his role in the so-called **Teapot Dome** scandal, named for the Wyoming oil reserve he handed to the Mammoth Oil Company.

By mid-1923, Harding had become disillusioned by these scandals. On a speaking tour that summer, he became ill and died in San Francisco on August 2. Although his death preceded revelation of the Teapot Dome scandal, some speculated that Harding committed suicide to avoid impeachment or was poisoned by his wife. Most evidence, however, points to death from natural causes, probably heart disease.

Calvin Coolidge: 30th President of the United States; took office after the death of President Warren Harding in 1923.

Coolidge Prosperity

Vice President **Calvin Coolidge**, who became president, was less outgoing than Harding. As governor of Massachusetts, Coolidge attracted national attention in 1919 with his stand against striking Boston policemen and won business support and the vice-presidential nomination in 1920.

Respectful of private enterprise and aided by Andrew Mellon, who was retained as treasury secretary, Coolidge's administration reduced federal debt, lowered income-tax rates (especially for the wealthy), and began construction of a national highway system. With farm prices falling, Congress twice passed bills to establish government-backed price supports for staple crops (the McNary-Haugen bills of 1927 and 1928). Resembling the 1890s Farmers' Alliances subtreasury scheme, these bills would have established a system whereby the government would buy surplus farm products and either hold them until prices rose or sell them abroad. Coolidge, however, vetoed the measures as improper government interference in the market economy.

"Coolidge prosperity" was the decisive issue in the 1924 presidential election. Both major parties ran candidates who favored private initiative over government intervention. At their national convention, Democrats voted 542 to 541 against condemning the revived Ku Klux Klan, and deadlocked for 103 ballots between southern prohibitionists, who supported former treasury secretary William G. McAdoo, and antiprohibition easterners, who backed New York's governor, Alfred E. Smith. They finally compromised on John W. Davis, a New York corporate lawyer.

Remnants of the Progressive movement, along with farm, labor, and socialist groups, formed a new Progressive Party and nominated Robert M. La Follette, the aging Wisconsin reformer. The new party stressed public ownership of railroads and power plants, conservation of natural resources, aid to farmers, rights for organized labor, and regulation of business. Coolidge beat Davis by 15.7 million to 8.4 million popular votes and 382 to 136 electoral votes. La Follette received 4.8 million popular votes and 13 electoral votes.

Extensions of Progressive Reform

The urgency for political and economic reform that inspired the previous Progressive generation faded in the 1920s. Much reform, however, occurred at state and local levels. Following pre–World War I initiatives, thirty-four states instituted or expanded workers' compensation laws and public welfare programs in the 1920s. By 1926, every major city and many smaller ones had planning and zoning commissions to harness physical growth to the common good. A new generation of reformers who later influenced national affairs acquired experience in statehouses, city halls, and universities.

Indian Affairs and Politics

Organizations such as the Indian Rights Association, the Indian Defense Association, and the General Federation of Women's Clubs worked to obtain justice and social services for Native Americans, including better education and return of tribal lands. But like other minorities, Indians met discrimination and pressure to assimilate. Severalty, the federal policy created by the Dawes Act of 1887, allotting land to individuals rather than to tribes, failed to make Indians self-supporting. Attached to their land, they showed little inclination to move to cities. Whites still hoped to convert native peoples into "productive" citizens, typically ignoring indigenous cultures. Reformers were especially critical of Indian women, who rejected middle-class homemaking habits and balked at sending their children to boarding schools.

Citizenship status remained unclear. The Dawes Act had conferred citizenship on Indians who accepted land allotments, but not those who remained on reservations. After several court challenges, Congress passed an Indian Citizenship Act (Snyder Act) in 1924, granting citizenship to all Indians. President Hoover reinforced this measure's intent by stating that citizenship was the best means for Indians to assimilate.

Women and Politics

Ratification of the Nineteenth Amendment in 1920 gave women the vote, but they remained excluded from local and national power structures. Instead, they worked through voluntary organizations to lobby legislators on issues such as birth control, peace, education, Indian affairs, or opposition to lynching.

In 1921, women's groups persuaded Congress to pass the **Sheppard-Towner Act**, allotting funds to states to create maternity and pediatric clinics to reduce infant mortality. (The measure ended in 1929, when Congress, pressured by physicians, canceled funding.) The Cable Act of 1922 reversed the law under which an American woman who married a foreigner assumed her husband's citizenship, allowing her to retain U.S. citizenship. At the state level, women achieved some rights, such as the ability to serve on juries.

As new voters, however, women pursued diverging goals. Women in the National Association of Colored Women, for example, fought for the rights of minorities. Other groups, such as the National Woman's Party, pressed for an equal rights amendment to ensure women's equality under the law. But such activity alienated the National Consumers League, the Women's Trade Union League, the League of Women Voters, and other organizations that supported protective legislation to limit hours and improve conditions for employed women.

Sheppard-Towner Act: Sought to reduce infant mortality by providing matching funds to states to create prenatal and child health clinics. It was repealed in 1929.

A Consumer Society

How did the emergence of a consumer society change American life?

The consumerism depicted in *Why Change Your Wife?* reflected important economic changes affecting the nation. Between 1919 and 1929, the gross national product—the total value of goods and services produced in the United States—swelled by 40 percent. Wages and salaries also grew (though not as drastically), while the cost of living remained stable. People had more purchasing power (see Table 24.1). By 1929, two-thirds of all Americans had electricity, compared with one-sixth in 1912. In 1929, one-fourth of all families owned vacuum cleaners. Many could afford such goods as radios, cosmetics, and movie tickets because several

TABLE 24.1   Consumerism in the 1920s

1900	
2 bicycles	$ 70.00
Wringer and washboard	5.00
Brushes and brooms	5.00
Sewing machine (mechanical)	25.00
TOTAL	$ 105.00
1928	
Automobile	$ 700.00
Radio	75.00
Phonograph	50.00
Washing machine	150.00
Vacuum cleaner	50.00
Sewing machine (electric)	60.00
Other electrical equipment	25.00
Telephone (per year)	35.00
TOTAL	$1,145.00

Source: From an article in *Survey Magazine* in 1928 reprinted in *Another Part of the Twenties*, by Paul Carter. Copyright 1977 by Columbia University Press. Reprinted with permission of the publisher.

family members worked or because the breadwinner took a second job. Nevertheless, new products and services were available to more than just the rich.

Effects of the Automobile

During the 1920s, automobile registrations soared from 8 million to 23 million, and by 1929 there was one car for every five Americans. Mass production and competition made cars affordable. A Ford Model T cost less than $300, and a Chevrolet sold for $700 by 1926—when factory workers earned about $1,300 a year and clerical workers about $2,300. At those prices, people could consider the car a necessity rather than a luxury.

Cars altered American life. Owners abandoned crowded streetcars; roads became cleaner as autos replaced horses. Women drivers achieved newfound independence. By 1927, most autos were enclosed (they previously had open tops), creating new private space for courtship and sex. Mostly, the car was the ultimate social equalizer. As one writer observed in 1924, "It is hard to convince Steve Popovich, or Antonio Branca, or plain John Smith that he is being ground into the dust by Capital when at will he may drive the same highways…and get as much enjoyment from his trip as the modern Midas."

After World War I, motorists joined farmers and bicyclists in their decades-old campaign for improved roads. In 1921, Congress passed the Federal Highway Act, providing funds for state roads, and in 1923 the Bureau of Public Roads planned a national highway system. Roadbuilding inspired such technological developments as mechanized graders and concrete mixers. The oil-refining industry, which produced gasoline, became powerful. In 1920, the United States produced about 65 percent of the world's oil. Public officials to pay more attention to traffic control, with General Electric Company producing the first timed stop-and-go traffic light in 1924.

Advertising

By 1929, more money was spent on advertising than on formal education. Blending psychological theory with practical cynicism, advertising theorists asserted that any people's tastes could be manipulated. For example, cosmetics manufacturers like Max Factor, Helena Rubenstein, and African American entrepreneur Madame C. J. Walker used movie stars and beauty advice in magazines to entice female customers. Other advertisers hired baseball star Babe Ruth to endorse food and sporting goods.

Radio

Radio became an influential advertising medium. By 1929, over 10 million Americans owned radios, spending $850 million annually on radio equipment. In the early 1920s, Congress decided that broadcasting should be a private enterprise, not a tax-supported public service as in Great Britain. American programming focused on entertainment rather than educational content, because entertainment attracted larger audiences and therefore higher advertising profits. Station KDKA in Pittsburgh, owned by Westinghouse Electric Company, pioneered commercial radio in 1920. In 1922, an AT&T-run station in New York City broadcast advertisements—commercials. By late 1922, there were 508 commercial stations.

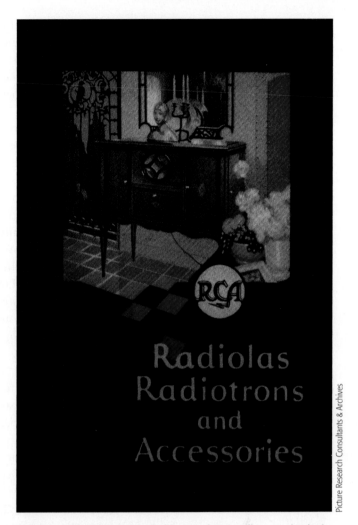

As large as today's big-screen television sets, luxury radios served as both entertainment machines and decorative furniture. The RCA "Radiola" was an early radio receiver combined with speakers and housed in an attractive wood cabinet.

Radio transformed American society. In 1924, both political parties broadcast their presidential nominating conventions, enabling candidates to reach more Americans. And radio's mass marketing and standardized programming blurred ethnic boundaries and helped create a homogeneous American culture, which television and other mass media expanded throughout the twentieth century.

Cities, Migrants, and Suburbs

What fueled the growth of cities in the 1920s?

The 1920 federal census revealed that, for the first time, a majority of Americans lived in urban areas (places with 2,500 or more people). Growth in manufacturing and services helped propel urbanization. Industries like steel, oil, and auto production energized Birmingham, Houston, and Detroit; services and retail trades boosted Seattle, Atlanta, and Minneapolis.

During the 1920s, 6 million Americans left farms for the city. Many young people, seeking excitement and openness, moved to regional centers like Kansas City or to the West. Between 1920 and 1930, California's population increased 67 percent, and California became a highly urbanized state while retaining its status as a leader in agricultural production.

African American Migration

African Americans, in what has come to be called the Great Migration, made up a sizable portion of people on the move during the 1920s. Pushed from cotton farming by a boll weevil plague and lured by industrial jobs, 1.5 million blacks moved, doubling the African American populations of New York, Chicago, Detroit, and Houston. They found jobs not unlike those in the South—janitors, longshoremen, and domestic servants for whites.

Forced by low wages and discrimination to seek cheap housing, black newcomers squeezed into ghettos like Chicago's South Side. But blacks found better neighborhoods closed to them. They could either crowd into densely populated black neighborhoods or spill into nearby white neighborhoods. Fears of "invasion" sparked violence and prompted neighborhood associations to adopt restrictive covenants, whereby white homeowners pledged not to sell or rent to blacks.

Marcus Garvey

In response to discrimination and violence, thousands of urban blacks joined movements that glorified racial independence. The most influential of these black nationalist groups was the Universal Negro Improvement Association (UNIA), led by **Marcus Garvey**, a Jamaican immigrant who believed blacks should separate from corrupt white society. Unlike the NAACP, formed by elite African American and white liberals (see page 553), the UNIA was comprised exclusively of blacks, largely from the lower classes.

Marcus Garvey: Charismatic black leader who promoted racial pride and independence and believed blacks should separate from white society.

Garvey furthered Booker T. Washington's ideas of economic independence (see page 552) by promoting black-owned businesses that would manufacture and sell products to black consumers. His newspaper, *Negro World,* preached black independence, and he founded the Black Star steamship line to transport manufactured goods among black businesses in North America, the Caribbean, and Africa. In 1919, the U.S. Bureau of Investigation (BOI), forerunner to the FBI, began monitoring Garvey's radical activities, and the BOI's deputy head, J. Edgar Hoover, proclaimed Garvey to be one of the most dangerous blacks in America.

The UNIA declined in the mid-1920s after mismanagement plagued Garvey's plans. In 1923, Garvey was deported for mail fraud involving the bankrupt Black Star line. His prosecution, however, was politically motivated. Middle-class African American leaders, such as W. E. B. Du Bois, opposed the UNIA, fearing that its extremism would undermine their efforts. Nevertheless, for years the UNIA attracted a large following (contemporaries estimated 500,000; Garvey claimed 6 million), and Garvey's speeches instilled in many African Americans a heightened sense of racial pride.

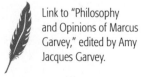

Link to "Philosophy and Opinions of Marcus Garvey," edited by Amy Jacques Garvey.

Newcomers from Mexico and Puerto Rico

The newest immigrants came from Mexico and Puerto Rico, where declining fortunes pushed people off the land. During the 1910s, Anglo farmers' associations encouraged Mexicans to provide cheap labor, and by the 1920s Mexican migrants constituted three-fourths of farm labor in the American West. Growers treated Mexican laborers as slaves, paying them extremely low wages. Although some achieved middle-class status, most crowded into urban low-rent districts plagued by poor sanitation, poor police protection, and poor schools. Mexicans moved back and forth across the border, creating a way of life that Mexicans called *sin fronteras*—without borders.

The 1920s also witnessed an influx of Puerto Ricans to the mainland, as a shift in the island's economy from sugar to coffee production created a labor surplus. Attracted by contracts from employers seeking cheap labor, they created *barrios* (communities) and found jobs in factories, hotels, restaurants, and domestic service. Like Mexicans, Puerto Ricans maintained customs and developed businesses—*bodegas* (grocery stores), cafés, boarding houses—and social organizations to help them adapt to American society. Educated elites—doctors, lawyers, and business owners—became community leaders.

Suburbanization   As urbanization peaked, suburban growth accelerated. Prosperity and automobile transportation in the 1920s made suburbs more accessible to those wishing to leave urban neighborhoods. Between 1920 and 1930, suburbs of Chicago (such as Oak Park and Evanston), Cleveland (Shaker Heights), and Los Angeles (Burbank and Inglewood) grew five to ten times faster than nearby central cities. Los Angeles builders alone erected 250,000 homes for auto-owning suburbanites. Most suburbs were middle- and upper-class bedroom communities; some, like Highland Park (near Detroit) were industrial satellites.

Suburbanites wanted to escape big-city crime, grime, and taxes, and they fought to preserve control over police, schools, and water and gas services. Particularly in the Northeast and Midwest, the suburbs' independence prevented central cities from accessing the resources and tax bases of wealthier suburban residents. Population dispersal spread the environmental problems of city life—trash, pollution, noise—across the metropolitan area.

Most of the consumers who jammed shops, movie houses, and sporting arenas, and who embraced fads like crossword puzzles and miniature golf, lived in or around cities. People defied older morals by patronizing speakeasies (illegal saloons during prohibition), wearing outlandish clothes, and dancing to jazz, while others reminisced about the simplicity of a world gone by.

New Rhythms of Everyday Life

How did technological advances impact social life in America in the 1920s?

Amid changes, people increasingly split their day into distinct time compartments: work, family, and leisure. For many, mechanization and higher productivity enabled employers to shorten the work week for many industrial laborers from six days to five and a half. White-collar employees often worked a forty-hour week, enjoyed the weekend off, and received annual vacations.

Family size decreased between 1920 and 1930 as birth control became more widely practiced. Over half the women married in the 1870s and 1880s had five or more children; in the 1920s, only 20 percent did. Meanwhile, divorce rates rose from 1 divorce for every 7.5 marriages in 1920 to 1 in 6 by 1929.

Links to the World

Pan American Airways

The Pan American Heritage Web Site

Providing air transport connections to the Caribbean, Central America, and South America, Pan American Airways established the first major passenger and cargo links between the United States and other nations. By the early 1930s, flights were so numerous that the timetable announced in this illustration consisted of twelve pages.

Air transportation and airmail service between the United States and Latin America began in the 1920s, but anti-American hostility in the region made establishing connections difficult. In 1926, the U.S. government, fearful that German aircraft might bomb the Panama Canal in future conflicts, signed a treaty with Panama giving American airplanes exclusive rights to Panamanian airports. Charles Lindbergh (see page 639) and a formerly obscure pilot, Juan Trippe, played key roles in expanding American air service throughout Latin America.

With help from his father-in-law, a banking partner of J. P. Morgan, Trippe established Pan American Airways (informally known as Pan Am) in 1927 and won a contract to carry mail between Florida and Cuba. In December of that year, Lindbergh charmed the Mexicans into accepting airline links to the United States. The next year, Lindbergh joined Pan Am and began flying company planes to Central and South America, helping Trippe initiate mail and passenger service to Panama, Mexico, and other Latin American countries in 1929. Trippe advertised to wealthy Americans the opportunity to escape prohibition and enjoy Caribbean beaches via Pan Am.

Pan Am built airports that became essential connections between Latin America and the rest of the world. Trippe's employees created aerial maps that provided navigational aids. Pan Am linked Latin America more closely with the United States and helped unite parts of Latin America that had previously been divided by impenetrable mountain ranges. Yet Pan Am would resort to almost any tactic to build an airport: it cooperated with unsavory dictators, engaged in bribery, and violated human rights, in one case helping Bolivian police corral local Indians behind barbed wire for days to clear land for an airport.

Still, Pan Am enabled Americans (mostly the wealthy) to travel abroad and brought more foreigners to the United States. In 1942, its aircraft became the first to fly around the world. In the 1940s, the company began offering flights to Europe and Africa. Until its demise in 1991, Pan Am provided a leading link between the United States and the rest of the world.

630

Expansion of Suburbs in the 1920s

An outburst of housing and highway construction made possible the rapid growth of suburbs in the 1920s. The Chicago suburb of Niles Centre, later renamed Niles Center and ultimately called the Village of Skokie, was incorporated in 1888. Aided by the service of commuter railroads, the village began to grow in the early 1900s, and in 1913 the first permanently paved road in Cook County was built in Niles Center. After 1920, a real estate boom began, and by the mid 1920s the village had its own water, sewer, and street lighting services, along with many more paved roads. Wealthy Chicagoans such as utilities and railroad investor Samuel Insull built lavish homes in Niles Center, and soon commercial and office buildings sprang up along the major thoroughfares. Population grew so rapidly that the community boasted that it was "The World's Largest Village." The Great Depression halted the boom in 1929, but significant growth resumed after the Second World War. How do you think daily life changed as a result of the growth of suburbs?

Skokie Historical Society

In some areas, real estate developers laid out streets and blocks in burgeoning suburbs, enticing offices, stores, and institutions before residences were even built. This photograph of Niles Center, Illinois, taken from an airplane around 1927, reveals how roads and automobiles had become essential to suburban expansion.

Skokie Historical Society

As the 1920s proceeded, suburban housing construction accelerated. These private homes, one still under construction, along Brown Street in Niles Center, Illinois, in 1926 reveal how an open prairie was converted into a residential community. Note the presence of autos, a flatbed truck, and electrical wires, all critical to suburban life.

Household Management

Machines lightened some household tasks. Especially in middle-class households, electric irons and washing machines simplified wives' chores. Gas- and oil-powered central heating and hot-water heaters eliminated the hauling of wood, coal, and water; maintaining a kitchen fire; and removing ashes.

But technology and economic change also created new demands on women's time. Daughters of working-class families stayed in school longer, making them less available to help with housework. Advertisers of washing machines, vacuum cleaners, and commercial soap tried to make women feel guilty for homes that weren't spotlessly clean. No longer a producer of food and clothing as her ancestors were, a housewife became the family's shopper and chauffeur. One survey found that urban housewives spent seven and one-half hours per week driving to shop and transport children.

Health and Life Expectancy

With the discovery of vitamins between 1915 and 1930, nutritionists advocated certain foods to prevent illness, and giant companies advertised products as filled with vitamins and minerals. Producers of milk, canned fruits and vegetables, and other foods made claims that were hard to dispute because little was known about these invisible, tasteless ingredients. Welch's Grape Juice, for example, avoided mentioning its excess sugars when it advertised that it was "Rich in Health Values."

Better diets and improved hygiene made Americans healthier. Life expectancy at birth increased from fifty-four to sixty years between 1920 and 1930, and infant mortality decreased by two-thirds. Public sanitation and research in bacteriology reduced life-threatening diseases, such as tuberculosis and diphtheria. But medical progress did not benefit everyone equally; infant mortality rates were 50 to 100 percent higher among nonwhites than among whites, and tuberculosis in inner-city slums remained alarmingly common. Nevertheless, the total population over age sixty-five grew 35 percent between 1920 and 1930.

Older Americans and Retirement

Industrialism put premiums on youth and agility, pushing older people into poverty from forced retirement and reduced income. Most European countries established state-supported pension systems in the early 1900s. Many Americans, however, believed that pensions smacked of socialism and that individuals should prepare for old age by saving in their youth.

Most inmates in state poorhouses were older people, and almost one-third of Americans age sixty-five and older depended financially on someone else. Few employers, including the federal government, provided for retired employees. Resistance to pension plans broke at the state level in the 1920s. Led by the physician Isaac Max Rubinow and the journalist Abraham Epstein, reformers persuaded voluntary associations, labor unions, and legislators to endorse old-age assistance. By 1933, almost every state provided at least minimal support to needy elderly, opening the door to a national program of old-age insurance.

Social Values

New influences altered habits and values. Women and men wore more casual and colorful styles than their parents' generation. The line between acceptable and inappropriate behavior blurred as smoking, drinking, and frankness about sex became fashionable. Birth control gained a large following in respectable circles. Newspapers, magazines, motion pictures (such as *Why Change Your Wife?*), and popular songs (such as "I Don't Care") made certain that Americans did not suffer from "sex starvation."

Because state child-labor laws and compulsory-attendance rules kept children in school longer, peer groups played a more influential role in socializing youngsters than parents. School classes, sports, and clubs constantly brought together children of the same age, separating them from the influence of adults.

Between 1890 and the mid-1920s, ritualized middle- and upper-class courtship, consisting of men's formally "calling on" women and chaperoned social engagements, faded in favor of "dating," without supervision. Unmarried young people, living away from family restraints, eagerly went on dates to new commercial amusements, such as movies and nightclubs. Automobiles made dating more extensive. A woman's job seldom provided sufficient income for entertainments, but she could enjoy them if a man "treated" her. Romance, and at times sexual exploitation, accompanied the practice, especially when a woman was expected to trade sexual favors for being treated. Under the courtship system, a woman controlled who could "call" on her, but reliance on a man's money for entertainment presented difficult moral choices.

Women in the Work Force

After World War I, women continued to stream into the labor force. By 1930, 10.8 million women held paying jobs, an increase of 2 million since war's end. Although the proportion of women working in agriculture shrank, their proportion in categories of urban jobs grew or held steady (see Figure 24.1). Sex segregation persisted; most women took jobs that men seldom sought. Thus, over 1 million women worked as teachers and nurses. Some 2.2 million women were typists, bookkeepers, and filing clerks, a tenfold increase since 1920. Another 736,000 were store clerks,

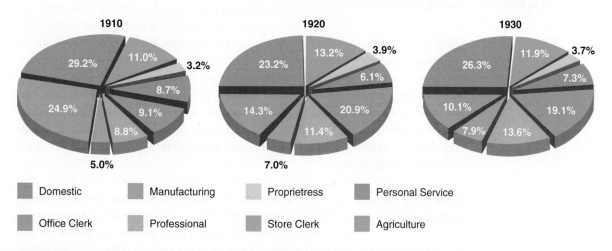

FIGURE 24.1

Changing Dimensions of Paid Female Labor, 1910–1930

These charts reveal the extraordinary growth in clerical and professional occupations among employed women and the accompanying decline in agricultural labor in the early twentieth century. Notice that manufacturing employment peaked in 1920 and that domestic service fluctuated as white immigrant women began to move out of these jobs and were replaced by women of color.

George Eastman House

The expansion of service-sector jobs and new technology opened new opportunities for women in the 1920s. This telephone operator handled scores of phone calls and monitored a huge switchboard at the same time. Her dress and jewelry contrasted with the simpler styles worn by factory women, who had to be more careful in working with dangerous machines.

and growing numbers were personal service workers, such as waitresses and hairdressers. Although almost 2 million women worked in manufacturing, their numbers grew little over the decade. Women's wages seldom exceeded half of those paid to men.

Family economic needs were paramount among women's reasons for working. Consumerism tempted working- and middle-class families to live beyond their means or expand their incomes with women's wages. Although most married women did not hold paying jobs (only 12 percent were employed in 1930), married women as a proportion of the work force rose by 30 percent during the 1920s, and the number of employed married women swelled from 1.9 million to 3.1 million.

Employment of Minority Women

The proportion of nonwhite women in paid labor was double that of white women. Often, they entered the work force because husbands were unemployed or underemployed. The majority of employed African American women held domestic jobs. The few who held factory jobs performed the least desirable, lowest-paying tasks. Some opportunities opened for educated African American women in social work, teaching, and nursing, but these women also faced discrimination and low incomes. More than white mothers, employed black mothers called on female relatives to help with childcare.

Next to African American women, Japanese American women were the most likely to hold paying jobs, similarly working as field hands and domestics, facing racial bias and low pay. Economic necessity also drew thousands of Mexican American women into the labor force, although their traditions resisted female employment. Most worked as domestic servants, operatives in garment factories, and agricultural laborers.

Alternative Images of Femininity

Women remade the image of femininity, casting aside the heavy, floor-length dresses and long hair of previous generations. Instead, many opted for the independence and sexual freedom of the 1920s flapper with her short skirts and bobbed hair. Although few women lived the flapper life, office workers, store clerks, and college coeds adopted the look. As Cecil B. DeMille's movies showed, new female icons included movie temptresses, such as Clara Bow, known as the "It Girl," and Gloria Swanson, notorious for torrid love affairs on and off the screen. Many women asserted new social equality with men. One observer described "the new woman" as intriguingly independent.

She takes a man's point of view as her mother never could....She will never make you a hatband or knit you a necktie, but she'll drive you from the station...in her own little sports car. She'll don knickers and go skiing with you,...she'll dive as well as you, perhaps better, she'll dance as long as you care to...

Gay and Lesbian Culture

The era's sexual openness enabled the underground homosexual culture to surface somewhat. In nontraditional city neighborhoods, such as New York's Greenwich Village, cheap rents and a relative tolerance attracted gay men and lesbians, who patronized dance halls, speakeasies, and cafés. Still, gay establishments remained targets for police raids, demonstrating that there was little acceptance from the larger society.

These trends represented a break with the nineteenth century's more restrained culture. But social change rarely proceeds smoothly. As the decade advanced, groups mobilized to defend older values.

Lines of Defense

Early in 1920, the leader of a newly formed organization hired two public relations experts, Edward Clarke and Elizabeth Tyler. They canvassed the South, Southwest, and Midwest, where they found countless people eager to pay a $10 membership fee and $6 for a white uniform. Clarke and Tyler pocketed $2.50 from each membership and secured 5 million members by 1923.

> How did various groups seek to hold the line on social change in the 1920s?

Ku Klux Klan

This was the Ku Klux Klan, a revived version of the hooded order that terrorized southern communities after the Civil War. Reconstituted in 1915 by William J. Simmons, an Atlanta, Georgia, evangelist and insurance salesman, the Klan adopted the hoods, intimidating tactics, and the mystical terminology of its forerunner (its leader was the Imperial Wizard; its book of rituals, the Kloran).

The new Klan fanned outward from the Deep South, wielding power in places as diverse as Oregon, where Portland's mayor was a Klan member, and Indiana, where Klansmen held the governorship and several legislative seats. Members included many from the urban middle class who feared losing social and economic gains and were nervous about a new youth culture that eluded family control. It included a women's adjunct with roughly a half-million members.

One phrase summed up Klan goals: "Native, white, Protestant supremacy." *Native* meant no immigration, no mongrelization of American culture. According to Imperial Wizard Hiram Wesley Evans, "The world has been so made so that each race must fight for its life, must conquer, accept slavery, or die." Evans accused the Catholic Church of discouraging assimilation and enslaving people to priests and a foreign pope.

Using threatening assemblies, violence, and political and economic pressure, the Klan meted out vigilante justice to suspected bootleggers, wife beaters, and adulterers; forced schools to stop teaching evolution; campaigned against Catholic and Jewish political candidates; and fueled racial tensions against Mexicans in Texas border cities. Klan women promoted native white Protestantism but also worked for moral reform and prohibition. Because the KKK vowed to protect women's virtue, housewives sometimes appealed to the Klan to punish abusive or irresponsible husbands. The Klan's method of justice was flogging.

By 1925, however, scandal undermined the Klan's moral base. Indiana grand dragon David Stephenson was convicted of second-degree murder after he kidnapped and raped a woman who later died. Eventually, the Klan's negative brand of patriotism and purity could not compete in a pluralistic society.

Intolerance pervaded American society in the 1920s. Nativists charged that Catholic and Jewish immigrants clogged city slums, flouted community norms, and stubbornly embraced alien religious and political beliefs. Fear of immigrant radicals also fueled a dramatic 1921 trial of two Italian anarchists, **Nicola Sacco and Bartolomeo Vanzetti**, convicted of murdering a paymaster and guard in Braintree, Massachusetts. Evidence for their guilt was flimsy.

Nicola Sacco and Bartolomeo Vanzetti: Italian immigrants found guilty of a Massachusetts murder and sentenced to death. Sacco and Vanzetti were also anarchists and much of their murder trial focused on their radicalism.

Immigration Quotas

Efforts to restrict immigration gathered support. Labor leaders warned that aliens would depress wages and raise unemployment. Business executives, who formerly desired cheap immigrant laborers, now realized that mechanization would keep wages low. Drawing support from such groups, Congress set yearly immigration allocations for each nationality in the Emergency Quota Act of 1921. By restricting annual immigration of a given nationality to 3 percent of immigrants from that nation already residing in the United States in 1910, the Act favored Anglo-Saxon Protestant immigrants. It discriminated against Catholics and Jews from southern and eastern Europe, whose numbers were comparatively small in 1910.

In 1924, Congress replaced the Quota Act with the **National Origins Act**. This law limited annual immigration to 150,000 people and set quotas at 2 percent of each nationality residing in the United States in 1890, except for Asians, who were banned completely. The act further restricted southern and eastern Europeans, since fewer of those groups lived in the United States in 1890 than in 1910, although it allowed foreign-born wives and children of U.S. citizens to enter as nonquota immigrants.

In 1927, a revised National Origins Act redefined quotas to be distributed among European countries in proportion to the national origins (country of birth or descent) of American inhabitants in 1920. People from the Western Hemisphere did not fall under the quotas (except for those whom the Labor Department defined as potential paupers) and became the largest immigrant groups (see Figure 24.2).

National Origins Act of 1924: Restricted annual immigration from any foreign country to two percent of each nationality residing in the United States in 1890 (but barred Asians); also limited total annual immigration to 150,000.

Fundamentalism

The pursuit of spiritual purity stirred religious fundamentalists, as millions sought salvation from what they perceived as the irreverence of a materialistic, hedonistic society. Resolutely believing that God's miracles created the world, they condemned the theory of evolution as heresy. Wherever fundamentalists constituted a majority of a community, they sought to determine what schools taught. Their enemies were modernists, who used social sciences, such as psychology, to interpret behavior. To modernists, God was important to the study of culture and history, but science advanced knowledge.

fundamentalism: Twentieth century movement within Protestantism that taught literal interpretation of the Bible.

Scopes trial: Trial that took place after high school teacher John Scopes challenged a Tennessee law that banned teaching the theory of evolution in public schools.

Scopes Trial

In 1925, Christian **fundamentalism** clashed with modernism in the **Scopes Trial** in Dayton, Tennessee. The state legislature banned public schools from teaching the theory that humans evolved

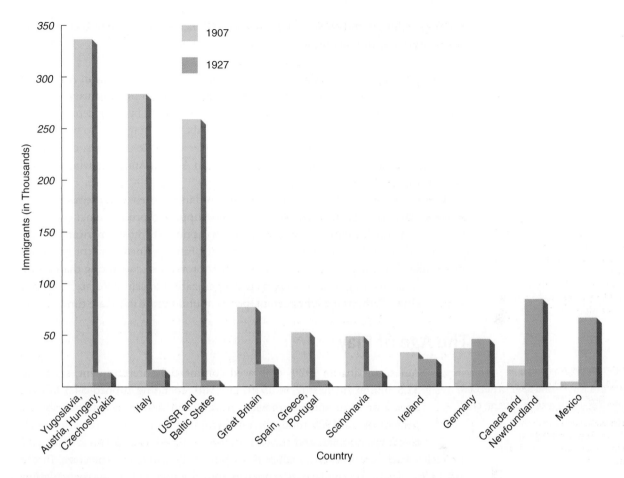

FIGURE 24.2
Sources of Immigration, 1907 and 1927

Immigration peaked in 1907 and 1908, when newcomers from southern and eastern Europe poured into the United States. After immigration restriction laws were passed in the 1920s, the greatest number of immigrants came from the Western Hemisphere (Canada and Mexico), which was exempted from the quotas, and the number coming from eastern and southern Europe shrank.

from lower forms of life rather than descending from Adam and Eve. High school teacher John Thomas Scopes volunteered to serve as a test case and was arrested for violating the law. William Jennings Bryan, former secretary of state and three-time presidential candidate, argued for the prosecution, and civil liberties lawyers headed by Clarence Darrow represented Scopes. News correspondents crowded into town, and radio stations broadcast the trial.

Although Scopes was convicted—clearly he had broken the law—modernists claimed victory. The testimony, they believed, showed fundamentalism to be illogical. The trial's climax occurred when Bryan testified as an expert on the Bible. He asserted that Eve really had been created from Adam's rib, that the Tower of Babel was responsible for the diversity of languages, and that Jonah had actually been swallowed by a big fish. Spectators in Dayton cheered Bryan, but the liberal press mocked him. Nevertheless, fundamentalists continued to pressure schools to stop teaching evolution and created an independent subculture with their own schools, radio ministries, and missionary societies.

Religious Revivalism   Urban Pentecostal churches attracted African Americans and whites struggling with economic insecurity, nervous about modernism's attack on old-time religion, and swayed by their depiction of a personal Savior. Using modern advertising and elaborately staged radio broadcasts, magnetic preachers, such as Aimee Semple McPherson of Los Angeles, the former baseball player Billy Sunday, and Father Divine (an African American who amassed an interracial following) stirred revivalist fervor.

Clergy and teachers of all faiths condemned dancing, new dress styles, and sex in movies and parked cars. Many urban dwellers supported prohibition, believing it would win the battle against poverty, vice, and corruption. Yet most Americans sought balance as they tried to adjust to the modern order. Few refrained from the radio and movies like *Why Change Your Wife?*—activities that proved less corrupting than critics feared. Americans sought fellowship in civic organizations, such as Rotary, Elks, and women's clubs. Perhaps most important, people found release in leisure time.

The Age of Play

> Why did movie and sports heroes become so important during the 1920s?

Americans in the 1920s embraced commercial entertainment, spending $2.5 billion on leisure in 1919; by 1929, spending topped $4.3 billion. Spectator amusements—movies, music, and sports—accounted for 21 percent of the 1929 total; the rest involved participatory recreation such as games, hobbies, and travel. Entrepreneurs fed an appetite for fads and spectacles. Early in the 1920s, mahjong, a Chinese tile game, was the craze. In the mid-1920s, devotees popularized crossword puzzles, printed in mass-circulation newspapers and magazines. By 1930, the nation boasted thirty thousand miniature golf courses. Dance crazes like the Charleston and recorded music on radio boosted the growing popularity of jazz.

Movies and Sports   Americans embraced movies and sports. In total capital investment, motion pictures became one of the nation's leading industries. In 1922, movies attracted 40 million viewers weekly; by 1929, nearly 100 million—at a time when the nation's population was 120 million and total weekly church attendance was 60 million. Between 1922 and 1927, the Technicolor Corporation developed a means of producing movies in color. That, along with the introduction of sound in 1927's *The Jazz Singer,* made movies more exciting.

Although DeMille's romantic comedies like *Why Change Your Wife?* explored worldly themes, his most popular films—*The Ten Commandments* (1923) and *The King of Kings* (1927)—were biblical. Lurid dramas like *Souls for Sale* (1923) and *A Woman Who Sinned* (1924) also drew big audiences, as did slapstick comedies starring Harold Lloyd and Charlie Chaplin. In 1927, producers—bowing to pressure from legislators and religious leaders—instituted self-censorship, forbidding nudity, rough language, and plots that did not end with justice and morality triumphant. Movies also reproduced social prejudices—the few black actors were limited to playing maids and butlers.

Spectator sports drew millions every year. In an age when technology and mass production robbed experiences of their uniqueness, sports provided the unpredictability that people craved. Newspapers and radio magnified this tension, glorifying events with such dramatic narrative that promoters did not need advertising.

Baseball's drawn-out suspense, diverse plays, and potential for keeping statistics attracted a huge following. After the 1919 "Black Sox scandal"—when eight members of the Chicago White Sox were banned for allegedly throwing the World Series to the Cincinnati Reds (even though a jury acquitted them)—baseball transformed itself. A record 300,000 people attended the six-game 1921 World Series between the New York Giants and New York Yankees. Millions enjoyed professional games on the radio. Although African American ballplayers were prohibited from the major leagues, they formed their own teams, and in 1920 the first successful Negro League was founded in Kansas City, Missouri.

Sports Heroes

As technology and mass society made the individual less significant, people clung to heroic personalities. Athletes like Bill Tilden in tennis, Gertrude Ederle in swimming (in 1926, she became the first woman to swim across the English Channel), and Bobby Jones in golf were famous. But boxing, football, and baseball produced the most popular sports heroes. Heavyweight champion Jack Dempsey, the "Manassa (Colorado) Mauler," attracted the first of several million-dollar gates in his fight with Frenchman Georges Carpentier in 1921.

Link to a video showing the success of Gertrude Ederle swimming the English Channel.

Baseball's foremost hero was George Herman "Babe" Ruth, who began as a pitcher but broke records hitting home runs. Ruth hit twenty-nine homers in 1919, fifty-four in 1920 (the year the Boston Red Sox traded him to the New York Yankees), fifty-nine in 1921, and sixty in 1927—each year a record. His talent and boyish grin endeared him to millions. Known for overindulgence in food, drink, and sex, he charmed fans into forgiving his excesses with by visiting hospitalized children.

Link to a video of the boxing match between Jack Dempsey and Georges Carpentier.

Movie Stars and Public Heroes

Americans fulfilled their yearning for romance and adventure through movie idols. One of the decade's most adored movie personalities was Rudolph Valentino, whose image exploited the era's sexual liberalism. In his most famous film, Valentino played a passionate sheik who carried away beautiful women to his tent. When he died at thirty-one of complications from ulcers and appendicitis, the press turned his funeral into a public extravaganza.

The era's most celebrated hero, however, was **Charles A. Lindbergh**, an indomitable aviator who in May 1927 flew a plane solo from New York to Paris. The flight riveted America, as newspaper and telegraph reports followed Lindbergh's progress. After the pilot landed successfully, President Coolidge dispatched a warship to bring "Lucky Lindy" home, where he was greeted with a parade. Lindbergh received the Distinguished Flying Cross and the Congressional Medal of Honor. Promoters offered him millions of dollars to tour the world and $700,000 for a movie contract. His flight epitomized individual achievement and courage—old-fashioned values that attracted public respect.

Charles A. Lindbergh: Popular aviator who flew solo across the Atlantic in his small single engine plane, the "Spirit of St. Louis," in May 1927.

Prohibition   The Eighteenth Amendment (1919) and subsequent federal law (the Volstead Act of 1920) prohibited the manufacture, sale, and transportation of alcoholic beverages. It worked well at first. Per capita consumption of liquor dropped, as did arrests for drunkenness. But it was barely enforced: in 1922, Congress gave the Prohibition Bureau less than $7 million for nationwide enforcement, and by 1927 most state budgets omitted funds to enforce prohibition.

After 1925, prohibition broke down as thousands made their own wine and gin illegally and bootleg importers evaded the few patrols that existed. Moreover, drinking was a business with willing customers, and criminal organizations capitalized on public demand. The most notorious of such mobs belonged to Al Capone, who seized control of illegal liquor and vice in Chicago, maintaining power over politicians and the vice business through intimidation, bribery, and violence. Americans wanted liquor, and until 1931, when a federal court convicted and imprisoned Capone for income-tax evasion (the only charge for which authorities could obtain hard evidence), he supplied them.

Cultural Currents

How did discontent with 1920s conformity give rise to important creative cultural movements?

Intellectuals were quick to expose the era's hypocrisies. Writers and artists felt at odds with society, and their rejection of materialism and conformity was biting and bitter.

Literature of Alienation   Several writers from the so-called Lost Generation, including novelist Ernest Hemingway and poets Ezra Pound and T. S. Eliot, abandoned the United States for Europe. Others, like novelists William Faulkner and Sinclair Lewis, remained in America but expressed disillusionment with the materialism they witnessed. F. Scott Fitzgerald's novels, *This Side of Paradise* (1920) and *The Great Gatsby* (1925), and Eugene O'Neill's plays scorned Americans' preoccupation with money. Edith Wharton explored the clash of old and new moralities in novels such as *The Age of Innocence* (1920). Hemingway's *A Farewell to Arms* (1929) interwove antiwar sentiment with critiques of the emptiness in modern relationships.

Harlem Renaissance   Discontent inspired a new generation of African American artists. Middle-class, educated, and proud of their African heritage, black writers rejected white culture and exalted the militantly assertive "New Negro." In the "Negro Mecca" of New York's Harlem, black intellectuals and artists, aided by a few white patrons, celebrated black culture during what became known as the Harlem Renaissance.

The popular 1921 musical comedy *Shuffle Along* is often credited with launching the Harlem Renaissance and showcased talented African American artists, such as the composer Eubie Blake and the singer Josephine Baker. The Harlem Renaissance also fostered several gifted writers, among them poets Langston Hughes, Countee Cullen, and Claude McKay and novelists Zora Neale Hurston, Jessie Fauset, and Alain Locke. Though cherishing their African heritage and folk culture of the slave

Collection of Archie Motley and Valerie Gerrard Browne. Photo courtesy of The Art Institute of Chicago

This painting by African American artist Archibald Motley represented the "Ash-Can" style, which considered no subject too undignified to paint, as well as the sensual relationship between jazz music and dancing in African American culture.

South, these artists and intellectuals realized that blacks had to come to terms with being free Americans. Langston Hughes wrote, "We younger Negro artists who create now intend to express our individual dark-skinned selves without fear or shame. If white people are pleased, we are glad. If they are not, it doesn't matter. We know we are beautiful."

Jazz

The Jazz Age, as the 1920s is sometimes called, owes its name to the music of the African American culture. Evolving from African and African American folk music, early jazz communicated exuberance, humor, and autonomy that African Americans seldom experienced in their public and political lives. Jazz's emotional rhythms and improvisation blurred the distinction between composer and performer. Urban dance halls and nightclubs, some of which included interracial audiences, featured performers like trumpeter Louis Armstrong and blues singer Bessie Smith. Music recorded by African American artists and aimed at African American consumers (sometimes called "race records") gave African Americans a place in commercial culture. More important, jazz endowed America with its own distinctive art form.

In many ways, the 1920s were the nation's most creative years. Painters such as Georgia O'Keeffe, Aaron Douglas, and John Marin forged a uniquely American style of visual art. Composer Henry Cowell pioneered electronic music, and Aaron Copland built orchestral works around native folk motifs. George Gershwin blended jazz rhythms, classical forms, and folk melodies in serious works (*Rhapsody in Blue,* 1924, and Piano Concerto in F, 1925, and hit tunes such as "The Man I Love"). In architecture, skyscrapers drew worldwide attention to American forms. The "emotional and aesthetic starvation" that essayist Harold Stearns lamented early in the decade were gone by 1929.

The Election of 1928 and End of the New Era

What were the early signs that the prosperity of the 1920s was coming to an end?

Intellectuals' uneasiness about materialism seldom affected the confident rhetoric of politics. Herbert Hoover voiced that confidence when he accepted the Republican nomination for president in 1928. "We in America today," Hoover boasted, "are nearer to the final triumph over poverty than ever before in the history of any land."

Herbert Hoover

As the Republican candidate in 1928 (Coolidge chose not to seek reelection), Hoover fused the traditional value of individual hard work with modern emphasis on corporate action. A Quaker from Iowa, orphaned at age ten, Hoover put himself through Stanford University and became a wealthy mining engineer. During and after World War I, he distinguished himself as U.S. food administrator.

As secretary of commerce under Harding and Coolidge, Hoover promoted associationalism. Recognizing that nationwide associations dominated commerce and industry, Hoover sought business and government cooperation. He made the Commerce Department a center for the promotion of business, encouraging trade associations, holding conferences, and issuing reports, all aimed at improving productivity and profits.

Al Smith

In sharp contrast, Democrats in 1928 chose New York's governor Alfred E. Smith. Hoover had rural, native-born, Protestant, and business roots, but had never run for public office. Smith was an urbane politician of Irish stock with a career embedded in New York City's Tammany Hall political machine. He relished the give-and-take of city streets.

Smith was the first Roman Catholic to run for president on a major party ticket. His religion enhanced his appeal among urban ethnics, who increasingly voted, but intense anti-Catholic sentiments lost him southern and rural votes. Smith had a strong record on Progressive reform and civil rights, but his campaign stressed issues unlikely to unite these groups, particularly his opposition to prohibition.

Hoover, who emphasized national prosperity under Republican administrations, won the popular vote by 21 million to 15 million and the electoral vote by 444 to 87. Smith carried the nation's twelve largest cities, formerly Republican strongholds. For the next forty years, the Democratic Party solidified this urban base, which in conjunction with its traditional strength in the South made the party a formidable force in national elections.

Hoover's Administration

At his inaugural, Hoover proclaimed a New Day, "bright with hope." His cabinet featured mostly businessmen, including six millionaires. To lower ranking posts, Hoover appointed young professionals who agreed that a scientific approach could solve national problems. Like Hoover, Americans widely believed that individual effort led to success and that poverty suggested personal weakness. Prevailing opinion also held that fluctuations of the business cycle were natural and therefore not to be tampered with by government.

Stock Market Crash

This trust dissolved on October 24, 1929, later known as Black Thursday, when stock market prices suddenly plunged, wiping out $10 billion in value (worth around $100 billion today). Panic set in. Prices of many stocks hit record lows; some sellers could find no buyers. At noon, leading bankers put up $20 million and ceremoniously began buying stocks. The mood brightened, and some stocks rallied.

But as news spread, frightened investors sold off to avoid further losses. On Black Tuesday, October 29, prices plummeted again. Hoover assured Americans that "the crisis will be over in sixty days." He shared the popular assumptions that the economy was strong enough to endure until the market righted itself. Instead, the crash ultimately unleashed a devastating worldwide depression.

In hindsight, the depression began long before the stock market crash. Prosperity in the 1920s was not as widespread as optimists believed. Agriculture had languished for decades, and many areas, especially in the South, were outside the new bounty of consumer society. Industries such as mining and textiles failed to sustain profits throughout the decade, and even the automotive and household goods industries had been stagnant since 1926. The fever of speculation included rash investment in California and Florida real estate, as well as in the stock market, and masked what was unhealthy in the national economy.

Declining Demand

The economic weakness that underlay the Great Depression had several interrelated causes. Since mid-1928, demand for new housing had faltered, reducing sales of building materials and unemployment. In growth industries, such as automobiles and electric appliances, demand leveled off, so factory owners cut production and workers. Retailers had amassed large inventories that were going unsold and started ordering less. Farm prices continued to sag, leaving farmers with less income for new machinery and goods. As wages and employment fell, families could not afford to buy consumer goods. Thus, by 1929, a sizable population of underconsumers was causing serious repercussions.

As the rich grew richer, middle- and lower-income Americans barely made modest gains. Although average per capita disposable income (income after taxes) rose about 9 percent between 1920 and 1929, income of the wealthiest 1 percent rose 75 percent. Much of this increase was put into stock market investments, not consumer goods.

Intercollegiate Athletics

In 1924 brutality, academic fraud, and illegal payments to recruits prompted the Carnegie Foundation for the Advancement of Higher Education to undertake a five-year investigation of college sports. Its 1929 report recommended the abolition of football and condemned coaches and alumni but had minimal effect. Football was immensely popular, and colleges and universities built stadiums to attract spectators, bolster alumni allegiance, and enhance revenues.

From the 1920s to the present, intercollegiate sports ranked as a major commercial entertainment. Still, American higher education has struggled to reconcile conflicts between the commercialism of athletic competition and the ideals of amateurism. But the economic potential of college sports coupled with expanding athletic departments—elaborate facilities as well as staffs—has created programs that compete with and sometimes overshadow an institution's academic mission.

Since the 1920s, recruiting scandals, academic fraud, and felonious behavior sparked controversy in college sports. In 1952, after revelations of point-shaving (fixing the outcome) of basketball games at several colleges, the American Council on Education undertook its own study. Its recommendations, including the elimination of football bowl games, went largely unheeded. In 1991, further abuses prompted the Knight Foundation Commission on Intercollegiate Athletics to urge college presidents to reform intercollegiate athletics. Few significant changes resulted, even after a follow-up study in 2001.

The most sweeping reforms followed court rulings in the 1990s, mandating that women's sports be treated equally with men's under Title IX of the Educational Amendments Act of 1972. Enforcement, however, provoked a backlash that resulted in efforts to prevent men's teams from being cut to satisfy Title IX. In recent years, the National College Athletic Association (NCAA) has attempted to regulate academic standards in college athletics, but its success depends on cooperation from member institutions. With millions of dollars involved, the system established in the 1920s has withstood most pressures for change.

Corporate Debt and Stock Market Speculation

Furthermore, many businesses overloaded themselves with debt. To obtain loans, they misrepresented their assets in ways that hid their inability to repay. Such practices, overlooked by lending agencies, put the nation's banking system on precarious footing.

Risky stock market speculation also precipitated the depression. Individuals and corporations bought millions of stocks on margin, meaning that they invested with a down payment of only a fraction of a stock's actual price and then used these partially paid-for stocks as collateral for more stock purchases. When stock prices stopped rising, investors tried to unload what they bought on margin. But with numerous investors selling simultaneously, prices plunged. Brokers demanded full payment for stocks bought on margin. The more obligations went unmet, the more the system tottered. Inevitably, banks and investment companies collapsed.

Economic Troubles Abroad; Federal Failures at Home

International economic conditions also contributed to the Depression. During and after World War I, Americans loaned billions to European nations. By the late 1920s, however, American investors instead kept their money in the lucrative U.S. stock market. Europeans, unable to borrow more or sell goods in the American market because of high tariffs, bought less from the United States. Moreover, the Allied nations depended on German war reparations to pay their debts to the United States, and the German government depended on American bank loans to pay those reparations. When the crash choked off American loans, the western economy ground to a halt.

The government refrained from regulating speculation. In supporting business expansion, the Federal Reserve Board pursued easy credit policies, charging low discount rates (interest on its loans to member banks) even though such loans were financing the speculative mania.

Neither experts nor people on the street realized what really happened in 1929. Conventional wisdom, based on previous depressions, held that economic problems had to run their course. So in 1929 people waited for the tailspin to ease, never realizing that the new era had ended and that the economy, politics, and society would have to be rebuilt.

Summary

Two critical events, the end of World War I and beginning of the Great Depression, marked the boundaries of the 1920s. After the war, traditional customs weakened as women and men sought new forms of self-expression and gratification. Modern science and technology touched the lives of rich and poor alike through mass media, movies, sports, automobiles, and electric appliances. Moreover, the decade's freewheeling consumerism enabled ordinary Americans to emulate wealthier people purchasing more and engaging in stock market speculation.

Beneath the new era's materialism, prejudice and ethnic tensions tainted the American dream. Klansmen and immigration restrictionists encouraged discrimination against racial minorities and ethnic groups. Meanwhile, the distinguishing forces of twentieth-century life—technological change, bureaucratization, mass culture, and growth of the middle class—accelerated, making the decade truly "new."

Chapter Review

Big Business Triumphant

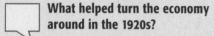

What helped turn the economy around in the 1920s?

Two factors helped transform the initial postwar World War I recession into recovery: the advent of electric energy in 1922 and new government pro-business initiatives. Electricity enabled goods to be produced more inexpensively, thereby driving consumer demand and stimulating the economy across the board. New installment or credit plans for purchasing big items such as cars also drove consumption. Business organizations successfully used new lobbying techniques to prompt government to implement pro-business policies that also stimulated growth. Congress cut taxes on corporations and wealthy individuals in 1921, and passed the Fordney-McCumber Tariff Act (1922). The Federal Trade Commission and the Interstate Commerce Commission tended to cooperate with corporations rather than regulate them. And several Supreme Court decisions sheltered business from government regulation and hindered organized labor.

Politics and Government

What happened to Progressive reform in the 1920s?

While Progressivism faded on a national level, its reform spirit continued to inspire local and state initiatives as well as those by women and ethnic groups. After the war, many states adopted or expanded workers' compensation laws and public welfare programs. Native American groups worked for better education and return of tribal lands, while white reformers held out hope of getting Indians to adopt white middle-class standards of work, family, and citizenship. Although women got the right to vote in 1920, their voluntary organizations became the tools for lobbying for various issues from birth control to protective labor legislation to questions of citizenship and equality.

A Consumer Society

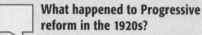

How did the emergence of a consumer society change American life?

In the 1920s, incomes increased, while new mass production methods kept the price of goods stable or made them more affordable. Consequently, greater numbers of Americans could afford products such as automobiles that once were the province of the wealthy. Car ownership led consumers to join with farmers in seeking improved roadways. At the same time, the emergence of advertising as a tool helped manipulate purchases and increasingly erased ethnic differences to create a more homogenous consumer society. And the growth of the radio, with its mass marketing and standardized programs, further blurred differences and heightened immigrants assimilation into American culture and ways of life.

Cities, Migrants, and Suburbs

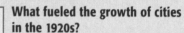

What fueled the growth of cities in the 1920s?

In 1920, for the first time in U.S. history, more people lived in urban areas than rural areas. In part, the shift was driven by young people, who left farms for the more exciting and varied life of cities. The demographic change was also driven by the migration of African Americans from poverty and a boll weevil plague on southern farms to seek better paying factory jobs in the North. Once there, they faced discrimination in housing. Immigrants from Mexico and Puerto Rico were similarly pushed off their land due to agricultural changes to find better opportunities in America. Many Mexicans became underpaid and exploited farm laborers in the West, while Puerto Ricans found jobs in factories and restaurants or as domestic servants. Both maintained customs and developed local businesses or social clubs to help them adapt.

New Rhythms of Everyday Life

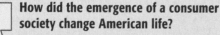

How did technological advances impact social life in America in the 1920s?

First, improved productivity and mechanization led to shorter workweeks, permitting the expansion of leisure activities and greater freedom, especially for young people. Industrialism privileged youth and agility over experience and forced older people to retire, which often meant economic hardship or poverty. Second, new appliances made housework less arduous and time-consuming and shifted women's roles from producer within the home to consumer for the family. Third, advances in nutrition helped people live longer and healthier lives. Birth control also enabled families to separate sexuality from reproduction, and family size decreased. Finally, as products and services became more widely available, an increasing number of married women moved into the work force to expand their families' purchasing power.

Lines of Defense

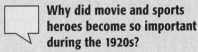

How did various groups seek to hold the line on social change in the 1920s?

Troubled by the liberal social influences of the era, several groups emerged seeking to restore what they considered to be traditional American values. The Ku Klux Klan was reconstituted in 1915 to re-establish native white American supremacy in the face of increasing immigration and black migration and to protect white women's virtue against so-called corrupting influences. They were joined in their anti-immigration sentiment by other nativist groups, who pressed Congress to establish immigration quotas. Similarly, fundamentalist Christian groups sought to replace the modern emphasis on science with a renewed centrality of God's role in creation and daily life. Hence, the Tennessee legislature banned the teaching of the theory of evolution, resulting in the pivotal Scopes trial in 1925. Religious revivalism likewise condemned the new social practices of dating, dancing, and fashion and the hint of sex in movies.

The Age of Play

Why did movie and sports heroes become so important during the 1920s?

As mass consumption took hold, Americans felt robbed of a sense of individual distinctiveness. To recover that lost sensibility, Americans gravitated toward leisure activities that celebrated individual achievement or that inspired a sense of adventure or romance. Sports provided drama, unpredictability, and a chance to celebrate a particular player's talent. Motion pictures not only let viewers live vicariously through the exciting lives of characters, but also inspired the hope for adventure in their own lives. Finally, national heroes such as aviator Charles Lindbergh made the possibility of greatness seem real and attainable, even if most Americans would never personally experience it for themselves.

Cultural Currents

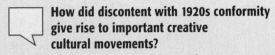

How did discontent with 1920s conformity give rise to important creative cultural movements?

Many artists and writers felt disillusioned with the materialism they witnessed in America during this age of mass consumption and innovation. While some, like Ernest Hemingway, left for Europe, others remained in the United States and transformed these feelings into novels and other creative works that explored the problems of modern society or proffered a particular political view. Middle-class, educated African Americans rejected white culture and celebrated their heritage in novels, poems, plays, and art, creating the literary and artistic movement known as the Harlem Renaissance. Black culture also produced the Jazz Age, creating a distinctly American musical form.

The Election of 1928 and the End of the New Era

What were the early signs that the prosperity of the 1920s was coming to an end?

While the 1929 stock market crash put a definitive ending on the era's seeming prosperity, in truth, the seeds of recession were sown many years before. First, so-called prosperity had never reached farmers; agriculture had lagged for decades. Mining, textiles, and other industries did not remain profitable the entire decade, and even the automobile industry was stagnant after 1926. As demand faltered, factories cut back on production and workers, which in turn meant less disposable income to purchase consumer goods, triggering further cutbacks in retail orders and production. Housing demand dropped off after mid-1928, and at the same time, businesses were overloaded with debt. Together, this made for a perfect economic storm when the market crashed in 1929.

Suggestions for Further Reading

Lynn Dumenil, *The Modern Temper: American Culture and Society in the 1920s* (1995)

Colin Grant, *Negro with a Hat: The Rise and Fall of Marcus Garvey* (2008)

Maury Klein, *Rainbow's End: The Crash of 1929* (2003)

Roland Marchand, *Advertising the American Dream: Making Way for Modernity, 1920–1940* (1985)

Nathan Miller, *New World Coming: The 1920s and the Making of Modern America* (2004)

David Montgomery, *The Fall of the House of Labor: The Workplace, the State, and American Activism, 1865–1925* (1987)

Mae M. Ngai, *Impossible Subjects: Illegal Aliens and the Making of Modern America* (2004)

George Sanchez, *Becoming Mexican American: Ethnicity, Culture and Identity in Chicano Los Angeles, 1900–1945* (1993)

Susan Thistle, *From Marriage to the Market: The Transformation of Women's Lives and Work* (2006)

Go to the CourseMate website for primary source links, study tools, and review materials for this chapter.
www.cengagebrain.com

The Great Depression and the New Deal

25

1929–1941

In 1931, the rain stopped in the Great Plains. Montana and North Dakota became as arid as the Sonora Desert. Temperatures reached 115 degrees in Iowa. The soil baked. Farmers watched rich black dirt turn to gray dust.

Then the winds began to blow. Farmers had stripped the Plains of native grasses in the 1920s, plowing up 50,000 acres of new land daily. Now, with nothing to hold the earth, it began to blow away. The dust storms began in 1934—and worsened in 1935. Dust obscured the sun. Cattle, blinded by blowing grit, ran in circles until they died. Clouds of dust filled the skies of Kansas, Colorado, Oklahoma, Texas, and New Mexico—the Dust Bowl.

In late 1937, on a farm near Stigler, Oklahoma, Marvin Montgomery counted his assets: $53 and a 1929 Hudson car. On December 29, 1937, Montgomery and his wife and four children—along with their furniture, bedding, pots, and pans—squeezed into the Hudson. Traveling west on Route 66, the Montgomerys headed for California.

At least a third of farms in the Dust Bowl were abandoned in the 1930s, and many families headed west, lured by advertisements promising work in California fields. Some 300,000 people migrated to California in the 1930s; many were white-collar workers seeking better opportunities in California's cities. But the plight of families like the Montgomerys, captured in federal government-sponsored Farm Security Administration (FSA) photographs, came to represent the human suffering of the Great Depression.

The Montgomerys ran out of money in Arizona and worked in the cotton fields there for five weeks before moving on. In California, wages were low and migrant families felt unwelcome. As they took over the agricultural labor formerly done by Mexicans and Mexican Americans, they forfeited their "whiteness" in the eyes of many Californians. "Negroes and Okies' upstairs," read a sign in a San Joaquin valley movie theater.

Most migrants to rural California lived in squalid camps, but the Montgomerys secured housing provided by the Farm

Chapter Outline

Hoover and Hard Times, 1929–1933
Farmers and Industrial Workers | Marginal Workers | Middle-Class Workers and Families | Hoover's Limited Solutions | Protest and Social Unrest | Bonus Army

Franklin D. Roosevelt and the Launching of the New Deal
Banking Crisis | First Hundred Days | National Industrial Recovery Act | Agricultural Adjustment Act | Relief Programs

Political Pressure and the Second New Deal
Business Opposition | Demagogues and Populists | Left-Wing Critics | Shaping the Second New Deal | Works Progress Administration | Social Security Act | Roosevelt's Populist Strategies

Labor
Rivalry Between Craft and Industrial Unions | Sit-Down Strikes | Memorial Day Massacre

VISUALIZING THE PAST *The Women's Emergency Brigade and the General Motors Sit-Down Strike*

Federal Power and the Nationalization of Culture
New Deal in the West | New Deal for Native Americans | New Deal in the South | Mass Media and Popular Culture

LINKS TO THE WORLD *The 1936 Olympic Games*

Security Administration. The FSA camp had 240 tents and 40 small houses. For nine months, the Montgomery family lived in a fourteen-by-sixteen-foot tent, which rented for 10 cents a day plus four hours of volunteer labor a month. Then they moved into an FSA house, "with water, lights, and everything, yes sir; and a little garden spot furnished." Soon, employment opportunities emerged in California's aircraft factories and shipyards mobilizing for World War II.

The Montgomerys' experience shows the human costs of the Great Depression that plunged the world into an economic crisis. Between 1929 and 1933, the U.S. gross national product was cut in half. Corporate profits fell from $10 billion to $1 billion; 100,000 businesses closed. Four million workers were unemployed in January 1930; by November, unemployment reached 6 million. When President Herbert Hoover left office in 1933, 13 million workers—about one-fourth of the labor force—were idle, and millions worked only part-time. There was no national safety net: no welfare system, no unemployment compensation, no Social Security. And, as thousands of banks failed, with no federally guaranteed deposit insurance, families' savings disappeared.

Herbert Hoover, who was elected president in the prosperous late 1920s, looked first to private enterprise for solutions. By the end of his term, he extended the federal government's role in managing an economic crisis further than his predecessors had. Still, the depression deepened, and Americans became desperate. The economic catastrophe exacerbated existing racial and class tensions in the United States, while in Germany, it propelled Adolf Hitler to power. By late 1932, many feared the depression was a crisis of capitalism, even of democracy itself.

In 1932, voters replaced Hoover with a man who promised a New Deal. Franklin Delano Roosevelt's programs did not end the depression (only the massive mobilization for World War II did that), but they did alleviate suffering. For the first time, the federal government assumed responsibility for the nation's economy and its citizens' welfare, thus strengthening its power in relation to states.

Although some Americans saw the depression as an opportunity for major economic change—even revolution—Roosevelt's goal was to save capitalism. New Deal programs increased federal government regulation without fundamentally altering the system or distribution of wealth. Despite pressure to attack racial discrimination, Roosevelt never directly challenged southern legal segregation—partly because he relied on southern Democrats in Congress to pass New Deal legislation.

Despite its limits, the New Deal preserved America's democratic experiment through uncertainty and crisis. By decade's end, a world war shifted America's focus from domestic to foreign policy. But the changes begun by the New Deal continued to transform the United States for decades.

As you read this chapter, keep the following questions in mind:

* How did economic hard times during the 1930s affect Americans, and what differences were there in the experiences of specific groups and regions?

* How and why did the power of the federal government expand during the Great Depression?

* What were the successes and the failures of the New Deal?

Link to photographs taken by FSA photographer Dorothea Lange that capture the suffering of the depression.

Hoover and Hard Times, 1929–1933

Why was Hoover reluctant to implement relief programs during the Great Depression?

By the early 1930s, as the depression deepened, tens of millions of Americans were desperately poor. In cities, the hungry lined up at soup kitchens; some scratched through garbage cans for food. In West Virginia and Kentucky, widespread hunger and limited resources led the American Friends Service Committee to distribute food only to those weighing 10 percent below the normal weight for their height. In November 1932, *The Nation* told readers that one-sixth of the American population risked starvation.

Families were evicted. The new homeless poured into shantytowns, called "Hoovervilles" in ironic tribute to the formerly popular president. Over a million men took to the road or the rails in search of work. Couples delayed marriage and married people put off having children. In 1933 the birth rate sank below replacement rates. More than a quarter of women ages twenty to thirty during the Great Depression never had children.

Farmers and Industrial Workers

The agricultural sector, which employed almost one-quarter of American workers and missed the good times of the 1920s, was hit hard. As urbanites cut spending and foreign competitors dumped agricultural surpluses into the global market, farm prices hit bottom. Farmers tried to compensate by producing more, thus adding to the surplus and further depressing prices. By 1932, a bushel of wheat that cost North Dakota farmers 77 cents to produce brought only 33 cents. Cash-strapped farmers could not pay property taxes or mortgages. Banks foreclosed. In Mississippi, on a single day in April 1932 approximately one-fourth of the states' farmland was auctioned to meet debts. By the middle of the decade, the Dust Bowl would also drive thousands of farmers from their land.

America's industrial workers had seen their standard of living improve during the 1920s, and their consumer spending bolstered the nation's economic growth. But as incomes declined, sales of manufactured goods plummeted and factories closed—more than seventy thousand went out of business by 1933. As car sales dropped from 4.5 million in 1929 to 1 million in 1933, Ford laid off more than two-thirds of its Detroit workers. Almost one-quarter of industrial workers were unemployed, and those with jobs saw the average wage fall by almost one-third.

Marginal Workers

For workers on the lowest rungs of the employment ladder, the depression was crushing. In the South, where African Americans faced the greatest discrimination, jobs that white men had considered below their dignity—bellhop, garbage collector—seemed suddenly

Chronology

1929	Stock market crash (October); Great Depression begins
1930	Hawley-Smoot Tariff raises rates on imports
1931	"Scottsboro Boys" arrested in Alabama
1932	Banks fail throughout nation
	Bonus Army marches on Washington
	Hoover's Reconstruction Finance Corporation tries to stabilize banks, insurance companies, railroads
	Roosevelt elected president
1933	13 million Americans unemployed
	"First Hundred Days" of Roosevelt administration offer major legislation for economic recovery and poor relief
	National bank holiday halts run on banks
	Agricultural Adjustment Act (AAA) encourages decreased farm production
	National Industrial Recovery Act (NIRA) attempts to spur industrial growth
	Tennessee Valley Authority (TVA) established
1934	Long starts Share Our Wealth Society
	Townsend proposes old-age pension plan

	Indian Reorganization (Wheeler-Howard) Act restores lands to tribal ownership
1935	National Labor Relations (Wagner) Act guarantees workers' right to unionize
	Social Security Act establishes insurance for the aged, the unemployed, and needy children
	Works Progress Administration (WPA) creates jobs in public works projects
	Revenue (Wealth Tax) Act raises taxes on business and the wealthy
1936	9 million Americans unemployed
	United Auto Workers win sit-down strike against General Motors
1937	Roosevelt's court-packing plan fails
	Memorial Day massacre of striking steelworkers
	"Roosevelt recession" begins
1938	10.4 million Americans unemployed
	80 million movie tickets sold each week
1939	Marian Anderson performs at Lincoln Memorial
	Social Security amendments add benefits for spouses and widows

desirable. In 1930, a short-lived fascist-style organization, the Black Shirts, recruited forty thousand members with the slogan "No Jobs for Niggers Until Every White Man Has a Job!" And as industry cut production in the North, blacks were typically the first fired. By 1932, African American unemployment reached almost 50 percent.

Mexican Americans and Mexican nationals in the Southwest were also hit hard. Their wages on California farms fell from a miserable 35 cents an hour in 1929 to 14 cents an hour by 1932. Throughout the Southwest, campaigns against "foreigners" hurt Mexican immigrants and American citizens of Hispanic descent whose families had lived in the Southwest for centuries, long before the land belonged to the United States. In 1931, the Labor Department announced plans to deport illegal immigrants to free jobs for Americans. This policy fell hardest on people of Mexican origin. Even those who immigrated legally often lacked full documentation. The U.S. government deported eighty-two thousand Mexicans between 1929 and 1935. Almost half a million people repatriated to Mexico during the 1930s. Some left voluntarily, but many were tricked into believing they had no choice.

Even before the economic crisis, women of all classes and races were barred from many jobs and paid significantly less than men. Most Americans believed that men should be breadwinners and women homemakers and worried that women who worked took jobs from men. In fact, men laid off from U.S. Steel would not have been hired as secretaries, "salesgirls," or maids. Nonetheless, when a 1936 Gallup poll asked whether wives should work if their husbands had jobs, 82 percent of respondents (including 75 percent of the women) answered no. Such beliefs influenced policy. In 1930 and 1931, 77 percent of urban school systems refused to hire married women as teachers.

The depression had a mixed impact on women workers. At first, women workers lost jobs faster than men. Women in low-wage manufacturing jobs were laid off before male employees. Almost one-quarter of domestic workers—many of them African American—lost jobs as middle class families economized. Despite discrimination and a poor economy, however, women's employment increased during the 1930s. "Women's jobs," such as teaching and clerical work, were not hit as hard as "men's jobs" in heavy industry, and women increasingly sought employment to keep their families afloat. Still, by 1940 only 15.2 percent of married women were employed.

Middle-Class Workers and Families

Although unemployment climbed to 25 percent, most Americans did not lose homes or jobs during the depression. Professional and white-collar workers fared better than industrial workers and farmers. Many middle-class families, however, "made do" with less. Women economized, using cheap ingredients to extend food further ("Cracker-Stuffed Cabbage"). Although most families' incomes fell, the impact was cushioned by the falling cost of consumer goods. Men who could no longer provide well for their families often deemed themselves "failures." But even for the relatively affluent, the psychological impact of the depression was inescapable. The human toll of the depression was visible everywhere, and no one took economic security for granted any more.

Hoover's Limited Solutions

Although **Herbert Hoover**, "the Great Engineer," had a reputation as a problem solver, no one, including Hoover, knew what to do about the crisis. Experts disagreed about the depression's causes and about potential solutions. Many business leaders believed financial panics and depressions, though painful, were part of a natural "business cycle." Economic depressions, according to this theory, brought down inflated prices and cleared the way for real growth.

Herbert Hoover: 31st President of the United States, 1929–1933.

Herbert Hoover disagreed. "The economic fatalist," he said, "believes that these crises are inevitable.... I would remind these pessimists that exactly the same thing was once said of typhoid, cholera, and smallpox." Hoover had faith in "associationalism": business and professional organizations, coordinated by the federal government, uniting to solve the nation's problems. The federal government would serve as a clearing-house for ideas that state and local governments and private industry could voluntarily implement.

While many Americans thought Hoover was doing nothing, in truth he stretched his beliefs about the role of government to their limit. He tried voluntarism, exhortation, and limited government intervention. First, he sought voluntary pledges from business groups to keep wages stable and renew investment. But when businesspeople looked at their own bottom lines, few could honor those promises.

As unemployment climbed, Hoover continued to encourage voluntary responses, creating the President's Organization on Unemployment Relief (POUR) to generate private contributions to aid the destitute. Although 1932 saw record charitable contributions, they were inadequate. By mid-1932, one-quarter of New York's private charities, funds exhausted, closed their doors. State and city officials found their treasuries drying up, too. Hoover feared that government "relief" would destroy self-reliance in the poor. Thus, he authorized federal funds to feed the drought-stricken livestock of Arkansas farmers but rejected a smaller grant providing food for impoverished farm families. Many Americans became angry at Hoover's seeming insensitivity. Two short years after his election, Hoover was the most hated man in America.

Hoover eventually endorsed limited federal action to combat the crisis, but it was too little. Federal public works projects, such as the Grand Coulee Dam in Washington, created some jobs. The Federal Farm Board, established in 1929, supported crop prices by lending money to cooperatives to buy crops and keep them off the market. But the board ran short of money, and unsold surpluses jammed warehouses.

Hoover also signed into law the Hawley-Smoot Tariff (1930) to support American farmers and manufacturers by raising import duties to a staggering 40 percent. Instead, it hampered international trade as other nations created their own protective tariffs. And, as other nations sold less to the United States, they had less money to repay their U.S. debts or buy American products. Fearing the collapse of the international monetary system, Hoover in 1931 announced a moratorium on the payment of First World War debts and reparations.

In January 1932, the administration took its most forceful action. The **Reconstruction Finance Corporation** (RFC) provided federal loans to banks, insurance companies, and railroads, which Hoover hoped would shore up those industries and halt the disinvestment in the American economy. Here, Hoover compromised his ideological principles. This was direct government intervention, not "voluntarism." If he would support direct assistance to private industries, why not relief to the millions of unemployed?

Reconstruction Finance Corporation: Agency set up under the Hoover administration during the Great Depression to make loans to shore up banks and other industries.

Protest and Social Unrest

More and more Americans asked that question. Social unrest and violence surfaced as the depression deepened. This raised the specter of popular revolt, and Chicago mayor Anton Cermak told Congress that if the federal government did not send his citizens aid, it would have to send troops instead.

Tens of thousands of farmers took the law into their own hands. Angry crowds forced auctioneers to accept just a few dollars for foreclosed property, and then returned it to the original owners. In August 1932, a new group, the Farmers' Holiday Association, encouraged farmers to hold back agricultural products to limit supply and drive prices up. In the Midwest, farmers barricaded roads to stop other farmers' trucks, and then dumped the contents in roadside ditches. In cities, the most militant actions came from Unemployed Councils, local groups for unemployed workers that were created and led by Communist Party members. Communist leaders believed that the depression demonstrated capitalism's failure and offered an opportunity for revolution. Few of the quarter-million Americans joining the local Unemployed Councils sought revolution, but they did demand

National Archives

In the summer of 1932, unemployed veterans of the First World War gathered in Washington, D.C. to demand payment of their soldiers' bonuses. After Congress rejected the appeal of the "Bonus Army," some refused to leave and President Hoover sent U.S. Army troops to force them out. Here, police battle Bonus Marchers in July 1932.

action. When three thousand members of Detroit Unemployment Councils marched on Ford's River Rouge plant in 1932, Ford security guards opened fire on the crowd, killing four men and wounding fifty. As social unrest spread, so did racial violence. Vigilante committees offered bounties to force African Americans off the Illinois Central Railroad's payroll: $25 for maiming and $100 for killing black workers. Ten men were murdered and at least seven wounded. The Ku Klux Klan reemerged, and white mobs tortured, hanged, and mutilated thirty-eight black men during the depression's early years. Racial violence was not restricted to the South; lynchings took place in Pennsylvania, Minnesota, Colorado, and Ohio as well.

Bonus Army   The worst confrontation happened in summer 1932. More than fifteen thousand unemployed World War I veterans and their families converged on the nation's capital as Congress debated a bill authorizing immediate payment of cash "bonuses" that veterans were scheduled to receive in 1945. Calling themselves the Bonus Army, they set up a sprawling "Hooverville" shantytown across the river from the Capitol. Concerned about the impact on the federal budget, President Hoover opposed the bonus bill, and the Senate voted it down.

Most of the Bonus Marchers left Washington, but several thousand stayed. Calling them "insurrectionists"—though many were simply destitute—the president set a deadline for their departure. On July 28, Hoover sent in the U.S. Army, led by General Douglas MacArthur. Four infantry companies, four troops of cavalry, a machine gun squadron, and six tanks converged on the veterans and their families. What followed shocked Americans: men and women chased by horsemen; children tear-gassed; shacks set afire. Hoover was unrepentant, insisting in a campaign speech, "Thank God we still have a government that knows how to deal with a mob."

As the depression worsened, the appeal of a strong leader—someone who would take decisive action—grew. In February 1933, the U.S. Senate passed a resolution calling for newly elected president **Franklin D. Roosevelt** to assume "unlimited power." The rise to power of Hitler and his National Socialist Party in depression-ravaged Germany was an obvious parallel.

Franklin D. Roosevelt: 32nd President of the United States, 1933–1945.

Franklin D. Roosevelt and the Launching of the New Deal

How did the federal government take on new roles during the period dubbed "The First Hundred Days"?

In the 1932 presidential campaign, Democratic challenger Franklin Delano Roosevelt insisted that the federal government had to play a greater role. Roosevelt supported direct relief payments for the unemployed, declaring that such governmental aid was "a matter of social duty." He pledged "a new deal for the American people," though he was never very explicit about its outlines. His most concrete proposals, in fact, were sometimes contradictory. But Roosevelt committed to use the power of the federal government to combat the paralyzing economic crisis. Voters chose Roosevelt over Hoover overwhelmingly.

Franklin Roosevelt, the twentieth-century president most beloved by America's "common people," was born into upper-class privilege. After graduating from Harvard College and Columbia Law School, he married **Eleanor Roosevelt**, Theodore Roosevelt's niece and his own fifth cousin, once removed. He served in the New York State legislature, was appointed assistant secretary of the navy by Woodrow Wilson, and, at age thirty-eight, ran for vice president in 1920 on the Democratic Party's losing ticket.

Eleanor Roosevelt: Widely popular and influential First lady of the United States from 1933 to 1945.

In 1921, Roosevelt was stricken with polio and was bedridden for two years. He lost the use of his legs but gained, according to his wife Eleanor, a new strength of character. By 1928, Roosevelt was sufficiently recovered to run for—and win—the governorship of New York, and then to accept the Democratic Party's presidential nomination in 1932.

Elected in November 1932, Roosevelt would not take office until March 4, 1933. (The Twentieth Amendment to the Constitution shifted future inaugurations to January 20.) In this long interregnum, the American banking system reached the verge of collapse.

Banking Crisis

The origins of the banking crisis lay in the flush years of World War I and the 1920s, when American banks made risky loans. After real-estate and stock market bubbles burst in 1929 and agricultural prices collapsed, these loans soured, leaving many banks without sufficient funds to cover customers' deposits. Fearful of losing their savings, depositors withdrew money from banks and put it into gold or under mattresses.

"Bank runs," in which crowds of frightened customers demanded their money, became common.

By the 1932 election, the bank crisis was escalating rapidly. Hoover, the lame-duck president, refused to take action without Roosevelt's support, while Roosevelt refused to endorse actions he could not control. By Roosevelt's inauguration on March 4, every state had either suspended banking operations or restricted depositors' access to their money. The new president understood that the total collapse of the U.S. banking system would threaten the nation's survival.

Roosevelt vowed in his inaugural address to face the crisis "frankly and boldly." The lines best remembered from his speech are words of comfort: "the only thing we have to fear is fear itself—nameless, unreasoning, unjustified terror." But the only loud cheers came when Roosevelt asserted that, if need be, "I shall ask the Congress for the one remaining instrument to meet the crisis—broad Executive power to wage a war against the emergency, as great as the power that would be given to me if we were in fact invaded by a foreign foe."

Link to the video and transcript of FDR's first inaugural address.

The next day Roosevelt, using powers legally granted by the World War I Trading with the Enemy Act, closed the nation's banks for a four-day "holiday" and summoned Congress to an emergency session. He introduced the Emergency Banking Relief Bill, which was passed sight unseen by unanimous House vote, approved 73 to 7 in the Senate, and immediately signed into law. It provided federal authority to reopen solvent banks and reorganize the rest, and authorized federal money to shore up private banks. Roosevelt had attacked "unscrupulous money changers," and critics of the failed banking system hoped he planned to remove the banks from private hands. Instead, Roosevelt's banking policy was like Hoover's—a fundamentally conservative approach that upheld the status quo.

The banking bill could save the U.S. banking system only if Americans were confident enough to deposit money in the reopened banks. In the first of his radio "Fireside Chats," Roosevelt asked Americans for support. The next morning when banks opened, people lined up to deposit money. It was an enormous triumph for the new president. It also demonstrated that Roosevelt, though unafraid to take bold action, was not as radical as some wished or as others feared.

First Hundred Days

During the ninety-nine-day-long special session of Congress, dubbed by journalists "The First Hundred Days," the federal government took on dramatically new roles. Roosevelt, aided by advisers—lawyers, university professors, and social workers collectively nicknamed "the Brain Trust"—and by the capable First Lady, sought to revive the American economy. These "New Dealers" had no single plan, and Roosevelt fluctuated between balancing the budget and massive deficit spending (spending more than is taken in in taxes and borrowing the difference). But with a mandate for action and the support of a Democrat-controlled Congress, the new administration produced a flood of legislation. Two basic strategies emerged during the First Hundred Days. New Dealers experimented with national economic planning, and they created a range of "relief" programs for the needy.

National Industrial Recovery Act (NIRA): Agency that brought together business leaders to draft codes of "fair competition" for their industries. These codes recognized workers' rights to establish unions, set production limits, prescribed wages and working conditions, and forbade pricecutting and unfair competitive practices.

Agricultural Adjustment Act (AAA): New Deal program that sought to curb the surplus farm production that depressed crop prices by offering payments for reducing production of seven farm products.

National Industrial Recovery Act

At the heart of the New Deal experiment were the **National Industrial Recovery Act (NIRA)** and the **Agricultural Adjustment Act (AAA)**. The NIRA was based on the belief that "destructive competition" worsened industry's economic woes. Skirting anti-trust regulation, the NIRA authorized competing businesses to cooperate in crafting industrywide codes that allowed manufacturers to establish industry-wide prices and wages. With wages and prices stabilized, the theory went, consumer spending would increase, thus allowing industries to rehire workers. Significantly, Section 7(a) guaranteed industrial workers the right to "organize and bargain collectively"—in other words, to unionize. Individual businesses' participation in this **National Recovery Administration** (NRA) program was voluntary, so though it was larger than previous government–private sector cooperation, it was not very different from Hoover-era "associationalism."

As small-business owners feared, big business dominated the NRA-mandated cartels. NRA staff lacked the experience to stand up to corporate representatives. The twenty-six-year-old NRA staffer who oversaw the creation of the petroleum industry code was "helped" by twenty highly paid oil industry lawyers. The majority of the 541 codes approved by the NRA reflected the interests of major corporations, not small-business owners, labor, or consumers. Fundamentally, the NRA did not deliver economic recovery. In 1935, the Supreme Court ended the fragile, floundering system when it ruled that the NRA extended federal power past its constitutional bounds.

National Recovery Administration: Agency responsible for administering the National Industrial Recovery Act and establishing fair-trade codes for industries with the goal of stimulating the economy.

Agricultural Adjustment Act

The Agricultural Adjustment Act (AAA) had a more enduring effect. Establishing a national system of crop controls, it offered subsidies to farmers who agreed to limit production of specific crops. (Overproduction drove crop prices down.) In 1933, the nation's farmers destroyed 8.5 million piglets and plowed under crops in the fields. Millions of hungry Americans found it difficult to understand this waste of food.

Government crop subsidies proved a disaster for tenant farmers and sharecroppers, who were turned off their land as landlords cut production. In the South, the number of sharecropper farms dropped by almost one-third between 1930 and 1940 and dispossessed farmers—many of them African American—headed to cities and towns. But the subsidies did help many. In the Dakotas, government payments accounted for almost three-quarters of the total farm income for 1934.

In 1936, the Supreme Court found that the AAA, like the NRA, was unconstitutional. But the AAA (unlike the NRA) was too popular with its constituency, American farmers, to disappear. The legislation was rewritten to meet the Supreme Court's objections, and farm subsidies continued into the twenty-first century.

Relief Programs

Roosevelt moved quickly to implement poor relief: $3 billion in federal dollars were allocated in 1935. New Dealers—like many other Americans—disapproved of direct relief payments. Thus, New Deal programs emphasized "work relief." By January 1934, the Civil Works Administration hired 4 million people, most earning $15 a week. And the **Civilian Conservation Corps** (CCC) paid unmarried young men $1 a day to do hard outdoor labor: building dams and reservoirs, creating trails in national parks. By 1942, the CCC employed 2.5 million men, including eighty thousand Native Americans working on western Indian reservations.

Work relief programs rarely included poor women. Mothers of young children were usually classified as "unemployable" and offered "mother's-aid" grants that,

Civilian Conservation Corps: Relief program that employed jobless young men in such government projects as reforestation, park maintenance, and erosion control.

as historian Linda Gordon explains, were miniscule compared to wages in federal works programs. While federal relief programs rejected the poor-law tradition that distinguished between the "deserving" and the "undeserving" poor, local officials did not. Journalist Lorena Hickok reported to Harry Hopkins that "a woman who isn't a good housekeeper is apt to have a pretty rough time of it."

The **Public Works Administration** (PWA), created by Title II of the National Industrial Recovery Act, appropriated $3.3 billion for PWA projects in 1933. New Deal public works programs built infrastructure nationwide, especially in underdeveloped regions.

But the PWA's main purpose was to pump federal money into the economy. As federal revenues for 1932 had totaled only $1.9 billion, this huge appropriation shows that the Roosevelt administration was willing to use the controversial technique of deficit spending to stimulate the economy.

In the three months until Congress adjourned on June 16, 1933, Roosevelt delivered fifteen messages proposing major legislation, and Congress passed fifteen significant laws (see Table 25.1). The United States rebounded from near collapse. As New Deal programs were implemented, unemployment fell steadily from 13 million in 1933 to 9 million in 1936. Farm prices rose, along with wages and salaries, and business failures abated (see Figure 25.1).

Public Works Administration: New Deal relief agency that appropriated $3.3 billion for large-scale public works projects to provide jobs and stimulate the economy.

TABLE 25.1 New Deal Achievements

Year	Labor	Agriculture and Environment	Business and Industrial Recovery	Relief	Reform
1933	Section 7(a) of NIRA	Agricultural Adjustment Act Farm Credit Act	Emergency Banking Relief Act Economy Act Beer-Wine Revenue Act Banking Act of 1933 (guaranteed deposits) National Industrial Recovery Act	Civilian Conservation Corps Federal Emergency Relief Act Home Owners Refinancing Act Public Works Administration Civil Works Administration	TVA Federal Securities Act
1934	National Labor Relations Board	Taylor Grazing Act			Securities Exchange Act
1935	National Labor Relations (Wagner) Act	Resettlement Administration Rural Electrification Administration		Works Progress Administration National Youth Administration	Social Security Act Public Utility Holding Company Act Revenue Act (wealth tax)
1937		Farm Security Administration		National Housing Act	
1938	Fair Labor Standards Act	Agricultural Adjustment Act of 1938			

Source: Adapted from Charles Sellers, Henry May, and Neil R. McMillen, *A Synopsis of American History*, 6th ed. Copyright © 1985 by Houghton Mifflin Company. Reprinted by permission.

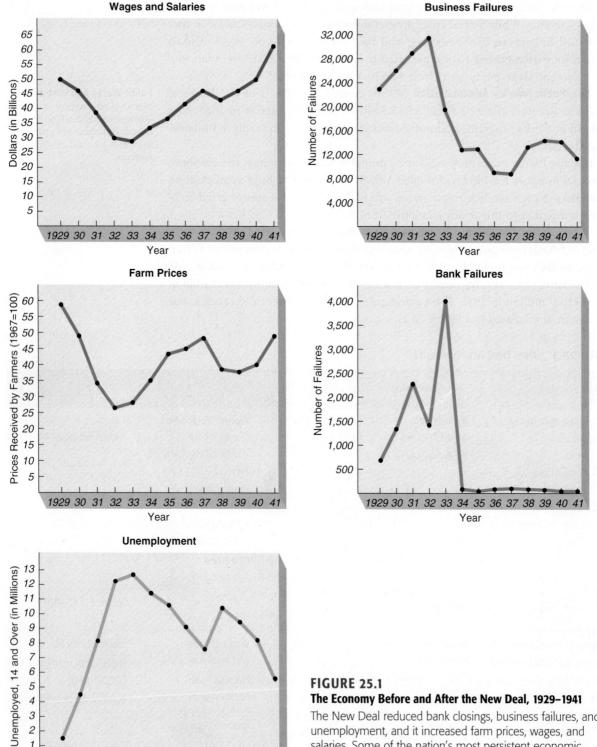

FIGURE 25.1

The Economy Before and After the New Deal, 1929–1941

The New Deal reduced bank closings, business failures, and unemployment, and it increased farm prices, wages, and salaries. Some of the nation's most persistent economic problems, however, did not disappear until the advent of the Second World War.

Political Pressure and the Second New Deal

What were the hallmarks of the Second New Deal?

The unprecedented popular and congressional support for Roosevelt's New Deal did not last. The seeming unity of the First Hundred Days masked deep divides within the nation, and once the immediate crisis was averted the struggle over solutions began. Some tried to stop the expansion of government power, others pushed for increased governmental action to combat continuing poverty and inequality.

Business Opposition As the economy partially recovered, many wealthy business leaders criticized the New Deal. They condemned government regulation and taxation, along with the use of deficit financing for public works. In 1934, several corporate leaders joined former presidential candidate Al Smith and disaffected conservative Democrats to establish the American Liberty League to campaign against New Deal "radicalism." Hoping to turn southern whites against the New Deal and splinter the Democratic Party, the Liberty League also secretly channeled funds to a racist group in the South, which tried to foster protest by circulating pictures of the First Lady with African Americans.

Demagogues and Populists Other Americans (sometimes called "populists") thought the government favored business over the people. Unemployment decreased—but 9 million people were still jobless. In 1934, a wave of strikes involving 1.5 million workers hit the nation. In 1935, enormous dust storms enveloped the southern plains, killing livestock and driving families like the Montgomerys from their land. As their dissatisfaction mounted, so did the appeal of various demagogues, who played to people's prejudices.

Father Charles Coughlin, a Roman Catholic priest whose weekly radio sermons reached 30 million listeners, spoke to those who felt they had lost control of their lives to distant elites. Increasingly anti–New Deal, he was also anti-Semitic, telling listeners that an international conspiracy of Jewish bankers caused their problems.

Another challenge came from Dr. Francis E. Townsend, a public health officer in Long Beach, California, who lost his job at age sixty-seven with only $100 in savings. His situation was common. With social welfare left to the states, only about 400,000 of the 6.6 million elderly Americans received any state-supplied pensions. As employment and savings disappeared, many older people fell into poverty. Townsend proposed that Americans over age sixty should receive a government pension of $200 a month, financed by a new "transaction" (sales) tax. Townsend's plan was fiscally impossible (almost three-quarters of working Americans earned $200 a month or less) and profoundly regressive (because sales tax rates are the same for everyone, they take a larger share of income from those who earn least). Nonetheless, 20 million Americans, or 1 in 5 adults, signed petitions supporting this plan.

Then there was Huey Long, perhaps the most successful populist demagogue in American history. As a U.S. senator, Long initially supported the New Deal but soon decided that Roosevelt had fallen captive to big business. In 1934, Long proposed that the government seize (by taxation) all income exceeding $1 million a year and wealth in excess of $5 million per family and use those funds to provide each American family an annual income of $2,000 and a one-time homestead allowance of $5,000. By mid-1935, Long's movement claimed 7 million members, and few doubted that he aspired to the presidency. But Long was killed by a bodyguard's bullet during an assassination attempt in September 1935.

Left-Wing Critics

The political left also gained ground. Socialists and communists alike criticized the New Deal for trying to save capitalism instead of lessening the inequality of power and wealth in America. In California, muckraker and socialist Upton Sinclair won the Democratic gubernatorial nomination in 1934 with the slogan "End Poverty in California" and the left-wing Progressive Party provided seven of Wisconsin's ten representatives to Congress. Even the U.S. Communist Party found new support as it campaigned for social welfare and relief. Disclaiming any intention of overthrowing the U.S. government, the party proclaimed that "Communism Is Twentieth Century Americanism" and cooperated with left-wing labor unions, student groups, and writers' organizations in a "**Popular Front**" against fascism abroad and racism at home. In the late 1920s, it established the League of Struggle for Negro Rights to fight lynching, and from 1931 on provided critical legal and financial support to the "Scottsboro Boys," who were falsely accused of raping two white women in Alabama (see page 673). In 1938, the party had fifty-five thousand members.

Popular Front: Coalition of communist and politically left groups against fascism and racism.

Shaping the Second New Deal

It was not only external critics who pushed Roosevelt to focus on social justice. Due to Eleanor Roosevelt's influence, the president's administration included many progressive activists. **Frances Perkins**, America's first woman cabinet member, came from a social work background, as did Roosevelt's close adviser Harold Ickes. Women social reformers who coalesced around the First Lady played important roles, and African Americans had an unprecedented voice in this White House. By 1936, at least fifty black Americans held relatively important positions in New Deal agencies and cabinet-level departments. Journalists called these officials—who met on Friday evenings at the home of Mary McLeod Bethune, Director of Negro Affairs for the National Youth Administration—the "black cabinet."

Frances Perkins: Served as Secretary of Labor from 1933 to 1945, former Progressive reformer, and first woman cabinet member.

As the election of 1936 neared, Roosevelt knew he had to appeal to seemingly contradictory desires. Americans hit hard by the depression looked to the New Deal for help. Those with a tenuous hold on the middle class wanted security and stability. Still others, frightened by populist promises of people like Long and Coughlin, wanted the New Deal to preserve American capitalism. With this in mind, Roosevelt took the initiative again.

During the period historians call the Second New Deal, Roosevelt introduced progressive programs aimed at providing "greater security for the average man than he has ever known before in the history of America." The first triumph of the Second New Deal was a law that Roosevelt called "the Big Bill." The Emergency Relief Appropriation Act provided $4 billion in new deficit spending, primarily for massive public works programs for the jobless. It also established the Resettlement Administration, which resettled destitute families and organized rural homestead communities and suburban greenbelt towns for low-income workers; the Rural

Electrification Administration, which brought electricity to isolated areas; and the National Youth Administration, which sponsored work-relief programs for young adults.

Works Progress Administration

The largest and best-known program was the **Works Progress Administration** (WPA), later renamed the Work Projects Administration. The WPA employed more than 8.5 million people who built 650,000 miles of highways and roads, and 125,000 public buildings, as well as bridges, reservoirs, irrigation systems, sewage treatment plants, parks, playgrounds, and swimming pools nationwide. WPA workers built or renovated schools and hospitals, operated nurseries for pre-school children, and taught 1.5 million adults to read and write.

The WPA also employed artists, musicians, writers, and actors in cultural programs. The WPA's Federal Theater Project brought vaudeville, circuses, and theater, including African American and Yiddish plays, to cities and towns. Its Arts Project hired painters and sculptors to teach in rural schools and commissioned artists to decorate post office walls with murals depicting American life. Perhaps the most ambitious program, the WPA's Federal Writers' Project (FWP) hired authors such as John Steinbeck and Richard Wright to create guidebooks for every state and write about the people of the United States. More than two thousand elderly former slaves told their stories to FWP writers as "slave narratives." Life stories of sharecroppers and textile workers were published as *These Are Our Lives* (1939). WPA arts projects were controversial, for many of the WPA artists, performers, and writers sympathized with the political struggles of workers and farmers, and some were communists.

Coit Tower, San Francisco

The Works Progress Administration commissioned twenty-six artists to create a mural depicting scenes of life in modern California for San Francisco's Coit Tower, which had been completed in 1933. "The Woman with Calla Lilies," a detail from the large fresco that filled the lobby, was painted by Maxine Albro.

Works Progress Administration: Massive public works program that hired people to construct highways, roads, buildings; it also provided jobs for artists, actors, and writers in cultural programs.

Social Security Act

Big Bill programs were part of a short-term "emergency" strategy, but Roosevelt's long-term strategy centered on the **Social Security Act**. This measure created, for the first time, a federal system to provide for the social welfare of American citizens. Its key provision was a pension system in which eligible workers paid Social Security taxes on wages and their employers contributed an equivalent amount; these workers then received federal retirement benefits. The Social Security Act also created welfare programs, including a cooperative federal-state system of unemployment compensation and Aid to Dependent Children (later renamed Aid to Families with Dependent Children, AFDC) for needy children in families without fathers present.

Social Security Act: New Deal relief measure that launched a federal retirement benefits system as well as unemployment compensation, aid to needy children and other welfare benefits.

Compared with the national systems of social security in most western European nations, the U.S. system was fairly conservative. First, the government did not pay for old-age benefits; workers and their bosses did. Second, the tax was regressive in that the more workers earned, the less they were taxed proportionally. Finally, the law did not cover agricultural labor, domestic service, and "casual labor not in the course of the employer's trade or business" (for example, janitorial work at a hospital). Thus, a disproportionately high number of people of color, who worked as farm laborers, domestic servants, or in service jobs, received no benefits. The act also excluded public-sector employees, so many teachers, nurses, librarians, and social workers (mostly women) went uncovered. (Although the original Social Security Act provided no retirement benefits for spouses or widows of covered workers, Congress added these benefits in 1939.) Despite these limitations, the federal government took some responsibility for the economic security of the aged, the temporarily unemployed, dependent children, and people with disabilities.

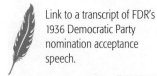 Link to a transcript of FDR's 1936 Democratic Party nomination acceptance speech.

Roosevelt's Populist Strategies

As the 1936 election approached, Roosevelt adopted the populist language of his critics. Denouncing the "unjust concentration of wealth and power," he proposed that government should "cut the giants down to size" through antitrust suits and heavy corporate taxes. He also supported the Wealth Tax Act, which helped redistribute income (see Figure 25.2).

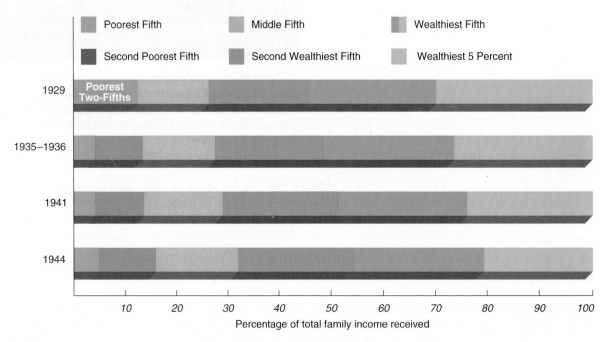

FIGURE 25.2
Distribution of Total Family Income Among the American People, 1929–1944 (percentage)
Although the New Deal provided economic relief to the American people, it did not, as its critics so often charged, significantly redistribute income downward from the rich to the poor.
Source: Adapted from U.S. Bureau of the Census, *Historical Statistics of the United States, Colonial Times to 1970.* Bicentennial Edition, Washington, D.C.: U.S. Government Printing Office, 1975, page 301.

In November 1936, Roosevelt won the presidency by a landslide. Democrats won such huge majorities in the House and Senate that some worried the two-party system might collapse. In fact, Roosevelt and the Democrats had forged a powerful "New Deal coalition," consisting of the urban working class (especially immigrants from southern and eastern Europe), organized labor, the eleven states of the Confederacy (the "Solid South"), and northern blacks. African Americans in northern cities now constituted voting blocs, and New Deal benefits drew them away from the Republican Party, which they had long supported as the party of Lincoln. This New Deal coalition ensured that Democrats would occupy the White House for most of the next thirty years.

Labor

During the depression's worst years, American workers struggled for the rights of labor. Management, however, resisted unionization, with some refusing to recognize unions and others hiring armed thugs to intimidate workers. When workers walked off the job, employers replaced them with strike-breakers. Workers tried to keep the strikebreakers from crossing picket lines, and the situation often turned violent. Local police or National Guard troops frequently intervened for management. As strikes spread, violence erupted in the steel, automobile, and textile industries, among lumber workers in the Pacific Northwest, and among teamsters in the Midwest.

> How did Roosevelt provide support for labor?

The Roosevelt administration supported labor with the 1935 **National Labor Relations (Wagner) Act**. It guaranteed workers the right to organize unions and bargain collectively. It outlawed "unfair labor practices," such as firing workers who joined unions, prohibited management from sponsoring company unions, and required employers to bargain with labor's elected union representatives on wages, hours, and working conditions. The Wagner Act created an enforcement mechanism: the National Labor Relations Board (NLRB). By decade's end, the NLRB played a key role in mediating disputes. With federal protection, union membership grew from 3.6 million in 1929 to 7 million in 1938.

National Labor Relations (Wagner) Act: Guaranteed workers the rights to organize and bargain collectively and outlawed unfair labor practices.

The Wagner Act further alienated business leaders from the New Deal. "No Obedience," proclaimed an editorial in a leading business magazine.

Rivalry Between Craft and Industrial Unions

The growth and increasing militancy of the labor movement exacerbated an existing division between "craft" and "industrial" unions. Craft unions represented labor's elite: skilled workers in a particular trade, such as carpentry. Industrial unions represented all the workers, skilled and unskilled, in a given industry. In the 1930s, industrial unions grew dramatically.

Craft unions dominated the American Federation of Labor, the powerful umbrella organization for specific unions. Most AFL leaders offered little support for industrial organizing. Many looked down on industrial workers, disproportionately immigrants from southern and eastern Europe. Skilled workers had economic interests different from those of unskilled workers, and more conservative craft unionists were alarmed at what they saw as the radicalism of industrial unions.

The Women's Emergency Brigade and the General Motors Sit-Down Strike

During the 1937 sit-down strike by automobile workers in Flint, Michigan, a women's "emergency brigade" of wives, daughters, sisters, and sweethearts demonstrated daily at the plant. When police tried to force the men out of Chevrolet Plant No. 9 by filling it with tear gas, the women used clubs to smash the plant's windows and let in fresh air. Sixteen people were injured that day in the riot between police and strikers. The following day the Women's Emergency Brigade marched again. Using this photograph as visual evidence, how did these women attempt to demonstrate the respectability and mainstream nature of their protest? How does that message fit with the clubs several still carry?

© Bettmann/Corbis

Gerenda Johnson, wife of a striker, leads a march past the GM Chevrolet small parts plant on the day following a violent conflict between police and strikers.

In 1935, John L. Lewis, head of the United Mine Workers and the nation's most prominent labor leader, resigned as vice president of the AFL. He and other industrial unionists created the Committee for Industrial Organization (CIO); the AFL then suspended all CIO unions. In 1938, the slightly renamed **Congress of Industrial Organizations** had 3.7 million members, slightly more than the AFL's 3.4 million. Unlike the AFL, the CIO included women and people of color, giving these "marginal" workers greater employment security and the benefits of collective bargaining.

Congress of Industrial Organizations: 3.7 million member association of industrial unions; included women and people of color.

Sit-Down Strikes
The most decisive labor conflict came when the United Auto Workers (UAW) demanded recognition from General Motors (GM), Chrysler, and Ford. When GM refused, UAW organizers and workers at the Fisher Body plant in Flint, Michigan, held a "sit-down strike" on December 30, 1936 *inside* the factory. Refusing to leave, they immobilized GM production. GM tried to force them out by turning off the heat. When police tried tear gas; strikers turned water hoses on them.

Link to songs, photographs, and video from the GM sit-down strike of 1936–1937.

As the sit-down strike spread to adjacent plants, auto production plummeted. General Motors obtained a court order to evacuate the plant, but the strikers stood firm, risking imprisonment and fines. In a critical decision, Michigan's governor refused to send in the National Guard. After forty-four days, GM agreed to recognize the union, and Chrysler followed. Ford held out until 1941.

Memorial Day Massacre
On the heels of this triumph, however, came a reminder of the costs of labor's struggle. On Memorial Day 1937, picnicking workers and their families marched toward the Republic Steel plant in Chicago, intending to support strikers picketing there. Police ordered them to disperse. One marcher threw something, and the police attacked. Ten men were killed, seven shot in the back. Thirty marchers were wounded, including a woman and three children. Many Americans, fed up with labor strife and violence, showed little sympathy for the workers.

Gradually violence receded, as the National Labor Relations Board successfully mediated disputes. Unionized workers—about 23 percent of the nonagricultural work force—saw their standard of living rise. By 1941, the average steelworker could afford to buy a pair of shoes for his children every other year.

Federal Power and the Nationalization of Culture

In what ways did the Depression inspire the emergence of a youth culture?

In the 1930s, national media, politics, and the federal government played an increasingly important role in the lives of Americans from different regions, classes, and ethnic backgrounds. In 1930, with the single exception of the post office, Americans had little direct contact with the federal government. By the end of the 1930s, almost 35 percent of the population received some federal government benefit, whether crop subsidies through the federal AAA or a WPA job or relief payments through FERA. Beginning with the New Deal, Americans expected the federal government to play a major role in the life of the nation.

New Deal in the West
The New Deal changed the American West more than any other region, as federally sponsored construction of dams and other public works projects reshaped the region's economy and environment. The Boulder Dam (later renamed for Herbert Hoover) harnessed the Colorado River, providing water to southern California municipalities and using hydroelectric power to produce electricity for Los Angeles and southern Arizona. The water from such dams opened new areas to agriculture and allowed western cities to expand; the

cheap electricity they produced attracted industry. After the completion of Washington State's Grand Coulee Dam in 1941, the federal government controlled a great deal of water and hydroelectric power in the region, which effectively meant control over the region's future.

The federal government also brought millions of acres of western land under its control in the 1930s. To combat the environmental disaster of the Dust Bowl and keep agriculture prices from falling further, federal programs worked to limit production. In 1934, the Taylor Grazing Act imposed new restrictions on ranchers' use of public lands for grazing stock. Federal stock reduction programs probably saved the western cattle industry, but they destroyed the Navajos' traditional economy by forcing them to reduce the size of sheep herds on federally protected reservation lands. Large western farms and ranches benefited from federal subsidies and crop supports, but such programs also increased federal government control in the region.

New Deal for Native Americans

New federal activism also extended to the West's people. Previous federal policy toward Native Americans, especially those on reservations, were disastrous. The Bureau of Indian Affairs (BIA) was riddled with corruption; in its attempts to "assimilate" Native Americans, it separated children from parents, suppressed native languages, and outlawed tribal religious practices. Division of tribal lands failed to promote individual land ownership. In the early 1930s, Native Americans were the poorest group in the nation, plagued with an infant mortality rate twice that of white Americans.

In 1933, Roosevelt named one of the BIA's most vocal critics to head the agency. John Collier, founder of the American Indian Defense Agency, meant to completely reverse America's Indian policy. The **Indian Reorganization Act** (1934) worked toward ending forced assimilation and restoring Indian lands to tribal ownership. Indian tribes regained their status as semisovereign nations, guaranteed "internal sovereignty" in matters not limited by acts of Congress.

Indian Reorganization Act: 1934 measure that sought to restore Indian lands to tribal ownership and provided federal recognition of tribes as semisovereign nations.

Some Indians denounced the IRA as a "back-to-the-blanket" measure based on romantic notions of "authentic" Indian culture. The tribal government structure specified by the IRA was culturally alien to tribes such as the Papagos, whose language had no word for "representative." The Navajo nation refused to ratify the IRA. Eventually, however, 181 tribes organized under the IRA, which laid the groundwork for future economic development and limited political autonomy among native peoples.

New Deal in the South

New Dealers did not set out to transform the American West, but they did intend to transform the South, which was long mired in poverty. In 1929, the South's per capita income of $365 per year compared to $921 in the West. More than half of southern farm families were tenants or sharecroppers. Almost 15 percent of South Carolina's people could not read or write.

Tennessee Valley Authority: Ambitious plan of economic development that centered on creating an extensive hydroelectric power project in the poor Appalachian area.

The largest federal intervention in the South was the **Tennessee Valley Authority** (TVA), authorized by Congress during Roosevelt's First Hundred Days. The TVA was created to develop a water and hydroelectric power project similar to the West's multipurpose dams of the West (see Map 25.1). However, confronted with the poverty

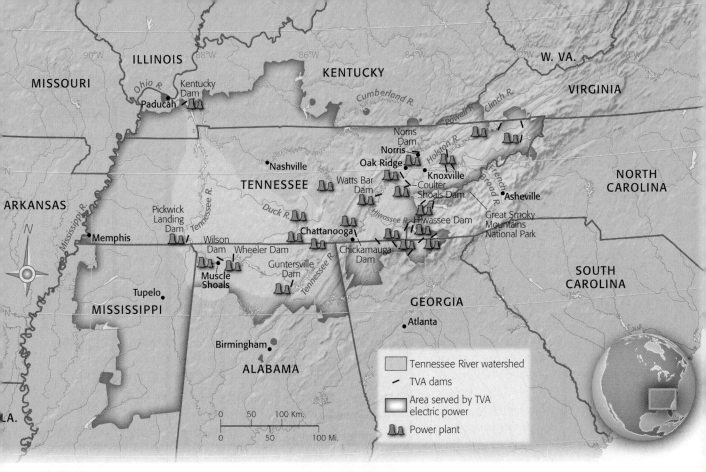

MAP 25.1

The Tennessee Valley Authority

To control flooding and generate electricity, the Tennessee Valley Authority constructed dams along the Tennessee River and its tributaries from Paducah, Kentucky, to Knoxville, Tennessee.

Source: Copyright © Cengage Learning

of the Tennessee River Valley region (which included parts of Virginia, North Carolina, Tennessee, Georgia, Alabama, Mississippi, and Kentucky), the TVA expanded to promote economic development, bring electricity to rural areas, restored fields worn out from overuse, and fight malaria.

Although it benefited many southerners, the TVA proved to be an environmental disaster. TVA strip mining caused soil erosion. Its coal-burning generators released sulfur oxides, which combined with water vapor to produce acid rain. Above all, the TVA degraded the water by dumping untreated sewage, toxic chemicals, and metal pollutants from strip mining into streams and rivers.

Southern senators benefited from federal dollars to their states. But they were also suspicious of federal intervention. When federal action threatened the South's racial hierarchy, they resisted. As the nation's poorest and least educated region, the South would not easily be integrated into the national culture and economy. But New Deal programs began that process and improved the lives of at least some of the region's people.

Mass Media and Popular Culture

America's national popular culture helped break down regional boundaries and foster national connections.

The 1936 Olympic Games

The 1936 Olympic Games, scheduled in Berlin under the Nazi regime, created a dilemma for the United States and other nations. Would participation in the Nazi-orchestrated spectacle lend credence to Hitler? Or would victories by other nations undermine Hitler's claims about the superiority of Germany's "Aryan race"?

From the first modern Olympic Games in 1896, international politics were always near the surface. Germany was excluded in 1920 and 1924 following its World War I defeat. The International Olympic Committee's choice (in 1931) of Berlin for the XI Olympiad was intended to welcome Germany back into the world community. However, with Hitler's rise to power in 1933, Germany determined to use the games as propaganda for the Nazi state. Soon thereafter, campaigns to boycott the Berlin Olympics emerged in several nations, including the United States.

Americans were divided over the boycott. Some U.S. Jewish groups led campaigns against U.S. participation in Berlin, while others took no public position, concerned

Leonard de Selva/Corbis

that their actions might lead to increased anti-Semitic violence within Germany. African Americans opposed the boycott and looked forward to demonstrating in Berlin how wrong Hitler's notions of Aryan superiority were. Some also pointed out the hypocrisy of American officials who criticized Germany while ignoring U.S. discrimination against black athletes.

The United States sent 312 athletes to Berlin; 18 were African Americans who won 14 medals, almost one-quarter of the U.S. total of 56. Track and field star Jesse Owens earned 4 gold medals. Jewish athletes won 13. But German athletes won 89. Despite the controversy, the XI Olympiad was a public relations triumph for Germany. The *New York Times,* impressed by the Germans' hospitality, proclaimed that the XI Olympiad put Germany "back in the fold of nations."

The idealistic vision of nations linked in peaceful athletic competition hit a low point at the 1936 Olympics. The 1940 Olympic Games, scheduled for Tokyo, were cancelled because of the escalating world war.

Corbis-Bettmann

The eleventh summer Olympic Games in Berlin were carefully crafted as propaganda for the Nazi state. And the spectacle of the 1936 games, as represented in the poster above, was impressive. But on the athletic fields, Nazi claims of Aryan superiority were challenged by athletes such as African American Jesse Owens, who is shown at left breaking the Olympic record in the 200-meter race.

Radio filled the days and nights of the depression era. As cheaper models became available, by 1937 people were buying radios at the rate of twenty-eight a minute. By decade's end, 27.5 million households owned radios, and families listened on average five hours a day. Roosevelt used radio to speak directly to the American people with "Fireside Chats."

In a time of uncertainty, radio gave citizens immediate access to political news and the actual voices of elected leaders. During hard times, radio offered escape: for children, the adventures of *Flash Gordon;* for housewives, new soap operas, such as *The Romance of Helen Trent.* Families gathered to listen to the comedy of ex-vaudevillians Jack Benny, George Burns, and Gracie Allen.

Listeners were carried to New York City for performances of the Metropolitan Opera on Saturday afternoons; to the Moana Hotel on the beach at Waikiki through the live broadcast of *Hawaii Calls;* to major league baseball games (begun by the St. Louis Cardinals in 1935) in distant cities. Millions shared the horror of the kidnapping of aviator Charles Lindbergh's son in 1932; black Americans in the urban North and rural South experienced the triumphs of African American boxer Joe Louis ("the Brown Bomber"). Radio lessened isolation and helped create a more homogeneous mass culture across class and regional lines.

The shared popular culture of 1930s America also centered on Hollywood movies. The film industry suffered in the initial years of the depression, but it rebounded after 1933. In a nation of fewer than 130 million people, between 80 and 90 million movie tickets were sold weekly by the mid-1930s, as Americans sought escape at the movies. Comedies were especially popular, from the slapstick of the Marx Brothers to the sophisticated banter of *My Man Godfrey.*

Link to clips from the Marx Brothers' film *Duck Soup.*

Yet as gangster movies (including *Little Caesar* and *Scarface*) drew crowds in the early 1930s, many Americans worried about their glamorization of crime. Faced with a boycott organized by the Roman Catholic Legion of Decency, in 1934 the film industry established a production code that would determine what American film audiences saw—and did not see—for decades.

Link to the film production code.

Finally, in an unintended consequence, federal policies to channel jobs to male heads of households strengthened the power of national popular culture. During Roosevelt's first two years in office, 1.5 million youths lost jobs; many young people who would have gone to work at age fourteen in better times decided to stay in school. By decade's end, three-quarters of American youth went to high school—up from one-half in 1920—and graduation rates doubled. As more young people went to high school, more participated in national youth culture, increasingly listening to the same music and adopting similar clothing, dances, and speech. Paradoxically, the hard times of the depression caused youth culture to spread more widely among America's young.

The Limits of the New Deal

Roosevelt began his second term with a strong mandate for reform. Almost immediately, however, the president's actions undermined his New Deal agenda. Labor strife and racial issues divided America. As the world inched toward war, domestic initiatives lost ground to foreign affairs and defense. By late 1938, New Deal reform ground to a halt.

How did Roosevelt undermine his New Deal agenda?

Court-Packing Plan   Following his landslide victory in 1936, Roosevelt sought to safeguard his progressive agenda. He saw the U.S. Supreme Court as its greatest threat. In ruling unconstitutional both the National Industrial Recovery Act (in 1935) and the Agricultural Adjustment Act (in 1936), the Court rejected specific legislative provisions and the expansion of presidential and federal power such legislation entailed. Only three of the nine justices were consistently sympathetic to New Deal "emergency" measures, and Roosevelt was convinced the Court would invalidate most of the Second New Deal legislation. Citing the advanced age and heavy workload of the nine justices, he asked Congress for authority to appoint up to six new justices. But in an era that had seen the rise of Hitler, Mussolini, and Stalin, many Americans saw Roosevelt's plan as an attack on constitutional government. Congress rebelled, and Roosevelt experienced his first major congressional defeat.

Ironically, during the long public debate over court packing, key swing-vote justices began to support pro–New Deal rulings. The Court upheld both the Social Security Act and the Wagner Act (*NLRB v. Jones & Laughlin Steel Corp.*), extending Congress's power to regulate interstate commerce. Moreover, a new judicial pension program encouraged older judges to retire, and the president appointed seven new associate justices. In the end, Roosevelt got what he wanted from the Supreme Court, but the court-packing plan damaged his credibility.

Roosevelt Recession   Another New Deal setback was the recession of 1937–1939, sometimes called the Roosevelt recession. In 1937, confident that the depression had reversed, Roosevelt reduced government spending. The Federal Reserve Board, concerned about a 3.6 percent inflation rate, tightened credit. These two actions sent the economy into a tailspin: unemployment climbed from 7.7 million in 1937 to 10.4 million in 1938.

New Dealers struggled over the direction of liberal reform. Some urged trust-busting; others advocated the resurrection of national economic planning. But Roosevelt instead chose deficit financing to stimulate consumer demand and create jobs. And in 1939, with conflict over the world war that had begun in Europe commanding more U.S. attention, the New Deal came to an end. Roosevelt sacrificed further domestic reforms in return for conservative support for his programs of military rearmament and preparedness.

Election of 1940   No president had served more than two terms, and Americans speculated about whether Franklin Roosevelt would seek a third term in 1940. Roosevelt seemed undecided until spring, when Adolf Hitler's military advances in Europe convinced him to stay on. Roosevelt promised Americans, "Your boys are not going to be sent into any foreign wars."

Roosevelt did not win this election in a landslide, but the New Deal coalition held. Roosevelt again won in the cities, supported by blue-collar workers, ethnic Americans, and African Americans. He also carried every southern state.

Race and the Limits of the New Deal   While the New Deal benefitted many Americans, it fell short of equality for people of color. National programs were implemented locally. In the South, African Americans received lower relief payments than whites and were paid less for WPA jobs. And in Tucson, Arizona, Federal Emergency Relief Agency officials divided applicants into four groups—Anglos, Mexican Americans, Mexican immigrants, and Indians—and allocated relief payments in descending order.

Such discriminatory practices were rooted in racism and served the economic interests of whites/Anglos. The majority of African American and Mexican American workers were paid so poorly that they *earned* less than impoverished whites got for "relief." Why would these workers take low-paying private jobs if government relief or government work programs provided more income? Local communities understood that federal programs threatened a political, social, and economic system based on racial hierarchies.

The case of the Scottsboro Boys illustrates racism in conflicts between local and national power in 1930s America. One night in March 1931, young black and white "hobos" starting fighting on a Southern Railroad freight train as it passed through Alabama. The black youths won and tossed the whites off the train. Afterward, a posse stopped the train, and threw the black youths in the Scottsboro, Alabama, jail. Two white women "riding the rails" claimed that the men raped them. Medical evidence later showed that the women were lying. But within two weeks, eight of the so-called Scottsboro Boys were convicted of rape by all-white juries and sentenced to death. The ninth, a boy of thirteen, was saved from the death penalty by one vote. The case—clearly a product of southern racism—became a cause célèbre, nationally and through the efforts of the Communist Party, worldwide.

The Supreme Court intervened, ruling that Alabama deprived black defendants of equal protection under the law by excluding African Americans from juries and denying defendants counsel. Alabama, however, staged new trials, convicting five of the young men (four would be paroled by 1950, and one escaped from prison). On issues of race, the South would not yield easily to federal power.

Marchers in Washington, D.C. demand freedom for the "Scottsboro Boys," young African American men who were falsely accused and convicted of raping two white women in Alabama in 1931. This 1933 march was organized by the International Labor Defense, the legal arm of the Communist Party of the United States of America, which waged a strong campaign on behalf of the nine young men.

Second, the gains made by people of color under the New Deal were limited by the political realities of southern resistance. For example, in 1938 southern Democrats blocked an antilynching bill with a six-week filibuster in the Senate. Roosevelt refused to use his political capital to break the filibuster and pass the bill. He knew that blacks would not desert the Democratic Party, but without southern senators, his legislative agenda was dead. Roosevelt wanted all Americans to experience democracy, but he had no strong commitment to civil rights.

African American Support   Why, then, did African Americans support Roosevelt and the New Deal? Because, despite discriminatory policies, the New Deal helped African Americans. By 1939, almost one-third of African American households survived on income from a WPA job. African Americans held significant positions in the Roosevelt administration, and the First Lady publically showed her commitment to racial equality. When the Daughters of the American Revolution refused to allow acclaimed black contralto Marian Anderson to perform in Washington's Constitution Hall, Eleanor Roosevelt arranged for Anderson to sing at the Lincoln Memorial instead.

Nonetheless, given the limits of New Deal reform, some African Americans concluded that self-help and direct-action movements were a surer alternative. In 1934, black tenant farmers and sharecroppers joined with poor whites to form the Southern Tenant Farmers' Union. In the North, African American consumers boycotted white merchants who refused to hire blacks. Their slogan was "Don't Buy Where You Can't Work." And the Brotherhood of Sleeping Car Porters, led by A. Philip Randolph, fought for the rights of black workers. Such actions helped improve the lives of black Americans during the 1930s.

An Assessment of the New Deal   Any analysis of the New Deal must begin with Roosevelt himself. Assessments of him varied widely during his presidency: he was passionately hated, and passionately loved. When he spoke to Americans in his Fireside Chats, hundreds of thousands wrote to him, asking for help and offering advice.

Eleanor Roosevelt played an unprecedented role in the Roosevelt administration. As First Lady, she worked for social justice, bringing reformers, trade unionists, and advocates for the rights of women and African Americans to the White House. Sometimes described as the New Deal's conscience, she took public positions—especially on African American civil rights—far more progressive than those of her husband's administration. She served as a lightning rod, deflecting conservative criticism from her husband to herself. And she cemented the allegiance of such groups as African Americans to the New Deal.

Most historians and political scientists consider Franklin Roosevelt a truly great president, citing his courage, his willingness to experiment, and his capacity to inspire the nation. Some, who see the New Deal as a squandered opportunity for true change, charge that Roosevelt lacked vision. They judge Roosevelt by goals that were not his own: Roosevelt was a pragmatist whose goal was to preserve the system. But even critics agree that he transformed the presidency. Some find this troubling, tracing the roots of "the imperial presidency" to the Roosevelt administration.

During his more than twelve years in office, Roosevelt strengthened the presidency and the federal government. Through New Deal programs, the government

Social Security

The New Deal's Social Security system has created a secure old age for millions of Americans. Although Social Security initially excluded some of America's neediest citizens such as farm and domestic workers, amendments expanded eligibility. Today, almost 99 percent of American workers are covered by Social Security. But today's Social Security system faces an uncertain future. Its troubles are due partly to decisions made during the 1930s. President Franklin Roosevelt did not want Social Security to be confused with poor relief. Instead, he created a system financed by payments from workers and employers. This system, however, presented a short-term problem. If benefits came from their contributions, workers who began receiving Social Security payments in 1940 would have received less than $1 a month. Therefore, Social Security payments from current workers paid the benefits of those already retired.

Over the years, this financing system has become increasingly unstable. In 1935, average life expectancy was under sixty-five years, the age one could collect benefits. Today, American men live almost sixteen years past the retirement, and women come close to twenty years past retirement age. In 1935, there were 16 current workers paying into the system for each person receiving benefits. In 2000, there were fewer than 3.5 workers per retiree. Unless the system is reformed, many argue, the retirement of the baby-boom cohort could even bankrupt the system.

While the stock market rose rapidly during the 1990s, some proposed that, because Social Security paid only a fraction of what individuals might have earned by investing their Social Security tax payments in stocks, let Americans do just that. Opponents declared this proposal too risky; others asked if current workers kept their money to invest, where would benefits for current retirees come from? The stock market's huge drop in 2001 and then in 2008 (and the losses sustained by private pension funds) slowed the push for privatization. Nonetheless, with the oldest baby boomers beginning to retire, questions about the future of Social Security remain an important part of the system's legacy.

expanded its regulatory responsibilities, including overseeing the nation's financial systems. For the first time, the federal government offered relief to the jobless and needy and used deficit spending to stimulate the economy. Millions of Americans benefited from government programs still operating today, among them Social Security.

However, as late as 1939, more than 10 million people remained jobless, and the nation's unemployment rate stood at 19 percent. It was not until 1941, as the nation mobilized for war that unemployment declined to 10 percent. By 1944, only 1 percent of the labor force was jobless. World War II, not the New Deal, reinvigorated the American economy.

Summary

In the 1930s, a major economic crisis threatened the nation. By 1933, almost one-quarter of America's workers were unemployed. Millions were hungry or homeless. Herbert Hoover, elected president in 1928, believed that government should play a limited role in managing the economy. He tried to solve the nation's economic problems through "associationalism," a voluntary partnership of businesses and the federal government. In the 1932 presidential election, voters turned to the candidate who promised them a "New Deal," Franklin Delano Roosevelt.

The New Deal was a liberal reform program that developed within America's capitalist and democratic system. It expanded the power of the federal government. New Deal reforms forced banks, utilities, stock markets, farms, and most businesses to adhere to federal rules. The government guaranteed workers' right to join, and federal law required employers to negotiate with workers' unions on wages, hours, and working conditions. Many unemployed workers, elderly and disabled Americans, and dependent children were protected by a national welfare system administered through the federal government. The New Deal had its detractors. Business leaders attacked its new regulations and support of organized labor. As the federal government expanded its role, tensions between national and local authority sometimes flared, and differences in regional social and economic structures challenged policymakers. Both the West and the South were transformed by federal government action, but citizens there were suspicious of federal intervention, and white southerners resisted challenges to the racial system of Jim Crow. The political realities of a fragile New Deal coalition and strong opposition shaped—and limited—New Deal programs. However, the New Deal fundamentally changed the way that the U.S. government would deal with future economic downturns and with the needs of its citizens.

Chapter Review

Hoover and Hard Times, 1929–1933

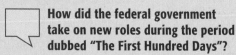

Why was Hoover reluctant to implement relief programs during the Great Depression?

Hoover believed in limited government and was afraid that government relief would promote entitlement and weaken self-reliance among the poor. When he made federal funds available to feed livestock, but not people, he was reviled by Americans everywhere. By the time he finally initiated federal jobs programs, it was too late to change public opinion. His public works projects, such as the Grand Coulee Dam, created some jobs, but nowhere near enough to have an impact. While the Federal Farm Board, established in 1929, supported farm prices and lent money to coops, it was poorly funded. Hoover's most direct government program—the Reconstruction Finance Corporation implemented at the end of his presidency in 1932—offered relief to businesses, but still provided no direct relief for the unemployed.

Franklin D. Roosevelt and the Launching of the New Deal

How did the federal government take on new roles during the period dubbed "The First Hundred Days"?

During this special session of Congress held just after his election in 1932, Roosevelt sought to revive the flagging economy through two types of federal initiatives: national economic planning and relief programs. Both would ultimately expand federal power. The planning portion of this "New Deal" focused on the National Industrial Recovery Act (NIRA) and the Agricultural Adjustment Act (AAA). The NIRA encouraged industries to adopt wage and price standards that could erase competition and increase consumer spending and, therefore, demand for workers. The AAA established crop controls and offered farm subsidies. Roosevelt also spent $3 billion on work relief programs, such as the Civilian Conservation Corps, which hired young men to help build dams, reservoirs, and trails in national parks; and the Public Works Administration, whose workers completed the Grand Coulee Dam and built New York City's Triborough Bridge and hundreds of other public facilities. Fifteen laws were passed, helping the United States to recover and unemployment to drop from 13 million in 1933 to 9 million in 1936.

Political Pressure and the Second New Deal

What were the hallmarks of the Second New Deal?

Responding to political pressure, the Roosevelt administration increased direct economic support for hard-hit and vulnerable Americans. The Emergency Relief Appropriation Act allocated $4 billion in deficit spending to provide public works jobs through the Works Progress Administration (WPA)—building roads, bridges, and parks and renovating schools and hospitals. It also implemented initiatives to teach illiterate Americans to read and write and employed artists, writers, and actors. The Resettlement Administration relocated poor families and organized homestead communities, while the Rural Electrification Administration brought electricity to rural areas. The hallmark of the "Second New Deal" was the Social Security Act, which created a federal pension system, unemployment benefits, and welfare for needy families.

Labor

How did Roosevelt provide support for labor?

Labor unrest and dissatisfaction with dwindling wages and harsh working conditions increased throughout the 1930s. Public support for strikes waned as violence escalated throughout the decade. But Roosevelt bolstered labor's rights with the 1935 National Labor Relations (Wagner) Act, which guaranteed workers the right to organize unions and bargain collectively. The Act made it illegal for businesses to fire workers who joined unions and banned management from sponsoring company unions. It also required firms to bargain with union representatives about wages, hours, and working conditions and created a National Labor Relations Board to mediate disputes. As the NLRB took hold, violence dissipated and workers' wages increased.

Federal Power and the Nationalization of Culture

In what ways did the Depression inspire the emergence of a youth culture?

Government policies focused on channeling jobs to the male heads of household. That meant that young boys who, at age 14, under normal economic conditions would have gone to work, could not find jobs. Hence, they stayed in school longer, and high school graduation rates by the end of the decade doubled. As young people spent more time in school, they developed a shared youth culture reflected in shared choices of music, clothing, and behavior.

The Limits of the New Deal

How did Roosevelt undermine his New Deal agenda and, ultimately, his legacy?

Roosevelt made two moves with serious consequences for the New Deal. Concerned that the Supreme Court, which had ruled both the NIRA and the AAA unconstitutional, would also rule against future initiatives, Roosevelt asked Congress to give him the authority to appoint six new justices, arguing that the present nine were getting old and were overworked. Congress refused and, although FDR was able to name seven new associate justices when a new pension program encouraged older judges to retire, his political credibility was damaged by his court-packing scheme. Second, in 1939, with war intensifying in Europe, Roosevelt traded further domestic reform for conservatives' support for military rearmament.

Suggestions for Further Reading

Anthony J. Badger, *The New Deal: The Depression Years, 1933–1940* (1989)

Alan Brinkley, *The End of Reform: New Deal Liberalism in Recession and War* (1995)

Alan Brinkley, *Voices of Protest: Huey Long, Father Coughlin, and the Great Depression* (1982)

Lizabeth Cohen, *Making a New Deal: Industrial Workers in Chicago* (1990)

Blanche Wiesen Cook, *Eleanor Roosevelt, Vols. 1 and 2* (1992, 1999)

Timothy Egan, *The Worst Hard Time* (2005)

Sidney Fine, *Sitdown: The General Motors Strike of 1936–37* (1969)

James E. Goodman, *Stories of Scottsboro* (1994)

David M. Kennedy, *Freedom from Fear: The American People in Depression and War* (1999)

Robert McElvaine, *The Great Depression: America, 1929–1941* (1984)

Donald Worster, *Dust Bowl: The Southern Plains in the 1930s* (2004)

Go to the CourseMate website for primary source links, study tools, and review materials for this chapter. www.cengagebrain.com

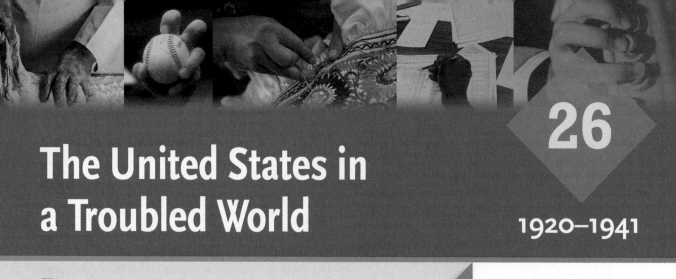

The United States in a Troubled World

26

1920–1941

I n 1921, the Rockefeller Foundation dedicated several million dollars for projects to control yellow fever in Latin America, beginning in Mexico. Carried by mosquitoes, the virus caused severe headaches, vomiting, jaundice (yellow skin), and often death. Learning from the pioneering work of Carlos Juan Finlay of Cuba, Oswaldo Cruz of Brazil, and U.S. Army surgeon Walter Reed, scientists sought to destroy the mosquito in its larval stage, before it became an egg-laying adult.

U.S. diplomats, military officers, and business executives agreed that the disease threatened public health, which in turn disturbed political and economic order. When outbreaks occurred, ports were closed and quarantined, disrupting trade and immigration. The infection struck American officials, merchants, investors, and soldiers stationed abroad. It incapacitated workers, reducing productivity. Throughout Latin America, insufficient official attention to yellow-fever epidemics stirred public discontent against regimes the United States supported. When the Panama Canal opened in 1914, leaders feared the disease would spread, even reinfecting the United States, which suffered its last epidemic in 1905.

Gradually overcoming strong local anti-U.S. feelings, Rockefeller personnel inspected breeding places and deposited larvae-eating fish in public waterworks. In 1924, La Fundación Rockefeller declared yellow fever eradicated in Mexico. Elsewhere in Latin America, the foundation's antimosquito campaign proved successful in maritime and urban areas but less so in rural and jungle regions. Politically, Rockefeller Foundation efforts in the 1920s and 1930s strengthened central governments by providing a public health infrastructure and diminished anti-U.S. sentiment.

The Rockefeller Foundation's campaign offers insights into Americans' fervent but futile effort to build a stable international order after World War I. Despite the "isolationist" tag sometimes applied to U.S. foreign relations during the interwar decades, Americans remained active in world affairs in the 1920s and

678

1930s—from gunboats on Chinese rivers, to negotiations in European financial centers, to marine occupations in Haiti and Nicaragua, to oil wells in the Middle East, to campaigns against diseases in Africa and Latin America. President Wilson rightly said after World War I that the United States had "become a determining factor in the history of mankind."

The most apt description of interwar U.S. foreign policy is "independent internationalism." Notwithstanding the nation's overseas projects—colonies, spheres of influence, naval bases, investments, trade, missionary activity, humanitarian projects—many Americans regarded themselves as isolationists, meaning they wanted no part of Europe's political squabbles, military alliances, or the League of Nations, which might drag them into war. Internationalist-minded Americans—including most senior officials—also wanted to stay out of future European wars but were more willing than isolationists to work to shape the world.

A stable world would better facilitate American prosperity and security. In the interwar years, American diplomats increasingly sought to exercise U.S. power through conferences, humanitarian programs, cultural penetration (Americanization), moral lectures and calls for peace, nonrecognition of disapproved regimes, arms control, and economic and financial ties under the Open Door principle.

But a stable world order proved elusive. Public health projects saved countless lives but could not address the low living standards and staggering poverty of dependent peoples around the globe. World War I debts and reparations bedeviled the 1920s. The Great Depression shattered world trade and threatened America's prominence in international markets. It also spawned political extremism, militarism, and war in Europe and Asia. As Nazi Germany marched to war, the United States adopted a neutrality policy. The United States sought to defend its interests in Asia against Japanese aggression by invoking the Open Door policy.

In the late 1930s, and especially after the outbreak of European war in September 1939, many Americans came to agree with President Franklin D. Roosevelt that Germany and Japan imperiled U.S. interests because they were building self-sufficient spheres of influence on the basis of military and economic domination. Roosevelt first pushed for U.S. military preparedness and then favored aiding Britain and France. A German victory, he reasoned, would destroy traditional economic ties, threaten U.S. influence in the Western Hemisphere, and place at the pinnacle of European power Adolf Hitler, whose ambitions and barbarities seemed limitless.

Meanwhile, Japan seemed determined to dismember America's Asian friend China, to destroy the Open Door principle, and endanger a U.S. colony—the Philippines. To deter Japanese expansion in the Pacific, the United States cut off supplies of vital American products, such as oil. Japan's surprise attack on Pearl Harbor, Hawai'i, in December 1941 brought the United States into World War II.

As you read this chapter, keep the following questions in mind:

* Why and by what means did Americans try to facilitate a stable world order in the interwar period?

* How did the Roosevelt administration respond to the growing Nazi German threat in the second half of the 1930s?

* Why did the United States enter World War II?

Chronology

1921–22	Washington Conference limits naval arms		1937	Sino-Japanese War breaks out
	Rockefeller Foundation begins battle against yellow fever in Latin America			Roosevelt makes "quarantine speech" against aggressors
1922	Mussolini comes to power in Italy		1938	Mexico nationalizes American-owned oil companies
1924	Dawes Plan eases German reparations			Munich Conference grants part of Czechoslovakia to Germany
1928	Kellogg-Briand Pact outlaws war		1939	Germany and Soviet Union sign nonaggression pact
1929	Great Depression begins			
	Young Plan reduces German reparations			Germany invades Poland; Second World War begins
1930	Hawley-Smoot Tariff raises duties		1940	Germany invades Denmark, Norway, Belgium, the Netherlands, and France
1931	Japan seizes Manchuria			
1933	Adolf Hitler becomes chancellor of Germany			Selective Training and Service Act starts first U.S. peacetime draft
	United States extends diplomatic recognition to Soviet Union		1941	Lend-Lease Act gives aid to Allies
	United States announces Good Neighbor policy for Latin America			Germany attacks Soviet Union
1934	Fulgencio Batista comes to power in Cuba			United States freezes Japanese assets
1935	Italy invades Ethiopia			Roosevelt and Churchill sign Atlantic Charter
	Congress passes first Neutrality Act			Japanese flotilla attacks Pearl Harbor, Hawai'i; United States enters Second World War
1936	Germany reoccupies Rhineland			
	Spanish Civil War breaks out			

Searching for Peace and Order in the 1920s

How did the peace movement influence U.S. foreign policy in the interwar years?

World War I left Europe in shambles. Between 1914 and 1921, Europe suffered tens of millions of casualties from world war, civil wars, massacres, epidemics, and famine. Germany and France lost 10 percent of their workers. The American Relief Administration and private charities delivered food to needy Europeans, including Russians wracked by famine in 1921 and 1922. Through food relief, Americans hoped to dampen any appeal political radicalism might have overseas. Secretary of State Charles Evans Hughes and other leaders expected U.S. economic expansion to promote international stability, believing prosperity would eliminate ideological extremes, revolution, arms races, aggression, and war.

Collective security, as envisioned by Woodrow Wilson (see page 615), elicited little enthusiasm among Republican leaders. Senator Henry Cabot Lodge gloated in 1920 that "we have destroyed Mr. Wilson's League of Nations." Not quite. The Geneva-headquartered League of Nations, envisioned as a peacemaker, proved feeble, not just because the United States did not join but also because members failed to utilize it to settle disputes. Still, starting in the mid-1920s, U.S. officials participated discreetly in League meetings on public health, prostitution, drug and arms trafficking, counterfeiting of currency, and other questions. The Rockefeller Foundation donated $100,000 a year to the League's public health ventures.

Peace Groups

Wilson's legacy was felt in other ways as well. During the interwar years, peace groups worked for international stability and drew widespread public support. Women gravitated to their own organizations because of the popular assumption that women—as nurturing mothers—had a unique aversion to war. Carrie Chapman Catt's moderate National Conference on the Cure and Cause of War, formed in 1924, and the U.S. section of the Women's International League for Peace and Freedom (WILPF), organized in 1915 by Jane Addams and Emily Greene Balch, became the largest women's peace groups. When Addams won the Nobel Peace Prize in 1931, she transferred her award money to the League of Nations.

Peace groups differed over strategies to ensure world order. Some urged cooperation with the League of Nations and the World Court. Others championed arbitration, disarmament and arms reduction, the outlawing of war, and strict neutrality during wars. The WILPF called for an end to U.S. economic imperialism, which it claimed compelled the United States to intervene militarily in Latin America to protect U.S. business interests. The Women's Peace Union (organized in 1921) lobbied for a constitutional amendment requiring a national referendum on a declaration of war. Quakers, YMCA officials, and Social Gospel clergy in 1917 created the American Friends Service Committee to identify pacifist alternatives to warmaking.

Washington Naval Conference

Peace advocates influenced Warren G. Harding's administration to convene the **Washington Naval Conference** of November 1921–February 1922. Delegates from Britain, Japan, France, Italy, China, Portugal, Belgium, and the Netherlands joined a U.S. team led by Secretary of State Charles Evans Hughes to discuss limiting naval armaments. American leaders worried that an expansionist Japan, with the world's third largest navy, would overtake the United States, ranked second behind Britain.

Hughes opened the conference with the stunning proposal to scrap thirty major U.S. ships, totaling 846,000 tons. He urged the British and Japanese delegations to do away with smaller amounts. The final limit was 500,000 tons each for the Americans and the British, 300,000 tons for the Japanese, and 175,000 tons each for the French and the Italians. These limits were agreed to in the Five-Power Treaty, which also set a ten-year moratorium on building capital ships (battleships and aircraft carriers). The governments further pledged not to build new fortifications in their Pacific possessions (such as the Philippines). Next, the Nine-Power Treaty reaffirmed the Open Door in China, recognizing Chinese sovereignty. Finally, in the Four-Power Treaty, the United States, Britain, Japan, and France agreed to respect one another's Pacific possessions. These treaties did not limit submarines, destroyers, or cruisers, nor did they provide enforcement powers for the Open Door. Still, Hughes achieved arms limitation and improved America's strategic position vis-à-vis Japan in the Pacific.

Washington Naval Conference: Multi-national conference led by U.S. Secretary of State Hughes to address the problem of the United States, Great Britain, and Japan edging toward a dangerous (and costly) naval-arms race.

Kellogg-Briand Pact

Peace advocates also welcomed the Locarno Pact of 1925, a set of agreements among European nations that sought to reduce tensions between Germany and France, and the Kellogg-Briand Pact of 1928. In the latter document, sixty-two nations agreed to "condemn recourse to war for the solution of international controversies, and renounce it as an instrument of national policy." The Kellogg-Briand Pact passed the U.S. Senate 85 to 1, but it lacked enforcement provisions. Although weak, it reflected popular opinion that war was barbaric. But arms limitations, peace pacts, and efforts by peace groups and international institutions failed to muzzle the dogs of war, which fed on the economic troubles that upended world order.

The World Economy, Cultural Expansion, and Great Depression

How did the Great Depression help push the world to the brink of war?

While Europe struggled to recover after World War I, the international economy wobbled and then collapsed. The Great Depression set off a political chain reaction that carried the world to war. Cordell Hull, U.S. secretary of state from 1933 to 1944, argued that political extremism and militarism sprang from maimed economies. Hull proved right.

Economic and Cultural Expansion

Because of World War I, the United States became a creditor nation and the financial capital of the world (see Figure 26.1). From 1914 to 1930, private investments abroad grew fivefold, to more than $17 billion. By the late 1920s, the United States produced nearly half of the world's industrial goods and ranked first among exporters ($5.2 billion worth of shipments in 1929). Britain and Germany lost ground to American businesses in Latin America, where Standard Oil operated in eight nations and the United Fruit Company became a huge landowner.

America's economic prominence facilitated the export of American culture. Hollywood movies saturated the global market and stimulated interest in all things American. Although some foreigners warned against Americanization, others aped U.S. mass-production methods and emphasis on efficiency and modernization. Coca-Cola opened a bottling plant in Essen, Germany; Ford built an automobile assembly plant in Cologne.

Adolf Hitler: German chancellor and Nazi dictator whose efforts to restore his nation's prominence included a brutal program to purify it of Jews and others he deemed "inferior race."

Germans marveled at Henry Ford's industrial techniques (*Fordismus*). In the 1930s, Nazi leader **Adolf Hitler** sent German car designers to Detroit before launching the Volkswagen. The Phelps-Stokes Fund further advertised the American capitalist model, exporting to black Africa Booker T. Washington's Tuskegee philosophy of education, while the Rockefeller Foundation supported colleges to train doctors in Lebanon and China and funded medical research in Europe.

The U.S. government assisted this expansion. The Webb-Pomerene Act (1918) excluded from antitrust prosecution those combinations set up for export trade; the Edge Act (1919) permitted American banks to open foreign-branch banks; and the overseas offices of the Department of Commerce distributed market information. The federal government also stimulated foreign loans by American investors. U.S. government support for the expansion of the telecommunications industry helped International Telegraph and Telephone (IT&T), Radio Corporation of America (RCA), and the Associated Press (AP) become international giants by 1930.

War Debts and German Reparations

Some Europeans branded the United States stingy for its handling of World War I debts and reparations. Twenty-eight nations became entangled in inter-Allied government debts totaling $26.5 billion ($9.6 billion of them owed to the U.S. government). Europeans owed private American creditors another $3 billion and urged Americans

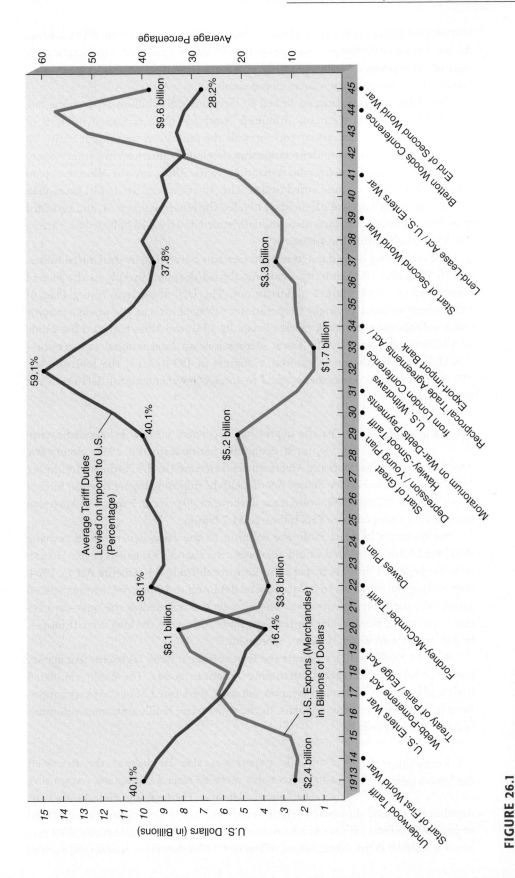

FIGURE 26.1
The United States in the World Economy

In the 1920s and 1930s, global depression and war scuttled the United States' hope for a stable economic order. This graph suggests, moreover, that high American tariffs meant lower exports, further impeding world trade. The Reciprocal Trade Agreements program initiated in the early 1930s was designed to ease tariff wars with other nations.

Source: U.S. Bureau of the Census, *Historical Statistics of the United States, Colonial Times to 1970* (Washington, D.C., 1975).

to erase government debts as a magnanimous contribution to the war effort. During the war, they angrily charged, Europe bled while America profited. American leaders insisted on repayment, some pointing out that the victorious European nations gained vast territory and resources as war spoils.

The debts question became linked to Germany's $33 billion reparations bill. Hobbled by inflation, Germany defaulted. American bankers loaned millions of dollars to keep Germany afloat and forestall the radicalism that might thrive on economic troubles. A triangular relationship developed: American investors' money flowed to Germany, Germany paid reparations to the Allies, and the Allies then paid some of their debts to the United States. The American-crafted 1924 Dawes Plan reduced Germany's annual payments, extended the repayment period, and provided more loans. The United States also gradually scaled down Allied obligations, cutting the debt by half during the 1920s.

But everything hinged on continued German borrowing in the United States, and in 1928 and 1929 American lending abroad dropped sharply in the face of more lucrative stock market opportunities. The U.S.-negotiated Young Plan of 1929, which reduced Germany's reparations, salvaged little as the world economy collapsed following the stock market crash. By 1931, the Allies had paid back only $2.6 billion. Staggered by the Great Depression—an international catastrophe—they defaulted on the rest. Annoyed, Congress in 1934 passed the Johnson Act, which forbade U.S. government loans to foreign governments in default to the United States.

Decline in Trade

As the depression deepened, tariff wars revealed a reinvigorated economic nationalism. By 1932, twenty-five nations retaliated against rising American tariffs (created in the Fordney-McCumber Act of 1922 and the Hawley-Smoot Act of 1930) by imposing higher rates on foreign imports. From 1929 to 1933, world trade declined by 40 percent. Exports of American merchandise slumped from $5.2 billion to $1.7 billion.

For Secretary of State Hull, the solution to the crisis depended on reviving world trade; this he insisted would also boost the chances for global peace. He successfully pressed Congress to pass the Reciprocal Trade Agreements Act in 1934, empowering the president to reduce U.S. tariffs by up to 50 percent through special agreements with foreign countries. The act's central feature was the most-favored-nation principle, whereby the United States was entitled to the lowest tariff rate set by any nation with which it had an agreement.

In 1934, Hull also helped create the Export-Import Bank, a government agency providing loans to foreigners purchasing American goods. The bank stimulated trade and became a diplomatic weapon, allowing the United States to exact concessions by approving or denying loans. In the short term, Hull's ambitious programs brought mixed results.

U.S. Recognition of the Soviet Union

Economic imperatives also lay behind the Roosevelt administration's move to extend diplomatic recognition to the Soviet Union. Throughout the 1920s, the Republicans refused diplomatic relations with the Soviet government, which failed to pay $600 million for confiscated American-owned property and repudiated pre-existing Russian debts. Nonetheless, in the late 1920s American businesses, such as

General Electric and International Harvester, entered the Soviet marketplace, and Henry Ford signed a contract to build an automobile plant there. By 1930, the Soviet Union was the largest buyer of American farm and industrial equipment.

Upon becoming president, Roosevelt speculated that closer Soviet-American relations might help the economy while deterring Japanese expansion. In 1933, he granted U.S. diplomatic recognition to the Soviet Union in return for Soviet agreement to discuss its debts and grant Americans in the Soviet Union religious freedom and legal rights.

U.S. Dominance in Latin America

Through the Platt Amendment, the Roosevelt Corollary, the Panama Canal, military intervention, and economic preeminence the United States had thrown an imperial net over Latin America in the early twentieth century. U.S. dominance in the hemisphere grew after World War I. A prominent State Department officer patronizingly remarked that Latin Americans were of "low racial quality" and "easy people to deal with if properly managed."

U.S.-made schools, roads, telephones, and irrigation systems dotted Caribbean and Central American nations. American "money doctors" in Colombia and Peru helped reform tariff and tax laws and invited U.S. companies to build public works. Washington forced private high-interest loans on the Dominican Republic and Haiti. Republican administrations curtailed U.S. military intervention in the hemisphere, withdrawing troops from the Dominican Republic (1924) and Nicaragua (1925). But marines returned to Nicaragua in 1926 to end fighting between conservative and liberal Nicaraguans and protect American property. In Haiti, the U.S. troop commitment lasted from 1915 until 1934, with soldiers there to keep pro-Washington governments in power.

> How was Roosevelt's Good Neighbor policy different from past dealings in Latin America?

PRIVATE WHARF, W. F. McLAUGHLIN & CO., SANTOS, BRAZIL.

© Curt Teich Postcard Archives, Lake County Museum

Among the U.S. companies with large holdings in Latin America in the interwar period was F. W. McLaughlin & Co. of Chicago. Here, workers on a private company wharf in Santos, Brazil, prepare to load coffee for shipment to the United States.

Link to a transcript of FDR's speech at the Inter-American Conference for the Maintenance of Peace in Buenos Airies, 1937.

Good Neighbor policy: Implemented by President Roosevelt, this Latin American policy stated that no nation had the right to intervene in the affairs of another; it substituted direct U.S. intervention with diplomacy and support for various leaders, businesses, and other programs.

Link to a political cartoon of the United States as the Good Neighbor.

American Economic Muscle

By 1929, American investments in Latin America (excluding bonds and securities) totaled $3.5 billion, and U.S. exports dominated the region's trade. Country after country experienced the repercussions of U.S. economic and political decisions. For example, the price that Americans set for Chilean copper determined the health of Chile's economy. Latin American nationalists protested that their resources were being drained away by U.S. companies, leaving many nations in a disadvantageous position. Unapologetic Americans believed they were bringing material improvements and the blessings of liberty to Latin American neighbors. Two years later, a Chilean newspaper warned that the American "Colossus" had "financial might" without "equal in history" and that its aim was "Americas for the Americans—of the North." In the United States, Senator William Borah of Idaho urged that Latin Americans be granted the right to decide their own futures.

Good Neighbor Policy

Renouncing unpopular military intervention, the United States tried new methods to maintain its influence in Latin America: Pan-Americanism (a fifty-year-old concept strengthening ties between North and South America), support for strong local leaders, the training of national guards, economic and cultural penetration, Export-Import Bank loans, financial supervision, and political subversion. Dubbed the **Good Neighbor policy** by Roosevelt in 1933, it meant that the United States would be less blatant in its domination—less willing to defend exploitative business practices and to launch military expeditions and less reluctant to consult with Latin Americans.

Most notably, Roosevelt ordered home the U.S. military forces stationed in Haiti (since 1915) and Nicaragua (since 1912, with a hiatus in 1925–1926), and he restored some sovereignty to Panama and increased that nation's income from the canal. Roosevelt's popularity in Latin America grew when, in a series of pan-American conferences, he joined in pledging that no nation in the hemisphere would intervene in the "internal or external affairs" of any other.

Roosevelt promised more than he was prepared to deliver. His administration continued to support dictators in the region, believing they would preserve U.S. economic interests. When a revolution brought a radical government to power in Cuba in 1933, FDR instructed the American ambassador in Havana to work with conservative Cubans to replace the new government with one friendlier to U.S. interests. With Washington's support, army sergeant Fulgencio Batista took power in 1934.

During the Batista era, which lasted until Fidel Castro ousted Batista in 1959, Cuba protected U.S. investments and aligned itself with U.S. foreign policy. In return, the United States provided military aid and Export-Import Bank loans, abrogated the unpopular Platt Amendment, and gave Cuban sugar a favored position in the U.S. market. American tourists flocked to Havana's nightlife of rum, rhumba, prostitution, and gambling. Nationalistic Cubans protested that their nation had become a mere extension of the United States.

Clash with Mexican Nationalism

In Mexico, Roosevelt again showed the restraint that his predecessors lacked. Since Woodrow Wilson sent troops to Mexico in 1914 and 1916, U.S.-Mexican relations struggled as the two governments wrangled over U.S. economic interests. Still, by 1934 the United States was Mexico's chief trading partner, accounting for 61 percent of

Mexico's imports and taking 52 percent of its exports. That year, however, a new government under Lázaro Cárdenas pledged "Mexico for the Mexicans" and strengthened trade unions to strike against foreign corporations.

In 1937, workers struck foreign oil companies for higher wages and recognition, but the companies, including Standard Oil, rejected union appeals, hoping to send a message across the hemisphere that economic nationalism could never succeed. The following year, the Cárdenas government expropriated the property of all foreign-owned petroleum companies, calculating that the approaching war in Europe would restrain the United States from attacking Mexico. The United States countered by reducing purchases of Mexican silver and promoting a multinational business boycott. But Roosevelt rejected appeals to intervene militarily, fearing that Mexicans would increase oil sales to Germany and Japan. Tense negotiations led to a 1942 agreement whereby the United States conceded that Mexico owned and controlled its raw materials, and Mexico compensated the companies for their lost property.

While the United States remained the dominant power in the hemisphere, the Good Neighbor policy filled Latin Americans with hope that a new era had dawned. The sober-minded nationalists in the region knew that deepening tensions in Europe and Asia might have influenced Washington's restraint. But these threats also created a sense that nations in the Western Hemisphere should stand together.

The Course to War in Europe

On March 5, 1933, one day after Roosevelt's inauguration, Germany's parliament granted dictatorial powers to the new chancellor, Adolf Hitler, leader of the **Nazi Party**. It was a stunning rise to power for Hitler, whose Nazis probably would have remained a fringe party had the Great Depression not hit Germany so hard. Production plummeted 40 percent, and unemployment ballooned to 6 million, meaning that two out of five people were jobless. A disintegrating banking system, which robbed millions of their savings, and widespread German resentment over the Versailles peace settlement fueled mass discontent. While the communists preached a workers' revolution, German businessmen and property owners supported Hitler and the Nazis, believing they could manipulate him once he had thwarted the communists. They were wrong.

Like Benito Mussolini, who gained control of Italy in 1922, Hitler was a fascist. Fascism (called Nazism, or National Socialism, in Germany) celebrated supremacy of the state over the individual, dictatorship over democracy, authoritarianism over freedom of speech, a state-regulated economy over a free market, and militarism over peace. The Nazis vowed to revive Germany, cripple communism, and "purify" the German "race" by destroying Jews and others, such as homosexuals and Gypsies, whom Hitler deemed inferior. The Nuremberg Laws of 1935 stripped Jews of citizenship and outlawed Jewish intermarriage with Germans. Half of all German Jews were without work.

German Aggression Under Hitler

Determined to get out from under the Versailles treaty, Hitler withdrew Germany from the League of Nations, ended reparations payments, and began to rearm. While secretly laying plans to conquer neighboring states, he watched admiringly as Mussolini's troops invaded Ethiopia in 1935. The next year, Hitler ordered his troops into the Rhineland, an area demilitarized by the Versailles treaty.

> Why did many Americans support isolationism at the outbreak of World War II?

Nazi Party: National Socialist German Workers' Party founded in Germany in 1919; it rose to prominence under the leadership of Adolf Hitler; stressed facism and anti-Semitism.

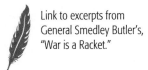

Link to excerpts from General Smedley Butler's, "War is a Racket."

In 1936, Italy and Germany formed an alliance called the Rome-Berlin Axis. Shortly thereafter, Germany and Japan united against the Soviet Union in the Anti-Comintern Pact. Britain and France responded with a policy of **appeasement**, hoping to curb Hitler's expansionism by permitting him a few territorial nibbles. Instead, the German leader continually raised his demands.

appeasement: The process of making concessions to pacify, quiet, or satisfy the other party.

The Spanish Civil War in 1936 upped the ante for Hitler. Beginning in July, about three thousand American volunteers, known as the Abraham Lincoln Battalion of the International Brigades, joined Spanish Loyalists in defending Spain's elected republican government against Francisco Franco's fascist movement. The Soviet Union also aided the Loyalists. Hitler and Mussolini sent military aid to Franco, who won in 1939, tightening fascism's grip on the European continent.

Early in 1938, Hitler again tested European tolerance when he sent soldiers to annex his birth nation, Austria. In September, he seized the Sudeten region of Czechoslovakia. France and Britain, without consulting the Czechs, agreed to allow Hitler this territorial bite, in exchange for a pledge that he would not take more. British Prime Minister Neville Chamberlain returned home proclaiming, "peace in our time." In March 1939, Hitler swallowed the rest of Czechoslovakia (see Map 26.2).

Isolationist Views in the United States

Many Americans sought to distance themselves from the tumult by embracing isolationism—which signified abhorrence of war and opposition to U.S. alliances with other nations. Americans learned powerful negative lessons from World War I: that war damages reform movements, undermines civil liberties, dangerously expands federal power, disrupts the economy, and accentuates racial and class tensions. In a 1937 Gallup poll, nearly two-thirds thought U.S. participation in World War I was a mistake.

Conservative isolationists feared higher taxes and increased executive power if the nation went to war. Liberal isolationists worried that domestic problems might go unresolved with increased military spending. Many isolationists predicted that, in attempting to spread democracy, Americans would lose freedoms at home. The vast majority of isolationists opposed fascism, but they did not think the United States should do what Europeans themselves refused to do: block Hitler.

Nye Committee Hearings

A congressional committee headed by Senator Gerald P. Nye held hearings from 1934 to 1936 on the role of business in the U.S. decision to enter World War I. The Nye committee did not prove that American munitions makers dragged the nation into that war, but it uncovered evidence that bribed foreign politicians to bolster arms sales in the 1920s and 1930s.

Isolationists grew suspicious of American business ties with Nazi Germany and fascist Italy. Twenty-six of the top American corporations, including DuPont, Standard Oil, and General Motors, had contracts in 1937 with German firms. After Italy attacked Ethiopia in 1935, American petroleum, copper, scrap iron, and steel exports to Italy increased substantially, despite Roosevelt's call for a moral embargo. Other businesses, such as the Wall Street law firm of Sullivan and Cromwell, severed lucrative ties with Germany to protest the Nazi persecution of Jews.

neutrality acts: Laws passed in mid-thirties to keep the United States out of any European wars.

Reflecting the popular desire for distance from Europe's distress, Roosevelt signed a series of **neutrality acts**. The Neutrality Act of 1935 prohibited arms shipments to either side in a war, once the president declared the existence of belligerency.

The Neutrality Act of 1936 forbade loans to belligerents. The Neutrality Act of 1937 introduced the cash-and-carry principle, which required warring nations to pay cash for nonmilitary purchases and carry goods from U.S. ports in their own ships. The act also forbade Americans from traveling on the ships of belligerent nations.

Roosevelt's Evolving Views

President Roosevelt shared isolationist views in the early 1930s. Although prior to World War I, he was an expansionist and interventionist, during the interwar period he talked more about the horrors of war. In a speech in August 1936 at Chautauqua, New York, Roosevelt appealed to pacifist voters in the upcoming election. The United States, he promised, would remain unentangled in the European conflict. During the crisis over Czechoslovakia in 1938, Roosevelt endorsed appeasement.

Meanwhile, Roosevelt grew troubled by the arrogance of Germany, Italy, and Japan—aggressors he tagged the "three bandit nations." He condemned the Nazi persecution of the Jews and Japan's expansionist actions in East Asia. In November 1938, Hitler launched *Kristallnacht* (or "Crystal Night," named for the shattered glass that littered the streets after the attack on Jewish synagogues, businesses, and homes) and sent tens of thousands of Jews to concentration camps. Shocked, Roosevelt recalled the U.S. ambassador to Germany and allowed fifteen thousand refugees on visitor permits to remain longer in the United States. But he would not break trade relations with Hitler or push Congress to loosen tough immigration laws. Congress rejected all measures, including a bill to admit twenty thousand children under the age of fourteen. Motivated by economic concerns and widespread anti-Semitism, more than 80 percent of Americans supported Congress's decision to uphold immigration restrictions.

Even the tragic voyage of the *St. Louis* did not change government policy. The vessel left Hamburg in mid-1939 carrying 930 desperate Jewish refugees. Denied entry to Havana, the *St. Louis* headed for Miami, where Coast Guard cutters prevented it from docking and forced it to return to Europe. Some refugees took shelter in countries that later were overrun by Hitler's legions.

Quietly, Roosevelt began readying for war. In early 1938 he successfully pressured the House of Representatives to defeat a constitutional amendment that would require a majority vote in a national referendum before a congressional declaration of war could take effect (unless the United States were attacked). Later, in the wake of the Munich crisis, Roosevelt asked Congress for funds to fortify the air force, which he believed essential to deter aggression. In January 1939, the president secretly decided to sell bombers to France. Although these five hundred combat planes did not deter war, French orders spurred the growth of the U.S. aircraft industry.

Hitler's swallowing of Czechoslovakia in March 1939 proved a turning point for Western leaders. Until then, they could explain away Hitler's actions by saying he was only trying to reunite German-speaking peoples. They now realized it would take force to stop him. When Hitler began eyeing Poland, London and Paris stood by the Poles. Undaunted, Berlin signed a nonaggression pact with Moscow in August 1939, including a top-secret protocol that carved eastern Europe into German and Soviet zones, and let the Soviets grab the eastern half of Poland and the three Baltic states of Lithuania, Estonia, and Latvia, formerly part of the Russian Empire.

German *Blitzkrieg* in Poland

World War II in Europe would drag on for almost six years. It began suddenly, however, with Nazi Germany's invasion of Poland in the predawn hours of September 1, 1939. The thundering tanks, the long line of German soldiers, and the headlines all present visual information about the German *blitzkrieg*. Together, these images convey Germany's technological and manpower superiority as well as the momentous consequences of the invasion. Which one speaks to you most powerfully, and why? How would you receive information about an important event like this today?

© Michael Nicholson/Corbis

German propaganda postcard showing Panzer tanks during the blitzkrieg.

STF/AFP/Getty Images

German troops entering Poland after the blitzkrieg.

Hulton Archive/Getty Images

The front page of London's Evening Standard newspaper on September 1, 1939, announcing the German invasion of Poland.

690

Poland and the Outbreak of World War II

Early on September 1, 1939, German tanks rolled into Poland. German fighter planes covered the advance, thereby launching a new type of warfare, the *blitzkrieg* ("lightning war")—highly mobile land forces and armor combined with tactical aircraft. Within forty-eight hours, Britain and France declared war on Germany.

When Europe descended into war in September 1939, Roosevelt declared neutrality and pressed for repeal of the arms embargo. After much debate, Congress in November lifted the embargo on contraband and approved cash-and-carry exports of arms. Using methods short of war, Roosevelt thus began to aid the Allies. Hitler sneered that a "half Judaized ... half Negrified" United States was "incapable of conducting war."

Japan, China, and a New Order in Asia

Meanwhile, Asia suffered the aggressive march of Japan. The United States had interests at stake in Asia: the Philippines and Pacific islands, religious missions, trade and investments, and the Open Door in China. In missionary fashion, Americans believed they were China's special friend and protector. Pearl Buck's bestselling novel and subsequent film, *The Good Earth* (1931), countered prevailing images of "heathen Chinee" by representing the Chinese as noble peasants. By contrast, the aggressive Japan loomed as a threat to American interests. The Tokyo government seemed bent on subjugating China and unhinging the Open Door doctrine of equal trade and investment.

> How did the United States perceive its interests to be threatened by Japanese expansionism?

The Chinese were uneasy about the U.S. presence in Asia and shared Japan's desire to reduce western influence. The 1911 Chinese Revolution still rumbled in the 1920s, as antiforeign riots damaged U.S. property and imperiled American missionaries. Chinese nationalists criticized the American imperialist practice of extraterritoriality (the exemption from Chinese legal jurisdiction of foreigners accused of crimes), and they demanded respect for Chinese sovereignty.

Jiang Jieshi

In the late 1920s, civil war broke out in China when Jiang Jieshi (Chiang Kai-shek) ousted Mao Zedong and his communist followers from the ruling Guomindang Party. Americans applauded this anti-Bolshevism and Jiang's conversion to Christianity in 1930. Jiang's new wife, American-educated Soong Meiling, won their hearts with her flawless English and western fashion. Warming to Jiang, U.S. officials signed a treaty in 1928 restoring control of tariffs to the Chinese.

Japan grew suspicious of U.S. ties with China. In the early twentieth century, Japanese-American relations deteriorated as Japan gained influence in Manchuria, Shandong, and Korea. The Japanese sought to dominate Asian territories that produced the raw materials that their import-dependent island nation required. The Japanese also resented the discriminatory immigration law of 1924, which excluded them from emigrating to the United States. Secretary Hughes called the law "a lasting injury" to Japanese-American relations. Despite the Washington Conference treaties, naval competition continued, as did commercial rivalry. In the United States the importation of inexpensive Japanese goods spawned "Buy America" campaigns and boycotts.

Manchurian Crisis Relations further soured in 1931 after the Japanese military seized Manchuria from China (see Map 26.1). Larger than Texas, Manchuria served Japan both as a buffer against the Soviets and as a vital source of coal, iron, timber, and food. More than half of Japan's foreign investments rested in Manchuria. Although the seizure of Manchuria violated the Nine-Power Treaty and the Kellogg-Briand Pact, the United States lacked the power to compel Japanese withdrawal, and the League of Nations merely condemned the Tokyo government. The American response came as a moral lecture known as the Stimson Doctrine: the United States would not recognize any impairment of China's sovereignty or of the Open Door policy, Secretary Stimson declared in 1932.

Japan continued to pressure China, triggering the Sino-Japanese War in mid-1937. Japanese forces seized Beijing and several coastal cities. The bombing of Shanghai intensified anti-Japanese sentiment in the United States. To help China by permitting it to buy American arms, Roosevelt refused to declare the existence of war, thus avoiding activation of the Neutrality Acts.

Roosevelt's Quarantine Speech On October 5, 1937, the president called for a quarantine to curb the "epidemic of world lawlessness." People who thought Washington had been too gentle with Japan cheered, while isolationists warned that Roosevelt was edging toward war.

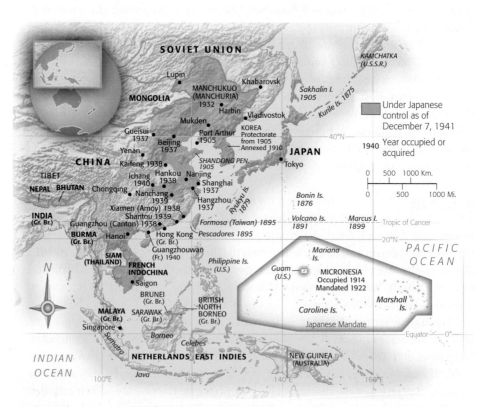

MAP 26.1

Japanese Expansion Before Pearl Harbor

The Japanese quest for predominance began at the turn of the century and intensified in the 1930s. China suffered the most at the hands of Tokyo's military. Vulnerable U.S. possessions in Asia and the Pacific proved no obstacle to Japan's ambitions for a Greater East Asia Co-Prosperity Sphere.

Source: Copyright © Cengage Learning

On December 12, Japanese aircraft sank the American gunboat *Panay,* an escort for Standard Oil Company tankers on the Yangtze River, killing two American sailors. Roosevelt was relieved when Tokyo apologized and offered to pay for damages.

Japan's declaration of a New Order in Asia, in the words of one American official, "banged, barred, and bolted" the Open Door. Alarmed, the Roosevelt administration during the late 1930s gave loans and sold military equipment to Jiang's Chinese government. In mid-1939, the United States abrogated its trade treaty with Tokyo, yet Americans continued to ship oil, cotton, and machinery to Japan. The administration hesitated to initiate economic sanctions because it might spark a Japanese-American war at a time when Germany posed a more serious threat and the United States was unprepared for war. When war broke out in Europe in late summer 1939, Japanese-American relations were stalemated.

U.S. Entry into World War II

A stalemate was fine with many Americans if it kept the United States out of war. But could it stay out? Roosevelt remarked in 1939 that the United States could not "draw a line of defense around this country and live completely and solely to ourselves." Polls showed that Americans favored the Allies and supported aid to Britain and France, but the great majority emphatically wanted the United States to remain at peace. Troubled by this conflicting advice—oppose Hitler, aid the Allies, but stay out of the war—the president gradually moved the nation from neutrality to undeclared war against Germany and then, after the Japanese attack on Pearl Harbor, to full-scale war.

> In what way did Roosevelt gradually move America into World War II?

Because the stakes were so high, Americans vigorously debated the direction of foreign policy from 1939 through 1941. The widespread use of radio, the nation's chief news source, helped stimulate public interest. So did ethnic affiliations with the various belligerents and victims. The American Legion, the League of Women Voters, labor unions, and local chapters of the Committee to Defend America by Aiding the Allies and of the isolationist America First Committee (both organized in 1940) provided outlets for citizen participation in the national debate. African American churches organized anti-Italian boycotts to protest Mussolini's pummeling of Ethiopia.

In March 1940, the Soviet Union invaded Finland. In April, Germany conquered Denmark and Norway (see Map 26.2). On May 10, 1940, Germany attacked Belgium, the Netherlands, and France, ultimately pushing French and British forces back to the English Channel. At Dunkirk, France, between May 26 and June 6, more than 300,000 Allied soldiers frantically escaped to Britain on a flotilla of small boats. The Germans occupied Paris a week later. A new French government in the town of Vichy collaborated with the Nazis and, on June 22, surrendered France to Berlin. The German Luftwaffe (air force) launched massive bombing raids against Great Britain.

Alarmed by the swift defeat of one European nation after another, Americans gradually shed their isolationism. Promising that New Deal reforms would not be sacrificed for military preparedness, the president aided the beleaguered Allies to prevent the fall of Britain. In May 1940, he ordered the sale of old surplus military equipment to Britain and France. In July, he cultivated bipartisan support by naming Republicans Henry L. Stimson and Frank Knox, backers of aid to the Allies, secretaries of war and the navy, respectively. In September, the president traded fifty

MAP 26.2

The German Advance

Hitler's drive to dominate Europe pushed German troops deep into France and the Soviet Union. Great Britain took a beating but held on with the help of American economic and military aid before the United States itself entered the Second World War in late 1941.

Source: Copyright © Cengage Learning

over-age American destroyers for leases to eight British military bases, including Newfoundland, Bermuda, and Jamaica.

Selective Training and Service Act: Law that required all men between twenty-one and thirty (later expanded to eighteen through forty-five) to register with local draft boards.

Lend-Lease bill: Program proposed by Roosevelt to supply war material to cash-strapped Britain.

First Peacetime Military Draft

Two weeks later, Roosevelt signed the hotly debated and narrowly passed **Selective Training and Service Act**, the first peacetime military draft in American history. The law called for the registration of all men between the ages of twenty-one and thirty-five; more than 16 million men signed up. Meanwhile, Roosevelt won reelection in November 1940 with promises of peace: "Your boys are not going to be sent into any foreign wars."

Roosevelt claimed that the United States could avoid war by enabling the British to win. In January 1941, Congress debated the president's **Lend-Lease bill**. Because Britain was broke, the president explained, the United States should lend rather than sell weapons. In March 1941, with pro-British sentiment running high, the House passed the Lend-Lease Act by 317 votes to 71; the Senate followed with a 60-to-31 tally. The initial appropriation was $7 billion, but by war's end, it reached $50 billion, more than $31 billion of it for Britain.

To ensure delivery of Lend-Lease goods, Roosevelt ordered the U.S. Navy to patrol halfway across the Atlantic, and he sent American troops to Greenland.

Links to the World

Radio News

In radio's early years, network executives believed their job was to entertain Americans and that left current affairs to newspapers. Yet radio could report news as it happened, something no previous medium could do.

Franklin Roosevelt was among the first to grasp radio's potential. As governor of New York, he occasionally went on the air, and after becoming president, he commenced his Fireside Chats, reassuring Americans during the depression that the government was working to help them. The broadcasts were so successful that one journalist remarked, "The President has only to look toward a radio to bring Congress to terms."

Across the Atlantic, Adolf Hitler also used the radio to carry speeches directly to the German people. His message: Germany had been wronged by enemies abroad and by Marxists and Jews at home. But under Hitler, the Nazis promised to restore the country's former greatness. As *Sieg Heil!* thundered over the airwaves, millions of Germans saw Hitler as their salvation.

In 1938, as events in Europe escalated, American radio networks increased news coverage. When Hitler annexed Austria in March, NBC and CBS broke into scheduled programs to deliver bulletins. Then, on March 13, CBS broadcast the first international news roundup, a half-hour show featuring live reports. A new era in American radio was born. In the words of author Joseph Persico, what made the broadcast revolutionary "was the listener's sensation of being on the scene" in far-off Europe. When leaders from France and Britain met with Hitler in Munich later that year, millions of Americans listened intently to live radio updates.

Correspondents became well known, none more than Edward R. Murrow of CBS. During the Nazi air blitz of London in 1940–1941, Murrow's understated, nicotine-scorched voice kept Americans spellbound, as he tried to "report suffering to people [Americans] who have not suffered."

Undoubtedly, Murrow's reports strengthened the interventionist voices in Washington by emphasizing Winston Churchill's greatness and England's bravery. And radio reports from Europe made Americans feel closely linked to people living an ocean away.

Library of Congress

Edward R. Murrow at his typewriter in wartime London.

In July, the president dispatched marines to Iceland, arguing that it was essential for safeguarding the Western Hemisphere. He also sent Lend-Lease aid to the Soviet Union, which Hitler attacked in June (thereby shattering the 1939 Nazi-Soviet nonaggression pact). If the Soviets could hold off two hundred German divisions in the east, Roosevelt calculated, Britain would gain some breathing time.

Atlantic Charter

In August 1941, **Winston Churchill** and Roosevelt met for four days on a British battleship off the coast of Newfoundland. The two leaders issued the **Atlantic Charter**, a set of war aims reminiscent of Wilsonianism: collective security, disarmament, self-determination, economic cooperation, and freedom of the seas. Churchill later recalled that the president told him that he could not ask Congress to declare war against Germany, but "he would wage war" and "become more and more provocative."

On September 4, a German submarine launched torpedoes at (but did not hit) the American destroyer *Greer*. Henceforth, Roosevelt said, the U.S. Navy would fire first when under threat. He also made good on a private promise that American warships would convoy British merchant ships across the ocean. Thus, the United States entered into an undeclared naval war with Germany. When in early October a German submarine torpedoed the U.S. destroyer *Kearny* off the coast of Iceland killing one hundred Americans, the president announced that "the shooting has started." Congress scrapped the cash-and-carry policy and revised the Neutrality Acts to permit transport of munitions to Britain on armed American merchant ships. The United States was edging close to being a belligerent.

U.S. Demands on Japan

It seems ironic, therefore, that World War II came to the United States by way of Asia. Roosevelt wanted to avoid war with Japan to concentrate on defeating Germany. In September 1940, after Germany, Italy, and Japan signed the Tripartite Pact (to form the Axis powers), Roosevelt slapped an embargo on shipments of aviation fuel and scrap metal to Japan. After Japanese troops occupied French Indochina in July 1941, Washington froze Japanese assets in the United States, virtually ending trade (including oil) with Japan. "The oil gauge and the clock stood side by side" for Japan, wrote one observer.

Tokyo recommended a summit meeting between President Roosevelt and Prime Minister Prince Konoye, but American officials insisted that the Japanese first agree to respect China's sovereignty and honor the Open Door policy. Roosevelt supported Secretary Hull's hard line against Japan's pursuit of the Greater East Asia Co-Prosperity Sphere—the name Tokyo gave to the vast Asian region it intended to dominate.

Roosevelt told his advisers to string out ongoing Japanese-American talks to gain time to fortify the Philippines and check the fascists in Europe. By deciphering intercepted messages through Operation MAGIC, American officials learned that Tokyo's patience with diplomacy was dissipating. In late November, the Japanese rejected American demands to withdraw from Indochina. An intercepted message decoded on December 3 instructed the Japanese embassy in Washington to burn codes and destroy cipher machines—suggesting that war was coming.

Surprise Attack on Pearl Harbor

In a daring raid on Pearl Harbor in Hawai'i, an armada of sixty Japanese ships, including six carriers bearing 360 airplanes, crossed 3,000 miles of the Pacific Ocean. To avoid detection, they maintained radio silence. Early on December 7, some 230 miles northwest of Honolulu, the carriers unleashed their planes, dropping torpedoes and bombs on an unsuspecting American naval base and nearby airfields.

The stricken USS *West Virginia* was one of eight battleships caught in the surprise Japanese attack at Pearl Harbor, Hawai'i, on December 7, 1941. In this photograph, sailors on a launch attempt to rescue a crew member from the water as oil burns around the sinking ship.

The battleship USS *Arizona* fell victim to a Japanese bomb that ignited explosives below deck, killing more than 1,000 sailors. The USS *Nevada* tried to escape by heading out to sea, but was hit in a second aerial attack. Altogether, the invaders sank or damaged eight battleships, many smaller vessels, and more than 160 aircraft on the ground. A total of 2,403 died; 1,178 were wounded. The Pearl Harbor tragedy, from the perspective of the war's outcome, amounted to a military inconvenience more than a disaster.

Explaining Pearl Harbor

American cryptanalysts may have broken the Japanese diplomatic code, but the intercepted messages never revealed naval or military plans and never mentioned Pearl Harbor specifically. Roosevelt did not, as some critics charged, conspire to leave the fleet vulnerable to attack so that the United States could enter World War II through the back door of Asia. The base at Pearl Harbor was not on red alert

Presidential Deception of the Public

Before U-652 launched two torpedoes at the *Greer*, heading for Iceland on September 4, 1941, the U.S. destroyer had stalked the German submarine for hours. After the attack, which missed its mark, the *Greer* also released depth charges. But when President Roosevelt described the encounter in a radio Fireside Chat on September 11, he declared that the German submarine fired the first shot and accused Germany of violating freedom of the seas.

Roosevelt misled the American people about the events of September 4. The incident had little to do with freedom of the seas—which related to merchant ships, not to U.S. warships in a war zone. Roosevelt's words were a call to arms, yet he never asked Congress for a declaration of war against Germany. The president believed that deceiving Americans would move them toward war as noble and necessary. The practice worked: polls showed that most Americans approved Roosevelt's shoot-on-sight policy following the *Greer* incident.

Over time, even those who agreed that Germany had to be stopped, questioned Roosevelt's methods as dangerous to the democratic process, which cannot work in an environment of dishonesty and a usurping of congressional powers. In the 1960s, during the Vietnam War, Senator J. William Fulbright of Arkansas recalled the *Greer* incident: "FDR's deviousness in a good cause made it easier for LBJ to practice the same kind of deviousness in a bad cause." In the mid-1980s, Reagan administration officials consciously lied about U.S. arms sales to Iran and covert aid to the Nicaraguan rebels. After the March 2003 U.S. invasion of Iraq, there were charges that President George W. Bush and his aides did the same in claiming that Iraq had weapons of mass destruction, which its leader, Saddam Hussein, intended to use. Bush, critics charged, had used "weapons of mass deception" to justify the invasion of Iraq.

Following Roosevelt, presidents have found it easier to distort, withhold, or lie about foreign relations to shape a public. One result: the growth of the "imperial presidency"—grabbing power from Congress and using questionable means to support presidential objectives. The practice of deception—even for a noble end—was one of Roosevelt's legacies for a people and a nation.

---

because a message from Washington warning of the imminence of war was transmitted by a slow method and arrived too late. Base commanders believed Hawai'i too far from Japan to be a target. Like Roosevelt's advisers, they expected an assault on British Malaya, Thailand, or the Philippines. The Pearl Harbor calamity stemmed from mistakes and insufficient information, not from conspiracy.

Link to the transcript, audio, and commentary of President Roosevelt's December 8, 1941, "Day of Infamy" speech.

On December 8, referring to the previous day as "a date which will live in infamy," Roosevelt asked Congress for a declaration of war against Japan. He noted that Japan had also attacked Malaya, Hong Kong, Guam, the Philippines, Wake, and Midway. A unanimous vote in the Senate and a 388-to-1 vote in the House thrust America into war. Representative Jeannette Rankin of Montana voted no, as she had for World War I. Britain declared war on Japan, but the Soviet Union did not. Three days later, Germany and Italy, honoring the Tripartite Pact they had signed with Japan in September 1940, declared war against the United States.

A fundamental clash of systems explains why war came. Germany and Japan preferred a world divided into closed spheres of influence. The United States sought a liberal capitalist world. American principles manifested respect for human rights; fascists in Europe and militarists in Asia did not. The United States prided itself on democracy; Germany and Japan embraced authoritarian regimes. When the United States protested against German and Japanese expansion, Berlin and Tokyo charged that Washington conveniently ignored its sphere of influence in Latin America and its history of military and economic aggrandizement. Such incompatible objectives obstructed diplomacy and made war likely.

Summary

In the 1920s and 1930s, Americans could not create a peaceful and prosperous world order. The Washington Conference treaties failed to curb a naval arms race or protect China, and both the Dawes Plan and the Kellogg-Briand Pact proved ineffective. U.S. trade policies, shifting from protectionist tariffs to reciprocal trade agreements, only minimally improved U.S. or international commerce during the Great Depression. Recognition of the Soviet Union barely improved relations. Most ominous, the aggressors Germany and Japan ignored repeated U.S. protests. Even where U.S. policies seemed to satisfy Good Neighbor goals in Latin America, nationalist resentments simmered and Mexico challenged U.S. dominance.

During the late 1930s and early 1940s, President Roosevelt hesitantly but steadily moved the United States from neutrality to aiding the Allies, to belligerency, and finally to war after the Pearl Harbor attack. Congress gradually revised and retired the Neutrality Acts in the face of growing danger.

World War II offered another opportunity for Americans to set things right in the world. As publisher Henry Luce wrote in *American Century* (1941), the United States must "exert upon the world the full impact of our influence." Isolationists joined the president's calls for victory. "We are going to win the war, and we are going to win the peace that follows," Roosevelt predicted.

Chapter Review

Searching for Peace and Order in the 1920s

How did the peace movement influence U.S. foreign policy in the interwar years?

In the wake of World War I, several peace organizations—some formed by female activists—emerged to ensure world order and prevent another war. Their strategies varied: some embraced alliances with the League of Nations and the World Court; others looked to arbitration, disarmament, arms reduction, making wars illegal, and observing strict neutrality. Peace activism helped lead President Harding to convene the Washington Naval Conference from November 1921 to February 1922 in which delegates from Britain, Japan, France, Italy, China, Portugal, Belgium, and the Netherlands agreed to limit naval armaments and set a ten-year moratorium on ship-building. Other policy developments included the Nine-Power Treaty, which reaffirmed the Open Door in China and recognized Chinese sovereignty; the Locarno Pact of 1925, which sought to reduce tensions between Germany and France; and the Kellogg-Briand Pact of 1928, in which sixty-two nations agreed to condemn war as the solution to international disputes.

The World Economy, Cultural Expansion, and Great Depression

> **How did the Great Depression help push the world to the brink of war?**

Economic tensions existed among world powers after World War I. The United States emerged as a creditor nation and Europeans—particularly Germany—largely as debtors. Europeans often accused the United States of stinginess and profiting from Europe's hardships. When the stock market crashed in 1929, Europeans defaulted on a large portion of what they owed. The Great Depression not only created an international economic crisis, it also inspired economic nationalism in countries that were already pushed financially to the edge. Secretary of State Charles Hull aptly predicted that maimed economies inspired militarism and extremism, and no country's economy was as hard-pressed as Germany's.

U.S. Dominance in Latin America

> **How was Roosevelt's Good Neighbor policy different from past dealings in Latin America?**

Prior to Roosevelt, U.S. leaders were quick to resort to military intervention in dealing with Latin America. The Good Neighbor policy took a more subtle approach: it centered on building friendship ties through Pan-Americanism; supporting strong local leaders; training national guards; penetrating the region through economic and cultural means; providing financial supervision and loans; and relying on political subversion. Roosevelt withdrew troops from Haiti and Nicaragua restored some sovereignty to Panama, and increased that nation's income from the canal. While the administration backed dictators who seemed supportive of U.S. economic interests, the Good Neighbor policy nonetheless convinced many Latin Americans that a new, more cooperative era had begun.

The Course to War in Europe

> **Why did many Americans support isolationism at the outbreak of World War II?**

Americans had long embraced isolationism largely because their long history of political independence that did not necessitate alliances with other nations.

That was fortified by the experience of World War I, which damaged reform movements at home, disrupted the U.S. economy, and expanded federal power. In fact, two-thirds of Americans surveyed thought entry into World War I had been a mistake. Many Americans similarly feared tax increases, the loss of freedom at home, and the shift of federal funds away from domestic problems toward military spending. Some also distrusted the role of business in pushing the nation toward war.

Japan, China, and a New Order in Asia

> **How did the United States perceive its interests to be threatened by Japanese expansionism?**

As Japan moved to lessen—and eliminate—western influence in the East and to dominate Asian territories producing beneficial raw materials, the United States worried about what this would mean to its geopolitical and economic interests in East Asia, including in the Philippines and the Pacific Islands. They also feared it portended Japanese control of China and Southeast Asia. The Japanese viewed the U.S. presence in the region as an intolerable check on their ambitions, and the two nations remained locked in a stalemate as World War II loomed.

U.S. Entry into World War II

> **In what way did Roosevelt gradually move America into World War II?**

Like most Americans, Roosevelt remained wary of intervening actively in the growing crisis, but as one European nation after another succumbed to the Nazis, staying out of the conflict proved increasingly difficult. Roosevelt was horrified by Germany's treatment of Jews and Japan's expansionism in East Asia, but Hitler's 1939 takeover of Czechoslovakia proved the turning point. FDR quietly began preparing for war, even while hoping that he could keep the United States out of it by ensuring that Britain did not fall. In May 1940 he ordered the sale of surplus military equipment to Britain and France. Because England had no money to pay for weapons, the president urged Congress to let it borrow the necessary arms. The president also signed the Selective Training and Service Act, the first peacetime military draft.

Suggestions for Further Reading

H. W. Brands, *Traitor to His Class: The Privileged Life and Radical Presidency of Franklin Delano Roosevelt* (2008)

Patrick Cohrs, *The Unfinished Peace After World War I: America, Britain and the Stabilization of Europe, 1919–1932* (2006)

Frank Costigliola, *Awkward Dominion: American Political, Economic, and Cultural Relations with Europe* (1984)

Justus D. Doenecke, *Storm on the Horizon: The Challenge to American Intervention, 1939–1941* (2000)

Akira Iriye, *The Origins of the Second World War in Asia and the Pacific* (1987)

David M. Kennedy, *Freedom from Fear: The American People in Depression and War, 1929–1945* (1999)

Walter LaFeber, *Inevitable Revolutions: The United States in Central America,* 2nd and extended ed. (1993)

Fredrick B. Pike, *FDR's Good Neighbor Policy* (1995)

Emily S. Rosenberg, *Spreading the American Dream: American Economic and Cultural Expansion, 1890–1945* (1982)

Linda A. Schott, *Reconstructing Women's Thoughts: The Women's International League for Peace and Freedom Before World War II* (1997)

Go to the CourseMate website for primary source links, study tools, and review materials for this chapter. www.cengagebrain.com

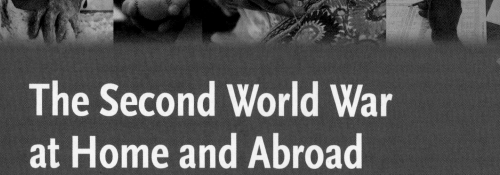

27

The Second World War at Home and Abroad

1941–1945

illiam Dean Wilson was only sixteen in 1942 when U.S. Marine Corps recruiters came to Shiprock, New Mexico, where he attended the Navajo boarding school. Five years too young to be drafted and a year too young to volunteer, he lied about his age, dropped out of school, and joined the Marine Corps.

Wilson was recruited for one of the most important projects of the war. Battles were won or lost because nations broke the codes enemies used to transmit messages. The marines were developing a code based on Diné, the highly complex Navajo language. In 1942, there was no written form and fewer than thirty non-Navajos in the world—none of them Japanese—who understood it. This code promised to be unbreakable.

Wilson and other Navajo recruits helped devise a basic code. Navajo words represented the first letter of their English translations; thus *wol-la-chee* ("ant") stood for the letter *A*. Each also memorized Navajo words that represented 413 basic military terms. *Dah-he-tih-hi* ("hummingbird") meant fighter plane; *ne-he-mah*, "our mother," was the United States.

Beginning with the Battle of Guadalcanal, Wilson and others of the 420 code talkers participated in every Marine assault in the Pacific. Usually, two code talkers were assigned to a battalion, one going ashore with assault forces and the other receiving messages on ship. Often under hostile fire, code talkers set up their equipment and transmitted enemy sightings or directed shelling by American detachments. "Were it not for the Navajos," declared Major Howard Conner, Fifth Marine Division signal officer, "the Marines would never have taken Iwo Jima. The entire operation was directed by Navajo code…."

Wartime service changed the Navajo code talkers' lives. For some, it broadened horizons and deepened ambitions; William Dean Wilson became a tribal judge. But in 1945 most Navajo war veterans simply wanted to return to their homes and traditional culture. They participated in purification ceremonies to dispel battlefield ghosts and invoke blessings for the future.

2222222222222

222222222

World War II marked a turning point in the lives of Americans and the history of the United States. Although the war began badly for the United States, by mid-1942 the Allies halted the Axis powers' advance. In June 1944, American troops, together with Canadian, British, and Free French units, launched a massive invasion across the English Channel, landing at Normandy and pushing into Germany the following spring. Battered by bombing raids, leaderless after Adolf Hitler's suicide, and pressed by a Soviet advance, the Nazis capitulated in May 1945. In the Pacific, Americans drove Japanese forces back toward Japan. America's devastating conventional bombing of Japanese cities, followed by the atomic bombs that demolished Hiroshima and Nagasaki in August 1945 and the Soviet Union's declaration of war on Japan, led to Japan's surrender. At war's end, prospects for international cooperation seemed bleak. The "Grand Alliance"—Britain, the Soviet Union, and the United States—had different visions of the postwar world, and the advent of the atomic age frightened everyone.

The war was fought far from the United States, but it had a major impact on American society. America's leaders committed the United States to become the "arsenal of democracy," producing vast quantities of arms. All economic sectors—industry, finance, agriculture, labor—were mobilized. America's big businesses got bigger, as did labor unions and farms. The federal government, which had the monumental task of managing the war, expanded its reach and power.

During the war, nearly one of every ten Americans moved to another state. Most headed for war-production centers, especially in northern and West Coast cities. Japanese Americans were forced from their homes and incarcerated in remote "relocation centers." While the war encouraged African Americans to demand full citizenship rights, competition for jobs and housing spawned race riots. For women, the war offered new job opportunities in the armed forces and war industries.

On the home front, the American people supported the war effort by collecting scrap iron, rubber, and newspapers for war use and planting "victory gardens." At war's end, although many Americans grieved for lost loved ones and worried about the postwar order, the United States had unprecedented power and prosperity.

As you read this chapter, keep the following questions in mind:

* What military, diplomatic, and social factors influenced decisions about how to fight the Second World War?
* Was the generation of Americans that fought World War II "the greatest generation"?
* How did World War II transform the United States?

The United States at War

As Japanese bombs fell on the U.S. territory of Hawai'i, American anti-war sentiment evaporated. Franklin Roosevelt declared war on Japan on December 8, 1941. When Germany declared war on the United States three days later, America joined British and Soviet Allied nations in battling the Axis powers of Japan, Germany, and Italy. Although the attack on Pearl Harbor was a surprise, America's embargo of shipments to Japan and refusal to accept Japan's expansionist policies had helped bring the two nations to the brink of war, and the United States was deeply involved in an undeclared naval war with Germany before Japan's attack

Was the United States prepared for war when it finally entered World War II?

Chronology

1941	Japan attacks Pearl Harbor
	United States enters World War II
1942	War Production Board created to oversee conversion to military production
	Allies losing war in Pacific to Japan; U.S. victory at Battle of Midway in June is turning point
	Office of Price Administration creates rationing system for food and consumer goods
	United States pursues "Europe First" war policy; Allies reject Stalin's demands for a second front and invade North Africa
	West Coast Japanese Americans relocated to internment camps
	Manhattan Project set up to create atomic bomb
	Congress of Racial Equality established
1943	Soviet army defeats German troops at Stalingrad
	Congress passes War Labor Disputes (Smith-Connally) Act following coal miners' strike
	"Zoot suit riots" in Los Angeles; race riots break out in Detroit, Harlem, and other cities

	Allies invade Italy
	Roosevelt, Churchill, and Stalin meet at Teheran Conference
1944	Allied troops land at Normandy on D-Day, June 6
	Roosevelt elected to fourth term as president
	United States retakes Philippines
1945	Roosevelt, Stalin, and Churchill meet at Yalta Conference
	British and U.S. forces firebomb Dresden, Germany
	Battles of Iwo Jima and Okinawa result in heavy Japanese and American losses
	Roosevelt dies; Truman becomes president
	Germany surrenders; Allied forces liberate Nazi death camps
	Potsdam Conference calls for Japan's "unconditional surrender"
	United States uses atomic bombs on Hiroshima and Nagasaki
	Japan surrenders

on Pearl Harbor. By December 1941, Roosevelt had instituted an unprecedented peacetime draft, created war mobilization agencies, and commissioned war plans for simultaneous struggle in Europe and the Pacific.

A Nation Unprepared   Nonetheless, the nation was not ready for war. Throughout the 1930s, military funding was a low priority. In September 1939 (when Hitler invaded Poland and began World War II), the U.S. Army ranked forty-fifth in size among the world's armies and could fully equip only one-third of its 227,000 men. A peacetime draft instituted in 1940 expanded the U.S. military to 2 million men, but Roosevelt's 1941 survey of war preparedness estimated that the United States could not be ready to fight before June 1943.

In December 1941, the Allies were losing the war (see Map 26.1). Hitler claimed Austria, Czechoslovakia, Poland, the Netherlands, Denmark, and Norway. Romania was lost, then Greece and Bulgaria. France fell in 1940. Britain fought on, but German planes rained bombs on London. More than 3 million German-led soldiers penetrated the Soviet Union and Africa. German U-boats controlled the Atlantic from the Arctic to the Caribbean. Within months of America's entry into the war, German submarines sank 216 vessels—some so close to American shores that people could see the glow of burning ships.

War in the Pacific   In the Pacific, the war was largely America's. The Soviets had not declared war on Japan, and there were too few British troops protecting England's Asian colonies to make much difference. By late spring 1942, Japan had captured most European colonial possessions in Southeast Asia. The Japanese attacked the Philippines hours after Pearl Harbor and destroyed U.S. air capability in the region. American and Filipino troops retreated to the Bataan Peninsula, hoping to hold the main island, Luzon, but Japanese forces were superior. In March 1942, General Douglas MacArthur, the commander of U.S. forces in the Far East, departed the Philippines, proclaiming, "I shall return."

Left behind were almost eighty thousand American and Filipino troops. Starving and sick, they held on for almost another month before surrendering. Japanese troops, lacking supplies, were unprepared to deal with this large number of prisoners, and most believed the prisoners forfeited honorable treatment by surrendering. In what came to be known as the Bataan Death March, the Japanese force-marched their captives to prison camps 80 miles away, denying them food and water and bayoneting or beating to death those who fell behind. Ten thousand Filipinos and six hundred Americans died on the march. Tens of thousands of Filipino civilians died under Japanese occupation.

The United States stuck back. On April 18, sixteen American B-25s appeared over Japan. The Doolittle raid (named after the mission's leader) did little harm but pushed Japanese commander Yamamoto to bold action. Japan moved to lure the weakened United States into a "decisive battle." The target was Midway—two tiny islands about 1,000 miles northwest of Honolulu, where the U.S. Navy had a base. If Japan could take Midway, it would have a secure defensive perimeter far from the home islands (see Map 27.2). By using Guam, the Philippines, and even Australia as hostages, Japan believed, it could negotiate a favorable peace agreement with the United States.

General Yamamoto did not know that America's MAGIC code-breaking machines could decipher Japanese messages. When the Japanese fleet arrived, it found the U.S. Navy lying in wait. The Battle of Midway in June 1942 was a turning point in the Pacific war. Japan's hope to force the United States to withdraw, leaving Japan to control the Pacific, vanished. Now Japan was on the defensive.

"Europe First" Strategy Despite the importance of these early Pacific battles, America's war strategy was "Europe First." American war planners believed that if Germany conquered the Soviet Union, it might directly threaten the United States. Roosevelt also feared that the Soviet Union, suffering heavy losses against Hitler, might pursue a separate peace with Germany and so undo the Allied coalition. Therefore, the United States would work with Britain and the USSR to defeat Germany, then deal with an isolated Japan.

British prime minister Winston Churchill and Soviet premier **Joseph Stalin** disagreed over strategy. By late 1941, German troops nearly reached Moscow and Leningrad (present-day St. Petersburg) and slashed into Ukraine, taking Kiev, claiming the lives of over a million Soviet soldiers. Stalin pressed for British and American troops to attack Germany from the west to draw Germans away from the Soviet front. Roosevelt agreed and promised to open a "second front" before the end of 1942. Churchill, however, blocked this plan. Churchill wanted to control the North Atlantic shipping lanes first and promoted air attacks on Germany. He also pushed for an attack on Axis positions in North Africa; halting the Germans there would protect British imperial possessions in the Mediterranean and the oil-rich Middle East.

Joseph Stalin: Soviet premier and dictator of the Soviet Union who came to power after the death of Vladimir Lenin in 1924 and ruled until his death in 1953.

MAP 27.1

The Allies on the Offensive in Europe, 1942–1945

The United States pursued a "Europe First" policy: first defeat Germany, then focus on Japan. American military efforts began in North Africa in late 1942 and ended in Germany in 1945 on May 8 (V-E Day).

Source: Copyright © Cengage Learning

Against his advisers' advice, Roosevelt accepted Churchill's plan. The U.S. military was not ready for a major campaign, and Roosevelt needed to show the American public some success in the European war. Thus, instead of rescuing the USSR, the British and Americans landed in North Africa in November 1942, winning quick victories in Algeria and Morocco. In Egypt, the British confronted General Erwin Rommel and his Afrika Korps in a struggle over the Suez Canal and the Middle East oil fields, with Rommel's army surrendering after six months. Meanwhile, the Soviet army hung on. The Soviet Union lost 1.1 million men in the Battle of Stalingrad but defeated the German Sixth Army there in early 1943. By spring 1943, Germany, like Japan, was on the defensive. Relations among the Allies remained precarious as the United States and Britain continued to resist Stalin's demand for a second front.

The Production Front and American Workers

Although the war would be fought on the battlefields of Europe and the Pacific, America's strategic advantage lay on the "production front" at home. By making the machines that would win the war for the Allies, the United States would prevail through a "crushing superiority of equipment," Roosevelt told Congress.

How did wartime production needs create a new relationship between government and business and government and science?

Goals for military production were staggering. In 1940, American factories built only 3,807 airplanes. Following Pearl Harbor, Roosevelt wanted 60,000 aircraft in 1942 and twice that in 1943. Plans called for the manufacture of 16 million tons of shipping and 120,000 tanks. The military needed supplies for a force that would reach almost 16 million men. During the war, military production superseded the manufacture of civilian goods. Automobile plants built tanks and airplanes instead of cars; dress factories sewed military uniforms. The **War Production Board**, established in early 1942, allocated resources and coordinated production among thousands of independent factories.

War Production Board: Government agency established during WWII which allocated resources, coordinated production among thousands of independent factories, and awarded government contracts for wartime production.

Businesses, Universities, and the War Effort

During the war, American businesses overwhelmingly cooperated with government war-production plans, inspired by patriotism and generous financial incentives. In 1940, as the United States produced armaments for the Allies, the American economy recovered from the depression. Rising consumer spending built industrial confidence. Auto manufacturers, for example, expected to sell 25 percent more in 1941 than in 1939. The massive retooling necessary to produce planes or tanks instead of cars would be expensive and leave manufacturers dependent on a single client—the federal government. The federal government, however, paid for retooling and factory expansions; it guaranteed profits by allowing corporations to charge the government for production costs plus a fixed profit. It created generous tax write-offs and exemptions from antitrust laws. Consequently, corporations doubled their net profits between 1939 and 1943.

Most military contracts went to America's largest corporations, which had the facilities to guarantee rapid production. From mid-1940 through September 1944, the government awarded contracts totaling $175 billion, with about two-thirds going to the top hundred corporations. General Motors received 8 percent of the total. This approach made sense for a nation that wanted enormous quantities of war goods manufactured quickly; most small businesses lacked the necessary capacity. However, wartime government contracts further consolidated American manufacturing in the hands of giant corporations.

Courtesy, Collection of Peter Kreitler

Unprepared to fight a war of such magnitude, the U.S. government turned to the nation's largest and most efficient corporations to produce the planes and ships and guns that would make America the "great arsenal of democracy," and General Motors received 8 percent of the value of all government war contracts. With no new cars to sell, GM continued to advertise in national magazines, proclaiming "Victory Is Our Business." Pictured here is GM's in-house magazine for employees, reminding these "production soldiers" of the importance of their work.

Manhattan Project

Wartime needs also created a new relationship between science and the U.S. military. Millions of dollars funded university research programs, which developed new technologies of warfare, such as vastly improved radar systems. The most important government-sponsored research program was the **Manhattan Project**, a $2 billion secret effort to build an atomic bomb. Roosevelt was convinced by scientists fleeing the Nazis in 1939 that Germany was developing an atomic weapon, and he resolved to beat them to it. The Manhattan Project achieved the world's first sustained nuclear chain reaction in 1942 at the University of Chicago. In 1943, the federal government established a secret community for atomic scientists and their families at Los Alamos, New Mexico, to develop the weapon that would change the world.

Manhattan Project: Secret program to develop the atomic bomb.

New Opportunities for Workers

America's new defense factories required millions of workers. At first workers were plentiful: 9 million Americans were still unemployed in 1940 when war mobilization began. But the armed forces took almost 16 million men, forcing industry to look more broadly for workers. Women, African Americans, Mexican Americans, and poor whites from Appalachia and the Deep South streamed into defense jobs.

In some cases, federal action eased their path. As many industries refused to hire African Americans, **A. Philip Randolph**, head of the Brotherhood of Sleeping Car Porters, proposed a march on Washington, D.C., to demand equal access to defense jobs. Roosevelt, fearing race riots, offered a deal. In exchange for canceling the march, the president issued Executive Order No. 8802, which prohibited discrimination in war industries and government jobs. Although enforcement was uneven, hundreds of thousands of black Americans migrated from the South to northern and western industrial cities on the strength of this guarantee of job equality.

A. Philip Randolph: Labor leader whose threatened march on Washington led to the creation of Executive Order No. 8802, which prohibited racial discrimination in war industries and government jobs.

Through the **bracero program**, Mexican workers also filled wartime jobs in the United States. About 200,000 Mexican farm workers, or *braceros*, were offered short-term contracts to fill vacant agricultural jobs as Americans sought well-paid war work. Mexican and Mexican American workers faced discrimination and segregation, but they seized these new economic opportunities. In 1941 not a single Mexican American worked in the Los Angeles shipyards; by 1944, 17,000 worked there.

bracero program: Wartime "temporary worker" measure that brought in seasonal farm laborers from Mexico.

Women at Work

Employers initially insisted that women were not suited for industrial jobs, but labor shortages changed their position. Posters and billboards urged women to "Do the Job HE Left Behind, and the government's War Manpower Commission glorified the invented worker **"Rosie the Riveter."**

Rosie the Riveter was an inspiring, albeit inaccurate, image of working women. Only 16 percent of women workers held defense plant jobs, and only 4.4 percent held "skilled" jobs (such as riveting). Nonetheless, during the war years, more than 6 million women entered the labor force, and the number of working women increased by 57 percent. More than 400,000 African American women left domestic service for higher-paying industrial jobs, often with union benefits.

Rosie the Riveter: Symbol of the woman war worker; the bulging muscles represented her strength as she aided the nation's war effort by taking jobs vacated by men who fought in the war.

Workers in defense plants were often expected to work ten days for every day off or to accept difficult night shifts. Businesses and the federal government provided workers new support to keep them on the job. The West Coast Kaiser shipyards offered high pay, childcare, subsidized housing, and healthcare: the Kaiser Permanente Medical Care Program, a forerunner of the health maintenance organization (HMO), supplied medical care for a weekly payroll deduction of 50 cents. The federal government also funded childcare centers, which 130,000 preschoolers and 320,000 school-age children attended.

Organized Labor During Wartime

Because America's war strategy relied on industrial production, the federal government attempted to ensure that labor strikes would not interrupt production. Days after Pearl Harbor, a White House labor-management conference agreed to a no-strike/no-lockout pledge. In 1942, Roosevelt created the National War Labor Board (NWLB) to settle disputes. The NWLB forged a temporary compromise between labor union demands for a "closed shop," in which only union members could work, and management's desire for "open" shops. Workers could not be required to join a union, but unions could enroll as many members as possible. Between 1940 and 1945, union membership ballooned from 8.5 million to 14.75 million.

The government did restrict union power if it threatened war production. When coal miners in the United Mine Workers union went on strike in 1943, following an NWLB attempt to limit wage increases to a cost-of-living adjustment, coal shortages halted railroads and closed steel mills. Few Americans supported this strike. As anti-labor sentiment grew, Congress passed the War Labor Disputes (Smith-Connally) Act, granting the president authority to seize and operate any strike-bound plant deemed necessary to the national security.

Success on the Production Front

For nearly four years, American factories operated twenty-four hours a day, seven days a week, turning out roughly 300,000 airplanes, 102,000 armored vehicles, 77,000 ships, 20 million small arms, 40 billion bullets, and 6 million tons of bombs. By war's end, the United States was producing 40 percent of the world's weaponry. This feat depended on transforming formerly skilled work into assembly-line mass production. Henry Ford, now seventy-eight years old, created a massive bomber plant outside Detroit with assembly lines almost a mile long producing one B-24 Liberator bomber every hour. On the West Coast, William Kaiser cut construction time for Liberty ships—the huge, 440-foot-long cargo ships transporting tanks, guns and bullets overseas—from 355 to 56 days. The ships were not well made; welded hulls sometimes split in rough seas. However, as the United States struggled to produce cargo ships faster than German U-boats could sink them, production speed counted more than quality.

Life on the Home Front

What was the impact of the war on family life?

The United States, protected by two oceans from its enemies, was spared the war that other nations experienced. Americans grieved the loss of loved ones abroad, but bombs did not fall on U.S. cities; invading armies did not burn and rape and kill. Instead, war mobilization ended the Great Depression and brought prosperity. American civilians experienced the paradox of good times amid global conflagration.

Supporting the War Effort

Still the war was a constant presence for Americans on "the home front." Civilians supported the war effort, though Americans were never as committed to shared sacrifice as images of "the greatest generation"—widely circulated in early twenty-first century popular history and culture—suggest. During the war, however, families planted 20 million "victory gardens" to free up food supplies for the military. Housewives saved cooking fat, which yieleded glycerin to make black powder used in shells or bullets. Children collected scrap metal; the iron in one old shovel blade could make four hand grenades.

Many consumer goods were rationed or unavailable. To save wool for military use, the War Production Board directed that men's suits would have narrow lapels, shorter jackets, and no vests or pant cuffs. Bathing suits, the WPB specified, must shrink by 10 percent. When silk and nylon were diverted from stockings to parachutes, women used makeup on their legs. The Office of Price Administration (OPA), created by Congress in 1942, established a nationwide rationing system for such goods as sugar, coffee, and gasoline. By early 1943, the OPA instituted a point system for rationing food. Every citizen received two ration books each month, and feeding a family required complex calculations. Sugar was tightly rationed, and people saved for months to make a birthday cake. A black market existed, but most Americans understood that sugar produced alcohol for weapons manufacture and meat fed "our boys" overseas.

Propaganda and Popular Culture

Despite near-unanimous support for the war, government leaders worried that, over time, public willingness to sacrifice might lag. In 1942, Roosevelt created the Office of War Information (OWI), which hired Hollywood filmmakers and New York copywriters to sell the war at home. OWI posters exhorted Americans to sacrifice, and reminded them to watch what they said, for "loose lips sink ships."

Link to World War II propaganda posters.

Popular culture also reinforced wartime messages. A *Saturday Evening Post* advertisement for vacuum cleaners (unavailable for the duration) urged women war workers to fight "for freedom and all that means to women everywhere. You're fighting for a little house of your own, and…the right to bring up your children without the shadow of fear." Songs urged Americans to "Remember December 7th" or to "Accentuate the Positive." Others made fun of America's enemies ("You're a sap, Mr. Jap / Uncle Sam is gonna spanky").

Link to World War II era anti-Axis cartoons.

Movies drew 90 million viewers a week in 1944—out of a total population of 132 million. During the war and Hollywood tried to meet Eleanor Roosevelt's challenge to "Keep 'em laughing." *A WAVE, a WAC, and a Marine* promised "no battle scenes, no message, just barrels of fun." Others, such as *Bataan* or *Wake Island*, portrayed actual—if sanitized—events. Even in comedies, however, the war was always present. Theaters held "plasma premieres," offering free admission to anyone donating blood to the Red Cross. Audiences rose to sing "The Star Spangled Banner," then watched newsreels with censored combat footage before the feature film. In movie theaters, Americans saw the horror of Nazi death camps in May 1945.

Wartime Prosperity

The war demanded sacrifices from Americans, but between 1939 and the end of the war, per capita income rose from $691 to $1,515, and salaries increased more than 135 percent. Price controls kept inflation down so that wage increases did not disappear to higher costs. With little to buy, savings rose.

Portraying the Enemy

Racial stereotyping affected how both the Americans and the Japanese waged war. The Americans badly underestimated the Japanese, leaving themselves open for the surprise attack on Pearl Harbor and American forces in the Philippines. And the Japanese, believing Americans were barbarians who lacked a sense of honor, mistakenly expected that the United States would withdraw from East Asia once confronted with Japanese power and determination. This cover for *Collier's* magazine, appearing shortly after the first anniversary of Japan's attack on Pearl Harbor, shows some of the most extreme racial imagery of the war, but it was scarcely alone. How is Japan portrayed here? How might the fact that Japan had launched an immensely successful surprise attack on the United States have shaped this image, or Americans' reactions to it?

American propaganda caricatured all the Axis powers, but the Japanese were most likely to be portrayed as subhuman.

World War II cost approximately $304 billion (more than $3 trillion in today's dollars), which the United States financed through deficit spending, borrowing money by selling war bonds. The national debt skyrocketed, from $49 billion in 1941 to $259 billion in 1945 (and was not paid off until 1970). However, wartime revenue acts increased the number of Americans paying personal income tax from 4 million to 42.6 million—at rates ranging from 6 to 94 percent—and introduced a new system in which employers "withheld" taxes from employee paychecks. For the first time, individual Americans paid more in taxes than corporations.

A Nation in Motion Despite hardships and fears, the war offered home-front Americans new opportunities. More than 15 million civilians moved during the war (see Map 27.2), including seven hundred thousand black Americans who left the South during the war years. The rapid influx of war workers to cities and towns strained community resources. Migrants crowded into substandard housing—even woodsheds, tents, or cellars—and into trailer parks without adequate sanitary facilities. Disease spread: scabies and ringworm, polio, tuberculosis. Many long-term residents found the newcomers—especially the unmarried male war workers—a rough bunch. In and around Detroit, where car factories now produced tanks and planes, residents called war workers freshly arrived from southern Appalachia "hillbillies" and "white trash." Many migrants knew little about urban life. One young man from rural Tennessee, unfamiliar with traffic lights and street signs, navigated by counting trees between his home and the war plant where he worked. Some Appalachian "trailer-ites" appalled their neighbors by building outdoor privies.

Racial Conflicts

As people from different backgrounds confronted one another under difficult conditions, tensions rose. In 1943, almost 250 racial conflicts exploded in forty-seven cities. In Detroit, white mobs—undeterred by police—roamed the city attacking blacks. Blacks hurled rocks at police and dragged white passengers off streetcars. After thirty hours of rioting, twenty-five blacks and nine whites lay dead.

In Los Angeles in 1943, young Mexican American gang members, or *pachucos,* wore zoot suits: long jackets with wide padded shoulders, loose pants "pegged" below the knee, wide-brimmed hats, and dangling watch chains. With cloth rationed, wearing pants requiring five yards of fabric was a political statement, and although a high percentage of Mexican Americans served in the military, many white servicemen believed otherwise. Rumors that *pachucos* had attacked white sailors set off four days of violence as mobs of white men—mainly soldiers and sailors—roamed the streets attacking and stripping zoot-suiters. Los Angeles outlawed zoot suits, but the riots ended only when naval personnel were removed from the city.

Families in Wartime

War profoundly transformed families. Despite policies exempting married men and fathers from the draft during most of the war, almost 3 million families were broken up. The divorce rate of 16 per 1,000 marriages in 1940 almost doubled to 27 per 1,000 in 1944. Still, the number of marriages rose from 73 per 1,000 unmarried women in 1939 to 93 in 1942. Some couples scrambled to marry before the man was sent overseas; others sought military deferments. Total births climbed from 2.4 million babies in 1939 to 3.1 million in 1943. Many were "goodbye babies," conceived to guarantee the family's continuation if the father died in war.

On college campuses, women complained, along with the song lyrics, "There is no available male." But other young women found plenty of male company, sparking concern about wartime threats to sexual morality. *Youth in Crisis,* a 1943 newsreel, featured a girl with "experience far beyond her age" necking with a soldier on the street. These "victory girls" were said to support the war effort by giving their all to men in uniform. Many young men and women behaved as they never would in peacetime, which often meant hasty marriages to virtual strangers, especially if a baby was on the way. Despite changes in behavior, taboos against unwed motherhood remained strong, and only 1 percent of births during the war were to unmarried women. Wartime mobility also increased opportunities for same-sex relationships, and gay communities grew in such cities as San Francisco.

In many ways, the war reinforced traditional gender roles that had weakened during the depression, when many men lost the breadwinner role. Now men defended their nation while women "kept the home fires burning," sometimes filling jobs vacated by soldiers "for the duration" of the war. Women who worked were frequently blamed for neglecting their children and creating an "epidemic" of juvenile delinquency Nonetheless, millions of women took on new responsibilities in wartime and enjoyed greater independence, and many husbands returned to find that their families' lives seemed complete without them.

The Limits of American Ideals

The U.S. government worked hard to explain to its citizens the reasons for their sacrifices. In 1941 Roosevelt had pledged America to defend "four essential human freedoms"—freedom of speech, freedom of religion, freedom from want, and freedom from fear. Government-sponsored films contrasted democracy and totalitarianism, freedom and fascism, equality and oppression.

In what ways were American notions of civil liberties and basic freedoms tested during the war years?

As America fought the totalitarian regimes of the Axis powers, the nation confronted tough questions. What limits on civil liberties were justified in the interest of national security? How freely could information flow without revealing military secrets and costing American lives? How could the United States protect itself against spies or saboteurs, especially from German, Italian, or Japanese citizens living in the United States? And what about America's ongoing race problem? The answers revealed tensions between the nation's democratic claims and its wartime practices.

Regarding civil liberties, American leaders embraced a "strategy of truth," declaring that citizens required a truthful accounting of the war's progress. However, the government closely controlled military information, as even seemingly unimportant details might tip off enemies about troop movements. While government-created propaganda sometimes dehumanized the enemy, especially the Japanese, such hate mongering was used much less than during World War I.

More complex was how to handle dissent and guard against enemy agents potentially operating within the nation's borders. The 1940 Alien Registration (Smith) Act made it unlawful to advocate the overthrow of the U.S. government by force or violence. After Pearl Harbor, the government arrested thousands of Germans, Italians, and other Europeans as suspected spies and potential traitors. The government interned 14,426 Europeans in Enemy Alien Camps and prohibited ten thousand Italian Americans from living or working in restricted zones along the California coast.

Internment of Japanese Americans In March 1942, Roosevelt ordered that all 112,000 foreign-born Japanese and Japanese Americans living in California, Oregon, and the state of Washington (the vast majority of the mainland population) be removed from the West Coast to "relocation centers." There were no individual charges, as was the case with Italian and German nationals; Japanese and Japanese Americans were imprisoned, under suspicion solely because they were of Japanese descent.

American anger at Japan's "sneak attack" on Pearl Harbor fueled calls for internment, as did fears that West Coast cities might be attacked. Long-standing racism was evident, but people in economic competition with Japanese Americans also supported internment. Although Japanese nationals were forbidden U.S. citizenship or property ownership, American-born Nissei (second generation) and Sansei (third

Links to the World

Tokyo Rose

Thousands of American soldiers fighting the Japanese in the Pacific found their closest link to home in American popular music on Japanese airwaves. Far less comforting, however, many servicemen wrote home about Tokyo Rose, the sultry-voiced, English-speaking announcer who taunted them with tales of wives' and girlfriends' infidelity and predicted, with alarming certainty, devastating attacks on American forces.

An American government investigation in summer 1945 concluded that Tokyo Rose did not exist. Most probably, historians have argued, Tokyo Rose was the creation of American servicemen rather than of Japanese propagandists. Tales of Tokyo Rose enabled soldiers to discuss fears that were too difficult to confront directly.

On the first day of September, however, Iva Toguri as "Tokyo Rose" held a press conference in Japan, most likely prompted by reporters' promise of $2000

for an exclusive interview (money she never received). An American citizen visiting a sick aunt in Japan when the war began, Toguri did host a radio show aimed at American servicemen during the war but as Orphan Ann, not Tokyo Rose. She threatened listeners to "creep up and annihilate them with [her] nail file" rather than with military bombardment and attacks with poison gas that American servicemen remembered hearing.

In this interview, Toguri had, by claiming the identity of Tokyo Rose, seemingly confessed to treason. The U.S. government imprisoned her for a year while they investigated her story. Released for lack of evidence, she attempted to return to the United States, prompting widespread protests. Veterans demanded a trial of the woman who had "betrayed" or caused American servicemen's deaths. In 1949, Toguri was convicted on the basis of perjured testimony and imprisoned for ten years. Toguri's conviction was shaped by the new cold war between the United States and the Soviet Union, as Americans worried about the loyalty of American citizens. America's new superpower status created links to a larger world that shaped national opinions and fears.

When reporters offered $2000 for an interview with "Tokyo Rose," recently married Iva Toguri D'Aquino stepped forward— even though Tokyo Rose did not exist. Shown here being interviewed by U.S. correspondents in Yokohama following the end of the war, Toguri never received the promised funds but was instead arrested and held in custody while the U.S. government investigated her actions during the war.

© Corbis

generation), all U.S. citizens, were successful in business and agriculture. The eviction order forced Japanese Americans to sell property valued at $500 million for a fraction of its worth.

The internees were sent to camps in Arkansas's Mississippi River floodplain; to Wyoming's intermountain terrain; the western Arizona desert; and to other desolate spots in the West. The camps were bleak: Behind barbed wire, families lived in a single room furnished only with cots, blankets, and a bare light bulb. Most had no running water. Toilets and dining and bathing facilities were communal. People nonetheless attempted to sustain community life, setting up schools, consumer cooperatives, and sports leagues. Betrayed by their government, many internees were ambivalent about their loyalty to the United States. Some sought legal remedy, but the Supreme Court upheld the government's action in *Korematsu v. U.S.* (1944). Almost 6,000 of the 120,000 internees renounced U.S. citizenship and demanded to be sent to Japan. Others sought to demonstrate their loyalty. The all–Japanese American 442nd Regimental Combat Team, drawn heavily from internees, was the most decorated unit of its size, receiving a Congressional Medal of Honor, 47 Distinguished Service Crosses, 350 Silver Stars, and more than 3,600 Purple Hearts. In 1988, Congress apologized and paid $20,000 to each of the 60,000 surviving Japanese American internees.

African Americans and "Double V"

African American leaders wanted the nation to confront the parallels between Nazi racist doctrines and Jim Crow segregation in the United States. Proclaiming a "Double V" campaign (victory at home and abroad), groups such as the National Association for the Advancement of Colored People (NAACP) hoped to "persuade, embarrass, compel and shame our government and our nation into a more enlightened attitude toward a tenth of its people." The NAACP, 50,000 strong in 1940, had 450,000 members by 1946. And in 1942, civil rights activists founded the Congress of Racial Equality (CORE), which stressed "nonviolent direct action" and staged sit-ins to desegregate restaurants and movie theaters in Chicago and Washington, D.C.

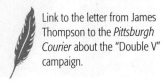

Link to the letter from James Thompson to the *Pittsburgh Courier* about the "Double V" campaign.

Military service was a key issue for African Americans, who understood the link between the military service and citizenship. But the U.S. military remained segregated by race and resisted using black units as combat troops. As late as 1943, less than 6 percent of the armed forces were African American. The marines initially refused to accept African Americans, and the navy approximated segregation by assigning black men to service positions in which they would rarely interact with nonblacks as equals or superiors.

A Segregated Military

The federal government and War Department decided that the world war was no time to integrate the military. The majority of Americans (approximately 89 percent of Americans were white) opposed integration. Racism was so entrenched that the Red Cross segregated blood plasma during the war. Integration of military installations, the majority of which were in the South, would have provoked a crisis as federal power contradicted state law. Government and military officials argued that wartime integration would create disorder within the military and hinder America's war effort. General George C. Marshall, Army Chief of Staff, proclaimed "The army is not a sociological laboratory." Hopes for racial justice, so long deferred, were another casualty of the war.

National Archives

During World War II, for the first time, the War Department sanctioned the training and use of African American pilots. These members of the 99th Pursuit Squadron—known as "Tuskegee Airmen" because they trained at Alabama's all-black Tuskegee Institute—joined combat over North Africa in June 1943. Like most African American units in the racially segregated armed forces, the men of the 99th Pursuit Squadron were under the command of white officers.

Despite discrimination, African Americans stood up for their rights. Lt. Jackie Robinson refused to move to the back of the bus at the army's Camp Hood, Texas, in 1944—and faced court-martial, even though military regulations forbade discrimination on military vehicles. Black sailors disobeyed orders to return to work after an explosion—caused by the navy practice of assigning untrained men to load bombs onto Liberty ships—destroyed two ships and killed 320 men. When they were court-martialed, future Supreme Court justice and chief counsel for the NAACP Thurgood Marshall claimed that "This is not fifty men on trial for mutiny. This is the Navy on trial for its whole vicious policy toward Negroes."

African American servicemen did eventually fight on the front lines. The "Tuskegee Airmen," pilots trained at the Tuskegee Institute in Alabama, saw heroic service in all-black units, such as the Ninety-ninth Pursuit Squadron, which won eighty Distinguished Flying Crosses. After the war, African Americans called on their wartime service to claim their civil rights. African Americans' wartime experiences were mixed, but the war was a turning point for equal rights.

America and the Holocaust

America's inaction in what we now call the Holocaust is tragic, though the consequences are clearer now than at the time. As the United States turned away refugees on the *St. Louis* (page 689) in early 1939 and refused to relax immigration quotas to admit European Jews and others fleeing Hitler's Germany, almost no one foresaw death camps like Auschwitz. Americans knew they were turning away people fleeing dire persecution, and anti-Semitism played a significant role, but it was not unusual to refuse those seeking refuge, especially during a major economic crisis.

In 1942, American newspapers reported the "mass slaughter" of Jews and other "undesirables" (Gypsies, homosexuals, the physically and mentally handicapped) under Hitler. Many Americans, having been duped by manufactured atrocity tales during World War I, wrongly discounted these stories. But Roosevelt knew about Nazi death camps capable of killing up to two thousand people an hour using the gas Zyklon-B.

In 1943, British and American representatives met in Bermuda but took no action. Appalled, Secretary of the Treasury Henry Morgenthau Jr. charged that the State Department's foot dragging made the United States an accessory to murder. In 1944, Roosevelt created the War Refugee Board, establishing refugee camps in Europe and helping to save 200,000 Jews. But it came too late. By war's end, the Nazis had systematically murdered almost 11 million people.

Life in the Military

How did racial and gender norms play out in the military during World War II?

More than 15 million men and approximately 350,000 women served in the U.S. armed forces during World War II. Eighteen percent of American families had a father, son, or brother in the military. Some men (and all of the women) volunteered. But more than 10 million were draftees. By presidential order, the military stopped accepting volunteers in December 1942 in an attempt to fill military positions while maintaining war production. The draft extended broadly and mostly equitably across the population during World War II.

Selective Service

The Selective Service Act allowed deferments, but they did not disproportionately benefit the wealthy. Almost ten thousand Princeton students or alumni served—as did all four of Franklin and Eleanor Roosevelt's sons. The small number of college deferments was balanced by deferments for many "critical occupations," including war workers and almost 2 million agricultural workers. Most exemptions were for men deemed physically or mentally unqualified to serve. Army physicians discovered the depression's impact as draftees arrived with rotted teeth and deteriorated eyesight—signs of malnutrition. Almost one-third of African American draftees were functionally illiterate. Forty-six percent of African Americans and almost one-third of European-Americans called for the draft were classified "4-F"—unfit for service.

Nonetheless, almost 12 percent of America's population served in the military. Ethnic and regional differences were profound, and northerners and southerners often could not understand one another. Differences among whites were often profound, and although African Americans and Japanese Americans served in separate units, Hispanics, Native Americans, and Chinese Americans served alongside whites. The result was often tension, but many Americans became less prejudiced as they served with men unlike themselves.

Fighting the War

Although military service was widespread, the burdens of combat were not equally shared. Women's roles in the U.S. military were much more restricted than in the British or Soviet militaries, where women served in combat-related positions. U.S. women served as nurses, in communications offices, and as typists or cooks. The recruiting slogan for the WACs (Women's Army Corps) was "Release a Man for Combat." However, most men never saw combat either; one-quarter never left the United States. One-third of U.S. military personnel served in clerical positions, filled mainly by well-educated men. African Americans, though assigned dirty and dangerous tasks, were largely kept from combat service. In World War II, lower-class, less-educated white men did most of the fighting.

Combat in World War II was horrible. Hollywood war films depicted men dying bravely, shot cleanly and comforted by buddies in their last moments. In reality, less than 10 percent of casualties were caused by bullets. Most men were killed or wounded by mortars, bombs, or grenades. Seventy-five thousand American men remained missing in action at war's end, blown into fragments too small to identify. Combat meant sliding down a mud-slicked hill into a pile of putrid corpses and using flamethrowers that burned at 2,000 degrees Fahrenheit on other human beings. It meant steering a landing craft through floating body parts, knowing that if you made it ashore, you could be blown apart by artillery. Service was for the war's duration. Only death, serious injury, or victory offered release.

Close to 300,000 American servicemen died in combat, and almost 1 million were wounded, half of them seriously. Medical advances, such as the development of penicillin and the use of blood plasma to prevent shock, helped wounded men survive—but many never fully recovered. Between 20 and 30 percent of combat casualties were psychoneurotic. The federal government censored images of American combat deaths, consigning them to a secret file known as "the chamber of horrors." Americans at home rarely understood what combat had been like.

Winning the War

Why did Truman opt to use the atomic bomb to help end the war, rather than negotiate a peace with Japan?

Axis hopes for victory depended on a short war. German and Japanese leaders knew that, if the United States had time to fully mobilize, flooding the theaters of war with armaments and reinforcing Allied troops with fresh, trained men, the war was lost, but many believed the United States would concede if met with early, decisive defeats. By mid-1942, the Axis powers understood that they had underestimated American resolve and other Allies' willingness to sacrifice their citizens to stop the Axis's advance (see Map 27.1). The chance of an Axis victory grew slim as months passed, but though the outcome was virtually certain after spring 1943, two years of fighting lay ahead.

Tensions Among the Allies

The Allies' suspicions of one another undermined cooperation. The Soviets pressed Britain and the United States to open a second front to draw German troops away from the USSR. The United States and Britain, however, continued to delay. With the alliance badly strained, the three Allied leaders met in Tehran, Iran, in December 1943. Stalin and Roosevelt dismissed Churchill's proposal for another peripheral attack, this time through the Balkans to Vienna. The three agreed to launch **Operation Overlord**—the cross-channel invasion of France—in early 1944. And the Soviet Union promised to aid the Allies against Japan once Germany was defeated.

Operation Overlord: Allied troops stormed a sixty-mile stretch of the Normandy coast in the largest amphibious invasion in history.

War in Europe

The second front opened in the dark morning hours of June 6, 1944: D-Day. In the largest amphibious landing in history, more than 140,000 Allied troops commanded by American general Dwight D. Eisenhower scrambled ashore at Normandy, France. Landing craft and soldiers immediately encountered the enemy; they triggered mines and were pinned down by fire from cliffside pillboxes. Although heavy bombardment and the clandestine work of saboteurs had softened the German defenses, the fighting was ferocious.

By late July, 1.4 million Allied troops spread across the countryside, liberating France and Belgium by the end of August, but leaving a path of devastation. Almost thirty-seven thousand Allied troops died in that struggle, and up to twenty thousand French civilians were killed, most by Allied bombing. German armored divisions counterattacked in Belgium's Ardennes Forest in December, hoping to reach Antwerp to halt Allied supplies through that Belgian port. After weeks of heavy fighting in the **Battle of the Bulge**, the Allies gained control in late January 1945.

Battle of the Bulge: Military offensive led by Germany. Named for the eighty-mile-long and fifty-mile-wide "bulge" that the German troops drove inside the American lines.

By that point, "strategic" bombing destroyed Germany's war production and devastated its economy. In early 1945, the British and Americans began "morale" bombing, killing tens of thousands of civilians in aerial attacks on Berlin and then Dresden. Meanwhile, Soviet troops marched through Poland to Berlin. American forces crossed the Rhine River in March 1945 and captured the industrial Ruhr valley. Several units entered Austria and Czechoslovakia, where they met Soviet soldiers.

Yalta Conference

In early 1945, Franklin Roosevelt, by this time very ill, called for a summit meeting to discuss plans for the postwar world. The three Allied leaders met at Yalta, in the Russian Crimea, in February 1945. Britain, its formerly powerful empire now vulnerable and shrinking, sought to protect its colonial possessions and limit Soviet power. The Soviet Union, with 21 million dead, wanted German reparations for its massive rebuilding effort. The Soviets hoped to expand their sphere of influence throughout eastern Europe and guarantee national security; Germany, Stalin insisted, must be permanently weakened.

The United States also sought to expand its influence and control the peace. Roosevelt lobbied for the United Nations Organization, approved in principle the previous year at Dumbarton Oaks in Washington, D.C., through which the United States hoped to exercise influence. The United States wanted to avoid the debts-reparations fiasco that plagued Europe after World War I. U.S. goals included self-determination for liberated peoples; gradual decolonization; and management of world affairs by what Roosevelt called the Four Policemen: the Soviet Union, Great Britain, the United States, and China. (Roosevelt hoped China might help stabilize Asia after the war. The United States abolished the Chinese Exclusion Act in 1943 to consolidate ties between the two nations.) The United States also wanted to limit Soviet influence in the postwar world.

Military positions during the Yalta conference helped shape the negotiations. Soviet troops occupied eastern European nations, including Poland, where Moscow installed a pro-Soviet regime despite a British-supported Polish government-in-exile in London. With Soviet troops in place, Britain and the United States were limited in negotiating this region's future. The Big Three agreed that some eastern German territory would be transferred to Poland and the remainder divided into four zones—the fourth to be administered by France. Berlin, within the Soviet zone, would also be divided among the four victors. In exchange for U.S. promises to support Soviet claims on territory lost to Japan in the Russo-Japanese War of 1904–1905, Stalin agreed to a treaty of friendship with Jiang Jieshi (Chiang Kai-shek), America's ally in China, rather than with the communist Mao Zedong (Mao Tse-tung), and to declare war on Japan within three months of Hitler's defeat.

Harry S Truman

Franklin D. Roosevelt, reelected to an unprecedented fourth term in November 1944, died on April 12, 1945, and Vice President Harry S Truman became president. Truman, who replaced former vice president Henry Wallace as Roosevelt's running mate in 1944, was inexperienced in foreign policy and was not informed about the top-secret atomic weapons project until he became president. Eighteen days into Truman's presidency, Adolf Hitler killed himself in a bunker in bomb-ravaged Berlin. On May 8, Germany surrendered.

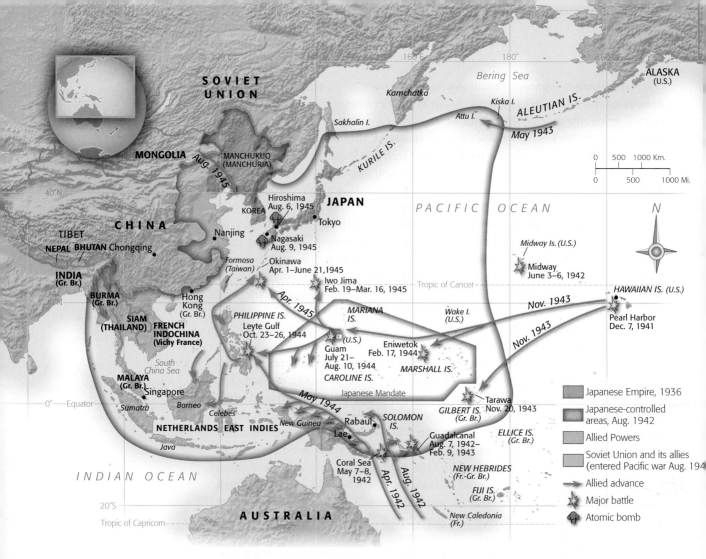

MAP 27.2

The Pacific War

The strategy of the United States was to "island-hop"—from Hawai'i in 1942 to Iwo Jima and Okinawa in 1945. Naval battles were also decisive, notably the Battles of the Coral Sea and Midway in 1942. The war in the Pacific ended with Japan's surrender on August 15, 1945 (V-J Day).

Source: Copyright © Cengage Learning

As the great powers jockeyed for influence after Germany's surrender, the Grand Alliance began to crumble. At the Potsdam Conference in mid-July, Truman was less patient with the Soviets than Roosevelt had been. Truman learned during the conference that a test of the new atomic weapon had been successful. The United States no longer needed the Soviet Union's help in the Pacific war. The Allies did agree that Japan must surrender unconditionally. But with the end of the European war, wartime bonds among the Allies were strained.

War in the Pacific   In the Pacific, the war continued. Since the Battle of Midway in June 1942, American strategy had been to "island-hop" toward Japan, skipping the most fortified islands whenever possible and taking the weaker ones, aiming to strand Japanese armies. To cut off supplies, Americans targeted the Japanese merchant marine. By 1944, Allied troops—from the United States, Britain, Australia, and New Zealand—secured the Solomon, Gilbert, Marshall, and Mariana Islands. General Douglas MacArthur landed at Leyte to retake the Philippines for the United States in October 1944.

In February 1945, while the Big Three were meeting at Yalta, U.S. and Japanese troops battled for Iwo Jima, a small island about 700 miles south of Tokyo. Twenty-one thousand Japanese defenders occupied the island's high ground. Hidden in a caves, trenches, and underground tunnels, they were protected from U.S. aerial bombardment supporting an amphibious landing. The island offered no cover, and marines were slaughtered as they came ashore. For twenty days, U.S. forces fought their way up Mount Suribachi, the highest and most heavily fortified point on Iwo Jima. Iwo Jima claimed 6,821 American and more than twenty thousand Japanese lives.

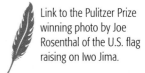

Link to the Pulitzer Prize winning photo by Joe Rosenthal of the U.S. flag raising on Iwo Jima.

A month later, American troops landed on Okinawa, an island at the southern tip of Japan, from which Allied forces planned to invade the main Japanese islands. Fighting raged for two months. The monsoon rains began in May, turning battle-fields into seas of mud filled with decaying corpses. The supporting fleet endured mass kamikaze (suicide) attacks, as Japanese pilots intentionally crashed bomb-laden planes into American ships. On Okinawa, 7,374 American soldiers and marines died in battle. Almost the entire Japanese garrison of 100,000 was killed. More than one-quarter of Okinawa's people, or approximately 80,000 civilians, perished.

Bombing of Japan

With American forces just 350 miles from Japan's main islands, a powerful Japanese military faction was determined to preserve the emperor's sovereignty and avoid an unconditional surrender. On the night of March 9, 1945, 333 American B-29 Superfortresses dropped explosives on a 4-by-3-mile area of Tokyo. They created a firestorm, a fierce blaze that sucked the oxygen from the air, creating hurricane-force winds and growing hot enough to melt concrete and steel. Almost 100,000 people were incinerated, suffocated, or boiled to death hiding in canals. Over the following five months, American bombers attacked sixty-six Japanese cities, leaving 8 million people homeless, killing almost 900,000.

Japan, meanwhile, was attempting to bomb the U.S. mainland. Thousands of bomb-bearing high-altitude balloons, constructed from rice paper and potato-flour paste by schoolgirls, were launched into the jet stream. Those that reached the United States fell on unpopulated areas, occasionally starting forest fires. The only mainland U.S. casualties in the war were five children and an adult on a Sunday school picnic in Oregon who accidentally detonated a balloon bomb. As General Yamamoto had realized at the war's beginning, American resources would far out-last Japan's.

Early in the summer of 1945, Japan put out peace feelers through the Soviets. Japan was not, however, willing to accept the "unconditional surrender" terms the Allied leaders agreed to at Potsdam, and Truman chose not to pursue a negotiated peace. U.S. troops were mobilizing to invade the Japanese home islands, but the Manhattan Project's success offered another option, and Truman took it. Using atomic bombs on Japan, Truman believed, would end the war quickly and save American lives. Concern about the postwar order also influenced Truman's decision;

Link to President Truman's announcement on the use of the atomic bomb.

Potsdam Declaration: Ultimatum Truman gave to Japan to surrender unconditionally or face "prompt and utter destruction."

the atomic bomb demonstrated American power and prevented the Soviets from entering the Pacific war and playing a role in the peace that followed.

Some historians argue that Japan was on the verge of unconditional surrender; others that the antisurrender faction was strong enough to prevail. No matter which is true, bombing (whether conventional or atomic) fit the established U.S. strategy of using machines rather than men whenever possible. The decision to use the atomic bomb did not seem as momentous to Truman as it does in retrospect. The moral line had already been crossed with wholesale bombing of civilian populations: the Japanese bombed Shanghai in 1937. Germans "terror-bombed" Warsaw, Rotterdam, and London. British and American bombers purposely created firestorms in German cities, killing 225,000 people on a single night in Dresden, Germany. The American bombing of Japanese cities with conventional weapons already killed nearly a million people. What distinguished the atomic bombs from conventional bombs was their power and efficiency—not that they killed huge numbers of civilians in unspeakably awful ways.

On July 26, 1945, the Allies delivered an ultimatum to Japan: promising that the Japanese people would not be "enslaved," the **Potsdam Declaration** called for

This scorched watch, found in the rubble at Hiroshima, stopped at the time of the blast—8:16. The shock waves and fires caused by the atomic bomb leveled great expanses of the city. Radiation released by the bomb caused lingering deaths for thousands who survived the explosion. The photo of Hiroshima shown above was taken eight months after the attack.

John Launois/Black Star

U.S. Air Force

Nuclear Proliferation

Virtually from the moment of the Hiroshima and Nagasaki atomic bombings, American strategists grappled with the problem of keeping others from the "nuclear club," particularly the Soviet Union. On September 23, 1949, President Truman informed shocked Americans that the Soviets had successfully tested an atomic device.

In the years thereafter, membership in the nuclear club grew, through huge national investments, espionage, and a black market selling raw materials and technologies. There were successful detonations by Great Britain (1952), France (1960), China (1964), India (1974), and Pakistan (1998). Israel crossed the nuclear weapon threshold on the eve of the 1967 Six-Day War but to this day has refused to confirm that it has the bomb. Recently, creditable reports indicate that North Korea has a small nuclear arsenal and that Iran is working to get one.

Still the number of nuclear states is fewer than experts predicted in the 1960s, when analysts warned that thirty nations might be so armed by the 1990s. It did not happen because the five existing nuclear powers committed themselves in the mid-1960s to promoting nonproliferation. Subsequently, twenty-two of thirty-one states that started down the nuclear path changed course and renounced the bomb. By late 2006, the Treaty on the Non-Proliferation of Nuclear Weapons (NPT), enacted on July 1, 1968, had 187 signatories and was hailed as one of the great international agreements of the post-1945 era.

Skeptics took a different view, noting that three states outside the NPT (Israel, India, and Pakistan) became nuclear powers. They charged the "original five" with preventing others from obtaining nuclear arms while keeping large stockpiles themselves. With the world in 2009 awash in some twenty-three thousand nuclear weapons (97 percent belonging to the United States and Russia), critics feared terrorist groups or other nonstate actor getting bombs. In that nightmare scenario, they warned, the de facto post-Nagasaki international moratorium on the use of nuclear weapons would be literally blown away.

unconditional surrender or "prompt and utter destruction." Tokyo radio announced that the government would respond with *mokusatsu* (literally, "kill with silence," or ignore the ultimatum). On August 6, 1945, a B-29 bomber, the *Enola Gay,* dropped an atomic bomb above Hiroshima, igniting a firestorm and killing 130,000 people. Tens of thousands more would suffer from radiation poisoning.

On August 8, the Soviet Union declared war on Japan. On August 9, the United States used a second atomic bomb on Nagasaki, killing sixty thousand people. Five days later, Japan surrendered. Recent histories argue that the Soviet declaration of war played a more significant role in Japan's surrender than America's use of atomic weapons. In the end, the Allies promised that the Japanese emperor could remain as the nation's titular head. World War II was over.

Summary

Hitler once prophesied, "We may be destroyed, but if we are, we shall drag a world with us." World War II devastated much of the globe. In Asia and Europe, ghostlike people wandered through rubble, searching for food. One out of nine people in the Soviet Union had perished: at least 21 million civilian and military war dead. The Chinese lost 10 million; the Germans and Austrians, 6 million; the Japanese,

2.5 million. Up to 1 million died of famine in Japanese-controlled Indochina. Almost 11 million people were murdered in Nazi death camps. Across the globe, World War II killed at least 55 million people.

War required Allied nations with different goals to cooperate. Tensions remained high, as the United States and Britain resisted Stalin's demands for a second front to draw Germans away from the Soviet Union. The United States, meanwhile, was fighting the Japanese in the Pacific. When Japan surrendered in August 1945, the strains between the Soviet Union and its English-speaking Allies made postwar stability unlikely.

American servicemen covered the globe, while on the home front, Americans worked around the clock to make weapons. Despite wartime sacrifices, many Americans found the war had improved their lives. Mobilization ended the Great Depression. Americans moved to war-production centers. The influx of workers strained community resources and sometimes led to social friction and violence. But many Americans—African Americans, Mexican Americans, women, poor whites from the South—found new opportunities in well-paid war jobs. The federal government became a stronger presence, regulating business and employment; overseeing military conscription, and even controlling what people could buy to eat or to wear.

At war's end, only the United States had the economic resources to spur international recovery; only the United States was more prosperous than when war began. In the coming struggle to fashion a new world—the Cold War—the United States held a commanding position. For better or worse—and clearly there were elements of each—World War II was a turning point in the nation's history.

Chapter Review

The United States at War

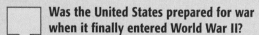 **Was the United States prepared for war when it finally entered World War II?**

No. The Roosevelt administration had begun efforts to prepare the nation to enter the war, despite strong opposition from much of the public, but those changes—including the institution of the first peacetime draft in the nation's history—were minor compared to the scale of the challenge ahead. The United States did not maintain a large standing army before World War II, and in 1939, the U.S. Army ranked forty-fifth among world armies, and there was only enough equipment for one-third of its troops. President Roosevelt's study of U.S. preparedness determined that the country would not be up to fighting before 1943–a luxury it would not have after the December 7, 1941 attack on Pearl Harbor pulled America officially into the war.

The Production Front and American Workers

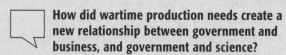 **How did wartime production needs create a new relationship between government and business, and government and science?**

Mobilizing for war required that factories shift from producing consumer goods to wartime necessities such as uniforms, arms, tanks, and so forth. The federal government enticed businesses to cooperate by offering generous tax write-offs and exemptions from antitrust laws. It also paid to retool or expand factories for war production and guaranteed the bottom line by allowing corporations to charge production costs plus a fixed profit. This enabled companies to double their net profits from 1939 to 1944. The government ensured that labor strikes would not disrupt production by having the newly formed National War Labor Board settle disputes. The government spent millions on university research programs that would develop new war technologies, most importantly, the $2 billion secret Manhattan Project to build an atomic bomb.

Life on the Home Front

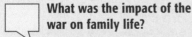

What was the impact of the war on family life?

Family life was transformed by the war. Nearly three million families were broken up during the war years, despite government policies that exempted married men and fathers from the draft. Although divorce rates doubled, marriage rates also increased from 73 per 1,000 unmarried women in 1939 to 93 in 1942—with couples scrambling to tie the knot before draftees were sent overseas. Birth rates rose, too, from 2.4 million babies in 1939 to 3.1 million in 1943, as families had children in the hopes of continuing the family should the father not return from war. Despite fears about the erosion of sexual mores, taboos against unwed motherhood remained strong, and only 1 percent of births during the war were to unmarried women. Wartime mobility also increased opportunities for same-sex relationships, and gay communities grew in such cities as San Francisco. Still, the war reinforced traditional gender roles—men served as the nation's defenders while women were to "keep the home fires burning," sometimes filling jobs vacated by soldiers, albeit just "for the duration." Nonetheless, millions of women enjoyed the independence that came with their new responsibilities, and many men returned to families that functioned without them.

The Limits of American Ideals

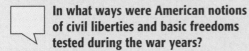

In what ways were American notions of civil liberties and basic freedoms tested during the war years?

Without question, tensions emerged between wartime practices and America's democratic ideals. Government propaganda films contrasted American democracy and freedom with totalitarianism and fascism. While U.S. leaders embraced a "strategy of truth" that promised to honestly report the war's progress to the public, the government nonetheless tightly controlled military information—even seemingly unimportant details. Freedoms were in fact curbed, as evident in passage of the 1940 Alien Registration (Smith Act), which made it illegal to advocate overthrowing the U.S. government. But the most grievous civil liberties violation was the treatment of ethnic Americans and resident aliens, notably the internment

of the Japanese. In March 1942, Roosevelt ordered that all 112,000 foreign-born Japanese and Japanese Americans living in California, Oregon, and the state of Washington be removed from the West Coast to "relocation centers"— camps in Arkansas, Wyoming, and Arizona. There were no individual charges; they were imprisoned under suspicion solely because they were of Japanese descent. In 1988, Congress issued a public apology, with included a $20,000 payment to each of the surviving 60,000 Japanese American internees.

Life in the Military

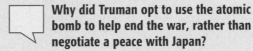

How did racial and gender norms play out in the military during World War II?

More than 15 million men and approximately 350,000 women served in the U.S. armed forces during World War II. The discrimination that existed throughout American society was replicated in the armed services: African Americans and Japanese Americans served in units segregated from whites (although Hispanics, Native Americans, and Chinese Americans were part of "white" units). African Americans were given the dirtiest and most dangerous assignments, though they were largely kept from combat service. Less-educated, lower-class white men did most of the fighting. Women who volunteered for the Women's Army Corps and other female military organizations served as nurses, in communications offices, as typists, and as cooks—all military extensions of their traditional gender roles.

Winning the War

Why did Truman opt to use the atomic bomb to help end the war, rather than negotiate a peace with Japan?

Historians continue to debate this question. From a military standpoint, Truman would only agree to an unconditional surrender of the Japanese, something the Japanese were unlikely to accept. Truman believed that using the atomic bomb would end the war quickly and save U.S. soldiers' lives. He was also concerned about the postwar order and believed the atomic bomb would demonstrate American power and keep the Soviets both from entering the Pacific war and later playing a role in the peace process. Because extensive bombing of Japanese civilian areas had already occurred, Truman did not see the use of the bomb as crossing a moral line the way it would later come to be understood. What distinguished the atomic bombs from conventional bombs, as Truman saw it, was their power and efficiency—not that they killed huge numbers of civilians in unspeakably awful ways.

Suggestions for Further Reading

Michael C. C. Adams, *The Best War Ever: America and World War II* (1993)

Tsuyoshi Hasegawa, *Racing the Enemy: Stalin, Truman, and the Surrender of Japan* (2005)

William I. Hitchcock, *The Bitter Road to Freedom: A New History of the Liberation of Europe* (2008)

John Howard, *Concentration Camps on the Homefront: Japanese Americans in the House of Jim Crow* (2008)

David M. Kennedy, *Freedom from Fear: The American People in Depression and War, 1929–1945* (1999)

Warren F. Kimball, *Forged in War: Roosevelt, Churchill, and the Second World War* (1997)

Nelson Lichtenstein, *Labor's War at Home: The CIO in World War II* (1983)

Gerald F. Linderman, *The World Within War: America's Combat Experience in World War II* (1997)

Leisa Meyers, *Creating G.I. Jane: Sexuality and Power in the Women's Army Corps During World War II* (1996)

George Roeder, Jr., *The Censored War: American Visual Experience During World War II* (1993)

Barbara Dianne Savage, *Broadcasting Freedom: Radio, War, and the Politics of Race, 1938–1948* (1999)

Ronald Takaki, *Double Victory: A Multicultural History of America in World War II* (2000)

28

The Cold War and American Globalism

1945–1961

On July 16, 1945, the "Deer" Team leader parachuted into northern Vietnam, near Kimlung, a village in a valley of rice paddies. Colonel Allison Thomas and five other members of his Office of Strategic Services (OSS) unit could not know that the end of the Second World War was weeks away. Their mission: to work with the Vietminh, a nationalist Vietnamese organization, to sabotage Japanese forces that in March seized Vietnam from France. A banner proclaimed, "Welcome to Our American Friends." Ho Chi Minh, head of the Vietminh, offered the OSS team supper. The next day, Ho denounced the French but remarked "We welcome 10 million Americans." "Forget the Communist Bogy," Thomas radioed OSS headquarters in China.

A communist dedicated to winning his nation's independence from France, Ho joined the French Communist Party after World War I. For the next two decades, living in China, the Soviet Union, and elsewhere, he planned and fought to free his nation from French colonialism. During World War II, Ho's Vietminh warriors harassed French and Japanese forces and rescued downed American pilots. In March 1945, Ho met with U.S. officials in China. Receiving no aid from his ideological allies in the Soviet Union, Ho hoped the United States would favor his nation's quest for liberation.

Other OSS personnel soon parachuted into Kimlung, including a male nurse who diagnosed Ho's ailments as malaria and dysentery. Quinine and sulfa drugs restored his health, but Ho remained frail. Everywhere the Americans went, impoverished villagers thanked them with gifts of food and clothing, interpreting the foreigners' presence as a sign of U.S. anticolonial and anti-Japanese sentiments. In early August, the Deer Team offered Vietminh soldiers weapons training. Ho hoped young Vietnamese could study in the United States and that U.S. technicians could help build an independent Vietnam.

A second OSS unit, the "Mercy" Team, headed by Captain Archimedes Patti, arrived in the city of Hanoi on August 22. But, unbeknownst to these OSS members, who believed that President Franklin D. Roosevelt's sympathy for eventual Vietnamese independence remained U.S. policy, the new Truman administration had decided to let France decide Vietnam's fate. That policy change explains why Ho never received answers to the letters and telegrams he sent to Washington beginning August 30, 1945.

On September 2, 1945, with OSS personnel present, Ho Chi Minh read his declaration of independence for the Democratic Republic of Vietnam: "All men are created equal; they are endowed by their Creator with certain unalienable Rights; among these are Life, Liberty, and the pursuit of Happiness." Borrowing from the internationally renowned 1776 American document, Ho itemized Vietnamese grievances against France.

In a last meeting with Captain Patti, Ho expressed sadness that the United States armed the French to reestablish their colonial rule in Vietnam. Sure, Ho said, U.S. officials in Washington judged him a Moscow puppet because he was a communist. But Ho claimed that he drew inspiration from the American struggle for independence. Ho insisted the Vietnamese would go it alone. And they did—first against the French and eventually against more than half a million U.S. troops in what became the United States' longest war.

Because Ho Chi Minh and many of his nationalist followers declared themselves communists, U.S. leaders rejected their appeal. Endorsing the containment doctrine against communism, American presidents from Truman to George H. W. Bush believed that a ruthless Soviet Union directed a worldwide communist conspiracy against peace, free-market capitalism, and democracy. Soviet leaders from Joseph Stalin to Mikhail Gorbachev protested that a militarized, economically aggressive United States sought world domination. This protracted contest between the United States and the Soviet Union acquired the name Cold War.

The primary feature of world affairs for more than four decades, the Cold War was fundamentally a contest between the United States and the Soviet Union over spheres of influence. The contest between the capitalist West and the communist East dominated international relations and eventually took the lives of millions, cost trillions of dollars, spawned doomsday fears, and destabilized several nations. Occasionally, the two superpowers negotiated and signed agreements to temper their dangerous arms race; at other times, they went to the brink of war and armed allies to fight vicious Third World conflicts. Sometimes these allies had their own ambitions and resisted pressure from one or both superpowers.

Vietnam was part of the *Third World*, a term for nations that in the Cold War era wore neither the West (the First World) nor the East (the Second World) label. Sometimes called developing countries, Third World nations were generally nonwhite, nonindustrialized, and located in the southern half of the globe—in Asia, Africa, the Middle East, and Latin America. Many had been colonies of European nations or Japan and were vulnerable to the Cold War rivalry. U.S. leaders often interpreted their anticolonialism as Soviet inspired rather than as expressions of indigenous nationalism. Vietnam became one among many sites where Cold War fears and Third World aspirations intersected, prompting U.S. intervention and a globalist foreign policy that regarded the world as the appropriate sphere for America's influence.

Critics in the United States challenged Cold War exaggerations of threats from abroad, meddlesome interventions in the Third World, and militarization of foreign policy. But when leaders like Truman described the Cold War as a life-and-death struggle against a monstrous enemy, critics were drowned out by charges that dissenters were soft on communism, if not un-American. U.S. leaders successfully cultivated a Cold War consensus that stifled debate and shaped the mindset of generations of Americans.

As you read this chapter, keep the following questions in mind:

* **Why did relations between the Soviet Union and the United States turn hostile soon after their victory in World War II?**

* **When and why did the Cold War expand from a struggle over the future of Europe and central Asia to one encompassing virtually the entire globe?**

* **By what means did the Truman and Eisenhower administrations seek to expand America's global influence in the late 1940s and the 1950s?**

From Allies to Adversaries

Was the Cold War inevitable?

World War II unsettled the international system. Germany was in ruins. Great Britain was overstrained, France was rent by internal division, and Italy was weakened. Japan was decimated and occupied, and China was headed toward renewed civil war. Throughout Europe and Asia, factories, transportation, and communications links were reduced to rubble, and agricultural production plummeted. The United States and the Soviet Union offered different solutions. The collapse of Germany and Japan, moreover, created power vacuums that drew the two major powers into collision as they sought influence where Axis aggressors had once held sway. For example, in Greece and China, where civil wars raged between leftists and conservative regimes, the two powers supported opposite sides.

Decolonization With empires disintegrating, a new Third World emerged. Financial constraints and nationalist rebellions forced the imperial states to set their colonies free. Britain exited India (and Pakistan) in 1947 and Burma and Sri Lanka (Ceylon) in 1948. The Philippines gained independence from the United States in 1946. After four years of battling nationalists in Indonesia, the Dutch left in 1949. In the Middle East, Lebanon (1943), Syria (1946), and Jordan (1946) gained independence, while in Palestine British officials faced pressure from Zionists intent on creating a Jewish homeland and from Arab leaders opposed to it. In Iraq, nationalist agitation increased against the British-installed government. Washington and Moscow saw these new or emerging Third World states as potential allies that might provide military bases, resources, and markets. Some new nations, however, chose nonalignment in the Cold War.

Chronology

1945	Roosevelt dies; Truman becomes president Atomic bombings of Japan	1951	United States signs Mutual Security Treaty with Japan
1946	Kennan's "long telegram" criticizes USSR Vietnamese war against France erupts	1953	Eisenhower becomes president Stalin dies United States helps restore shah to power in Iran Korean War ends
1947	Truman Doctrine seeks aid for Greece and Turkey Marshall offers Europe economic assistance National Security Act reorganizes government	1954	Geneva accords partition Vietnam CIA-led coup overthrows Arbenz in Guatemala
1948	Communists take power in Czechoslovakia Truman recognizes Israel United States organizes Berlin airlift	1955	Soviets create Warsaw Pact
		1956	Soviets crush uprising in Hungary Suez crisis sparks war in Middle East
1949	NATO founded as anti-Soviet alliance Soviet Union explodes atomic bomb Mao's communists win power in China	1957	Soviets fire first ICBM and launch *Sputnik*
		1958	U.S. troops land in Lebanon Berlin crisis
1950	NSC-68 recommends major military buildup Korean War starts in June; China enters in fall	1959	Castro ousts Batista in Cuba
		1960	Eighteen African colonies become independent

Stalin's Aims

The United States and Soviet Union assessed their most pressing tasks differently. The Soviets, though committed to victory over capitalist countries, were most concerned about preventing another invasion of their homeland. Its land mass was three times that of the United States, but it had only 10,000 miles of seacoast, which was under ice for much of the year. Russian leaders before and after the revolution made increased maritime access a chief foreign policy aim.

Worse, the USSR's geographical frontiers were hard to defend. Siberia, vital for mineral resources, lay 6,000 miles east of Moscow and was vulnerable to encroachment by Japan and China. In the west, the border with Poland generated violent clashes since World War I, and 25 million Russians died after Hitler's invasion in 1941. Henceforth, Soviet leaders wanted no dangers along their western borders.

Overall, however, Soviet territorial objectives were limited. Although Americans were quick to compare Stalin to Hitler, Stalin's aims were more limited and resembled those of tsars before him: he wanted to push the Soviet Union's borders to include the Baltic states of Estonia, Latvia, and Lithuania, along with the eastern part of prewar Poland. To the south, Stalin wanted a presence in northern Iran, and he pressed the Turks for naval bases and free access out of the Black Sea. Economically, the Soviets did not promote rapid rebuilding of the region's war-ravaged economies or expanded world trade.

U.S. Economic and Strategic Needs

The United States, by contrast, came out of the war secure in its borders. Separated from other world powers by two oceans, the U.S. home base was virtually immune from attack during the fighting. American casualties were fewer than any of the other major combatants. With its fixed capital intact, its resources more plentiful than

Stalin: Ally to Adversary

These two *Look* magazine portrayals of Soviet leader Stalin indicate how quickly the Grand Alliance of World War II disintegrated into the superpower confrontation of the Cold War. In the first piece, from mid 1944, correspondent Ralph Parker writes that Stalin spends half his time writing poetry and the other half reading it to the school children who clamor to sit on his knee. "Stalin," Parker adds, "is undoubtedly among the best-dressed of all world leaders making Churchill in his siren suit look positively shabby." Four years later, Louis Fischer paints a very different picture. "This small man with drooping shoulders tyrannizes one-fifth of the world," Fischer writes of the Soviet leader, adding that neither Hitler nor any Russian czar were as powerful or as menacing as the "Great Red Father." What do these two items suggest about American attitudes toward the outside world? What do they suggest about the role of the press in U.S. society?

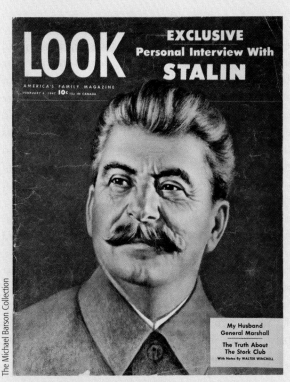

The Michael Barson Collection

"A Guy named Joe" cover story of Look Magazine by Ralph Parker, June 27, 1944.

The Michael Barson Collection

"Life Story of Stalin" by Louis Fischer in Look Magazine, June 8, 1948

ever, and in lone possession of the atomic bomb, the United States was the strongest power in the world at war's end.

But Washington officials worried about complacency. Some other power—almost certainly the Soviet Union—could take advantage of instability in war-torn Europe and Asia and seize control of these areas, with dire implications for the United States' security. Therefore, Washington sought bases overseas to keep an airborne enemy at bay. To enhance U.S. security, U.S. planners sought the quick reconstruction of nations—including former enemies Germany and Japan—and a world economy based on free trade.

The Soviets, on the other hand, refused to join the new World Bank and International Monetary Fund (IMF), created at the July 1944 Bretton Woods Conference by forty-four nations to stabilize trade and finance. They held that the United States dominated both institutions and used them to promote private investment and open international commerce, which Moscow saw as capitalist tools. With the United States as its largest donor, the World Bank opened in 1945 and made loans to finance members' reconstruction projects; the IMF, also heavily U.S.-backed, helped members meet their balance-of-payments problems through currency loans.

Stalin and Truman

Joseph Stalin, though hostile to the western powers and capable of ruthlessness against his people (his periodic purges since the 1930s took the lives of millions), did not want war. He was aware of his country's weakness vis-à-vis the United States and believed he must try to achieve his aspirations through cooperation. Stalin believed that Germany and Japan would eventually threaten the Soviet Union, and his suspicion of capitalist powers was boundless. Many concluded that Stalin was clinically paranoid. As historian David Reynolds has noted, this alleged paranoia, coupled with Stalin's xenophobia (fear of anything foreign) and his Marxist-Leninist ideology, created in him a mental map of them versus us that influenced his approach to world affairs.

Harry Truman had none of Stalin's capacity for ruthlessness, but to a lesser degree he, too, was also prone to a "them versus us" world-view. He often glossed over nuances, ambiguities, and counterevidence, preferring an either/or answer. Truman exaggerated, as when he declared in his undelivered farewell address that he "knocked the socks off the communists" in Korea. When Truman protested in 1945 during a meeting at the White House that the Soviets were not fulfilling the Yalta agreement on Poland, the Soviet commissar of foreign affairs, V. M. Molotov, stormed out. Truman self-consciously developed what he called his tough method, which became a trademark of U.S. Cold War diplomacy.

The Beginning of the Cold War

No precise start for the Cold War's beginning can be given. It resulted from an ongoing process that arguably began in 1917 with the Bolshevik Revolution and the western powers' hostile response. But in a more meaningful sense, it began in mid-1945, as World War II ended. By spring 1947, certainly, the struggle had begun.

One of the first Soviet-American clashes came in Poland in 1945, when the Soviets blocked the Polish government-in-exile in London from becoming part of the communist government that Moscow sponsored. The Soviets also extinguished civil liberties in Romania, arguing that the United States similarly manipulated Italy.

Moscow initially allowed free elections in Hungary and Czechoslovakia, but as the Cold War accelerated and U.S. influence in Europe expanded, the Soviets encouraged communist coups in Hungary (1947) and Czechoslovakia (1948). Yugoslavia was unique: its independent communist government, led by Josip Broz Tito, broke with Stalin in 1948.

To defend their actions, Moscow officials noted that the United States was reviving their traditional enemy, Germany, and was meddling in eastern Europe. The Soviets cited clandestine American meetings with anti-Soviet groups, repeated calls for elections likely to produce anti-Soviet regimes, and the use of loans to gain political influence (financial diplomacy). Moscow charged that the United States was pursuing a double standard—intervening in eastern Europe but demanding that the Soviet Union stay out of Latin America and Asia. The United States called for free elections in the Soviet sphere, Moscow noted, but not in the U.S. sphere in Latin America.

Atomic Diplomacy

The Soviets believed the United States was practicing "atomic diplomacy"—maintaining a nuclear monopoly to scare the Soviets into diplomatic concessions. Secretary of State James F. Byrnes thought that the atomic bomb could deter Soviet expansion, but Secretary of War Henry L. Stimson disagreed in 1945. If Americans continued to have "this weapon rather ostentatiously on our hip," he warned Truman, the Soviets' "suspicions and their distrust of our purposes and motives will increase."

In this atmosphere, Truman refused to turn over the weapon to an international authority. In 1946, he backed the Baruch Plan, named after its author, financier Bernard Baruch, which provided for U.S. abandonment of its atomic monopoly only after the world's fissionable materials were controlled by an international agency. The Soviets retorted that it would require them to shut down their atomic-bomb development project while the United States continued its own. Washington and Moscow soon became locked in a frightening nuclear arms race.

By the middle of 1946, Soviets and Americans clashed on every front. When the United States refused a Soviet request for a reconstruction loan but gave one to Britain, Moscow upbraided Washington for using its dollars to manipulate foreign governments. The two Cold War powers also backed different groups in Iran, where the United States helped bring the pro-West shah to the throne. Unable to agree on the unification of Germany, the former allies built up their zones independently.

After Stalin gave a speech in February 1946 depicting the world as threatened by capitalist acquisitiveness, the U.S. chargé d'affaires in Moscow, **George F. Kennan**, sent a pessimistic long telegram to Washington. His widely circulated report fed a growing belief among U.S. officials that only toughness would work with the Soviets. The following month, in Fulton, Missouri, former British prime minister Winston Churchill warned that a Soviet-erected iron curtain cut off eastern European countries from the West. With an approving Truman nearby, Churchill called for Anglo-American partnership to resist the new menace.

The growing Soviet-American tensions had major implications for the United Nations. The delegates who gathered in San Francisco in April 1945 to sign the U.N. charter agreed on an organization that included a General Assembly of all member states and a smaller Security Council spearheading peace and security issues. Five great powers were given permanent seats on the council—the United States, the Soviet Union, Great Britain, China, and France—and could each exercise a veto

George F. Kennan: American diplomat in Moscow, architect of the Cold War policy of containment.

against any proposed action. To be effective on the major issues of war and peace, therefore, the U.N. needed great power. Of the fifty-one founding states, twenty-two came from the Americas and another fifteen from Europe, which effectively gave the United States a large majority in the assembly. In retaliation, Moscow exercised its veto in the Security Council.

Some high-level U.S. officials were dismayed by the administration's harsh anti-Soviet posture. Secretary of Commerce Henry A. Wallace charged that Truman's get-tough policy substituted atomic and economic coercion for diplomacy. Wallace told a Madison Square Garden audience in September 1946 that "getting tough never brought anything real and lasting—whether for schoolyard bullies, or businessmen or world powers." Truman fired Wallace, blasting him privately as "a real Commy."

Truman Doctrine

East-West tensions escalated further in early 1947, when Britain requested American help in Greece defending their conservative client-government (a government dependent on the economic or military support of a more powerful country) in a civil war against leftists. The Republican Eightieth Congress wanted less spending; many of its members had little respect for the Democratic president who voters repudiated in the 1946 elections by giving the GOP ("Grand Old Party," the Republican Party) majorities in both houses of Congress. Republican senator Arthur Vandenberg of Michigan, a bipartisan leader, told the president that he would have to "scare hell out of the American people" to gain congressional approval.

Thus, the president delivered a speech laced with alarmist language staking out the United States' role in the postwar world. Truman claimed that communism imperiled the world. "If Greece should fall under the control of an armed minority," he concluded in an early version of the domino theory, "the effect upon its neighbor, Turkey, would be immediate and serious. Confusion and disorder might well spread throughout the entire Middle East." Truman articulated what became known as the **Truman Doctrine**: "It must be the policy of the United States to support free peoples who are resisting attempted subjugation by armed minorities or by outside pressures."

Critics correctly pointed out that the Soviet Union was little involved in the Greek civil war, that the communists in Greece were more pro-Tito than pro-Stalin, and that the resistance movement had noncommunist as well as communist members. Truman countered that, should communists gain control of Greece, they might open the door to Soviet power in the Mediterranean. The Senate approved Truman's request by 67 to 23 votes. Using U.S. dollars and military advisers, the Greek government defeated the insurgents in 1949, and Turkey became a U.S. ally on the Soviets' border.

Inevitable Cold War?

In the months after Truman's speech, the term *Cold War* slipped into the lexicon as a description of the Soviet-American relationship. Within two years of the victory over the Axis powers, the two Grand Alliance members were locked in a struggle for world dominance that would last almost half a century. Even before World War II ended, observers anticipated that the United States and the Soviet Union would seek to fill the power vacuum. The two countries had a history of hostility and were militarily powerful. Most of all, they were divided by sharply differing political economies with divergent needs and by a deep ideological chasm.

Link to the Truman Doctrine.

Truman Doctrine: U.S. policy designed to contain the spread of communism; began with President Truman's 1947 request to Congress for economic and military aid to the struggling countries of Greece and Turkey to prevent them from succumbing to Soviet pressure.

It is far less clear that the conflict had to result in a Cold War. The "cold peace" that had prevailed from the revolution in 1917 through World War II could conceivably have continued into the postwar years. Neither side's leadership wanted war. Both hoped—at least initially—that cooperation could be maintained. The Cold War resulted from decisions by individuals who might have done more to maintain diplomatic dialog and negotiate solutions to international problems. For decades, Americans would wonder if the high price they were paying for victory in the superpower confrontation was necessary.

Containment in Action

To counter Soviet and communist expansion, the Truman team chose a policy of **containment**. George Kennan, now at the State Department in Washington, published an influential statement of the containment doctrine. Writing as Mr. X in the July 1947 issue of *Foreign Affairs* magazine, Kennan advocated a "policy of firm containment, designed to confront the Russians with unalterable counterforce at every point where they show signs of encroaching upon the interests of a peaceful and stable world." Such counterforce, Kennan argued, would check Soviet expansion. Kennan's X article joined the Truman Doctrine as a key manifesto of Cold War policy.

> Was the U.S. containment policy successful?

containment: U.S. policy uniting military, economic, and diplomatic strategies to prevent the spread of Soviet communism and to enhance America's security and influence abroad.

Lippmann's Critique

The veteran journalist Walter Lippmann took issue with the containment doctrine in his powerful book *The Cold War* (1947), calling it a "strategic monstrosity" that failed to distinguish between areas vital and peripheral to U.S. security. Nor did Lippmann share Truman's conviction that the Soviet Union was plotting to take over the world. Ironically, Kennan agreed with much of Lippmann's critique and soon distanced himself from the doctrine he helped create.

Invoking the containment doctrine, the United States in 1947 and 1948 began to build an international economic and defensive network to protect American prosperity and security and to advance U.S. hegemony. In western Europe, the region of primary concern, American diplomats pursued economic reconstruction, the ouster of communists from governments, as occurred in 1947 in France and Italy, and blockage of "third force" or neutralist tendencies. Officials also kept the decolonization of European empires orderly. Meanwhile, American culture—consumer goods, music, consumption ethic, and production techniques—permeated European societies. Some Europeans resisted Americanization, but transatlantic ties strengthened.

Marshall Plan

Americans, who already spent billions of dollars on European relief and recovery by 1947, remembered too well the troubles of the 1930s: global depression, political extremism, and war born of economic discontent. Such cataclysms could not be allowed to happen again; communism must not replace fascism. Hence, in June 1947, Secretary of State George C. Marshall announced that the United States would finance a massive European recovery program. Launched in 1948, the **Marshall Plan** sent $12.4 billion to western Europe until 1951 (see Map 28.1). To stimulate business at home, the legislation required that Europeans spend this aid on American-made products. The Marshall Plan proved a mixed success; it caused inflation, failed to solve a balance-of-payments problem, took only tentative steps toward economic integration, and further divided Europe

Marshall Plan: The Truman administration's proposal for massive U.S. economic aid to speed the recovery of war-torn Europe.

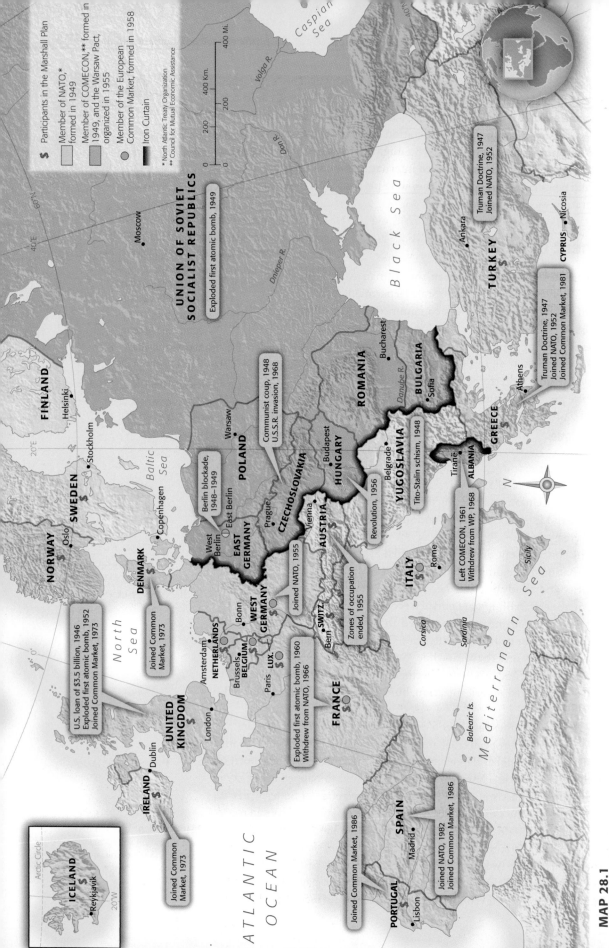

MAP 28.1

Divided Europe

After the Second World War, Europe broke into two competing camps. When the United States launched the Marshall Plan in 1948, the Soviet Union countered with its own economic plan the following year. When the United States created NATO in 1949, the Soviet Union answered with the Warsaw Pact in 1955. On the whole, these two camps held firm until the late 1980s.

Source: Copyright © Cengage Learning

Legend

$ Participants in the Marshall Plan

Member of NATO,* formed in 1949

Member of COMECON,** formed in 1949, and the Warsaw Pact, organized in 1955

Member of the European Common Market, formed in 1958

Iron Curtain

* North Atlantic Treaty Organization
** Council for Mutual Economic Assistance

400 Mi.
400 km.
0 200
0 200

Map labels

UNION OF SOVIET SOCIALIST REPUBLICS

Exploded first atomic bomb, 1949

Moscow

Volga R.
Don R.
Dnieper R.
Danube R.

Caspian Sea

Black Sea

Mediterranean Sea

Baltic Sea

North Sea

ATLANTIC OCEAN

TURKEY
Truman Doctrine, 1947
Joined NATO, 1952
Ankara

CYPRUS · Nicosia

GREECE
Truman Doctrine, 1947
Joined NATO, 1952
Joined Common Market, 1981
Athens

BULGARIA
Sofia

ROMANIA
Bucharest

YUGOSLAVIA
Tito-Stalin schism, 1948
Belgrade

ALBANIA
Left COMECON, 1961
Withdrew from WP, 1968
Tiranë

HUNGARY
Revolution, 1956
Budapest

POLAND
Warsaw

CZECHOSLOVAKIA
Communist coup, 1948
U.S.S.R. invasion, 1968
Prague

AUSTRIA
Zones of occupation ended, 1955
Joined NATO, 1955
Vienna

EAST GERMANY
Berlin blockade, 1948–1949
East Berlin
West Berlin

WEST GERMANY
Bonn

SWITZ.
Bern

ITALY
Rome

SPAIN
Joined NATO, 1982
Joined Common Market, 1986
Madrid

PORTUGAL
Joined Common Market, 1986
Lisbon

FRANCE
Exploded first atomic bomb, 1960
Withdrew from NATO, 1966
Paris

NETHERLANDS
Amsterdam

BELGIUM
Brussels

LUX.

DENMARK
Joined Common Market, 1973
Copenhagen

SWEDEN
Stockholm

NORWAY
Oslo

FINLAND
Helsinki

UNITED KINGDOM
U.S. loan of $3.5 billion, 1946
Exploded first atomic bomb, 1952
Joined Common Market, 1973
London

IRELAND
Joined Common Market, 1973
Dublin

ICELAND
Joined Common Market, 1973
Reykjavik
Arctic Circle

Corsica
Sardinia
Sicily
Balearic Is.

60°N
40°E
20°E
0°
20°W
40°N

N

between "East" and "West." But the program spurred impressive western European industrial production and investment, started the region toward self-sustaining economic growth, and—from the American perspective—contained communism.

National Security Act

Truman streamlined U.S. defense by working with Congress on the **National Security Act of July 1947**. The act created the Office of Secretary of Defense (which became the Department of Defense two years later) to oversee the armed services, the National Security Council (NSC) of high-level officials to advise the president, and the Central Intelligence Agency (CIA) to conduct spy operations and information gathering overseas. By the early 1950s, the CIA expanded to include covert (secret) operations aimed at overthrowing unfriendly foreign leaders. The National Security Act gave the president increased powers regarding foreign policy.

In response, Stalin forbade communist satellite governments in eastern Europe to accept Marshall Plan aid and ordered communist parties in western Europe to work to thwart it. He also created the Cominform, an organization designed to coordinate communist activities around the world. Whereas U.S. planners saw the Marshall Plan as protecting their European friends against a potential Soviet threat, to Stalin it raised anew the specter of capitalist penetration. He tightened his grip on eastern Europe—most notably, engineering a coup in Czechoslovakia in February 1948 that ensured full Soviet control, which heightened anxiety in the United States.

Berlin Blockade and Airlift

In June 1948, the Americans, French, and British agreed to fuse their German zones, and integrate West Germany (the Federal Republic of Germany) into the western European economy. Fearing a resurgent Germany tied to the American Cold War camp, the Soviets cut off western land access to the jointly occupied city of Berlin, located inside the Soviet zone. President Truman then ordered the **Berlin airlift**, a massive airlift of food, fuel, and other supplies to Berlin. The Soviets finally lifted the blockade in May 1949 and founded the German Democratic Republic, or East Germany.

The successful airlift may have saved Truman's political career; he narrowly defeated Republican Thomas E. Dewey in the November 1948 presidential election. Truman next formalized the military alliance among the United States, Canada, and western Europe. In April 1949, twelve nations signed a mutual defense treaty, agreeing that an attack on any one of them would be considered an attack on all, and establishing the **North Atlantic Treaty Organization** (NATO; see Map 28.1).

Not since 1778 had the United States entered a formal European military alliance, and some critics, such as Senator Robert A. Taft, Republican of Ohio, claimed that NATO would provoke rather than deter war. Administration officials responded that should the Soviets ever probe westward, NATO would bring the full force of the United States to bear on the Soviet Union. Truman officials also hoped that NATO would keep western Europeans from embracing communism or even neutralism in the Cold War. The Senate ratified the treaty by 82 votes to 13, and the United States began to spend billions of dollars under the Mutual Defense Assistance Act.

By summer 1949, Truman and his advisers were basking in the successes of their foreign policy. Containment was working, West Germany was recovering, the Berlin

National Security Act of July 1947: Act that unified the armed forces under a single agency, later called the Department of Defense. It also established the National Security Council to advise the president on matters of national security and created the Central Intelligence Agency (CIA).

Berlin airlift: American program to deliver food and supplies to the people of the blockaded city of Berlin, Germany.

North Atlantic Treaty Organization: A mutual defense pact between the United States and eleven other nations—including Europe and Canada—promising to stand united in the face of military aggression, specifically by the Soviet Union.

Mao Zedong: Chinese military and political leader who established the communist People's Republic of China.

Link to William Faulkner's Nobel Prize speech about nuclear war, fear, and the artist.

NSC-68: Secret report by the National Security Council that would characterize U.S. Cold War strategy for decades; it saw the clash between the United States and the Soviet Union as a fight between good and evil and reversed post World War military demobilization, focusing instead on military build-up.

How did the Cold War turn "hot" in Asia?

blockade had been defeated, and NATO had been formed. True, there was trouble in China, where the communists under **Mao Zedong** were winning a civil war. But that struggle would likely wax and wane for years to come. Just possibly, some dared to think, Harry Truman was on his way to winning the Cold War.

Twin Shocks

Then, suddenly, in late September, came two momentous developments that made Americans feel in even greater danger than ever before. First, a U.S. reconnaissance aircraft detected unusually high radioactivity in the atmosphere: the Soviets had exploded an atomic device. With the U.S. nuclear monopoly erased, western Europe seemed more vulnerable. Second, the communists in China completed their conquest sooner than many expected. Now the world's largest and most populous countries were ruled by communists, and one of them had the atomic bomb.

Rejecting calls for high-level negotiations, Truman in early 1950 gave the go-ahead for production of a hydrogen bomb, the "Super." Kennan bemoaned the militarization of the Cold War and was replaced at the State Department by Paul Nitze. The National Security Council delivered to the president in April 1950 a significant top-secret document tagged **NSC-68**. Predicting continued tension with expansionistic communists, the report, authored primarily by Nitze, urged a much enlarged military budget and the mobilization of public support. The Cold War was about to become vastly more expensive and far-reaching.

The Cold War in Asia

Asia gradually became ensnared in the Cold War. Indeed, the consequences of an expansive containment doctrine would exact its heaviest price on the United States, in the bloody wars in Korea and Vietnam. Though less important to both superpowers than Europe, Asia would be the continent where the Cold War most often turned hot.

From the start, Japan was crucial to U.S. strategy. The United States monopolized Japan's reconstruction through a military occupation directed by General Douglas MacArthur. Truman disliked "Mr. Prima Donna, Brass Hat" MacArthur, but MacArthur wrote a democratic constitution, gave women voting rights, revitalized the economy, and destroyed the nation's weapons. U.S. authorities Americanized Japan by censoring films critical of the United States (for the destruction of Hiroshima, for example) or depicting Japanese customs, such as suicide, arranged marriages, and swordplay. In 1951, the United States and Japan signed a separate peace that restored Japan's sovereignty and ended the occupation. A Mutual Security Treaty that year provided for the stationing of U.S. forces in Japan, including a U.S. base on Okinawa.

Chinese Civil War

The administration had less success in China. The United States had long backed the Nationalists of Jiang Jieshi (Chiang Kai-shek) against Mao Zedong's communists. But after World War II, Generalissimo Jiang's government had become corrupt, inefficient, and out of touch with discontented peasants, whom the communists enlisted with promises of land reform. Jiang also subverted American efforts to negotiate a cease-fire and a coalition government.

American officials divided on the question of whether Mao was an Asian Tito—communist but independent—or, as most believed, part of an international communist movement that might give the Soviets a springboard into Asia. Thus, when Chinese communists made secret overtures to the United States for diplomatic talks in 1945 and 1949, American officials rebuffed them. Mao leaned to the Soviet side in the Cold War. Because of China's fierce independence, a Sino-Soviet schism opened.

With his victory in September 1949, Mao proclaimed the People's Republic of China (PRC). Truman hesitated to extend diplomatic recognition to the new government. U.S. officials became alarmed by the 1950 Sino-Soviet treaty of friendship and the harassment of Americans in China. Truman also chose nonrecognition because vocal Republican critics, the so-called China lobby, pinned Jiang's defeat on Truman. The president argued that despite billions of dollars in American aid, Jiang proved a poor instrument of containment. Not until 1979 did official Sino-American relations resume.

Vietnam's Quest for Independence

Mao's victory in China drew urgent American attention to Indochina, the southeast Asian peninsula held by France for the better part of a century. The Japanese wrested control over Indochina during World War II, but the Vietnamese nationalists grew stronger. Their leader, Ho Chi Minh, hoped to use Japan's defeat to assert Vietnamese independence, and he sought U.S. support. American rejected Ho's appeals in favor of restoring French rule, mostly to ensure France's cooperation in the emerging Soviet-American confrontation. Ho, the State Department declared, was an "agent of international communism" who would assist Soviet and, after 1949, Chinese expansionism. Overlooking the native roots of the nationalist rebellion against French colonialism, Washington officials interpreted events in Indochina through a Cold War lens.

When war between the Vietminh and France broke out in 1946, the United States initially took a hands-off approach. But when Jiang's regime collapsed in China three years later, the Truman administration in February 1950 recognized the French puppet government of Bao Dai, a playboy and former emperor. To many Vietnamese, the United States thus became in essence a colonial power, an ally of the hated French. Second, in May, the administration agreed to send weapons and assistance to sustain the French in Indochina. From 1945 to 1954, the United States gave $2 billion of the $5 billion that France spent to keep Vietnam within its empire—to no avail (see Chapters 30 and 31). How Vietnam became the site of the United States' longest war is one of the most tragic stories of modern history.

The Korean War

What were the consequences of the Korean War for the United States?

Early on June 25, 1950, a large military force of the Democratic People's Republic of Korea (North Korea) moved into the Republic of Korea (South Korea). Colonized by Japan since 1910, Korea was divided in two after Japan's defeat in 1945. Although the Soviets armed the North and the Americans armed the South (U.S. aid had reached $100 million a year), the **Korean War** began as a civil war. Since its division, the two parts had been skirmishing while antigovernment (and anti-U.S.) guerrilla fighting flared in the South.

Korean War: War between North Korea and South Korea with heavy U.S. and Soviet involvement (1950–1953) with each seeking to undermine the other with economic pressure and military raids.

Both the North's communist leader, Kim Il Sung, and the South's president, Syngman Rhee, sought to reunify their nation. Kim's military gained strength when tens of thousands of Koreans returned home in 1949 after serving in Mao's army. Though President Truman claimed the Soviets had masterminded the North Korean attack, Stalin reluctantly approved the attack after Kim predicted an early victory and after Mao backed Kim. When the U.N. Security Council voted to defend South Korea, the Soviet representative was not present to veto because the Soviets were boycotting the United Nations for its refusal to admit the People's Republic of China. During the war, Moscow gave limited aid to North Korea and China, reneging on promised Soviet airpower. Aware of his strategic inferiority vis-à-vis the United States, Stalin did not want war.

U.S. Forces Intervene

The president first ordered General Douglas MacArthur to send arms and troops to South Korea. He did not seek congressional approval—fearing lawmakers would initiate a lengthy debate—and thereby set the precedent of waging war on executive authority alone. After the Security Council voted to assist South Korea, MacArthur became commander of U.N. forces in Korea. Sixteen nations contributed troops, but 40 percent were South Korean and about 50 percent American. In the war's early weeks, North Korean tanks and superior firepower sent the South Korean army into retreat. The first American soldiers, taking heavy casualties, could not stop the North Korean advance. Within weeks, the South Koreans and Americans were pushed into the tiny Pusan perimeter at South Korea's tip.

General MacArthur planned a daring amphibious landing at heavily fortified Inchon, several hundred miles behind North Korean lines. After U.S. bombs pounded Inchon, marines sprinted ashore on September 15, 1950, liberating the South Korean capital of Seoul and pushing the North Koreans back. Truman meanwhile redefined the U.S. war goal from the containment of North Korea to the reunification of Korea by force.

Chinese Entry into the War

In September, U.N. forces drove deep into North Korea, and American aircraft began strikes against bridges on the Yalu River, the border between North Korea and China. Mao publicly warned that China could not permit the bombing of its transportation links with Korea and would not accept annihilation of North Korea. MacArthur shrugged off the warnings, and Washington officials agreed, confident that the Soviets were not preparing for war.

MacArthur was right about the Soviets, but wrong about the Chinese. On October 25, the Chinese sent soldiers into the war near the Yalu River. Perhaps to lure U.S. forces into a trap or to signal willingness to negotiate, they pulled back after a successful offensive against South Korean troops. Then, on November 26, tens of thousands of Chinese troops surprised U.S. forces and drove them southward. One U.S. officer described "the men of a whole United States Army fleeing from a battlefield, abandoning their wounded, running for their lives."

Truman's Firing of MacArthur

By 1951, the front had stabilized around the 38th parallel. Both Washington and Moscow welcomed negotiations, but MacArthur called for an attack on China and Jiang's return. Denouncing the concept of limited war (war without nuclear weapons, confined to one place), MacArthur hinted that the president was practicing appeasement. In April, backed by the Joint Chiefs of Staff (the heads of the various armed services), Truman fired MacArthur, who nonetheless returned home a hero. Truman's popularity sagged, but he weathered scattered demands for his impeachment.

Armistice talks began in July 1951, but the fighting continued for two more years. Defying the Geneva Prisoners of War Convention (1949), U.S. officials announced that only those North Korean and Chinese prisoners of war (POWs) who wished to go home would be returned. While Americans resisted forced repatriation, the North Koreans denounced forced retention. Both sides undertook "reeducation" or "brainwashing" on POWs.

Peace Agreement   As the POW issue stalled negotiations, U.S. officials made deliberately vague public statements about using atomic weapons in Korea. Not until July 1953 was an armistice signed. Stalin's death in March and new leaders in Moscow and Washington facilitated a settlement. The combatants agreed to hand over the POW question to a special panel of neutral nations, which later gave prisoners their choice of staying or leaving. The North Korean–South Korean borderline was set near the 38th parallel, the prewar boundary, and a demilitarized zone was created between them.

American casualties totaled 54,246 dead and 103,284 wounded. Nearly 5 million Asians died: 2 million North Korean civilians and 500,000 soldiers; 1 million South Korean civilians and 100,000 soldiers; and at least 1 million Chinese soldiers—ranking Korea as one of the costliest wars of the twentieth century.

© Bettmann/Corbis

Soldiers from Company D First Marine Division, mounted on a M-26 tank, spearheaded a patrol in search of guerrillas during the Korean War.

Consequences of the War

The Korean War carried major domestic political consequences. The failure to achieve victory and the public's impatience undoubtedly helped to elect Republican Dwight Eisenhower to the presidency in 1952, as the former general promised to end the war. The powers of the presidency grew as Congress repeatedly deferred to Truman. The president never asked Congress for a declaration of war, believing that, as commander-in-chief, he had the authority to send troops wherever he wished. He saw no need to consult Congress, except to get the $69.5 billion Korean War bill paid. In addition, Republican lawmakers, including Wisconsin senator Joseph McCarthy, accused Truman and Secretary of State Dean Acheson of being soft on communism; this pushed the administration into an uncompromising position in the negotiations.

Moreover, the Sino-American hostility generated by the war made U.S. reconciliation with the Beijing government impossible and made South Korea and Formosa major recipients of American foreign aid. The alliance with Japan strengthened as its economy boomed after filling large U.S. procurement orders. Australia and New Zealand joined the United States in a mutual defense agreement, the ANZUS Treaty (1951). The U.S. Army sent four divisions to Europe and initiated plans to rearm West Germany. The military budget jumped from $14 billion in 1949 to $44 billion in 1953; it remained between $35 billion and $44 billion a year throughout the 1950s. The Soviet Union matched this military buildup, resulting in an arms race. Truman's legacy was a highly militarized U.S. foreign policy on a global scale.

Unrelenting Cold War

How did Dulles and Eisenhower raise the stakes in the Cold War?

President Eisenhower and Secretary of State **John Foster Dulles** largely sustained Truman's Cold War policies. As a World War II general, Eisenhower negotiated with world leaders. After the war, he served as army chief of staff and NATO supreme commander. Dulles had been closely involved with U.S. diplomacy since the first decade of the century.

John Foster Dulles: Secretary of State under Dwight D. Eisenhower. He spoke of a holy war against "atheistic communism" and rejected the policy of containment.

Eisenhower and Dulles accepted the Cold War consensus about the threat of communism and the need for global vigilance. Although Democrats promoted an image of Eisenhower as a bumbling, passive, aging hero, deferring most foreign policy matters to Dulles, the president in fact commanded the policymaking process and occasionally tamed the more hawkish proposals of Dulles and Vice President Richard Nixon. Even so, the secretary of state was influential. Few Cold Warriors rivaled Dulles's impassioned anticommunism, often expressed in biblical terms. Though articulate, he impressed people as arrogant and hectoring and averse to compromise, an essential ingredient in successful diplomacy. His assertion that neutrality was an "immoral and short-sighted conception" did not sit well with Third World leaders, who resented being told they had to choose between East and West.

"Massive Retaliation"

Considering containment too defensive, Dulles called instead for liberation, freeing eastern Europe from Soviet control. *Massive retaliation* was the administration's plan for the nuclear obliteration of the Soviet state or its assumed client, the People's Republic of China, if either one took aggressive action.

Militarily, Eisenhower and Dulles emphasized airpower and nuclear weaponry. The president's preference for heavy weapons stemmed partly from his desire to trim the federal budget (and get "more bang for the buck," as the saying went). Galvanized by the successful test of the world's first hydrogen bomb in November 1952, Eisenhower oversaw a massive stockpiling of nuclear weapons—from 1,200 at the start of his presidency to 22,229 at the end. With this huge military arsenal, the United States could practice "brinkmanship": not backing down in a crisis, even if it meant taking the nation to the brink of war. Eisenhower also popularized the "**domino theory**": that small, weak, neighboring nations would fall to communism like dominoes if they were not supported by the United States.

CIA as Foreign Policy Instrument

Eisenhower increasingly utilized the Central Intelligence Agency as an instrument of foreign policy. The CIA put foreign leaders (such as King Hussein of Jordan) on its payroll; subsidized foreign labor unions, newspapers, and political parties; planted false stories in newspapers through disinformation projects; and trained foreign military officers in counterrevolution. It hired American journalists and professors, used business executives as fronts, and conducted experiments on unsuspecting Americans to determine the effects of mind control drugs (the MKULTRA program). The CIA also launched covert operations (including assassination schemes) to subvert Third World governments, helping to overthrow the governments of Iran (1953) and Guatemala (1954), but failing in attempts to topple regimes in Indonesia (1958) and Cuba (1961).

The U.S. intelligence community followed the principle of plausible deniability: covert operations should be conducted in such a way and the decisions that launched them concealed so well that the president could deny any knowledge of them. Thus, President Eisenhower disavowed any U.S. role in Guatemala, even though he ordered the operation. He and his successor, John F. Kennedy, also denied instructing the CIA to assassinate Cuba's Fidel Castro, whose regime after 1959 became stridently anti-American.

Nuclear Buildup

Leaders in Moscow quickly became aware of Eisenhower's covert actions, as well as his stockpiling of nuclear weapons. They increased their intelligence and tested their first H-bomb in 1953. Four years later, they fired the world's first intercontinental ballistic missile (ICBM) and propelled the satellite *Sputnik* into outer space. Americans felt more vulnerable to air attack, even though in 1957 the United States had 2,460 strategic weapons and a nuclear stockpile of 5,543, compared with the Soviet Union's 102 and 650. The administration deployed intermediate-range missiles in Europe, targeted against the Soviet Union. At the end of 1960, the United States added Polaris missile-bearing submarines to its navy. To foster future technological advancement, the National Aeronautics and Space Administration (NASA) was created in 1958.

Overall, though, Eisenhower sought to avoid military confrontation with the Soviet Union and China, content to follow Truman's *containment* of communism. Eisenhower refused to use nuclear weapons and proved more reluctant than other Cold War presidents to send soldiers into battle. Convinced that the struggle against Moscow would be largely decided by international public opinion, he wanted to win the "hearts and minds" of people overseas. The "People-to-People" campaign, launched in 1956, used ordinary Americans and nongovernmental organizations to enhance the international image of the United States.

domino theory: Eisenhower's prediction that if Vietnam went communist, then smaller, neighboring communities of Thailand, Burma, Indonesia, and ultimately all of Asia would fall like dominos.

Sputnik: Soviet satellite that was the world's first successful launch in space in 1957; it dashed the American myth of unquestioned technological superiority.

Links to the World

The People-to-People Campaign

Just after the Cold War began, U.S. officials determined that the Soviet-American confrontation was as much psychological and ideological as military and economic. One result was the People-to-People campaign, a state-private venture initiated by the United States Information Agency (USIA) in 1956, which aimed to win the "hearts and minds" of people around the world. In this program, American propaganda experts used ordinary Americans, businesses, civic organizations, labor groups, and women's clubs to promote confidence abroad in American goodness. The People-to-People campaign, one USIA pamphlet said, made "every man an ambassador."

Campaign activities resembled the home-front mobilization efforts of World War II. Americans were told that $30 could send a ninety-nine-volume portable library of American books to schools and libraries overseas. Publishers donated magazines and books for free distribution to foreign countries. People-to-People committees organized sister-city affiliations and pen-pal letter exchanges, hosted exchange students,

and organized travelling People-to-People delegations. The travellers were urged to behave like goodwill ambassadors and "help overcome any feeling that America is a land that thinks money can buy everything."

Camp Fire Girls in more than three thousand communities took photographs on the theme "This is our home. This is how we live. These are my People." The photographs were sent to girls in Latin America, Africa, Asia, and the Middle East. The Hobbies Committee connected people with interests in radio, photography, coins, stamps, and horticulture.

The persistence to this day of the widespread impression that Americans are a provincial, materialistic people prompts skepticism about the People-to-People campaign's success. But alongside this negative image is a positive one that sees Americans as admirably open, friendly, optimistic, and pragmatic. Whatever role the People-to-People campaign played in the larger Cold War struggle, it certainly linked ordinary Americans more closely to people around the world.

Dwight D. Eisenhower Library

"Make a friend this trip," urges this framed People-to-People poster, delivered to President Eisenhower in May 1957, "for yourself, for your business, for your country." With the president are two of the campaign's leaders, John W. Hanes Jr. and Edward Lipscomb.

Sometimes the propaganda war was waged on the Soviets' turf. In 1959, Vice President Richard Nixon traveled to Moscow for a U.S. products fair. In the display of a modern American kitchen, Nixon extolled capitalist consumerism, while Soviet premier Nikita Khrushchev, Stalin's successor, touted the merits of communism. The encounter became famous as the kitchen debate.

Rebellion in Hungary   In February 1956, Khrushchev called for peaceful coexistence between capitalists and communists, denounced Stalin, and suggested that Moscow would tolerate different brands of communism. Testing Khrushchev's permissiveness, revolts erupted in Poland and Hungary. After a new Hungarian government in 1956 withdrew from the Warsaw Pact (the Soviet military alliance formed in 1955 with communist countries of eastern Europe), Soviet troops and tanks crushed the rebellion.

Although the Eisenhower administration's propaganda encouraged liberation efforts, U.S. officials could not aid the rebels without igniting a world war. Instead, they promised only to welcome more Hungarian immigrants than American quota laws allowed. The West could have reaped some propaganda advantage had not British, French, and Israeli troops—U.S. allies—invaded Egypt during the Suez crisis just before the Soviets smashed the Hungarian uprising (see page 750).

The turmoil had hardly subsided when the divided city of Berlin again became a Cold War flash point. The Soviets railed against American bombers capable of carrying nuclear warheads in West Germany, and they complained that West Berlin had become an escape route for disaffected East Germans. In 1958, Khrushchev announced that the Soviet Union would recognize East German control of all of Berlin unless the United States and its allies began talks on German reunification and rearmament. The United States refused; Khrushchev backed down but promised to press the issue again.

U-2 Incident   Two weeks before a summit in Paris on May 1, 1960, a U-2 spy plane carrying high-powered cameras crashed 1,200 miles inside the Soviet Union. Moscow admitted shooting down the plane and promptly displayed captured CIA pilot Francis Gary Powers and the pictures he had snapped of Soviet military sites. Khrushchev demanded an apology for the U.S. violation of Soviet airspace. When Washington refused, the Soviets left the Paris summit.

Meanwhile, both sides kept a wary eye on the People's Republic of China. Despite evidence of a widening Sino-Soviet split, most U.S. officials treated communism as a monolithic movement. In 1954, in a dispute over Jinmen (Quemoy) and Mazu (Matsu), two tiny islands off the Chinese coast, the United States and the People's Republic of China lurched toward the brink. Taiwan's Jiang Jieshi used these islands to raid the mainland. Communist China bombarded the islands in 1954. Thinking that U.S. credibility was at stake, Eisenhower defended the outposts, hinting that he might use nuclear weapons. "Let's keep the Reds guessing," advised John Foster Dulles.

Formosa Resolution   In early 1955, Congress passed the Formosa Resolution, authorizing the president to deploy troops to defend Formosa and adjoining islands. In so doing, Congress formally surrendered to the president what it informally gave up in the 1950 Korea decision: the constitutional power to declare war. The crisis passed, but war loomed again in 1958 over Jinmen and Mazu. This time, as Jiang withdrew some troops, China relaxed its bombardments. But Eisenhower's nuclear threats persuaded the Chinese that they, too, needed nuclear arms. In 1964, China exploded its first nuclear bomb.

The Struggle for the Third World

How did racism in America interfere with U.S. leaders' ability to win Cold War allies among developing nations?

In much of the Third World, the process of decolonization that began during the World War I accelerated after World War II, when the economically wracked imperial countries proved incapable of resisting their colonies' demands for freedom (see Map 28.2). From 1943 to 1994, a total of 125 countries became independent (including the former Soviet republics that departed the USSR in 1991). The emergence of so many new states after the 1940s shook the foundations of the international system. In the traditional U.S. sphere of influence, Latin America, nationalists once again challenged Washington's dominance.

Interests in the Third World

By the late 1940s, Soviet-American rivalry shifted increasingly to the Third World. The new nations could buy U.S. goods, supply strategic raw materials, and invite investments (more than one-third of the United States' private foreign investments were in Third World countries in 1959). Both great powers looked to these new states for votes in the United Nations and for military and intelligence bases. But many new nations sought to end the economic, military, and cultural hegemony of the West and played the two superpowers against each other to garner more aid and arms. U.S. interventions—military and otherwise—in the Third World, American leaders believed, became necessary to impress Moscow with Washington's might and to counter other potential threats to U.S. interests.

To thwart nationalist, radical, and communist challenges, more than 90 percent of U.S. foreign aid was going to developing nations by 1961. Washington also allied with undemocratic but anticommunist regimes, meddled in civil wars, and unleashed CIA covert operations. When some of the larger Third World states—notably India, Ghana, Egypt, and Indonesia—refused to take sides in the Cold War, Secretary of State Dulles declared that neutralism was a step toward communism, insisting with Eisenhower that every nation should take sides in this life-or-death struggle.

American leaders argued that technologically "backward" Third World countries needed western-induced capitalist development to enjoy economic growth and political moderation U.S. officials often ascribed stereotyped race-, age-, and gender-based characteristics to Third World peoples, seeing them as dependent and irrational, and therefore dependent on the fatherly tutelage of the United States.

Racism and Segregation as U.S. Handicaps

Racism influenced U.S. relations with Third World countries. In 1955, G. L. Mehta, the Indian ambassador to the United States, was refused service in the whites-only section of a restaurant at Houston International Airport. The insult stung, as did similar indignities experienced by other Third World diplomats. Dulles apologized to Mehta and thought racial segregation in the United States was a "major international hazard," spoiling U.S. efforts to win friends in Third World countries and giving the Soviets a propaganda advantage.

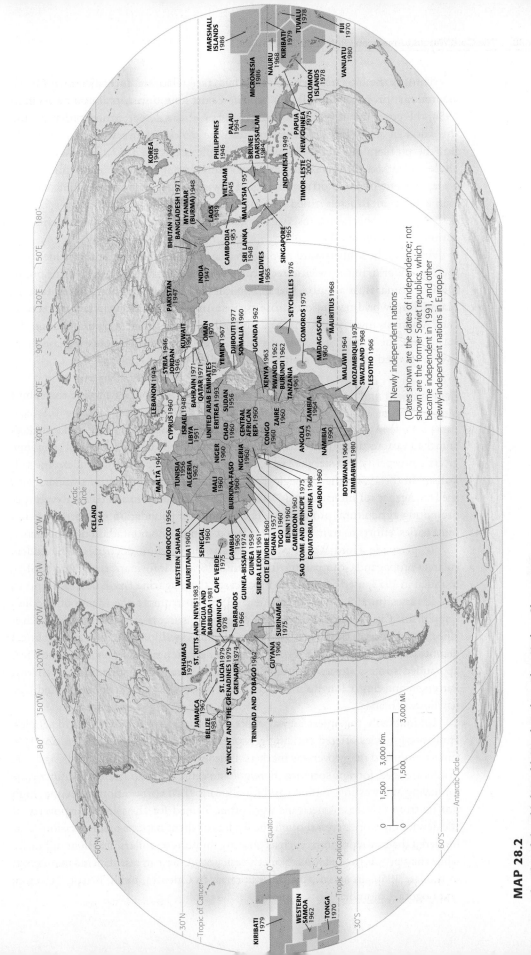

MAP 28.2

The Rise of the Third World: Newly Independent Nations Since 1943

Accelerated by the Second World War, decolonization liberated many peoples from imperial rule. New nations emerged in the postwar international system dominated by the Cold War rivalry of the United States and the Soviet Union. Many newly independent states became targets of great-power intrigue but chose nonalignment in the Cold War.

Source: Copyright © Cengage Learning

Thus, as the U.S. attorney general noted, race relations "furnished grist for the Communist propaganda mills." When the Court announced its *Brown* decision in 1954, the government quickly broadcast news of the desegregation order around the world in thirty-five languages on its *Voice of America* overseas radio network. But the problem did not go away. For example, after the 1957 Little Rock crisis, Dulles remarked that racial bigotry was "ruining our foreign policy." Still, when a Department of State office countered Soviet propaganda with a 1958 World's Fair exhibit in Brussels titled "The Unfinished Work"—on U.S. strides toward desegregation—southern conservatives kicked up such a furor that the Eisenhower administration closed the display.

American hostility toward revolution also obstructed the quest for influence in the Third World. In the twentieth century, the United States opposed revolutions in Mexico, China, Russia, Cuba, Vietnam, Nicaragua, and Iran, among other nations. Many Third World revolutions arose against America's Cold War allies and threatened American investments, markets, and military bases. Preferring to maintain the status quo, the United States usually supported its European allies or the conservative, propertied classes in the Third World.

Development and Modernization

Yet idealism also inspired U.S. policy. Believing that Third World peoples craved modernization and the U.S. economic model of private enterprise, U.S. policymakers launched various development projects. Such projects promised sustained economic growth, prosperity, and stability, which the benefactors hoped would undermine radicalism. In the 1950s, the Carnegie, Ford, and Rockefeller Foundations worked with the U.S. Agency for International Development (AID) to sponsor a Green Revolution promoting agricultural production. The Rockefeller Foundation supported foreign universities' efforts to train national leaders committed to nonradical development.

To persuade Third World peoples to abandon radical doctrines, U.S. leaders created propaganda campaigns. The United States Information Agency (USIA), founded in 1953, used films, radio broadcasts, the magazine *Free World,* exhibitions, and libraries (in 162 cities worldwide by 1961) to trumpet the theme of People's Capitalism. Citing the United States' economic success—contrasted with "slave-labor" conditions in the Soviet Union—it showcased well-paid U.S. workers, political democracy, and religious freedom. To counter ugly pictures of segregation, the USIA applauded success stories of individual African Americans, such as boxers Floyd Patterson and Sugar Ray Robinson. In 1960, some 13.8 million people visited U.S. pavilions abroad.

Undoubtedly, the American way of life had appeal for some Third World peoples. Hollywood movies offered enticing glimpses of middle-class materialism, and U.S. films dominated many overseas markets. Blue jeans, advertising billboards, and soft drinks flooded foreign societies. Foreigners often envied and resented Americans for having and wasting so much and for allowing their corporations to extract high profits from overseas. Americans were often blamed for the persistent poverty of the developing world, even though the leaders of those nations made decisions that hindered their own progress, such as pouring millions of dollars into their militaries while their people needed food. Nonetheless, anti-American resentments manifested in the late 1950s in attacks on USIA libraries in Calcutta, India; Beirut, Lebanon; and Bogotá, Colombia.

Intervention in
Guatemala

When the more benign techniques of containment—aid, trade, cultural relations—proved insufficient to get Third World nations to line up on the American side in the Cold War, the Eisenhower administration often showed a willingness to press harder, by covert or overt means. Guatemala was an early test case. In 1951, leftist Jacobo Arbenz Guzmán was elected president of Guatemala, a poor country whose largest landowner was the American-owned United Fruit Company. United Fruit was an economic power throughout Latin America, where it owned 3 million acres of land and operated railroads, ports, ships, and telecommunications facilities. To fulfi ll his promise of land reform, Arbenz expropriated United Fruit's unculti-vated land and offered compensation. The company dismissed the offer and charged that Arbenz posed a communist threat—a charge that CIA officials had already fl oated because Arbenz employed some communists in his government. The CIA began a secret plot to overthrow Arbenz. He turned to Moscow for mili-tary aid, thus reinforcing American suspicions. The CIA airlifted arms into Guatemala, dropping them at United Fruit facilities, and in mid-1954, CIA-supported Guatemalans struck from Honduras. U.S. planes bombed the capital city, and the invaders drove Arbenz from power. The new pro-American regime returned United Fruit's land, but an ensuing civil war staggered the Central American nation for decades.

The Cuban Revolution and Fidel Castro

Eisenhower also worried as turmoil gripped Cuba in the late 1950s. In early 1959, Fidel Castro's rebels, or *barbudos* ("bearded ones"), driven by anti-American nationalism, ousted Fulgencio Batista, a long-time U.S. ally whose corrupt, dictatorial regime turned Havana into a haven for gambling, prostitution, and organized crime. Cubans resented U.S. domination since the early twentieth century, when the Platt Amendment com-promised their independence. Castro sought to break the U.S. grasp on Cuban trade and roll back American business, which had invested some $1 billion on the island.

In early 1960, after Cuba signed a trade treaty with the Soviet Union, Eisenhower ordered the CIA to organize Cuban exiles to overthrow the Castro government. The agency also plotted the Cuban leader's assassination. When the president drastically cut U.S. sugar purchases, Castro seized North American–owned companies that had not yet been nationalized. Castro appealed to the Soviet Union, which offered loans and expanded trade. Before leaving office in early 1961, Eisenhower broke diplo-matic relations with Cuba and advised president-elect John F. Kennedy to advance plans for the invasion, which came—and failed—in early 1961 (see page 791).

Arab-Israeli Conflict

In the Middle East, meanwhile, ongoing tensions between Arabs and Jews posed additional challenges (see Map 33.1). Before the end of World War II, only France and Britain had been concerned with this region of the world. But the dissolution of empires and the rise of Cold War tensions drew Washington in, as did tensions in British-held Palestine. From 1945 to 1947, Britain tried to enlist U.S. officials to help resolve how to split Palestine between Arabs and Jews. The Truman administration declined, and the British in 1947 turned the issue over to the United Nations, which voted to partition Palestine into separate Arab and Jewish states. Arab leaders opposed the decision, but in May 1948 Jewish leaders announced the creation of Israel.

The United States, which lobbied to secure the U.N. vote, extended recognition to the new state mere minutes after its founding. A moral conviction that Jews deserved a homeland after the Holocaust and that Zionism would create a democratic Israel influenced Truman, as did the belief that Jewish votes might swing some states to the Democrats in the 1948 election. These beliefs trumped concerns that Arab oil producers might turn against the United States. The Soviet Union recognized the new nation, but Israel kept Moscow at arm's length. Palestinian Arabs, displaced from land they considered theirs, joined with Israel's Arab neighbors to make immediate war on the new state. The Israelis fought for six months until a U.N.-backed truce was called.

Thereafter, U.S. Middle East policy centered on ensuring Israel's survival and cementing ties with Arab oil producers. U.S. companies produced about half of the region's petroleum in the 1950s. Oil-rich Iran became a special friend as its shah granted American oil companies a 40 percent interest in a new petroleum consortium in return for CIA help in the successful overthrow, in 1953, of his rival, Mohammed Mossadegh.

American officials faced a more formidable foe in Egypt's Gamal Abdul Nasser, a towering figure in a pan-Arabic movement, who vowed to expel the British from the Suez Canal and the Israelis from Palestine. The United States wished neither to anger the Arabs, for fear of losing valuable oil supplies, nor to alienate its ally Israel, supported at home by politically active American Jews. When Nasser declared neutrality in the Cold War, Dulles lost patience.

Suez Crisis

In 1956, the United States reneged on its offer to help Egypt finance the Aswan Dam, which would provide inexpensive electricity and water for Nile valley farmland. Nasser responded by nationalizing the British-owned Suez Canal, intending to use its profits to build the dam. Fully 75 percent of western Europe's oil came from the Middle East, most of it via the Suez Canal. Fearing an interruption, the British and French conspired with Israel to bring down Nasser. On October 29, 1956, the Israelis invaded Suez, joined two days later by British and French forces.

Eisenhower fumed. Washington's allies had not consulted him, and the president feared the invasion would cause Nasser to seek help from the Soviets, inviting them into the Middle East. Eisenhower sternly demanded that London, Paris, and Tel Aviv pull their troops out, and they did. Egypt took possession of the canal, the Soviets built the Aswan Dam, and Nasser became a hero. The United States countered Nasser by supporting the notoriously corrupt conservative King Ibn Saud of Saudi Arabia, who renewed America's lease of an air base.

Eisenhower Doctrine

Washington officials worried that a power vacuum existed in the Middle East and that the Soviets might fill it. To protect U.S. interests, the president proclaimed in the 1957 **Eisenhower Doctrine** that the United States would intervene in the Middle East if any government threatened by a communist takeover asked for help. In 1958 fourteen thousand American troops scrambled to quell an internal political dispute in Lebanon that Washington feared might be exploited by pro-Nasser groups or communists.

Cold War concerns also drove Eisenhower's policy toward Vietnam. Despite substantial U.S. aid, the French lost steadily to the Vietminh. Finally, in early 1954, Ho's forces surrounded the French fortress at Dienbienphu in northwest Vietnam (see Map 30.1). Some advisers advocated military intervention, but Eisenhower

Eisenhower Doctrine: 1957 proclamation that the United States would send military aid and, if necessary, troops to any Middle Eastern nation threatened by "Communist aggression."

The National Security State

For decades, America's Cold War religion has been national security; its texts, the Truman Doctrine, the X article, and NSC-68; and its cathedral, the national security state. The word *state* in this case means "civil government." During the Cold War, embracing preparedness for total war, the U.S. government essentially transformed itself into a huge military headquarters that interlocked with corporations and universities.

Overseen by the president and his National Security Council, the national security state's core—once called the National Military Establishment—in 1949 became the Department of Defense. This department is a leading employer; its payroll by 2007 included 1.4 million people on active duty and almost 600,000 civilian personnel. Almost 700,000 of these troops and civilians served overseas, in 177 countries. Although national defense spending declined after the Cold War, it never fell below $290 billion. In the aftermath of the 9/11 terrorist attacks and the invasion of Iraq, the military budget rose again, reaching $439 billion in 2007. That does not include tens of billions of dollars in supplementary funds allocated by Congress to pay for operations in Afghanistan and Iraq.

Joining the Department of Defense as instruments of national security policy were the Joint Chiefs of Staff, the Central Intelligence Agency, and dozens more government bodies. The focus of these entities was finding the best means to combat real and potential threats from foreign governments. But what about threats from within? The terrorist attacks of September 2001 made starkly clear that enemies existed who, while perhaps beholden to a foreign entity, launched their attacks from inside the nation's borders.

Accordingly, in 2002 President George W. Bush created the Department of Homeland Security (DHS), with 170,000 employees encompassing all or part of twenty-two agencies, including the Coast Guard, the Customs Service, the Federal Emergency Management Administration (FEMA), and the Internal Revenue Service. It would involve the biggest overhaul of the federal bureaucracy since the Department of Defense was created, and it signified a more expansive notion of national security. By 2008, the number of DHS employees had risen to 208,000.

In 1961, President Eisenhower warned against a military-industrial complex, while others feared a warfare state. Still, the national security state remained vigorous in the early twenty-first century, a lasting legacy of the initial Cold War period for a people and a nation.

---

moved cautiously. The United States had advised and bankrolled the French, but had not committed troops to the war.

Eisenhower pressed the British to help form a coalition to address the Indochinese crisis, but they refused. At home, influential members of Congress—including Lyndon Baines Johnson of Texas, who as president would wage large-scale war in Vietnam—told Eisenhower they wanted "no more Koreas" and warned him against any U.S. military commitment. The issue became moot on May 7, when the weary French defenders at Dienbienphu surrendered.

Link to the Eisenhower Doctrine.

Geneva Accords on Vietnam

Peace talks, already under way in Geneva, brought Cold War and nationalist contenders together—the United States, the Soviet Union, Britain, the People's Republic of China, Laos, Cambodia, and the competing Vietnamese regimes of Bao Dai and Ho Chi Minh. The 1954 Geneva accords, signed by France and Ho's Democratic Republic of Vietnam, temporarily divided Vietnam at the 17th parallel; Ho's government was confined to the North, Bao Dai's to the South. The 17th parallel was meant as a truce line, not a national boundary; the country was scheduled to be reunified after national elections in 1956. Meanwhile, neither North nor South was to join a military alliance or permit foreign bases on its soil.

National Liberation Front

Diem proved a difficult ally. He abolished village elections and appointed people beholden to him. He threw dissenters in jail and shut down newspapers that criticized him. Noncommunists and communists alike struck back at Diem's repressive government. In Hanoi, Ho's government in the late 1950s sent aid to southern insurgents, who assassinated hundreds of Diem's village officials. In late 1960, southern communists, acting at Hanoi's direction, organized the National Liberation Front (NLF), known as the Vietcong. The Vietcong attracted other anti-Diem groups in the South. The Eisenhower administration, aware of Diem's shortcomings, affirmed its commitment to an independent, noncommunist South Vietnam.

Summary

The United States emerged from World War II as the preeminent world power. Washington officials nevertheless worried that the unstable international system, an unfriendly Soviet Union, and the decolonizing Third World could upset U.S. plans for the postwar peace. Locked with the Soviet Union in a Cold War, U.S. leaders marshaled their nation's superior resources to influence other countries. Foreign economic aid, atomic diplomacy, military alliances, client states, covert operations, propaganda, and cultural infiltration became the instruments of the Cold War, which began as a conflict over the Europe's future but soon encompassed the globe.

The United States' international leadership was welcomed by those who feared Stalin's intentions. The reconstruction of former enemies Japan and West Germany helped those nations recover swiftly and become staunch members of the western alliance. But U.S. policy also sparked resistance. Communist countries condemned financial and atomic diplomacy, while Third World nations sought to undermine the United States' European allies and sometimes identified the United States as an imperial coconspirator. Occasionally, even the United States' allies bristled at a United States that boldly proclaimed itself economic master and global policeman.

At home, critics protested that Presidents Truman and Eisenhower exaggerated the communist threat, wasting U.S. assets on immoral foreign ventures. Still, these presidents and their successors held to creating a nonradical, capitalist, free-trade international order. Determined to contain Soviet expansion, fearful of domestic charges of being soft on communism, they enlarged the U.S. sphere of influence and held the line against the Soviet Union and the People's Republic of China and against revolution everywhere. One consequence was a dramatic increase in presidential power over foreign affairs—what the historian Arthur M. Schlesinger Jr. called "the Imperial Presidency."

The United States' globalist perspective prompted Americans to interpret troubles in the developing world as Cold War conflicts, inspired by Soviet-backed communists. The intensity of the Cold War obscured for Americans the indigenous roots of most Third World troubles, as the wars in Korea and Vietnam attested. Nor could the United States abide developing nations' drive for economic independence—for controlling their own raw materials and economies. Intertwined in the global economy as importer, exporter, and investor, the United States read challenges from this periphery as threats to the American standard of living. Overall, the rise of the Third World introduced new actors to the world stage, challenging the bipolarity of the international system. All the while, the threat of nuclear war unsettled Americans and foreigners alike.

Chapter Review

From Allies to Adversaries

Was the Cold War inevitable?

Historians have long debated this question. Aside from their alliance during World War II, the United States and Soviet Union had a tense relationship dating back to the 1917 Bolshevik Revolution. Since leaders of each country did not want war, their decades-old "cold peace" arguably could have continued and inspired future cooperation. Some believe, however, that each nation's desire to fill the power vacuum left by the World War II defeat of Germany and Japan, along with their disparate goals and political ideologies, led individual leaders to make decisions that exacerbated tensions to the point of Cold War. While both nations clashed on most fronts by 1946, some argue that leaders could have done more to keep diplomatic negotiations open. Both countries backed different groups in Iran, could not agree on German reunification, and took many other opposing foreign policy positions. And the U.S. nuclear monopoly only escalated strife, first because the Soviets believed the United States used their nuclear superiority to bully them into concessions, and later when the Soviets had their own nuclear bomb, by advancing an arms race.

Containment in Action

Was the U.S. containment policy successful?

In 1947, Truman and his aides adopted what they called the containment policy, which meant challenging the Soviets every time they attempted to spread communism beyond their borders. The policy was successful in building an international network by aiding European reconstruction and having communists removed from governments, as in Italy and France. The policy also led the

United States to a twelve-nation mutual defense treaty in 1949 and the establishment of NATO (the North Atlantic Treaty Organization). Truman hoped NATO would keep Europeans from turning communist and would deter Soviets from expansion. But containment failed when China, the world's most populous nation, became communist in 1949. Containment similarly could not keep the Soviet Union from becoming a nuclear power.

The Cold War in Asia

How did the Cold War turn "hot" in Asia?

U.S. foreign policy sought to keep communism from spreading to Asia. That often led to decisions that alienated potential allies. The United States rejected an offer for diplomatic talks with China, and later refused diplomatic recognition to the People's Republic of China in 1949, fearing the nation was ultimately a likely Soviet ally. The U.S. also intervened militarily in Korea, to thwart what it saw a Soviet-sponsored attack by the North against the South. After the Sino-Soviet treaty of friendship in 1950, U.S. policy focused on keeping Indochina from falling to the communists. Rather than recognizing tensions in Vietnam as a rebellion against French colonial rule, Truman and his aides blamed the Soviets for stirring up insurrection to expand communism. As such, the United States lent military aid to the French, becoming increasingly engaged in what would develop into the Vietnam War.

The Korean War

What were the consequences of the Korean War for the United States?

Along with heavy casualties (54,246 Americans died and 103,284 were wounded), the conflict greatly influenced politics in the United States. First, the powers of the U.S. president expanded, as Truman never sought congressional permission to declare war, believing that as commander-in-chief, he could dispatch troops at will. Consequently, he only turned to Congress for funding, and Congress also deferred to Truman rather than exercise its authority. As Republicans accused Truman of being soft on communism, he took an increasingly uncompromising position in negotiations for peace. But public frustration over U.S. failure in the war led to Eisenhower's election in 1952. Finally, the war generated increased hostilities between the United States and China, stoked the arms race with the Soviet Union, and strengthened the U.S. alliance with Japan.

Unrelenting Cold War

How did Dulles and Eisenhower raise the stakes in the Cold War?

While President Eisenhower and Secretary of State Dulles continued the containment policy, they also added more aggressive tactics to their Cold War politics. Militarily, Eisenhower increased the nuclear arsenal, seeing it as a way to get more bang for the buck. Possessing the atomic bomb and the hydrogen bomb enabled the United States to practice brinkmanship, not backing down against the spread of communism, even to the brink of war. Eisenhower also popularized the domino theory—that neighboring countries would fall to communism like dominoes without U.S. assistance. At the same time, however, Eisenhower worked to avoid engaging in hot war. Instead, he increasingly utilized the Central Intelligence Agency, training foreign military officers in counter-revolutions, subverting Third World governments, and attempting to influence international opinion with disinformation and pro-U.S. campaigns. Brinkmanship and espionage prompted a similar Soviet response, as the USSR tested its own H-bomb in 1953, fired the first intercontinental ballistic missile in 1957, and increased

intelligence operations—all of which made Americans feel increasingly vulnerable to attack.

The Struggle for the Third World

How did racism in America interfere with U.S. leaders' ability to win Cold War allies among developing nations?

Racism influenced U.S. relations with Third World countries, whose leaders were often people of color. With segregation and discrimination persisting in the United States, it was difficult for U.S. leaders to claim a moral advantage over communism and win friends in new and developing nations. Matters were made worse when there were incidents of discrimination against visiting leaders, as when Indian ambassador G. L Mehta was refused service in the whites-only section of a Houston restaurant. To counter this image, the U.S. government broadcast the positive news of the Supreme Court's desegregation ruling in the *Brown vs. Board of Education* in 1954, using its Voice of America overseas radio network to get the word out around the world in thirty-five languages.

Suggestions for Further Reading

Campbell Craig and Fredrik Logevall, *America's Cold War: The Politics of Insecurity* (2009)

Nick Cullather, *Secret History: The CIA's Classified Account of Its Operations in Guatemala, 1952–1954* (1999)

Mary L. Dudziak, *Cold War Civil Rights: Race and the Image of American Democracy* (2000)

John Lewis Gaddis, *Strategies of Containment,* 2nd ed. (2005)

Walter LaFeber, *America, Russia, and the Cold War, 1945–2006,* 10th ed. (2006)

Douglas Little, *American Orientalism: The United States and the Middle East Since 1945* (2002)

Robert J. McMahon, *The Limits of Empire: The United States and Southeast Asia Since World War II* (1999)

Geoffrey Roberts, *Stalin's Wars: From World War to Cold War, 1939–1953* (2007)

Marc Trachtenberg, *A Constructed Peace: The Making of the European Settlement, 1945–1963* (1999)

Go to the CourseMate website for primary source links, study tools, and review materials for this chapter.
www.cengagebrain.com

America at Midcentury

29

1945–1960

I saac and Oleta Nelson wrapped themselves in blankets that morning in late January, 1951 as they joined a hundred or so friends and neighbors from Cedar City, Utah, to watch the first atomic test on U.S. soil since the end of World War II. "We wanted to…show our patriotism," Isaac remembered. The red-orange flare of the bomb lit up the trees across the valley, more than ten miles away.

In the years immediately following World War II, the United States tested atomic weapons on isolated islands in the south Pacific. U.S. officials knew the dangers of radioactivity. But as the USSR developed an atomic weapon and hostilities in Korea escalated the Cold War, Atomic Energy Commission (A.E.C.) members argued that testing outside the national borders might compromise national security. The danger to American public health and safety, they concluded (in a phrase from 1957 legal testimony), was offset by the threat of "total annihilation" by the Soviet enemy.

President Truman selected land in Nevada, already a bombing and gunnery range, for nuclear testing. Advisors portrayed the land, which stretched across portions of Nevada, Arizona, and Utah and was downwind of Los Angeles and Las Vegas, as "virtually uninhabitable." Yet almost 100,000 people lived there, including descendants of Mormons who had arrived in the 1840s and members of the Western Shoshone Nation, on whose land the test site lay. As radioactive clouds drifted over the towns and farms, children played in the fallout as if it were snow.

After fallout from "Harry," a 32-kiloton blast, saturated the region in 1953, 4,500 of the 14,000 sheep on local ranches died. The A.E.C. blamed the "unprecedented cold weather." Lambs were born that spring without wool or skin, their organs covered only by a thin membrane. The commission suppressed veterinary reports documenting lethal levels of radiation. In 1955, A.E.C. medical staff told residents that radiation from tests was only "about one-twentieth of that in an X-ray." Within hours of watching a fallout cloud, Oleta Nelson became nauseous, with violent diarrhea; her exposed skin turned bright red. A month later, her hair fell out. Oleta was diagnosed with a brain tumor in 1962. She died in 1965. By that time, the cancer rate for "downwinders" was one and a half times the rest of the U.S. population.

The Cold War did not affect most Americans so directly. Nonetheless, Cold War fears and policies shaped American life during the postwar era, even as many people labored to leave the difficult years of depression and war behind and create good lives for their families.

The United States emerged from World War II stronger and more prosperous. Europe and Asia had been devastated, but America's farms, cities, and factories were intact. U.S. production capacity had increased during the war, and fighting fascism gave Americans a unified purpose. But memories of sixteen years of depression and war would continue to shape the choices Americans made in their private lives, their domestic policies, and their relations with the world.

In the postwar era, the federal government's actions and individuals' choices profoundly reconfigured American society. Postwar social policies—often shaped by Cold War concerns—that sent millions of veterans to college on the GI Bill, linked the nation with high-speed interstate highways, fostered the growth of suburbs and the Sunbelt, and disrupted regional isolation helped to create a national middle-class culture encompassing an unprecedented majority of citizens. Countless individual decisions—to go to college, marry young, have a large family, move to the suburbs, start a business—were made possible by federal initiatives. Americans in the postwar era defined a new American Dream—one that centered on the family, greater material comfort and consumption, and a shared sense of a common culture. Elite cultural critics roundly denounced this ideal of suburban comfort as "conformism," but many Americans found satisfaction in this new way of life.

Nonetheless, almost one-quarter of Americans did not share in the postwar prosperity. Rural poverty continued, and inner cities became increasingly impoverished as more-affluent Americans moved to the suburbs and new migrants—poor black and white southerners, immigrants from Mexico and Puerto Rico, and Native Americans resettled by the federal government from tribal lands—arrived.

As class and ethnicity became less important in suburbia, race continued to divide Americans. African Americans faced discrimination nationwide, but the war marked a turning point in the struggle for equal rights. African Americans' initiatives led to important federal actions, including the Supreme Court's school desegregation decision in *Brown v. Board of Education*. In 1955, the year-long Montgomery bus boycott launched the modern civil rights movement.

Postwar domestic politics took second place to the foreign policy challenges of the Cold War and anticommunism shaped domestic politics. Truman pledged to expand the New Deal but was stymied by a conservative Congress, and Eisenhower offered a solid Republican platform, seeking—though rarely attaining—a balanced budget, reduced taxes, and lower levels of government spending. The economic boom that began after World War II lasted twenty-five years, bringing new prosperity to Americans. Although fears—of nuclear war, of returning hard times—lingered, prosperity bred complacency by the late 1950s. At decade's end, people sought satisfaction in their families and in the consumer pleasures newly available to so many.

As you read this chapter, keep the following questions in mind:

* **How did the Cold War affect American society and politics?**

* **How did federal government actions following World War II change the nation?**

* **During the 1950s, many people began to think of their country as a middle-class nation. Were they correct?**

Shaping Postwar America

Americans faced many challenges at the end of World War II. The nation had to reintegrate war veterans into civilian society and transform a wartime economy to peacetime functions. It also had to contend with the Cold War and new global balance of power. Though unemployment rose and a wave of strikes rocked the nation, the economy soon flourished. This strong economy, along with new federal programs, transformed American society.

What drove the mass migration of Americans to the suburbs after World War II?

The Veterans Return

In 1945, as Germany and Japan surrendered, the United States faced a new challenge: demobilizing almost 15 million servicemen. Veterans' homecomings were often joyful, but not always easy. Many veterans returned to wives whose lives had gone on without them, to children they barely knew. Some had serious physical injuries. Almost half a million veterans were diagnosed with neuropsychiatric disabilities, and the National Mental Health Act of 1946 passed largely because of the war's psychological toll on veterans.

Americans also worried about how the economy would absorb millions of returning veterans. As the end of the war approached, factories began to lay off workers. Ten days after the Allied victory over Japan, 1.8 million people nationwide received pink slips, and 640,000 filed for unemployment compensation.

The GI Bill

The federal government planned for demobilization during the war. In the spring of 1944, Congress unanimously passed the Servicemen's Readjustment Act, known as the **GI Bill** of Rights. It showed the nation's gratitude to servicemen but also attempted to keep demobilized veterans from swamping the U.S. economy. Approximately half of all veterans received unemployment benefits, meant to stagger their entry into the job market. The GI Bill also provided low-interest home or business loans and stipends to cover the cost of college or technical school tuition and living expenses.

GI Bill: Popular name for the Servicemen's Readjustment Act (1944), which sought to aid returning veterans—and maintain economic stability—by providing college tuition, job training, unemployment benefits, low-interest home and farm loans.

Chronology

1945	World War II ends	1953	Korean War ends
1946	Marriage and birth rates skyrocket		Congress adopts termination policy for Native American tribes
	More than 1 million veterans enroll in colleges under GI Bill		Rosenbergs executed as atomic spies
	More than 5 million U.S. workers go on strike	1954	*Brown v. Board of Education* decision reverses "separate but equal" doctrine
1947	Taft-Hartley Act limits power of unions		Senate condemns McCarthy
	Truman orders loyalty investigation of 3 million government employees	1955	Montgomery bus boycott begins
	Mass-production techniques used to build Levittown houses	1956	Highway Act launches interstate highway system
1948	Truman issues executive order desegregating armed forces and federal government		Eisenhower reelected
	Truman elected president		Elvis Presley appears on *Ed Sullivan Show*
1949	Soviet Union explodes atomic bomb	1957	King elected first president of Southern Christian Leadership Conference
1950	Korean War begins		School desegregation crisis in Little Rock, Arkansas
	McCarthy alleges communists in government		Congress passes Civil Rights Act
	"Treaty of Detroit" creates model for new labor-management relations		Soviet Union launches *Sputnik*
1951	Race riots in Cicero, Illinois, as white residents oppose residential integration	1958	Congress passes National Defense Education Act
1952	Eisenhower elected president	1959	Alaska and Hawai'i become forty-ninth and fiftieth states

The GI Bill applied equally to all veterans, regardless of race or gender, as long as they were not less-than-honorably discharged. But because of congressional wrangling, implementation fell to state and local agencies, which enabled racial discrimination to occur. And because people charged with homosexuality were not honorably discharged, they were denied benefits.

Nonetheless, almost half of returning veterans used GI education benefits. Roughly 2.2 million veterans attended college, graduate, or professional school. In 1947, about two-thirds of America's college students were veterans. While racial segregation persisted, Negro colleges grew. The flood of students and federal dollars into colleges and universities created a golden age for higher education, and the resulting increase in educated workers benefited the economy.

Education created social mobility: children of menial laborers became white-collar professionals. The G.I. Bill fostered a new national middle-class culture. As colleges exposed people to new ideas, students became less rooted in ethnic or regional cultures.

Economic Growth

American concerns that economic depression would return with war's end proved unfounded. The postwar economy recovered quickly, fueled by consumer spending. Although Americans brought home steady paychecks during the war, there was little to buy. No new cars, for example, had been built since 1942. Americans saved for four years, and they were ready to spend. Companies like General Motors, which expanded operations after the war, found millions of eager customers. Because most factories around the world were in ruins, U.S.

corporations expanded their global dominance. Farming was also revolutionized. New machines, such as crop dusting planes and mechanical cotton, tobacco, and grape pickers, along with increased use of fertilizers and pesticides greatly increased the total value of farm output, as the productivity of farm labor tripled. The potential for profit drew large investors, and the average size of farms increased from 195 to 306 acres.

Baby Boom

During the Great Depression, people delayed marriage, and America's birth rate plummeted. War's end brought a boom in marriage and birth rates. In 1946, the U.S. marriage rate was higher than that of any record-keeping nation (except Hungary). The soaring birth rate reversed the downward trend of the previous 150 years. "Take the 3,548,000 babies born in 1950," wrote Sylvia F. Porter in her syndicated newspaper column. "Bundle them into a batch, bounce them all over the bountiful land that is America. What do you get?" Porter's answer: "Boom. The biggest, boomiest boom ever known in history. Just imagine how much these extra people, these new markets, will absorb—in food, clothing, in gadgets, in housing, in services." Although the **baby boom** peaked in 1957, more than 4 million babies were born every year until 1965 (see Figure 29.1). As this vast cohort aged, it had successive impacts on housing, nursery schools, grade schools, and high schools, fads and popular music, colleges, the job market, and retirement funds, including Social Security.

baby boom: The soaring birth rate that occurred in the United States from 1946 through the early 1960s.

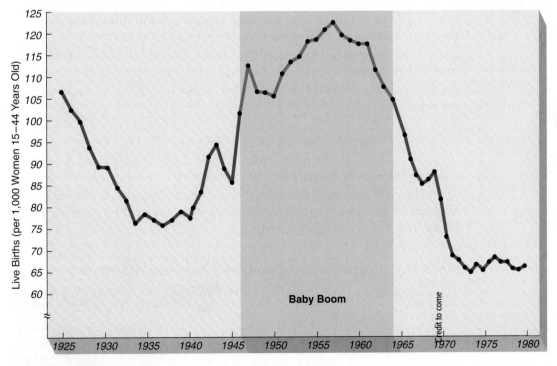

FIGURE 29.1
Birth Rate, 1945–1964

The birth rate began to rise in 1942 and 1943, but it skyrocketed during the postwar years beginning in 1946, reaching its peak in 1957. From 1954 to 1964, the United States recorded more than 4 million births every year.

Source: Adapted from U.S. Bureau of the Census, Historical Statistics of the United States, Colonial Times to 1970, *Bicentennial Edition (Washington, D.C.: U.S. Government Printing Office, 1975), p. 49.*

Scarcely any new housing had been built since the 1920s. Almost 2 million families were doubled up with relatives in 1948; 50,000 people lived in quonset huts, and in Chicago housing was so tight that 250 used trolley cars were sold as homes.

Suburbanization

A combination of market forces, government actions, and individual decisions solved the housing crisis and, in so doing, changed the way large numbers of Americans lived. In the postwar years, white Americans moved to the suburbs. Some white families moved out of urban neighborhoods because African American families were moving in. Most, however, simply wanted their own home, and suburban developments were affordable. Although suburban development predated World War II, the massive migration of 18 million Americans to the suburbs between 1950 and 1960 was on a wholly different scale (see Table 29.1).

In 1947, builder William Levitt adapted Henry Ford's assembly-line methods to revolutionize home building. By 1949, instead of four or five custom homes per year, Levitt's company built 180 houses a week. They were very basic—four and a half rooms on a 60-by-100-foot lot, all with identical floor plans disguised by four different exteriors. By rotating seven paint colors, Levitt guaranteed that only 1 in every 28 houses would be identical. The basic house sold for $7,990. Other homebuilders quickly adopted Levitt's techniques.

Suburban development happened on such a large scale because federal policies encouraged it. Federal Housing Administration (FHA) offered low-interest GI mortgages and loans. Congress authorized construction of a 37,000-mile chain of highways in 1947 and in 1956 passed the Highway Act to create a 42,500-mile interstate highway system. Intended to facilitate commerce and rapid mobilization of the military, these highways allowed workers to live farther from their jobs in central cities.

Inequality in Benefits

Postwar federal programs did not benefit Americans equally. First, federal policies often assisted men at the expense of women. As industry laid off civilian workers to make room for veterans, women lost jobs at a rate 75 percent higher than men. Many women still worked but were pushed into lower-paying jobs. Universities made room for veterans on the GI Bill by excluding qualified women students.

TABLE 29.1   Geographic Distribution of the U.S. Population, 1930–1970 (in percentages)

Year	Central Cities	Suburbs	Rural Areas and Small Towns
1930	31.8	18.0	50.2
1940	31.6	19.5	48.9
1950	32.3	23.8	43.9
1960	32.6	30.7	36.7
1970	31.4	37.6	31.0

Source: Adapted from U.S. Bureau of the Census, *Decennial Censuses,* 1930–1970 (Washington, D.C.: U.S. Government Printing Office).

Inequities were also based on race. Like European American veterans, African American, Native American, Mexican American, and Asian American veterans received educational benefits and hiring preference in civil service jobs. But war workers from these groups were among the first laid off. Federal loan officers and bankers often labeled African American or racially mixed neighborhoods "high risk," denying mortgages to racial minorities regardless of individual creditworthiness. This practice, called "redlining" because such neighborhoods were outlined in red on lenders' maps, kept African Americans and many Hispanics from sharing the postwar economic explosion. White families who bought homes with federally guaranteed mortgages saw their investments grow dramatically over the years.

Domestic Politics in the Cold War Era

> What happened to New Deal style liberalism after World War II?

The United States' social and economic transformations in the postwar era were largely due to federal policies and programs, but politically, foreign affairs were paramount, given the challenges of the expanding Cold War. Domestically, Truman attempted to build on the New Deal's liberal agenda, while Eisenhower sought balanced budgets and business-friendly policies. Neither administration approached the level of political and legislative activism of the 1930s New Deal.

Harry S Truman and Postwar Liberalism

Harry Truman, the plain-spoken former haberdasher from Missouri, never expected to be president. In 1944, when Franklin Roosevelt asked him to be his vice-presidential candidate, Truman almost refused. With the war in its fourth year, the president had little time for his new vice president and left Truman in the dark about everything from the Manhattan Project to plans for postwar domestic policy. When Roosevelt died, suddenly, in April 1945, Truman was left unprepared.

Truman stepped up, however, placing a sign on his desk that proclaimed, "The Buck Stops Here." Most of Truman's presidency focused on foreign relations, as he led the nation through the end of World War II and into the Cold War with the Soviet Union. Domestically, he oversaw reconversion from war to peace and attempted to keep a liberal agenda—the legacy of Roosevelt's New Deal—alive.

In his 1944 State of the Union address, President Roosevelt offered Americans a "Second Bill of Rights": the right to employment, healthcare, education, food, and housing. This declaration of government responsibility for citizens' welfare was the cornerstone of postwar liberalism. Truman's legislative program similarly promoted the federal government's active role in guaranteeing social welfare, promoting social justice, managing the economy, and regulating business. Truman proposed an increase in the minimum wage and the **Full Employment Act**, introduced by congressional Democrats in the winter of 1945, which guaranteed work to the able and willing, through public-sector employment if necessary. Truman's gamble that full employment would generate sufficient tax revenue and that consumer spending would fuel

Full Employment Act: Postwar liberal initiative that sought to stimulate economic growth by raising the minimum wage and guaranteeing jobs to those willing and able to work, through public-sector employment if necessary. The act passed without either of these provisions, which were blocked in Congress.

economic growth paid off, but a conservative coalition of Republicans and southern Democrats in Congress refused to raise the minimum wage and gutted the Full Employment Act, which passed in 1946 without provisions regarding guaranteed work. But it did create a Council of Economic Advisers to help the president prevent economic downturns.

Postwar Strikes and the Taft-Hartley Act

Converting to a peacetime economy hit workers hard, as inflation skyrocketed once wartime price controls were lifted. More than 5 million workers walked off the job. Unions shut down the coal, automobile, steel, and electric industries, and halted railroad and maritime transportation. The strikes were so disruptive that Americans began hoarding food and gasoline.

By the spring of 1946, Americans grew impatient with the strikes and partly blamed the Democratic administration. When unions threatened a national railway strike, President Truman announced that if strikers in an industry deemed vital to national security refused a presidential order to return to work, he would ask Congress to draft them into the armed forces. The Democratic Party would not offer unlimited support to organized labor.

Taft-Hartley Act: 1947 law that amended some of the pro-labor provisions of the 1935 Wagner Act. It permitted states to outlaw the closed shop—workplaces where only union members could be hired—outlawed secondary boycotts, required union officials to sign loyalty oaths, and permitted the president to call a cooling-off period to delay any strike that might endanger national safety or health.

Then, in 1947 in an effort to restrict the power of labor unions, pro-business Republicans and conservative Democratic allies passed the **Taft-Hartley Act**. It allowed states to adopt right-to-work legislation outlawing "closed shops," in which all workers were required to join the union if a majority favored a union shop. The law also mandated an eighty-day cooling-off period before unions initiated strikes imperiling national security. These restrictions limited unions' ability to expand their membership. Truman did not want to see union power limited, but Congress passed the Taft-Hartley Act over his veto.

As Truman presided over the rocky transition from a wartime to a peacetime economy, he had to deal with massive inflation (briefly hitting 35 percent), shortages of consumer goods, and postwar strikes that slowed production of consumer goods and further increased prices. Truman's approval rating plunged from 87 percent in late 1945 to 32 percent in 1946.

1948 Election

By 1948, it seemed that Republicans would win the White House in November. The party nominated Thomas Dewey, the man Roosevelt defeated in 1944, as its candidate. Republicans hoped schisms in the Democratic Party would ensure victory. Former New Dealer Henry A. Wallace was running on the **Progressive Party** ticket, advocating friendly relations with the Soviet Union, racial desegregation, and nationalization of basic industries. And when the Democratic Party adopted a pro-civil rights plank in 1948, some white southerners created the States' Rights Democratic Party (the Dixiecrats), which nominated the fiercely segregationist governor Strom Thurmond of South Carolina.

Progressive Party: Party formed from a splintering within the Democratic Party in 1948 by those dissatisfied with Truman. It advocated friendly relations with the Soviet Union, racial desegregation, a ban on monopolies, and nationalization of basic industries.

Truman refused to give up. He resorted to red-baiting, denouncing "Henry Wallace and his communists." He also sought support from African American voters in northern cities, becoming the first presidential candidate to campaign in Harlem. Truman prevailed, with the help of African American voters. Roosevelt's New Deal coalition—African Americans, union members, northern urban voters, and most southern whites—endured.

Truman's Fair Deal

In his 1949 State of the Union message, Truman stated: "I expect to give every segment of our population a **fair deal**." Truman, unlike Roosevelt, pushed legislation supporting African American civil rights, including antilynching bills. He proposed a national health insurance program and federal aid for education. Southern conservatives in Congress destroyed his civil rights legislation. The American Medical Association denounced his health insurance plan as "socialized medicine," and the Roman Catholic Church opposed educational assistance because it would not include parochial schools.

fair deal: Agenda proposed by President Truman that included civil rights, national healthcare legislation, and federal aid to education.

When Truman ordered troops to Korea in June 1950, many reservists and national guardsmen resented being called to active duty. Inflation rose, as people—remembering the previous war's shortages—stockpiled sugar, coffee, and canned goods. Charges of influence peddling by Truman's cronies, along with the unpopular war, pushed the president's approval rating to an all-time low of 23 percent in 1951.

Eisenhower's Dynamic Conservatism

"It's Time for a Change" was the Republican presidential campaign slogan in 1952, and voters agreed. Americans hoped that Republican candidate General **Dwight D. Eisenhower**, the popular World War II hero, could end the Korean War. And Eisenhower appealed to moderates in both parties (Democrats tried to recruit him as their presidential candidate).

Dwight D. Eisenhower: Republican President of United States (1953–1961) known for his moderate politics, steering a middle course between Democratic liberalism and traditional Republican conservatism.

With a Republican in the White House for the first time in twenty years, conservatives hoped to roll back such New Deal liberal programs as Social Security. As a moderate, Eisenhower embraced what he called "dynamic conservatism": being "conservative when it comes to money and liberal when it comes to human beings." In 1954, Eisenhower signed legislation that raised Social Security benefits and added 7.5 million workers, mostly self-employed farmers, to its rolls. Eisenhower's administration, motivated by Cold War fears, also increased funding for education. In 1957, when the Soviet Union successfully launched *Sputnik,* the first earth-orbiting satellite, and America's first satellite exploded seconds after liftoff, politicians and policy makers worried about the nation's scientific vulnerability. The resulting National Defense Education Act (NDEA) funded elementary and high-school programs in mathematics, foreign languages, and the sciences and offered fellowships and loans to college students.

Growth of the Military-Industrial Complex

Overall, however, Eisenhower's administration was fiscally conservative and pro-business. The president tried to reduce federal spending and to balance the budget. However, faced with three recessions (in 1953–1954, 1957–1958, and 1960–1961) and the cost of America's global activities, Eisenhower turned to deficit spending. In 1959, federal expenditures climbed to $92 billion, about half of which went to support a large standing military of 3.5 million men and to develop new weapons.

Link to text and audio excerpts of Eisenhower's farewell address.

Eisenhower, however, feared the impact of such developments. In his farewell address in early 1961, the outgoing president condemned this new "conjunction of an immense military establishment and a large arms industry" and warned that its "total influence—economic, political, even spiritual" threatened the nation's democratic process. Eisenhower, the former five-star general and war hero, urged Americans to "guard against...the **military-industrial complex**."

military-industrial complex: Term made famous by President Eisenhower's farewell speech in 1961; it refers to the U.S. military, arms industries, and related government and business interests, which together grew in power, size, and influence in the decades after World War II.

Cold War Fears and Anticommunism

How did Cold War fears inspire a
Red Scare in the United States?

International relations had a profound influence on America's domestic politics after World War II. Americans were frightened by the Cold War tensions between the United States and the Soviet Union, but such reasonable fears spilled over into anticommunist demagoguery and witch hunts, which trampled civil liberties, suppressed dissent, and resulted in the persecution of thousands of innocent Americans.

Anticommunism was not new: a Red Scare swept the nation following the 1917 Russian Revolution, and opponents of America's labor movement used charges of communism to block unionization through the 1930s. Many saw the Soviet Union's virtual takeover of eastern Europe in the late 1940s as an alarming parallel to Nazi Germany's takeover of neighboring states. People remembered the failure of "appeasement" at Munich and worried about being "too soft" toward the Soviet Union.

Espionage and Nuclear Fears

U.S. intelligence officers in a top-secret project, code-named "Venona," decrypted almost three thousand Soviet telegraphic cables that proved Soviet spies had infiltrated U.S. government agencies and nuclear programs. (The United States also had spies within the Soviet Union). Intelligence officials withheld this evidence from the American public so that the Soviets would not realize their codes had been compromised.

Fear of nuclear war also contributed to American anticommunism. In 1949, when the Soviet Union joined the United States in possessing atomic weapons, President Truman initiated a national atomic civil defense program, advising Americans, "I cannot tell you when or where the attack will come or that it will come at all. I can only remind you that we must be ready." Children practiced "duck-and-cover" positions in classrooms, learning how to shield their faces from the atomic flash. *Life* magazine featured backyard fallout shelters. Americans worried that the United States was newly vulnerable to attack.

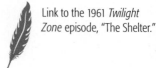

Link to the 1961 *Twilight Zone* episode, "The Shelter."

Politics of Anticommunism

American leaders did not always draw a sufficient line between attempts to prevent Soviet spies from infiltrating government agencies and anticommunist scare-mongering. Republican politicians "red-baited" Democratic opponents, eventually targeting the Truman administration. In 1947, President Truman ordered investigations into the loyalty of more than 3 million government employees. As anticommunist hysteria grew, the government discharged people deemed "security risks," among them alcoholics, homosexuals, and debtors thought susceptible to blackmail. Leading the anticommunist crusade was the **House Un-American Activities Committee** (popularly known as HUAC). Created in 1938 to investigate "subversive and un-American propaganda," the committee lost credibility by charging that film stars—including eight-year-old Shirley Temple—were Communist Party dupes. In 1947, HUAC attacked Hollywood again, using Federal Bureau of Investigation (FBI) files and the testimony of people like Screen Actors Guild president Ronald Reagan (a secret FBI informant). Screenwriters and directors known as the "Hollywood Ten" were sent to prison for contempt of Congress when they refused to "name names" of suspected communists.

House Un-American Activities Committee (HUAC): Influential Congressional committee, originally created in 1938, which investigated communist influence in America and contributed to anti-communist hysteria in the postwar United States.

At least a dozen others committed suicide. Studios blacklisted hundreds of actors, screenwriters, directors, even makeup artists suspected of communist affiliations. With no evidence of wrongdoing, people's careers were ruined.

McCarthyism and the Growing "Witch Hunt"

University professors became targets of the growing "witch hunt" in 1949, when HUAC demanded lists of textbooks used at eighty-one universities. When the board of regents at the University of California, Berkeley, instituted a loyalty oath for faculty, firing twenty-six who resisted on principle, protests nationwide forced the regents to back down. But many professors began to downplay controversial material in their courses. In the labor movement, the CIO expelled eleven unions, with more than 900,000 members, for alleged communist domination. The red panic reached its nadir in February 1950, when **Joseph R. McCarthy**, a relatively obscure, Republican U.S. senator from Wisconsin, charged that the U.S. State Department was "thoroughly infested with Communists." Not an especially credible source, McCarthy first claimed that there were 205 communists in the State Department, then 57, then 81. He had a severe drinking problem and a record of dishonesty as a lawyer and judge. But McCarthy crystallized Americans' anxieties, and such anticommunist excesses came to be known as McCarthyism.

Joseph R. McCarthy:
Wisconsin senator who launched a massive public campaign against Communism and the Soviet spies and sympathizers that he claimed were inside the federal government. He was later discredited.

Anticommunism in Congress

In such a climate, most public figures found it risky to stand up against McCarthyist tactics. In 1950, Congress passed the Internal Security (McCarran) Act, which

Robert Phillips/Getty Images

Senator Joseph McCarthy's downfall came in 1954 during the televised Army-McCarthy hearings, when army counsel Joseph Welsh (left) confronted McCarthy on national TV. McCarthy's wild accusations and abusive treatment of witnesses disgusted millions of viewers.

required members of "Communist-front" organizations to register with the government and prohibited them from holding government jobs or traveling abroad. In 1954, the Senate passed the Communist Control Act, sponsored by Democratic senator Hubert H. Humphrey of Minnesota, which effectively made membership in the Communist Party illegal.

In 1948, Congressman Richard Nixon of California, a member of HUAC, was propelled onto the national stage when he accused former State Department official Alger Hiss of espionage. That same year, **Ethel and Julius Rosenberg** were arrested for passing atomic secrets to the Soviets; they were found guilty of treason and executed in 1953. For decades, many historians believed the Rosenbergs were victims of a witch hunt, but there was strong evidence of Julius Rosenberg's guilt uncovered at the time (and evidence that Ethel Rosenberg was less involved). This evidence was not presented at trial for national security reasons and remained top secret until 1995, when a Clinton administration initiative opened the files.

Ethel and Julius Rosenberg:
Couple found guilty of conspiracy to commit espionage and executed in 1953.

Waning of the Red Scare

The worst excesses of Cold War anticommunism waned when Senator McCarthy was discredited on national television in 1954. McCarthy was a master at using the press, making sensational accusations—front-page material—just before reporters' deadlines. When McCarthy's charges proved untrue, retractions appeared in the back pages of the newspapers. But McCarthy's crucial mistake was charging on television that the U.S. Army was shielding communists, citing the case of one army dentist. In the so-called Army-McCarthy hearings, held by a Senate subcommittee in 1954, McCarthy, apparently drunk, alternately ranted and slurred his words. In December 1954, the Senate voted to "condemn" McCarthy for sullying the dignity of the Senate. He remained a senator, but exhaustion and alcohol took their toll and he died in 1957 at age forty-eight. With McCarthy discredited, the most virulent anticommunism had run its course. However, the use of fear tactics for political gain, and the narrowing of American freedoms and liberties were chilling legacies of the Cold War.

Link to the video of the exchange between Joseph Welch and McCarthy.

The Struggle for Civil Rights

The Cold War also shaped African American struggles for social justice and the nation's responses to them. As the Soviet Union pointed out, the United States could hardly pose as the leader of the free world or condemn the denial of human rights in eastern Europe and the Soviet Union while practicing segregation. Nor could the United States convince new African and Asian nations of its dedication to human rights if African Americans were subjected to segregation, discrimination, disfranchisement, and racial violence. Many Americans viewed any criticism of the United States as a Soviet-inspired attempt to weaken the nation. In this heated environment, African Americans struggled to seize the political initiative.

What facilitated the emergence of a renewed civil rights movement?

Link to the 1950s documentary on racism in Levittown, Penn., focusing on the African American Myers family.

Growing Black Political Power

African Americans who helped win World War II were determined to enjoy better lives in postwar America, and politicians like Harry Truman were heeding black aspirations, especially as black voters in some urban-industrial states began to influence the political balance of power.

President Truman supported African American civil rights because he genuinely believed that every American should enjoy equal citizenship rights. Truman was disturbed by a resurgence of racial terrorism, as a revived Ku Klux Klan burned crosses and murdered blacks seeking civil rights after World War II. But what really horrified Truman was the report that police in Aiken, South Carolina, gouged out the eyes of a black sergeant three hours after his army discharge. In December 1946, Truman signed an executive order establishing the President's Committee on Civil Rights. Its report, *To Secure These Rights,* would become the civil rights movement agenda for the next twenty years. It called for antilynching and antisegregation legislation and for laws guaranteeing voting rights and equal employment opportunity.

In 1948, Truman issued two executive orders. One proclaimed a policy of "fair employment throughout the federal establishment" and created the Employment Board of the Civil Service Commission to hear discrimination charges. The other ordered the racial desegregation of the armed forces. Despite strong opposition to desegregation within the military, segregated units were being phased out by the beginning of the Korean War.

Changing social attitudes and experiences in postwar America facilitated these changes. A new and visible black middle class was emerging, composed of college-educated activists, war veterans, and union workers. White awareness of social injustice was heightened by Gunnar Myrdal's social science study *An American Dilemma* (1944) and by Richard Wright's novel *Native Son* (1940) and autobiography *Black Boy* (1945). Blacks and whites worked together in CIO unions and service organizations, such as the National Council of Churches. In 1947, a black baseball player, **Jackie Robinson**, broke the major league color barrier and electrified Brooklyn Dodgers fans.

Jackie Robinson: First African American to play major-league baseball (1947).

Supreme Court Victories and School Desegregation

African Americans were successfully challenging racial discrimination in the courts and in state and local legislatures. Northern state legislatures, pressured by civil rights activists, passed prohibitions against employment discrimination in the 1940s and 1950s. During the 1940s, Thurgood Marshall, head of the NAACP's Legal Defense and Educational Fund, and his colleagues worked to destroy the separate-but-equal doctrine established in *Plessy v. Ferguson* (1896). In higher education, the NAACP calculated, the cost of equality in racially separate schools would be prohibitive. "You can't build a cyclotron for one student," acknowledged one university president. Through NAACP lawsuits, African American students won admission to professional and graduate schools at formerly segregated state universities. The NAACP also won victories through the Supreme Court in *Smith v. Allwright* (1944), which outlawed the whites-only primaries held by the Democratic Party in some southern states; *Morgan v. Virginia* (1946), which struck down segregation in interstate bus transportation; and *Shelley v. Kraemer* (1948), which held that racially restrictive covenants (private agreements among white homeowners not to sell to blacks) could not legally be enforced.

Even so, blacks continued to suffer disfranchisement, job discrimination, and violence. But in 1954, the NAACP won a historic Supreme Court victory:

Brown v. Board of Education of Topeka: Landmark Supreme Court case (1954) that overturned *Plessy v. Ferguson* (1896); it desegregated public schools by arguing that racially separate schools are inherently unequal.

Brown v. Board of Education of Topeka. Written by Chief Justice Earl Warren, the court's unanimous decision concluded that "Separate educational facilities are inherently unequal." But the ruling that overturned *Plessy v. Ferguson* did not demand immediate compliance. A year later, the Court ordered school desegregation, but only "with all deliberate speed."

Montgomery Bus Boycott

By the mid-1950s, African Americans were engaged in a grassroots struggle for civil rights in both the north and the south, though southern struggles drew the most national attention. In 1955, Rosa Parks, a department store seamstress and NAACP activist, was arrested for refusing to give up her seat to a white man on a public bus in Montgomery, Alabama. Her arrest enabled local black women's organizations and civil rights groups to organize a boycott of the city's bus system. They selected **Martin Luther King Jr.**, a twenty-six year-old, recently ordained Baptist minister with a Ph.D. from Boston University, as their leader. Schooled in the teachings of India's leader Mohandas K. Gandhi, King believed in nonviolent civil disobedience as a vehicle to focus the nation's attention on the immorality of Jim Crow.

Martin Luther King, Jr.: African American minister whose philosophy of civil disobedience fused the spirit of Christianity with the strategy of achieving racial justice by nonviolent resistance.

Link to Martin Luther King's words and legacy.

During the year-long Montgomery bus boycott, blacks rallied in their churches. They maintained their boycott through heavy rains and the steamy summer heat, often walking miles a day. With the bus company near bankruptcy and downtown merchants suffering from declining sales, city officials adopted harassment tactics to end to the boycott. But the black people of Montgomery persevered: thirteen months later, the Supreme Court declared Alabama's bus segregation laws unconstitutional.

White Resistance

White reactions to civil rights gains varied. Some communities in border states like Kansas and Maryland quietly implemented school desegregation, and southern moderates advocated a gradual rollback of segregation. But others urged defiance. The Klan experienced another resurgence, and white violence against blacks increased. In 1955, white men in Mississippi beat, mutilated, and murdered Emmett Till, a fourteen-year-old from Chicago, because they took offense at how he spoke to a white woman; an all-white jury took only 67 minutes to acquit those charged with the crime. Business and professional people created White Citizens' Councils (known familiarly as "uptown Ku Klux Klans") to resist school desegregation and use economic power against civil rights activists. When FBI director J. Edgar Hoover briefed President Eisenhower on southern racial tensions in 1956, he warned of communist influences among civil rights activists and suggested that Citizens' Councils might "control the rising tension."

White resistance also mounted in large northern cities. Chicago's African American population increased from 275,000 in 1940 to 800,000 in 1960, and their numbers gave them political power. Though most found good jobs in industry, they also found racism and housing segregation. So racially divided was Chicago that the U.S. Commission on Civil Rights in 1959 described it as "the most residentially segregated city in the nation." Other northern cities were not far behind.

Federal Authority and States' Rights

Although he disapproved of racial segregation, President Eisenhower objected to "compulsory federal law," for he believed that race relations would improve "only if [desegregation] starts locally." He also feared that rapid desegregation would jeopardize Republican inroads in the South. Thus, Eisenhower did not state forthrightly that the federal government would enforce the *Brown* decision as the nation's law.

Events in Little Rock, Arkansas, forced the president to act. In September 1957, Arkansas governor Orval E. Faubus defied a court-supported desegregation plan for Little Rock's Central High School, saying on television that "blood would run in the streets" if black students tried to enter the high school. On the second day of school, eight black teenagers tried to enter Central High, but they were turned away by Arkansas National Guard troops. The ninth student was surrounded by jeering whites and narrowly escaped the mob with the help of a sympathetic white woman.

The "Little Rock Nine" first entered Central High more than two weeks later and only after a federal judge intervened. As an angry crowd surrounded the school television broadcast the scene to the world, Eisenhower decided to nationalize the Arkansas National Guard (placing it under federal, not state, control) and dispatch one thousand army paratroopers to guard the students for the rest of the year. Eisenhower's use of federal power was a critical step toward racial equality, for he directly confronted the conflict between federal authority and states' rights. However, state power triumphed the following year, when Faubus closed public high schools in Little Rock rather than desegregate them.

In 1957, Congress passed the first Civil Rights Act since Reconstruction, creating the Commission on Civil Rights to investigate systemic discrimination, such as in voting. Although this measure was not fully effective, it lent federal recognition

© Bettmann/Corbis

For leading the movement to gain equality for blacks riding city buses in Montgomery, Alabama, Martin Luther King Jr. (1929–1968) and other African Americans, including twenty-three other ministers, were indicted by an all-white jury for violating an old law banning boycotts. In late March 1956, King was convicted and fined $500. A crowd of well-wishers cheered a smiling King (here with his wife, Coretta) outside the courthouse, where King producly declared, "The protest goes on!" King's arrest and conviction made the bus boycott front-page news across America.

to civil rights. Most important, however, was growing grassroots activism. In 1957, Martin Luther King Jr. became the first president of the Southern Christian Leadership Conference (SCLC), organized to coordinate civil rights activities. With the success in Montgomery and gains through the Supreme Court, African Americans were poised to launch a national civil rights movement.

Creating a Middle-Class Nation

What led to the emergence of a middle-class culture in the 1950s?

Despite resistance to civil rights during the 1950s, the United States was becoming increasingly inclusive. National prosperity offered ever greater numbers of Americans material comfort and security through entrance into an economic middle class. Old European ethnic identities faded, as an ever smaller percentage of America's people were first- or second-generation immigrants.

In the new suburbs, people from different backgrounds created communities. Middle-class Americans increasingly looked to national media for advice on matters ranging from how to celebrate Thanksgiving to how to raise children. New opportunities for consumption—whether teenage fads or suburban ranch-style homes—also tied disparate Americans together. In the postwar years, a new middle-class way of life transformed the United States.

Prosperity for More Americans

During the 1950s, strong economic growth made more Americans than ever economically secure. This economic boom was driven by consumer spending, as Americans bought consumer goods unavailable during the war, and industries expanded production. As the Cold War deepened, government defense spending created jobs and stimulated the economy.

Cold War military and aerospace programs fueled the need for highly educated scientists, engineers, and other white-collar workers. Universities received billions of dollars to fund research, expanding their roles in American life. Government-funded research went beyond military weapon systems and the space race: the transistor, invented during the 1950s, was used in radios and sparked the computer revolution.

A new era of labor relations helped bring economic prosperity to more Americans. The United Auto Workers (UAW) and General Motors led the way for other corporations in providing workers with health insurance, pension plans, and guaranteed cost-of-living adjustments, or COLAs. A 1950 agreement gave GM's workers a five-year contract with regular wage increases tied to corporate productivity. With wage increases tied to corporate productivity, labor cast its lot with management: workplace stability and efficiency, not strikes, would bring higher wages. During the 1950s, wages and benefits propelled union families into the economic middle class.

Sunbelt and Economic Growth

In the 1930s, Roosevelt called the South "the nation's No. 1 economic problem." During World War II, new defense plants and military training camps channeled federal money to the region, stimulating economic growth. In the postwar era, massive defense spending continued to shift economic development to the South and Southwest—the **Sunbelt** (see Map 29.1). Government actions—including tax breaks

Sunbelt: Southern and southwestern states whose rapid economic development brought many new residents during the postwar years.

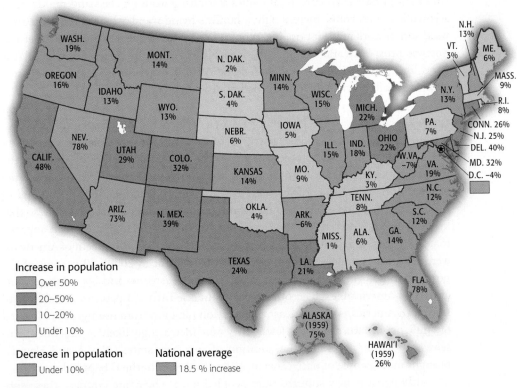

MAP 29.1

Rise of the Sunbelt, 1950–1960

The years after the Second World War saw a continuation of the migration of Americans to the Sunbelt states of the South, Southwest, and West Coast.

Source: Copyright © Cengage Learning

for oil companies, siting of military bases, and defense and aerospace contracts—were crucial to the region's new prosperity.

The Sunbelt's spectacular growth was also due to agribusiness, the oil industry, real-estate development, and recreation. Sunbelt states successfully sought foreign investment and drew industry with lower taxes and heating bills, along with right-to-work laws banning closed shops. The development of air conditioning was also crucial, making the hottest days bearable. Houston, Phoenix, Los Angeles, San Diego, Dallas, and Miami all boomed, and by 1963 California was the most populous state in the Union.

A New Middle-Class Culture

By the 1950s, it seemed that America was becoming a middle-class nation. Unionized blue-collar workers gained middle-class incomes, and veterans with GI Bill college educations swelled the managerial and professional class. In 1956, for the first time, the United States had more white-collar than blue-collar workers, and 60 percent of families had incomes in the middle-class range (approximately $3,000 to $9,000 a year in the mid-1950s).

Paradoxically, the strength of unions in the postwar era contributed to a decline in working-class identity: as large numbers of blue-collar workers participated in suburban middle-class culture, the lines separating working class and middle class seemed less important. Increasingly, a family's living standard mattered more than what sort of work made it possible. People of color did not share equally in America's postwar prosperity and were usually invisible in American representations of "the good life." However, many middle-income African Americans, Latinos, and Asian Americans did participate in the broad middle-class culture.

Whiteness and National Culture

The emergence of a national middle-class culture was possible partly because America's population was more homogeneous in the 1950s than before or since. In the nineteenth and early twentieth centuries, the United States restricted or prohibited immigration from Asia, Africa, and Latin America while accepting millions of Europeans. This large-scale European immigration was shut off in the 1920s, so that by 1960 only 5.7 percent of Americans were foreign-born (compared with approximately 15 percent in 1910 and 12.4 percent in 2005). In 1950, 88 percent of Americans were of European ancestry (compared with 69 percent in 2000); 10 percent of the population was African American; 2 percent was Hispanic; and Native Americans and Asian Americans each accounted for about one-fifth of 1 percent. But almost all European Americans were at least a generation removed from immigration. Instead of "Italians" or "Russians" or "Jews," they were increasingly likely to describe themselves as "white." In 1959, the addition of two new states, Alaska and Hawai'i, brought more people of native, Asian, or Pacific origin to the U.S. population.

Although the new suburbs were peopled mostly by white families, these suburbs were more diverse than the communities from which their residents had come. America's small towns and urban ethnic enclaves were homogeneous and usually intolerant of challenges to tradition. In the suburbs, many people encountered different customs and beliefs. But new suburbanites often traded the provincial homogeneity of specific ethnic or regional cultures for a new sort of homogeneity: a national middle-class culture.

Television

Because many white Americans were new to the middle class, they were uncertain about what was expected of them. They found instruction in the national mass media. Women's magazines helped housewives replace ethnic dishes with "American" recipes created from national brandname products—such as casseroles made with Campbell's Cream of Mushroom soup. Television also fostered America's shared culture. Although television sets cost about $300—the equivalent of $2,000 today—almost half of American homes had TVs by 1953. Television ownership rose to 90 percent by 1960, when more American households had a television set than a washing machine.

On television, suburban families like the Cleavers (*Leave It to Beaver*) ate dinner at a properly set dining room table. June Cleaver did housework in a carefully ironed dress. Every crisis was resolved through paternal wisdom. These popular family situation comedies reinforced the suburban middle-class ideal many American families sought.

The "middle-classness" of television programming was due partly to advertising. Corporations buying airtime did not want to offend potential consumers. Thus, although African American musician Nat King Cole drew millions of viewers to his NBC television show, it never found a sponsor. National corporations feared being linked to a black performer would hurt sales among whites—especially in the South. Because African Americans made up about 10 percent of the population and many had little disposable income, they had little influence. The *Nat King Cole Show* was canceled within a year; it was a decade before the networks again anchored a show around a black performer.

With only network television available—ABC, CBS, and NBC (and, until 1956, DuMont)—70 percent or more of all viewers might be watching the same popular program. (In the early twenty-first century, the most popular shows might attract 12 percent of the audience.) Television gave Americans shared experiences and helped create a more homogeneous, white-focused, middle-class culture.

Consumer Culture

Americans also found common ground through consumer goods. After decades of scarcity, Americans had a dazzling array of choices, and even the most utilitarian objects got two-tone paint jobs or rocket-ship details. People used purchases to express their personal identities and claim status. Cars more than anything else embodied consumer fantasies. Expensive Cadillacs were the first to develop tail fins, soon added to midrange Chevys, Fords, and Plymouths. Americans spent $65 billion on automobiles in 1955—a figure equivalent to almost 20 percent of the gross national product. To pay for cars, suburban houses and modern appliances, consumer debt rose from $5.7 billion in 1945 to $58 billion in 1961.

Religion

Church membership (primarily in mainline Christian churches) doubled between 1945 and the early 1960s. The mass media probably played a role, as preachers like Billy Graham created national congregations from television audiences with a message combining the promise of salvation with Cold War patriotism. But local churches and synagogues also offered new suburbanites a sense of community, celebrating life's rituals and supporting those far from their extended families.

Men, Women, and Youth at Midcentury

How did the economic and social structure of the 1950s influence gender roles?

Having survived the Great Depression and a world war, many Americans sought fulfillment in private life. They saw their commitment as an expression of faith in the future. Despite the satisfactions many found in family life, men and women found their life choices limited by social pressures to conform to narrowly defined gender roles.

Marriage and Families

During the 1950s, few Americans remained single, and most people married young. By 1959, almost half of American brides were under age nineteen; their husbands were usually only a year or so older. Early marriage was endorsed by experts and approved by most parents, partly to prevent premarital sex. One popular women's magazine argued, "When two people are ready for sexual intercourse at the fully human level they are ready for marriage.... And society has no right to stand in their way."

Many young couples found freedom from parental authority by marrying. Most newlyweds quickly had babies—an average of three—completing their family while in their twenties. Birth control (condoms and diaphragms) was widely available and

Moving to Levittown

Builder William Levitt's assembly-line methods created affordable homes for young families—although initially only "Caucasians" were allowed to buy homes in Levittown. This family, shown here on their moving day, would have received a copy of the Levittown *Homeowner's Guide,* which contained a list of "dos" and "don'ts": for example, residents were not to hang laundry on Sundays, when their neighbors were "most likely to be relaxing on the rear lawn." What does this photograph reveal about the new Levittown family, and why might the community rule book promise to help residents "enjoy their new home"? From looking carefully at the map, including street names and public spaces, how did developers try to create neighborhood and community in a development of inexpensive and virtually identical homes?

Urban Archives, Temple University, Philadelphia

The State Museum of Pennsylvania, Pennsylvania Historical and Museum Commission

The State Museum of Pennsylvania, Pennsylvania Historical and Museum Commission

774

widely used, as couples planned family size. Two children were the American ideal in 1940; by 1960, most couples wanted four. About 88 percent of children under eighteen lived with two parents (in 2000, the figure was 69 percent). Fewer children were born outside marriage; only 3.9 percent of births were to unmarried women in 1950 (compared with more than one-third of births in 2000). As late as 1960, there were only 9 divorces per 1,000 married couples.

Gender Roles in 1950s Families

In 1950s families, men and women usually took distinct roles, with male breadwinners and female homemakers. Contemporary commentators insisted this was based on essential differences between the sexes. In truth, the economic and social structure and cultural values of postwar America determined what choices were available to American men and women.

Dr. Spock: Physician and author of *Baby and Child Care*, the bestselling childrearing manual for parents of the baby boom generation.

During the 1950s, it was possible for many families to live in modest middle-class comfort on one (male) salary. There were incentives for women to stay home, especially while children were young. Good childcare was rarely available, and fewer families lived close to relatives. Childcare experts, including **Dr. Spock**, whose 1946 *Baby and Child Care* sold millions of copies, insisted that a mother's full-time attention was necessary for her children's well-being. Because of hiring discrimination, women who could afford to stay home often did not find the available jobs attractive enough to justify juggling paid employment with housework. Instead, schools and religious institutions benefited from women's volunteer labor.

Women and Work

Suburban domesticity left many women feeling isolated from the larger world their husbands inhabited. The popular belief that one should find complete emotional satisfaction in private life put unrealistic pressures on marriages. And finally, despite near-universal celebration of women's domestic roles, many women were managing both job and family responsibilities (see Figure 29.2). Twice as many women were employed in 1960 as in 1940, including 39 percent of women with children between age six and seventeen. Most worked part-time for a specific family goal: a new car; college tuition. They saw these jobs as service to the family, not independence from it.

Still, women faced discrimination in the work force. Want ads were divided into "Help Wanted—Male" and "Help Wanted—Female" categories. Female full-time workers earned, on average, 60 percent of what men were paid and were restricted to lower-paid "female" fields, as maids, secretaries, teachers, and nurses. A popular book, *Modern Woman: The Lost Sex,* claimed that ambitious women and "feminists" suffered from "penis envy." College psychology

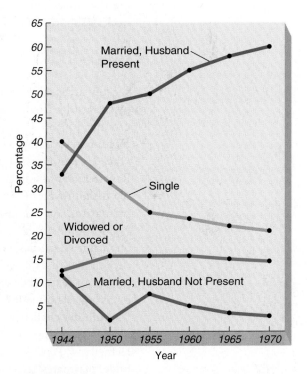

FIGURE 29.2
Marital Distribution of the Female Labor Force, 1944–1970
The composition of the female labor force changed dramatically from 1944 to 1970. In 1944, 41 percent of women in the labor force were single; in 1970, only 22 percent were single. During the same years, the percentage of the female labor force who had a husband in the home jumped from 34 to 59. The percentage who were widowed or divorced remained about the same from 1944 to 1970.
Source: Adapted from U.S. Bureau of the Census, Historical Statistics of the United States, Colonial Times to 1970, *Bicentennial Edition (Washington, D.C.: U.S. Government Printing Office, 1975) p. 133.*

textbooks warned women not to "compete" with men; magazine articles described "career women" as a "third sex." Medical schools commonly limited female admission to 5 percent of each class. In 1960, less than 4 percent of lawyers and judges were female. When future Supreme Court Justice Ruth Bader Ginsburg graduated at the top of her Columbia Law School class in 1959, she could not find a job.

"Crisis of Masculinity"

Academics and mass media critics devoted equal attention to the plight of the American male. American men faced a "crisis of masculinity," proclaimed the nation's mass-circulation magazines. In a bestselling book, sociologist William H. Whyte explained that postwar corporate employees had become "organization men," succeeding through cooperation and conformity, not initiative and risk. Experts claimed women's "natural" desire for security and comfort was stifling men's instinct for adventure. Men who did not conform to standards of male responsibility—husband, father, breadwinner—were socially condemned. Some linked concerns about masculinity to the Cold War, arguing that unless American men recovered masculinity diminished by white collar work or suburban family life, the nation's future was at risk.

Sexuality

Sexuality was complicated terrain in postwar America. Only heterosexual intercourse within marriage was socially acceptable. Women who became pregnant outside marriage were often ostracized by friends and family and expelled from school. Homosexuality was grounds for job dismissal, expulsion from college, even jail. In his major works on human sexuality, *Sexual Behavior in the Human Male* (1948) and *Sexual Behavior in the Human Female* (1953), Dr. Alfred Kinsey, director of the Institute for Sex Research at Indiana University, noted that, while 80 percent of his female sample disapproved of premarital sex on "moral grounds," half of them had had premarital sex. He also reported that 37 percent of American men had had "some homosexual experience." Americans made bestsellers of Kinsey's dry, quantitative studies, while the *Chicago Tribune* called him a "menace to society." Although Kinsey's research did not provide a completely accurate picture of American sexual behavior, it told many Americans that they were not alone in breaking certain rules.

Another challenge to the sexual rules came from Hugh Hefner, who launched *Playboy* magazine in 1953. Within three years, its circulation reached 1 million. Hefner saw *Playboy* as an attack on America's "ferocious anti-sexuality" and his nude "playmates" as a means for men to combat what he considered the increasingly "blurred distinctions between the sexes" in American life.

Youth Culture

The sheer numbers of "baby boom" youth made them a force in American society. As this group moved from childhood to youth, a distinctive youth culture developed. Its customs and rituals were created within peer groups and shaped by national media—teen magazines, movies, radio, advertising, and music. America's corporations quickly learned the power of youth, as children's fads launched multimillion-dollar industries. Mr. Potato Head—probably the first toy advertised on television—had $4 million in sales in 1952. In the mid-1950s, when Walt Disney's television show *Disneyland*

Barbie

Barbie, the all-American doll, is—like many Americans—an immigrant. Although introduced in 1959 by the American toy company Mattel, Barbie's origins lie in Germany, where she was called Lilli.

The German Lilli doll was a novelty toy for adult men (as evidenced by her proportions, equivalent to 39-21-31 in human terms and her sexy outfits). She was based on a character that cartoonist Reinhard Beuthien drew for the German tabloid *Das Bild* in 1952. Lilli was so popular that she became a regular feature, later made three-dimensional as *Bild* Lilli, an eleven-and-a-half-inch-tall blonde doll with the figure Barbie would make famous.

Lilli came to America with Ruth Handler, one of the founders and codirectors of the Mattel toy company. When she glimpsed Lilli while vacationing in Europe, Handler bought three—and gave one to her daughter Barbara, after whom Lilli would be renamed. Mattel bought the rights to Lilli and unveiled Barbie in March 1959. Despite mothers' hesitations about buying a doll that looked like Barbie, within the year Mattel had sold 351,000 Barbies at $3 each (or about $17 in 2000 dollars). The billionth Barbie was sold in 1997.

Within the United States, Barbie has been controversial—at least among adults. Some have worried that Barbie's wildly unrealistic figure fosters girls' dissatisfaction with their own body—a serious problem in a culture plagued with eating disorders. Others claim that, despite Barbie's 1980s "Girls Can Do Anything" makeover, Barbie represents empty-headed femininity, focused on endless consumption. And many have noted that blonde, blue-eyed Barbie fails to represent the diversity of America's people.

In 2002, international labor-rights groups called for a boycott of Barbie. They cited studies showing that half of all Barbies are made by exploited young women in mainland China: of the $10 retail, Chinese factories receive only 35 cents per doll to cover their costs, including labor. Saudi Arabia banned Barbie in 2003, arguing that her skimpy outfits and the values she represents are not suitable for a Muslim nation. Still, the eleven-and-a-half-inch doll remains popular worldwide, selling in more than 150 countries. Today, the average American girl has ten Barbies—and the typical German girl owns five. For better or worse, Barbie continues to link the United States and the rest of the world.

Before Barbie became an American child's toy, she was "Lilli," a German sex symbol. Mattel transformed the doll into a wholesome American teenager with a new wardrobe to match.

Foto: © Ivan Steiger, Toy Museum Munich & Prague

featured Davy Crockett, "King of the Wild Frontier," every child (and more than a few adults) *had* to have a coonskin cap. As these baby-boom children grew up, their buying power shaped American popular culture.

By 1960, America's 18 million teenagers were spending $10 billion a year. Seventy-two percent of movie tickets in the 1950s were sold to teenagers, and Hollywood created teen films ranging from forgettable B-movies to controversial films such as James Dean's *Rebel Without a Cause*. Adults worried that teens would copy the delinquency romanticized in *Rebel Without a Cause*, and teenage boys did emulate Dean's rebellious look. The film, however, blamed parents for teenage confusion, drawing on popular psychological theories about sexuality and the "crisis of masculinity." Nothing defined youth culture as much as music. Young Americans were electrified by the driving energy of Bill Haley and the Comets, Chuck Berry, Little Richard, and Buddy Holly. **Elvis Presley**'s 1956 appearance on TV's *Ed Sullivan Show* touched off a frenzy of teen adulation—and a flood of letters from parents scandalized by his "gyrations." Although few white musicians acknowledged it, the roots of rock 'n' roll lay in African American rhythm and blues. The raw energy and sometimes sexually suggestive lyrics of early rock music faded as the music industry sought white performers, like Pat Boone, to do blander, more acceptable "cover" versions of music by black artists.

Elvis Presley: Popular rock 'n' roll musician who melded country, gospel, and rhythm and blues influences; his sexually charged style drew young fans and alarmed many adults.

This distinct youth culture made many adults uneasy. Parents worried that "going steady" might encourage teens to "go too far" sexually. Juvenile delinquency was a major concern. Crime rates for young people had risen dramatically after World War II, but much of it was "status" crime—curfew violations, sexual experimentation, underage drinking—activities that were criminal because of the person's age. Congress held hearings on juvenile delinquency, with experts testifying to the corrupting power of youth-oriented popular culture, comic books in particular. Most youthful behavior, however, fit squarely into the consumer culture that youth shared with their parents. "Rebellious youth" rarely questioned the logic of postwar American culture.

Challenges to Middle-Class Culture

Beats: Nonconformist writers, such as Allen Ginsberg and Jack Kerouac, who expressed scorn for the middle-class ideals of conformity, religion, family values, and materialism.

The growth of middle-class culture inspired pockets of cultural dissent. **Beat** (a word that suggested both "down and out" and "beatific") writers rejected middle-class social decorum and contemporary literary conventions. The Beat Generation embraced spontaneity in their art, sought escape from the demands of everyday life, and enjoyed open sexuality and drug use. Perhaps the most significant beat work was Allen Ginsberg's angry, incantational poem "Howl" (1956), the subject of an obscenity trial whose verdict opened American publishing to a broader range of works. The mainstream press ridiculed the beats, dubbing them "beatniks" (after *Sputnik*, suggesting their un-Americanness). Still, they laid the groundwork for the 1960s counterculture.

The Limits of the Middle-Class Nation

What were the limits of middle class culture that began to emerge?

During the 1950s, America's popular culture and mass media celebrated new opportunities. But influential critics condemned middle-class culture as a wasteland of conformity, homogeneity, and ugly consumerism.

Critics of Conformity

These critics were not lone figures crying out in the wilderness. Americans, obsessed with self-criticism even as most participated wholeheartedly in the celebratory "consensus" culture of their age, rushed to buy books like J.D. Salinger's *The Catcher in the Rye* and Norman Mailer's *The Naked and the Dead,* which were profoundly critical of American society. Americans even made bestsellers of difficult academic works, such as David Riesman's *The Lonely Crowd* (1950) and William H. Whyte's *The Organization Man* (1955), both of which criticized conformity. These critiques also appeared in mass-circulation magazines like *Ladies' Home Journal* and *Reader's Digest.* Steeped in such cultural criticism, many Americans understood *Invasion of the Body Snatchers*—a 1956 film in which zombielike aliens grown in pods gradually replace a town's human inhabitants—as criticism of suburban conformity and of postwar cultural homogeneity.

Most critics were attempting to understand large-scale and significant changes in American society. Americans did lose some autonomy in work as large corporations replaced smaller businesses; they experienced the homogenizing force of mass production and a national consumer culture; they saw distinctions among ethnic groups and even among socioeconomic classes fade. Critics, however, were often elitist and antidemocratic, seeing only bland conformity and sterility in the emerging middle-class suburban culture and not understanding that inexpensive suburban housing gave healthier, possibly happier, lives to millions raised in dank, dark tenements or ramshackle farmhouses without indoor plumbing.

Environmental Degradation

The new consumer culture encouraged wasteful habits and harmed the environment. *BusinessWeek* noted that corporations need not rely on "planned obsolescence," purposely designing a product to wear out. Americans replaced products because they were "out of date," not because they did not work, and automakers, encouraging the trend, revamped designs annually. America's new consumer society used an ever larger share of the world's resources. By the 1960s, the United States, with only 5 percent of the world's population, consumed more than one-third of its goods and services.

The rapid economic growth exacted environmental costs. Steel mills, coal-powered generators, and internal-combustion car engines burning lead-based gasoline polluted the atmosphere and imperiled people's health. As suburbanites commuted greater distances to work and neighborhoods were built without public transportation, Americans relied on private automobiles, consuming the nonrenewable resources of oil and gasoline and filling cities and suburbs with smog. Water was diverted from lakes and rivers to service burgeoning Sunbelt cities, including the swimming pools and golf courses that dotted parched Arizona and southern California.

Defense contractors and farmers were among the country's worst polluters. Refuse from nuclear weapons facilities at Hanford, Washington and at Colorado's Rocky Flats arsenal poisoned soil and water resources. Agriculture used pesticides and other chemicals. DDT, a chemical used on Pacific islands during the war to kill mosquitoes and lice, was used widely in the United States until after 1962, when wildlife biologist Rachel Carson indicted DDT for the deaths of mammals, birds, and fish in her bestselling book *Silent Spring.*

In the midst of prosperity, few understood the consequences of the economic transformation taking place. The nation was moving toward a postindustrial economy in which providing goods and services to consumers was more important than producing goods. Therefore, though union members prospered during the 1950s, union membership grew slowly—because most new jobs were created in the union-resistant white-collar service trades. Technological advances increased productivity and also pushed people from well paid blue-collar jobs into the growing and lower-paid service sector.

Continuing Racism   Racial discrimination stood unchallenged in most of 1950s America. Suburbs, North and South, were almost always racially segregated. Many white Americans had little or no contact with people of different races, in part because the relatively small populations of non-white Americans were not dispersed equally nationwide. In 1960, there were 68 people of Chinese descent and 519 African Americans living in Vermont; 181 Native Americans lived in West Virginia; and Mississippi had just 178 Japanese American residents. Most white Americans in the 1950s—especially those outside the South—gave little thought to race. Instead, they regarded the emerging middle-class culture not as "white," but as "American," marginalizing people of color in image as in reality.

In an age of abundance, more than one in five Americans lived in poverty. One-fifth of the poor were people of color, including almost half of the nation's African Americans and more than half of all Native Americans. Two-thirds of the poor lived in households headed by a person with an eighth-grade education or less, one-fourth in households headed by a single woman. More than one-third of the poor were under age eighteen; one-fourth were over age sixty-five. Social Security payments helped, but many retirees were not yet covered, and medical costs drove many older Americans into poverty.

Poverty in an Age of Abundance   As millions of Americans (most of them white) settled in suburbs, the poor were concentrated in inner cities. African American migrants from the South were joined by poor whites from the southern Appalachians, moving to Chicago, Cincinnati, Baltimore, and Detroit. Latin Americans arrived in growing numbers from Mexico, the Dominican Republic, Colombia, Ecuador, and Cuba. Because of the strong economy, many newcomers gained a higher standard of living. But discrimination limited their advances, and they endured crowded and decrepit housing and poor schools. Federal programs that helped middle-class Americans sometimes made the lives of poor people worse. For example, the National Housing Act of 1949, passed to make available "a decent home . . . for every American family," provided for "urban redevelopment." Redevelopment meant slum clearance, replacing poor neighborhoods with luxury high-rise buildings, parking lots, and even highways.

In rural areas, the growth of large agribusinesses pushed tenant farmers and small farm owners off the land. From 1945 to 1961, the nation's farm population declined from 24.4 million to 14.8 million. When the harvesting of cotton in the South was mechanized in the 1940s and 1950s, more than 4 million people were displaced. Southern tobacco growers dismissed tenant farmers, bought tractors, and hired migratory workers. In the West and Southwest, Mexican citizens became cheap migrant labor under the *bracero* program. Almost 1 million Mexican workers came

After the war, American Indians lost sacred land to both big corporations and the federal government. In 1948 George Gillette (*left*), chairman of the Fort Berthold, North Dakota, Indian Tribal Council, covers his face and weeps as Secretary of the Interior J. A. Krug signs a contract buying 155,000 acres of tribal land for a reservoir.

legally to the United States in 1959. Entire families labored, enduring conditions little better than in the Great Depression.

Native Americans were America's poorest people, with an average annual income barely half that of the poverty level. Conditions worsened under termination, a federal policy implemented during Eisenhower's administration. Termination reversed the Indian Reorganization Act of 1934, allowing Indians to terminate their tribal status and remove reservation lands from federal protection prohibiting their sale. Sixty-one tribes were terminated between 1954 and 1960. Termination could only occur with a tribe's agreement, but pressure was sometimes intense—especially when reservation land was rich in natural resources. Enticed by cash payments, almost four-fifths of the Klamaths of Oregon voted to sell their shares of the forest land. Many Indians left reservation land for the city. By the time termination ceased in the 1960s, observers compared the situation of Native Americans to the devastation their forebears had endured in the nineteenth century.

Overall, many Americans enjoyed relative prosperity in the postwar era. But those who had made it to the comfortable middle class often ignored the plight of those left behind. Their children—the baby-boom generation—would see racism, poverty, and the self-satisfaction of postwar suburban culture as a failure of American ideals.

The Pledge of Allegiance

The Pledge of Allegiance Americans recite today was shaped by the Cold War. Congress added the phrase "under God" to the pledge in 1954 to emphasize the difference between the god-fearing United States and the "godless communists" of the Soviet Union.

The Pledge of Allegiance was not always an important part of American life. The original version was written in 1892 by Francis Bellamy, editor of *The Youth's Companion*, to commemorate the four-hundredth anniversary of Columbus's arrival in North America. In 1942, Congress officially adopted a revised version as an act of wartime patriotism. The Supreme Court ruled in 1943, however, that schoolchildren could not be forced to say the Pledge to the Flag.

During the Cold War years, the pledge became an increasingly important symbol of U.S. loyalty. Cold War fears fueled a campaign by the Knights of Columbus, a Catholic men's service organization, to include "under God" in the pledge. Supporting the bill, President Eisenhower proclaimed that

in this way we shall constantly strengthen those spiritual weapons which forever will be our country's most powerful resource in peace and war. From this day forward, the millions of our schoolchildren will daily proclaim in every city and town, every village and every rural schoolhouse, the dedication of our nation and our people to the Almighty.

Some Americans, citing the doctrine of separation of church and state, have protested including "under God." In June 2002, the Ninth District Court (covering California and eight western states) sparked a controversy by ruling that the 1954 pledge was unconstitutional because it conveyed "state endorsement" of a religious belief. Questions about the proper role of religion in the United States remain controversial, a legacy for a people and a nation becoming more diverse in the twenty-first century.

Summary

In the years following World War II, Americans married and had children in record numbers. Millions of veterans used the GI Bill to attend college, buy homes, and start businesses. Although American leaders feared that the nation would lapse back into economic depression after wartime government spending ended, consumer spending brought growth. Sustained economic growth lifted a majority of Americans into an expanding middle class.

The Cold War presidencies of Truman and Eisenhower focused more on international relations than on domestic politics. Within the United States, Cold War fears provoked an extreme anticommunism that stifled political dissent and diminished Americans' civil liberties and freedoms.

The continuing African American struggle for civil rights drew national attention during the Montgomery bus boycott. African Americans won victories in the Supreme Court, including the landmark *Brown v. Board of Education* decision. Truman and Eisenhower used federal power to guarantee the rights of African Americans, as a national civil rights movement coalesced.

Despite continued racial divisions, the United States became a more inclusive nation in the 1950s, as a majority of Americans participated in a national, consumer-oriented, middle-class culture. This culture largely ignored the poverty in the nation's cities and rural areas, but for the growing number in the middle-class, the American Dream seemed a reality.

Chapter Review

Shaping Postwar America

What drove the mass migration of Americans to the suburbs after World War II?

Two factors facilitated massive migration to the suburbs: first, demand for affordable, single-family homes, and second, federal policies. Few new houses or apartments were built during the Great Depression and World War II, and many young couples were forced to move in with relatives or find creative solutions to the housing shortage. In the postwar years, developers applied assembly-line techniques to home construction, creating new suburbs on relatively inexpensive land outside cities. At the same time, the Federal Housing Authority offered low-interest mortgages and loans, and Congress authorized the construction of major roadways and interstate highways in the late 1940s and 1950s. These roads linked the new suburbs to jobs in the cities.

Domestic Politics in the Cold War Era

What happened to New Deal style liberalism after World War II?

President Harry S Truman embraced the same government responsibility for citizens' welfare that drove FDR's New Deal programs, but with limited success. He sought an increase in the minimum wage, national housing legislation offering mortgage loans, national health insurance, and federal aid for education. He additionally supported the Full Employment Act and civil rights legislation for African Americans. But conservative Republicans and southern Democrats in Congress gutted the Full Employment Act and refused to raise the minimum wage, while southern conservatives destroyed his civil rights legislation. His medical insurance and educational funding also met with resistance. A moderate Republican, Eisenhower signed amendments to the Social Security Act that increased benefits and made 7.5 million workers eligible for the program. He also increased government funding for education. Still, neither Truman nor Eisenhower came close to the liberalism of the New Deal.

Cold War Fears and Anticommunism

How did Cold War fears inspire a Red Scare in the United States?

In the 1940s and 1950s, as Cold War tensions escalated between the U.S. and its rival superpower, the Soviet Union, Americans became increasingly nervous that communist power might reach their shores. Many Americans regarded the Soviet Union's virtual takeover of eastern Europe in the late 1940s as frighteningly similar to Nazi Germany's takeover of neighboring states during the war. Fear of a nuclear war with the Soviets also inspired anticommunism in the United States, especially after 1949 when the Soviet Union possessed atomic weapons. Normal fears, however, were replaced by irrational ones at every level of society, fueling anticommunist venom and witch hunts that violated people's civil rights and led to the persecution of thousands of innocent Americans. Mainstream Americans built bomb shelters; government employees could be deemed "security risks" (and fired) for such flimsy reasons as alcoholism, homosexuality, and high levels of debt—often without evidence of disloyalty. The House Un-American Activities Committee (HUAC) conducted public investigations that targeted Hollywood, university professors, and others. Consequently, studios blacklisted actors, screenwriters, and others suspected of communist affiliations, and university professors were fired based on the books they used or their unwillingness to take a loyalty oath. Fears drove the CIO to purge itself of eleven unions—900,000 labor union members—for alleged, but unproven, communist domination. The red scare waned after 1954 when Republican Senator Joseph McCarthy was discredited on national television for his claims about communist party members infiltrating the state department.

The Struggle for Civil Rights

What facilitated the emergence of a renewed civil rights movement?

African Americans who helped win World War II were determined to improve their status and end discrimination in the United States. That sentiment, along with the growth of a new and visible black middle class of college educated activists, war veterans, and union workers, helped reinvigorate civil rights activism among blacks and raise awareness of social injustice among white politicians and mainstream Americans. President Truman established the President's Commission on Civil Rights in 1946, which produced a report that became the civil rights' movement agenda for the next twenty years—calling for legislation to end lynching and segregation and guarantee voting rights and equality in employment. Academics and authors such as Gunnar Myrdal and Richard Wright produced powerful works that educated Americans about ongoing racial injustice. African Americans mounted successful challenges to racial discrimination in the courts, most notably the end of segregated schools in the 1954 landmark *Brown v. Board of Education of Topeka* case. At the grassroots level, blacks fought discrimination, most visibly in the year-long Montgomery Bus Boycott, which began in 1955 when Rosa Parks, a seamstress and NAACP activist, was arrested for refusing to give up her seat on a city bus to a white man. Martin Luther King, Jr., a recently ordained minister, led the successful boycott and in 1957 became the first president of the Southern Christian Leadership Conference (SCLC), organized to coordinate civil rights activities.

Creating a Middle-Class Nation

What led to the emergence of a middle-class culture in the 1950s?

In the postwar era, Americans enjoyed national prosperity on an unprecedented level. That meant that there were more and better-paying jobs that enabled greater numbers of people to move into the ranks of middle class, complete with its material comfort and security. Veterans who took advantage of G.I. Bill educational opportunities were able to swell the professional and managerial job classifications, while previously blue-collar manufacturing jobs now paid well-enough to make these families middle class, too. People of varying ethnic backgrounds came together via home ownership in the new suburbs, which, although still largely white, were far more diverse than the communities where people previously resided. An assortment of newly affordable goods from cars to clothing reached a wider segment of the population. And an emerging national mass media—magazines, newspapers, film, and television—taught all Americans how to behave and live like a single, unified, national middle-class—with American foods replacing ethnic dishes, national brands

replacing homemade products, and nationalized notions about how to raise children. Television shows reinforced ideas about how proper people dressed, arranged their homes, and raised children, thereby reinforcing white middle-class ideals to those watching across class, racial, and ethnic lines.

Men, Women, and Youth at Midcentury

How did the economic and social structure of the 1950s influence gender roles?

In the 1950s, men and women occupied separate gender roles. Economically, middle-class families could survive on one income, typically the man's. Most Americans believed that men should be breadwinners and women homemakers. Culturally, women's domestic roles were hailed as their true vocation, even though in reality they left many feeling isolated and unfulfilled. While many married women did work outside the home, it was often part-time and for a specific goal, such as a new car. There were other disincentives that kept many women from seeking full-time work or careers: childcare was virtually nonexistent; popular childcare experts such as Dr. Spock argued that children required a mother's full-time care; and hiring discrimination meant that there were few well-paying jobs open to women to make it worth juggling home and work responsibilities. Employment ads were sex segregated into Help Wanted—Male and Help Wanted—Female categories, and on average women earned only 60 percent of what men earned. Men who did not conform to standards of male responsibility—husband, father, breadwinner—were also socially condemned, and experts worried about the crisis in masculinity of a new generation of "organization men," corporate employees who succeeded through cooperation and conformity rather than initiative and risk.

The Limits of the Middle-Class Nation

What were the limits of middle class culture that began to emerge?

Influential critics pointed out several negative consequences of the middle class culture that emerged in the 1950s. First, consumerism encouraged wasteful and environmentally unsound purchasing habits. Instead of Americans replacing products when they wore out, now they replaced them when they seemed outdated. Worse, by the 1960s the United States, with only 5 percent of the world's population, consumed more than one-third of its goods and services. All of this production generated increased pollution and health concerns. Americans' growing dependence on the automobile to led to increased reliance on gasoline, and water was shifted from lakes to swimming pools as the Sunbelt developed. Even in the age of affluence, more than one-fifth of Americans were poor, often people of color (especially Native Americans and African Americans), many of whom were concentrated in inner cities. Racial discrimination continued, resulting in racially segregated suburbs. Programs that helped the middle class often hurt the poor, such as the National Housing Act of 1949, which promised decent housing via urban redevelopment; for the poor, that meant slum clearance, replacing their neighborhoods with luxury high-rise buildings, parking lots, and even highways.

Suggestions for Further Reading

Glenn C. Altschuler and Stuart M. Blumin, *The GI Bill: A New Deal for Veterans* (2009)

Taylor Branch, *Parting the Waters: America in the King Years, 1954–1963* (1988)

Lizabeth Cohen, *A Consumer's Republic: The Politics of Mass Consumption in Postwar America* (2003)

Stephanie Coontz, *The Way We Never Were: American Families and the Nostalgia Trap* (1992)

Thomas Patrick Doherty, *Cold War, Cool Medium: Television, McCarthyism, and American Culture* (2003)

Mary Dudziak, *Cold War Civil Rights: Race and the Image of American Democracy* (2000)

James Gregory, *The Southern Diaspora: How the Great Migrations of Black and White Southerners Transformed the Nation* (2007)

Thomas Hine, *Populuxe* (1986)

Grace Palladino, *Teenagers* (1996)

Michael Sherry, *In the Shadow of War* (1995)

Thomas J. Sugrue, *Sweet Land of Liberty: The Forgotten Struggle for Civil Rights in the North* (2008)

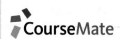

Go to the CourseMate website for primary source links, study tools, and review materials for this chapter. www.cengagebrain.com

The Tumultuous Sixties

30

1960–1968

I was late, and Ezell Blair had an exam the next day. But he and his friends in the dormitory sat talking—as they often did—about injustice, about living in a nation that proclaimed equality for all but denied full citizenship to some because of the color of their skin. They were complaining about the do-nothing adults, condemning the black community of Greensboro when Franklin McCain said, as if he meant it, "It's time to fish or cut bait." Joe McNeil and McCain's roommate, David Richmond, agreed.

The next day, February 1, 1960, after their classes at North Carolina Agricultural and Technical College, the four freshmen walked into town. At the F.W. Woolworth's on South Elm Street, one of the most profitable stores in the national chain, each bought a few small things. Then, nervously, they sat down at the lunch counter and tried to order coffee. These seventeen- and eighteen-year-olds were prepared to be arrested, even physically attacked. But nothing happened. The counter help ignored them as long as possible; finally one worker reminded them, "We don't serve colored here." An elderly white woman told the boys how proud she was of them. The store closed; the manager turned out the lights. After forty-five minutes, the four men who began the sit-in movement left the store.

They returned the next day with twenty fellow students. By February 3, sixty-three of the sixty-five seats were taken. On February 4, the sit-in spread to the S.H. Kress store across the street. By February 7, there were sit-ins in Winston-Salem; by February 8, in Charlotte; on February 9, in Raleigh. By the third week in February, students were picketing Woolworth's stores in the North. On July 26, 1960, they won. F.W. Woolworth's ended segregation in all its stores.

The sit-in at the Greensboro Woolworth's signaled the beginning of a decade of public activism unmatched in U.S. history. During the 1960s, millions of Americans—many of them young—marched for civil rights or against the war in Vietnam. Passion over contemporary issues revitalized democracy and threatened to tear the nation apart.

John F. Kennedy, the nation's youngest president, told Americans as he took office in 1961, "The torch has been passed to a new generation." Despite his inspirational language, Kennedy had only modest success implementing his domestic agenda. In his third year as president, however, Kennedy offered greater support for civil rights and proposed ambitious domestic policies. When Kennedy was assassinated in November 1963, his death seemed, to many, the end of an era of hope.

Lyndon Johnson, Kennedy's successor, invoked the memory of the martyred president to launch an ambitious program of civil rights and liberal legislation. Calling his vision the Great Society, Johnson meant to use federal power to eliminate poverty and guarantee equal rights to all Americans.

Despite liberal triumphs and civil rights gains, social tensions escalated during the mid-1960s. A revitalized conservative movement emerged, and Franklin Roosevelt's old New Deal coalition fractured as white southerners abandoned the Democratic Party. Angry that poverty and discrimination persisted despite landmark civil rights laws, many African Americans rioted. White youth culture increasingly rejected the values and lifestyle of its elders, creating what Americans have called the generation gap.

Developments overseas also contributed to a growing national instability. After the 1962 Cuban missile crisis brought the Soviet Union and the United States close to nuclear disaster, President John F. Kennedy and Soviet leader Nikita Khrushchev moved to reduce bilateral tensions in 1963. Cold War pressures in Europe lessened appreciably. Everywhere else, however, the superpowers competed frantically. Throughout the 1960s, the United States tried various of approaches—including foreign aid, CIA covert actions, military assaults, cultural penetration, economic sanctions, and diplomacy—to win the Cold War. In Vietnam, Kennedy expanded U.S. involvement significantly. Johnson "Americanized" the war, increasing U.S. troops to more than half a million in 1968.

By 1968, the war in Vietnam divided Americans and undermined Johnson's Great Society. With the assassinations of Martin Luther King Jr. and Robert Kennedy—two of America's brightest leaders—with cities in flames and tanks in Chicago streets in August, the fate of the nation seemed to hang in the balance.

As you read this chapter, keep the following questions in mind:

* **What were the successes and failures of American liberalism in the 1960s?**

* **Why did the United States expand its participation in the war in Vietnam and continue in the war so long?**

* **By 1968, many believed the fate of the nation hung in the balance. What did they think was at stake? What divided Americans, and how did they express their differences?**

Chronology

1960	Sit-ins begin in Greensboro
	Birth-control pill approved
	John F. Kennedy elected president
	Young Americans for Freedom write Sharon Statement
1961	Freedom Rides protest segregation in transportation
1962	Students for a Democratic Society issues Port Huron Statement
	Cuban missile crisis courts nuclear war
1963	Civil rights March on Washington for Jobs and Freedom draws more than 250,000
	South Vietnamese leader Diem assassinated following U.S.-sanctioned coup d'état
	John F. Kennedy assassinated; Lyndon B. Johnson becomes president
1964	Civil Rights Act passed by Congress
	Race riots break out in first of the "long, hot summers"
	Gulf of Tonkin Resolution passed by Congress
	Free Speech Movement begins at University of California, Berkeley
	Lyndon B. Johnson elected president
1965	Lyndon Johnson launches Great Society programs
	United States commits ground troops to Vietnam and initiates bombing campaign
	Voting Rights Act outlaws practices preventing most African Americans from voting in southern states
	Immigration and Nationality Act lowers barriers to immigration from Asia and Latin America
	Malcolm X assassinated
1966	National Organization for Women founded
1967	"Summer of love" in San Francisco's Haight-Ashbury district
	Race riots erupt in Newark, Detroit, and other cities
1968	Tet Offensive deepens fear of losing war in Vietnam
	Martin Luther King Jr. assassinated
	Robert Kennedy assassinated
	Violence erupts at Democratic National Convention
	Richard Nixon elected president

Kennedy and the Cold War

How was the Cuban missile crisis a watershed in U.S.–Soviet relations?

John F. Kennedy: President from 1961 until his assassination in 1963.

Young, handsome, and intellectually curious, **John F. Kennedy** brought wit and sophistication to the White House. His Irish American grandfather had been mayor of Boston, and his millionaire father, Joseph P. Kennedy, served as ambassador to Great Britain. In 1946, the young Kennedy returned from World War II a naval hero (the boat he commanded was sunk by a Japanese destroyer in 1943, and Kennedy saved his crew) and campaigned to represent Boston in the U.S. House of Representatives. He served three terms, and in 1952 was elected to the Senate.

John Fitzgerald Kennedy

As a Democrat, Kennedy inherited the New Deal commitment to America's social welfare system. He generally voted with the pro-labor sentiments of his low-income, blue-collar constituents. But he avoided controversial issues, such as civil rights and the censure of Joseph McCarthy. Kennedy won a Pulitzer Prize for his *Profiles in Courage* (1956), a study of principled politicians, but he shaded the truth in claiming sole authorship, as it was written largely by aide Theodore Sorensen (from more than one hundred pages of notes dictated by Kennedy). In foreign policy, Senator

Kennedy endorsed the Cold War policy of containment. Despite an unimpressive legislative record, he enjoyed an enthusiastic following, especially after his landslide reelection to the Senate in 1958.

Kennedy cultivated an image as a happy, healthy family man. But he was a chronic womanizer, even after his 1953 marriage to Jacqueline Bouvier. Nor was he the picture of physical vitality: as a child he nearly died of scarlet fever and later developed severe back problems, worsened by his participation in World War II. Kennedy was diagnosed with Addison's disease, an adrenalin deficiency that required daily cortisone injections and often left him in pain. As president he would require plenty of bed rest and frequent therapeutic swims in the White House pool.

Election of 1960

Kennedy beat Republican Richard Nixon in the 1960 presidential election by a narrow 118,000 votes of nearly 69 million cast. Kennedy achieved mixed success in the South but ran well in the Northeast and Midwest. His Roman Catholic faith hurt him in states where voters feared he would take direction from the pope, but helped in states with large Catholic populations. As the sitting vice president, Nixon had to answer for sagging economic figures and the Soviet downing of a U-2 spy plane. In televised debates against the telegenic Kennedy, Nixon looked nervous and surly, and the camera made him appear unshaven. Perhaps worse, when asked to list Nixon's significant decisions as vice president, Eisenhower replied, "If you give me a week, I might think of one."

Many Americans were enchanted with the youthful and photogenic Kennedys. Here, the president and his family pose outside the Palm Beach, Florida, home of the president's father after a private Easter Service, April 14, 1963.

The new president surrounded himself with young advisers whom writer David Halberstam called "the best and the brightest." Secretary of Defense Robert McNamara (age forty-four) was an assistant professor at Harvard at twenty-four and later the whiz-kid president of the Ford Motor Company. Kennedy's special assistant for national security affairs, McGeorge Bundy (age forty-one) became a Harvard dean at thirty-four with only a bachelor's degree. Secretary of State Dean Rusk (fifty-two) had been a Rhodes scholar in his youth. Kennedy was only forty-three, and his brother Robert, the attorney general, was thirty-five.

Kennedy gave top priority to waging the Cold War. In the campaign, he accused Eisenhower of pursuing an unimaginative foreign policy that failed to reduce the threat of nuclear war with the Soviet Union and weakened America's standing in the Third World.

Nation Building in the Third World

Kennedy understood, sooner than his advisers, that there were limits to American power abroad. More than his predecessor, he proved willing to initiate dialog with the Soviets, sometimes using his brother Robert as a secret channel to Moscow. Yet Kennedy also sought victory in the Cold War. After Soviet leader Nikita Khrushchev endorsed "wars of national liberation," such as the one in Vietnam, Kennedy called for "peaceful revolution" through nation building. The administration helped developing nations with aid to improve agriculture, transportation, and communications. Kennedy thus oversaw the creation of the multibillion-dollar Alliance for Progress in 1961 to spur economic development in Latin America. That year, too, he created the Peace Corps, dispatching American teachers, agricultural specialists, and health workers to assist authorities in developing nations.

Cynics then and later dismissed the Alliance and the Peace Corps as Kennedy's Cold War tools for countering anti-Americanism and defeating communism in the developing world. True enough, but the programs were also born of genuine humanitarianism. As the historian Elizabeth Cobbs Hoffman has written, "the Peace Corps broached an age-old dilemma of U.S. foreign policy: how to reconcile the imperatives and temptations of power politics with the ideals of freedom and self-determination for all nations."

The Alliance for Progress was only partly successful; infant mortality rates improved, but Latin American economies registered unimpressive growth and class divisions widened, exacerbating political unrest. Although many foreign peoples welcomed U.S. economic assistance and craved American material culture, they resented interference. And because aid was usually transmitted through a self-interested elite, it often never reached the poor.

Although Kennedy and his aides were supportive of social revolution in the Third World, they disapproved of communist involvement in these uprisings. Therefore, the administration relied on counterinsurgency to defeat revolutionaries who challenged pro-U.S. Third World governments. U.S. military and technical advisers trained native troops and police to quell unrest.

Soviet-American Tensions

The new president struggled in relations with the Soviet Union. A summit meeting with Soviet leader Nikita Khrushchev in Vienna in June 1961 went poorly, as the two leaders disagreed over preconditions for peace and stability in the world. Consequently, the administration's first year witnessed little movement on controlling the nuclear arms race or getting a superpower ban on testing nuclear weapons in the atmosphere or underground. Instead, both superpowers accelerated their arms production. In 1961, the U.S. military budget shot up 15 percent; by mid-1964, U.S. nuclear weapons increased by 150 percent. Government advice to citizens to build fallout shelters in their backyards intensified public fear of devastating war.

If war occurred, many believed Berlin would be the cause. In mid-1961, Khrushchev demanded an end to western occupation of West Berlin and a reunification of East and West Germany stood by U.S. commitment to West Berlin and West Germany. In August the Soviets, at the urging of the East German regime, erected a concrete and barbed-wire barricade to halt the exodus of East Germans into the more prosperous and politically free West Berlin. The Berlin Wall inspired protests throughout the noncommunist world, but Kennedy privately sighed that "a wall is a hell of a lot better than a war." The barrier shut off the flow of refugees, and the crisis passed.

Bay of Pigs Invasion   Yet Kennedy knew that Khrushchev would continue to press for advantage elsewhere, and he was particularly rankled by growing Soviet assistance to Fidel Castro's Cuban government. The Eisenhower administration contested the Cuban revolution and bequeathed to the Kennedy administration a partially developed CIA plan to overthrow Fidel Castro: CIA-trained Cuban exiles would land and secure a beachhead; the Cuban people would rise up against Castro and welcome a new U.S.-backed government.

The attack took place on April 17, 1961, as twelve hundred exiles landed at the swampy Bay of Pigs in Cuba. Instead of meeting discontented Cubans, they were greeted by Castro's troops and quickly captured. Kennedy tried to keep the U.S. participation in the operation hidden but the CIA's role swiftly became public. Anti-American sentiment swept through Latin America. Castro, concluding that the United States might launch another invasion, looked increasingly toward the Soviet Union for military and economic assistance.

Embarrassed by the Bay of Pigs fiasco, Kennedy vowed to bring Castro down. The CIA soon hatched a project called Operation Mongoose to disrupt the island's trade, support raids on Cuba from Miami, and kill Castro. The agency's assassination schemes included providing Castro with cigars laced with explosives and poison. The United States also tightened its economic blockade and undertook military maneuvers in the Caribbean. The Joint Chiefs of Staff sketched plans to spark a rebellion in Cuba that would be followed by an invasion of U.S. troops.

Cuban Missile Crisis   Both Castro and Khrushchev believed an invasion was coming, which partly explains the Soviet leader's risky decision in 1962 to secretly deploy nuclear missiles in Cuba as a deterrent. But Khrushchev also hoped the move would improve the Soviet position in the nuclear balance of power and force Kennedy to finally resolve the German problem. Khrushchev wanted the West out of Berlin, and he worried that Washington might provide West Germany with nuclear weapons. He thought he could prevent it by putting Soviet missiles just 90 miles off the coast of Florida. The world soon faced brinkmanship at its most frightening.

In mid-October 1962, a U-2 plane flying over Cuba photographed missile sites. The president immediately organized a special Executive Committee (ExComm) to force the missiles and their nuclear warheads out of Cuba. Options considered ranged from full-scale invasion to limited bombing to quiet diplomacy. Defense Secretary Robert McNamara proposed a solution acceptable to the president: a naval quarantine of Cuba.

Kennedy addressed the nation on television on October 22, demanding that the Soviets retreat. U.S. warships began crisscrossing the Caribbean, while B-52s with nuclear bombs took to the skies. Khrushchev agreed to withdraw the missiles if the United States pledged never to attack Cuba and removed Jupiter missiles aimed at the Soviet Union from Turkey. For days the world teetered on the brink of disaster. Then, on October 28, came a compromise. The United States agreed to Soviet demands in exchange for the withdrawal of Soviet offensive forces from Cuba. Fearing Castro might make matters worse, Khrushchev settled without consulting the Cubans.

Cuban missile crisis:
Confrontation between the
Soviet Union and the United
States in 1962 regarding the
Soviet deployment of nuclear
missiles in Cuba. It put the world
on the brink of nuclear disaster
until the two nations reached a
compromise.

The **Cuban missile crisis** was a watershed in the Soviet-American relationship. Kennedy and Khrushchev acted with greater prudence in its aftermath, taking steps toward improved relations. In August 1963, the adversaries signed a treaty banning nuclear tests in the atmosphere, the oceans, and outer space. They also installed a coded wire-telegraph "hot line" staffed around the clock to allow near-instant communication between the capitals. They refrained from further confrontation in Berlin.

Together, these small steps began to build much-needed mutual trust. By autumn 1963, the Cold War in Europe was fading as both sides accepted the status quo of a divided continent and fortified border. Still, the arms race continued and accelerated, and the superpower competition in the Third World remained intense.

Marching for Freedom

What was Kennedy's reaction to
growing civil rights activism?

President Kennedy regarded the Cold War as the most important issue Americans faced. But in the early 1960s, young civil rights activists seized the national stage and demanded that the federal government mobilize behind them.

Students and the Movement

In 1960, six years after the *Brown* decision declared "separate but equal" unconstitutional, only 10 percent of southern public schools had begun desegregation. Fewer than one in four adult African Americans in the South could vote, and water fountains were still labeled White Only and Colored Only. But within one year after the young men sat down at the all-white lunch counter in Greensboro, more than seventy thousand Americans—mostly college students—had participated in sit-ins.

**Student Nonviolent
Coordinating Committee
(SNCC):** Civil rights organization
founded by young people that
played a key role in grassroots
organizing in the south in the
early 60s.

The young people who created the **Student Nonviolent Coordinating Committee (SNCC)** in spring 1960 to coordinate the sit-in movement were committed to nonviolence. In the years to come, such young people would risk their lives in the struggle for social justice.

Freedom Rides and Voter Registration

On May 4, 1961, thirteen members of the Congress of Racial Equality (CORE), a nonviolent civil rights organization formed during World War II, purchased bus tickets in Washington, D.C., for a 1,500-mile trip through the South to New Orleans. Calling themselves Freedom Riders, this racially mixed group meant to demonstrate that, despite Supreme Court rulings ordering the desegregation of interstate buses, Jim Crow still ruled in the South. They knew they were risking their lives. One bus was firebombed outside Anniston, Alabama. Riders were badly beaten in Birmingham. In Montgomery, a thousand whites attacked riders with baseball bats and steel bars. Police stayed away; the police commissioner called the freedom riders troublemakers.

News of the violent attacks made headlines worldwide. Soviet commentators highlighted the "savage nature of American freedom and democracy." One southern business leader, in Tokyo to promote Birmingham as a site for international business development, saw Japanese interest evaporate when photographs of the Birmingham attacks appeared in Tokyo newspapers.

In America, the violence forced many to confront racial discrimination and hatred in their nation. Many middle- and upper-class white southerners resisted integration following the *Brown* decision, and the Freedom Rides made some think differently. The *Atlanta Journal* editorialized: "[I]t is time for the decent people…to muzzle the jackals." The global outcry pushed a reluctant President Kennedy to send federal marshals to safeguard Freedom Riders in Alabama. But bowing to white southern pressure, he allowed the Freedom Riders to be arrested in Mississippi.

Beginning in 1961, thousands of SNCC volunteers, many of them high school and college students, risked their lives encouraging African Americans in rural Mississippi to register to vote. Some SNCC volunteers were white, and some were northerners, but many were black southerners, often from low-income families. They experienced first-hand the intersection of racism, powerlessness, and poverty.

Kennedy and Civil Rights

Kennedy was sympathetic—though not terribly committed—to the civil rights movement, and he realized that racial oppression hurt the United States in the Cold War struggle for international opinion. However, like Franklin D. Roosevelt, he understood that if he alienated conservative southern Democrats in Congress, his legislative programs would founder. Thus, he appointed five die-hard segregationists to the federal bench in the Deep South and delayed fulfilling his campaign pledge to end segregation in federally subsidized housing (by executive order) until late 1962. He allowed FBI director J. Edgar Hoover to harass Martin Luther King and other activists, using wiretaps and surveillance to gather personal information and circulating rumors of communist connections and personal improprieties to discredit them.

But grassroots civil rights activism—and the violence of white mobs—forced Kennedy's hand. In September 1962, the president ordered 500 U.S. marshals to protect James Meredith, the first African American to attend the University of Mississippi. Thousands of whites attacked the marshals with guns, gasoline bombs, bricks, and pipes, killing two and seriously wounding 160 federal marshals. The marshals did not back down, nor did James Meredith.

Birmingham and the Children's Crusade

In 1961, the Freedom Riders captured the attention of the nation and the larger Cold War world. Martin Luther King Jr., having risen through the Montgomery bus boycott to leadership in the movement, concluded that only by provoking a crisis would the civil rights struggle advance. King and the SCLC planned a 1963 campaign in Birmingham, Alabama. Anticipating a violent response, they called their plan Project C—for confrontation. King wanted Americans to see the racist hate and violence that marred their nation.

Through April 1963, nonviolent protests in Birmingham led to hundreds of arrests. Then, on May 2, in a controversial action, King and Birmingham parents put children on the front lines. As about a thousand African American children, some as young as six, marched, police commissioner Eugene "Bull" Connor ordered police to train "monitor" water guns—powerful enough to strip bark from a tree at 100 feet—on them. The water guns mowed the children down, and police loosed attack dogs as the nation watched in horror on TV. President Kennedy demanded that Birmingham's white business and political elite negotiate a settlement. The Birmingham movement won and, more importantly, pushed civil rights to the fore of Kennedy's agenda.

"Segregation Forever!" On June 11, defiant Alabama governor George C. Wallace fulfilled a promise to "bar the schoolhouse door" himself to prevent desegregation of the University of Alabama. Hearing echoes of Wallace's inaugural pledge "Segregation now, segregation tomorrow, segregation forever!" and facing a nation rocked by civil rights protests, Kennedy committed the federal government to guarantee racial justice—even over the opposition of individual states. On June 12, in a televised address, Kennedy said, "Now the time has come for this nation to fulfill its promise." Hours later, civil rights leader Medgar Evers was murdered in his driveway in Jackson, Mississippi. The next week, the president asked Congress to pass a comprehensive civil rights bill ending legal racial discrimination.

March on Washington On August 28, 1963, a quarter-million Americans gathered on the Washington Mall to show support for Kennedy's civil rights bill. Behind the scenes, organizers from major civil rights groups—SCLC, CORE, SNCC, the NAACP, the Urban League, and A. Philip Randolph's Brotherhood of Sleeping Car Porters—grappled with growing tensions within the movement. SNCC activists saw Kennedy's proposed legislation as too little, too late. King and other older leaders counseled moderation. The movement was splintering.

What most Americans saw, however, was a celebration of unity. Black and white celebrities joined hands; folk singers sang freedom songs. Television aired Martin Luther King Jr.'s prophesy of a day when "all God's children, black men and white men, Jews and Gentiles, Protestants and Catholics, will be able to join hands and sing in the words of the old Negro spiritual, Free at last! Free at last! Thank God Almighty, we are free at last!" The 1963 March on Washington for Jobs and Freedom was a triumph, powerfully demonstrating African Americans' commitment to equality and justice. Days later, white supremacists bombed the Sixteenth Street Baptist Church in Birmingham, killing four black girls.

Freedom Summer During the summer of 1964, more than one thousand white students joined the voter mobilization project in Mississippi. They formed Freedom Schools, teaching literacy and constitutional rights, and helped organize the Mississippi Freedom Democratic Party as an alternative to the white-only Democratic Party. SNCC organizers also believed that large numbers of white volunteers would focus national attention on Mississippi repression and violence. Project workers were arrested over a thousand times and were shot at, bombed, and beaten. On June 21, local black activist James Cheney and two white volunteers, Michael Schwerner and Andrew Goodman, were murdered by a Klan mob. That summer, black and white activists risked their lives together, challenging the Deep South's racial caste system.

Liberalism and the Great Society

What made the War on Poverty controversial?

By 1963, Kennedy seemed to be taking a new path. Campaigning in 1960, he promised to lead Americans into a New Frontier, with the federal government working to eradicate poverty, guarantee healthcare to the elderly, and provide decent schools for all children. But few of Kennedy's domestic initiatives were passed into law. Lacking a popular mandate in the 1960 election, fearful of alienating southern Democrats in Congress, Kennedy let his social policy agenda languish.

"Project C" and National Opinion

This photograph of a police dog attacking a 17-year-old demonstrator during a civil rights march in Birmingham, Alabama, appeared on the front page of the *New York Times* on May 4, 1963, just above a second photograph of a fireman spraying a group that included three teenage girls with a high pressure fire hose. The following day President Kennedy discussed this photo in a meeting in the White House. Some historians argue that photographs not only document history, they make it. Is that statement true in this case? How does this photograph fit into Martin Luther King's plans for "Project C" (see page 793)? What difference might it make that the *New York Times* editors chose to run this photograph rather than one of the many others taken that day?

AP Photo/Bill Hudson

Mass media coverage helped galvanize public opinion in support of civil rights protesters.

Instead, Kennedy focused on the economy, believing that continued prosperity would solve social problems. Kennedy's vision was perhaps best realized in the United States's space program. As the Soviets moved ahead in the space race, Kennedy vowed in 1961 to put a man on the moon before decade's end. With billions in new funding, the National Aeronautics and Space Administration (NASA) began the Apollo program. And in February 1962, astronaut John Glenn orbited the earth in the space capsule *Friendship 7.*

Kennedy Assassination   The nation would not learn what sort of president John Kennedy might have become. On November 22, 1963, riding with his wife, Jackie, in an open-top limousine in Dallas, Texas, Kennedy was cheered by thousands along the motorcade's route. Suddenly, shots rang out. The president crumpled, shot in the head. Tears ran down the cheeks of CBS anchorman Walter Cronkite as he told the nation the president was dead.

That same day, police captured a suspect: Lee Harvey Oswald, a former U.S. marine (dishonorably discharged) who once attempted to gain Soviet citizenship. Two days later, Oswald was shot dead by nightclub owner Jack Ruby. Shocked Americans wondered if Ruby was silencing Oswald to prevent him from implicating others. The seven-member Warren Commission, headed by U.S. Supreme Court Chief Justice Earl Warren, concluded that Oswald acted alone. Millions of Americans watched their president's funeral: the brave young widow; a riderless horse; three-year-old "John-John" saluting his father's casket. In one awful moment in Dallas, the reality of the Kennedy presidency had been transformed into myth, the man into martyr. In the post-assassination national grief, **Lyndon Johnson** invoked Kennedy's memory to push through the most ambitious legislative program since the New Deal.

Lyndon Johnson: 36th President of the United States; champion of civil rights legislation and the war on poverty.

Johnson and the Great Society

Where Kennedy came from wealth and was educated at Harvard, Johnson grew up in modest circumstances in the Texas hill country and graduated from Southwest Texas State Teachers' College. He was as earthy as Kennedy was elegant, prone to curses and willing to use his physical size to his advantage. Johnson first came to Congress in 1937. As Senate majority leader from 1954 to 1960, he learned how to manipulate people and wield power. As president, he used these skills to unite the nation.

Johnson, a liberal in the style of Franklin D. Roosevelt, believed the federal government must actively improve Americans' lives. In a 1964 University of Michigan commencement address, he described his vision of "abundance and liberty for all…demand[ing] an end to poverty and racial injustice…where men are more concerned with the quality of their goals than the quantity of their goods." Johnson called this vision **"The Great Society."**

Link to President Johnson's "Great Society" speech.

The Great Society: President Johnson's vision for America; LBJ believed the federal government must act to alleviate poverty, end racial injustice, and improve the lives of all Americans.

Civil Rights Act of 1964: The most significant civil rights law in U.S. history; ended legal discrimination and segregation in public accommodations.

Civil Rights Act

Johnson signed into law the **Civil Rights Act of 1964**, which ended *legal* discrimination on the basis of race, color, religion, or national origin, in federal programs, voting, employment, and public accommodation. The original bill did not include sex discrimination; that was introduced by a southern congressman who hoped it would engender opposition to torpedo the bill. But a bipartisan group of women members of the House of Representatives ensured its passage with sex as a protected category. Significantly, the Civil Rights Act of 1964 gave the government authority to withhold federal funds from public agencies or federal contractors that discriminated and established the Equal Employment Opportunity Commission (EEOC) to investigate and judge job discrimination claims. However, the EEOC largely ignored sex discrimination, prompting women's equality activists in 1966 to form the **National Organization for Women (NOW)**.

Many Americans did not believe it was the federal government's job to end racial discrimination or poverty. Many white southerners resented federal intervention in local customs and, millions of conservative Americans believed that since the New Deal the federal government had overstepped its constitutional boundaries. They sought a return to local control and states' rights. In the 1964 election, this conservativism was championed by Republican candidate, Arizona senator Barry Goldwater.

Election of 1964

Goldwater voted against the 1964 Civil Rights Act and opposed Social Security. Like many conservatives, he believed that individual *liberty*, not equality, mattered most. Goldwater further believed that the United States needed a more powerful national military to fight communism; in campaign speeches, he suggested that the United States should use tactical nuclear weapons against its enemies.

Goldwater's campaign slogan, "In your heart you know he's right," was turned against him by Lyndon Johnson supporters: "In your heart you know he's right...far right," one punned. Johnson campaigned on an unemployment rate below 4 percent and economic growth above 6 percent. But, as he told an aide, his support for African American civil rights had "delivered the south to the Republican Party for my lifetime and yours."

Tensions exploded at the 1964 Democratic National Convention. Two delegations from Mississippi demanded to be seated. The Democratic Party's official delegation was exclusively white; the Mississippi Freedom Democratic Party (MFDP) was racially mixed. White southern delegates threatened to leave if the MFDP delegates were seated. Johnson sought a compromise, but the MFDP declined. "We didn't come all this way for no two seats," MFDP delegate Fannie Lou Hamer said, and the delegation walked out.

Johnson won the election by a landslide, but he lost the Deep South—the first Democrat since the Civil War to do so. Voters also elected the most liberal Congress in history. With the mandate provided by a record 61.1 percent of the popular vote, Johnson launched his Great Society. Congress passed the most sweeping reform legislation since 1935.

In late 1964, the SCLC made voting rights its top priority. Martin Luther King Jr. and other leaders turned to Selma, Alabama, seeking another public confrontation that would mobilize national support and federal action. It came on March 6, when state troopers turned electric cattle prods, chains, and tear gas against peaceful marchers. On March 15, the president supported a second monumental civil rights bill, the **Voting Rights Act**. It outlawed practices that prevented most blacks in the Deep South from voting and provided for federal election oversight in districts with evidence of past discrimination. Within two years, African Americans registered to vote in Mississippi jumped from 7 percent to almost 60 percent. Black elected officials became increasingly common in southern states over the following decade.

National Organization for Women (NOW): Civil-rights group for women that lobbied for equal opportunity, filed lawsuits against gender discrimination, and mobilized public opinion against sexism. (see page 820).

Voting Rights Act: Law that outlawed practices that prevented blacks in the South from voting.

Improving American Life

Seeking to improve American life, the Johnson administration established new student loan and grant programs to help low- and moderate-income Americans attend college, and created the National Endowment for the Arts and the National Endowment for the Humanities. The **Immigration Act of 1965** ended racially based quotas. And Johnson supported consumer protection legislation, including the 1966 National Traffic and Motor Vehicle Safety Act, inspired by Ralph Nader's expos of the automobile industry, *Unsafe at Any Speed* (1965). Johnson signed "preservation" legislation protecting America's wilderness and supported laws addressing environmental pollution.

Immigration Act of 1965: Law that abolished the national-origins quotas of the 1920s and transformed America's racial and ethnic kaleidoscope.

War on Poverty

At the heart of Johnson's Great Society was the **War on Poverty**, which included major legislation beginning in 1964. Johnson and other liberals believed that, in a time of affluence, the nation should use its resources to end "poverty, ignorance and hunger as intractable, permanent features of American society." (see Table 30.1).

War on Poverty: Name of campaign launched by Lyndon B. Johnson to bring the poor into mainstream society by promoting greater opportunity through public works and training programs.

Johnson's goal was "to offer the forgotten fifth of our people opportunity, not doles." Municipalities and school districts received billions of federal dollars to improve opportunities for the poverty-stricken, from preschoolers (Head Start) to high schoolers (Upward Bound) to young adults (Job Corps). The Model Cities program offered federal funds to upgrade employment, housing, education, and health in targeted urban neighborhoods, and Community Action Programs involved poor Americans in creating local grassroots antipoverty programs.

TABLE 30.1   Great Society Achievements, 1964–1966

	1964	1965	1966
Civil Rights	Civil Rights Act Equal Employment Commission Twenty-fourth Amendment	Voting Rights Act	
War on Poverty	Economic Opportunity Act Office of Economic Opportunity Job Corps Legal Services for the Poor VISTA		Model Cities
Education		Elementary and Secondary Education Act Head Start Upward Bound	
Environment		Water Quality Act Air Quality Act	Clean Water Restoration Act

New Government Agencies		Department of Housing and
		   Urban Development
		National Endowments for the
		   Arts and Humanities
			Department of Transportation

Other		Medicare and Medicaid Immigration and Nationality Act	

Note: The Great Society of the mid-1960s saw the biggest burst of reform legislation since the New Deal of the 1930s.

The Johnson administration also expanded the Food Stamp program and earmarked billions for constructing public housing and subsidizing rents. Two new federal programs guaranteed healthcare: **Medicare** for those sixty-five and older, and **Medicaid** for the poor. Finally, Aid to Families with Dependent Children (AFDC), the welfare program created during the New Deal, broadened benefits and eligibility.

The War on Poverty was controversial. Leftists believed that the government was doing too little to change structural inequality. Conservatives argued that Great Society programs created dependency among America's poor. Policy analysts noted that specific programs were ill conceived and badly implemented. Decades later, most historians judge the War on Poverty a mixed success. Its programs improved the quality of housing, healthcare, and nutrition available to the poor. Between 1965 and 1970, federal spending for Social Security, healthcare, welfare, and education more than doubled, with the number of Americans receiving food stamps increasing from 600,000 (in 1965) to 17 million in 1975. Poverty among the elderly fell from 40 percent in 1960 to 16 percent in 1974, due largely to increased Social Security benefits and Medicare. The War on Poverty improved many Americans' lives (see Figure 30.1).

But War on Poverty programs less successfully addressed the causes of poverty. Neither the Job Corps nor Community Action Programs showed significant results. Economic growth was primarily responsible for the dramatic decrease in poverty rates during the 1960s—from 22.4 percent of Americans in 1959 to 11 percent in 1973.

Political compromises created long-term problems. For example, Congress accommodated doctors and hospitals in its Medicare legislation by allowing federal reimbursements of hospitals' "reasonable costs" and doctors' "reasonable charges" in treating elderly patients. With no incentives for doctors or hospitals to hold prices down, national healthcare expenditures as a percentage of gross national product rose by almost 44 percent from 1960 to 1971. Problems aside, Johnson's Great Society was a moment in which many Americans believed they could and should solve the problems of poverty, disease, and discrimination.

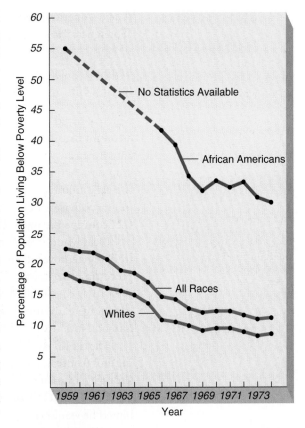

FIGURE 30.1
Poverty in America for Whites, African Americans, and All Races, 1959–1974
Because of rising levels of economic prosperity, combined with the impact of Great Society programs, the percentage of Americans living in poverty in 1974 was half as high as in 1959. African Americans still were far more likely than white Americans to be poor. In 1959, more than half of all blacks (55.1 percent) were poor; in 1974, the figure remained high (30.3 percent). The government did not record data on African American poverty for the years 1960 through 1965.
Source: © Cengage Learning

Medicare: Program created by President Johnson to provide government health insurance for those sixty-five and older.

Medicaid: Program created by President Johnson to provide health care for the poor.

Johnson and Vietnam

How did the war in Vietnam become Americanized?

In foreign policy, Johnson upheld ideas about U.S. superiority and the communist menace. International affairs had never much interested him, and he had little appreciation for foreign cultures. At the Taj Mahal in India, Johnson tested the monument's echo with a Texas cowboy yell. On a trip to Senegal, he ordered that an American bed, a special showerhead, and cases of Cutty Sark be sent with him. "Foreigners," Johnson quipped, only half-jokingly, "are not like the folks I am used to."

Kennedy's Legacy in Vietnam

Yet Johnson knew that foreign policy, especially regarding Vietnam, would demand his attention. Since the late 1950s, hostilities in Vietnam increased, as Ho Chi Minh's North assisted the Vietcong guerrillas in the South in reunifying the country under a communist government. President Kennedy increased aid to the Diem regime in Saigon, airdropped more raid teams into North Vietnam, and launched herbicide crop destruction to starve the Vietcong out of hiding. Kennedy also strengthened the U.S. military presence in South Vietnam: by 1963, more than sixteen thousand military advisers were there, some authorized to participate in combat alongside the U.S.-equipped Army of the Republic of Vietnam (ARVN).

Meanwhile, opposition to Diem's repressive regime increased. Peasants objected to being removed from their villages for their own safety, and Buddhist monks, protesting the Roman Catholic Diem's religious persecution, poured gasoline over their robes and ignited themselves in the streets of Saigon. Eventually U.S. officials encouraged ambitious South Vietnamese generals to remove Diem. They murdered him on November 1, 1963, just three weeks before Kennedy was killed.

The timing of Kennedy's assassination weeks later ensured that Vietnam would be the most controversial aspect of his legacy. He expanded U.S. involvement and approved a coup against Diem, but despite the urgings of top advisers, he refused to commit U.S. ground forces. Over time he became skeptical about South Vietnam's prospects and hinted he would end the U.S. commitment after winning reelection in 1964. What he would have done had he lived can never be known, but what seems clear is that Kennedy arrived in Dallas that fateful day uncertain about how to solve the Vietnam problem.

Tonkin Gulf Incident and Resolution

Lyndon Johnson, too, was unsure on Vietnam, wanting to do nothing there that could jeopardize his chances of winning the 1964 election. Yet Johnson also sought victory in the struggle, and throughout 1964 the administration secretly planned to expand the war to North Vietnam.

In early August 1964, U.S. destroyers reported coming under attack twice in three days from North Vietnamese patrol boats in the Gulf of Tonkin (see Map 30.1). Despite a lack of evidence that the second attack occurred, Johnson ordered retaliatory air strikes against North Vietnamese patrol boat bases and an oil depot. By a vote of 416 to 0 in the House and 88 to 2 in the Senate, Congress quickly passed the Gulf of Tonkin Resolution, giving the president the authority to "take all necessary measures to repel any armed attack against the forces of the United States and to prevent further aggression." In so doing, Congress essentially surrendered its war-making powers to the executive branch.

Decision for Escalation

President Johnson also appreciated how the Gulf of Tonkin affair boosted his public approval ratings and removed Vietnam as a campaign issue for GOP presidential nominee Barry Goldwater. On the ground in South Vietnam, however, the outlook remained grim. As the Vietcong made gains, U.S. officials secretly planned to escalate U.S. involvement.

In February 1965, in response to Vietcong attacks on U.S. installations in South Vietnam that killed thirty-two Americans, Johnson ordered Operation Rolling Thunder, a bombing program that continued, more or less uninterrupted, until

MAP 30.1

Southeast Asia and the Vietnam War

To prevent communists from coming to power in Vietnam, Cambodia, and Laos in the 1960s, the United States intervened massively in Southeast Asia. The interventions failed, and the remaining American troops made a hasty exit from Vietnam in 1975, when the victorious Vietcong and North Vietnamese took Saigon and renamed it Ho Chi Minh City

Source: Copyright © Cengage Learning

October 1968. On March 8, the first U.S. combat battalions came ashore near Danang. The North Vietnamese responded by increasing infiltration into the South. In Saigon, meanwhile, coups and countercoups by self-serving military leaders undermined U.S. efforts.

In July 1965, Johnson convened a series of high-level discussions about U.S. policy. Though the escalation of the war had by then already begun, these deliberations confirmed that America's commitment would be more or less open-ended. On July 28, Johnson publicly announced a significant troop increase, with others to follow. By the end of 1965, more than 180,000 U.S. ground troops were in South Vietnam. In 1966 the figure climbed to 385,000. In 1967 alone, U.S. warplanes flew 108,000 sorties and dropped 226,000 tons of bombs on North Vietnam. In 1968 U.S. troop strength reached 536,100. Each American escalation brought a new North Vietnamese escalation and increased assistance to Hanoi from the Soviet Union and China.

Opposition to Americanization

Rolling Thunder and the U.S. troop commitment Americanized the war, transforming it from a civil war between North and South into a U.S. war against the communist Hanoi government. In the key months of decision, Democratic leaders in the Senate, major newspapers such as the *New York Times* and the *Wall Street Journal,* and columnists such as Walter Lippmann warned against deepening involvement, as did Vice President Hubert H. Humphrey and Undersecretary of State George W. Ball. Virtually all of the United States's allies—including France, Britain, Canada, and Japan—cautioned against escalation and urged a political settlement. Remarkably, top U.S. officials knew that the odds of success were small but hoped new measures would cause Hanoi to end the insurgency in the South.

U.S. leaders feared that if the United States failed in Vietnam, other countries would find U.S. power less credible. The Soviets and Chinese would challenge U.S. interests elsewhere, and allied governments might conclude they could not depend on Washington. Johnson worried that failure in Vietnam would harm his domestic agenda and cause personal humiliation. As for the stated objective of helping a South Vietnamese ally repulse external aggression, that did not figure into the equation as much as it would have had the Saigon government—racked with infighting and possessing little popular support—done more in its own defense.

American Soldiers in Vietnam

To minimize publicity about the war, Johnson refused to call up reserve forces. This forced the military to rely heavily on the draft, which made Vietnam a young man's war—the average age of soldiers was twenty-two, compared with twenty-six in World War II. It also became a war of the poor and the working class. Through the years of heavy escalation (1965–1968), college students could get deferments, as could teachers and engineers. (In 1969, the draft was changed so that some students were called up through a lottery system.) The armed services recruited hard in poor communities, many of them heavily African American and Latino, advertising the military as an avenue of training and advancement; very often, the pitch worked. Once in uniform, those with fewer skills were far more likely to see combat, and hence to die.

Infantrymen maneuvered into thick jungles, where booby traps and land mines were a constant threat. Boots and human skin rotted from the rains, which alternated with the withering suns. The enemy was hard to find, often burrowed into elaborate underground tunnels or melded into the population, where any Vietnamese might be a Vietcong.

Larry Burrows/Getty Images

Wounded American soldiers after a battle in Vietnam.

The American forces fought well, and their entry helped stave off a South Vietnamese defeat, thereby achieving Americanization's most immediate and basic objective. But as the North Vietnamese matched each U.S. escalation with their own, the war became a stalemate. The U.S. commander, General William Westmoreland, mistakenly believed that a strategy of attrition represented the key to victory. Thus, the measure of success became the body count, the number of North Vietnamese and Vietcong corpses found after battle. But counts were manipulated by officers eager to demonstrate an operation's success. Worse, the U.S. reliance on massive military technology—including carpet bombing, napalm (jellied gasoline), and crop defoliants that destroyed forests—alienated many South Vietnamese and brought new recruits to the Vietcong.

Divisions at Home   As television coverage brought the war into homes nightly, the number of opponents grew. College professors and students organized debates and lectures on American policy, which became a form of protest, called "teach-ins" after the sit-ins of the civil rights movement. Pacifist groups, such as the American Friends Service Committee and the Women's International League for Peace and Freedom, organized early protests.

In early 1966, Senator William Fulbright held televised hearings on whether the national interest was served by the war. To the surprise of some, George F. Kennan testified that his containment doctrine was meant for Europe, not volatile Southeast Asia. America's "preoccupation" with Vietnam, Kennan asserted, was undermining its global obligations. The Fulbright hearings provoked Americans to think about the conflict and the nation's role in it and revealed deep divisions on Vietnam among public officials.

Defense secretary Robert McNamara, who championed the Americanization of the war in 1965, became increasingly troubled by the killing and bombing. In November 1965, he expressed skepticism that victory could ever be achieved. American credibility, far from being protected by the commitment, was suffering grievous damage, McNamara feared. But Johnson was determined to prevail in Vietnam. Although he occasionally halted the bombing to encourage Ho Chi Minh to negotiate (on America's terms), and to disarm critics, such pauses often were accompanied by increases in American troop strength. Ho steadfastly rejected American terms, which amounted to abandonment of his lifelong dream of an independent, unified Vietnam.

A Nation Divided

What were the hallmarks of the youth movement in the 1960s?

As Johnson struggled in Vietnam, his Great Society faced challenges at home. The United States was fracturing along many lines: black and white, youth and age, radical and conservative.

Urban Unrest

In 1964, shortly after President Johnson signed the landmark Civil Rights Act, racial violence erupted in northern cities. Angry Harlem residents took to the streets after a white police officer shot a black teenager. The following summer, in the predominantly black Watts section of Los Angeles, crowds burned, looted, and battled police for five days. The riot, which began when a white police officer attempted to arrest a black resident on suspicion of drunken driving, left thirty-four dead. In July 1967, twenty-six people were killed in street battles between African Americans and police and army troops in Newark, New Jersey. A week later, in Detroit, forty-three died as 3 square miles of the city went up in flames. In 1967 alone, there were 167 violent outbreaks in 128 cities.

The "long, hot summers" of urban unrest differed from previous race riots, which were typically started by whites. Here, black residents exploded in anger and frustration over the conditions of their lives. They looted and burned stores, most of them white-owned, while also devastating their own neighborhoods.

In 1968, the National Advisory Commission on Civil Disorders, chaired by Governor Otto Kerner of Illinois, warned that America was "moving towards two societies, one white, one black—separate and unequal," and blamed white racism for the riots. "What white Americans have never fully understood—but what the Negro can never forget—is that white society is deeply implicated in the ghetto. White institutions created it, white institutions maintain it, and white society condones it," concluded the Kerner Commission. Some white Americans disagreed, while others wondered why African Americans were venting their frustration just when they were making real progress in civil rights.

The answer stemmed partly from regional differences. The civil rights movement focused mostly on fighting *legal* disenfranchisement and discrimination in the South and largely ignored problems in the North. Increasingly concentrated in the deteriorating inner-city ghettos, most northern African Americans faced discrimination in housing, credit, and employment. The median income of northern African Americans was roughly half that of northern whites, and their unemployment rate was twice as high. Many northern African Americans had given up on the civil rights movement and the Great Society.

Black Power

In this climate, a new voice urged African Americans to seize freedom "by any means necessary." Malcolm X, a onetime pimp and street hustler who converted in prison to the Nation of Islam faith, offered African Americans new leadership. Members of the Nation of Islam, known as Black Muslims, espoused black pride and separatism from white society. Their faith combined traditional Islam with a belief that whites were subhuman devils whose race would soon be destroyed and emphasized sobriety, thrift, and social responsibility. By the early 1960s, Malcolm X had become the Black Muslims' chief spokesperson. But his murder in 1965 by members of the Nation of Islam who felt betrayed when he started his own, more racially tolerant organization, transformed Malcolm X into a powerful symbol of black defiance and self-respect.

A year after Malcolm X's death, Stokely Carmichael, SNCC chairman, denounced "the betrayal of black dreams by white America." To end white oppression, Carmichael proclaimed, blacks had to "stand up and take over" by electing black candidates, and organizing their own schools and institutions to embrace "**Black Power**." That year, SNCC expelled its white members and repudiated nonviolence and integration. CORE followed suit in 1967.

The best-known black radicals were the Black Panthers, an organization formed in Oakland, California, in 1966. Blending black separatism and revolutionary communism, the Panthers focused on destroying capitalism and its "military arm," the police. Male Panthers dressed in commando gear, carried weapons, and talked about killing "pigs" and did kill eleven police officers by 1970. Police responded in kind; most infamously, Chicago police murdered the local Panther leader Fred Hampton in his bed. However, the Panthers also worked to improve life in their neighborhoods by instituting free breakfast and healthcare programs for ghetto children, offering courses in African American history, and demanding jobs and housing. Before the end of the decade, a vocal minority of the United States's young would join in calls for revolution.

Black Power: Advocated in 1966 by SNCC president Stokley Carmichael; it advocated black nationalism, self-determination and greater militance as a means of self-defense.

Youth and Politics

By the mid-1960s, 41 percent of the American population was under age twenty. These young people spent more time with peers than any previous generation, as three-quarters of them graduated from high school (up from one-fifth in the 1920s) and almost half of them went to college (up from 16 percent in 1940). As this large baby-boom generation came of age, many believed they must provide democratic leadership for their nation. Inspired by the sit-in movement at black colleges, some white college students—from both political left and right—committed to changing the system.

In fall 1960, a group of conservative college students met at William F. Buckley's estate in Sharon, Connecticut, to form Young Americans for Freedom (YAF). Their manifesto, the Sharon Statement, endorsed Cold War anticommunism and a vision of limited government directly opposed to New Deal liberalism. The YAF planned to capture the Republican Party and move it to the political right; Goldwater's selection as the Republican candidate for president in 1964 demonstrated their early success.

Link to the Sharon Statement.

At the other end of the political spectrum, an emerging "New Left" also rejected liberalism. Whereas conservatives believed liberalism's activist government encroached on individual liberty, the New Left believed that liberalism was not enough to bring equality to all Americans. Meeting in Port Huron, Michigan, in 1962, founding members of Students for a Democratic Society (SDS) drafted their "Port Huron Statement," condemning racism, poverty in the midst of plenty, and

Link to the Port Huron Statement.

the Cold War. Calling for "participatory democracy," SDS sought to wrest power from the corporations, the military, and the politicians and return it to "the people."

Link to Mario Savio's "Machine" speech.

Free Speech Movement

The rise of activist white youth crystallized at the University of California, Berkeley. In the fall of 1964, the university administration banned political activity—including recruiting volunteers for civil rights work in Mississippi—from its traditional place along a university-owned sidewalk bordering the campus. When police tried to arrest a CORE worker who defied the order, four thousand students surrounded the police car. Berkeley graduate student and Mississippi Freedom Summer veteran Mario Savio encouraged the students: "You've got to put your bodies upon the levers...[and] you've got to indicate to the people who run it, to the people who own it, that unless you're free, the machine will be prevented from working at all."

Free Speech Movement (FSM): Coalition of student groups that insisted on the right to campus political activity. Began at the University of California, Berkeley.

Student political groups, left and right, united to create the **Free Speech Movement (FSM)**. The FSM won back the right to political speech, but not before state police had arrested almost eight hundred student protesters. Many saw the administration's actions as a failure of America's democratic promises, but the FSM also demonstrated to students their potential power. By decade's end, the activism born at Berkeley would spread to hundreds of colleges and universities.

Student Activism

Student protesters sought greater control over their education, demanding more relevant class offerings, more freedom in course selection, and a greater voice in the running of universities. Students protested against the doctrine of in loco parentis, which put universities legally "in the place of parents," allowing control over student behavior that went beyond the law. In loco parentis fell heaviest on women, who had strict curfew regulations called parietals, while men did not. Along with an end to sex discrimination, protesters like those at the University of Kansas wanted administrators to explain how statements that "college students are assumed to have maturity of judgment necessary for adult responsibility" squared with the minute regulation of students' nonacademic lives. One young man complained that "a high school dropout selling cabbage in a supermarket" had more rights and freedoms than successful university students.

Youth and the War in Vietnam

It was the war in Vietnam, however, that mobilized a nationwide student movement. Believing that learning and speaking out about issues was their civic duty, in 1965 university students and faculty held teach-ins about U.S. involvement in Vietnam. SDS sponsored the first major antiwar march that year, drawing twenty thousand protesters to Washington, D.C. On campuses everywhere, students borrowed civil rights movement tactics, picketing ROTC buildings and protesting military research and recruiting done on their campuses. Despite the antiwar protests' visibility, most students did not yet oppose the war: in 1967, only 30 percent of male students were **doves** on Vietnam, while 67 percent were **hawks**. But as the war escalated, more students distrusted the government as well as the seemingly arbitrary authority of university administrations.

doves: Term for opponents of American military involvement in Vietnam.

hawks: Term for those who supported American goals in the Vietnam War.

Youth Culture and the Counterculture

The large baby-boom generation changed the nation's culture more than its politics. Although many protested the war and marched for social justice, most did not.

Hundreds of thousands of young people came together for the Woodstock Music and Art Fair in August 1969. In its coverage, *Time* magazine warned adults that "the children of the welfare state and the atom bomb do indeed march to the beat of a different drummer, as well as to the tune of an electric guitarist," but the local sheriff called them "the nicest bunch of kids I've ever dealt with."

Fraternity and sorority life stayed strong even as radicalism flourished. And although there was some crossover, black, white, and Latino youth had different cultural styles, music, and clothes. Nonetheless, as potential consumers, young people exercised tremendous cultural authority and drove American popular culture in the late 1960s.

The most unifying element of youth culture was music. The Beatles captured American teenagers—73 million viewers watched their first television appearance on the Ed *Sullivan Show* in 1964. Bob Dylan promised revolutionary answers in "Blowin' in the Wind"; Janis Joplin brought the sexual power of the blues to white youth; James Brown and Aretha Franklin proclaimed black pride; and the psychedelic rock of Jefferson Airplane and the Grateful Dead—along with hallucinogenic drugs— redefined reality. At the Woodstock Festival in upstate New York in 1969, more than 400,000 people reveled in the music and a world of their own making, living in rain and mud for four days without shelter and without violence.

Some hoped to turn youth rebellion into social revolution, rejecting what they saw as hypocritical middle-class values. They crafted an alternative way of life, or **counterculture**, liberated from competitive materialism and celebrating pleasure. "Sex, drugs, and rock 'n' roll" became a mantra of sorts, offering these hippies

counterculture: Youth movement that promoted drugs, free love and an alternative way of life opposing what it saw as the materialism and conformity of mainstream American society.

Links to the World

The British Invasion

The British invasion began in earnest on February 7, 1964. Three thousand screaming American teenagers were waiting when Pan Am's *Yankee Clipper* touched down at Kennedy Airport with four British "moptops" aboard. "I Want to Hold Your Hand" was at the top of the U.S. charts, and the largest television audience in history watched the Beatles on the *Ed Sullivan Show* the following Sunday night.

Although the Beatles led the invasion, they did not conquer America alone. The Rolling Stones' first U.S. hit single also came in 1964. The Dave Clark Five appeared on *Ed Sullivan* eighteen times. And there were many others, Herman's Hermits, the Animals, the Yardbirds, the Hollies, the Kinks, and Petula Clark.

The British invasion was, at least partly, the triumphal return of American music, a transatlantic exchange that reinvigorated both nations. American rock 'n roll had lost much of its early energy by the early 1960s,

and the London-centered popular music industry was pumping out a saccharine version of American pop. But by the late 1950s, young musicians in England's provincial cities were listening to the music of African American bluesmen Muddy Waters and Howlin' Wolf; and the early rock 'n' roll of Buddy Holly and Chuck Berry. None of this music had a large audience in the United States, where *Billboard* magazine's number one hit for 1960 was Percy Faith's "Theme from *A Summer Place*" (a movie starring Sandra Dee and Troy Donahue).

Young British musicians, including John Lennon, Eric Clapton, and Mick Jagger, re-created American musical forms and reinvented rock 'n' roll. By the mid-1960s, the Beatles and the other British invasion bands were at the heart of a youth culture that transcended national boundaries. This music linked America's youth with young people throughout the world.

AP Images

The Beatles perform on the Ed Sullivan Show *in February 1964. Although Britain's Queen Mother thought the Beatles "young, fresh, and vital," American parents were appalled when the "long" Beatles haircut swept the nation.*

a path to a new consciousness. Many did the hard work of creating communes and intentional communities, whether in cities or in hidden stretches of the rural United States. Although the New Left criticized the counterculture as apolitical, many hippies did envision revolutionary change through mind-altering drugs, sex, or music.

The nascent counterculture first entered the national consciousness during summer 1967, when tens of thousands poured into the Haight-Ashbury district of San Francisco, the heart of the United States's psychedelic culture, for the summer of love. As an older generation of "straight" (or establishment) Americans watched with horror, white youth adopted countercultural ways. Coats and ties disappeared, as did stockings and bras. Young men grew long hair, and parents complained, "You can't tell the boys from the girls." Millions used marijuana or hallucinogenic drugs, read underground newspapers, and thought of themselves as alienated from straight culture even though as high school or college students, they were not completely dropping out.

Some of the most lasting cultural changes involved attitudes about sex. The mass media were fascinated with "free love," and while some people embraced promiscuous sexuality, more importantly, premarital sex no longer destroyed a woman's "reputation." The birth-control pill, widely available to single women by the late 1960s, greatly lessened the risk of unplanned pregnancy, and venereal diseases were easily cured by antibiotics. The number of couples living together increased 900 percent from 1960 to 1970. While many young people no longer hid that they were sexually active, 68 percent of American adults disapproved of premarital sex in 1969.

The adult generation that grew up in the hard decades of depression and war and saw middle-class respectability as crucial to success and stability did not understand. How could young people risk their futures by having sex without marriage, taking drugs, or protesting the war in Vietnam?

1968

What made 1968 distinctive?

By 1968, it seemed that the nation was coming apart. Divided over the war in Vietnam, frustrated by the slow pace of social change, or angry about racial violence, Americans faced the most serious domestic crisis of the postwar era.

The Tet Offensive

On January 31, 1968, the first day of the Vietnamese New Year (Tet), Vietcong and North Vietnamese forces struck South Vietnam, capturing provincial capitals (see Map 30.1). During the carefully planned offensive, the Saigon airport, the presidential palace, and the ARVN headquarters were attacked. U.S. and South Vietnamese units eventually regained control, inflicting heavy casualties and devastating villages.

Although the Tet Offensive was not the resounding battlefield victory its strategists sought, the heavy fighting called into question U.S. military leaders' predictions that the war would soon be won. Had not the Vietcong and North Vietnamese demonstrated that they could strike when and where they wished? If the United States's airpower, dollars, and half a million troops could not now defeat

Lyndon B. Johnson Presidential Library

Lyndon Johnson, 1968. The war in Vietnam gradually destroyed his presidency and divided the nation.

the Vietcong, could they ever do so? Top presidential advisers sounded notes of despair. Clark Clifford, the new secretary of defense, told Johnson the war could not be won, even with the 206,000 additional soldiers Westmoreland requested. Aware that the nation was suffering a financial crisis prompted by rampant deficit spending, Johnson's advisors knew that taking the initiative in Vietnam would cost billions more, further derail the budget, panic foreign owners of dollars, and wreck the economy.

Johnson's Exit

Controversy over the war split the Democratic Party, just as a presidential election loomed in November. Senator Eugene McCarthy of Minnesota and Robert F. Kennedy (now a senator from New York), both strong opponents of Johnson's war policies, forcefully challenged the president in early primaries. During a March 31 television address, Johnson announced a halt to most of the bombing, asked Hanoi to negotiate, and stunned listeners by withdrawing from the presidential race. His presidency had become a casualty of war. Peace talks began in May in Paris, but the war ground on.

Assassinations

Days after Johnson's shocking announcement, Martin Luther King Jr. was murdered in Memphis. It remains unclear why James Earl Ray, a white forty-year-old drifter and petty criminal, shot King or whether he acted alone. King had become an outspoken critic of the Vietnam War and of U.S. capitalism by 1968, and while some Americans hated what he stood for, most Americans mourned his death, and African American rage and grief exploded in 130 cities. The violence provoked a backlash from whites—primarily urban, working-class people who were had no sympathy for African Americans' increasing demands. In Chicago, Mayor Richard Daley ordered police to shoot rioters.

An already shaken nation watched in disbelief only two months later when antiwar Democratic presidential candidate Robert Kennedy was shot and killed after winning the California primary. His assassin, Sirhan Sirhan, an Arab nationalist, targeted Kennedy because he supported Israel.

Chicago Democratic National Convention

Violence erupted again in August at the Democratic National Convention in Chicago. Thousands of protesters converged on the city: students who'd gone Clean for Gene, cutting long hair and donning "respectable" clothes to campaign for antiwar candidate Eugene McCarthy; members of the United States's counterculture, drawn

The Immigration Act of 1965

When President Johnson signed the 1965 Immigration Act in a ceremony at the Statue of Liberty, he believed its importance was that it "repair[ed] a very deep and painful flaw in the fabric of American justice" by ending national-origins quotas that all but excluded "Polynesians, orientals, and Negroes." Nevertheless, the president mistakenly saw it as primarily symbolic. In fact, this act may have had greater long-term impact on Americans than any other Great Society legislation.

The 1965 Immigration Act ended blatant discrimination against potential immigrants from Asia, Africa, and Third World nations by substituting Eastern and Western Hemispheric "caps" for national quotas and allowing family reunification. The architects of the Immigration Act did not expect immigration to change, but world events decreed otherwise. Political instability, along with rapidly growing population in many poorer nations, created a large pool of potential immigrants who were drawn by U.S. prosperity.

By the 1990s, immigration accounted for almost 60 percent of America's population growth. By 2000, more Americans were foreign-born than at any time since the 1930s. The majority now came not from Europe but from Mexico, the Philippines, Vietnam, China, the Dominican Republic, Korea, India, the former USSR, Jamaica, and Iran.

More than two-thirds of the new immigrants settled in six states—New York, California, Florida, New Jersey, Illinois, and Texas—and later diversified other regions. By the late twentieth century, Spanish-language signs appeared in South Carolina, and Hmong farmers from the mountains of southeast Asia offered produce at the farmers' market in Missoula, Montana. The legacy of the 1965 Immigration Act was unintended but profound: the people and the nation are today more diverse than they otherwise would have been.

---

by the anarchist Yippies' promise of a Festival of Life to counter the Convention of Death; and antiwar groups. Mayor Daley assigned twelve thousand police to twelve-hour shifts and had twelve thousand army troops with bazookas, rifles, and flamethrowers as backup. Police attacked peaceful antiwar protesters and journalists. "The whole world is watching," chanted protesters, as police beat people.

Global Protest   Upheavals spread around the world that spring and summer. In France, university students protested rigid academic policies and the Vietnam War. They received support from French workers, who occupied factories and paralyzed public transport; the turmoil contributed to the collapse of Charles de Gaulle's government the following year. In Italy, Germany, England, Ireland, Sweden, Canada, Mexico, Chile, Japan, and South Korea, students held similar protests. In Czechoslovakia, hundreds of thousands of demonstrators flooded Prague streets, demanding democracy and an end to Soviet repression. This so-called Prague Spring developed into a full-scale national rebellion before being crushed by Soviet tanks.

Why so many uprisings occurred simultaneously is unclear. The postwar baby boom produced by the late 1960s a huge mass of young adults, many who grew up in relative prosperity with high expectations for the future. Technological advances allowed the nearly instantaneous transmittal of televised images worldwide, so protests in one country could readily inspire similar actions in others. Demonstrations might have occurred in any case, but news footage showing the wealthiest nation carpet bombing a poor country surely helped fuel the agitation.

Nixon's Election The presidential election of 1968 did little to heal the nation. Democratic nominee Hubert Humphrey, Johnson's vice president, seemed a continuation of old politics. Republican candidate Richard Nixon appealed to people tired of social unrest. He reached out to those he called "the great, quite forgotten majority—the nonshouters and the nondemonstrators." On Vietnam, Nixon vowed he would "end the war and win the peace." Governor George Wallace of Alabama, a segregationist who proposed using nuclear weapons on Vietnam, ran as a third-party candidate. Wallace carried five southern states, drawing almost 14 percent of the popular vote. Nixon won with slim margins. Divisions among Americans deepened.

Yet on Christmas Eve 1968—in a step toward fulfilling John Kennedy's pledge—*Apollo 8* entered lunar orbit. Looking down on a troubled world, the astronauts broadcast photographs of a fragile blue orb floating in darkness and read aloud the opening passages of Genesis, "In the beginning, God created the heaven and the earth…and God saw that it was good." Many listeners found themselves in tears.

Summary

The 1960s began with high hopes for a more democratic United States. Civil rights volunteers, often risking their lives, carried the quest for racial equality across the nation. The 1964 Civil Rights Act and the 1965 Voting Rights Act were major milestones. The United States was shaken by the assassination of President John Kennedy in 1963, but under President Johnson, the liberal vision of government working to improve citizens' lives inspired legislation designed to create a Great Society.

The Cold War between the United States and the USSR intensified during the 1960s, and the 1962 Cuban missile crisis almost brought nuclear war. Determined not to let Vietnam "fall" to communists, the United States sent military forces to prevent the victory of communist Vietnamese nationalists led by Ho Chi Minh. By 1968, there were more than half a million American ground troops in Vietnam, which divided Americans at home, undermined Great Society programs, and destroyed Lyndon Johnson's presidency.

Despite civil rights gains, many African Americans turned away from the movement, seeking more immediate change. Poor African American neighborhoods burned as riots spread nationwide. Vocal young people—and some of their elders—questioned whether democracy truly existed in the United States. Large numbers of the nation's white youth rebelled by embracing a "counterculture" that rejected white middle-class respectability. 1968 was a year of crisis, of assassinations and violence in the streets. The decade that started with promise ended in fierce political polarization.

Chapter Review

Kennedy and the Cold War

How was the Cuban missile crisis a watershed in U.S.–Soviet relations?

Tensions had long existed between the two super-powers, which both had nuclear weapons and disagreed over preconditions for peace and disarmament. In 1962, when the Soviets moved to place nuclear missiles in Cuba, 90 miles from the Florida coast, the U.S. and Soviet Union were on the brink of a nuclear disaster. Stressful negotiations between the two countries eventually led the Soviets to remove the missiles if the United States promised never to attack Cuba and remove missiles aimed at the Soviet Union from Turkey. The event forced both leaders to take small steps toward improving their relationship and operating with greater trust. In August 1963, they signed a treaty banning nuclear tests in the atmosphere, oceans, and outer space.

Marching for Freedom

What was Kennedy's reaction to growing civil rights activism?

President Kennedy was sympathetic to civil rights and recognized that U.S. racism damaged the nation's international reputation. But he also worried about alien-ating southern white Democrats in Congress. He kept their allegiance—and thwarted civil rights—by appointing segregationist judges to federal courts in the Deep South and held off signing an executive order forbidding segrega-tion in federally subsidized housing. He also permitted the FBI to harass civil rights leaders—Martin Luther King Jr. in particular—with wiretaps, surveillance, and efforts to dam-age their reputations. But continued African American activism and the often-violent responses of whites to actions such as the Freedom Rides and voter registration efforts—all of which were covered by national and interna-tional media—helped push Kennedy to finally and formally support the civil rights struggle. He ordered U.S. marshals to protect James Meredith, the first African American to attend the University of Mississippi, and in 1963, he asked Congress to pass a comprehensive civil rights bill.

Liberalism and the Great Society

What made the War on Poverty controversial?

As part of his Great Society programs, President Johnson believed he could use the nation's prosperity to end poverty once and for all. War on Poverty programs included public housing and subsidized rents, Medicare and Medicaid, Food Stamps, Head Start, Job Corps, and Community Action Programs to involve the poor in cre-ating antipoverty efforts. While a noble idea, the War on Poverty triggered intense reactions on both sides of the political spectrum. Those on the left felt the government had treated the surface-level problems resulting from poverty, without analyzing poverty's causes or address-ing the structural inequalities that caused it in the first place. Those on the right feared the programs would cre-ate dependency rather than inspire initiative among the poor. Analysts, too, thought many of the programs were poorly implemented.

Johnson and Vietnam

How did the war in Vietnam become Americanized?

In 1965, with the South Vietnamese govern-ment teetering on the brink of defeat, Lyndon Johnson dramatically expanded U.S. involvement in the conflict. Specifically, he launched Operation Rolling Thunder, a sustained bombing program that would last for three years, and he dispatched U.S. ground forces to the con-flict; by the end of the year, 180,000 U.S. troops were on the ground, and the number would reach more than half a million by 1968. As the U.S. presence in South Vietnam grew, so did that of North Vietnam, and so did the assistance to the North from the Soviet Union and China.

A Nation Divided

What were the hallmarks of the youth movement in the 1960s?

Whether via politics or culture, the baby boom generation of young Americans came of age determined to make a difference in shaping the future of the nation. Some were inspired by the civil rights movement. Many committed themselves to political change, both on the left and right. Conservative college students met in 1960 at William F. Buckley's family estate to form Young Americans for Freedom, with a goal of limited govern-ment and opposition to New Deal style liberalism. On the left, students who felt that liberalism had not gone far enough to bring equality to all Americans, founded the Students for a Democratic Society (SDS) in 1962.

Students protested a range of issues, from efforts to block free speech on campus to gender inequality and sexism to—most significantly—the Vietnam War. Other young Americans hoped to turn youth rebellion into social revolution, rejecting what they saw as hypocritical middle-class values. They crafted an alternative way of life, or counterculture, liberated from competitive materialism and celebrating pleasure and personal freedom.

1968

What made 1968 distinctive?

Around the world, 1968 was a year of violent protest and political disillusionment. In the United States, people became increasingly frustrated with the war in Vietnam, as the Tet Offensive demonstrated that the war's end was nowhere in sight.. Two national leaders—Martin Luther King and Robert Kennedy—were assassinated, dousing the hopes held by African Americans, political activists, and young voters for a different, more progressive America, and sparking violent protests in 130 cities. Demonstrations at the Democratic National Convention in Chicago turned violent, as police and army troops attacked peaceful antiwar protesters and journalists. Upheavals in

the U.S. spread worldwide. In France, students protested the war and rigid school policies, supported by workers who occupied factories and shut down public transportation. Within a year, similar student rebellions occurred in Italy, Germany, England, Ireland, Sweden, Canada, Mexico, Chile, Japan, and South Korea, while in Prague, Czechoslovakia, thousands of protesters demanded democracy and an end to Soviet repression, before their rebellion was crushed by Soviet tanks.

Suggestions for Further Reading

Beth Bailey, *Sex in the Heartland* (1999)
David Farber, *Chicago '68.* (1988)
Lawrence Freedman, *Kennedy's Wars: Berlin, Cuba, Laos, and Vietnam* (2000)
George C. Herring, *LBJ and Vietnam: A Different Kind of War* (1994)
Michael Kazin and Maurice Isserman, *America Divided: The Civil War of the 1960s* (1999)
Fredrik Logevall, *Choosing War: The Lost Chance for Peace and the Escalation of War in Vietnam* (1999)
Lisa McGirr, *Suburban Warriors: The Origins of the New American Right* (2001)
Charles Payne, *I've Got the Light of Freedom: The Organizing Tradition and the Mississippi Freedom Struggle* (1995)

 **CourseMate** Go to the CourseMate website for primary source links, study tools, and review materials for this chapter. www.cengagebrain.com

31

Continuing Divisions and New Limits

1969–1980

In 1969, Daniel Ellsberg was a thirty-eight-year-old former aide to Assistant Secretary of Defense John McNaughton. At the Pentagon, Ellsberg worked on a top-secret study of U.S. decision making in Vietnam. When he left office after Richard Nixon's election, Ellsberg accessed a copy of the study stored at the Rand Corporation, where he would resume his pregovernment research career. He spent six months poring over the seven thousand pages that comprised the Pentagon Papers.

Initially supportive of U.S. military intervention in Vietnam, Ellsberg had grown disillusioned. A Harvard-trained Ph.D., former marine officer, and Cold Warrior, he spent from 1965 to 1967 in South Vietnam, assessing the war's progress for his superiors in Washington. He went on combat patrols and interviewed military officials, U.S. diplomats, and Vietnamese leaders. The war, he concluded, was—in military, political, and moral respects—a lost enterprise.

Loyal to the president, Ellsberg was initially reluctant to act. But when in 1969 it became clear that Nixon had no intention of ending the war, Ellsberg boldly decided to risk imprisonment by making the Pentagon Papers public. The study, he believed, showed that presidents had escalated the American commitment in Vietnam despite pessimistic estimates from advisers—and that they had repeatedly lied to the public about their actions and the results. Ellsberg hoped disclosing this information would generate sufficient uproar to force a dramatic policy change.

Aided by a Rand colleague, Ellsberg surreptitiously photocopied the study, then spent months pleading with antiwar senators and representatives to release it. When they refused, he went to the press. On June 13, 1971, the *New York Times* published a front-page article on the Pentagon Papers. Other newspapers soon published excerpts, too.

Ellsberg's leak became controversial. Nixon tried to stop the papers' publication—among the first efforts to muzzle the press since the American Revolution—and to discredit Ellsberg and deter other leakers through the illegal actions of petty operatives. Many Americans saw Ellsberg as a hero who acted to shorten an illegitimate war. To others, he was a publicity-seeking traitor.

815

The 1970s would be, for Americans, a decade of division and limits. The chaos of 1968 continued in Nixon's early presidency. Antiwar sentiment became more extreme, and as government deceptions were exposed, Americans were increasingly divided over Vietnam. The movements for racial equality and social justice also became more radical by the early 1970s. Although some continued to work for racial integration, many embraced cultural nationalism and sought separatist cultures and societies. Even the women's movement, which won victories against sex discrimination in the 1970s, had a polarizing effect. Opponents, many of them women, understood feminism as an attack on their way of life and mobilized a conservative grassroots movement that would gain political importance in subsequent decades.

This divided America faced great challenges abroad. Richard Nixon and his national security adviser, Henry Kissinger, understood that the United States and the Soviet Union, weakened by the costs of their competition and challenged by other nations, faced a world where power was diffused. Accordingly, even as they stubbornly sought victory in Vietnam, Nixon and Kissinger sought improved relations with the People's Republic of China and the Soviet Union.

Ultimately, Richard Nixon's illegal acts in the political scandal known as "Watergate" shook the faith of Americans. By the time Nixon, under threat of impeachment, resigned, Americans were cynical about politics. Neither of Nixon's successors, Gerald Ford or Jimmy Carter, could restore that lost faith. Carter's presidency was undermined by international events beyond his control. In the Middle East—a region of increasing importance in U.S. foreign policy—Carter helped broker a peace between Egypt and Israel but proved powerless to end a lengthy hostage crisis in Iran. Meanwhile, the Soviet invasion of Afghanistan in 1979 revived Cold War tensions.

A deepening economic crisis added to Carter's woes. In the 1970s, middle-class Americans saw their savings disappearing to double-digit inflation and their jobs vanishing overnight. The downturn was largely caused by changes in the global economy and international trade, worsened by the oil embargo launched by Arab members of the Organization of Petroleum Exporting Countries in 1973. Americans realized their vulnerability to decisions made in far-off lands.

As you read this chapter, keep the following questions in mind:

* How did American foreign policy change as a result of involvement in Vietnam?

* Why did Americans see this era as an age of limits?

* Some historians describe the period between 1968 and 1980 as a time when many Americans lost faith—in their government, in the possibility of joining together in a society that offered equality to all, in the possibility of consensus instead of conflict. Do you agree, or were the struggles and divisions of this era similar to those of previous decades?

Chronology

1969	Stonewall Inn uprising begins gay liberation movement
	Apollo 11 Astronaut Neil Armstrong becomes first person to walk on moon's surface
	National Chicano Liberation Youth Conference held in Denver
	"Indians of All Tribes" occupy Alcatraz Island
	Nixon administration begins affirmative-action plan
1970	United States invades Cambodia
	Students at Kent State and Jackson State Universities shot by National Guard troops
	First Earth Day celebrated
	Environmental Protection Agency created
1971	Pentagon Papers published
1972	Nixon visits China and Soviet Union
	CREEP stages Watergate break-in
	Congress approves ERA and passes Title IX, which creates growth in women's athletics
1973	Peace agreement in Paris ends U.S. involvement in Vietnam
	OPEC increases oil prices, creating U.S. energy crisis

	Roe v. Wade legalizes abortion
	Agnew resigns; Ford named vice president
1974	Nixon resigns under threat of impeachment; Ford becomes president
1975	In deepening economic recession, unemployment hits 8.5 percent
	New York City saved from bankruptcy by federal loan guarantees
	Congress passes Indian Self-Determination and Education Assistance Act in response to Native American activists
1976	Carter elected president
1978	*Regents of the University of California v. Bakke* outlaws quotas but upholds affirmative action
	California voters approve Proposition 13
1979	Three Mile Island nuclear accident raises fears
	Camp David accords signed by Israel and Egypt
	American hostages seized in Iran
	Soviet Union invades Afghanistan
	Consumer debt doubles from 1975 to hit $315 billion

The New Politics of Identity

How did identity politics reshape political activism in the late 1960s and 1970s?

By the end of the 1960s, as divisions among Americans deepened, movements for social justice and racial equality became stronger, louder, and often more radical. The civil rights movement, begun in a quest for equality and integration, splintered, as many young African Americans rejected nonviolence and integration in favor of separatism, and embraced a distinct African American culture. Mexican Americans and Native Americans, inspired by the civil rights movement, created powerful "Brown Power" and "Red Power" movements by the early 1970s. They, too, demanded equal rights and cultural recognition. These movements fueled a new "identity politics," which saw group identity as the basis for political action and argued that social policy should be based on the needs, not of individuals, but of different identity-based groups.

African American Cultural Nationalism

By 1970, most African American activists no longer sought political power and racial justice by emphasizing the shared humanity of all people. Instead, they attracted a large following by highlighting the distinctiveness of black culture. Many African Americans, disillusioned by the racism that outlasted the end of legal segregation, believed that integration would mean subordination in a white-dominated society.

United Farm Workers leaders César Chávez and Dolores Huerta talk during the 1968 grape pickers' strike. The statue of the Virgin Mary, poster for presidential candidate Robert Kennedy, and photograph of Mahatma Gandhi suggest the guiding religious, political, and philosophical understandings of the movement.

Arthur Schatz/Time Life Pictures/Getty Images

In the early 1970s, though mainstream groups like the NAACP continued to seek equality through the courts and ballot boxes, many African Americans looked to culture rather than to narrow political action for social change. Rejecting current European American standards of beauty, young people let their hair grow into "naturals" and "Afros," claiming the power of black "soul." Seeking strength in their cultural heritage, black students and faculty fought successfully to create black studies departments in universities. African traditions were reclaimed—or sometimes invented. The new holiday Kwanzaa, created in 1966 by Maulana Karenga, a professor of black studies, celebrated African heritage.

Mexican American Activism

In 1970, the nation's 9 million Mexican Americans (4.3 percent of the United States's population) were concentrated in the Southwest and California. Although the federal census counted all Hispanics as white, discrimination in hiring, pay, housing, schools, and the courts was commonplace. Almost half of Mexican Americans were functionally illiterate, and in 1974, only 21 percent of Mexican American males graduated high school. Although more Mexican Americans were middle class, almost one-quarter remained below the poverty level in the 1970s.

The national Mexican American movement for social justice began with migrant farm workers. From 1965 to 1970, labor organizers **César Chávez** and Dolores Huerta led migrant workers in a strike (*huelga*) against large grape growers in California's San Joaquin Valley.

Chávez and the AFL-CIO–affiliated United Farm Workers (UFW) drew national attention to the working conditions of migrant laborers, who received as little as 10 cents an hour (the minimum wage in 1965 was $1.25) and were often lodged by employers in squalid housing without running water or indoor toilets. A national consumer boycott of table grapes brought the growers to the bargaining table, and in 1970 the UFW won better wages and working conditions. The union resembled nineteenth-century Mexican *mutualistas,* or cooperative associations. Its members founded cooperative groceries, a Spanish-language newspaper, and a theater group.

César Chávez: Labor leader who founded the United Farm Workers and was the driving force in creating the Latino civil rights movement of the 1960s and 1970s; he fused nonviolence (using boycotts, strikes and demonstrations) with the dignity of farm workers and of Hispanic heritage.

Chicano Movement

During the same period, in northern New Mexico, Reies Tijerina created the Alianza Federal de Mercedes (Federal Alliance of Grants). The group wanted the return of land it claimed belonged to local *hispano* villagers, whose ancestors occupied the territory before the United States annexed it under the 1848 Treaty of Guadalupe Hidalgo. In Denver, former boxer Rudolfo "Corky" Gonzáles drew more than one thousand Mexican Americans for the National Chicano Liberation Youth Conference in 1969. They adopted a manifesto, *El Plan Espiritual de Aztlan,* condemning the "brutal 'Gringo' invasion of our territories."

Link to *El Plan Espiritual de Aztlan.*

These young activists called for the liberation of *La Raza* (from *La Raza de Bronze,* "the brown people") from oppressive U.S. society, not for equal rights. They also rejected a hyphenated Mexican-American identity. The "Mexican American," they explained in *El Plan Espiritual de Aztlán,* "lacks respect for his culture." Instead, they called themselves Chicanos or Chicanas—barrio slang associated with *pachucos,* the hip, sometimes criminal young men who symbolized what "respectable" Mexican Americans despised.

Many middle-class and older Mexican Americans never embraced the term *Chicano* or the separatist, cultural agenda of *el movimiento.* Younger activists succeeded in introducing Chicano studies into local high school and college curricula and in creating a unifying cultural identity for Mexican American youth. La Raza Unida (RUP), a Southwest-based political party, registered tens of thousands of voters and won local elections. Although never as influential nationally as the African American civil rights movement, the Chicano movement effectively challenged discrimination locally and created a basis for political action.

Native American Activism

Between 1968 and 1975, Native American activists forced American society to hear their demands and to reform U.S. government policies toward native peoples. Young Native American activists were influenced by cultural nationalist beliefs. Seeking a return to the "old ways," they joined with "traditionalists" to challenge tribal leaders who advocated assimilation.

In November 1969, an activist group called Indians of All Tribes occupied Alcatraz Island in San Francisco Bay, demanding that the land be returned to native peoples for an Indian cultural center. The protest, which lasted nineteen months and involved more than four hundred people from fifty different tribes, marked the consolidation of pan-Indian activism, which claimed a shared "Indian" identity that transcended tribal differences. Although the protesters did not reclaim Alcatraz Island, they drew attention to the growing Red Power movement. In 1972, the radical U.S. Indian Movement occupied a Bureau of Indian Affairs office in Washington, D.C., and then in 1973 a trading post in Wounded Knee, South Dakota, where U.S. Army troops had massacred three hundred Sioux men, women, and children in 1890.

Link to photos from the 1969–1971 occupation of Alcatraz Island by Indians of All Tribes.

Meanwhile, moderate activists, working through such pan-tribal organizations as the National Congress of American Indians and the Native American Rights Fund, lobbied Congress for greater rights and resources to govern themselves. In response, Congress and the federal courts returned millions of acres of land, and in 1975 Congress passed the **Indian Self-Determination and Education Assistance Act**. Still, during the 1970s and 1980s, American Indians had a higher rate of tuberculosis, alcoholism, and suicide than any other group. Nine of ten lived in substandard housing, and unemployment approached 40 percent.

Indian Self-Determination and Education Assistance Act: 1975 act that granted Native American tribes control of federal aid programs on the reservations and oversight of their own schools.

Affirmative Action

As activists made Americans aware of inequality, policy-makers struggled to frame remedies. As early as 1965, President Johnson acknowledged the limits of civil rights legislation, calling for "not just legal equality...but equality as a fact and equality as a result." Johnson joined his belief that the federal government must help *individuals* attain competitive skills to a new concept: equality could be measured by *group* outcomes.

Practical issues helped shift emphasis to group outcomes. The 1964 Civil Rights Act outlawed discrimination but seemingly stipulated that action could be taken only when an employer "intentionally engaged" in discrimination against an individual. The tens of thousands of cases filed with the Equal Employment Opportunity Commission (EEOC) suggested a pervasive pattern of racial and sexual discrimination in education and employment, but each required proof of "intentional" actions against an individual. Some argued that it was possible, instead, to prove discrimination by "results"—by the relative number of African Americans or women an employer hired or promoted.

In 1969, the Nixon administration implemented the first major government affirmative action program. The Philadelphia Plan (so called because it targeted government contracts in that city) required businesses contracting with the federal government to show (in Nixon's words) "affirmative action to meet the goals of increasing minority employment" and set specific numerical "goals," or quotas, for employers. All major government contracts soon required affirmative action for women and racial and ethnic minorities, and many corporations and educational institutions began similar programs.

Supporters saw affirmative action as a remedy for the effects of past discrimination. Critics argued that creating proportional representation for women and minorities meant discrimination against others who had not created past discrimination and that group-based remedies violated the principle of judging individuals on their merits. As programs to bring members of underrepresented groups into college classrooms, law firms, and firehouses nationwide, a deepening recession made jobs scarce. Thus, increasing the number of minorities and women hired often meant reducing the number of white men, which triggered resentment.

The Women's Movement and Gay Liberation

What were the successes of the women's movement?

During the 1960s, a "second wave" of the American women's movement emerged, and by the 1970s mainstream and radical activists waged a multifront battle for "women's liberation." In 1963, the popularity of Betty Friedan's *The Feminine Mystique* signaled fuel for a revived women's movement. Writing as a housewife (though she had a long history of political activism), Friedan described "the problem with no name," the dissatisfaction of educated, middle-class wives and mothers like herself, who—looking at their homes and families—wondered guiltily if that was all there was to life. Instead of blaming women for failing to adapt to women's proper role, as 1950s magazines often did, Friedan blamed the role itself and the society that created it.

National Organization for Women (NOW): Women's rights organization founded in 1966 that lobbied for equal opportunity, filed lawsuits against gender discrimination, and mobilized public opinion against sexism.

Liberal and Radical Feminism

The organized, liberal wing of the women's movement emerged in 1966, with the founding of the **National Organization for Women** (NOW). Consisting primarily of educated, professional women, NOW began as a lobbying group seeking to pressure the EEOC to enforce the 1964 Civil Rights Act. (Racial discrimination was the EEOC's focus, and sex discrimination a low priority.) By 1970, NOW had one hundred chapters with more than three thousand members nationwide.

Another strand of the women's movement developed from the nation's increasingly radical social justice movements. Many women working for civil rights or against the Vietnam War were treated as second-class citizens, making coffee, not policy. As they analyzed inequality, these women recognized women's oppression. In 1968, a group of women protested the "degrading mindless-boob girlie symbol" represented by the Miss America Pageant in Atlantic City. Although nothing was burned, the pejorative term for feminists, *bra-burners*, came from this event, in which women threw items of "enslavement" (girdles, high heels, curlers, and bras) into a Freedom Trashcan.

Feminism was never a single set of beliefs. Most radical feminists, however, practiced "personal politics," believing, as feminist author Charlotte Bunch explained, that "there is no private domain of a person's life that is not political, and there is no political issue that is not ultimately personal." In the early 1970s, women meeting in suburban kitchens, college dorm rooms, and churches or synagogues created consciousness-raising groups, where they explored topics such as power relationships in marriage, sexuality, abortion, healthcare, work, and family.

Accomplishments of the Women's Movement

During the 1970s, the women's movement claimed significant achievements: the right of a married woman to obtain credit in her own name; the right of an unmarried woman to obtain birth control; the right of women to serve on juries; the end of sex-segregated help wanted ads. They challenged attitudes about rape that blamed the victim for the attack and established rape crisis centers, educated police and hospital officials about procedures for protecting rape survivors, and changed laws.

In 1971, the Boston Women's Health Collective published *Our Bodies, Ourselves* to help women understand and take charge of their sexual and reproductive health. Women who sought the right to safe and legal abortions won a major victory in 1973 when the Supreme Court, in a 7-to-2 decision on **Roe v. Wade**, ruled that privacy rights protected a woman's choice to end a pregnancy.

Women's organizations united to promote an **Equal Rights Amendment**, ending discrimination on the basis of sex, first proposed in the 1920s. On March 22, 1972, the Senate approved the amendment, which stated that "equality of rights under the law shall not be denied or abridged by the United States or by any State on account of sex" by a vote of 82 to 8. By the end of the year, 22 states (of the 38 necessary to amend the Constitution) ratified the ERA. Also in 1972, Congress passed Title IX of the Higher Education Act, which barred federal funds from colleges or universities that discriminated against women. Universities began channeling money to women's athletics, and women's participation in sports boomed.

Women's applications to graduate programs also boomed. In 1970, only 8.4 percent of medical school graduates and 5.4 percent of law school graduates were women. By 1979, those figures climbed to 23 percent and 28.5 percent respectively.

Roe v. Wade: 1973 Supreme Court ruling that privacy rights protected a woman's decision to end a pregnancy.

Equal Rights Amendment: Proposed constitutional amendment guaranteeing equal rights for women was passed with strong support of both Democrats and Republicans in Congress but fell short of ratification by the states by the 1982 deadline.

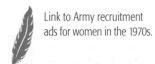

Link to Army recruitment ads for women in the 1970s.

The 1940s comic book heroine Wonder Woman appeared on the cover of *Ms.* magazine's first regular issue in July 1972. Wonder Woman represented feminist belief in "womanpower," but the choice of Wonder Woman had a practical justification as well: The main financial investor in *Ms.*, Warner Communications, was about to re-launch Wonder Woman comics.

Opposition to the Women's Movement

The women's movement met with powerful opposition, much of it from women. Many did not want equality if that meant giving up traditional gender roles in marriage or working at low-wage jobs. African and Hispanic American women, many of whom were active in movements for the liberation of their people and some of whom helped create second-wave feminism, often regarded feminism as a white movement that ignored their cultural traditions and diverted attention from the fight for racial equality.

Organized opposition to feminism came primarily from conservative, often religiously motivated men and women. As one conservative Christian writer claimed,

"The Bible clearly states that the wife is to submit to her husband's leadership." Such beliefs, along with fears about changing gender roles, fueled the STOP-ERA movement led by Phyllis Schlafly, a lawyer and conservative political activist. Schlafly attacked the women's movement as "a total assault on the role of the American woman as wife and mother." Schlafly's group argued that the ERA would decriminalize rape, force Americans to use unisex toilets, and make women subject to the military draft.

In fighting the ERA, tens of thousands of women became politically experienced; they fed a growing grassroots conservative movement that would blossom in the 1980s. By the mid-1970s, the STOP-ERA movement stalled the Equal Rights Amendment. Despite Congress's deadline extension, the amendment fell three states short of ratification and expired in 1982.

Gay Liberation

In the early 1970s, gay men and lesbians faced widespread discrimination. Consensual sexual intercourse between people of the same sex was illegal in almost every state, and until 1973 the American Psychiatric Association labeled homosexuality a mental disorder. Homosexual couples did not receive partnership benefits, such as health insurance; they not could adopt children. The issue of gay and lesbian rights divided even progressive organizations: in 1970, the New York City chapter of NOW expelled its lesbian officers. Gay men and lesbians could avoid harassment and discrimination by hiding their sexual identity, but that also made it difficult to organize politically.

There were small homophile organizations, such as the Mattachine Society and the Daughters of Bilitis, that worked for gay rights since the 1950s. But the symbolic beginning of the gay liberation movement came on June 28, 1969, when New York City police raided the Stonewall Inn, a gay bar in Greenwich Village, for violating a city law that made it illegal for more than three homosexual patrons to occupy a bar at the same time. That night, patrons stood up to the police, and hundreds joined them. The next morning, New Yorkers found a new slogan spray-painted on neighborhood walls: Gay Power.

Inspired by the Stonewall riot, some people worked openly and militantly for gay rights. They focused on legal equality and the promotion of Gay Pride. Some rejected the notion of fitting into straight (heterosexual) culture and created distinctive gay communities. By 1973, there were about eight hundred gay organizations in the United States. Centered in big cities and on college campuses, most organizations created supportive environments for gay men and lesbians to come out of the closet and push for reform. By decade's end, gay men and lesbians were a political force in cities including New York, Miami, and San Francisco.

The End in Vietnam

No issue divided Americans as pervasively as the Vietnam War. Although Richard Nixon said he was going to end the war fast, he did not. Like Johnson, he feared that a precipitous withdrawal would harm U.S. credibility on the world stage, as well as his own standing at home. Anxious to get American troops out of Vietnam, Nixon was equally committed to preserving an independent, noncommunist South Vietnam. Hence, he adopted a policy that at once contracted and expanded the war.

What kept Nixon from ending the Vietnam War as quickly as he had hoped?

Invasion of Cambodia   Nixon's policy centered on Vietnamization—building up South Vietnamese forces to replace U.S. forces. Accordingly, the president decreased U.S. troops from 543,000 in the spring of 1969 to 156,800 by the end of 1971, and to 60,000 by the fall of 1972. Vietnamization helped limit domestic dissent, but it did not end the stalemate in the Paris peace talks underway since 1968. Therefore, Nixon intensified the bombing of North Vietnam and enemy supply depots in neighboring Cambodia, hoping to pound Hanoi into concessions (see Map 30.1 on page 801).

The bombing of neutral Cambodia commenced in March 1969. For fourteen months, B-52 pilots flew 3,600 missions and dropped over 100,000 tons of bombs, initially in secret. When the North Vietnamese refused to buckle, Nixon turned up the heat: in April 1970, South Vietnamese and U.S. forces invaded Cambodia. The president announced publicly that he would not allow "the world's most powerful nation" to act "like a pitiful, helpless giant."

Protests and Counter-Demonstrations   Instantly, the antiwar movement emerged, as students on about 450 college campuses went out on strike and hundreds of thousands of demonstrators in various cities protested the administration's policies. The crisis atmosphere intensified on May 4, when National Guardsmen in Ohio fired into a crowd of fleeing students at Kent State University, killing 4 and wounding 11. Ten days later, police armed with automatic weapons blasted a women's dormitory at the historically black Jackson State University in Mississippi, killing 2 and wounding 9 students. Police claimed they had been shot at, but no such evidence could be found. Nixon's widening of the war sparked outrage, and in June the Senate terminated the 1964 Tonkin Gulf Resolution. After two months, U.S. troops withdrew from Cambodia.

Although a majority of Americans told pollsters they thought the original troop commitment to Vietnam was a mistake, 50 percent said they believed Nixon's claim that the Cambodia invasion would shorten the war, and some were angered by antiwar protests. In Washington, an "Honor America Day" program attracted more than 200,000 people who heard Billy Graham and Bob Hope laud administration policy. Nevertheless, the tumult over the invasion reduced Nixon's options on the war. Henceforth, solid majorities opposed any new missions for U.S. ground troops in Southeast Asia.

Morale Problems in the Military   Equally troubling, morale and discipline among troops was declining before Nixon took office. There were reports of drug addiction, desertion, racial discord, even the murder of unpopular officers by enlisted men (called fragging). The 1971 court-martial and conviction of Lieutenant William Calley, charged with overseeing the killing of more than three hundred unarmed South Vietnamese civilians in **My Lai** in 1968, got particular attention when an army photographer captured the horror in graphic pictures.

My Lai: South Vietnamese village and site of an intended search-and-destroy mission by U.S. soldiers that evolved into a brutal massacre of more than 300 unarmed civilians, including women and children; some were lined up in ditches and shot, with their village then burned to the ground.

Paris Peace Accords   The Nixon administration, meanwhile, stepped up efforts to pressure Hanoi into a settlement. When the North Vietnamese launched a major offensive into South Vietnam in March 1972, Nixon responded with a massive aerial onslaught. In December 1972, after an apparent peace agreement collapsed, the United States launched another air strike on the North—the so-called Christmas bombing.

A diplomatic agreement was close. Months earlier, Kissinger and his North Vietnamese counterpart, Le Duc Tho, resolved many outstanding issues. Notably, Kissinger agreed that North Vietnamese troops could remain in the South after the settlement, while Tho abandoned Hanoi's insistence that the Saigon government of Nguyen Van Thieu be removed. On January 27, 1973, Kissinger and Le Duc Tho signed a cease-fire agreement, and Nixon compelled a reluctant Thieu to accept it by threatening to cut off U.S. aid. The United States promised to withdraw its troops within sixty days. North Vietnamese troops could stay in South Vietnam, and a coalition government that included the Vietcong would be formed in the South.

The United States pulled its troops out of Vietnam, leaving behind some military advisers. Soon, full-scale war erupted again. Just before the South Vietnamese surrendered, hundreds of Americans and Vietnamese who worked for them were hastily evacuated from Saigon. On April 29, 1975, the South Vietnamese government collapsed, and Vietnam was reunified under a communist government in Hanoi. Saigon was renamed Ho Chi Minh City for the persevering patriot who died in 1969.

Costs of the Vietnam War

More than 58,000 Americans and between 1.5 and 2 million Vietnamese died in the war. Civilian deaths in Cambodia and Laos reached hundreds of thousands. The war cost the United States at least $170 billion, and billions more in subsequent veterans' benefits. Money spent on the war was unavailable for domestic programs. The nation suffered inflation, political schism, and abuses of executive power. The war also delayed accommodation with the Soviet Union and the People's Republic of China, fueled friction with allies, and alienated Third World nations.

In 1975, communists established repressive governments in Vietnam, Cambodia, and Laos, but beyond Indochina the domino effect once predicted by U.S. officials never occurred. Acute hunger afflicted the people of those devastated lands. Soon refugees—boat people—crowded aboard unsafe vessels to escape. Many emigrated to the United States, where they were received with mixed feelings by Americans reluctant to be reminded of defeat and their responsibility for the plight of the southeast Asian peoples.

Debate over the Lessons of Vietnam

Americans seemed angry and confused about the war. Hawkish observers claimed that failure in Vietnam undermined the nation's credibility. They pointed to a "Vietnam syndrome"—an American suspicion of foreign entanglements—which they feared would inhibit the future exercise of U.S. power. America lost in Vietnam, they asserted, because Americans lost their guts at home.

Dovish analysts, meanwhile, blamed the war on an imperial presidency that permitted strong-willed men to act without restraint and on a weak Congress that conceded too much power to the executive branch. Make the president adhere to the checks-and-balances system—make him go to Congress for a declaration of war—these critics counseled. This view found expression in the War Powers Act of 1973, which limited the president's warmaking freedom and required Congressional approval before committing U.S. forces to combat lasting more than sixty days.

The Image of War

The Vietnam War has been called the first "television war." More than ever before (or arguably since) news clips and photos brought Americans and others around the world face-to-face with the fighting and its victims. On June 8, 1972, as children and their families fled the village of Trang Bang, their bodies seared by napalm, Huynh Cong "Nick" Ut took this iconic photograph that became an antiwar rallying point and symbol of hope. The girl in the center, Phan Thi Kim Phuc, survived the attack but had to endure fourteen months of painful rehabilitation to treat the third-degree burns that covered more than half of her body. Kim later became a Canadian citizen and a Goodwill Ambassador for the United Nations Educational, Scientific and Cultural Organization (UNESCO). Some analysts have argued that a single image can become the voice of popular protest; others say that even indelible images such as this one cannot have that power. What do you think?

AP Images/Huynh Cong 'Nick' Ut

Vietnam Veterans Veterans' calls for help in dealing with posttraumatic stress disorder, which afflicted thousands of the 2.8 million Vietnam veterans, stimulated public discussion. Doctors reported that the disorder, which included nightmares and extreme nervousness, stemmed from soldiers having seen many children, women, and elderly killed. Some GIs inadvertently killed these people; some killed them vengefully and later felt guilt. Other veterans publicized their deteriorating health from the defoliant Agent Orange and other herbicides they handled or were accidentally sprayed with in Vietnam.

Nixon, Kissinger, and the World

The difficulties of the Vietnam war signified to Nixon and Kissinger that American power was limited and, in relative terms, in decline. This reality necessitated a new approach to the Cold War. In particular, they believed the United States had to adapt to a new, multipolar international system no longer defined by the Soviet-American rivalry. Western Europe was becoming a major player in its own right, as was Japan. The Middle East loomed increasingly large, due largely to America's growing dependence on oil. Mostly, Americans had to come to grips with China by rethinking its policy of hostile isolation.

> How did the Vietnam War influence Nixon's approach to foreign policy?

They were an unlikely duo—the reclusive, ambitious Californian, born of Quaker parents, and the sociable Jewish intellectual who fled Nazi Germany as a child. Nixon, ten years older, was a career politician, while Kissinger made his name as a Harvard professor and foreign policy consultant. What the two men shared was a paranoia about rivals and a capacity to think in broad conceptual terms about America's place in the world.

Nixon Doctrine In July 1969, Nixon and Kissinger acknowledged the limits of American power and resources in the Nixon Doctrine. The United States, they said, would provide economic aid to allies, but these allies should not count on American troops. Washington could not afford to sustain its overseas commitments and would have to rely on regional allies—including authoritarian regimes—to maintain an anticommunist world order. Nixon's doctrine partially retreated from the 1947 Truman Doctrine's promise to support noncommunist governments facing threats.

Détente The other pillar of the new foreign policy was **détente**: measured cooperation with the Soviets through negotiations within an environment of rivalry. Détente's primary purpose, like that of containment, was to check Soviet expansion and limit the Soviet arms buildup, but through diplomacy and mutual concessions. The second part of the strategy sought to curb revolution and radicalism in the Third World and quash threats to U.S. interests. Specifically, expanded trade with friendlier Soviets and Chinese might reduce the huge U.S. balance-of-payments deficit. Improving relations with both communist giants, when Sino-Soviet tensions were increasing, might weaken communism.

détente Nixon's foreign policy initiative with the Soviet Union; it focused on mutual cooperation and sought to check expansion and reduce arms buildup through diplomacy and negotiation.

The Soviet Union, too, found that the Cold War drained its resources, with defense needs and consumer demands at odds. Improved ties with Washington would also allow the USSR to focus on its increasingly fractious relations with China and might generate progress on outstanding European issues, including the status of Germany and Berlin. In May 1972, the United States and the USSR agreed in the ABM Treaty (officially the Treaty on the Limitation of Anti-Ballistic Missile Systems) to slow the arms race by limiting intercontinental ballistic missiles and antiballistic missile defenses.

Opening to China　　Meanwhile, the United States took dramatic steps to end two decades of Sino-American hostility. The Chinese wanted to spur trade and hoped that friendlier Sino-American relations would make their onetime ally and now enemy, the Soviet Union, more cautious. In early 1972, Nixon made a historic trip to Red China, where he and the venerable Chinese leaders Mao Zedong and Zhou Enlai agreed to disagree on many issues, except one: the Soviet Union should not be permitted to make gains in Asia. Sino-American relations improved slightly, and official diplomatic recognition came in 1979.

The opening to communist China and the policy of détente with the Soviet Union reflected Nixon's and Kissinger's belief in the importance of maintaining stability among the great powers. In the Third World, too, they sought stability, though there they hoped to get it by maintaining the status quo. As it happened, events in the Third World would provide the Nixon-Kissinger approach with its greatest test.

This was the week that changed the world, " Richard Nixon said of his visit to China in February 1972. Many historians agree and consider the China opening Nixon's greatest achievement as president. When he and wife Pat visited the Great Wall the president reportedly remarked: "This is a great wall."

OPEC and the 1973 Oil Embargo

I f one date can mark the decline of American power in the Cold War era and the arrival of Arab nations on the world stage, it would be October 20, 1973. That day, the Arab members of the Organization of Petroleum Exporting Countries (OPEC)—Saudi Arabia, Iraq, Kuwait, Libya, and Algeria—imposed an embargo on oil shipments to the United States and other Israeli allies. The move was in retaliation against U.S. support of Israel in the two-week-old Yom Kippur War. The embargo followed an OPEC price hike days earlier from $3.01 to $5.12 per barrel. In December, the five Arab countries, joined by Iran, raised prices again, to $11.65 per barrel, almost a fourfold increase from early October.

Gasoline prices surged across America, and some dealers ran low on supplies. Americans endured endless lines at the pumps and shivered in underheated homes. When the embargo ended in March 1974, oil prices stayed high, and the aftereffects of the embargo would linger through the decade. It confirmed how much America's economic destiny was beyond its control.

Just twenty years before, in the early 1950s, Americans produced at home all the oil they needed. By the early 1960s, the picture changed, as Americans depended on foreign sources for one of every six barrels of oil they used. As author Daniel Yergin has put it, "The shortfall struck at fundamental beliefs in the endless abundance of resources... that a large part of the public did not even know, up until October 1973, that the United States imported any oil at all."

When the embargo ended, Americans resumed their wastefulness, but in a changed world the United States had become a dependent nation, its economic future linked to decisions by Arab leaders half a world away.

In 1976, OPEC sharply raised the price of oil a second time, prompting this editorial cartoon by Don Wright of the Miami News.

Wars in the Middle East

In the Middle East, the situation grew more volatile after the Arab-Israeli Six-Day War in 1967. Israel scored victories against Egypt and Syria, seizing the Sinai Peninsula and the Gaza Strip from Egypt, the West Bank and East Jerusalem from Jordan, and the Golan Heights from Syria (see Map 33.1). Israel gained 28,000 square miles and could henceforth defend itself against invading forces. But with Gaza and the West Bank as the ancestral home to hundreds of thousands of Palestinians (see Chapter 28), Israel found itself governing people who wanted to see it destroyed. When the Israelis established Jewish settlements in their newly won areas, Arab resentment grew. Terrorists associated with the Palestinian Liberation Organization (PLO) made hit-and-run raids on Jewish settlements, hijacked jetliners, and murdered Israeli athletes at the 1972 Olympic Games in Munich, West Germany. The Israelis retaliated by assassinating PLO leaders.

In October 1973, on the Jewish High Holy Day of Yom Kippur, Egypt and Syria attacked Israel, primarily seeking revenge for the 1967 defeat. Surprised, Israel reeled before launching an effective effective counteroffensive against Soviet-armed Egyptian forces in the Sinai. To punish Americans for their pro-Israel stance, the Organization of Petroleum Exporting Countries (OPEC), a group of mostly Arab nations that united to raise oil prices, embargoed oil shipments to the United States and other Israeli supporters. An energy crisis rocked the nation. Kissinger arranged a cease-fire in the war, but OPEC did not lift the oil embargo until March 1974. The next year, Kissinger persuaded Egypt and Israel to accept a U.N. peacekeeping force in the Sinai. But Arabs still vowed to destroy Israel, and Israelis built more Jewish settlements in occupied lands.

Antiradicalism in Latin America and Africa

In Latin America, meanwhile, the Nixon administration sought to thwart radical leftist challenges to authoritarian rule. In Chile, after voters in 1970 elected a Marxist president, Salvador Allende, the CIA secretly encouraged military officers to stage a coup. In 1973, a military junta ousted Allende and installed an authoritarian regime under General Augusto Pinochet. (Allende was subsequently murdered.) Washington publicly denied any role.

In Africa, too, Washington preferred the status quo, backing the white-minority regime in Rhodesia (now Zimbabwe) and activating the CIA in a failed effort to defeat a Soviet- and Cuban-backed faction in Angola's civil war. In South Africa, Nixon tolerated the white rulers who imposed segregationist apartheid on blacks and mixed-race "coloureds" (85 percent of the population), keeping them poor, disfranchised, and ghettoized in prisonlike townships. After the leftist government assumed power in Angola, however, Washington paid attention to the rest of Africa, building economic ties and sending arms to friendly black nations, such as Kenya and the Congo, while distancing the United States from the white governments of Rhodesia and South Africa.

Presidential Politics and the Crisis of Leadership

How did Watergate bring down the Nixon administration?

Nixon's foreign policy accomplishments were overshadowed by domestic failures. He betrayed the public trust and broke laws. That, combined with Americans' belief that their leaders had lied repeatedly about the war in Vietnam, shook Americans' faith in government. This new mistrust joined with conservatives' traditional suspicion of big, activist government to create a crisis of leadership and undermine liberal policies that governed the nation since the New Deal. Suspicion of the government, exacerbated by Watergate, would limit what Nixon's successors, Gerald Ford and Jimmy Carter, could accomplish.

Nixon's Domestic Agenda

Richard Nixon was brilliant, politically cunning, yet also crude, prejudiced against Jews and African Americans, happy to use dirty tricks and presidential power against his enemies, and driven by a resentment that bordered on paranoia. The son of a grocer from an agricultural region of southern California, Nixon loathed the liberal establishment, which loathed him back, and his presidency was driven by that as much as by strong philosophical commitment to conservative principles.

Any of Nixon's domestic policy initiatives seemed liberal. The Nixon administration pioneered affirmative action. It doubled the budgets of the new National Endowment for the Humanities (NEH) and National Endowment for the Arts (NEA). Nixon supported the ERA, signed major environmental legislation, created the Occupational Safety and Health Administration (OSHA), used deficit spending to manage the economy, and proposed a guaranteed minimum income for all Americans.

Yet, Nixon pursued a conservative agenda that involved devolution, shifting federal government authority to states and localities. He promoted revenue-sharing programs that distributed federal funds back to the states, thus appealing to those who saw high taxes as supporting liberal giveaway programs for poor and minority Americans. Nixon worked to equate the Republican Party with law and order and the Democrats with permissiveness, crime, drugs, radicalism, and the hippie lifestyle. He used his outspoken vice president, Spiro Agnew, to attack war protesters as "naughty children." He appointed four conservative justices to the Supreme Court: Warren Burger, Harry Blackmun, Lewis Powell Jr., and William Rehnquist.

Determining whether Nixon was liberal, conservative, or simply pragmatic is complicated. For example, when the Nixon administration proposed a guaranteed minimum income for all Americans, his larger goal was to dismantle the welfare system and its liberal bureaucracy of social workers. And though Nixon doubled NEA funding, he redirected awards from the northeastern art establishment—the "elite" that he considered an enemy—toward local and regional art groups.

Nixon additionally sought to attract white southerners to the Republican Party. He nominated two southerners to the Supreme Court—one of whom had a segregationist record. When Congress declined to confirm either nominee, Nixon protested angrily. After the Supreme Court upheld a school desegregation plan requiring a highly segregated North Carolina school system to achieve racial integration by busing both black and white children throughout the county (*Swann v. Charlotte-Mecklenburg*, 1971), Nixon denounced busing. (Resistance to busing was not purely southern, as Boston residents protested—sometimes violently—court-ordered busing to combat school segregation in 1974.)

Enemies and Dirty Tricks

Nixon was almost sure of reelection in 1972. His Democratic opponent was **George McGovern**, a progressive senator from South Dakota and strong opponent of the Vietnam War, who appealed to the left. Alabama governor George Wallace, running on a third-party ticket, withdrew after an assassination attempt left him paralyzed. The Nixon campaign, however, took no chances. On June 17, five men from the

George McGovern: Liberal Senator from South Dakota and Democratic candidate for president in 1972.

Committee to Re-elect the President, or CREEP were caught breaking into Democratic National Committee offices at the Watergate complex in Washington, D.C. The break-in got little attention, and Nixon swept into office in November with 60 percent of the popular vote. McGovern carried only Massachusetts and the District of Columbia. But as Nixon triumphed, his downfall had begun.

From the beginning of his presidency, Nixon obsessively believed he was surrounded by enemies. On Nixon's order, his aide Charles Colson formed a secret group called "the Plumbers." Their first job was to break into the office of the psychiatrist treating Daniel Ellsberg, the former Pentagon employee who made the **Pentagon Papers** public, looking for material to discredit him. During the 1972 presidential campaign, the Plumbers bugged phones, infiltrated campaign staffs, and wrote anonymous letters falsely accusing Democratic candidates of sexual misconduct. They were going back to plant more surveillance equipment at the Democratic National Committee offices when they were caught by the D.C. police at the Watergate complex.

Pentagon Papers: 47-volume U.S. government study from the end of WW II to the Vietnam War, and tracing U.S. involvement in Southeast Asia. Released to the press by former Pentagon employee Daniel Ellsberg, they revealed military mistakes and a long history of White House lies to Congress, foreign leaders and the American people.

Link to "The Watergate Files" from the Ford Library and Museum.

Watergate Cover-Up and Investigation

Nixon was not directly involved in the Watergate affair. But instead of distancing himself and firing those responsible, he covered up their connection to the break-ins. He had the CIA stop the FBI's investigation, claiming it imperiled national security. At this point, Nixon obstructed justice—a felony and an impeachable crime—but he also halted the investigation. However, two relatively unknown reporters for the *Washington Post,* Carl Bernstein and Bob Woodward, stayed on the story. Aided by an anonymous, highly placed government official whom they code-named Deep Throat (the title of a notorious 1972 X-rated film), they followed a money trail leading straight to the White House. (W. Mark Felt, second in command at the FBI in the early 1970s, identified himself as Watergate's Deep Throat in 2005.)

From May to August 1973, the Senate held televised public hearings on the Watergate affair. White House Counsel John Dean, fearful that he was becoming the fall guy for the Watergate fiasco, gave damning testimony. On July 13, a White House aide told the Senate Committee that Nixon regularly recorded his conversations in the Oval Office. Nixon refused to turn the tapes over to Congress.

Link to *The Washington Post's* collection of Nixon's White House tapes.

Impeachment and Resignation

Nixon faced scandals on other fronts. In October 1973, Vice President Spiro Agnew resigned, following charges that he accepted bribes while governor of Maryland. Nixon appointed and Congress approved Michigan's **Gerald Ford**, the House minority leader, as Agnew's replacement. Meanwhile, Nixon's staff was increasingly concerned about his excessive drinking and seeming mental instability. Then, on October 24, 1973, the House of Representatives began impeachment proceedings.

Gerald Ford: Michigan Congressman who took the place of Vice President Spiro Agnew when Agnew resigned following charges of corruption. Ford became the 38th president of the nation when Nixon resigned in 1974.

Under court order, Nixon released edited portions of the Oval Office tapes. Although the first tapes revealed nothing criminal, the public was shocked by Nixon's obscenities and racist slurs. In July 1974, the Supreme Court ruled that Nixon must release all the tapes. Despite erasures on two key tapes, the House Judiciary Committee found evidence to impeach Nixon on three grounds: obstruction of justice, abuse of power, and contempt of Congress. On August 9, 1974, facing certain impeachment and conviction, Richard Nixon became the first president of the United States to resign.

The Watergate scandal shook Americans' confidence in government. It also prompted Congress to pass several bills aimed at restricting presidential power, including the War Powers Act.

Ford's Presidency

Gerald Ford, the nation's first unelected president, faced a cynical nation. The presidency was discredited. The economy was in decline. Ford was an honorable man who tried to end the long national nightmare. But when he issued a full pardon to Richard Nixon, his approval ratings plummeted from 71 to 41 percent.

Ford accomplished little domestically during his two and a half years in office. The Democrats gained a large margin in the 1974 congressional elections, and after Watergate, Congress was willing to exercise its power. Ford almost routinely vetoed its bills—thirty-nine in one year—but Congress often overrode his veto. Ford was often portrayed as a buffoon and klutz in political cartoons, comedy monologs, and on the new hit television show *Saturday Night Live*. Ford caught the fallout of disrespect that Nixon's actions had unleashed. No longer would respect for the presidency prevent the media from reporting presidential stumbles or misconduct.

Carter as "Outside" President

Jimmy Carter, who was elected in 1976 by a slim margin, initially benefited from Americans' suspicion of politicians. Carter was a one-term Georgia governor, one of the new southern leaders committed to racial equality. He grew up on his family's peanut farm in rural Plains, Georgia, graduated from the Naval Academy, then served as an engineer in the navy's nuclear submarine program. Carter, a born-again Christian, promised Americans, "I will never lie to you."

Jimmy Carter: 39th President of the United States (1977–1981).

From his inauguration, when he broke with the convention of a motorcade and walked down Pennsylvania Avenue holding hands with his wife and close adviser, Rosalynn, and their daughter, Amy, Carter emphasized his populist, outsider appeal. But that status proved problematic as president. Though an astute policymaker, he scorned the deal-making that was necessary to pass legislation in Congress.

Carter faced problems that would have challenged any leader: continued economic decline, unabated energy shortages, and public distrust of government. More than any other postwar U.S. leader, Carter was willing to tell Americans things they did not want to hear. As shortages of natural gas forced schools and businesses to close during the bitterly cold winter of 1977, Carter, wearing a cardigan sweater, called for sacrifice and implemented energy conservation measures at government buildings. In the defining speech of his presidency, Carter told Americans that the nation suffered from a crisis of the spirit. He talked about the false lures of self-indulgence and consumption. He called for a "new commitment to the path of common purpose." But he offered few solutions for the national malaise.

Carter eased burdensome government regulations without destroying consumer and worker safeguards and created the Departments of Energy and Education. He also established a $1.6 billion "superfund" to clean up abandoned chemical-waste sites and placed more than 100 million acres of Alaskan land under federal protection as national parks, forests, and wildlife refuges.

Economic Crisis

What were the long-term effects
of the 1970s recession?

Since World War II, except for a few brief downturns, prosperity dominated American life. Prosperity made possible the great liberal initiatives of the 1960s and improved the lives of America's poor and elderly. But in the early 1970s, that long period of economic expansion ended. In 1974 alone, the gross national product dropped 2 percentage points. Industrial production fell 9 percent. Inflation—the increase in costs of goods and services—skyrocketed, and unemployment grew.

Stagflation and Its Causes

Throughout most of the 1970s, the U.S. economy floundered in what economists dubbed "stagflation": a stagnant economy characterized by high unemployment combined with out-of-control inflation. Stagflation was almost impossible to manage with traditional economic remedies. When the federal government increased spending to stimulate the economy and reduce unemployment, inflation grew. When it tried to control inflation by cutting government spending or tightening money supply, the recession deepened and unemployment escalated.

The causes of the economic crisis were complex. President Johnson created inflationary pressure by waging an expensive war in Vietnam while greatly expanding domestic spending in his Great Society programs. But fundamental problems also came from the United States' changing role in the global economy. By the early 1970s, both of the United States's wartime adversaries, Japan and Germany, had become major economic powers and competitors in global trade that the United States once dominated. In 1971, for the first time since the nineteenth century, the United States imported more than it exported, beginning an era of U.S. trade deficits.

Corporate actions also contributed to the growing trade imbalance. During the years of global dominance, few U.S. companies improved production techniques or educated workers. Consequently, U.S. productivity—the average output of goods per hour of labor—declined. But wages rarely did. The combination of falling productivity and high labor costs meant that U.S. goods became increasingly expensive. Worse, U.S. companies allowed the quality of their goods to decline. From 1966 to 1973, for example, U.S. car and truck manufacturers recalled almost 30 million vehicles because of serious defects.

The United States's global economic vulnerability was driven home by the energy crisis in 1973. The country depended on imported oil for almost one-third of its energy. When OPEC cut off shipments to the United States, prices rose 350 percent and increased heating costs, shipping costs, and manufacturing costs, as well as the cost of goods and services. Inflation jumped from 3 percent in 1973 to 11 percent in 1974. Sales of gas-guzzling U.S. cars plummeted as people switched to energy-efficient subcompacts from Japan and Europe. GM laid off 6 percent of its domestic work force and put larger numbers on rolling unpaid leaves. As the ailing automobile industry quit buying steel, glass, and rubber, manufacturers of these goods laid off workers, too.

Attempts to Fix the Economy

American leaders tried desperately to manage the economic crisis, but their actions often exacerbated it. As America's rising trade deficit undermined international confidence in the dollar, the Nixon administration ended the dollar's link to the gold standard; free-floating exchange rates increased prices of foreign goods in the United States and stimulated inflation. President Ford followed the tenets of monetary theory, which held that, with less money available to "chase" the supply of goods, price increases would gradually slow down, ending the inflationary spiral. He curbed federal spending and encouraged the Federal Reserve Board to tighten credit, which prompted the worst recession in forty years. In 1975, unemployment reached 8.5 percent.

Carter's larger economic policies, including his 1978 deregulation of airline, trucking, banking, and communications industries, would eventually foster economic growth—but not soon enough. After a decade of decline, Americans were losing faith in the economy and their leaders' ability to manage it.

Impacts of the Economic Crisis

The 1970s economic crisis accelerated the transition from an industrial to a service economy. During the 1970s, the American economy "deindustrialized." Automobile companies laid off workers. Steel plant closings left communities devastated. Other manufacturing concerns moved overseas, seeking lower labor costs and fewer government regulations. New jobs were created—27 million of them—overwhelmingly in the "service sector": retail sales, restaurants, and other service providers. These jobs paid much lower wages than union manufacturing and often lacked healthcare benefits.

Formerly successful blue-collar workers saw their middle-class standards of life slipping away. More married women joined the work force because they had to. High school or college graduates in the 1970s, raised with high expectations, found limited possibilities, if they found jobs at all.

As the old industrial North and Midwest regions declined, people headed for the Sunbelt, which was booming (see Map 31.1). The federal government invested heavily in the South and West during the postwar era, especially in military and defense industries. The Sunbelt was primed for the rapid growth of modern industries and services—aerospace, defense, electronics, transportation, research, banking and finance, and leisure. City and state governments competed for business dollars, partly by preventing the growth of unions. Atlanta, Houston, and other southern cities marketed themselves as cosmopolitan and racially tolerant; they bought sports teams and built museums.

This population shift south and west, combined with the flight of middle-class taxpayers to the suburbs, created disaster in northern and midwestern cities. New York City, near financial collapse by late 1975, was saved only when the House and Senate Banking Committees approved federal loan guarantees. Cleveland defaulted on its debts in 1978, the first major city to do so since Detroit declared bankruptcy in 1933.

Tax Revolts

Meanwhile, a tax revolt movement emerged in the West. In California, inflation had driven property taxes up rapidly, hitting middle-class taxpayers hard. Instead of calling for wealthy citizens and major corporations to pay a larger share, voters rebelled against taxation itself. California's Proposition 13, passed by a landslide in 1978, rolled back property taxes and restricted future increases. Thirty-seven states similarly cut property taxes, and twenty-eight lowered their state income taxes.

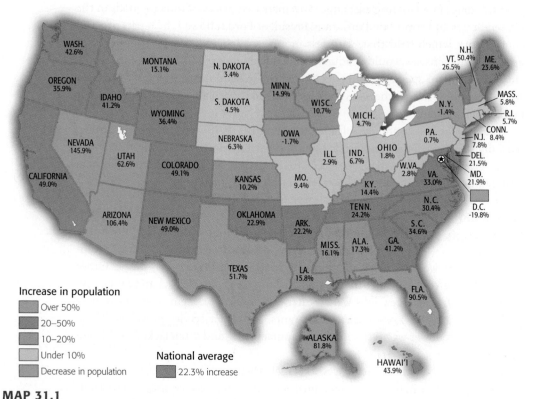

MAP 31.1

The Continued Shift to the Sunbelt in the 1970s and 1980s

Throughout the 1970s and 1980s, Americans continued to leave economically declining areas of the North and East in pursuit of opportunity in the Sunbelt. States in the Sunbelt and in the West had the largest population increases.

Source: Copyright © Cengage Learning.

The impact of Proposition 13 and similar initiatives was initially cushioned by state budget surpluses, but as those turned to deficits, states cut services—closing fire stations and public libraries, ending or limiting mental health services and programs for the disabled. Public schools were hit especially hard.

Credit and Investment   Before the runaway inflation of the 1970s, home mortgages and auto loans were the only major debt most Americans had. National credit cards had become common only in the late 1960s, and few Americans—especially those who remembered the Great Depression—were willing to spend money they did not have. In the 1970s, however, double-digit inflation rates made it economically smarter to buy goods before prices went up, even if it meant borrowing the money. Because debt was paid off later with devalued dollars, the consumer came out ahead. In 1975, consumer debt hit a high of $167 billion; it almost doubled to $315 billion by 1979.

In the 1970s, Americans became investors rather than savers. Because banking regulations capped interest paid on individual savings accounts, with inflation, a savings account bearing 5 percent interest actually *lost* more than 20 percent of its value from 1970 through 1980. That same money, invested at market rates, would have grown dramatically. Fidelity Investments, a mutual fund company, saw an opportunity: its money market accounts combined many smaller investments to purchase large-denomination Treasury bills and certificates of deposit, thus providing small investors the high interest rates normally available only to major investors. Money market investments grew from $1.7 billion in 1974 to $200 billion in 1982. Deregulation of the New York Stock Exchange spawned discount brokerage houses, whose low commission rates were affordable for middle-class investors.

An Era of Cultural Transformation

As Americans struggled with economic recession, governmental betrayal, and social division, major strands of late-twentieth-century culture developed. The current environmental movement, the growth of technology, the rise of born-again Christianity and a "therapeutic culture," contemporary forms of sexuality and the family, and America's emphasis on diversity all have roots in this odd decade sandwiched between the political vibrancy of the 1960s and the conservatism of the 1980s.

> How did the new social mores of the 1970s impact family life?

Environmentalism

A series of ecological crises drove home the fragility of the environment. In 1969, a major oil spill took place off the coast of Santa Barbara, California; that same year, the polluted Cuyahoga River, flowing through Cleveland, caught fire. In 1979, human error contributed to a nuclear accident at the Three Mile Island nuclear power plant near Harrisburg, Pennsylvania, and in 1980 President Carter declared a federal emergency at New York State's Love Canal, a dump site for a local chemical manufacturer, after it was discovered that 30 percent of local residents had suffered chromosome damage. Public activism produced major environmental initiatives, from the Environmental Protection Agency (EPA), created (under strong public pressure) in 1970 by the Nixon administration, to eighteen major environmental laws enacted by Congress during the decade.

When almost 20 million Americans—half of them schoolchildren—celebrated the first Earth Day on April 22, 1970, they signaled the triumph of a new understanding of environmentalism. Central to this movement was a recognition that the earth's resources were finite and must be conserved and protected. Many also identified rapid global population growth as a problem, and state public health offices frequently dispensed contraceptives to stem this new "epidemic."

Ken Regan/Regan Pictures, Inc.

Celebrants of the first Earth Day, on April 22, 1970, gather in an urban park. More than 20 million Americans across the nation participated in local teach-ins, celebrations, and protests to draw attention to environmental issues. By 1990, Earth Day was celebrated globally, drawing 200 million participants from 141 countries.

Technology

Neil Armstrong: First man to set foot on the moon.

During these years, Americans became uneasy about the science and technology that had been one source of America's might. Americans watched with pride as astronaut **Neil Armstrong** stepped onto the lunar surface on July 20, 1969, but technology could not cope with earth-bound problems of poverty, crime, pollution, and urban decay. The failure of technological warfare to deliver victory in Vietnam came as antiwar protesters were questioning the morality of such technology. Although some Americans joined a movement for human-scale development, the nation depended on complex technological systems. And it was during the 1970s that America's computer revolution began: the integrated circuit was created in 1970, and by 1975 the MITS Altair 8800—boasting 256 bytes of memory and taking about thirty hours to assemble—could be mail-ordered from Albuquerque, New Mexico.

Religion and the Therapeutic Culture

As Americans confronted material limits, they increasingly sought spiritual fulfillment Although Methodist, Presbyterian, and Episcopalian churches lost members during this era, evangelical and fundamentalist Christian churches grew dramatically. Protestant evangelicals, describing themselves as "born again," emphasized the daily presence of God in their lives. Even some Catholics, such as the Mexican Americans who embraced the *cursillo* movement (a "little course" in faith), sought a personal relationship with God. The New Age movement drew from and often combined nonwestern spiritual and religious practices, including Zen Buddhism, yoga, and shamanism, along with insights from western psychology and spiritually oriented environmentalism.

During the 1970s, the United States saw the emergence of a therapeutic culture. Although some were disgusted with the self-centeredness of the Me-Decade, bestselling books by therapists and self-help gurus insisted that individual feelings offered the ultimate measure of truth. Self-help books with titles like *I'm OK—You're OK* made up 15 percent of all bestselling books.

Sexuality and the Family

Link to news coverage of the 1979 Disco Demolition night at Comiskey Park in Chicago.

One such self-help book was *The Joy of Sex* (1972), which sold 3.8 million copies in two years. Sex became more visible in public culture during the 1970s, as television loosened its regulation of sexual content. In the early 1960s, married couples in television shows were required to occupy twin beds; in the 1970s, hit television shows included *Three's Company,* a comedy based on the then-scandalous premise that a single man shared an apartment with two beautiful female roommates—and got away with it by pretending he was gay. Donna Summers's 1975 disco hit "Love to Love You Baby" contained sixteen minutes of sexual moaning. Discos were sites of sexual display, both for gay men and for macho working-class cultures. Though few Americans participated in heterosexual orgies at New York City's Plato's Retreat, many read about them in *Time* magazine.

Sexual behaviors also changed. The seventies were the era of singles bars and gay bathhouses, but for most Americans, the sexual revolution meant broader public acceptance of premarital sex and limited acceptance of homosexuality, especially among educated Americans. More heterosexual young people lived together without marriage during the 1970s; the Census Bureau even coined the term *POSSLQ* (persons of opposite sex sharing living quarters) to describe the relationship.

Changes in sexual mores and women's roles altered the American family, too. By the late 1970s, the birth rate dropped 40 percent from its 1957 peak. Almost one-quarter of young single women in 1980 said they did not plan to have children. And a rising percentage of babies were born to unmarried women, as the number of families headed by never-married women rose 400 percent. The divorce rate also rose, partly because states implemented "no fault" divorce. Americans also developed greater acceptance of various family forms (symbolized by the blended family of television's *Brady Bunch*).

Youth

Young people gained new freedoms and responsibilities in American society during the 1970s. In 1971, recognizing that the 18-year-old men who were eligible for the draft could not vote, Congress passed and the states quickly ratified the 26th Amendment, which lowered the voting age to 18. Similarly, 29 states lowered their drinking age. Marijuana use skyrocketed, and several states moved toward decriminalization. In the early 1970s, some young people established communes and attempted to create countercultural worlds outside "the system." Later in the decade, others created the punk movement, which offered new physical and cultural spaces for youth through music and its do-it-yourself ethic.

Diversity

The racial-justice and identity movements of the late 1960s and 1970s made Americans more aware of differences among the nation's peoples, as an influx of new immigrants from Latin America and Asia increased the visibility of Hispanic and Asian Americans. The challenge was figuring out how to acknowledge the new importance of "difference" in public policy. The 1970s solution was the idea of "diversity." Difference was not a problem but a strength; the nation should not seek policies to diminish differences among its peoples but should instead seek to foster the "diversity" of its schools, workplaces, and public culture.

Link to the Supreme Court's decision in *Regents of the University of California v. Bakke*.

The 1978 Supreme Court decision in *Regents of the University of California v. Bakke* was a crucial early step. Allan Bakke, a thirty-three-year-old white man with a strong academic record, was denied admission to the medical school of the University of California at Davis. Bakke sued, charging he had been denied equal protection because the medical school's affirmative-action program reserved 16 percent of its slots for racial-minority candidates, who were held to lower standards. In 1978, the Supreme Court, in a split decision, decided in favor of Bakke. Four justices argued that any race-based decision violated the Civil Rights Act of 1964; four saw affirmative-action programs as constitutionally acceptable. The deciding vote, though for Bakke, contained an important qualification. A "diverse student body," Justice Lewis Powell wrote, is "a constitutionally permissible goal for an institution of higher education." To achieve diversity, educational institutions could consider race in admissions.

Renewed Cold War and Middle East Crisis

What was Carter's record regarding the Middle East?

When Jimmy Carter took office in 1977, he asked Americans to abandon their "inordinate fear of Communism." Carter vowed to reduce the U.S. military presence overseas, to cut back arms sales, and slow the nuclear arms race. More than 400,000 U.S. military personnel were stationed abroad, the United States had military links with ninety-two nations, and the CIA was active on every continent. Carter promised to avoid new Vietnams and give more attention to environmental issues. He especially determined to improve human rights abroad—the freedom to vote, worship, travel, speak out, and get a fair trial. Like his predecessors, however, Carter identified revolutionary nationalism as a threat to the United States's global prominence.

Carter's Divided Administration

Carter spoke and acted inconsistently, partly because in the post-Vietnam years no consensus existed in foreign policy and partly because his advisers squabbled among themselves. One source of the problem was Zbigniew Brzezinski, a Polish-born political scientist who became Carter's national security adviser. An old-fashioned Cold Warrior, Brzezinski blamed foreign crises on Soviet expansionism. Carter gradually listened more to Brzezinski than to Secretary of State Cyrus Vance, an experienced public servant who advocated quiet diplomacy. Under Carter, détente deteriorated and the Cold War deepened. Initially, Carter maintained fairly good relations with Moscow and secured some foreign policy successes. The United States signed two treaties with Panama in 1977. One provided for the return of the Canal Zone to Panama in 2000, and the other guaranteed the United States the right to defend the canal after that time. With conservatives denouncing the deal as a sellout, the Senate narrowly endorsed both agreements in 1978. The majority agreed with Carter's argument that relinquishing the canal would improve U.S. relations with Latin America.

Wally McNamee/CORBIS

Egyptian president Anwar al-Sadat, U.S. President Jimmy Carter, and Israeli Prime Minister Menachem Begin sit together outside the White House on March 26, 1979, ready to sign the peace treaty based on the Camp David Accords of September 1978. The treaty ended the longstanding state of war between Egypt and Israel.

Camp David Accords

The crowning accomplishment of Carter's presidency was the **Camp David accords**, the first mediated peace treaty between Israel and an Arab nation. In September 1978, the president persuaded Israel and Egypt to agree to a peace treaty, gained Israel's promise to withdraw from the Sinai Peninsula, and forged a provisional agreement that provided for continued negotiations on the future status of Palestinians living in the occupied territories of Jordan's West Bank and Egypt's Gaza Strip. Other Arab states denounced the agreement for not requiring Israel to relinquish all occupied territories and not guaranteeing a Palestinian homeland. But the accord, signed on March 26, 1979, by Israeli prime minister Menachem Begin and Egyptian president Anwar al-Sadat, at least ended warfare along one frontier.

Camp David accords: Agreements that were signed by Egypt's President Sadat and Israel's Prime Minister Begin following twelve days of secret negotiations—arranged by President Carter—at Camp David.

Soviet Invasion of Afghanistan

Meanwhile, relations with Moscow deteriorated. U.S. and USSR officials sparred over the Kremlin's reluctance to lift restrictions on Jewish emigration and over the Soviet decision to deploy new intermediate-range ballistic missiles aimed at western Europe. Then, in December 1979, the Soviets invaded Afghanistan, a remote country whose strategic position made it a source of great-power conflict. Following World War II, Afghanistan struggled with ongoing ethnic and factional squabbling; in the 1970s, it spiraled into anarchy. In late 1979, the Red Army entered Afghanistan to shore up a faltering communist government under siege by Muslim rebels. Moscow officials calculated they could be in and out of the country before anyone noticed, including the Americans.

Carter not only noticed but reacted forcefully. He suspended shipments of grain and high-technology equipment to the Soviet Union, withdrew a major arms control treaty from Senate consideration, and initiated an international boycott of the 1980 Summer Olympics in Moscow. He also secretly authorized the CIA to distribute aid, including arms and military support, to the Mujahidin (Islamic guerillas) fighting the communist government and sanctioned military aid to their backer, Pakistan. Announcing the Carter Doctrine, the president asserted that the United States would intervene, unilaterally and militarily, should Soviet aggression threaten the petroleum-rich Persian Gulf. Carter warned aides that the Soviets, unless checked, would likely attack elsewhere in the Middle East, but declassified documents confirm what critics said: that the Soviet invasion was limited and did not presage a push into the Persian Gulf.

Iranian Hostage Crisis

Carter simultaneously faced a tough foreign policy test in neighboring Iran. The shah, long favored by the United States, was dethroned by a coalition of Iranians, who resented the dislocation of their traditional ways by the shah's attempts at modernization. Riots led by anti-American Muslim clerics erupted in late 1978. The shah went into exile, and in April 1979 Islamic revolutionaries, led by the Ayatollah Khomeini, an elderly cleric who denounced the United States as the stronghold of capitalism and western materialism, proclaimed a Shi'ite Islamic Republic. In November, with the exiled shah in the United States for medical treatment, mobs stormed the U.S. embassy in Teheran. They took American personnel as hostages, demanding the return of the shah to stand trial. The Iranians eventually released a few American prisoners, but fifty-two others suffered solitary confinement, beatings, and terrifying mock executions.

The All-Volunteer Force

On June 30, 1973, the United States ended its military draft and turned to an all-volunteer force (AVF). The nation never had a peacetime draft before 1940, when it began looking ahead to the coming war. But as the country embraced global leadership after World War II and faced a heightened Cold War, the draft became part of American life. More than 50 million American men had been inducted into the military between World War II's end and 1973.

Richard Nixon promised to end the draft during his 1968 presidential campaign, realizing that it was a focus for widespread protest against the Vietnam War. Ending the draft was not feasible during the war, but Nixon began planning for an all-volunteer force once in office. Many Americans supported the shift because they believed a president could not rely on a draft to compel people to fight a war they did not support.

The military, however, disliked Nixon's plan. The war in Vietnam shattered morale and left the military—particularly the army—in disarray. Public opinion of the military was at an all-time low. How would they attract volunteers?

As the largest of the four services, the army required the most volunteers. To draw volunteers, it ended make-work ("chickenshit") tasks and enhanced professionalism. It also turned to market research and advertising. Discovering that many men were afraid to lose their individuality, the army launched a campaign telling potential volunteers, "Today's Army Wants to Join You."

The army needed about 225,000 recruits annually (compared to about 65,000 per year in 2009) and had difficulty attracting them. Within a decade, however, America's military boasted a higher rate of high school graduates than the comparable age population. During an era of relative peace, many young people found opportunities for education and training through military service, particularly the economically disadvantaged, a high percentage of whom were African American.

The proportion of women in the military increased from 1.9 percent in 1972 to about 15 percent currently, with a wider range of available roles. The nation's understanding of military service changed from an obligation of (male) citizenship to a voluntary choice. The implications seemed less urgent in peacetime. But in wartime, the legacy of the move to an AVF raises the question: What does it mean when only a small number of volunteers bears the burden of warfare and most Americans never have to consider the possibility of going to war?

Unable to gain the hostages' freedom through diplomatic intermediaries, Carter took steps to isolate Iran economically, freezing Iranian assets in the United States. When the hostage takers paraded their blindfolded captives before television cameras, Americans felt taunted and humiliated. In April 1980, Carter broke diplomatic relations with Iran and ordered a daring rescue mission. But equipment failed and two aircraft collided, killing eight American soldiers. The hostages were not freed until January 1981, after Carter left office.

The Iranian revolution, together with the rise of the Mujahidin in Afghanistan, signified the emergence of Islamic fundamentalism as a force in world affairs. Socialism and capitalism, the answers that the two superpowers offered to the problems of modernization, failed to solve the problems in Central Asia and the Middle East. Consequently, Islamic orthodoxy found growing support for its message: that secular leaders such as Nasser in Egypt and the shah in Iran had taken their peoples down the wrong path, necessitating a return to conservative Islamic values and Islamic law. The Iranian revolution expressed a deep and complex mixture of discontents within many Islamic societies.

Rise of Saddam Hussein

U.S. officials took some consolation from Iran's troubles with the avowedly secular government in neighboring Iraq. Ruled by the Ba'athist Party, Iraq won favor in Washington for its pursuit and execution of Iraqi communists. When a Ba'athist leader named Saddam Hussein took over as president of Iraq in 1979 and threatened the Teheran government, U.S. officials worried that Saddam could offset the Iranian danger in the Persian Gulf. As border clashes between Iraqi and Iranian forces escalated into war 1980, Washington policymakers were officially neutral but soon tilted toward Iraq.

Carter earned some diplomatic successes in the Middle East, Africa, and Latin America, but the revived Cold War and prolonged Iranian hostage crisis hurt the administration politically. Contrary to Carter's goals, more U.S. military personnel were stationed overseas in 1980 than in 1976; the defense budget climbed and arms sales grew to $15.3 billion in 1980. On human rights, the president practiced a double standard, applying the human-rights test to some nations (the Soviet Union, Argentina, and Chile) but not to U.S. allies (South Korea, the shah's Iran, and the Philippines). Still, Carter's human-rights policy saved the lives of some political prisoners and institutionalized concern for human rights worldwide. But his inability to restore economic and military dominance dashed his reelection prospects. He lost in 1980 to the hawkish Ronald Reagan, former Hollywood actor and governor of California.

Summary

From the crisis year of 1968 on, Americans were increasingly polarized—over the Vietnam War, over the best path to racial equality and equal rights, and over the meaning of America itself. As many activists turned to "cultural nationalism," or group-identity politics, notions of American unity seemed a relic of the past. And though a new women's movement won victories against sex discrimination, powerful opposition arose in response.

During this era, Americans became increasingly disillusioned with politics and presidential leadership. Richard Nixon's abuses of power in the Watergate scandal and cover-up, combined with growing awareness that the administration had lied repeatedly about the United States's role in Vietnam, produced a profound suspicion of government. A major economic crisis ended the post–World War II expansion, and Americans struggled with the effects of stagflation: rising unemployment rates coupled with high inflation.

Overseas, a string of setbacks—defeat in Vietnam, the oil embargo, and the Iranian hostage crisis—signified the waning of U.S. power. Détente with the Soviet Union had flourished for a time; however, by 1980 Cold War tensions escalated. And the Middle East became an increasing focus of U.S. foreign policy.

Plagued by political, economic, and foreign policy crises, by the late 1970s America's age of liberalism was over; the elements for a conservative resurgence were in place.

Chapter Review

The New Politics of Identity

How did identity politics reshape political activism in the late 1960s and 1970s?

By the late 1960s, social justice movements were becoming more vocal and radical; they were also shifting their activist agendas to focus on racial, ethnic, and cultural distinctiveness. Younger, newer members to the struggle for black, Hispanic, and Native American civil rights wanted more than simply integration into mainstream U.S. society—they also wanted to embrace and celebrate the cultural heritage and history that made them distinct and find acceptance for these differences within society writ large. As such, their activism shifted to "identity politics," which saw group identity as the basis of social action. Through the Black Power movement, for example, African Americans embraced a black standard of beauty, celebrated their heritage, and founded black studies programs in universities—all while seeking social and political equality, too. Most importantly, movements like Black Power, Red Power (Native American), or Brown Power (Mexican American), which embraced identity politics as their modus operandi, argued that social policy should be based not on what might empower an individual, but rather on what would most benefit an entire identity group.

The Women's Movement and Gay Liberation

What were the successes of the women's movement?

The women's movement made major gains in the 1960s and 1970s: the right of a married woman to obtain credit in her own name; the right of an unmarried woman to obtain birth control; women's right to serve on juries; and the end of sex-segregated help wanted ads. Activists established rape crisis centers, educated law enforcement, and challenged definitions of rape that blamed the victim for the attack. Many worked for legalized abortion at the state level and won a major victor with the 1973 Supreme Court decision in *Roe v. Wade,* which ruled that privacy rights protected a woman's decision not to continue a pregnancy. The women's movement also achieved greater opportunities for women in sports via passage of Title IX of the Higher Education Act, which barred federal funds from colleges or universities discriminating against women. Likewise, the movement sparked the creation of women's studies programs in colleges nationwide.

The End in Vietnam

What kept Nixon from ending the Vietnam War as quickly as he had hoped?

Nixon's policy in Vietnam was driven by a goal to end the war fast, partly so that it would not ruin his political career as it had Johnson's. But at the same time, he did not want to hurt American credibility as a world leader, and he still sought to prevent South Vietnam's defeat. Consequently, although he dramatically decreased the number of American troops from 543,000 in 1969 to 60,000 in 1970, he increased bombing of North Vietnam and neutral Cambodia, hoping to force the enemy into concessions. The North Vietnamese stood firm. A cease-fire was agreed to in 1973, and shortly after U.S. troops left, a large-scale war developed between North and South Vietnam, with the latter falling and the communists claiming control of the entire country in 1975.

Nixon, Kissinger, and the World

How did the Vietnam War influence Nixon's approach to foreign policy?

The drawn-out struggle in Vietnam signified to Nixon that American power was limited. The war must be wound down, and similar commitments must be avoided in the future. Accordingly, he adopted the Nixon Doctrine, which said the United States would provide economic aid but not troops to allies. In addition, he implemented détente, a policy aimed at creating improved Soviet-American relations and a reduced arms race within an environment of rivalry. With his historic trip to China in early 1972, he moved to end two decades of Sino-American hostility. Chinese leaders Mao Zedong and Zhou Enlai agreed with Nixon that the Soviet Union should be kept from making gains in Asia.

Presidential Politics and the Crisis of Leadership

How did Watergate bring down the Nixon administration?

Sometimes paranoid, Nixon kept long lists of so-called enemies and directed aide Charles Colson to form a secret group called the Plumbers to dig up dirt on various groups, individuals and political rivals. During Nixon's 1972 reelection campaign, the Plumbers were arrested while breaking into the Democratic National Campaign headquarters in the Watergate complex to plant surveillance equipment. While Nixon was not directly involved in this effort, he made the mistake of blocking the CIA and FBI investigations into it—which constituted an obstruction of justice (an impeachable offense). He also initially refused to turn over his audiotape conversations to congressional hearings. Eventually, he relinquished the tapes, although several contained significant gaps. Congress began impeachment hearings, and facing certain conviction and impeachment, on August 9, 1974, Nixon became the first U.S. president to resign from office.

Economic Crisis

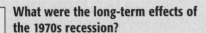

What were the long-term effects of the 1970s recession?

The 1970s recession accelerated the nation's shift from an industrial to a service-based economy. As manufacturers in leading industries, such as automobiles and steel, laid off large numbers of workers or shifted to cheaper overseas production, new jobs opened in the lower-paid service sector, such as cashiers and waiters. Increasing numbers of married women went to work to keep their families afloat. Older industrial cities suffered decay, while the Sunbelt was well-positioned to prosper with the growth of modern industries such as defense, aerospace, and finance. Double-digit inflation in the 1970s led people to buy up goods before prices would rise, often on credit, fueling a major rise in consumer indebtedness. Finally, with interest rates capped on savings accounts, people increasingly shifted to new forms of investment in mutual funds and the stock market.

An Era of Cultural Transformation

How did the new social mores of the 1970s impact family life?

Increasing tolerance and openness about sex in the 1970s facilitated major changes in traditional notions of what constituted a family. There was a broader acceptance of premarital sex and limited acceptance of homosexuality. As a result, more heterosexual couples opted to live together without marrying. Though most did still marry, they married later and had fewer children. By decade's end, the birth rate dropped nearly 40 percent from its all-time high, and roughly 25 percent of single women said they did not intend to have children at all. Divorce rates also shot up as a result of new no-fault laws that enabled couples to end their marriages without proving adultery, abandonment, or other cause. Americans also developed a greater acceptance for a variety of family forms, including new blended families resulting from divorce and remarriage.

Renewed Cold War and Middle East Crisis

What was Carter's record regarding the Middle East?

On the one hand, Carter achieved great success in mediating a peace treaty between Israel and Egypt in 1978. Although Arab states felt it fell short in not providing a Palestinian homeland and allowing Israel to maintain some of its occupied territories, it was a major first step toward a lasting settlement in the region. On the other hand, Carter angered Iranians when he provided protection for the exiled shah in the United States to seek medical treatment. Mobs stormed the U.S. embassy in Iran and took hostages to press for the shah to stand trial. Carter's inability to free the U.S. hostages contributed to his political downfall and defeat in his reelection bid in 1980.

Suggestions for Further Reading

Donald T. Critchlow, *Phyllis Schlafly and Grassroots Conservatism: A Woman's Crusade* (2005)

Daniel Ellsberg, *Secrets: A Memoir of Vietnam and the Pentagon Papers* (2002)

David Farber, *Taken Hostage: The Iran Hostage Crisis and America's First Encounter with Radical Islam* (2004)

Nancy MacLean, *Freedom Is Not Enough: The Opening of the American Workplace* (2006)

Rick Perlstein, *Nixonland: The Rise of a President and the Fracturing of America* (2008)

Ruth Rosen, *The World Split Open: How the Modern Women's Movement Changed America* (2000)

Hal Rothman, *The Greening of a Nation: Environmentalism in the U.S. Since 1945* (1997)

Edward D. Berkowitz, *Something Happened: A Political and Cultural Overview of the Seventies* (2007)

John D. Skrentny, *The Minority Rights Revolution* (2002)

Odd Arne Westad, *The Global Cold War: Third World Interventions and the Making of Our Times* (2005)

Conservatism Revived

32

1980–1992

I t was hot and there was a lot of desert," Luisa Orellana remembered about crossing the Mexican border into the United States in the early 1980s. "All of us started running, each one with a child in our arms.... It rained so hard we couldn't see where we were going, but it helped because the Border Patrol couldn't see us either."

Three months earlier Luisa's father was murdered. Tanis Stanislaus Orellana had worked in El Salvador with Archbishop Óscar Romero, the most powerful critic of the ruling military dictatorship whose death squads killed thirty thousand Salvadorans between 1979 and 1981. Romero was assassinated in 1980—shot as he consecrated the Eucharist during Mass. The civil war that followed lasted twelve years, leading an estimated 4 million Salvadorans to seek refuge elsewhere from the threat of torture, rape, and murder.

Luisa's family joined that exodus; after Orellana's murder, they fled, leaving almost everything behind. Taking a bus through Guatemala, they crossed illegally into Mexico and, sheltered by churches, made their way from Chiapas to Mexico City to Agua Prieta, on the U.S.-Mexico border.

There, Luisa's family ran two miles through blinding rain. Cold, hungry, and scared, they were met by the Sanctuary movement, Americans who believed that the U.S. government's refugee policy, which offered asylum to those fleeing violent repression and possible death or torture, must include those who escaped the deadly civil wars ravaging Central America in the 1980s. The U.S. government instead designated them "economic refugees" and denied them asylum.

The U.S. Sanctuary movement used church networks and human rights groups to investigate Central American refugees' stories of rape, torture, and murder. Many members belonged to faith-based communities, although secular institutions, including universities and the state of New Mexico, also participated. Some movement members went to prison, charged with transporting or harboring fugitives.

Luisa's family went from the sanctuary offered by Tucson churches at the center of the movement to live in the basement of a Spokane, Washington, Catholic church. In 1989, the U.S. government granted protection and work permits to Central American refugees. Luisa stayed in Washington, where she became a teacher of English as a second language. Luisa Orellana's family were part of the "new immigration" that began in the early 1970s and grew throughout the 1980s, as record numbers of immigrants came to the United States from Asia, Mexico, Central and South America, and the Caribbean. Many from Central America, Vietnam, the Soviet Union, and Cuba were political refugees. The Orellanas found safety and peace in the United States, but not all immigrants—or all Americans—fared so well in the 1980s. Divisions between rich and poor increased; social problems—drugs, violence, homelessness, the growing AIDS epidemic—made life more difficult for the urban poor, while those on the other side of the economic divide, enjoyed an era of luxury and ostentation.

Ronald Reagan's election in 1980 began twelve years of Republican rule, as Reagan was succeeded by his vice president, George H. W. Bush, in 1988. Reagan was a popular president who seemed to restore the confidence shaken by the 1970s social, economic, and political crises. Wealthy people liked Reagan's pro-business economic policies; the religious New Right shared his vision of "God's America"; white middle- and working-class Americans admired Reagan's charisma and his embrace of "old-fashioned" values.

Reagan supported New Right social issues: he was anti-abortion, embraced prayer in schools, and reversed the GOP's support of the Equal Rights Amendment. Most important, Reagan appointed Supreme Court and federal judges whose rulings strengthened social-conservative agendas. Reagan's primary focus was on the conservative issues of reducing the size and power of the federal government and creating favorable conditions for business. The U.S. economy recovered from the 1970s stagflation and boomed through much of the 1980s. But corruption flourished in financial institutions freed from government oversight. By the end of the Reagan-Bush era, a combination of tax cuts and massive increases in defense caused the budget deficit to jump fivefold.

Overseas, meanwhile, the Cold War intensified, then ended. The key figure in the intensification was Reagan, who promised to stand up to the Soviet Union. The key figure in ending the Cold War was Soviet leader Mikhail Gorbachev, who came to power in 1985 determined to end the USSR's economic decline, which required a more amicable superpower relationship. Gorbachev hoped to reform the Soviet system, not eradicate it, but lost control of events as revolutions in eastern Europe toppled one

LINKS TO THE WORLD *CNN*

LEGACY FOR A PEOPLE AND A NATION *The Americans with Disabilities Act*

SUMMARY

communist regime after another. In 1991, the Soviet Union itself disappeared. The Persian Gulf War of that same year demonstrated America's unrivaled world power and the unprecedented importance of the Middle East.

As you read this chapter, keep the following questions in mind:

* Ronald Reagan, campaigning for president in 1984, told voters, "It's morning again in America." How might Americans from different backgrounds judge the accuracy of his claim?

* What issues, beliefs, backgrounds, and economic realities divided Americans in the 1980s, and how do those divisions shape the culture and politics of contemporary America?

* Why did the Cold War intensify and then wane during the decade of the 1980s?

Reagan and the Conservative Resurgence

What groups made up the new Republican coalition of the 1980s?

The 1970s were hard for Americans: defeat in Vietnam, the resignation of a president in disgrace, the energy crisis, economic stagflation, and the Iranian hostage crisis. In 1980, President Carter's approval rating stood at 21 percent, lower than Richard Nixon's during the Watergate crisis. The time was ripe for a challenge to Carter's leadership, the Democratic Party, and the liberalism that had essentially governed the United States since Franklin Roosevelt's New Deal.

Ronald Reagan

Ronald Reagan: Former actor and California governor (1967–1975) who became the 40th President of the United States from 1981–1989.

In 1980, several conservative Republican politicians entered the presidential race, including **Ronald Reagan**, former movie star and two-term governor of California. In the 1940s, as president of Hollywood's Screen Actors Guild, Reagan was a New Deal Democrat. But in the 1950s, as a corporate spokesman for General Electric, he became increasingly conservative. In 1964, Reagan's televised speech supporting Republican presidential candidate Barry Goldwater catapulted him to the forefront of conservative politics.

Elected governor of California two years later, Reagan became known for his right-wing rhetoric: The United States should "level Vietnam, pave it, paint stripes on it, and make a parking lot out of it." And in 1969, when student protestors occupied People's Park near the University of California in Berkeley, he threatened a "bloodbath," dispatching National Guard troops. Reagan was often pragmatic; he denounced welfare but presided over reform of the state's social welfare bureaucracy. And he signed one of the nation's most liberal abortion laws.

The New Conservative Coalition

neoconservatives: A small but influential group of intellectuals—typically former Democrats disillusioned with the party after Vietnam—who became part of Republican Ronald Reagan's conservative coalition.

In the 1980 election, Reagan contrasted incumbent Jimmy Carter with an optimistic vision for America's future. With his Hollywood charm, he forged different sorts of American conservatives into a new coalition. Political conservatives wanted to strengthen national defense, limit federal power, and roll back the liberal programs of the 1930s New Deal and 1960s Great Society. Reagan similarly attracted economic conservatives, promising deregulation and tax policies benefiting corporations, wealthy investors, and entrepreneurs. He also drew **neoconservatives**, a small but

Chronology

1980	Reagan elected president	1986	Iran-contra scandal erupts
1981	AIDS first observed in United States	1987	Stock market drops 508 points in one day
	Economic problems continue; prime interest rate reaches 21.5 percent		Palestinian *intifada* begins
	"Reaganomics" plan of budget and tax cuts approved by Congress	1988	George H. W. Bush elected president
1982	Unemployment reaches 10.8 percent, highest rate since Great Depression	1989	Tiananmen Square massacre in China
			Berlin Wall torn down
			U.S. troops invade Panama
	ERA dies after STOP-ERA campaign prevents ratification in key states		Gulf between rich and poor at highest point since 1920s
1983	Reagan introduces SDI	1990	Americans with Disabilities Act passed
	Terrorists kill U.S. marines in Lebanon		Communist regimes in eastern Europe collapse
	U.S. invasion of Grenada		Iraq invades Kuwait
1984	Reagan aids contras despite congressional ban		South Africa begins to dismantle apartheid
	Economic recovery; unemployment rate drops and economy grows without inflation	1991	Persian Gulf War
			USSR dissolves into independent states
	Reagan reelected		United States enters recession
	Gorbachev promotes reforms in USSR	1992	Annual federal budget deficit reaches high of $300 billion at end of Bush presidency

influential group of intellectuals—typically former Democrats disillusioned with the party after Vietnam.

Reagan further tapped into the sentiments that fueled the 1970s tax revolt movement, drawing voters from traditionally Democratic constituencies, such as labor unions and urban ethnic groups. Many middle- and working-class whites resented what they saw as tax-funded welfare for people who did not work. These "Reagan Democrats" found the Republican critique of tax-funded social programs and "big government" appealing, even though Reagan's policies would benefit the wealthy at their expense.

Finally, Reagan drew the increasingly powerful, religiously based New Right. Many of them were evangelical Christians who believed (in Moral Majority founder Jerry Falwell's words) that America's "internal problems are the direct result of her spiritual condition."

Reagan's Conservative Agenda Reagan won the election with 51 percent of the popular vote. Jimmy Carter carried only six states. Reagan served two terms as president, and like Franklin Roosevelt, defined the era over which he presided. Reagan was not especially focused on the details of governing. When Carter briefed him on foreign and domestic policy, Reagan took no notes. Critics argued that his lack of knowledge could prove dangerous—as when he insisted that intercontinental ballistic missiles carrying nuclear warheads could be called back once launched.

But supporters insisted that Reagan focused on the big picture. When he spoke to the American people, he offered what seemed to be simple truths. While even supporters winced at his willingness to reduce complex policy issues to basic (and often misleading)

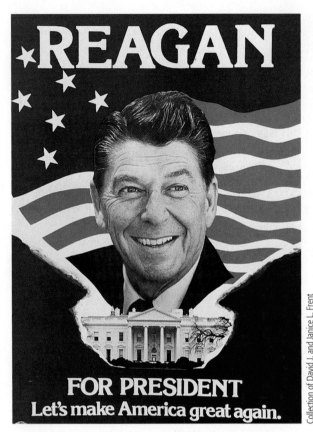

REAGAN

FOR PRESIDENT
Let's make America great again.

Collection of David J. and Janice L. Frent

Ronald Reagan, the Republican presidential candidate in 1980, campaigned for "family values," an aggressive anti-Soviet foreign and military policy, and tax cuts. He also exuded optimism and appealed to Americans' patriotism. This poster issued by the Republican National Committee included Reagan's favorite campaign slogan, "Let's make America great again."

stories, Reagan was to most Americans the Great Communicator. He won admiration for his courage after he was seriously wounded in an assassination attempt sixty-nine days into his presidency. Most important, Reagan had a clear vision for the United States' future. He wanted to roll back the liberalism of the past fifty years that made government responsible for the nation's economic health and the social welfare of its citizens.

Attacks on Social Welfare Programs

Reagan, like traditional conservatives, believed that the federal government could not solve social problems. He tapped into a backlash against such Great Society programs. Many Americans who struggled to make ends meet during the economic crises of the 1970s and early 1980s resented paying taxes that, they believed, funded government handouts. Lasting racial tensions also fueled public resentment: Reagan fed a stereotype of welfare recipients as unwed, black, teenage mothers who kept having babies to collect larger checks.

In 1981, the administration cut social welfare funding by $25 billion. But welfare programs benefiting the poor (Aid to Families with Dependent Children and food stamp programs) were small compared with Social Security and Medicare—welfare programs benefiting Americans across income levels. The Reagan administration did shrink the *proportion* of the federal budget devoted to social welfare programs (including Social Security and Medicare) from 28 to 22 percent by the late 1980s, but only because of a $1.2 trillion increase in defense spending.

Pro-Business Policies and the Environment

Reagan also attacked federal environmental, health, and safety regulations as reducing business profits and discouraging economic growth. Administration officials claimed that removing government regulation would restore the creativity of America's free-market system. However, they did not so much end government's role as deploy government power to aid corporate America. The president even appointed opponents of federal regulations to head agencies charged with enforcing them.

Environmentalists were appalled when Reagan appointed James Watt, a well-known antienvironmentalist, as secretary of the interior. Watt was a leader in the Sagebrush Rebellion, which sought the return of publicly owned lands in the West, such as national forests, to state control. The federal government controlled more than half of western lands, including 83 percent of the land in Nevada, 66 percent in Utah, and 50 percent in Wyoming. But state control was not the sole issue; Watt's group wanted to open western public lands to businesses for logging, mining, and ranching.

Telling Congress in 1981, "I don't know how many generations we can count on until the Lord returns," Watt dismissed concerns about protecting resources and public lands and allowed private corporations to acquire oil, mineral, and timber rights to federal lands for minuscule payments. He was forced to resign in 1983 after he referred to a federal advisory panel as "a black…a woman, two Jews, and a cripple." Even before Watt's resignation, his actions reenergized the nation's environmental movement and provoked opposition from business leaders in western states who understood that uncontrolled strip-mining and clear-cut logging could destroy lucrative tourism and recreation industries.

Attacks on Organized Labor

The pro-business Reagan administration undercut organized labor's ability to negotiate wages and working conditions. Union power was already waning; labor union membership declined in the 1970s as jobs in heavy industry disappeared, and efforts to unionize the high-growth electronics and service sectors failed. In August 1981, Reagan intervened in a strike by the Professional Air Traffic Controllers Organization (PATCO). The air traffic controllers—federal employees, for whom striking was illegal—protested working conditions they believed compromised the safety of air travel. Forty-eight hours into the strike, Reagan fired the 11,350 strikers, stipulating that they could never be rehired by the Federal Aviation Administration.

With the support of Reagan appointees to the National Labor Relations Board, businesses took an increasingly hard line with labor during the 1980s, and unions failed to mount effective opposition. Yet roughly 44 percent of union families voted for Reagan in 1980, drawn to his espousal of old-fashioned values and vigorous anticommunist rhetoric.

The New Right

It is surprising that the religious New Right was drawn to Reagan, a divorced man without strong ties to religion or, seemingly, his own children. But Reagan supported New Right social issues: the anti-abortion cause and prayer in public schools.

Reagan's judicial nominations also pleased the religious New Right. The Senate, in a bipartisan vote, refused to confirm Supreme Court nominee Robert Bork, but Congress eventually confirmed Anthony M. Kennedy. Reagan also appointed Anton Scalia, who would become a key conservative force, and Sandra Day O'Connor (the first woman appointee), and elevated Nixon appointee William Rehnquist to chief justice. In 1986, the increasingly conservative Supreme Court upheld a Georgia law that punished consensual sex between men with up to twenty years in jail (*Bowers v. Hardwick*); in 1989, justices ruled that a Missouri law restricting the right to an abortion was constitutional (*Webster v. Reproductive Health Services*), thus encouraging further challenges to *Roe v. Wade*. Overall, however, the Reagan administration did not push a conservative social agenda as strongly as some in the new Republican coalition had hoped.

Reaganomics

The centerpiece of Reagan's domestic agenda was the economic program that took his name: Reaganomics. The U.S. economy was faltering in the early 1980s. Stagflation proved resistant to traditional remedies: when the government increased spending to stimulate a stagnant economy, inflation skyrocketed; when it cut spending or tightened the money supply to reduce inflation, the economy plunged deeper into recession and unemployment jumped.

Why was the 1980s' economic boom a mixed blessing?

Reagan offered a simple answer. Instead of focusing on the complexities of global competition, deindustrialization, and OPEC's control of oil, Reagan argued that U.S. economic problems were caused by intrusive government regulation of business and industry, expensive social programs, high taxes, and deficit spending—in short, government itself. Reagan sought to unshackle the free-enterprise system from government regulation, slash social programs, and balance the budget by reducing the role of the federal government.

Supply-Side Economics   Reagan's economic policy was based largely on supply-side economics, the theory that tax cuts (rather than government spending) stimulate growth. Economist Arthur Laffer proposed one hypothesis—his soon-to-be-famous Laffer curve. It stated that at some point rising tax rates discourage people from engaging in taxable activities (such as investing). As people invest less, the economy slows, and there is less tax revenue to collect. Cutting taxes, in contrast, reverses the cycle.

Although economists accepted the larger principle behind Laffer's curve, almost none believed that U.S. tax rates approached the point of disincentive. Even conservative economists were suspicious of supply-side principles. Reagan and his staff, however, sought a massive tax cut, arguing that American corporations and individuals would invest funds freed up by lower tax rates, producing new plants, jobs, and products. And as prosperity returned, profits at the top would "trickle down" to the middle classes and even to the poor.

David Stockman, head of the Office of Management and Budget, proposed a five-year plan to balance the federal budget through economic growth (created by tax cuts) and deep spending cuts, primarily in social programs. Congress cooperated with a three-year, $750 billion tax cut, the largest in American history. Stockman's plan assumed $100 billion in cuts from government programs, including Social Security and Medicare, which Congress rejected. Reagan, meanwhile, canceled out gains from domestic spending cuts by dramatically increasing defense spending.

Major tax cuts, big increases in defense spending, small cuts in social programs: the federal budget deficit exploded from $59 billion in 1980 to more than $100 billion in 1982 to almost $300 billion by the end of George Bush's presidency in 1992. The federal government borrowed money to make up the difference, transforming the United States from the world's largest creditor to its largest debtor (see Figure 32.1). The national debt grew to almost $3 trillion.

Harsh Medicine for Inflation   In 1981, the Federal Reserve Bank, an autonomous federal agency, raised interest rates for bank loans to an unprecedented 21.5 percent, battling inflation by tightening the money supply and slowing the economy. The nation plunged into recession. By year's end, the gross national product (GNP) fell 5 percent and sales of cars and houses dropped sharply. Unemployment soared to 8 percent.

By late 1982, unemployment reached 10.8 percent, the highest rate since 1940. For African Americans, it was 20 percent. Reagan promised that consumers would lift the economy from the recession by spending their tax cuts. But as late as April 1983, unemployment remained at 10 percent, and people were angry.

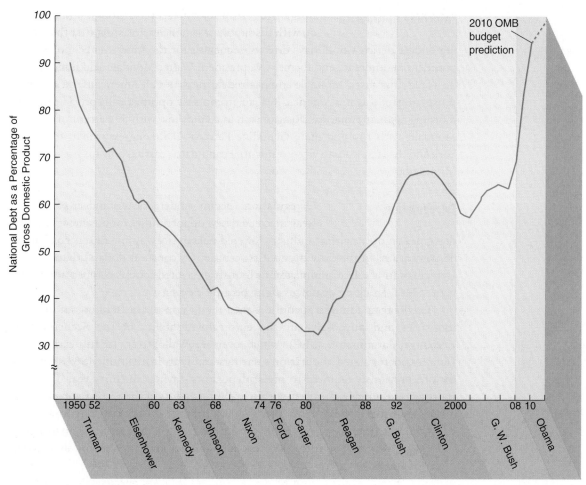

FIGURE 32.1
America's Rising National Debt, 1974–1989

America's national debt, which rose sporadically throughout the 1970s, soared to record heights during the 1980s. Under President Reagan, large defense expenditures and tax cuts caused the national debt to grow by $1.5 trillion.

Source: Adapted from U.S. Bureau of the Census, *Statistical Abstract of the United States* (Washington, D.C.: 1992), p. 315.

Along with industries such as steel and automobiles, agriculture, too, was faltering as farmers suffered from falling crop prices, floods, droughts, and burdensome debts at high interest rates. Many lost their property through mortgage foreclosures; others filed for bankruptcy. As the recession deepened, poverty rose to its highest level since 1965.

It was harsh medicine, but the Federal Reserve Bank's plan to end stagflation worked. High interest rates helped drop inflation from 12 percent in 1980 to less than 7 percent in 1982. The economy also benefited from OPEC's 1981 decision to increase oil production, thus lowering prices. In 1984, the GNP rose 7 percent, the sharpest increase since 1951, and midyear unemployment fell to a four-year low of 7 percent.

Link to a collection of campaign ads from the 1984 election.

"Morning in America"

Reagan got credit for the recovery, though it had little to do with his supply-side policies. Insisting that the escalating budget deficit would have dire consequences for the American economy, 1984 presidential candidate and former vice president Walter Mondale said honestly that he would raise taxes. Mondale emphasized fairness; not all Americans, he said, were prospering in Reagan's America. Reagan, in contrast, optimistically proclaimed, "It's morning again in America." Reagan won in a landslide, with 59 percent of the vote. Mondale, with running mate Geraldine Ferraro—U.S. congresswoman from New York and the first woman vice-presidential candidate—carried only his home state of Minnesota.

Deregulation

Deregulation, begun under Carter and expanded by Reagan, created new opportunities for business. The 1978 deregulation of the airline industry lowered ticket prices; airline tickets cost almost 45 percent less in the early twenty-first century (in constant dollars) than in 1978. Deregulation of telecommunications industries created serious competition for the giant AT&T, and long-distance calling became inexpensive.

The Reagan administration loosened regulation of the banking and finance industries and purposely cut the enforcement ability of the Securities and Exchange Commission (SEC), which oversees Wall Street. In the early 1980s, Congress deregulated the nation's savings-and-loan institutions (S&Ls), organizations previously required to invest depositors' savings in thirty-year, fixed-rate mortgages secured by property within a 50-mile radius of the S&L's main office. By ending government oversight of investment practices, while covering losses from bad S&L investments, Congress left no penalties for failure. S&Ls increasingly put depositors' money into high-risk investments and engaged in shady—even criminal—deals.

Junk Bonds and Merger Mania

Risky investments typified Wall Street as well, as Michael Milken, a reclusive bond trader, pioneered the junk bond industry and created lucrative investment possibilities. Milken offered financing to debt-ridden corporations unable to get traditional, low-interest bank loans, using bond issues that paid investors high interest rates because they were high-risk (thus junk bonds). Many of these corporations were attractive targets for takeover by other corporations or investors, who, in turn, could finance takeovers with junk bonds. Such predators could use the first corporation's existing debt as a tax write-off, sell off unprofitable units, and lay off employees to create a more profitable corporation.

By the mid-1980s, hundreds of major corporations—including giants Walt Disney and Conoco—fell prey to merger mania and hostile takeovers. Profits for investors were staggering, and by 1987 Milken, the guru of junk bonds, was earning $550 million a year—about $1,046 a minute.

Deregulation helped smaller corporations challenge the virtual monopolies of giant corporations in fields like telecommunications. And the American economy boomed. Although the stock market plunged 508 points on a single day in October 1987—losing 22.6 percent of its value, or almost double the percentage loss in the 1929 crash—it rebounded quickly. The high-risk boom of the 1980s, however, had

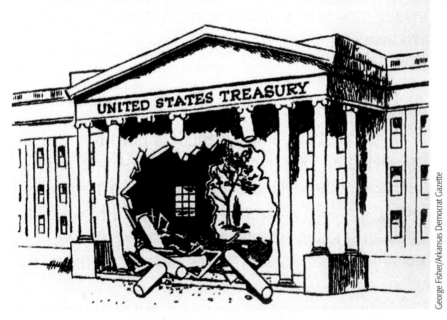

S & L s' new drive-through window

The 1980s savings-and-loan crisis led to the greatest collapse of U.S. financial institutions since the Great Depression. The federal bailout of S&Ls would cost American taxpayers at least $124 billion.

George Fisher/Arkansas Democrat Gazette

significant costs. Corporate downsizing meant layoffs for white-collar workers and management personnel, many of whom had difficulty finding comparable positions. The wave of mergers and takeovers left American corporations increasingly burdened by debt. It also helped to consolidate sectors of the economy—such as the media—under the control of a few players.

The Rich Get Richer The high-risk, deregulated boom of the 1980s was rotten with corruption. By the late 1980s, insider trading scandals—in which people used "inside" corporate information unavailable to the general public to make huge profits trading stocks—rocked financial markets and sent some of the most prominent Wall Street figures to jail. Savings and loans lost billions in bad investments, sometimes turning to fraud to cover them up. Scandal reached to the White House: Vice President Bush's son Neil was involved in shady S&L deals. The Reagan-Bush administration's bailout of the S&L industry cost taxpayers half a trillion dollars.

During the 1980s, the rich got richer, and the poor got poorer (see Figure 32.2). The number of Americans reporting an annual income of $500,000 increased tenfold between 1980 and 1989. The average compensation of corporate executive officers increased from 35 times an average worker's pay in 1978 to 71 times workers' average pay in 1989 (in 2005 the ratio was 262 to 1). In 1987, the United States had forty-nine billionaires—up from one in 1978. Middle-class incomes, however, remained stagnant.

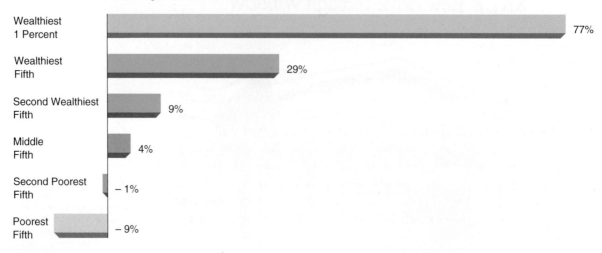

FIGURE 32.2
While the Rich Got Richer in the 1980s, the Poor Got Poorer
Between 1977 and 1989, the richest 1 percent of American families reaped most of the gains from economic growth. In fact, the average pretax income of families in the top percentage rose 77 percent. At the same time, the typical family saw its income edge up only 4 percent. And the bottom 40 percent of families had actual declines in income.
Source: Data from the *New York Times*, March 5, 1992.

Reagan's economic policies benefited the wealthy at the expense of other Americans. Reagan's tax policies decreased the total effective tax rates—income taxes plus Social Security taxes—for the top 1 percent of American families by 14.4 percent. But they increased taxes for the poorest 20 percent of families by 16 percent. By 1990, the richest 1 percent controlled 40 percent of the nation's wealth.

Reagan and the World

What characterized Reagan's approach to foreign policy?

A key element in Reagan's winning strategy in the 1980 election was his call for the United States to assert itself in the world. Though lacking a firm grasp of world issues, history, and geography, Reagan adhered to a few core principles. One was a deep anticommunism; a second was an underlying optimism about the United States' power and ability to positively affect the world. Together, these elements help explain Reagan's aggressive anticommunist foreign policy and his positive response in his second term to Soviet leader Mikhail Gorbachev's call for "new thinking" in world affairs.

Soviet-American Tension

Initially, embracing the strident anticommunism of early U.S. Cold War foreign policy, Reagan rejected Nixon's détente and Carter's human rights focus. Where Nixon and Carter perceived an increasingly multipolar international system, the Reagan team reverted to a bipolar perspective defined by the Soviet-American relationship. When Poland's pro-Soviet leaders in 1981 cracked down on an independent labor organization, Solidarity, Washington restricted Soviet-American trade and hurled angry words at Moscow. In March 1983, Reagan told evangelical Christians in Florida that the Soviets were "an evil empire." That year, Reagan restricted commercial flights to the Soviet Union after a Soviet fighter pilot mistakenly shot down a South Korean commercial jet that strayed 300 miles off course into Soviet airspace, killing 269 passengers.

Reagan believed that a substantial military buildup would thwart the Soviet threat. Accordingly, the administration launched the largest peacetime arms buildup in history. In 1985, when the military budget hit $294.7 billion (a doubling since 1980), the Pentagon spent an average of $28 million an hour. Assigning low priority to arms control talks, Reagan announced in 1983 his desire for a space-based defense shield against incoming ballistic missiles: the **Strategic Defense Initiative** (SDI). His critics tagged it "Star Wars" and said such a system could never work—some enemy missiles would get through. Moreover, the critics warned, SDI would elevate the arms race to dangerous levels. Still, SDI research and development consumed tens of billions of dollars.

Reagan Doctrine

Because he attributed Third World disorders to Soviet intrigue, the president declared the Reagan Doctrine: the United States would openly support anticommunist movements—freedom fighters battling the Soviets or Soviet-backed governments. In Afghanistan, Reagan continued providing covert assistance, through Pakistan, to the Mujahidin rebels fighting Soviet occupation. When the Soviets stepped up the war in 1985, the Reagan administration sent more high-tech weapons, particularly anti-aircraft Stinger missiles. Easily transportable and fired by a single soldier, the Stingers turned the tide in Afghanistan by making Soviet jets and helicopters vulnerable below eleven thousand feet.

The administration also applied the Reagan Doctrine aggressively in the Caribbean and Central America (see Map 32.1). In October 1983, the president sent troops into the tiny Caribbean island of Grenada to oust a pro-Marxist government. In El Salvador, he provided military and economic assistance to a military-dominated government struggling with left-wing revolutionaries. The regime used right-wing death squads, from which Luisa Orellana and her family fled. By decade's end, the death squads had killed forty thousand dissidents and citizens, as well as several U.S. missionaries. By the late 1980s, the United States spent more than $6 billion there in a counterinsurgency war. In January 1992, the Salvadoran combatants finally negotiated a U.N.-sponsored peace.

Contra War in Nicaragua

The Reagan administration also meddled in the Nicaraguan civil war. In 1979, leftist insurgents overthrew Anastasio Somoza, a long-time U.S. ally. The revolutionaries called themselves Sandinistas in honor of César Augusto Sandino, who headed the anti-imperialist Nicaraguan opposition against U.S. occupation in the 1930s and was finally assassinated by Somoza supporters. When the Sandinistas aided rebels in El Salvador, bought Soviet weapons, and invited Cubans to help reorganize the Nicaraguan army, Reagan officials charged that Nicaragua was becoming a Soviet client. In 1981, the CIA began to train, arm, and direct more than ten thousand counterrevolutionaries, known as contras, to overthrow the Nicaraguan government.

Strategic Defense Initiative (SDI): Reagan's proposed program for developing a high-tech, space-based defense shield that would protect the United States against incoming ballistic missiles; nicknamed "Star Wars" by critics.

Many Americans, including Democratic leaders in Congress, were skeptical about the communist threat and warned that Nicaragua could become another Vietnam. Congress in 1984 voted to stop U.S. military aid to the contras. Secretly, the Reagan administration lined up other countries, including Saudi Arabia, Panama, and South Korea, to funnel money and weapons to the contras, and in 1985 Reagan imposed an economic embargo against Nicaragua. Reagan rejected a plan from Costa Rica's president Oscar Arias Sanchez in 1987 to obtain a cease-fire in Central America through negotiations and cutbacks in military aid to rebel forces. (Arias won the 1987 Nobel Peace Prize.) Three years later after Reagan left office, Central American presidents brokered a settlement; in the national election that followed, the Sandinistas lost to a U.S.-funded party. After a decade of civil war, thirty thousand Nicaraguans had died, and the ravaged economy was one of the poorest in the hemisphere.

Oliver North: U.S. Marine colonel who became a central figure in the Iran-Contra, arms-for-hostages scandal.

Iran-Contra Scandal Reagan's obsession with defeating the Sandinistas almost caused his political undoing. In November 1986 it became known that the president's national security adviser, John M. Poindexter, and an aide, Marine lieutenant colonel **Oliver North**, in collusion with CIA director Casey, covertly

MAP 32.1

The United States in the Caribbean and Central America

The United States has often intervened in the Caribbean and Central America. Geographical proximity, economic stakes, political disputes, security links, trade in illicit drugs, and Cuban leader Fidel Castro's long-time defiance of Washington have kept U.S. eyes fixed on events in the region.

Source: Copyright © Cengage Learning

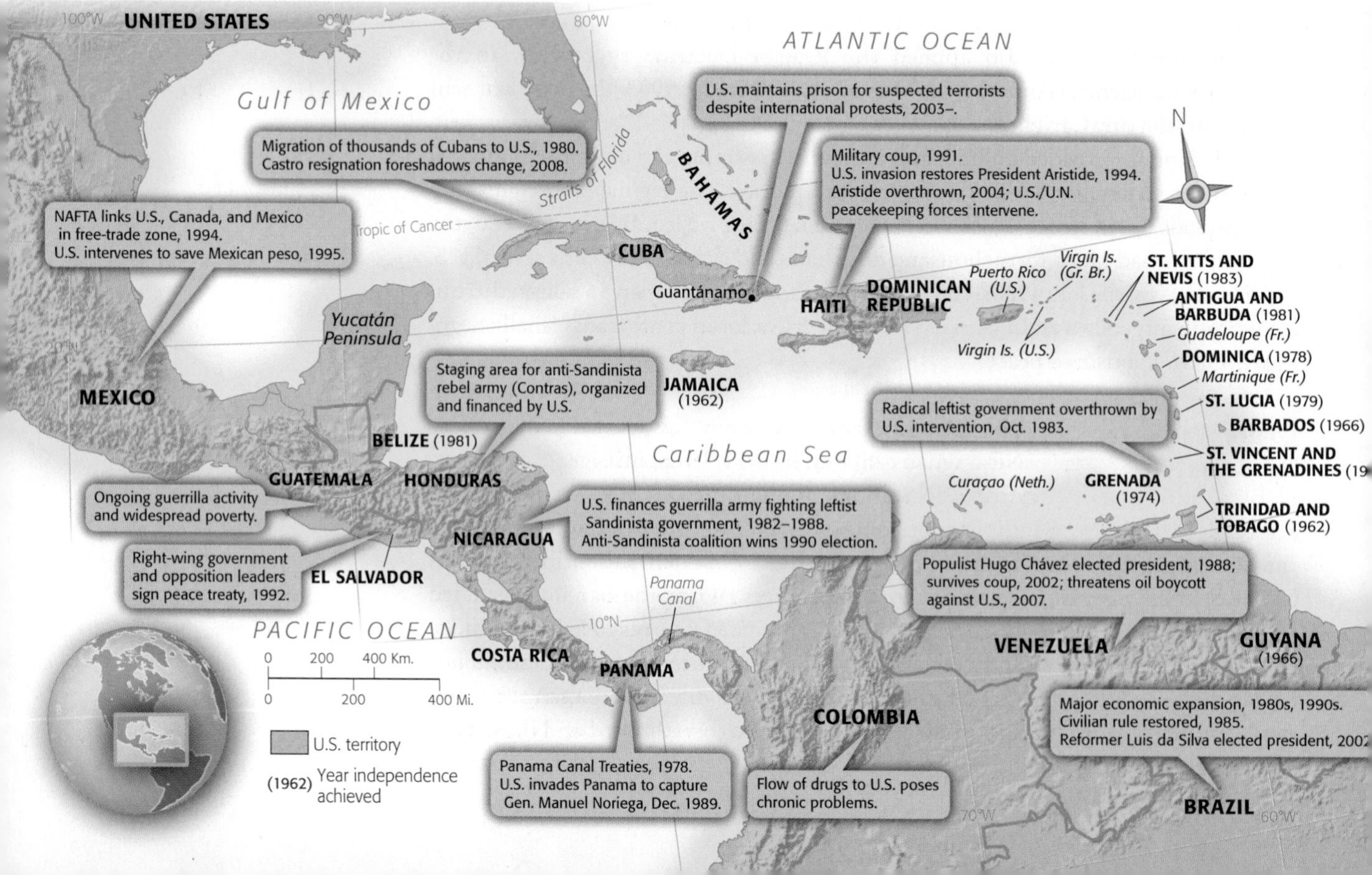

sold weapons to Iran in an unsuccessful attempt to win the release of Americans held hostage by Islamic fundamentalist groups in the Middle East. Washington had condemned Iran as a terrorist nation and demanded that allies cease trade there. More damaging was the revelation that money from the Iran arms deal was illegally diverted to the contras. North later admitted that he illegally destroyed government documents and lied to Congress to keep the operation clandestine.

Although Reagan survived the **Iran-contra scandal**, his popularity declined, and Congress reasserted its authority over foreign affairs. In late 1992, outgoing president George W. H. Bush pardoned several former government officials convicted of lying to Congress. Critics smelled a cover-up, for Bush himself, as vice president, participated in high-level meetings on Iran-contra deals. As for North, his conviction was overturned on a technicality.

Iran-contra scandal: Scandal in which Reagan administration illegally sold weapons to Iran to finance contras in Nicaragua.

U.S. Interests in the Middle East

Iran-contra also pointed to the increased importance in U.S. foreign policy of the Middle East and terrorism (see Map 33.1). The main U.S. goals in the Middle East remained preserving access to oil and supporting its ally Israel, while checking Soviet influence. In addition, American leaders faced new pressures from a deepened Israeli-Palestinian conflict and an anti-American and anti-Israeli Islamic fundamentalist movement that spread after the 1979 ouster of the shah of Iran.

The 1979 Camp David accords between Israel and Egypt raised hopes of a lasting settlement involving self-government for the Palestinian Arabs living in the Israeli-occupied Gaza Strip and West Bank. Instead, Israel and the Palestinian Liberation Organization (PLO) remained at odds. In 1982, in retaliation for Palestinian shelling of Israel from Lebanon, Israeli troops invaded Lebanon. The beleaguered PLO and various Lebanese factions called on Syria to contain the Israelis. Thousands of civilians died. Soon after Reagan sent Marines to Lebanon to join a peacekeeping force, U.S. troops became embroiled in a war between Christian and Muslim factions. In October 1983, terrorist bombs demolished a barracks, killing 241 U.S. servicemen. Four months later, Reagan pulled the remaining Marines out.

Terrorism

The attack on the Marine barracks showed the growing danger of terrorism to the United States and other western countries. In the 1980s, numerous otherwise powerless groups, many of them associated with the Palestinian cause or with Islamic fundamentalism, relied on terrorism to further their aims. Often they targeted U.S. citizens and property, because of Washington's support of Israel and U.S. involvement in the Lebanese civil war. Of the 690 hijackings, kidnappings, bombings, and shootings around the world in 1985, for example, 217 were against Americans, most originating in Iran, Libya, Lebanon, and the Gaza Strip. Three years later, a Pan American passenger plane was destroyed over Scotland, and many suspected pro-Iranian terrorists.

Washington, allied with Israel, continued to propose plans for Israelis to give back occupied territories and for Arabs to stop trying to push the Jews out of the Middle East. As the peace process stalled in 1987, Palestinians in the West Bank began an *intifada* (Arabic for "uprising") against Israeli forces. Israel refused to negotiate, but the United States talked with PLO chief Yasir Arafat after he renounced terrorism and accepted Israel's right to live in peace. For the PLO to recognize Israel and the United States to recognize the PLO were major developments in the Arab-Israeli conflict.

In South Africa, too, American diplomacy became more aggressive. At first, the Reagan administration followed a policy of constructive engagement, asking the increasingly isolated government to reform its white supremacist apartheid system. But many Americans demanded cutting off imports from South Africa and pressuring 350 U.S. companies to cease operations there. Some U.S. cities and states passed divestment laws, withdrawing dollars from U.S. companies active in South Africa. Public protest and congressional legislation forced the Reagan administration in 1986 to impose economic restrictions. Within two years, about half of the U.S. companies in South Africa left.

Enter Gorbachev

Many on the right disliked the South Africa sanctions policy; they believed the main black opposition group, the African National Congress (ANC), was dominated by communists, and they doubted the efficacy of sanctions. They also balked when Reagan, his popularity declining, entered negotiations with the Soviet Union. At a 1985 Geneva summit meeting, Reagan agreed in principle with new Soviet leader Mikhail S. Gorbachev's contention that strategic weapons should be substantially reduced, and at a 1986 Reykjavik, Iceland, meeting, they came close to a major reduction agreement. SDI stood in the way: Gorbachev insisted it should be shelved, and Reagan refused.

But Reagan and Gorbachev got along well. As General Colin Powell commented, though the Soviet leader was far superior to Reagan in mastery of specifics, he understood that Reagan was, as Powell put it, "the embodiment of his people's down-to-earth character, practicality, and optimism." And Reagan toned down his strident anti-Soviet rhetoric.

Perestroika and *Glasnost*

The turnaround in Soviet-American relations stemmed more from changes abroad than from Reagan's decisions. Under Gorbachev, a younger generation of Soviet leaders came to power in 1985. They modernized the highly bureaucratized, decaying economy through a reform program known as *perestroika* ("restructuring") and liberalized the authoritarian political system through *glasnost* ("openness"). For these reforms to work, Soviet military expenditures had to be reduced.

Intermediate-Range Nuclear Forces (INF) Treaty: Treaty signed by U.S. President Reagan and Soviet leader Mikhail Gorbachev banning all land-based intermediate-range nuclear missiles in Europe, and resulting in the destruction of 2,800 missiles.

In 1987, Gorbachev and Reagan signed the **Intermediate-Range Nuclear Forces (INF) Treaty** banning all land-based intermediate-range nuclear missiles in Europe. About 2,800 missiles were destroyed. Gorbachev also reduced his nation's armed forces, helped settle regional conflicts, and began the withdrawal of Soviet troops from Afghanistan. The Cold War was coming to an end.

American Society in the 1980s

What divided Americans in the 1980s?

As the Cold War waned, the belief in a United States united by shared middle-class values also lost its force. By the 1980s, after years of social struggle and division, few Americans believed in the reality of that vision; many rejected it as undesirable. Although the 1980s were never as contentious as the 1960s and 1970s, deep social divides split Americans. A newly powerful group of Christian conservatives challenged the secular culture. A growing class of affluent Americans seemed a society apart from the urban poor, whom sociologists and journalists began calling the underclass. And the composition of the

U.S. population was changing dramatically, as people immigrated to the United States from more and different nations than ever before.

Growth of the Religious Right

Since the 1960s, America's mainline liberal Protestant churches—Episcopalian, Presbyterian, Methodist—had lost members, while Southern Baptists and other denominations offering the experience of being "born again" through belief in Jesus Christ and the literal truth of the Bible (fundamentalism) grew rapidly. Fundamentalist preachers reached out through television: by the late 1970s, televangelist Oral Roberts was drawing 3.9 million viewers. Nearly 20 percent of Americans self-identified as fundamentalist Christians in 1980.

Most fundamentalist Christian churches stayed out of the social and political conflicts of the 1960s and early 1970s. But in the late 1970s, some influential preachers mobilized for political struggle. In a 1980 Washington for Jesus rally, fundamentalist leader Pat Robertson told crowds, "We have enough votes to run the country." The Moral Majority, founded in 1979 by Jerry Falwell, sought to create a Christian America, partly by supporting political candidates. Falwell's defense of socially conservative values and his condemnation of feminism (he called NOW the National Order of Witches), homosexuality, pornography, and abortion resonated with many Americans.

Throughout the 1980s, the coalition of conservative Christians known as the New Right campaigned against America's secular culture. Rejecting "multiculturalism"—that different cultures and lifestyle choices were equally valid—the New Right worked to make "God's law" the basis for American society. Concerned Women for America, founded by Beverly LaHayes in 1979, wanted elementary school readers containing "unacceptable" religious beliefs (including excerpts from *The Diary of Anne Frank* and *The Wizard of Oz*) removed from classrooms, and fundamentalist Christian groups again challenged teaching evolutionary theory in public schools. The Reagan administration frequently turned to James Dobson, founder of the conservative Focus on the Family organization, for policy advice.

Link to President Reagan's remarks at the Baptist Fundamentalism Annual Convention on April 13, 1984.

"Culture Wars"

Many Americans vigorously opposed the New Right's seeming intolerance and threat to basic freedoms, including freedom of religion for those whose beliefs differed from the conservative Christianity of the New Right. In 1982, politically progressive television producer Norman Lear, influential former congresswoman Barbara Jordan, and other prominent figures from the fields of business, religion, politics, and entertainment founded People for the American Way to support American civil liberties, the separation of church and state, and the values of tolerance and diversity. The struggle between the religious right and their opponents for the nation's future came to be known as the culture wars.

Many beliefs of Christian fundamentalists ran counter to the way most Americans lived—especially regarding women's roles. By the 1980s, a generation of girls had grown up expecting opportunities their mothers never had. Legislation such as the Civil Rights Act of 1964 and Title IX opened both academic and athletic programs to females. By 1985, more than half of married women with children under three worked outside the home—many from economic necessity. The religious right's insistence that women's place was in the home, subordinated to her husband, contradicted the gains made toward sexual equality and the reality of many women's lives.

The New Inequality   As Americans fought the "culture wars" of the 1980s, another social divide threatened the nation. A 1988 national report on race relations looked back to the 1968 Kerner Commission report to claim, "America is again becoming two separate societies," white and black. The majority of the United States' poor were white, and the black middle class was expanding. But people of color were disproportionately poor. In 1980, 33 percent of African Americans and 26 percent of Hispanic Americans lived in poverty, compared with 10 percent of whites (see Figure 32.3).

Reasons for poverty varied. The legacies of racism played a role. The changing job structure was partly responsible, as well-paid jobs decreased, replaced by lower-paid service jobs. In addition, families headed by a single mother were five times more likely to be poor than families maintained by a married couple. By 1992, 59 percent of African American children and 17 percent of white children lived in female-headed households, and almost half of African American children lived in poverty.

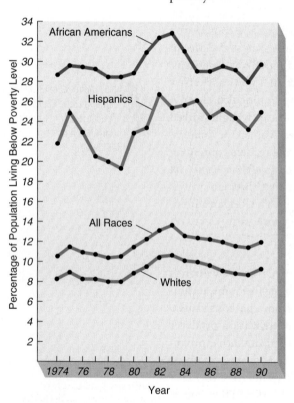

FIGURE 32.3
Poverty in America by Race, 1974–1990

Poverty in America rose in the early 1980s but subsided afterward. Many people of color, however, experienced little relief during the decade. Notice that the percentage of African Americans living below the poverty level was three times higher than that for whites. It was also much higher for Hispanics.

Source: Adapted from U.S. Bureau of the Census, *Statistical Abstract of the United States* (Washington, D.C.: 1992), p. 461.

Social Crises in American Cities   In impoverished inner-city neighborhoods, violent crime—particularly homicides and gang warfare—grew alarmingly, as did school dropout rates, crime rates, and child abuse. Some people sought escape in drugs, especially crack, a derivative of cocaine, which first struck New York City's poorest neighborhoods in 1985. Gang shootouts over drugs were deadly: the toll in Los Angeles in 1987 was 387 deaths, more than half of them innocent bystanders. Many states instituted mandatory prison sentences for possessing small amounts of crack equivalent to those for 100 grams of cocaine, the drug of more-affluent, white Americans. Such policies increased America's prison population almost fourfold from 1980 to the mid-1990s, with black and Latino youth arrested in disproportionate numbers. By 2000, young black men were more likely to have been arrested than to have graduated from college.

Homelessness also grew during the 1980s. Some homeless were impoverished families; many had drug or alcohol problems. About one-third were former psychiatric patients. By 1985, 80 percent of the total number of beds in state mental hospitals had been eliminated on the premise that neighborhood programs would better serve people than state institutions. Such local programs never materialized. Consequently, many of America's mentally ill citizens wandered the streets.

The AIDS Epidemic   Another social crisis confronting Americans in the 1980s was the global spread of acquired immune deficiency syndrome,

Combating the Spread of AIDS

During the 1960s and 1970s, with penicillin offering a quick and painless cure for venereal diseases and dependable contraceptives, such as the birth control pill, widely available, non-monogamous sex had fewer physical risks than at any time in history. But new sexually transmitted diseases appeared during the 1980s. By far the most serious was HIV/AIDS (Human Immunodeficiency Virus/Acquired Immune Deficiency Syndrome). Because AIDS initially was diagnosed in communities of gay men, many heterosexual Americans were slow to understand that they, too, might be at risk. Public health agencies and activist groups worked to raise awareness and promote safe sex. How is the couple in this ad portrayed? How does this image complicate widespread assumptions about who is at risk? And how does this public service advertisement make the case for "safe sex"?

Campaigns for "safe sex," such as this New York City subway ad, urged people to use condoms.

or **AIDS**. Caused by the human immunodeficiency virus (HIV), AIDS leaves its victims susceptible to deadly infections and cancers. The human immunodeficiency virus is spread through the exchange of blood or body fluids, often through sexual intercourse or needle sharing by intravenous drug users.

AIDS was first diagnosed in the United States in 1981. Between 1981 and 1988, of the 57,000 AIDS cases reported, nearly 32,000 resulted in death. Politicians were slow to devote resources to AIDS, partly because it was initially perceived as a "gay man's disease." "A man reaps what he sows," declared the Reverend Jerry Falwell of the Moral Majority. AIDS, and other sexually transmitted diseases such as genital herpes and chlamydia, ended an era defined by penicillin and "the pill," in which sex was freed from the threat of serious disease or unwanted pregnancy.

AIDS: Acquired Immune Deficiency Syndrome first diagnosed in the United States in 1981; had a very high mortality rate in the 1980s.

Link to the text and video of Vito Russo's "Why We Fight" speech.

New Immigrants from Asia

Social divisions were further complicated by the arrival of new immigrants from regions barely represented in the United States. Between 1970 and 1990, the United States absorbed more than 13 million new arrivals, most from Latin America and Asia. Before the 1965 immigration reforms, Americans of Asian ancestry made up less than 1 percent of the population; by 1990, that figure tripled.

Before 1965, most Asian Americans were of Japanese ancestry (about 52 percent in 1960), followed by Chinese and Filipino. There were only 603 Vietnamese residents of the United States in 1964. By 1990, the United States had absorbed almost 800,000 refugees from Indochina, casualties of the Vietnam war. Immigrants flooded in from South Korea, Thailand, India, Pakistan, Bangladesh, Indonesia, Singapore, Laos, Cambodia, and Vietnam. Japanese Americans were now only 15 percent of the Asian American population.

Immigrants from Asia were typically highly skilled or unskilled. Unsettled conditions in the Philippines in the 1970s and 1980s created an exodus of well-educated Filipinos to the United States. India's abundance of physicians and healthcare workers increasingly emigrated, as did educated, skilled workers from Korea, Taiwan, and China. Other Chinese immigrants, however, had few job skills and spoke little English. Many crowded into neighborhoods like New York City's Chinatown, where women worked under terrible conditions in the city's nonunion garment industry.

But even highly educated immigrants had limited options. A 1983 study found that Korean Americans owned three-quarters of the approximately twelve hundred greengroceries in New York City. Though often cited as a success story, Korean greengrocers usually descended the professional ladder: 78 percent had college or professional degrees.

The Growing Latino Population

Unprecedented immigration coupled with a high birth rate made Hispanic Americans the fastest-growing group of Americans. In 1970, Hispanic Americans made up 4.5 percent of the nation's population; that jumped to 9 percent by 1990, when one out of three Los Angelenos and Miamians were Hispanic. Mexican Americans, concentrated in California and the Southwest, made up most of this population, but Puerto Ricans, Cubans, Dominicans, and other Caribbean immigrants also lived in the United States, clustered principally in East Coast cities.

During the 1980s, people from Guatemala and El Salvador, like Luisa Orellana, fled civil war and government violence for the United States. Although the U.S. government commonly refused them political asylum (about 113,000 Cubans received political refugee status during the 1980s, compared with fewer than 1,400 El Salvadorans), a national Sanctuary movement of Christian churches defied the law to protect refugees from deportation. Economic troubles in Mexico and throughout Central and South America also produced a flood of undocumented workers who crossed the poorly guarded 2,000-mile border between the United States and Mexico, seeking economic opportunities. Some were sojourners, who moved back and forth across the border. A majority meant to stay.

Many Americans believed new arrivals threatened jobs and economic security, and nativist violence and bigotry increased. In 1982 twenty-seven-year-old Vincent Chin was beaten to death in Detroit by an unemployed auto worker and his uncle. American automobiles were losing to Japanese imports, and the two men seemingly mistook the Chinese American Chin for Japanese. In New York, Philadelphia, and Los Angeles, inner-city African Americans boycotted Korean groceries. Riots broke out in Los Angeles schools between black students and newly arrived Mexicans. In Dade County, Florida, voters passed an antibilingual measure that removed Spanish-language signs on public transportation, while at the state and national level people debated declaring English the "official" U.S. language. Public school classrooms, however, struggled with practical issues: in 1992, more than one thousand school districts in the United States enrolled students from at least eight different language groups.

Concerned about illegal aliens, Congress passed the **Immigration Reform and Control (Simpson-Rodino) Act** in 1986. Its purpose was to discourage illegal immigration by imposing sanctions on employers who hired undocumented workers, but it also provided amnesty to millions who immigrated illegally before 1982.

Immigration Reform and Control (Simpson-Rodino) Act: 1986 law that sought to discourage illegal immigration by fining employers who hired undocumented workers, but that also provided amnesty and a path to citizenship for millions who immigrated illegally before 1982.

New Ways of Life

Many Americans found their lifestyles transformed during the 1980s due to new technologies and new models of distribution and consumption. American businesses made huge capital investments in technology as computers became workplace staples. With new communications technology, large office parks could be located outside cities, where building costs were low, fostering "edge cities" or "technoburbs" filled with residents who lived, worked, and shopped beyond the old city centers. New single family homes grew larger; home prices rose from two and a half times the median household salary in 1980 to more than four times the median salary in 1988.

While the rich embraced ostentation (Donald Trump's $29 million yacht had gold-plated bathroom fixtures), people of more modest means also consumed more. Between 1980 and 1988, Walmart's sales jumped from $1.6 billion to $20.6 billion. The number of American shopping malls increased by two-thirds. Eating out became common. The percentage of overweight or obese Americans increased dramatically during the 1980s, even as more people began to run marathons, take aerobics classes or buy actress Jane Fonda's aerobics exercise videos.

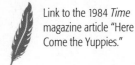

Link to the 1984 *Time* magazine article "Here Come the Yuppies."

Almost half of American families owned a home computer by 1990. About half of all families subscribed to cable television by the mid 1980s. MTV (Music Television), launched in 1981, quickly became a national phenomenon. Early MTV stars included Michael Jackson, whose fourteen-minute "Thriller" video premiered there in 1983, and Madonna, whose creative manipulation of her image, from "Boy Toy" sexuality to "Express Yourself" celebration of female empowerment, infuriated both sides in the decade's culture wars. Movie attendance dropped as Americans bought newly affordable VCRs and rented movies.

The End of the Cold War and Global Disorder

What were the highs and lows of Bush's presidency?

The end of Ronald Reagan's presidency coincided with world events that brought the dawn of a new international system. Reagan's vice president, **George H.W. Bush**, would become president and oversee the transition. The scion of a Wall Street banker and U.S. senator from Connecticut, Bush attended an exclusive boarding school and then Yale. He had the advantage in seeking the Republican presidential nomination in having been a loyal vice president. And he possessed a

George H.W. Bush: 41st president (1989–1993).

formidable résumé, including ambassador to the United Nations, chairman of the Republican Party, special envoy to China, and director of the CIA. He had also been a war hero, flying fifty-eight combat missions in the Pacific in World War II and receiving the Distinguished Flying Cross.

George Herbert Walker Bush

Bush entered the 1988 presidential campaign trailing his Democratic opponent, Massachusetts governor Michael Dukakis. Republicans turned that around by waging one of the most negative campaigns in U.S. history. Dukakis, while not personally attacking Bush, ran an uninspired campaign. Bush won by 8 percentage points in the popular vote and received 426 electoral votes to Dukakis's 112. The Democrats, however, retained control of both houses of Congress.

Bush's main interest was foreign policy, but he was naturally cautious and reactive in world affairs, much to the chagrin of neoconservatives. Mikhail Gorbachev's reforms in the Soviet Union were now stimulating reforms in eastern Europe that ultimately led to revolution. In 1989, thousands in East Germany, Poland, Hungary, Czechoslovakia, and Romania startled the world by repudiating their communist governments and staging mass protests for increased freedom. In November 1989, Germans scaled the Berlin Wall and tore it down; the following October, the two Germanys reunited. By then, other eastern European communist governments had fallen or were near collapse.

Pro-Democracy Movements

Challenges to communist rule in China met with less success. In June 1989, Chinese armed forces slaughtered hundreds—perhaps thousands—of unarmed students and citizens holding peaceful pro-democracy rallies in Beijing's Tiananmen Square. The Bush administration, anxious to preserve influence in Beijing, simply denounced the action, allowing the Chinese government to emphatically reject political liberalization.

Elsewhere, however, democratization efforts proved too powerful to resist. In South Africa, a new government under F. W. de Klerk began a cautious retreat from apartheid. In February 1990, de Klerk legalized all political parties in South Africa, including the ANC, and released Nelson Mandela, a hero to black South Africans, after a twenty-seven-year imprisonment. Then, the government repealed its apartheid laws over several years, allowing all citizens to vote. Mandela, who became South Africa's first black president in 1994, called the transformation a small miracle.

AP Images/John Parkin

African National Congress (ANC) leader Nelson Mandela gestures after casting his vote at Ohlange High School hall in Inanda, on April 27, 1994, for South Africa's first all-race elections. When results were announced later in the week, Mandela had been elected South Africa's first black president.

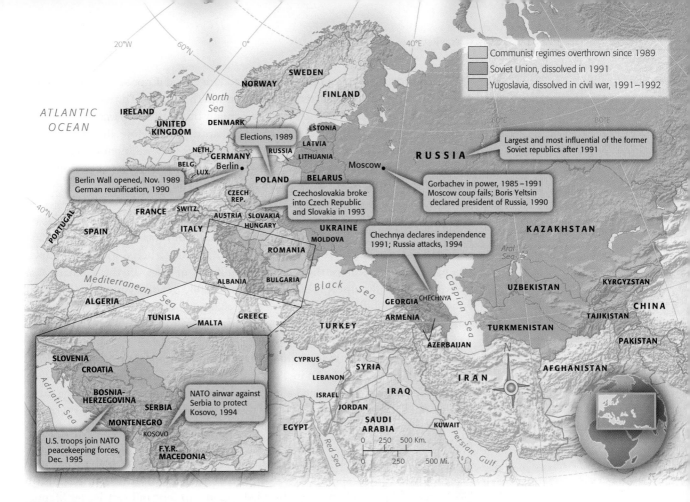

MAP 32.2

The End of the Cold War in Europe

When Mikhail Gorbachev came to power in the Soviet Union in 1985, he initiated reforms that ultimately undermined the communist regimes in eastern Europe and East Germany and led to the breakup of the Soviet Union itself, ensuring an end to the Cold War.

Source: Copyright © Cengage Learning

Collapse of Soviet Power

In 1990, the Soviet Union began to disintegrate. First the Baltic states of Lithuania, Latvia, and Estonia declared independence from Moscow. The following year, the Soviet Union ceased to exist, disintegrating into successor states—Russia, Ukraine, Tajikistan, and many others (see Map 32.2). Muscled aside by Russian reformers who thought he was moving too slowly toward democracy and free-market economics, Gorbachev lost power. The breakup of the Soviet empire, the dismantling of the Warsaw Pact (the Soviet military alliance formed in 1955 with communist countries of eastern Europe), the repudiation of communism by its leaders, German reunification, and a significantly reduced risk of nuclear war signaled the end of the Cold War.

The United States and its allies had won. The containment policy followed by nine presidents—from Truman through Bush—had many critics over the years, but succeeded at containing communism for four-plus decades without blowing up the world and obliterating freedom at home. Over time, the Soviet socialist economy proved less able to compete with the American free-market, less able to cope with the demands of the Soviet and eastern European citizenry.

Yet the Soviet empire might have survived longer had it not been for Gorbachev, one of the most influential figures of the twentieth century. Through unexpected overtures and decisions, Gorbachev fundamentally transformed the superpower relationship in ways that could scarcely have been anticipated before. Ronald Reagan's role was less central but still important because of his later willingness to negotiate and treat Gorbachev more as a partner than as an adversary. Just as personalities mattered in starting the Cold War, they mattered in ending it.

Costs of Victory

The victory in the Cold War elicited little celebration among Americans. The confrontation may never have become a hot war globally, but the period after 1945 nevertheless witnessed numerous Cold War–related conflicts claiming millions of lives. In the Vietnam War alone, up to 2 million people died, more than 58,000 of them Americans. Military budgets ate up billions of dollars, shortchanging domestic programs. Some Americans wondered whether the communist threat was ever as grave as officials had claimed.

Bush proclaimed a new world order and signed important arms reduction treaties with the Soviet Union in 1991 and with the post-breakup Russia in 1993. But the United States sustained a large defense budget and stationed large numbers of military forces overseas. As a result, Americans were denied the peace dividend that they hoped would reduce taxes and free up funds for domestic problems.

In Central America, the Bush administration cooled the zeal with which Reagan meddled, but showed no reluctance to intervene to further U.S. aims. In December 1989, American troops invaded Panama to oust military leader Manuel Noriega. A long-time drug trafficker, Noriega stayed in Washington's favor in the mid-1980s by providing logistical support for the Nicaraguan contras. In the early 1990s, exposés of his sordid record changed Bush's mind. Noriega was captured and taken to Miami, where, in 1992, he was convicted of drug trafficking and imprisoned. Devastated Panama, meanwhile, became increasingly dependent on the United States.

Saddam Hussein's Gamble

The strongest test of Bush's foreign policy came in the Middle East. The Iran-Iraq War ended inconclusively in August 1988, after eight years and almost 400,000 dead. The Reagan administration assisted the Iraqis with weapons and intelligence, as had many NATO countries. In mid-1990, Iraqi president Saddam Hussein, facing massive war debts, invaded neighboring Kuwait, hoping to enhance his regional power and oil revenues. George Bush condemned the invasion and vowed to defend Kuwait, partly fearing that Iraq might threaten U.S. oil supplies in Kuwait and petroleum-rich Saudi Arabia.

Within weeks, Bush convinced every important government, including most Arab and Islamic states, to economically boycott Iraq. Then, in Operation Desert Shield, Bush dispatched more than 500,000 U.S. forces to the region, joined by more than 200,000 from allied countries. Likening Saddam to Hitler and declaring it the first post-Cold War "test of our mettle," Bush rallied a deeply divided Congress to authorize "all necessary means" to oust Iraq from Kuwait (a vote of 250 to 183 in the House and 52 to 47 in the Senate). Many Americans believed that economic

Bruno Barbey/Magnum Photos, Inc.

In the Persian Gulf War of early 1991, Operation Desert Storm forced Iraqi troops out of Kuwait. Much of that nation's oil industry was destroyed by bombs and by the retreating Iraqis, who torched oil facilities as they left. Oil wells burned for months, darkening the sky over these American forces and causing environmental damage.

sanctions should be given more time to work, but Bush would not wait. Victory would come swiftly and cleanly.

Operation Desert Storm   Operation Desert Storm began on January 16, 1991, with the greatest air armada in history pummeling Iraqi targets. U.S. missiles reinforced round-the-clock bombing raids on Baghdad, Iraq's capital. It was a television war, in which CNN reporters broadcast live from a Baghdad hotel as bombs fell. In late February, coalition forces under General Norman Schwartzkopf launched a ground war that quickly routed the Iraqis from Kuwait. When the war ended on March 1, at least 40,000 Iraqis had been killed, while allied troops lost 240 (148 of them Americans).

Bush rejected suggestions from advisers to take Baghdad and topple Hussein's regime. Coalition members would not have agreed to such a plan, and it was unclear who would replace Iraq's dictator. So Saddam Hussein remained, though with his authority curtailed. The United Nations maintained an arms and economic embargo, and the Security Council issued Resolution 687, demanding full disclosure of Iraq's program to develop weapons of mass destruction and ballistic missiles. In Resolution 688, the Security Council condemned the Iraqi regime's brutal crackdown against Kurds in northern Iraq and Shi'ite Muslims in the south and demanded access for humanitarian groups. The United States, Britain, and France seized on Resolution 688 to create a northern no-fly zone, prohibiting Iraqi aircraft flights. A similar no-fly zone was set up in southern Iraq in 1992 and expanded in 1996.

Links to the World

CNN

When Ted Turner launched CNN, his Cable News Network, on June 1, 1980, few people took it seriously. CNN, with a staff of three hundred—mostly young, mostly inexperienced—operated from the basement of a converted Atlanta country club. CNN was initially known for its on-air errors, as when a cleaning woman emptied anchor Bernard Shaw's trash during his live newscast. But by 1992, CNN was seen in more than 150 nations, and *Time* magazine named Ted Turner its "Man of the Year."

Throughout the 1980s, CNN built relations with local news outlets worldwide. Millions watched as CNN reporters broadcast live from Baghdad in the 1991 Gulf War. When the Soviet Union wanted to denounce the 1989 U.S. invasion of Panama, officials called CNN's Moscow bureau instead of the U.S. embassy. During the Gulf War, Saddam Hussein reportedly kept televisions in his bunker tuned to CNN, and in 1992 President George H. W. Bush noted, "I learn more from CNN than I do from the CIA."

Despite its global mission, CNN's American origins were often apparent. During the U.S. invasion of Panama, CNN cautioned correspondents not to refer to the American military forces as "our" troops. What CNN offered was a global experience: people throughout the world watching the major moments in contemporary history as they unfolded. America's CNN created new links among the world's people. But, as *Time* magazine noted (while praising Turner as the "Prince of the Global Village"), such connections "did not produce instantaneous brotherhood, just a slowly dawning awareness of the implications of a world transfixed by a single TV image."

© Bettmann/Corbis

An employee at the CNN studios in Jerusalem dons a gas mask after an alarm sounds indicating an Iraqi missile attack on Israeli targets, January 19, 1991. CNN changed media history in the way its live coverage reported events as they unfolded.

The Americans with Disabilities Act

The Americans with Disabilities Act (ADA), passed by large bipartisan majorities in Congress and signed into law by President George H.W. Bush on July 26, 1990, built on the legacy of the United States' civil rights movement. Beyond prohibiting discrimination, it mandated that public and private entities—schools, stores, restaurants and hotels, government provide "reasonable accommodations" to allow people with disabilities to participate fully in the life of their communities and their nation.

The equal-access provisions of the ADA have changed the U.S. landscape. Steep curbs and stairs once blocked access to wheelchair users; now ramps and lifts are common. Buses "kneel" for passengers with limited mobility; crosswalks and elevators use audible signals for the sight-impaired; colleges and universities offer qualified students a wide range of assistance. People with various disabilities have traveled into the Grand Canyon and other parks, thanks to the National Park Service's accessibility programs.

At the same time, ADA employment regulations have generated difficult legal questions. Which conditions are covered by the ADA? (The Supreme Court ruled that asymptomatic HIV infection is a covered disability and carpal tunnel syndrome is not.) Employers may not discriminate against qualified people who can, with "reasonable" accommodation, perform the "essential" tasks of a job—but what is "reasonable" and what is "essential"? The specific provisions of the ADA will likely continue to be contested and redefined in the courts. But as Attorney General Janet Reno noted, as she celebrated the ADA's tenth anniversary, its true legacy is the determination "to find the best in everyone and to give everyone equal opportunity."

Although many would later question President Bush's decision to stop short of Baghdad, initially there were few objections. In the wake of Desert Storm, the president's popularity soared to 91 percent, beating the record 89 percent set by Harry Truman in June 1945 after Germany surrendered. Cocky advisers thought Bush could ride his popularity through the 1992 election.

Domestic Issues   Bush could also claim domestic achievements that seemed to affirm his pledge to lead a "kinder, gentler nation." In 1990, for example, Bush signed the **Americans with Disabilities Act**. Also in 1990, the president signed the Clean Air Act, which sought to reduce acid rain by limiting factory and automobile emissions.

Yet Bush's poll numbers started falling and kept falling, largely because of his ineffectual response to the weakening economy. He was slow to grasp the implications of the national debt and massive federal deficit. When the nation entered a full-fledged recession after the Gulf War, Bush merely proclaimed that things were not that bad. Business shrank, despite low interest rates that theoretically should have encouraged investment. Real-estate prices plummeted. American products faced tougher competitors, especially Japan and Asian nations. As unemployment climbed to 8 percent, consumer confidence sank. By late 1991, fewer than 40 percent of the American people felt comfortable about the nation's direction.

Americans with Disabilities Act: Law that barred discrimination against disabled persons in employment, transportation, public accommodation, communications, and governmental activities.

Clarence Thomas: 1991 African American nominee for the Supreme Court who was appointed despite accusations of sexual harassment by an attorney he had supervised. As a justice, he has interpreted the Constitution narrowly, championing conservative social issues.

Clarence Thomas Nomination

Bush's credibility was diminished further in fall 1991 by the confirmation hearings for **Clarence Thomas**, his Supreme Court nominee. The Bush administration hoped that those who opposed the nomination of another conservative to the high court might support an African American justice. But in October, Anita Hill, an African American law professor at the University of Oklahoma, charged that Thomas had sexually harassed her when she worked for him during the early 1980s. The televised Judiciary Committee hearings turned ugly, and some Republican members suggested that Hill was either lying or mentally ill. Thomas described himself as the "victim" of a "high-tech lynching." However, Hill's testimony focused the nation's attention on issues of power, gender, race, and the workplace. And the Senate's confirmation of Thomas, along with the attacks on Hill, angered many, further increasing the gender gap in American politics.

Summary

When Ronald Reagan left the White House in 1988, the *New York Times* wrote: "Ronald Reagan leaves no Vietnam War, no Watergate, no hostage crisis. But he leaves huge question marks—and much to do." George H.W. Bush met the foreign policy promises of the 1980s, as the Soviet Union collapsed and America won the Cold War. He also led the United States into war with Iraq, which ended swiftly but left Saddam Hussein in power.

During the 1980s, the United States moved from recession to economic prosperity. However, deep tax cuts and massive increases in defense spending boosted the national debt from $994 billion to more than $2.9 trillion. Pro-business policies, such as deregulation, created opportunities for economic growth but also opened the door to corruption. Policies that benefited the wealthy at the expense of middle-class or poor Americans widened the gulf between the rich and everyone else. Drug addiction, crime, and violence grew, especially in impoverished areas. The 1980s also saw the coalescence of "culture wars" between fundamentalist Christians who sought to "restore" America to God and opponents who championed separation of church and state and embraced liberal values. The nation shifted politically to the right, though the coalitions of economic and social conservatives that supported Reagan were fragile.

Finally, during the 1980s, America became more racially and ethnically varied. The nation's Latino and Asian population grew in size and visibility. During the Reagan-Bush years, America became more divided and more diverse. In the years to come, Americans and their leaders would struggle with the legacies of the "Reagan era."

Chapter Review

Reagan and the Conservative Resurgence

What groups made up the new Republican coalition of the 1980s?

In his 1980 and 1984 presidential campaigns (and as president), Ronald Reagan appealed to, and ultimately united, a broad range of previously fragmented groups nationwide, transforming them into a strong Republican base. First, Reagan drew those who wanted to strengthen the military, minimize federal power, and weaken liberal social programs stemming from the 1930s New Deal and 1960s Great Society. Second, Reagan attracted economic conservatives with his stand on deregulation, weaker unions, and tax policies benefiting corporations and investors. Third, Reagan drew support from disillusioned Democrats—intellectual neoconservatives who fell away from the party after Vietnam as well as members of unions and ethnic groups who resented what they saw as their hard-earned tax dollars funding welfare hand-outs to those who did not work. Finally, though divorced, Reagan also drew the growing religious New Right into his coalition by embracing causes that were important to them, such as the anti-abortion movement and prayer in public schools.

Reaganomics

Why was the 1980s' economic boom a mixed blessing?

On the one hand, by 1984, the Federal Reserve's policy of increasing interest rates and tightening money supply ended stagflation and reversed the economic downturn. And President Reagan's pro-business policies and deregulation helped smaller companies make inroads into fields previously dominated by major corporations. On the other hand, deregulation allowed many businesses—particularly the financial services industry—to operate without accountability to governing authorities such as the SEC. Consequently, corruption was widespread, as some investors became rich via insider trading, the illegal practice of buying stocks with information not available to the public. Shady deals in the savings and loan industry caused its collapse and required a federal bail-out of half a trillion dollars. The high-risk investment climate of the latter half of the decade not only fueled a stock market crash in 1987, but also led to corporate downsizing and layoffs for middle managers. Finally, Reagan's tax cuts and other policies benefited the rich at the expense of other Americans, enabling the rich to get richer while the poor became poorer.

Reagan and the World

What characterized Reagan's approach to foreign policy?

In foreign policy, Reagan was both aggressive and flexible. In dealing with the Soviets, he initially adopted a strident anticommunist position, implementing the Reagan Doctrine to aid anticommunist freedom fighters around the world. He branded the Soviet Union as "an evil empire" and helped arm counter-revolutionaries to overthrow the Nicaraguan government when he thought it

was becoming communist. Believing that a solid defense would thwart the Soviet threat, Reagan launched the largest peacetime arms buildup in U.S. history, spending $294.7 billion in 1985 (twice as much as in 1980). But his optimism about the power of the United States to positively affect world events also led him in his second term to accept Soviet leader Mikhail Gorbachev's call for disarmament and new thinking in world affairs that led to the end of the Cold War.

American Society in the 1980s

What divided Americans in the 1980s?

Americans continued to feel the tug of unresolved racial and ethnic tensions, especially as the immigrant groups who arrived in the 1960s and 1970s (the majority from Asia and Latin America) changed the demographic composition of American society. The gulf—both economic and cultural—widened between well-off Americans and the urban poor. New lines were also being drawn between secular and religious forces, as a powerful new group of Christian conservatives sought to reverse what they regarded as society's increased permissiveness, restore conservative family values, and shape the nation's future around their core Christian beliefs. The resulting battle, dubbed the culture wars, pitted those who supported the separation of church and state and celebrated tolerance and diversity against this new religious right.

The End of the Cold War and Global Disorder

What were the highs and lows of Bush's presidency?

George H. W. Bush's popularity ratings soared to 91 percent after the United States' success in Operation Desert Storm. He scored kudos for passing the Americans with Disabilities Act, banning job discrimination against those with disabilities who can reasonably perform a job's task with minor accommodations. He also signed the Clean Air Act in 1990, which sought to reduce acid rain by restricting factory and auto emissions. But his blind-spot about the weakening economy and recession that emerged after the Gulf War turned voters off. He dismissed the rising jobless rates, shrinking number of businesses, and plummeting real estate prices as not that bad, leading many Americans to distrust the nation's future in Bush's hands.

Suggestions for Further Reading

Elijah Anderson, *Streetwise: Race, Class, and Change in an Urban Community* (1992)

Lou Cannon, *President Reagan: The Role of a Lifetime* (2000)

Robert M. Collins, *Transforming America: Politics and Culture During the Reagan Years* (2006)

John Ehrman, *The Eighties: America in the Age of Reagan* (2005)

Jack F. Matlock, *Reagan and Gorbachev: How the Cold War Ended* (2004)

John Micklethwait and Adrian Wooldridge, *The Right Nation: Conservative Power in America* (2004)

James A. Morone, *Hellfire Nation: The Politics of Sin in American History* (2003)

James Patterson, *The Restless Giant: The United States from Watergate to Bush vs. Gore* (2005)

Mary Elise Sarotte, *1989: The Struggle to Create Post-Cold War Europe* (2009)

 **CourseMate**

Go to the CourseMate website for primary source links, study tools, and review materials for this chapter.
www.cengagebrain.com

Into the Global Millennium

America Since 1992

33

At 8:46 a.m. on that fateful Tuesday morning, Jan Demczur, a window washer, stepped into an elevator in the North Tower of the World Trade Center in New York City. The elevator started to climb, but before it reached its next landing, one of the six occupants recalled, "We felt a muted thud. The whole building shook. And the elevator swung from side to side like a pendulum." None of the occupants knew it, but American Airlines Flight 175 had just crashed into the building, at a speed of 440 miles per hour.

The elevator started plunging. Someone pushed the emergency stop button, and the descent stopped. Then a voice came over the intercom: there had been an explosion. As smoke seeped into the elevator, several men used the wooden handle of Demczur's squeegee to force open the doors but discovered they were on the fiftieth floor, where this elevator did not stop. In front of them was a wall.

Demczur, a Polish immigrant and former builder, saw that the wall was made of sheetrock, a plasterboard he knew could be cut. Using the squeegee, the men took turns scraping and poking, and finally burst through to a men's bathroom. Startled firefighters guided them to a stairwell. They finally reached the street at 10:23 a.m. Five minutes later, the tower collapsed.

It was September 11, 2001.

Later that day, Demczur learned that terrorists had hijacked four airliners and turned them into missiles. Two were flown into the World Trade Center; one slammed into the Pentagon in Washington, D.C.; and one crashed in a Pennsylvania field after passengers tried to retake the plane from the hijackers. Both World Trade Center towers collapsed, killing nearly three thousand people.

It was the deadliest attack the United States ever suffered on its soil. The events sent shock waves around the globe, revealing how interconnected the world had become in the early twenty-first century. At the World Trade Center alone, nearly five hundred foreigners from more than eighty countries perished.

Many of the victims were, like Demczur, immigrants who came to New York seeking a better life; others were on temporary work visas. But all made the World Trade Center a kind of global city within a city, where some 50,000 people worked and another 140,000 visited daily.

A symbol of U.S. financial power, the World Trade Center towers also represented the globalization of trade that marked the 1980s and 1990s. The towers housed the offices of more than four hundred businesses, including the world's leading financial institutions—Bank of America, Switzerland's Credit Suisse Group, Germany's Deutsche Bank, and Japan's Dai-Ichi Kangyo Bank.

Globalization was a 1990s buzzword and went beyond trade and investment to include connections in commerce, communications, and culture. While terrorists—tied to a radical Islamic group called Al Qaeda—sought to bring down that globalization, their attack used the same international technological, economic, and travel infrastructure that fueled global integration. Cell phones, computers, intercontinental air travel—all instruments of globalization—were crucial in the terrorists' plot to turn four jetliners into lethal weapons.

Islamic militants had bombed the World Trade Center's underground parking garage before, in 1993, but Americans at the time paid only fleeting attention. President Bill Clinton took office in 1993 and concentrated less on foreign policy and more on domestic issues such as healthcare and deficit reduction. Clinton also sought to harness globalization to the United States' benefit.

For most Americans, the 1990s brought good times. The stock market soared, unemployment dropped, and more Americans owned homes. But the 1990s were also marked by violence and cultural conflict—the first multiethnic uprising in Los Angeles, domestic terrorism in Oklahoma City, school shootings, and hate crimes.

These were also politically volatile years. From the first days of Clinton's presidency, conservative Republicans blocked Democrats' legislative programs, and the GOP routed Democrats in the 1994 midterm elections. But Republicans alienated voters by shutting down the federal government during the winter of 1995–1996 in a budget standoff, and Clinton was reelected in 1996. However, scandal plagued the Clinton White House, compromising the president's ability to lead.

Clinton's successor, George W. Bush, successful in a close and controversial election, responded to the 9/11 attacks by declaring a "war on terrorism." Bush ordered U.S. forces into large-scale military action, first in Afghanistan, where Al Qaeda was headquartered with the blessing of the ruling Taliban regime, then in Iraq to oust Saddam Hussein's government. Militarily, the Taliban and the Iraqi government were quickly beaten. Al Qaeda, however, remained a threat, and in Afghanistan fighting resumed.

In Iraq, U.S. occupying forces battled a major insurgency. Bush's high approval ratings dropped, and though he won reelection in 2004, his second term was undermined by continued bloodshed in Iraq and scandal at home. In 2008, Democratic candidate Barack Obama won the presidency on a platform of hope and change. As the nation's first African American president, his election was symbolically important, but Obama, who inherited two wars and a major recession, struggled to deliver the domestic transformations he had promised.

As you read this chapter, keep the following questions in mind:

* **What was "The New Economy" of the 1990s, and how did it contribute to the globalization of business?**

* **Did the attacks of September 11, 2001, change America in fundamental ways? Explain.**

* **Why did the United States invade Iraq in 2003, and why did its occupying forces subsequently face a drawn-out and bloody insurgency?**

Social Strains and New Political Directions

Although the 1990s would be remembered for relative peace and prosperity, the decade did not start that way. Drugs, homelessness, and crime plagued U.S. cities. Racial tensions worsened; the gulf between rich and poor widened. The economy tipped into recession. Public disillusionment with political leaders ran strong. As the 1992 presidential election began, Americans wanted a change.

Turmoil in L.A. Racial tensions that troubled the nation erupted in the South Central neighborhood of Los Angeles in 1992. There was an immediate cause: A jury with no African American members had acquitted four white police officers charged with beating a black man, Rodney King, who fled a pursuing police car at speeds exceeding 110 miles per hour.

The roots of the violence, however, went deeper. Almost one-third of South Central residents lived in poverty—a rate 75 percent higher than for the city as a whole—after well-paid jobs disappeared during the deindustrialization of the 1970s and 1980s. Tensions increased as new immigrants arrived—Latinos from Mexico and Central America, who competed with African Americans for jobs, and Koreans who established small businesses such as grocery stores. Outside the legitimate economy, the 40 Crips (an African American gang) and the 18th Street gang (Latino) struggled over territory as the crack epidemic further decimated the neighborhood and the homicide rate soared. Many African American and Latino residents saw high prices in Korean-owned shops as exploitation, while Korean shopkeepers complained of frequent shoplifting, robberies, even beatings.

The violence in Los Angeles was a multiethnic uprising that left at least fifty-three people dead and symbolized fundamental conflicts in American society. In addition, the economy had grown slowly or not at all during the Bush administration. In 1978, California's Proposition 13—the first in a series of tax revolts nationwide—cut property taxes while the population boomed, and the state faced bankruptcy in mid-1992. Thirty states were in financial trouble in the early 1990s. Factory employment plummeted, and corporate downsizing cost well-educated

Chronology

1992	Violence erupts in Los Angeles over Rodney King verdict
	Major economic recession
	Clinton elected president
1993	Congress approves North American Free Trade Agreement (NAFTA)
1994	Contract with America helps Republicans win majorities in House and Senate
	Genocide in Rwanda
	U.S. intervention in Haiti
1995	Domestic terrorist bombs Oklahoma City federal building
	U.S. diplomats broker peace for Bosnia
1996	Welfare reform bill places time limits on welfare payments
	Clinton reelected
1998	House votes to impeach Clinton
1999	Senate acquits Clinton of impeachment charges
	NATO bombs Serbia over Kosovo crisis
	Antiglobalization demonstrators disrupt World Trade Organization (WTO) meeting in Seattle

2000	Nation records longest economic expansion in its history
	Supreme Court settles contested presidential election in favor of Bush
2001	Economy dips into recession; period of low growth and high unemployment begins
	Bush becomes president
	Al Qaeda terrorists attack World Trade Center and Pentagon
	United States attacks Al Qaeda positions in Afghanistan, topples ruling Taliban regime
2003	United States invades Iraq, ousts Saddam Hussein regime
2004	Bush reelected
2005	Hurricane Katrina strikes Gulf Coast
2006	Iraq War continues; by end of year, U.S. deaths reach three thousand
	Democrats take both houses of Congress in midterm elections
2007	Major economic recession begins in December
2008	Barack Obama elected president
2009	Obama announces increased U.S. military commitment to Afghanistan; U.S. continues troop drawdown in Iraq

white-collar workers their jobs, too. In 1991, median household incomes severely declined; in 1992, the number of poor people in America reached the highest level since 1964.

Clinton's Victory

As the American economy suffered, so did President George H. W. Bush's approval rating. Despite the credit Bush gained for ending the Cold War and the quick victory in the Gulf War, economic woes and a lack of what he once called the "vision thing" left him vulnerable in the 1992 presidential election.

The Democratic nominee, Arkansas governor **Bill Clinton**, offered a profound contrast to Bush. Clinton's campaign headquarters bore signs with the four-word reminder "It's the economy stupid." In a town hall–format presidential debate, a woman asked how the economic troubles affected each candidate, and Clinton replied, "Tell me how it's affected you again?" George Bush was caught on camera looking at his watch.

On election day, Clinton and his running mate, Tennessee Senator Al Gore, swept New England, the West Coast, and much of the industrial Midwest, even making inroads into an almost solidly Republican South and drawing "Reagan Democrats" back to the fold.

Bill Clinton: 42nd U.S. President, from 1993–2001. Clinton served as the Governor of Arkansas for twelve years prior to his election to the U.S. Presidency.

Presidential candidate Bill Clinton campaigns in Jackson, Mississippi, in 1992. Describing Clinton's campaign appearance the night before the election, a *New York Times* journalist wrote: "Bill Clinton, a middling amateur saxophonist, is playing his true instrument, the crowd."

Clinton and the "New Democrats"

A journalist described Bill Clinton in a 1996 *New York Times* article as "one of the biggest, most talented, articulate, intelligent, open, colorful characters ever to inhabit the White House," while noting that Clinton "can also be an undisciplined, fumbling, obtuse, defensive, self-justifying rogue." Larger than life, Clinton was a born politician from a small town called Hope who had wanted to be president most of his life. At Georgetown University in Washington, D.C., during the 1960s he protested the Vietnam War and (like many of his generation) maneuvered to keep himself out of it. Clinton won a Rhodes scholarship to Oxford, earned his law degree from Yale, and returned to his home state of Arkansas, where he was elected governor in 1978 at age thirty-two. Bill Clinton's wife, **Hillary Rodham Clinton**, was the first First Lady to have a significant career of her own. They met when they were both law students at Yale, where Hillary Rodham had made Law Review (an honor not shared by her husband).

Politically, Bill Clinton was a "new Democrat," advocating a more centrist—though still socially progressive—position for the Democratic Party. Clinton and his colleagues emphasized private-sector economic development, focusing on job training and other policies they believed would promote opportunity, not dependency. They championed a global outlook in foreign policy and economic development, along with an ethic of "mutual responsibility" and "inclusiveness."

Hillary Rodham Clinton: Wife of President Bill Clinton, she was directly involved in policymaking during her husband's presidency. She later served as a New York senator (2001–2009), ran for president, and served as Secretary of State.

Clinton began his presidency with an ambitious program of reform and revitalization, including appointing a cabinet that "looks like America" in all its diversity. Republicans did not allow Clinton the traditional honeymoon period and maneuvered him into fulfilling his pledge to end the ban on gays in the military before he secured congressional or military support. Amid controversy, Clinton accepted a "don't ask, don't tell" compromise that alienated liberals and conservatives, the gay community and the military.

Clinton's major goal was affordable healthcare. But special interests mobilized in opposition: the insurance industry worried about lost profits; the business community feared higher taxes; the medical community worried about more regulation, lower government reimbursement rates, and reduced healthcare quality. The healthcare task force, cochaired by Hillary Rodham Clinton, could not defeat these forces and healthcare failed.

"Republican Revolution" and Political Compromise

New-style Republicans challenged the beleaguered Clinton. In September 1994, more than three hundred Republican candidates for the House of Representatives endorsed the Contract with America. Developed under the leadership of Georgia representative **Newt Gingrich**, the Contract promised "the end of [big] government... [and] the beginning of a Congress that respects the values and shares the faith of the American family." It called for a balanced-budget amendment to the Constitution, reduction of the capital gains tax, a two-year limit on welfare payments (while making unmarried mothers under eighteen ineligible), and increased defense spending.

In the midterm elections, the Republican Party mobilized socially conservative voters to take control of both houses of Congress for the first time since 1954. Many Republicans believed attempts to weaken federal power and dismantle the welfare state would succeed.

But while they supported reducing government spending, many Americans opposed cuts to specific programs, including Medicare and Medicaid, education and college loans, highway construction, farm subsidies, veterans' benefits, and Social Security. Republicans made a bigger mistake when they issued Clinton an ultimatum on the federal budget and forced the government to suspend all nonessential action during the winter of 1995–1996.

Such struggles led Clinton to make compromises that moved American politics to the right. For example, he signed the 1996 Personal Responsibility and Work Opportunity Act, a welfare reform measure mandating that heads of families on welfare must find work within two years (though states could exempt 20 percent of recipients), limiting welfare benefits to five years over an individual's lifetime, and making many legal immigrants ineligible. The Telecommunications Act of 1996, signed by Clinton, reduced diversity in media by permitting companies to own more television and radio stations.

Clinton was reelected in 1996 (defeating Republican Bob Dole and Reform Party candidate Ross Perot), partly because Clinton stole some of the conservatives' thunder. He declared that "the era of big government is over" and invoked family values, a centerpiece of the Republican campaign. Sometimes Clinton's actions were true compromises; other times, he reclaimed issues from the conservatives, as when he redefined family values as "fighting for the family-leave law."

Newt Gingrich: Republican Congressman who co-authored the 1994 "Contract with America" pledging tax cuts, congressional term limits, tougher crime laws, anti-pornography measures, a balanced-budget amendment, and other reforms.

Link to the 1994 Republican Party's "Contract with America."

Clinton's legislative accomplishments were modest but included the Family and Medical Leave Act, guaranteeing 91 million workers the right to take time off to care for ailing relatives or newborn children. The Health Insurance Portability and Accountability Act ensured that, when Americans changed jobs, they would not lose health insurance because of preexisting medical conditions. Clinton created national parks that protected 3.2 million acres of American land and made progress cleaning up toxic waste dumps. However, the 1990s will most likely be remembered for its prosperity and economic growth.

Political Partisanship and Scandal

Political battles were divisive and ugly as the political right attacked Clinton with vehemence. Hillary Clinton was a frequent target; when she told a hostile interviewer during her husband's first presidential campaign, "I suppose I could have stayed home and baked cookies ... But what I decided to do was pursue my profession." The *New York Post* called her "an insult to most women." And an independent counsel's office headed by Kenneth Starr, a conservative Republican and former judge, would spend $72 million investigating allegations of wrongdoing by the Clintons. Starr was originally charged with investigating Whitewater, a 1970s Arkansas real-estate deal in which the Clintons had invested. He found no evidence against the Clintons, but Starr expanded his investigation and proved that Clinton lied to a grand jury when he testified that he had not engaged in sexual relations with twenty-two-year-old White House intern Monica Lewinsky.

In a 445-page report to Congress, Starr outlined eleven possible grounds for impeachment, accusing Clinton of lying under oath, obstruction of justice, witness tampering, and abuse of power. In December 1998, the House of Representatives, voting along party lines, concluded that the president committed perjury and obstructed justice. Clinton became the second president to face a trial in the Senate, which has the constitutional responsibility to decide (by two-thirds vote) whether to remove a president from office.

But the American people did not want Clinton removed from office. Polls showed that large majorities approved of his job performance, even while condemning his personal behavior. Many did not believe his actions constituted "high crimes and misdemeanors" (normally acts such as treason) required by the Constitution for impeachment. The Republican-controlled Senate, responding partly to popular opinion, did not vote to convict Clinton.

Politics, the Media, and Celebrity Culture

Clinton was not the first president to engage in illicit sex. President John F. Kennedy had numerous sexual affairs, including one with a nineteen-year-old intern. But after the 1970s Watergate scandals, the media no longer turned a blind eye to presidential misconduct. The fiercely competitive news networks relied on scandal, spectacle, and crisis to lure viewers. The 1990s partisan political wars created a take-no-prisoners climate. Both Republican Speaker of the House Newt Gingrich and his successor, Robert Livingston, resigned when evidence of their extramarital affairs surfaced. Finally, as former Clinton aide Sidney Blumenthal writes, the impeachment struggle was part of the culture wars: "a monumental battle over ... cultural mores and the position of women in American society, and about the character of the American people."

Violence and Anger in American Society

Political extremism exploded on April 19, 1995, when 168 people were killed in a bomb blast that destroyed the nine-story Alfred P. Murrah Federal Building in Oklahoma City.

At first, many blamed Middle Eastern terrorists. But a charred piece of truck axle two blocks away, with a still legible vehicle identification number, revealed that the bomber was Timothy McVeigh, a white American and Persian Gulf War veteran. He sought revenge for the deaths of Branch Davidian religious sect members, whom he believed the FBI deliberately slaughtered in a standoff over firearms charges two years before in Waco, Texas.

In subsequent months, reporters and investigators discovered militias, tax resisters, and white-supremacist groups nationwide. These groups believed that the federal government was controlled by "sinister forces," including Zionists, cultural elitists, and the United Nations. After McVeigh's act of domestic terrorism, many groups lost members.

On April 20, 1999, eighteen-year-old Eric Harris and seventeen-year-old Dylan Klebold opened fire on classmates and teachers at Columbine High School in Littleton, Colorado, killing thirteen before killing themselves. No clear reason why two academically successful students in a middle-class suburb would commit mass murder emerged. Students in Paducah, Kentucky; Springfield, Oregon; and Jonesboro, Arkansas, also massacred classmates.

Then, two hate crimes shocked the nation. In 1998, James Byrd Jr., a forty-nine-year-old African American, was murdered by three white supremacists who dragged him with a chain from the back of a pickup truck in Jasper, Texas. Later that year, Matthew Shepherd, a gay college student, was beaten and left tied to a wooden fence in freezing weather outside Laramie, Wyoming. His killers said they were humiliated when he flirted with them at a bar. To some, these murders signified the strength of racism and homophobia in the United States. Others saw Americans' horror over these murders as a sign of positive change.

Clinton's Diplomacy

Internationally, the United States occupied a uniquely powerful position in the 1990s. The demise of the Soviet Union created a one-superpower world in which the United States stood far above other powers in political, military, and economic might. Yet in his first term Clinton was more wary in traditional aspects of foreign policy—great-power diplomacy, arms control, regional disputes—than in facilitating American cultural and trade expansion. Recalling the public's impatience in the Vietnam debacle, he was suspicious of foreign military involvements.

Clinton's mistrust of foreign interventions was cemented by the difficulties in Somalia. In 1992, Bush sent U.S. Marines to the East African nation as part of a U.N. effort to ensure that humanitarian supplies reached starving Somalis. But in summer 1993, when Americans were attacked there, Clinton withdrew U.S. troops. And he did not intervene in Rwanda, where in 1994 the majority Hutus butchered 800,000 of the minority Tutsis in a brutal civil war.

Balkan Crisis

Many administration officials argued for using America's power to contain ethnic hatreds, support human rights, and promote democracy worldwide. That notion was tested in the Balkans, where

Bosnian Muslims, Serbs, and Croats were killing one another. Clinton talked tough against Serbian aggression and atrocities in Bosnia-Herzegovina, especially the Serbs' "ethnic cleansing" of Muslims through massacres and rape camps. He occasionally ordered air strikes, but he primarily emphasized diplomacy. In late 1995, American diplomats brokered a fragile peace.

But Yugoslav president Slobodan Milosevic continued the anti-Muslim and anti-Croat fervor. When Serb forces moved to violently rid Kosovo of its majority ethnic Albanians, reports of Serbian atrocities and a major refugee crisis stirred world opinion and pressed Clinton to intervene. In 1999, U.S.-led NATO forces launched a massive aerial bombardment of Serbia. Milosevic withdrew from Kosovo, where U.S. troops joined a U.N. peacekeeping force.

Agreements in the Middle East

In the Middle East, Clinton tried to help the PLO and Israel settle their differences. In September 1993, the PLO's Yasir Arafat and Israel's prime minister, Yitzhak Rabin, signed an agreement at the White House for Palestinian self-rule in the Gaza Strip and the West Bank's Jericho. The following year Israel signed a peace accord with Jordan, further reducing the chances of another Arab-Israeli war. Radical anti-Arafat Palestinians, however, continued terrorist attacks on Israelis, while extremist Israelis killed Palestinians and, in November 1995, Rabin himself. Only after American-conducted negotiations and renewed violence in the West Bank did Israel agree in early 1997 to withdraw troops from the Palestinian city of Hebron. Thereafter, the peace process alternately sagged and spurted.

International environmentalism also gathered pace in the 1990s. The George H. W. Bush administration had opposed many provisions of the 1992 Rio de Janeiro Treaty protecting the diversity of plant and animal species and resisted stricter rules to reduce **global warming**. Clinton, urged on by his environmentalist vice president Al Gore, signed the 1997 Kyoto protocol, which aimed to combat carbon dioxide and other emissions. But facing strong opposition, Clinton never submitted the protocol for ratification to the Republican-controlled Senate.

global warming: Worldwide surge in average temperatures most scientists attribute to greenhouse-gas emissions.

Bin Laden and Al Qaeda

Meanwhile, the threat to U.S. interests by Islamic fundamentalism loomed. Senior White House officials worried **Al Qaeda** (Arabic for "the base"), an international terrorist network led by Osama bin Laden, wanted to purge Muslim countries of what it considered the profane influence of the West.

The son of a Yemen-born construction tycoon in Saudi Arabia, bin Laden had supported the Afghan Mujahidin in their struggle against Soviet occupation. He then founded Al Qaeda and financed terrorist projects with his substantial inheritance. Then he focused on American targets. In 1995, a car bomb in Riyadh killed 7 people, 5 of them Americans. In 1998, bombings at the American embassies in Kenya and Tanzania killed 224 people, including 12 Americans. In Yemen in 2000, a boat laden with explosives hit the destroyer USS *Cole*, killing 17 American sailors. Although bin Laden masterminded and financed these attacks, he eluded U.S. attempts to apprehend him. In 1998, Clinton approved a plan to assassinate bin Laden, but it failed.

Al Qaeda: A radical Islamic group founded in the late 1980s and headed by Osama bin Laden; it relies on an international network of cells to carry out terrorist attacks against the West, particularly the United States and its allies, in the name of Islamic fundamentalism.

Globalization and Prosperity

For most Americans, the late 1990s marked unprecedented peace and prosperity. Between 1991 and 1999, the Dow Jones Industrial Average climbed from 3,169 to a high of 11,497. The booming market benefited the middle class and the wealthy, as mutual funds, 401(k) plans, and other new investment vehicles drew a majority of Americans into the stock market. In 1952, only 4 percent of U.S. households owned stocks; by 2000, almost 60 percent did.

At the end of the 1990s, unemployment was 4.3 percent—the lowest peacetime rate since 1957. That made it easier to implement welfare reform, and welfare rolls declined 50 percent. Both the richest 5 percent and poorest 20 percent of American households saw their incomes rise almost 25 percent. That translated to an average gain of $50,000 for the top 5 percent and only $2,880 for the bottom 20 percent, further widening the gap between rich and poor. Still, by 1999, more than two-thirds of Americans were homeowners—the highest percentage in history.

The roots of the 1990s boom were in the 1970s, when corporations began investing in new technologies, retooling plants, and cutting labor costs. Specifically, companies reduced the influence of organized labor by moving operations to the union-weak South and West and to countries such as China and Mexico, with cheap labor and lax pollution controls.

Digital Revolution   The rapid development of information technology—computers, fax machines, cell phones, and the Internet—had a huge economic impact in the 1980s and 1990s. New companies and industries sprang up, many headquartered in California's Silicon Valley. By the late 1990s, the *Forbes* list of the 400 Richest Americans featured high-tech leaders such as Microsoft's

Students and their teacher gather around a laptop at an elementary school in Hebei Province, China. This innovative tool for learning connects these students to resources that were not easily accessible in the past.

© Bettmann/Corbis

Bill Gates, the wealthiest person in the world with worth approaching $100 billion, as his company produced the operating software for most personal computers.

The heart of this technological revolution was the microprocessor. Introduced in 1970 by Intel, it miniaturized a computer's central processing unit, enabling small machines to perform calculations previously requiring large machines. Computing chores that took a week in the early 1970s took only a minute by 2000; the cost of storing one megabyte of information fell from $5,000 in 1975 to $.17 in 1999.

Clinton and his advisers helped further spur economic growth by abandoning the middle-class tax cut and making deficit reduction a top priority. White House officials rightly concluded that, if the deficit—which topped $500 billion—could be brought under control, interest rates would drop and the economy would rebound. And that is what happened. By 1997, the budget deficit had been erased, and the gross national product rose by an average of 3.5–4 percent annually.

Globalization of Business

The journalist Thomas L. Friedman asserted that the post–Cold War world was the age of **globalization**, characterized by the integration of markets, finance, and technologies. U.S. officials lowered trade and investment barriers, completing the **North American Free Trade Agreement (NAFTA)** with Canada and Mexico in 1993, and in 1994 concluding the Uruguay Round of the General Agreement on Tariffs and Trade (GATT), which lowered tariffs for the seventy member nations that accounted for about 80 percent of world trade. The Clinton administration also endorsed the 1995 creation of the **World Trade Organization** (WTO), to administer and enforce agreements made at the Uruguay Round. Finally, the president formed a National Economic Council to promote trade missions around the world.

globalization: The removal of barriers to flow of capital, goods, and ideas across national borders.

North American Free Trade Association (NAFTA): Pact that admitted Mexico to the free-trade zone that the United States and Canada had created earlier.

World Trade Organization: International organization that regulates the global trading system and provides dispute resolution between member nations.

Multinational corporations were the hallmark of this global economy. By 2000, there were 63,000 parent companies worldwide and 690,000 foreign affiliates. Some, such as Nike and Gap, Inc., subcontracted some production to developing countries with the lowest labor costs. World exports totaled $5.4 trillion in 1998, twice that of 1978. U.S. exports reached $680 billion in 1998, but imports rose to $907 billion (for a trade deficit of $227 billion). Sometimes the multinationals affected foreign policy, as when Clinton in 1995 extended full diplomatic recognition to Vietnam under pressure from such corporations as Coca-Cola, Citigroup, General Motors, and United Airlines, which wanted to enter that emerging market.

Critics of Globalization

While the administration promoted open markets, labor unions argued that free-trade agreements exacerbated the trade deficit and exported American jobs. Average wages for American workers declined after 1973, from $320 per week to $260 by the mid-1990s. Other critics maintained that globalization widened the gap between rich and poor countries, creating a mass of "slave laborers" in poor countries working under conditions that would be intolerable in the West. Environmentalists charged that globalization exported pollution to countries unprepared to deal with it. Still others warned about the power of multinational corporations over traditional cultures.

Antiglobalization fervor reached a peak in the fall of 1999, when thousands of protesters disrupted the WTO meeting in Seattle. In the months that followed, there were sizable protests at meetings of the International Monetary Fund (IMF) and the World Bank.

Target: McDonald's

Activists also targeted corporations, such as the Gap, Starbucks, Nike, and, especially, McDonald's, which by 1995 was serving 30 million customers daily in over one hundred countries. Critics assailed the company's alleged exploitation of workers, its high-fat menu, and its role in creating an increasingly homogeneous world culture. For six years starting in 1996, McDonald's endured hundreds of often-violent protests, including bombings in Rome, Prague, London, Macao, Rio de Janeiro, and Jakarta.

Others decried the violence and the arguments of the antiglobalization campaigners. True, some economists acknowledged, statistics showed that global inequality had grown. But if one included quality-of-life measurements, such as literacy and health, global inequality had declined. Some studies found that wage and job losses for U.S. workers were caused not primarily by globalization factors, such as imports, production outsourcing, and immigration, but by technological change that made production more efficient. Some researchers saw no evidence that governments' sovereignty had been compromised or that there was a "race to the bottom" in labor and environmental standards from globalization.

As for creating a homogeneous global culture, McDonald's, others said, tailored its menu and operating practices to local tastes. And although American movies, TV programs, music, computer software, and other intellectual property dominated world markets, foreign competition also arrived in the United States. American children were gripped by the Japanese fad Pokemon, for example, and satellite television created a worldwide following for European soccer teams.

The Bush-Gore Race

Al Gore: Long-time Democratic Senator from Tennessee and vice president under Bill Clinton (1993–2001); unsuccessfully ran for president in the highly contested 2000 race; won a 2007 Nobel Peace Prize for his advocacy and expertise on environmental issues, particularly global warming.

George W. Bush: 43rd President of the United States, from 2001 to 2008; son of 41st president George H. W. Bush

The strong economy should have given Vice President **Al Gore** an advantage in the 2000 presidential election. But Gore failed to inspire voters. Earnest and highly intelligent, with a resume that included service in Vietnam and six terms in Congress, he appeared to be a well-informed policy wonk rather than a charismatic leader.

Gore's Republican opponent was the son of former president George H. W. Bush. An indifferent student, **George W. Bush** graduated from Yale in 1968 and pulled strings to jump ahead of a one-and-a-half-year waiting list for the Texas Air National Guard, thus avoiding service in Vietnam. He had a rocky career in the oil business, but Bush's fortunes improved during his father's presidency, and in 1994 he was elected to the first of two terms as governor of Texas.

The Contested Election of 2000

Al Gore narrowly won the popular vote, but not the presidency. It all came down to Florida (where Bush's brother Jeb was governor) and its twenty-five electoral votes. In the initial tally, Bush narrowly edged Gore out in Florida, but the close margin legally required a recount. In several heavily African American counties, tens of thousands of votes went uncounted because voters failed to fully dislodge the "chads," small perforated squares, when punching the paper ballots. Lawyers struggled over whether "hanging chads" (partially detached) and "pregnant chads" (punched but not detached) were sufficient signs of voter intent. In Palm Beach County, many elderly Jewish residents were confused by a poorly designed ballot and accidentally selected the allegedly anti-Semitic Pat Buchanan instead of Gore. After thirty-six days, with court cases at the state and federal levels, the Supreme Court voted 5 to 4 along narrowly partisan lines to end the recount process. Florida's electoral votes—and the presidency—went to George Bush. Struggles over the election further polarized the nation.

With the close election, many believed Bush would govern from the center. Some also thought he moved to the right during the election only to ensure conservative evangelical Christian votes. But Bush governed from the right, arguably further to the right than any other modern administration.

9/11 and the War in Iraq

In international affairs, the administration charted a unilateralist course. Given America's preponderant power, senior Bush officials reasoned, it did not need other countries' help. Accordingly, Bush withdrew the United States from the 1972 Anti-Ballistic Missile Treaty with Russia to develop a National Missile Defense system similar to Reagan's "Star Wars." The White House renounced the 1997 **Kyoto protocol** on controlling global warming and opposed a protocol strengthening the 1972 Biological and Toxin Weapons Convention. These decisions and the administration's hands-off policy toward the Israeli-Palestinian peace process caused consternation in Europe.

Kyoto protocol: A protocol setting strict emission targets for industrialized nations. President Bush refused to sign the agreement, making the United States one of only four nations that declined participation.

9/11

Then came September 11, 2001. On that sunny Tuesday morning, nineteen hijackers seized control of four commercial jets departing from East Coast airports. At 8:46 a.m. one plane crashed into the 110-story North Tower of the World Trade Center in New York City. At 9:03 a.m., a second plane flew into the South Tower. In under two hours, both buildings collapsed, killing thousands of office workers, firefighters, and police officers. At 9:43, the third plane crashed into the Pentagon. The fourth plane was also headed toward Washington, but several passengers, learning of the World Trade Center attacks through cell-phone conversations, stormed the cockpit; in the scuffle, the plane crashed in Somerset County, Pennsylvania, killing all aboard.

More than three thousand people died in the deadliest act of terrorism in history. The hijackers—fifteen Saudi Arabians, two Emiratis, one Lebanese, and an Egyptian—had ties to Al Qaeda. Officials in the Clinton and Bush administrations had warned that an Al Qaeda attack was inevitable, but neither administration made counterterrorism a foreign policy priority.

Afghanistan War

In an instant, counterterrorism was priority number one. President Bush responded with military force. Al Qaeda operated out of Afghanistan with the blessing of the ruling Taliban, a repressive Islamic fundamentalist group that gained power in 1996. In early October, the United States launched a sustained bombing campaign against Taliban and Al Qaeda positions, and sent special operations forces to help a resistance organization in northern Afghanistan. Within two months, the Taliban was driven from power, although bin Laden and top Taliban leaders eluded capture.

As administration officials acknowledged, military victory did not end the terrorist threat. Bush spoke of a long struggle against evil forces, in which the nations of the world were either with the United States or against it. Some questioned whether a war on terrorism could ever be won in a meaningful sense, given that the foe was a nonstate actor. Stunned by September 11, most Americans experienced a renewed sense of national unity and pride. Flag sales soared, and Bush's approval ratings skyrocketed.

The attacks on 9/11 brought forth an outpouring of sympathy for the victims and their families, and for the United States generally, from people around the world. Here firefighters in Taipei, Taiwan, attend a prayer service during a global day of mourning.

PATRIOT Act

But the new patriotism had a dark side. Congress passed the **USA PATRIOT Act** (Uniting and Strengthening America by Providing Appropriate Tools Required to Intercept and Obstruct Terrorism), making it easier for law enforcement to conduct searches, wiretap telephones, and obtain electronic records on individuals. Attorney General John Ashcroft approved giving FBI agents new powers to monitor the Internet, mosques, and rallies. Civil libertarians charged that the Justice Department overstepped, and some judges ruled against the tactics. Yet, according to a June 2002 Gallup poll, 80 percent of Americans were willing to exchange some freedoms for security.

Weeks after the attacks, 71 percent surveyed said that they felt depressed, and one-third had trouble sleeping. Yet people continued shopping in malls, visiting amusement parks, and working in skyscrapers. Although airline bookings dropped significantly early on, people returned to the skies. In Washington, Democrats and Republicans again sparred over judicial appointments, energy policy, and the proposed new **Department of Homeland Security**, approved by Congress in November 2002 to coordinate defense against terrorism.

Economic Uncertainty

Economically, the months before September 11 witnessed a collapse of the "dot-coms," Internet companies that were the darlings of Wall Street in the 1990s. In 2001, some five hundred dot-coms declared bankruptcy or closed. There were other economic warning signs as well,

USA PATRIOT Act: Controversial anti-terrorist law that extended the government's legal surveillance power to allow monitoring of telephone and internet communications and library searches.

Department of Homeland Security: Cabinet-level department created by Congress to coordinate anti-terrorism efforts. Various agencies were placed under its jurisdiction including the Coast Guard, the Customs Service, the Federal Emergency Management Agency (FEMA), and the Immigration and Naturalization Service.

notably a meager 0.2 percent growth rate in goods and services for 2001's second quarter. Corporate revenues were also down.

Economic concerns deepened after 9/11 with a four-day closing of Wall Street and sharp drop in stock prices. The Dow Jones Industrial Average plunged 14.26 percent. The markets eventually rebounded, but questions remained about the economy's health. Neither economic uncertainty nor the failure to capture **Osama bin Laden** dented Bush's popularity. In the 2002 midterm elections, Republicans retook the Senate and increased their majority in the House.

International Responses

Overseas, the president's standing was not nearly so high. Immediately after September 11, governments worldwide announced they would work with Washington against terrorism. But within a year, Bush's good-versus-evil stance put off foreign observers. When the president hinted that the United States might unilaterally strike Saddam Hussein's Iraq or deal forcefully with North Korea or Iran—Bush's "axis of evil"—many allied governments strongly objected.

Bush and other top officials argued that in an age of terrorism, the United States would not wait for a potential security threat to become real; it would strike first. Americans, Bush declared had to be "ready for preemptive action when necessary to defend our liberty and to defend our lives." Critics, among them world leaders, called it recklessly aggressive and contrary to international law.

But Bush was determined, particularly on Iraq. Several of his top advisers, including Secretary of Defense Donald Rumsfeld and Vice President Dick Cheney, had wanted to oust Saddam Hussein since the 1991 Gulf War. After the Twin Towers fell, they folded Iraq into the war on terrorism—even though counterterrorism experts saw no link between Saddam and Al Qaeda. Initially, Secretary of State **Colin Powell**, the first African American in that post, kept the focus on Afghanistan, but gradually the White House shifted. By spring 2002 a secret consensus was reached: Saddam Hussein would be removed by force.

Why Iraq?

In September 2002, Bush challenged the United Nations to enforce its resolutions against Iraq, or the United States would act itself. He and his aides offered shifting reasons for getting tough with Iraq. They said Saddam was a major threat to the United States and its allies, a leader who possessed and would use banned biological and chemical "weapons of mass destruction" (WMDs) and who sought nuclear weapons. They claimed, contrary to their own intelligence, that he had ties to Al Qaeda and could be linked to the 9/11 attacks.

But there were other motivations as well. Neoconservatives claimed that ousting Saddam would enhance the security of Israel, the United States' key Middle East ally, and start a chain reaction extending democracy throughout the region. White House political strategists believed a swift removal of a hated dictator would assure Bush's reelection. And Bush wanted to prevent an Iraq armed with WMDs from destabilizing an oil-rich region.

Congressional Approval

Bush claimed he did not need congressional authorization for military action against Iraq, but sought it anyway. In early October 2002, the House of Representatives voted 296 to 133 and the Senate 77-23 to authorize force against Iraq. Many who voted in favor were unwilling to

Osama bin Laden: A wealthy Islamic fundamentalist militant who had been expelled from his native Saudi Arabia in 1991 and took refuge in Sudan, where he financed large-scale construction and agricultural projects and amassed followers to his Al Qaeda terrorist organization, masterminding several attacks, among them September 11, 2001, attack on the United States.

Colin Powell: Four-star general who served as National Security Adviser (1987–1989), Chairman of the Joint of Chiefs of Staff (1989–1993), and Secretary of State (2001–2005).

defy Bush so close to midterm elections, even though they opposed military action without U.N. sanction. Critics complained that the president had not presented evidence that Saddam Hussein constituted an imminent threat or was connected to the 9/11 attacks. Bush switched to a less hawkish stance, and in early November, the U.N. Security Council unanimously approved Resolution 1441, imposing rigorous arms inspections on Iraq.

But the Security Council was divided over the next move. In late January 2003, the weapons inspector's report castigated Iraq for failing to complete "the disarmament that was demanded of it" but also said it was too soon to tell whether inspections would succeed. Whereas U.S. and British officials said the time for diplomacy was up, France, Russia, and China called for more inspections. As the U.N. debate continued, Bush sent about 250,000 soldiers to the region. Britain sent about 45,000 troops.

Fall of Baghdad

In late February, the United States floated a resolution to the U.N. that proposed issuing an ultimatum to Iraq, but only three of the fifteen Security Council members agreed. Bush abandoned the resolution and diplomatic efforts on March 17, when he ordered Saddam Hussein to leave Iraq within forty-eight hours or face an attack. Saddam ignored the ultimatum, and on March 19 the United States and Britain launched an aerial bombardment of Baghdad and other areas. A ground invasion followed (see Map 33.1). On April 9, Baghdad fell.

Thus, when violence soon erupted, U.S. planners seemed powerless to respond. The plight of ordinary Iraqis deteriorated as the occupation authority proved unable to maintain order. Decisions by the Coalition Governing Council (CPA), headed by Ambassador Paul Bremer, made matters worse, notably Bremer's move in May to disband the Iraqi army. A multisided insurgency of Saddam loyalists, Iraqi nationalists, and foreign Islamic revolutionaries took shape; soon, U.S. occupying forces faced frequent ambushes. By October 2003, more troops died from these attacks than had perished in the initial invasion.

The chaos in Iraq and the failure to find weapons of mass destruction had critics questioning the war's validity. Prewar claims of a "rush to war" resounded again. Even defenders of the invasion castigated the administration for its failure to anticipate the occupation problems. In spring 2004, photos showing Iraqi detainees being abused by American guards at Abu Ghraib prison were broadcast worldwide, generating international condemnation.

Election of 2004

Facing reelection, President Bush expressed disgust at Abu Ghraib and denied charges that he and top aides condoned the abuse. The White House also claimed the transfer of sovereignty to an interim Iraqi government in June would flatten the insurgency. Bush's Democratic opponent, Senator **John Kerry** of Massachusetts, a Vietnam veteran who had voted for the Iraq resolution, never articulated a clear alternative strategy on the war. Bush won reelection with 51 percent of the popular vote to Kerry's 48 percent and 279 electoral votes to Kerry's 252. The GOP also increased its majorities in the House and Senate.

John Kerry: Senator from Massachusetts and Vietnam War veteran; Democratic nominee for president in 2004.

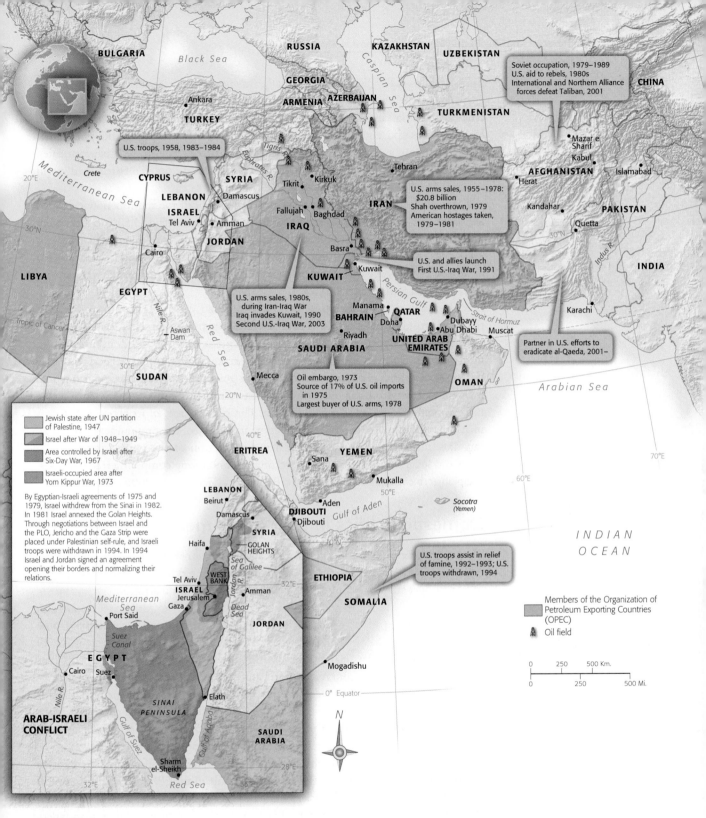

MAP 33.1

The Middle East

Middle East nations maintained precarious relations with the United States. To protect its interests, the United States extended large amounts of economic and military aid and sold them weapons. The Arab-Israeli dispute particularly upended order, although the peace process moved forward intermittently.

Source: Copyright © Cengage Learning

America Isolated   Internationally, Bush faced criticism because of Iraq, Abu Ghraib, his administration's lack of engagement in the Israeli-Palestinian dispute, and seeming disdain for diplomacy generally. The White House, critics said, rightly sought to prevent North Korea and Iran from joining the nuclear club but seemed incapable of making it happen. In Europe, Bush continued to be depicted as a gun-slinging cowboy whose aggressive policies threatened world peace.

Iraq, though, remained the chief problem. The bill for the war now exceeded $1 billion per week. In March 2005, American war dead reached 1,500; in December 2006, it reached 3,000. Meanwhile, by mid-2006, estimates of Iraqi civilian deaths ranged from 60,000 to 655,000. Iraqi casualties resulted from insurgent suicide attacks, U.S. bombing of suspected insurgent hideouts, and increasing sectarian violence between Sunnis and Shi'ites.

The Bush administration denied that Iraq had degenerated into civil war or that the struggle had become a Vietnam-like quagmire, but it seemed uncertain how to end the fighting. In Congress and the press, calls for withdrawal from Iraq multiplied, but skeptics cautioned it could make things worse, triggering sectarian bloodshed and a collapse of the Baghdad government. The power and regional influence of neighboring Iran would increase, and American credibility would be undermined throughout the Middle East. The 2007 "surge" of increased U.S. forces in Iraq contributed to a drastic reduction in violence, as commanders shifted to a counterinsurgency strategy emphasizing protection of the population. But the surge did little to promote political reconciliation among competing Iraqi factions. That objective remained elusive when Bush left office in early 2009.

Domestic Politics in Post 9/11 America

The centerpiece Bush's domestic agenda, achieved before the 9/11 attacks, was a $1.3 trillion tax cut—the largest in U.S. history. As Bush intended, it wiped out the $200 billion budget surplus he inherited from the Clinton administration.

The Presidency of George W. Bush   Much of Bush's agenda fit with conservative principles. Religious conservatives liked the newly prominent role of religion in politics. The president spoke frequently of his faith; Attorney General John Ashcroft, a Pentecostal Christian, held prayer meetings every morning in the Justice Department. And Bush appointed the medical director of a Christian pregnancy-counseling center whose website claimed that the "distribution of birth control is demeaning to women … and adverse to human health and happiness" to head the nation's federal family planning program.

Bush also advocated economic deregulation. His administration dismantled environmental restrictions on the oil, timber, and mining industries, and as Wall Street developed an array of risky financial instruments, he remained hands-off. While his plan to partially privatize Social Security or reform immigration failed, Bush did reshape the Supreme Court. Fifty-year-old conservative U.S. Circuit Court judge John Roberts was confirmed as chief justice after Chief Justice William Renquist died, and another strong conservative, 55-year-old Samuel Alito, became junior associate justice when Sandra Day O'Connor resigned.

But Bush often turned to a form of "big government" conservatism. Bush dramatically increased the federal government's role in public education through his "**No Child Left Behind**" initiative. Meant to fix a "broken system of education that dismisses certain children and classes of children as unteachable," the legislation linked federal funding to state action: to receive federal education dollars, states had to set "high standards," evaluating students through standardized tests and holding schools accountable. While conservatives traditionally argued against federally subsidized medical care, the Bush administration created an expensive entitlement program covering prescription drugs for American seniors under Medicare.

No Child Left Behind: Label for Bush law mandating standardized testing in reading and math in grades four and eight.

Hurricane Katrina

Growing perceptions of administrative incompetence began to undermine Americans' confidence in Bush's administration. In late August, 2005, a major hurricane hit the U.S. Gulf Coast and New Orleans. **Hurricane Katrina** destroyed the levees that kept low-lying parts of New Orleans from being swamped by Lake Pontchartrain and surrounding canals. Floodwater covered 80 percent of New Orleans, and more than eighteen hundred people died.

Tens of thousands of people who lacked the resources to flee New Orleans sought shelter at the Superdome. Food and water quickly ran low and toilets backed up; people wrapped the dead in blankets and waited for rescue. Those outside the Gulf region, watching the suffering crowd of mainly poor, black New

Hurricane Katrina: Worst natural disaster in U.S. history; resulting flooding destroyed much of New Orleans and Gulf Coast in August 2005; poor handling of the crisis fueled cries of racism and tarnished the Bush administration.

AP Photo/Ben Sklar

Rescuers save a family from floodwaters in Bay St. Louis, Mississippi, after Hurricane Katrina. Katrina destroyed not only New Orleans, but much of the U.S. Gulf Coast from Louisiana into Alabama. The federal government designated 90,000 square miles as disaster area. More than 1,800 people lost their lives in the storm.

Orleanians at the Superdome, discussed what Democratic party leader Howard Dean called the "ugly truth": that poverty remains linked to race. The public also worried about administrative mismanagement and the president's seeming indifference.

Economic Recession

But larger troubles were brewing: American home prices—a "housing bubble"—were about to collapse. After initial deregulation in the 1980s, financial institutions sought new ways to expand their profits and experimented with "subprime" mortgages for people who previously would not have qualified for credit. By 2006, one-fifth of all home loans were subprime. As demand for homes kept rising, so did prices. Because housing prices kept going up, lenders saw little risk. If a family defaulted on their mortgage and lost their house, the property could be sold for more than it was worth. Wall Street firms bought up mortgages, bundling them together, good and bad, into multibillion dollar packages to sell to investors. These mortgage-backed securities—made possible by deregulation—were complex and risky.

This unstable structure began to fail in 2007, as more borrowers defaulted on mortgages. People tried to escape unaffordable mortgages by selling their houses, but housing prices plummeted. Increasingly, mortgages were larger than a home's value. And the financial institutions that gambled on mortgage-backed securities did not have enough capital to sustain such losses. Worldwide, banks were on the verge of collapse.

This crisis paralyzed the credit markets. Businesses couldn't get loans to buy raw materials or inventory; consumers couldn't get credit to buy large items, such as cars. Many Americans were already deeply in debt. In 2005, the average family spent more than it earned—and for those under 35, the savings rate was minus 16 percent. As credit tightened, people bought less. Businesses laid off workers, and unemployment climbed. The Bush administration attempted to prevent the financial system's collapse by bailing out those deemed "too big too fail." The Troubled Asset Relief Program (TARP) eventually provided $700 billion dollars in loans to failing institutions, but Americans on "main street" were angry that tax dollars rescued wealthy bankers on "Wall Street."

Election of 2008

In the 2008 presidential election, the hard-fought Democratic primary pitted New York senator Hillary Clinton against Illinois senator **Barack Obama**, forcing Americans to confront the meaning of race and gender in American society. Obama, who won the Democratic nomination, ran against Arizona senator John McCain, a Vietnam veteran who survived five years in a P.O.W. camp. McCain never drew enthusiastic support from socially conservative Republicans, though some embraced his choice of running mate, Alaska Governor Sarah Palin. Obama mobilized the grassroots: young people, African Americans, people who had never voted before. More than any previous candidate, he used technology to reach voters, who contributed millions of dollars through his website.

Republican vice presidential candidate Sarah Palin drew crowds, but appeared uninformed on key issues. Critics argued that McCain's choice of Palin showed weak judgment that could be disastrous in the presidency. The economy was the deciding

Barack Obama: 44th president (elected 2008) and the nation's first African American president who took office in the midst of the worst economic crisis since the Great Depression.

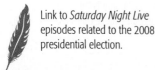

Link to *Saturday Night Live* episodes related to the 2008 presidential election.

factor: McCain's claim, in the midst of Wall Street's September 2008 meltdown, that "the fundamentals of our economy are strong" backfired, giving Obama victory in November.

Barack Obama

Link to the March 18, 2008, "Race Speech" by, at the time, presidential candidate, Barack Obama.

Barack Hussein Obama, the nation's forty-fourth president, was born in Hawai'i in 1961. His mother was a white woman from Kansas; his father a Kenyan graduate student at the University of Hawai'i. (The couple divorced when their child was two years old and each married again, giving Barack both African and Indonesian half-siblings.) Obama spent part of his childhood in Indonesia with his mother and attended high school in Hawai'i. After graduating from Harvard Law School, Obama became a community organizer in Chicago. He married fellow Harvard Law graduate Michelle Robinson, working as a civil rights lawyer and law professor at the University of Chicago before entering state politics in 1997. He gained national acclaim as a first-term senator for his keynote speech at the 2004 Democratic national convention.

Obama began his presidency with ambitious goals. He vowed to pass a comprehensive healthcare reform bill within the year, but he also had to confront his inheritance: two unresolved wars, a massive federal deficit, and a major recession. In February 2009, Obama signed legislation creating a $787 billion economic stimulus package to jumpstart the economy and supported expanding TARP and bailing out failing auto giants GM and Chrysler. The economy began a slow recovery in 2009, but unemployment rates remained high, reaching 10.2 percent. One in eight Americans received food stamps from the government, and Walmart pointed to evidence of hard times: a big jump in the purchase of kitchen storage containers for leftovers.

© Bettmann/Corbis

More than 75,000 people gathered in Chicago's Grant Park to celebrate Barack Obama's election on November 4, 2008.

Fierce partisan bickering stalled healthcare reform and job creation. Some saw the gridlock as proof that U.S. leaders were unable to address long-term social and economic challenges; others countered that the system was designed by the Founders to function slowly and cautiously.

Link to President Obama's West Point speech announcing troop increase in Afghanistan.

In foreign affairs, Obama had more latitude. In Iraq, U.S. casualty figures continued to decline in 2009, and Obama planned to withdraw combat forces from the country by August 2010. After deliberating in fall 2009, Obama announced that he would boost U.S. troop numbers in Afghanistan by about 30,000, bringing the total to 100,000. To allay concerns that the war would stretch on indefinitely, Obama simultaneously declared that the United States would begin withdrawing its forces in 2011. Critics were unmoved, calling Afghanistan "Obama's War."

Americans in the First Decade of the New Millennium

At the beginning of the twenty-first century, the United States is a nation of extraordinary diversity. Immigration reform in the mid-1960s opened U.S. borders to people from a wider variety of nations than previously. At the same time, new technologies—the Internet, cable and satellite television—replaced mass markets with niche markets. Everything from television shows to cosmetics to cars could be targeted toward specific groups defined by age, ethnicity, class, gender, or lifestyle choices. These changes helped to make Americans' understandings of identity more fluid and complex.

Race and Ethnicity in Recent America

In the 2000 U.S. government census, for the first time Americans could identify themselves as belonging to more than one race. The change acknowledged the growing number of Americans born to parents of different racial backgrounds. Critics, however, worried that, because census data are used for allocating resources, the new "multiracial" option would reduce the clout of minority groups. Thus, the federal government counted those who identified both as white and a racial or ethnic minority as belonging to the minority group. Consequently, the official population of some groups increased. Others rejected racial and ethnic categories altogether: 20 million people identified themselves simply as "American."

On October 17, 2006, the United States population passed 300 million. During the 1990s, the population of people of color grew twelve times as fast as the white population, fueled by immigration and birth rates. In 2003, Latinos passed African Americans to become the second largest ethnic or racial group (after non-Hispanic whites), making the United States the fifth largest "Latino" country in world (see Figure 33.1). Immigration from Asia also remained high, and in 2007, 5 percent of the U.S. population was Asian or Asian American. Most of this immigration is legal, but in 2005 an estimated 11.1 million people were in the United States without official documentation, up from 3 million in 1980.

The Changing American Family

Americans were increasingly divided over changing family structure (see Figure 33.2). The median age at marriage continued to rise, reaching 28.1 for men and 25.9 for women in 2009. In 2006, when households composed of married couples slipped below 50 percent for the first time, unmarried, opposite-sex partners made up about

MAP 33.2

Mapping America's Diversity

Aggregate figures (more than 12 percent of the U.S. population was African American and about 4 percent Asian American in 2000, for example) convey America's ethnic and racial diversity. However, as this map shows, members of racial and ethnic groups are not distributed evenly throughout the nation.

Source: Adapted from the *New York Times National Edition,* April 1, 2001, "Portrait of a Nation," p. 18. Copyright 2001 by The New York Times Co. Reprinted with permission.

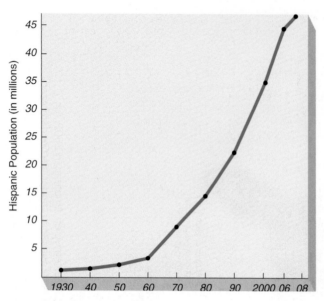

FIGURE 33.1
The Growth of the U.S. Hispanic Population

"Hispanic" combines people from a wide variety of national origins or ancestries—including all the nations of Central and South America, Mexico, Cuba, Puerto Rico, the Dominican Republic, Spain—as well as those who identify as Californio, Tejano, Nuevo Mexicano, and Mestizo.

Source: Adapted from the U.S. Department of Commerce, Economics and Statistics Information, Bureau of the Census, 1993 report "We, the American…Hispanics"; also recent Census Bureau figures for the Hispanic population.

5 percent of households, and same-sex couples accounted for just under 1 percent. One-third of female-partner households and one-fifth of male-partner households had children, and in 2002 the American Academy of Pediatrics endorsed adoption by gay couples. An antigay movement coexisted with support for the legal equality of gay, lesbian, trans-gendered, and bisexual Americans. Although many states and corporations extended domestic-partner benefits to gay couples, the federal Defense of Marriage Act, passed in 1996, defined marriage as a union between one man and one woman.

The birth rate to unmarried women increased to four of every ten babies in 2007. (In Sweden, the rate was 55 percent; in Japan 2 percent.) In the major-ity of married-couple families with children under eighteen, both parents held jobs. Although almost one-third of families with children had only one par-ent present—usually the mother—children also lived in blended families created by second marriages or moved between parents with joint custody. In 2006, the leading edge of the baby-boom generation turned sixty. As life expectancy increases, the growing num-ber of elderly Americans will put enormous pressure on the nation's healthcare system and strain Social Security and Medicare.

Other health issues have become increasingly important. More than two-thirds of American adults are now overweight or obese—conditions linked to hypertension, car-diovascular disease, and diabetes. In 1995, no state had an adult obesity rate that hit 20 percent. By 2009, only Colorado fell below that 20 percent mark. Childhood obesity rates exceeded 30 percent in twenty-nine states. Cigarette smoking continues to slowly decline. About one-fifth of adults smoked in 2008, down from about one-third in 1980. Approximately 440,000 people die annu-ally from smoking-related illnesses, and medical costs and lost productivity total about $157 billion a year.

Medicine, Science, and Religion

Rapid advances in biogenetics offer new possibilities and raise ethical conundrums. During in vitro fertilizations—in which sperm and egg combine in a sterile dish and the fertilized egg or eggs are then transferred to the uterus—five-or six-cell blastocytes are formed. These blastocytes contain stem cells, unspecialized cells that can be induced to become cells with specialized func-tions. For example, stem cells might become insulin-producing cells of the pancreas, and thus a cure for diabetes.

President Bush in 2001 called embryonic stem cell research "the leading edge of a series of moral hazards," because extracting stem cells destroys the blastocyte's

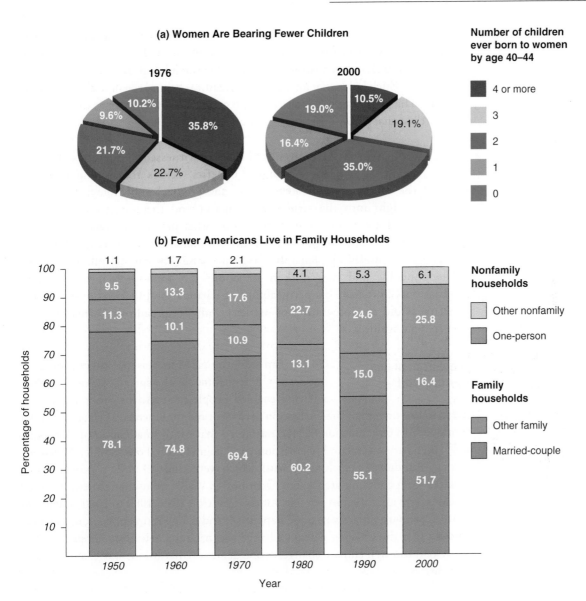

FIGURE 33.2
The Changing American Family

American households became smaller in the latter part of the twentieth century, as more people lived alone and women had, on average, fewer children.

Source: Adapted from U.S. Bureau of the Census, www.census.gov/prod/2002pubs/censr-4.pdf and www.census.gov/population/pop-profile/2000/chap04.pdf.

"potential for life." He limited federally funded research to the existing seventy-eight stem cell lines, most of which turned out not to be viable. However, most Americans support stem cell research, believing that the moral good of curing diseases outweighs the moral good of preserving the potential life of blastocytes. In early 2009, President Obama signed an executive order ending the Bush restrictions.

Still, for many there remains a conflict between religious belief and scientific study. Fundamentalist Christians sought to prevent the teaching of evolution in the nation's science classes or to introduce instruction of biblical creationism or intelligent design, which holds that an intelligent creator is behind the development of life on earth. The percentage of Americans who accept scientific evidence for evolution is lower than that in any other major nation except Turkey.

Century of Change   The twentieth century witnessed momentous changes, some bringing benefits, others threatening the existence of the human species. Research in the physical and biological sciences provided insight into the structure of matter and the universe. Technology enabled Americans to be more connected to other people worldwide than ever. This was perhaps the most powerful product of globalization. In 1955, 51 million people a year traveled by plane. By the turn of the century, 1.6 billion were airborne annually, and 530 million—or about 1.5 million each day—crossed international borders. This permeability of national boundaries brought many benefits, as did the integration of markets and the spread of information that occurred alongside it.

Globalization and World Health   On the flip side, the rapid increase in international air travel was a potent force for the spread of global disease, as flying enabled people to reach the other side of the world in less time than the incubation period for many ailments. Worse, in 2003 the World Health Organization (WHO) estimated that nearly one-quarter of global disease and injury was related to environmental degradation. For example, 90 percent of diarrheal diseases (such as cholera), which were killing 3 million people a year, resulted from contaminated water. According to WHO, more than thirty infectious diseases were identified in humans for the first time from 1980 to 2000—including AIDS, Ebola virus, hantavirus, and hepatitis C and E. Environmentalists, meanwhile, insisted that the growing global exchange was having a deleterious impact on the ecosystem through climate change, ozone depletion, hazardous waste, and damage to fisheries.

Confronting Terrorism   The 9/11 attacks brought home what Americans had previously only dimly perceived: that globalization shrunk the buffers that distance and two oceans provided the United States. Al Qaeda used the increasingly open, globalized world to expand its reach. It had shown that small terrorist cells could become transnational threats without a state sponsor or home base. According to U.S. intelligence, Al Qaeda operated in more than ninety countries.

How would one go about vanquishing such a foe? Was a decisive victory even possible? These remained open questions nine years after the World Trade Center collapsed. Unchallenged militarily, the United States felt few constraints about intervening in Afghanistan and then Iraq. It continued to spend colossal sums on its military. (The Pentagon in 2010 spent more than $680 billion, or roughly $77 million dollars per hour.) America had military commitments around the globe, from the Balkans and Iraq to Afghanistan and Korea (see Table 33.1).

Links to the World

The "Swine Flu" Pandemic

When United flight 803 from Washington DC landed at Tokyo's Narita airport on May 20, 2009, Japanese health officials boarded the plane. Wearing respirator masks, goggles, and disposable scrubs, they used thermal scanners to check passengers for elevated temperatures. If any symptoms were discovered, the plane would be quarantined. Japan had already closed its borders to travelers from Mexico, where the H1N1 "swine flu" virus emerged about three weeks earlier. Mexico closed schools and businesses. Nevertheless, the H1N1 virus had, by mid-May, already spread to more than 22 countries.

After several deaths in Mexico in late April, the World Health Organization raised its alert level to stage 5, expecting the virus to create the first major flu pandemic in more than forty years. Health analysts believed that the "right" pathogen emerging in the "right" place might spread worldwide in a day.

But global connections also offered new tools to combat pandemics. Global surveillance of disease might head off developing health threats, for example, and individual nations and global organizations can pool expertise as they develop vaccines and techniques to cope with pandemics. In addition, some believe that a global culture where borders present little barrier may facilitate the growth of global immunities to infectious diseases.

People everywhere were relieved when swine flu was ultimately no more deadly than a seasonal flu. Previously, SARS (severe, acute respiratory syndrome) and the H5N1 "bird flu" also failed become worldwide heath threats. But the World Heath Organization and the U.S. Centers for Disease Control and Prevention cautioned that the emergence of a major pandemic was simply a matter of time. In the era of globalization, diseases do not stop at borders or respect wealth and power, and the links between Americans and the rest of the world's peoples cannot be denied.

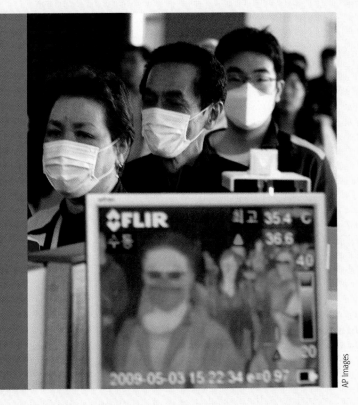

As the H1N1 virus—"swine flu"—spread rapidly in the spring of 2009, nations around the world attempted to prevent the spread of infection. Here, thermal cameras check the body temperatures of passengers arriving at Incheon International Airport in South Korea.

AP Images

TABLE 33.1   U.S. Military Personnel on Active Duty in Foreign Countries, 2009[1]

Region/Country[2]	Personnel	Region/Country[2]	Personnel
United States and Territories		Diego Garcia	253
Continental U.S.	959,508	Egypt	265
Alaska	21,597	Iraq	164,000
Hawai'i	36,890	Israel	45
Guam	2,970	Oman	34
Puerto Rico	179	Pakistan	39
Europe		Qatar	463
Belgium*	1,267	Saudi Arabia	269
France*	58	United Arab Emirates	105
Germany*	52,658	**Sub-Saharan Africa**	
Greece*	361	Djibouti	1,207
Greenland*	144	Kenya	41
Hungary	60	South Africa	30
Italy*	9,707	**Western Hemisphere**	
Netherlands*	510	Bahamas, The	45
Norway*	70	Brazil	37
Portugal*	716	Canada	128
Russia	57	Chile	30
Spain*	1,365	Colombia	77
Turkey*	1,616	Cuba (Guantanamo)	926
United Kingdom*	9,199	Honduras	416
East Asia and Pacific		Peru	45
Australia	139	**Total Foreign Countries[2]**	262,793
China (includes Hong Kong)	68	**Ashore**	242,291
Japan	35,965	**Afloat**	20,502
Korea, Rep. of	[Figures not available]	**Total Worldwide[2]**	1,418,542
Philippines	117	**Ashore**	1,313,308
Singapore	125	**Afloat**	105,234
Thailand	95		
North Africa, Near East, and South Asia			
Afghanistan	66,400		
Bahrain	1,507		

*NATO countries

[1] Only countries with 30 or more U.S. military personnel are listed.

[2] Includes all regions/countries, not simply those listed.

Source: U.S. Department of Defense, Defense Manpower Data Center.

The Internet

"Google it"—the phrase, essentially unknown before the new century, had within its first years become a household expression. Google was the popular Internet search engine that went from obscurity in the mid-1990s to handling more than 300 million queries daily from around the world—almost 40 percent of all Internet search requests.

While widespread Internet use was a recent phenomenon, its history went back four decades. In the mid-1960s, the U.S. military's Advanced Research Projects Agency (ARPA) wanted a communications network for government and university researchers across the nation. In 1969, early portions of the experimental system, called ARPANET, went online at UCLA; the University of California, Santa Barbara; Stanford Research Institute; and the University of Utah. By 1971,

twenty-three computers were connected, and the numbers reached a thousand by 1984. Renamed the Internet, this system transmitted only words, but in 1990 computer scientists developed the World Wide Web to send graphic and multimedia information. Then in 1993, the first commercial "browser" for Web navigation hit the market, followed in 1994 and 1995 by two superior browsers: Netscape and Internet Explorer.

By the end of 2009, there were more than 1.7 billion Internet users worldwide, including 230 million Americans. With technological advances and new forms of "broadband" access with high-speed connections, users could send and receive e-mail, join online discussion groups, read newspapers, download books and music, shop, and do their banking—all through a computer at home. For Americans in the new globally connected millennium, the Internet was a fitting legacy of the twentieth century.

Summary

The 1990s were, for most Americans, good times. A digitized revolution in communications and information generated prosperity and transformed life in America and worldwide. The longest economic expansion in American history—from 1991 to 2001—meant that most Americans who wanted jobs had them, that the stock market boomed, that the nation had a budget surplus, and that more Americans owned homes. And with no formidable rival, the United States stood as the world's lone superpower.

Yet unsettling events troubled the nation. Minutes before midnight on December 31, 1999, President Clinton called on Americans not to fear the future, but to "welcome it, create it, and embrace it." The challenges ahead would include the contested 2000 presidential election that was decided by the Supreme Court in a partisan 5-to-4 vote and the end of a ten-year economic expansion in 2001.

Then, on September 11, 2001, radical Islamic terrorists attacked the World Trade Center and the Pentagon, killing thousands. The new president, George W. Bush, declared a war on terrorism. While U.S. forces went after targets in Afghanistan, Congress created the Department of Homeland Security and passed the USA PATRIOT Act, expanding the federal government's surveillance powers. In March 2003, Bush initiated a war in Iraq, not expecting the full-blown insurgency that followed. Bush won reelection in 2004, but his fortunes waned. Two costly wars abroad and a severe economic crisis paved the way for Barack Obama's historic election in 2008.

Arizona's Immigration Law

In April 2010, the state of Arizona enacted a controversial immigration law, by far the toughest in the nation. Intended to help identify and deport undocumented immigrants, it required immigrants to carry their immigration documents and authorized police to question anyone suspected of wrongdoing about his or her immigration status. Those without papers could be detained until their status was verified. Opponents of the bill argued that it would lead to harassment of Hispanics, whether they were undocumented, legal immigrants, or US citizens, and President Obama called it a threat to "basic notions of fairness that we cherish as Americans." This bill—one of 222 state immigration laws enacted between 2007 and early 2010—provoked a national debate. What case against the law does this editorial cartoon make? How does the cartoonist use iconic images? Does the cartoon suggest problems with the wording of the law or with its possible implementation?

"I CAN TELL BY THE COLOR OF YOUR SKIN YOU'RE NOT FROM AROUND HERE, ARE YOU?"

© 2010 Joe Heller, The Green Bay Press-Gazette, and PoliticalCartoons.com

Dozens of editorial cartoons took on the Arizona Immigration law. This one, by Joe Heller, appeared in the Green Bay Press.

The first decade of the twenty-first century was different from what Americans imagined on New Year's Eve 1999. The terror attacks of September 11, 2001, shook America to its core. Then came two lengthy wars, followed by the most severe economic downturn since the Great Depression. By decade's end, Americans were deeply divided over how to respond to the nation's problems. As a new decade dawned, Americans continued to struggle over foreign and domestic priorities with the passion and commitment that keeps democracy alive.

Chapter Review

Social Strains and New Political Directions

What political struggles complicated Bill Clinton's first presidency?

As a "New Democrat" or centrist, Bill Clinton faced members of his own party who found some of his policies—such as his emphasis on private sector economic development—too conservative. Worse, from the start, a new breed of conservative Republicans challenged many of Clinton's campaign goals, and ultimately took control of both houses of Congress after the mid-term elections in 1994. This group successfully blocked Clinton's attempts at healthcare reform and compromised his position on gays in the military. These increasing partisan roadblocks led the beleaguered president to make compromises that pushed the nation further to the right—most notably, signing the 1996 Personal Responsibility and Work Opportunity Act (also known as "Welfare Reform"), which limited federal assistance for the needy to two years, and the Telecommunications Act, which allowed greater concentration of media ownership in fewer hands.

Globalization and Prosperity

What concerns did critics raise about globalization?

The so-called "age of globalization" that emerged in the late 1990s was characterized by greater worldwide integration of markets, finance, and technology. Labor unions feared losing jobs to less expensive overseas production, while critics argued that globalization widened the gap between rich and poor nations, fueling the creation of an underclass of "slave laborers" in poor countries and a race to the bottom. Environmentalists charged that globalization resulted in greater pollution of developing countries, and others feared the power of multinational corporations over traditional cultures. Anti-global protests targeted McDonald's as symbolizing the creation of a homogeneous global culture, and demonstrations turned violent at World Trade Organization meetings in 1999 and those of the International Monetary Fund in 2001.

9/11 and the War in Iraq

How did the events of Sept. 11 change America's relationship to the world?

Immediately after the attacks, the world community united in support of the United States, promising to work with Washington to fight terrorism. But before long, as President Bush took a firm good-vs.-evil stance that dictated countries were either with the United States or against it, he began to alienate allies and other friendly nations. Bush and his aides felt that the United States could not wait for threats to materialize; they had to strike first. And Bush differed with much of the U.N. Security Council over how to deal with Saddam Hussein's Iraq. The Council wanted to give arms inspections more time to succeed; the United States, backed by Britain, felt the time for diplomacy was over. The discord increased when Bush opted to launch an invasion. Bush also faced sharp international criticism for the military's abuse of war prisoners at Abu Ghraib.

Domestic Politics in Post-9/11 America

What was the decisive factor in the 2008 election?

In a word, the economy. While Americans were increasingly unhappy about the war in Iraq and disliked the Bush administration's handling of Hurricane Katrina, the biggest issue fueling voters rejection of the Republican Party and its presidential candidate John McCain was the deepening economic crisis. Years of deregulation led to risky investment practices in America's financial sector—particularly in housing and credit—that ultimately triggered a dangerous spiral of plummeting home values, foreclosures, and banking and credit problems. As credit tightened, businesses laid off workers and unemployment skyrocketed. The Bush administration provided $700 billion in loans to failing institutions, angering many Americans. When John McCain misspoke in the midst of the financial meltdown that "the fundamentals of our economy are strong," many questioned how in touch he was, and elected Barack Obama.

Americans in the First Decade of the New Millennium

What demographic changes are Americans beginning to face in the 21st century?

As the American population reached the 300 million mark in 2006, the country was more racially and ethnically diverse than ever. The population of people of color grew twelve times faster than that of whites, and Latinos became the second largest ethnic or racial group after non-Hispanic whites. Family structure has become increasingly varied, with households composed of married couples representing less than 50 percent of the population, and one-third of all children born to single women. The country also faces an aging population, as the leading edge of the baby boom generation turned 60 in 2006. That, combined with greater life expectancy, presents new concerns of healthcare and additional family pressures. Meanwhile, debates about balancing science and religion—particularly over the teaching of evolution and biblical creationism—continue to divide the nation.

Suggestions for Further Reading

Derek Chollet and James Goldgeier, *America Between the Wars: From 11/9 to 9/11* (2008)

Barbara Ehrenreich, *Nickled and Dimed: On (Not) Getting by in America* (2002)

David Halberstam, *War in a Time of Peace: Bush, Clinton, and the Generals* (2001)

John F. Harris, *The Survivor: Bill Clinton in the White House* (2005)

Jennifer L. Hochschild, *Facing up to the American Dream: Race, Class, and the Soul of the Nation* (1995)

James Mann, *Rise of the Vulcans: The History of Bush's War Cabinet* (2004)

Alejandro Portes and Reuben G. Rumbaut, *Immigrant America: A Portrait*, 3d ed. (2006)

Thomas E. Ricks, *The Gamble: General David Paterus and the American Military Adventure in Iraq, 2006-2008* (2009)

Joseph E. Stiglitz, *Globalization and Its Discontents* (2002)

Go to the CourseMate website for primary source links, study tools, and review materials for this chapter.
www.cengagebrain.com

Appendix

Declaration of Independence in Congress, July 4, 1776

When, in the course of human events, it becomes necessary for one people to dissolve the political bonds which have connected them with another, and to assume, among the powers of the earth, the separate and equal station to which the laws of nature and of nature's God entitle them, a decent respect to the opinions of mankind requires that they should declare the causes which impel them to the separation.

We hold these truths to be self-evident: That all men are created equal; that they are endowed by their Creator with certain unalienable rights; that among these are life, liberty, and the pursuit of happiness; that, to secure these rights, governments are instituted among men, deriving their just powers from the consent of the governed; that whenever any form of government becomes destructive of these ends, it is the right of the people to alter or to abolish it, and to institute new government, laying its foundation on such principles, and organizing its powers in such form, as to them shall seem most likely to effect their safety and happiness. Prudence, indeed, will dictate that governments long established should not be changed for light and transient causes; and accordingly all experience hath shown that mankind are more disposed to suffer, while evils are sufferable, than to right themselves by abolishing the forms to which they are accustomed. But when a long train of abuses and usurpations, pursuing invariably the same object, evinces a design to reduce them under absolute despotism, it is their right, it is their duty, to throw off such government, and to provide new guards for their future security. Such has been the patient sufferance of these colonies; and such is now the necessity which constrains them to alter their former systems of government. The history of the present King of Great Britain is a history of repeated injuries and usurpations, all having in direct object the establishment of an absolute tyranny over these states. To prove this, let facts be submitted to a candid world.

He has refused his assent to laws, the most wholesome and necessary for the public good.

He has forbidden his governors to pass laws of immediate and pressing importance, unless suspended in their operation till his assent should be obtained; and, when so suspended, he has utterly neglected to attend to them.

He has refused to pass other laws for the accommodation of large districts of people, unless those people would relinquish the right of representation in the legislature, a right inestimable to them, and formidable to tyrants only.

He has called together legislative bodies at places unusual, uncomfortable, and distant from the depository of their public records, for the sole purpose of fatiguing them into compliance with his measures.

He has dissolved representative houses repeatedly, for opposing, with manly firmness, his invasions on the rights of the people.

He has refused for a long time, after such dissolutions, to cause others to be elected; whereby the legislative powers, incapable of annihilation, have returned to the people at large for their exercise; the state remaining, in the mean time, exposed to all the dangers of invasions from without and convulsions within.

He has endeavored to prevent the population of these states; for that purpose obstructing the laws for naturalization of foreigners; refusing to pass others to encourage their migration hither, and raising the conditions of new appropriations of lands.

He has obstructed the administration of justice, by refusing his assent to laws for establishing judiciary powers.

He has made judges dependent on his will alone, for the tenure of their offices, and the amount and payment of their salaries.

He has erected a multitude of new offices, and sent hither swarms of officers to harass our people and eat out their substance.

He has kept among us, in times of peace, standing armies, without the consent of our legislatures.

He has affected to render the military independent of, and superior to, the civil power.

He has combined with others to subject us to a jurisdiction foreign to our constitution, and unacknowledged by our laws, giving his assent to their acts of pretended legislation:

For quartering large bodies of armed troops among us;

For protecting them, by a mock trial, from punishment for any murders which they should commit on the inhabitants of these states;

For cutting off our trade with all parts of the world;

For imposing taxes on us without our consent;

For depriving us, in many cases, of the benefits of trial by jury;

For transporting us beyond seas, to be tried for pretended offenses;

For abolishing the free system of English laws in a neighboring province, establishing therein an arbitrary government, and enlarging its boundaries, so as to render it at once an example and fit instrument for introducing the same absolute rule into these colonies;

For taking away our charters, abolishing our most valuable laws, and altering fundamentally the forms of our governments;

For suspending our own legislatures, and declaring themselves invested with power to legislate for us in all cases whatsoever.

He has abdicated government here, by declaring us out of his protection and waging war against us.

He has plundered our seas, ravaged our coasts, burned our towns, and destroyed the lives of our people.

He is at this time transporting large armies of foreign mercenaries to complete the works of death, desolation, and tyranny already begun with circumstances of cruelty and perfidy scarcely paralleled in the most barbarous ages, and totally unworthy the head of a civilized nation.

He has constrained our fellow-citizens, taken captive on the high seas, to bear arms against their country, to become the executioners of their friends and brethren, or to fall themselves by their hands.

He has excited domestic insurrection among us, and has endeavored to bring on the inhabitants of our frontiers the merciless Indian savages, whose known rule of warfare is an undistinguished destruction of all ages, sexes, and conditions.

In every stage of these oppressions we have petitioned for redress in the most humble terms; our repeated petitions have been answered only by repeated injury. A prince, whose character is thus marked by every act which may define a tyrant, is unfit to be the ruler of a free people.

Nor have we been wanting in our attentions to our British brethren. We have warned them, from time to time, of attempts by their legislature to extend an unwarrantable jurisdiction over us. We have reminded them of the circumstances of our emigration and settlement here. We have appealed to their native justice and magnanimity; and we have conjured them, by the ties of our common kindred, to disavow these usurpations, which would inevitably interrupt our connections and correspondence. They, too, have been deaf to the voice of justice and of consanguinity. We must, therefore, acquiesce in the necessity which denounces our separation, and hold them, as we hold the rest of mankind, enemies in war, in peace friends.

We, therefore, the representatives of the United States of America, in General Congress assembled, appealing to the Supreme Judge of the world for the rectitude of our intentions, do, in the name and by the authority of the good people of these colonies, solemnly publish and declare, that these United Colonies are, and of right ought to be, FREE AND INDEPENDENT STATES; that they are absolved from all allegiance to the British crown, and that all political connection between them and the state of Great Britain is, and ought to be, totally dissolved; and that, as free and independent states, they have full power to levy war, conclude peace, contract alliances, establish commerce, and do all other acts and things which independent states may of right do. And for the support of this declaration, with a firm reliance on the protection of Divine Providence, we mutually pledge to each other our lives, our fortunes, and our sacred honor.

Articles of Confederation

Whereas the Delegates of the United States of America in Congress assembled did on the fifteenth day of November in the Year of our Lord One Thousand Seven Hundred and Seventy seven, and in the Second Year of the Independence of America agree to certain articles of Confederation and perpetual Union between the States of Newhampshire, Massachusetts Bay, Rhode Island and Providence Plantations, Connecticut, New York, New Jersey, Pennsylvania, Delaware, Maryland, Virginia, North Carolina, South Carolina and Georgia in the Words following, viz. "Articles of Confederation and perpetual Union between the states of Newhampshire, Massachusetts Bay, Rhode Island and Providence Plantations, Connecticut, New York, New Jersey, Pennsylvania, Delaware, Maryland, Virginia, North Carolina, South Carolina and Georgia.

Article I

The Stile of this confederacy shall be "The United States of America."

Article II

Each state retains its sovereignty, freedom and independence, and every Power, Jurisdiction and right, which is not by this confederation expressly delegated to the United States, in Congress assembled.

Article III

The said states hereby severally enter into a firm league of friendship with each other, for their common defence, the security of their Liberties, and their mutual and general welfare, binding themselves to assist each other, against all force offered to, or attacks made upon them, or any of them, on account of religion, sovereignty, trade, or any other pretence whatever.

Article IV

The better to secure and perpetuate mutual friendship and intercourse among the people of the different states in this union, the free inhabitants of each of these states, paupers, vagabonds and fugitives from Justice excepted, shall be entitled to all privileges and immunities of free citizens in the several states; and the people of each state shall have free ingress and regress to and from any other state, and shall enjoy therein all the privileges of trade and commerce, subject to the same duties, impositions and restrictions as the inhabitants thereof respectively, provided that such restriction shall not extend so far as to prevent the removal of property imported into any state, to any other state of which the Owner is an inhabitant; provided also that no imposition, duties or restriction shall be laid by any state, on the property of the united states, or either of them.

If any Person guilty of, or charged with treason, felony, or other high misdemeanor in any state, shall flee from Justice, and be found in any of the united states, he shall upon demand of the Governor or executive power, of the state from which he fled, be delivered up and removed to the state having jurisdiction of his offence.

Full faith and credit shall be given in each of these states to the records, acts and judicial proceedings of the courts and magistrates of every other state.

Article V

For the more convenient management of the general interests of the united states, delegates shall be annually appointed in such manner as the legislature of each state shall direct, to meet in Congress on the first Monday in November, in every year, with a power reserved to each state, to recall its delegates, or any of them, at any time within the year, and to send others in their stead, for the remainder of the Year.

No state shall be represented in Congress by less than two, nor by more than seven Members; and no person shall be capable of being a delegate for more than three years in any term of six years; nor shall any person, being a delegate, be capable of holding any office under the united states, for which he, or another for his benefit receives any salary, fees or emolument of any kind.

Each state shall maintain its own delegates in a meeting of the states, and while they act as members of the committee of the states.

In determining questions in the united states, in Congress assembled, each state shall have one vote.

Freedom of speech and debate in Congress shall not be impeached or questioned in any Court, or place out of Congress, and the members of congress shall be protected in their persons from arrests and imprisonments, during the time of their going to and from, and attendance on congress, except for treason, felony, or breach of the peace.

Article VI

No state without the Consent of the united states in congress assembled, shall send any embassy to, or receive any embassy from, or enter into any conference, agreement, or alliance or treaty with any King, prince or state; nor shall any person holding any office of profit or trust under the united states, or any of them, accept of any present, emolument, office or title of any kind whatever from any king, prince or foreign state; nor shall the united states in congress assembled, or any of them, grant any title of nobility.

No two or more states shall enter into any treaty, confederation or alliance whatever between them, without the consent of the united states in congress assembled, specifying accurately the purposes for which the same is to be entered into, and how long it shall continue.

No state shall lay any imposts or duties, which may interfere with any stipulations in treaties, entered into by the united states in congress assembled, with any king, prince or state, in pursuance of any treaties already proposed by congress, to the courts of France and Spain.

No vessels of war shall be kept up in time of peace by any state, except such number only, as shall be deemed necessary by the united states in congress assembled, for the defence of such state, or its trade; nor shall any body of forces be kept up by any state, in time of peace, except such number only, as in the judgment of the united states, in congress assembled, shall be deemed requisite to garrison the forts necessary for the defence of such state; but every state shall always keep up a well regulated and disciplined militia, sufficiently armed and accoutred, and shall provide and constantly have ready for use, in public stores, a due number of field pieces and tents, and a proper quantity of arms, ammunition and camp equipage.

No state shall engage in any war without the consent of the united states in congress assembled, unless such state be actually invaded by enemies, or shall have received certain advice of a resolution being formed by some nation of Indians to invade such state, and the danger is so imminent as not to admit of a delay, till the united states in congress assembled can be consulted: nor shall any state grant commissions to any ships or vessels of war, nor letters of marque or reprisal, except it be after a declaration of war by the united states in congress assembled, and then only against the kingdom or state and the subjects thereof, against which war has been so declared, and under such regulations as shall be established by the united states in congress assembled, unless such state be infested by pirates, in which case vessels of war may be fitted out for that occasion, and kept so long as the danger shall continue, or until the united states in congress assembled shall determine otherwise.

Article VII

When land-forces are raised by any state for the common defence, all officers of or under the rank of colonel, shall be appointed by the legislature of each state respectively by whom such forces shall be raised, or in such manner as such state shall direct, and all vacancies shall be filled up by the state which first made the appointment.

Article VIII

All charges of war, and all other expences that shall be incurred for the common defence or general welfare, and allowed by the united states in congress assembled, shall be defrayed out of a common treasury, which shall be supplied by the several states, in proportion to the value of all land within each state, granted to or surveyed for any Person, as such land and the buildings and improvements thereon shall be estimated according to such mode as the united states in congress assembled, shall from time to time direct and appoint. The taxes for paying that proportion shall be laid and levied by the authority and direction of the legislatures of the several states within the time agreed upon by the united states in congress assembled.

Article IX

The united states in congress assembled, shall have the sole and exclusive right and power of determining on peace and war, except in the cases mentioned in the sixth article—of sending and receiving ambassadors—entering into treaties and alliances, provided that no treaty of commerce shall be made whereby the legislative power of the respective states shall be restrained from imposing such imposts and duties on foreigners, as their own people are subjected to, or from prohibiting the exportation or importation of any species of goods or commodities whatsoever—of establishing rules for deciding in all cases, what captures on land or water shall be legal, and in what manner prizes taken by land or naval forces in the service of the united states shall be divided or appropriated—of

granting letters of marque and reprisal in times of peace—appointing courts for the trial of piracies and felonies committed on the high seas and establishing courts for receiving and determining final appeals in all cases of captures, provided that no member of congress shall be appointed a judge of any of the said courts.

The united states in congress assembled shall also be the last resort on appeal in all disputes and differences now subsisting or that hereafter may arise between two or more states concerning boundary, jurisdiction or any other cause whatever; which authority shall always be exercised in the manner following. Whenever the legislative or executive authority or lawful agent of any state in controversy with another shall present a petition to congress, stating the matter in question and praying for a hearing, notice thereof shall be given by order of congress to the legislative or executive authority of the other state in controversy, and a day assigned for the appearance of the parties by their lawful agents, who shall then be directed to appoint by joint consent, commissioners or judges to constitute a court for hearing and determining the matter in question: but if they cannot agree, congress shall name three persons out of each of the united states, and from the list of such persons each party shall alternately strike out one, the petitioners beginning, until the number shall be reduced to thirteen; and from that number not less than seven, nor more than nine names as congress shall direct, shall in the presence of congress be drawn out by lot, and the persons whose names shall be so drawn or any five of them, shall be commissioners or judges, to hear and finally determine the controversy, so always as a major part of the judges who shall hear the cause shall agree in the determination: and if either party shall neglect to attend at the day appointed, without showing reasons, which congress shall judge sufficient, or being present shall refuse to strike, the congress shall proceed to nominate three persons out of each state, and the secretary of congress shall strike in behalf of such party absent or refusing; and the judgment and sentence of the court to be appointed, in the manner before prescribed, shall be final and conclusive; and if any of the parties shall refuse to submit to the authority of such court, or to appear to defend their claim or cause, the court shall nevertheless proceed to pronounce sentence, or judgment, which shall in like manner be final and decisive, the judgment or sentence and other proceedings being in either case transmitted to congress, and lodged among the acts of congress for the security of the parties concerned: provided that every commissioner, before he sits in judgment, shall take an oath to be administered by one of the judges of the supreme or superior court of the state, where the cause shall be tried, "well and truly to hear and determine the matter in question, according to the best of his judgment, without favour, affection or hope of reward:" provided also that no state shall be deprived of territory for the benefit of the united states.

All controversies concerning the private right of soil claimed under different grants of two or more states, whose jurisdictions as they may respect such lands, and the states which passed such grants are adjusted, the said grants or either of them being at the same time claimed to have originated antecedent to such settlement of jurisdiction, shall on the petition of either party to the congress of the united states, be finally determined as near as may be in the same manner as is before prescribed for deciding disputes respecting territorial jurisdiction between different states.

The united states in congress assembled shall also have the sole and exclusive right and power of regulating the alloy and value of coin struck by their own authority, or by that of the respective states—fixing the standard of weights and measures throughout the united states—regulating the trade and managing all affairs with the Indians, not members of any of the states, provided that the legislative right of any state within its own limits be not infringed or violated—establishing and regulating post-offices from one state to another, throughout all the united states, and exacting such postage on the papers passing thro' the same as may be requisite to defray the expences of the said office—appointing all officers of the land forces, in the service of the united states, excepting regimental officers—appointing all the officers of the naval forces, and commissioning all officers whatever in the service of the united states—making rules for the government and regulation of the said land and naval forces, and directing their operations.

The united states in congress assembled shall have authority to appoint a committee, to sit in the recess of congress, to be denominated "A Committee of the States," and to consist of one delegate from each state; and to appoint such other committees and civil officers as may be necessary for managing the general affairs of the united states under their direction—to appoint one of their number to preside, provided that no person be allowed to serve in the office of president more than one year in any term of three years; to ascertain the necessary sums of Money to be raised for the service of the united states, and to appropriate and apply the same for defraying the public expences—to borrow money, or emit bills on the credit of the united states, transmitting every half year to the respective states an account of the sums of money so borrowed or emitted—to build and equip a navy—to agree upon the number of land forces, and to make requisitions from each state for its quota, in proportion to the number of white inhabitants in such state; which requisition shall be binding, and thereupon the legislature of each state shall appoint the regimental officers, raise the men and cloath, arm and equip them in a soldier like manner, at the expence of the united states, and the officers and men so cloathed, armed and equipped shall march to the place appointed, and within the time agreed on by the united states in congress assembled: But if the united states in congress assembled shall, on consideration of circumstances judge proper that any state should not raise men, or should raise a smaller number than its quota, and that any other state should raise a greater number of men than the quota thereof, such extra number shall be raised, officered, cloathed, armed and equipped in the same manner as the quota of such state, unless the legislature of such state shall judge that such extra number cannot be safely spared out of the same, in which case they shall raise, officer, cloath, arm and equip as many of such extra number as they judge can be safely spared. And the officers and men so cloathed, armed and equipped, shall march to the place appointed, and within the time agreed on by the united states in congress assembled.

The united states in congress assembled shall never engage in a war, nor grant letters of marque and reprisal in time of peace, nor enter into any treaties or alliances, nor coin money, nor regulate the value thereof, nor ascertain the sums and expences necessary for the defence and welfare of the united states, or any of them, nor emit bills, nor borrow money on the credit of the united states, nor appropriate money, nor agree upon the number of vessels of war, to be built or purchased, or the number of land or sea forces to be raised, nor appoint a commander in chief of the army or navy, unless nine states assent to the same: nor shall a question on any other point, except for adjourning from day to day be determined, unless by the votes of a majority of the united states in congress assembled.

The congress of the united states shall have power to adjourn to any time within the year, and to any place within the united states, so that no period of adjournment be for a longer duration than the space of six Months, and shall publish the Journal of their proceedings monthly, except such parts thereof relating to treaties, alliances or military operations as in their judgment require secresy; and the yeas and nays of the delegates of each state on any question shall be entered on the Journal, when it is desired by any delegate; and the delegates of a state, or any of them, at his or their request shall be furnished with a transcript of the said Journal, except such parts as are above excepted, to lay before the legislatures of the several states.

Article X

The committee of the states, or any nine of them, shall be authorised to execute, in the recess of congress, such of the powers of congress as the united states in congress assembled, by the consent of nine states, shall from time to time think expedient to vest them with; provided that no power be delegated to the said committee, for the exercise of which, by the articles of confederation, the voice of nine states in the congress of the united states assembled is requisite.

Article XI

Canada acceding to this confederation, and joining in the measures of the united states, shall be admitted into, and entitled to all the advantages of this union: but no other colony shall be admitted into the same, unless such admission be agreed to by nine states.

Article XII

All bills of credit emitted, monies borrowed and debts contracted by, or under the authority of congress, before the assembling of the united states, in pursuance of the present confederation, shall be deemed and considered as a charge against the united states, for payment and satisfaction whereof the said united states, and the public faith are hereby solemnly pledged.

Article XIII

Every state shall abide by the determinations of the united states in congress assembled, on all questions which by this confederation are submitted to them. And the Articles of this confederation shall be inviolably observed by every state, and the union shall be perpetual; nor shall any alteration at any time hereafter be made in any of them; unless such alteration be agreed to in a congress of the united states, and be afterwards confirmed by the legislatures of every state.

AND WHEREAS it hath pleased the Great Governor of the World to incline the hearts of the legislatures we respectively represent in congress, to approve of, and to authorize us to ratify the said articles of confederation and perpetual union. Know Ye that we the under-signed delegates, by virtue of the power and authority to us given for that purpose, do by these presents, in the name and in behalf of our respective constituents, fully and entirely ratify and confirm each and every of the said articles of confederation and perpetual union, and all and singular the matters and things therein contained: And we do further solemnly plight and engage the faith of our respective constituents, that they shall abide by the determinations of the united states in congress assembled, on all questions, which by the said confederation are submitted to them. And that the articles thereof shall be inviolably observed by the states we respectively represent, and that the union shall be perpetual. In Witness whereof we have hereunto set our hands in Congress. Done at Philadelphia in the state of Pennsylvania the ninth Day of July in the Year of our Lord one Thousand seven Hundred and Seventy-eight, and in the third year of the independence of America.

Constitution of the United States of America and Amendments*

Preamble

We the people of the United States, in order to form a more perfect union, establish justice, insure domestic tranquillity, provide for the common defense, promote the general welfare, and secure the blessings of liberty to ourselves and our posterity, do ordain and establish this Constitution for the United States of America.

Article I

Section 1 All legislative powers herein granted shall be vested in a Congress of the United States, which shall consist of a Senate and a House of Representatives.

Section 2 The House of Representatives shall be composed of members chosen every second year by the people of the several States, and the electors in each State shall have the qualifications requisite for electors of the most numerous branch of the State Legislature.

No person shall be a Representative who shall not have attained to the age of twenty-five years, and been seven years a citizen of the United States, and who shall not, when elected, be an inhabitant of that State in which he shall be chosen.

Representatives and direct taxes shall be apportioned among the several States which may be included within this Union, according to their respective numbers, *which shall be determined by adding to the whole number of free persons, including those bound to service for a term of years and excluding Indians not taxed, three-fifths of all other persons.*

*Passages no longer in effect are printed in italic type.

The actual enumeration shall be made within three years after the first meeting of the Congress of the United States, and within every subsequent term of ten years, in such manner as they shall by law direct. The number of Representatives shall not exceed one for every thirty thousand, but each State shall have at least one Representative; *and until such enumeration shall be made, the State of New Hampshire shall be entitled to choose three, Massachusetts eight, Rhode Island and Providence Plantations one, Connecticut five, New York six, New Jersey four, Pennsylvania eight, Delaware one, Maryland six, Virginia ten, North Carolina five, South Carolina five, and Georgia three.*

When vacancies happen in the representation from any State, the Executive authority thereof shall issue writs of election to fill such vacancies.

The House of Representatives shall choose their Speaker and other officers; and shall have the sole power of impeachment.

Section 3 The Senate of the United States shall be composed of two Senators from each State, chosen by the legislature thereof, for six years; and each Senator shall have one vote.

Immediately after they shall be assembled in consequence of the first election, they shall be divided as equally as may be into three classes. The seats of the Senators of the first class shall be vacated at the expiration of the second year, of the second class at the expiration of the fourth year, and of the third class at the expiration of the sixth year, so that one-third may be chosen every second year; and if vacancies happen by resignation or otherwise, during the recess of the legislature of any State, the Executive thereof may make temporary appointments until the next meeting of the legislature, which shall then fill such vacancies.

No person shall be a Senator who shall not have attained to the age of thirty years, and been nine years a citizen of the United States, and who shall not, when elected, be an inhabitant of that State for which he shall be chosen.

The Vice-President of the United States shall be President of the Senate, but shall have no vote, unless they be equally divided.

The Senate shall choose their other officers, and also a President *pro tempore,* in the absence of the Vice-President, or when he shall exercise the office of President of the United States.

The Senate shall have the sole power to try all impeachments. When sitting for that purpose, they shall be on oath or affirmation. When the President of the United States is tried, the Chief Justice shall preside: and no person shall be convicted without the concurrence of two-thirds of the members present.

Judgment in cases of impeachment shall not extend further than to removal from the office, and disqualification to hold and enjoy any office of honor, trust or profit under the United States: but the party convicted shall nevertheless be liable and subject to indictment, trial, judgment and punishment, according to law.

Section 4 The times, places and manner of holding elections for Senators and Representatives shall be prescribed in each State by the legislature thereof; but the Congress may at any time by law make or alter such regulations, except as to the places of choosing Senators.

The Congress shall assemble at least once in every year, and such meeting shall be on the first Monday in December, unless they shall by law appoint a different day.

Section 5 Each house shall be the judge of the elections, returns and qualifications of its own members, and a majority of each shall constitute a quorum to do business; but a smaller number may adjourn from day to day, and may be authorized to compel the attendance of absent members, in such manner, and under such penalties, as each house may provide.

Each house may determine the rules of its proceedings, punish its members for disorderly behavior, and with the concurrence of two-thirds, expel a member.

Each house shall keep a journal of its proceedings, and from time to time publish the same, excepting such parts as may in their judgment require secrecy; and the yeas and nays of the members of either house on any question shall, at the desire of one-fifth of those present, be entered on the journal.

Neither house, during the session of Congress, shall, without the consent of the other, adjourn for more than three days, nor to any other place than that in which the two houses shall be sitting.

Section 6 The Senators and Representatives shall receive a compensation for their services, to be ascertained by law and paid out of the treasury of the United States. They shall in all cases except treason, felony and breach of the peace, be privileged from arrest during their attendance at the session of their respective houses, and in going to and returning from the same; and for any speech or debate in either house, they shall not be questioned in any other place.

No Senator or Representative shall, during the time for which he was elected, be appointed to any civil office under the authority of the United States, which shall have been created, or the emoluments whereof shall have been increased, during such time; and no person holding any office under the United States shall be a member of either house during his continuance in office.

Section 7 All bills for raising revenue shall originate in the House of Representatives; but the Senate may propose or concur with amendments as on other bills.

Every bill which shall have passed the House of Representatives and the Senate, shall, before it become a law, be presented to the President of the United States;

if he approve he shall sign it, but if not he shall return it with objections to that house in which it originated, who shall enter the objections at large on their journal, and proceed to reconsider it. If after such reconsideration two-thirds of that house shall agree to pass the bill, it shall be sent, together with the objections, to the other house, by which it shall likewise be reconsidered, and, if approved by two-thirds of that house, it shall become a law. But in all such cases the votes of both houses shall be determined by yeas and nays, and the names of the persons voting for and against the bill shall be entered on the journal of each house respectively. If any bill shall not be returned by the President within ten days (Sundays excepted) after it shall have been presented to him, the same shall be a law, in like manner as if he had signed it, unless the Congress by their adjournment prevent its return, in which case it shall not be a law.

Every order, resolution, or vote to which the concurrence of the Senate and House of Representatives may be necessary (except on a question of adjournment) shall be presented to the President of the United States; and before the same shall take effect, shall be approved by him, or being disapproved by him, shall be repassed by two-thirds of the Senate and House of Representatives, according to the rules and limitations prescribed in the case of a bill.

Section 8   The Congress shall have power

To lay and collect taxes, duties, imposts, and excises, to pay the debts and provide for the common defense and general welfare of the United States; but all duties, imposts and excises shall be uniform throughout the United States;

To borrow money on the credit of the United States;

To regulate commerce with foreign nations, and among the several States, and with the Indian tribes;

To establish an uniform rule of naturalization, and uniform laws on the subject of bankruptcies throughout the United States;

To coin money, regulate the value thereof, and of foreign coin, and fix the standard of weights and measures;

To provide for the punishment of counterfeiting the securities and current coin of the United States;

To establish post offices and post roads;

To promote the progress of science and useful arts by securing for limited times to authors and inventors the exclusive right to their respective writings and discoveries;

To constitute tribunals inferior to the Supreme Court;

To define and punish piracies and felonies committed on the high seas and offenses against the law of nations;

To declare war, grant letters of marque and reprisal, and make rules concerning captures on land and water;

To raise and support armies, but no appropriation of money to that use shall be for a longer term than two years;

To provide and maintain a navy;

To make rules for the government and regulation of the land and naval forces;

To provide for calling forth the militia to execute the laws of the Union, suppress insurrections, and repel invasions;

To provide for organizing, arming, and disciplining the militia, and for governing such part of them as may be employed in the service of the United States, reserving to the States respectively the appointment of the officers, and the authority of training the militia according to the discipline prescribed by Congress;

To exercise exclusive legislation in all cases whatsoever, over such district (not exceeding ten miles square) as may, by cession of particular States, and the acceptance of Congress, become the seat of government of the United States, and to exercise like authority over all places purchased by the consent of the legislature of the State, in which the same shall be, for erection of forts, magazines, arsenals, dockyards, and other needful buildings;—and

To make all laws which shall be necessary and proper for carrying into execution the foregoing powers, and all other powers vested by this Constitution in the government of the United States, or in any department or officer thereof.

Section 9   *The migration or importation of such persons as any of the States now existing shall think proper to admit shall not be prohibited by the Congress prior to the year 1808; but a tax or duty may be imposed on such importation, not exceeding $10 for each person.*

The privilege of the writ of habeas corpus shall not be suspended, unless when in cases of rebellion or invasion the public safety may require it.

No bill of attainder or ex post facto law shall be passed.

No capitation, or other direct, tax shall be laid, unless in proportion to the census or enumeration herein before directed to be taken.

No tax or duty shall be laid on articles exported from any State.

No preference shall be given by any regulation of commerce or revenue to the ports of one State over those of another; nor shall vessels bound to, or from, one State, be obliged to enter, clear, or pay duties in another.

No money shall be drawn from the treasury, but in consequence of appropriations made by law; and a regular statement and account of the receipts and expenditures of all public money shall be published from time to time.

No title of nobility shall be granted by the United States: and no person holding any office of profit or trust under them, shall, without the consent of the Congress, accept of any present, emolument, office, or title, of any kind whatever, from any king, prince, or foreign state.

Section 10 No State shall enter into any treaty, alliance, or confederation; grant letters of marque and reprisal; coin money; emit bills of credit; make anything but gold and silver coin a tender in payment of debts; pass any bill of attainder, ex post facto law, or law impairing the obligation of contracts, or grant any title of nobility.

No State shall, without the consent of Congress, lay any imposts or duties on imports or exports, except what may be absolutely necessary for executing its inspection laws: and the net produce of all duties and imposts, laid by any State on imports or exports, shall be for the use of the treasury of the United States; and all such laws shall be subject to the revision and control of the Congress.

No State shall, without the consent of Congress, lay any duty of tonnage, keep troops or ships of war in time of peace, enter into any agreement or compact with another State, or with a foreign power, or engage in war, unless actually invaded, or in such imminent danger as will not admit of delay.

Article II

Section 1 The executive power shall be vested in a President of the United States of America. He shall hold his office during the term of four years, and, together with the Vice-President, chosen for the same term, be elected as follows:

Each State shall appoint, in such manner as the legislature thereof may direct, a number of electors, equal to the whole number of Senators and Representatives to which the State may be entitled in the Congress; but no Senator or Representative, or person holding an office of trust or profit under the United States, shall be appointed an elector.

The electors shall meet in their respective States, and vote by ballot for two persons, of whom one at least shall not be an inhabitant of the same State with themselves. And they shall make a list of all the persons voted for, and of the number of votes for each; which list they shall sign and certify, and transmit sealed to the seat of government of the United States, directed to the President of the Senate. The President of the Senate shall, in the presence of the Senate and House of Representatives, open all the certificates, and the votes shall then be counted. The person having the greatest number of votes shall be the President, if such number be a majority of the whole number of electors appointed; and if there be more than one who have such majority, and have an equal number of votes, then the House of Representatives shall immediately choose by ballot one of them for President; and if no person have a majority, then from the five highest on the list said house shall in like manner choose the President. But in choosing the President the votes shall be taken by States, the representation from each State having one vote; a quorum for this purpose shall consist of a member or members from two-thirds of the States, and a majority of all the States shall be necessary to a choice. In every case, after the choice of the President, the person having the greatest number of votes of the electors shall be the Vice-President. But if there should remain two or more who have equal votes, the Senate shall choose from them by ballot the Vice-President.

The Congress may determine the time of choosing the electors and the day on which they shall give their votes; which day shall be the same throughout the United States.

No person except a natural-born citizen, *or a citizen of the United States at the time of the adoption of this Constitution,* shall be eligible to the office of President; neither shall any person be eligible to that office who shall not have attained to the age of thirty-five years, and been fourteen years a resident within the United States.

In cases of the removal of the President from office or of his death, resignation, or inability to discharge the powers and duties of the said office, the same shall devolve on the Vice-President, and the Congress may by law provide for the case of removal, death, resignation, or inability, both of the President and Vice-President, declaring what officer shall then act as President, and such officer shall act accordingly, until the disability be removed, or a President shall be elected.

The President shall, at stated times, receive for his services a compensation, which shall neither be increased nor diminished during the period for which he shall have been elected, and he shall not receive within that period any other emolument from the United States, or any of them.

Before he enter on the execution of his office, he shall take the following oath or affirmation:—"I do solemnly swear (or affirm) that I will faithfully execute the office of the President of the United States, and will to the best of my ability preserve, protect and defend the Constitution of the United States."

Section 2 The President shall be commander in chief of the army and navy of the United States, and of the militia of the several States, when called into the actual service of the United States; he may require the opinion, in writing, of the principal officer in each of the executive departments, upon any subject relating to the duties of their respective offices, and he shall have power to grant reprieves and pardons for offenses against the United States, except in cases of impeachment.

He shall have power, by and with the advice and consent of the Senate, to make treaties, provided two-thirds of the Senators present concur; and he shall nominate, and by and with the advice and consent of the Senate, shall appoint ambassadors, other public ministers and consuls, judges of the Supreme Court, and all other officers of the United States, whose appointments are not herein otherwise provided for, and which shall be established by law: but Congress may by law vest the appointment of such inferior officers, as they think proper, in the President alone, in the courts of law, or in the heads of departments.

The President shall have power to fill up all vacancies that may happen during the recess of the Senate, by granting commissions which shall expire at the end of their next session.

Section 3 He shall from time to time give to the Congress information of the state of the Union, and recommend to their consideration such measures as he shall judge necessary and expedient; he may, on extraordinary occasions, convene both houses, or either of them, and in case of disagreement between them, with respect to the time of adjournment, he may adjourn them to such time as he shall think proper; he shall receive ambassadors and other public ministers; he shall take care that the laws be faithfully executed, and shall commission all the officers of the United States.

Section 4 The President, Vice-President and all civil officers of the United States shall be removed from office on impeachment for, and on conviction of, treason, bribery, or other high crimes and misdemeanors.

Article III

Section 1 The judicial power of the United States shall be vested in one Supreme Court, and in such inferior courts as the Congress may from time to time ordain and establish. The judges, both of the Supreme and inferior courts, shall hold their offices during good behavior, and shall, at stated times, receive for their services a compensation which shall not be diminished during their continuance in office.

Section 2 The judicial power shall extend to all cases, in law and equity, arising under this Constitution, the laws of the United States, and treaties made, or which shall be made, under their authority;—to all cases affecting ambassadors, other public ministers and consuls;—to all cases of admiralty and maritime jurisdiction;—to controversies to which the United States shall be a party;—to controversies between two or more States;—*between a State and citizens of another State;*—between citizens of different States;—between citizens of the same State claiming lands under grants of different States, and between a State, or the citizens thereof, and foreign states, citizens or subjects.

In all cases affecting ambassadors, other public ministers and consuls, and those in which a State shall be party, the Supreme Court shall have original jurisdiction. In all the other cases before mentioned, the Supreme Court shall have appellate jurisdiction, both as to law and fact, with such exceptions, and under such regulations, as the Congress shall make.

The trial of all crimes, except in cases of impeachment, shall be by jury; and such trial shall be held in the State where said crimes shall have been committed; but when not committed within any State, the trial shall be at such place or places as the Congress may by law have directed.

Section 3 Treason against the United States shall consist only in levying war against them, or in adhering to their enemies, giving them aid and comfort. No person shall be convicted of treason unless on the testimony of two witnesses to the same overt act, or on confession in open court.

The Congress shall have power to declare the punishment of treason, but no attainder of treason shall work corruption of blood, or forfeiture except during the life of the person attainted.

Article IV

Section 1 Full faith and credit shall be given in each State to the public acts, records, and judicial proceedings of every other State. And the Congress may by general laws prescribe the manner in which such acts, records, and proceedings shall be proved, and the effect thereof.

Section 2 The citizens of each State shall be entitled to all privileges and immunities of citizens in the several States.

A person charged in any State with treason, felony, or other crime, who shall flee from justice, and be found in another State, shall on demand of the executive authority of the State from which he fled, be delivered up, to be removed to the State having jurisdiction of the crime.

No person held to service or labor in one State, under the laws thereof, escaping into another, shall, in consequence of any law or regulation therein, be discharged from such service or labor, but shall be delivered up on claim of the party to whom such service or labor may be due.

Section 3 New States may be admitted by the Congress into this Union; but no new State shall be formed or erected within the jurisdiction of any other State; nor any State be formed by the junction of two or more States, or parts of States, without the consent of the legislatures of the States concerned as well as of the Congress.

The Congress shall have power to dispose of and make all needful rules and regulations respecting the territory or other property belonging to the United States; and nothing in this Constitution shall be so construed as to prejudice any claims of the United States, or of any particular State.

Section 4 The United States shall guarantee to every State in this Union a republican form of government, and shall protect each of them against invasion; and on application of the legislature, or of the executive (when the legislature cannot be convened), against domestic violence.

Article V

The Congress, whenever two-thirds of both houses shall deem it necessary, shall propose amendments to this Constitution, or, on the application of the legislatures of two-thirds of the several States, shall call a convention for proposing amendments, which, in either case, shall be valid to all intents and purposes, as part of this Constitution, when ratified by the legislatures of three-fourths of the several States, or by conventions in three-fourths thereof, as the one or the other mode of ratification may be proposed by the Congress; provided *that no amendments which may be made prior to the year one thousand eight hundred and eight shall in any manner affect the first and fourth clauses in the ninth section of the first article;* and that no State, without its consent, shall be deprived of its equal suffrage in the Senate.

Article VI

All debts contracted and engagements entered into, before the adoption of this Constitution, shall be as valid against the United States under this Constitution, as under the Confederation.

This Constitution, and the laws of the United States which shall be made in pursuance thereof; and all treaties made, or which shall be made, under the authority of the United States, shall be the supreme law of the land; and the judges in every State shall be bound thereby, anything in the Constitution or laws of any State to the contrary notwithstanding.

The Senators and Representatives before mentioned, and the members of the several State legislatures, and all executive and judicial officers, both of the United States and of the several States, shall be bound by oath or affirmation to support this Constitution; but no religious test shall ever be required as a qualification to any office or public trust under the United States.

Article VII

The ratification of the conventions of nine States shall be sufficient for the establishment of this Constitution between the States so ratifying the same.

Done in Convention by the unanimous consent of the States present, the seventeenth day of September in the year of our Lord one thousand seven hundred and eighty-seven and of the Independence of the United States of America the twelfth. In witness whereof we have hereunto subscribed our names.

Amendments to the Constitution*

Amendment I

Congress shall make no law respecting an establishment of religion, or prohibiting the free exercise thereof; or abridging the freedom of speech, or of the press; or the right of the people peaceably to assemble, and to petition the government for a redress of grievances.

Amendment II

A well-regulated militia being necessary to the security of a free State, the right of the people to keep and bear arms shall not be infringed.

Amendment III

No soldier shall, in time of peace, be quartered in any house without the consent of the owner, nor in time of war, but in a manner to be prescribed by law.

Amendment IV

The right of the people to be secure in their persons, houses, papers, and effects, against unreasonable searches and seizures, shall not be violated, and no warrants shall issue but upon probable cause, supported by oath or affirmation, and particularly describing the place to be searched, and the persons or things to be seized.

Amendment V

No person shall be held to answer for a capital, or otherwise infamous crime, unless on a presentment or indictment of a grand jury, except in cases arising in the land or naval forces, or in the militia, when in actual service in time of war or public danger; nor shall any person be subject for the same offense to be twice put in jeopardy of life or limb; nor shall be compelled in any criminal case to be a witness against himself, nor be deprived of life, liberty, or property, without due process of law; nor shall private property be taken for public use without just compensation.

Amendment VI

In all criminal prosecutions, the accused shall enjoy the right to a speedy and public trial, by an impartial jury of the State and district wherein the crime shall have been committed, which district shall have been previously ascertained by law, and to be informed of the nature and cause of the accusation; to be confronted with the witnesses against him; to have compulsory process for obtaining witnesses in his favor, and to have the assistance of counsel for his defense.

---

*The first ten Amendments (the Bill of Rights) were adopted in 1791.

Amendment VII

In suits at common law, where the value in controversy shall exceed twenty dollars, the right of trial by jury shall be preserved, and no fact tried by a jury shall be otherwise reexamined in any court of the United States, than according to the rules of the common law.

Amendment VIII

Excessive bail shall not be required, nor excessive fines imposed, nor cruel and unusual punishments inflicted.

Amendment IX

The enumeration in the Constitution, of certain rights, shall not be construed to deny or disparage others retained by the people.

Amendment X

The powers not delegated to the United States by the Constitution, nor prohibited by it to the States, are reserved to the States respectively, or to the people.

Amendment XI

[Adopted 1798]

The judicial power of the United States shall not be construed to extend to any suit in law or equity, commenced or prosecuted against one of the United States by citizens of another State, or by citizens or subjects of any foreign state.

Amendment XII

[Adopted 1804]

The electors shall meet in their respective States, and vote by ballot for President and Vice-President, one of whom, at least, shall not be an inhabitant of the same State with themselves; they shall name in their ballots the person voted for as President, and in distinct ballots the person voted for as Vice-President, and they shall make distinct lists of all persons voted for as President, and of all persons voted for as Vice-President, and of the number of votes for each, which lists they shall sign and certify, and transmit sealed to the seat of government of the United States, directed to the President of the Senate;—the President of the Senate shall, in the presence of the Senate and House of Representatives, open all the certificates and the votes shall then be counted;—the person having the greatest number of votes for President shall be the President, if such number be a majority of the whole number of electors appointed; and if no person have such majority, then from the persons having the highest numbers not exceeding three on the list of those voted for as President, the House of Representatives shall choose immediately, by ballot, the President. But in choosing the President, the votes shall be taken by States, the representation from each State having one vote; a quorum for this purpose shall consist of a member or members from two-thirds of the States, and a majority of all the States shall be necessary to a choice. And if the House of Representatives shall not choose a President whenever the right of choice shall devolve upon them, before *the fourth day of March* next following, then the Vice-President shall act as President, as in the case of the death or other constitutional disability of the President.

The person having the greatest number of votes as Vice-President shall be the Vice-President, if such number be a majority of the whole number of electors appointed; and if no person have a majority, then from the two highest numbers on the list the Senate shall choose the Vice-President; a quorum for the purpose shall consist of two-thirds of the whole number of Senators, and a majority of the whole number shall be necessary to a choice. But no person constitutionally ineligible to the office of President shall be eligible to that of Vice-President of the United States.

Amendment XIII

[Adopted 1865]

Section 1 Neither slavery nor involuntary servitude, except as a punishment for crime whereof the party shall have been duly convicted, shall exist within the United States, or any place subject to their jurisdiction.

Section 2 Congress shall have power to enforce this article by appropriate legislation.

Amendment XIV

[Adopted 1868]

Section 1 All persons born or naturalized in the United States, and subject to the jurisdiction thereof, are citizens of the United States and of the State wherein they reside. No State shall make or enforce any law which shall abridge the privileges or immunities of citizens of the United States; nor shall any State deprive any person of life, liberty, or property, without due process of law; nor deny to any person within its jurisdiction the equal protection of the laws.

Section 2 Representatives shall be apportioned among the several States according to their respective numbers, counting the whole number of persons in each State, excluding Indians not taxed. But when the right to vote at any election for the choice of Electors for President and Vice-President of the United States, Representatives in Congress, the executive and judicial officers of a State, or the members of the legislature thereof, is denied to any of the male inhabitants of such State, being twenty-one years of age and citizens of the United States, or in any way abridged, except for participation in rebellion, or other crime, the basis of representation therein shall be reduced in the proportion which the number of such male citizens shall bear to the whole number of male citizens twenty-one years of age in such State.

Section 3 No person shall be a Senator or Representative in Congress, or Elector of President and Vice-President, or hold any office, civil or military, under the United States, or under any State, who, having previously taken an oath, as a member of Congress, or as an officer of the United States, or as a member of any State legislature, or as an executive or judicial officer of any State, to support the Constitution of the United States, shall have engaged in insurrection or rebellion against the same, or given aid or comfort to the enemies thereof. Congress may, by a vote of two-thirds of each house, remove such disability.

Section 4 The validity of the public debt of the United States, authorized by law, including debts incurred for payment of pensions and bounties for services in suppressing insurrection or rebellion, shall not be questioned. But neither the United States nor any State shall assume or pay any debt or obligation incurred in aid of insurrection or rebellion against the United States, or any claim for the loss of emancipation of any slave; but all such debts, obligations, and claims shall be held illegal and void.

Section 5 The Congress shall have power to enforce, by appropriate legislation, the provisions of this article.

Amendment XV
[Adopted 1870]

Section 1 The right of citizens of the United States to vote shall not be denied or abridged by the United States or by any State on account of race, color, or previous condition of servitude.

Section 2 The Congress shall have power to enforce this article by appropriate legislation.

Amendment XVI
[Adopted 1913]

The Congress shall have power to lay and collect taxes on incomes, from whatever source derived, without apportionment among the several States, and without regard to any census or enumeration.

Amendment XVII
[Adopted 1913]

Section 1 The Senate of the United States shall be composed of two Senators from each State, elected by the people thereof, for six years; and each Senator shall have one vote. The electors in each State shall have the qualifications requisite for electors of [voters for] the most numerous branch of the State legislatures.

Section 2 When vacancies happen in the representation of any State in the Senate, the executive authority of such State shall issue writs of election to fill such vacancies: Provided, that the Legislature of any State may empower the executive thereof to make temporary appointments until the people fill the vacancies by election as the Legislature may direct.

Section 3 This amendment shall not be so construed as to affect the election or term of any Senator chosen before it becomes valid as part of the Constitution.

Amendment XVIII
[Adopted 1919; Repealed 1933]

Section 1 After one year from the ratification of this article the manufacture, sale, or transportation of intoxicating liquors within, the importation thereof into, or the exportation thereof from the United States and all territory subject to the jurisdiction thereof, for beverage purposes, is hereby prohibited.

Section 2 The Congress and the several States shall have concurrent power to enforce this article by appropriate legislation.

Section 3 This article shall be inoperative unless it shall have been ratified as an amendment to the Constitution by the legislatures of the several States, as provided by the Constitution, within seven years from the date of the submission thereof to the States by the Congress.

Amendment XIX
[Adopted 1920]

Section 1 The right of citizens of the United States to vote shall not be denied or abridged by the United States or by any State on account of sex.

Section 2 The Congress shall have power to enforce this article by appropriate legislation.

Amendment XX
[Adopted 1933]

Section 1 The terms of the President and Vice-President shall end at noon on the 20th day of January, and the terms of Senators and Representatives at noon on the 3rd day of January, of the years in which such terms would have ended if this article had not been ratified; and the terms of their successors shall then begin.

Section 2 The Congress shall assemble at least once in every year, and such meeting shall begin at noon on the 3d day of January, unless they shall by law appoint a different day.

Section 3 If, at the time fixed for the beginning of the term of the President, the President-elect shall have died, the Vice-President-elect shall become President. If a President shall not have been chosen before the time fixed for the beginning of his term, or if the President-elect shall have failed to qualify, then the Vice-President-elect shall act as President until a President shall have qualified; and the Congress may by law provide for the case wherein neither a President-elect nor a Vice-President-elect shall have qualified, declaring who shall then act as President, or the manner in which one who is to act shall be selected, and such persons shall act accordingly until a President or Vice-President shall have qualified.

Section 4 The Congress may by law provide for the case of the death of any of the persons from whom the House of Representatives may choose a President whenever the right of choice shall have devolved upon them, and for the case of the death of any of the persons from whom the Senate may choose a Vice-President whenever the right of choice shall have devolved upon them.

Section 5 Sections 1 and 2 shall take effect on the 15th day of October following the ratification of this article.

Section 6 This article shall be inoperative unless it shall have been ratified as an amendment to the Constitution by the Legislatures of three-fourths of the several States within seven years from the date of its submission.

Amendment XXI

[Adopted 1933]

Section 1 The eighteenth article of amendment to the Constitution of the United States is hereby repealed.

Section 2 The transportation or importation into any State, Territory, or Possession of the United States for delivery or use therein of intoxicating liquors, in violation of the laws thereof, is hereby prohibited.

Section 3 This article shall be inoperative unless it shall have been ratified as an amendment to the Constitution by conventions in the several States, as provided in the Constitution, within seven years from the date of submission thereof to the States by the Congress.

Amendment XXII

[Adopted 1951]

Section 1 No person shall be elected to the office of President more than twice, and no person who has held the office of President, or acted as President, for more than two years of a term to which some other person was elected President shall be elected to the office of President more than once. But this article shall not apply to any person holding the office of President when this article was proposed by the Congress, and shall not prevent any person who may be holding the office of President, or acting as President, during the term within which this article becomes operative from holding the office of President or acting as President during the remainder of such term.

Section 2 This article shall be inoperative unless it shall have been ratified as an amendment to the Constitution by the legislatures of three-fourths of the several States within seven years from the date of its submission to the States by the Congress.

Amendment XXIII

[Adopted 1961]

Section 1 The District constituting the seat of Government of the United States shall appoint in such manner as the Congress may direct:

A number of electors of President and Vice-President equal to the whole number of Senators and Representatives in Congress to which the District would be entitled if it were a State, but in no event more than the least populous State; they shall be in addition to those appointed by the States, but they shall be considered for the purposes of the election of President and Vice-President, to be electors appointed by a State; and they shall meet in the District and perform such duties as provided by the twelfth article of amendment.

Section 2 The Congress shall have the power to enforce this article by appropriate legislation.

Amendment XXIV

[Adopted 1964]

Section 1 The right of citizens of the United States to vote in any primary or other election for President or Vice-President, for electors for President or Vice-President, or for Senator or Representative in Congress, shall not be denied or abridged by the United States or any State by reason of failure to pay any poll tax or other tax.

Section 2 The Congress shall have the power to enforce this article by appropriate legislation.

Amendment XXV

[Adopted 1967]

Section 1 In case of the removal of the President from office or of his death or resignation, the Vice-President shall become President.

Section 2 Whenever there is a vacancy in the office of the Vice-President, the President shall nominate a Vice-President who shall take office upon confirmation by a majority vote of both Houses of Congress.

Section 3 Whenever the President transmits to the President pro tempore of the Senate and the Speaker of the House of Representatives his written declaration that he is unable to discharge the powers and duties of his office, and until he transmits to them a written declaration to the contrary, such powers and duties shall be discharged by the Vice-President as Acting President.

Section 4 Whenever the Vice-President and a majority of either the principal officers of the executive departments or of such other body as Congress may by law provide, transmit to the President pro tempore of the Senate and the Speaker of the House of Representatives their written declaration that the President is unable to discharge the powers and duties of his office, the Vice-President shall immediately assume the powers and duties of the office as Acting President.

Thereafter, when the President transmits to the President pro tempore of the Senate and the Speaker of the House of Representatives his written declaration that no inability exists, he shall resume the powers and duties of his office unless the Vice-President and a majority of either the principal officers of the executive department[s] or of such other body as Congress may by law provide, transmit within four days to the President pro tempore of the Senate and the Speaker of the House of Representatives their written declaration that the President is unable to discharge the powers and duties of his office. Thereupon Congress shall decide the issue, assembling within forty-eight hours for that purpose if not in session. If the Congress, within twenty-one days after receipt of the latter written declaration, or, if Congress is not in session, within twenty-one days after Congress is required to assemble, determines by two-thirds vote of both Houses that the President is unable to discharge the powers and duties of his office, the Vice-President shall continue to discharge the same as Acting President; otherwise, the President shall resume the powers and duties of his office.

Amendment XXVI

[Adopted 1971]

Section 1 The right of citizens of the United States, who are eighteen years of age or older, to vote shall not be denied or abridged by the United States or by any State on account of age.

Section 2 The Congress shall have power to enforce this article by appropriate legislation.

Amendment XXVII

[Adopted 1992]

No law, varying the compensation for the services of the Senators and Representatives, shall take effect, until an election of Representatives shall have intervened.

Presidential Elections

Year	Number of States	Candidates	Parties	Popular Vote	% of Popular Vote	Electoral Vote	% Voter Participation[a]
1789	10	**George Washington**	No party			69	
		John Adams	designations			34	
		Other candidates				35	
1792	15	**George Washington**	No party			132	
		John Adams	designations			77	
		George Clinton				50	
		Other candidates				5	
1796	16	**John Adams**	Federalist			71	
		Thomas Jefferson	Democratic-Republican			68	
		Thomas Pinckney	Federalist			59	
		Aaron Burr	Democratic-Republican			30	
		Other candidates				48	
1800	16	**Thomas Jefferson**	Democratic-Republican			73	
		Aaron Burr	Democratic-Republican			73	
		John Adams	Federalist			65	
		Charles C. Pinckney	Federalist			64	
		John Jay	Federalist			1	
1804	17	**Thomas Jefferson**	Democratic-Republican			162	
		Charles C. Pinckney	Federalist			14	
1808	17	**James Madison**	Democratic-Republican			122	
		Charles C. Pinckney	Federalist			47	
		George Clinton	Democratic-Republican			6	
1812	18	**James Madison**	Democratic-Republican			128	
		DeWitt Clinton	Federalist			89	
1816	19	**James Monroe**	Democratic-Republican			183	
		Rufus King	Federalist			34	
1820	24	**James Monroe**	Democratic-Republican			231	
		John Quincy Adams	Independent Republican			1	
1824	24	**John Quincy Adams**	Democratic-Republican	108,740	30.5	84	26.9
		Andrew Jackson	Democratic-Republican	153,544	43.1	99	
		Henry Clay	Democratic-Republican	47,136	13.2	37	
		William H. Crawford	Democratic-Republican	46,618	13.1	41	
1828	24	**Andrew Jackson**	Democratic	647,286	56.0	178	57.6
		John Quincy Adams	National Republican	508,064	44.0	83	
1832	24	**Andrew Jackson**	Democratic	701,780	54.2	219	55.4
		Henry Clay	National Republican	484,205	37.4	49	
		Other candidates		107,988	8.0	18	

Presidential Elections (continued)

Year	Number of States	Candidates	Parties	Popular Vote	% of Popular Vote	Electoral Vote	% Voter Participation[a]
1836	26	**Martin Van Buren**	Democratic	764,176	50.8	170	57.8
		William H. Harrison	Whig	550,816	36.6	73	
		Hugh L. White	Whig	146,107	9.7	26	
1840	26	**William H. Harrison**	Whig	1,274,624	53.1	234	80.2
		Martin Van Buren	Democratic	1,127,781	46.9	60	
1844	26	**James K. Polk**	Democratic	1,338,464	49.6	170	78.9
		Henry Clay	Whig	1,300,097	48.1	105	
		James G. Birney	Liberty	62,300	2.3		
1848	30	**Zachary Taylor**	Whig	1,360,967	47.4	163	72.7
		Lewis Cass	Democratic	1,222,342	42.5	127	
		Martin Van Buren	Free Soil	291,263	10.1		
1852	31	**Franklin Pierce**	Democratic	1,601,117	50.9	254	69.6
		Winfield Scott	Whig	1,385,453	44.1	42	
		John P. Hale	Free Soil	155,825	5.0		
1856	31	**James Buchanan**	Democratic	1,832,955	45.3	174	78.9
		John C. Frémont	Republican	1,339,932	33.1	114	
		Millard Fillmore	American	871,731	21.6		
1860	33	**Abraham Lincoln**	Republican	1,865,593	39.8	180	81.2
		Stephen A. Douglas	Democratic	1,382,713	29.5	12	
		John C. Breckinridge	Democratic	848,356	18.1	72	
		John Bell	Constitutional Union	592,906	12.6	39	
1864	36	**Abraham Lincoln**	Republican	2,206,938	55.0	212	73.8
		George B. McClellan	Democratic	1,803,787	45.0	21	
1868	37	**Ulysses S. Grant**	Republican	3,013,421	52.7	214	78.1
		Horatio Seymour	Democratic	2,706,829	47.3	80	
1872	37	**Ulysses S. Grant**	Republican	3,596,745	55.6	286	71.3
		Horace Greeley	Democratic	2,843,446	43.9	b	
1876	38	**Rutherford B. Hayes**	Republican	4,036,572	48.0	185	81.8
		Samuel J. Tilden	Democratic	4,284,020	51.0	184	
1880	38	**James A. Garfield**	Republican	4,453,295	48.5	214	79.4
		Winfield S. Hancock	Democratic	4,414,082	48.1	155	
		James B. Weaver	Greenback-Labor	308,578	3.4		
1884	38	**Grover Cleveland**	Democratic	4,879,507	48.5	219	77.5
		James G. Blaine	Republican	4,850,293	48.2	182	
		Benjamin F. Butler	Greenback-Labor	175,370	1.8		
		John P. St. John	Prohibition	150,369	1.5		
1888	38	**Benjamin Harrison**	Republican	5,447,129	47.9	233	79.3
		Grover Cleveland	Democratic	5,537,857	48.6	168	
		Clinton B. Fisk	Prohibition	249,506	2.2		

Presidents and Vice Presidents (continued)

Year	Number of States	Candidates	Parties	Popular Vote	% of Popular Vote	Electoral Vote	% Voter Participation[a]
		Anson J. Streeter	Union Labor	146,935	1.3		
1892	44	**Grover Cleveland**	Democratic	5,555,426	46.1	277	74.7
		Benjamin Harrison	Republican	5,182,690	43.0	145	
		James B. Weaver	People's	1,029,846	8.5	22	
		John Bidwell	Prohibition	264,133	2.2		
1896	45	**William McKinley**	Republican	7,102,246	51.1	271	79.3
		William J. Bryan	Democratic	6,492,559	47.7	176	
1900	45	**William McKinley**	Republican	7,218,491	51.7	292	73.2
		William J. Bryan	Democratic; Populist	6,356,734	45.5	155	
		John C. Wooley	Prohibition	208,914	1.5		
1904	45	**Theodore Roosevelt**	Republican	7,628,461	57.4	336	65.2
		Alton B. Parker	Democratic	5,084,223	37.6	140	
		Eugene V. Debs	Socialist	402,283	3.0		
		Silas C. Swallow	Prohibition	258,536	1.9		
1908	46	**William H. Taft**	Republican	7,675,320	51.6	321	65.4
		William J. Bryan	Democratic	6,412,294	43.1	162	
		Eugene V. Debs	Socialist	420,793	2.8		
		Eugene W. Chafin	Prohibition	253,840	1.7		
1912	48	**Woodrow Wilson**	Democratic	6,296,547	41.9	435	58.8
		Theodore Roosevelt	Progressive	4,118,571	27.4	88	
		William H. Taft	Republican	3,486,720	23.2	8	
		Eugene V. Debs	Socialist	900,672	6.0		
		Eugene W. Chafin	Prohibition	206,275	1.4		
1916	48	**Woodrow Wilson**	Democratic	9,127,695	49.4	277	61.6
		Charles E. Hughes	Republican	8,533,507	46.2	254	
		A. L. Benson	Socialist	585,113	3.2		
		J. Frank Hanly	Prohibition	220,506	1.2		
1920	48	**Warren G. Harding**	Republican	16,143,407	60.4	404	49.2
		James M. Cox	Democratic	9,130,328	34.2	127	
		Eugene V. Debs	Socialist	919,799	3.4		
		P. P. Christensen	Farmer-Labor	265,411	1.0		
1924	48	**Calvin Coolidge**	Republican	15,718,211	54.0	382	48.9
		John W. Davis	Democratic	8,385,283	28.8	136	
		Robert M. La Follette	Progressive	4,831,289	16.6	13	
1928	48	**Herbert C. Hoover**	Republican	21,391,993	58.2	444	56.9
		Alfred E. Smith	Democratic	15,016,169	40.9	87	
1932	48	**Franklin D. Roosevelt**	Democratic	22,809,638	57.4	472	56.9
		Herbert C. Hoover	Republican	15,758,901	39.7	59	
		Norman Thomas	Socialist	881,951	2.2		

Presidential Elections (continued)

Year	Number of States	Candidates	Parties	Popular Vote	% of Popular Vote	Electoral Vote	% Voter Participation[a]
1936	48	Franklin D. Roosevelt	Democratic	27,752,869	60.8	523	61.0
		Alfred M. Landon	Republican	16,674,665	36.5	8	
		William Lemke	Union	882,479	1.9		
1940	48	Franklin D. Roosevelt	Democratic	27,307,819	54.8	449	62.5
		Wendell L. Willkie	Republican	22,321,018	44.8	82	
1944	48	Franklin D. Roosevelt	Democratic	25,606,585	53.5	432	55.9
		Thomas E. Dewey	Republican	22,014,745	46.0	99	
1948	48	Harry S Truman	Democratic	24,179,345	49.6	303	53.0
		Thomas E. Dewey	Republican	21,991,291	45.1	189	
		J. Strom Thurmond	States' Rights	1,176,125	2.4	39	
		Henry A. Wallace	Progressive	1,157,326	2.4		
1952	48	Dwight D. Eisenhower	Republican	33,936,234	55.1	442	63.3
		Adlai E. Stevenson	Democratic	27,314,992	44.4	89	
1956	48	Dwight D. Eisenhower	Republican	35,590,472	57.6	457	60.6
		Adlai E. Stevenson	Democratic	26,022,752	42.1	73	
1960	50	John F. Kennedy	Democratic	34,226,731	49.7	303	62.8
		Richard M. Nixon	Republican	34,108,157	49.5	219	
1964	50	Lyndon B. Johnson	Democratic	43,129,566	61.1	486	61.7
		Barry M. Goldwater	Republican	27,178,188	38.5	52	
1968	50	Richard M. Nixon	Republican	31,785,480	43.4	301	60.6
		Hubert H. Humphrey	Democratic	31,275,166	42.7	191	
		George C. Wallace	American Independent	9,906,473	13.5	46	
1972	50	Richard M. Nixon	Republican	47,169,911	60.7	520	55.2
		George S. McGovern	Democratic	29,170,383	37.5	17	
		John G. Schmitz	American	1,099,482	1.4		
1976	50	James E. Carter	Democratic	40,830,763	50.1	297	53.5
		Gerald R. Ford	Republican	39,147,793	48.0	240	
1980	50	Ronald W. Reagan	Republican	43,904,153	50.7	489	52.6
		James E. Carter	Democratic	35,483,883	41.0	49	
		John B. Anderson	Independent	5,720,060	6.6		
		Ed Clark	Libertarian	921,299	1.1		
1984	50	Ronald W. Reagan	Republican	54,455,075	58.8	525	53.3
		Walter F. Mondale	Democratic	37,577,185	40.6	13	
1988	50	George H. W. Bush	Republican	48,886,097	53.4	426	50.1
		Michael S. Dukakis	Democratic	41,809,074	45.6	111c	
1992	50	William J. Clinton	Democratic	44,909,326	43.0	370	55.2
		George H. W. Bush	Republican	39,103,882	37.4	168	
		H. Ross Perot	Independent	19,741,048	18.9		

Justices of the Supreme Court (continued)

Year	Number of States	Candidates	Parties	Popular Vote	% of Popular Vote	Electoral Vote	% Voter Participation[a]
1996	50	William J. Clinton	Democratic	47,402,357	49.2	379	49.1
		Robert J. Dole	Republican	39,196,755	40.7	159	
		H. Ross Perot	Reform	8,085,402	8.4		
		Ralph Nader	Green	684,902	0.7		
2000	50	George W. Bush	Republican	50,455,156	47.9	271	51.2
		Albert Gore	Democratic	50,992,335	48.4	266	
		Ralph Nader	Green	2,882,955	2.7		
2004	50	George W. Bush	Republican	62,039,073	50.7	286	55.3
		John F. Kerry	Democratic	59,027,478	48.2	251	
		Ralph Nader	Independent	240,896	0.2		
2008	50	Barack Obama	Democratic	69,498,459	53.0	365	61.7
		John McCain	Republican	59,948,283	46.0	173	
		Ralph Nader	Independent	739,165	0.55		

Candidates receiving less than 1 percent of the popular vote have been omitted. Thus the percentage of popular vote given for any election year may not total 100 percent.

Before the passage of the Twelfth Amendment in 1804, the electoral college voted for two presidential candidates; the runner-up became vice president.

Before 1824, most presidential electors were chosen by state legislatures, not by popular vote.

[a]Percent of voting-age population casting ballots.
[b]Greeley died shortly after the election; the electors supporting him then divided their votes among minor candidates.
[c]One elector from West Virginia cast her electoral college presidential ballot for Lloyd Bentsen, the Democratic Party's vice-presidential candidate.

Presidents and Vice Presidents

1. President	**George Washington**	1789–1797
Vice President	John Adams	1789–1797
2. President	**John Adams**	1797–1801
Vice President	Thomas Jefferson	1797–1801
3. President	**Thomas Jefferson**	1801–1809
Vice President	Aaron Burr	1801–1805
Vice President	George Clinton	1805–1809
4. President	**James Madison**	1809–1817
Vice President	George Clinton	1809–1813
Vice President	Elbridge Gerry	1813–1817
5. President	**James Monroe**	1817–1825
Vice President	Daniel Tompkins	1817–1825
6. President	**John Quincy Adams**	1825–1829
Vice President	John C. Calhoun	1825–1829
7. President	**Andrew Jackson**	1829–1837
Vice President	John C. Calhoun	1829–1833
Vice President	Martin Van Buren	1833–1837
8. President	**Martin Van Buren**	1837–1841
Vice President	Richard M. Johnson	1837–1841
9. President	**William H. Harrison**	1841
Vice President	John Tyler	1841
10. President	**John Tyler**	1841–1845
Vice President	None	
11. President	**James K. Polk**	1845–1849
Vice President	George M. Dallas	1845–1849
12. President	**Zachary Taylor**	1849–1850
Vice President	Millard Fillmore	1849–1850
13. President	**Millard Fillmore**	1850–1853
Vice President	None	
14. President	**Franklin Pierce**	1853–1857
Vice President	William R. King	1853–1857
15. President	**James Buchanan**	1857–1861
Vice President	John C. Breckinridge	1857–1861
16. President	**Abraham Lincoln**	1861–1865
Vice President	Hannibal Hamlin	1861–1865
Vice President	Andrew Johnson	1865
17. President	**Andrew Johnson**	1865–1869
Vice President	None	
18. President	**Ulysses S. Grant**	1869–1877
Vice President	Schuyler Colfax	1869–1873
Vice President	Henry Wilson	1873–1877
19. President	**Rutherford B. Hayes**	1877–1881
Vice President	William A. Wheeler	1877–1881
20. President	**James A. Garfield**	1881
Vice President	Chester A. Arthur	1881
21. President	**Chester A. Arthur**	1881–1885
Vice President	None	
22. President	**Grover Cleveland**	1885–1889
Vice President	Thomas A. Hendricks	1885–1889
23. President	**Benjamin Harrison**	1889–1893
Vice President	Levi P. Morton	1889–1893
24. President	**Grover Cleveland**	1893–1897
Vice President	Adlai E. Stevenson	1893–1897
25. President	**William McKinley**	1897–1901
Vice President	Garret A. Hobart	1897–1901
Vice President	Theodore Roosevelt	1901
26. President	**Theodore Roosevelt**	1901–1909
Vice President	Charles Fairbanks	1905–1909
27. President	**William H. Taft**	1909–1913
Vice President	James S. Sherman	1909–1913
28. President	**Woodrow Wilson**	1913–1921
Vice President	Thomas R. Marshall	1913–1921
29. President	**Warren G. Harding**	1921–1923
Vice President	Calvin Coolidge	1921–1923
30. President	**Calvin Coolidge**	1923–1929
Vice President	Charles G. Dawes	1925–1929
31. President	**Herbert C. Hoover**	1929–1933
Vice President	Charles Curtis	1929–1933
32. President	**Franklin D. Roosevelt**	1933–1945
Vice President	John N. Garner	1933–1941
Vice President	Henry A. Wallace	1941–1945
Vice President	Harry S Truman	1945
33. President	**Harry S Truman**	1945–1953
Vice President	Alben W. Barkley	1949–1953
34. President	**Dwight D. Eisenhower**	1953–1961
Vice President	Richard M. Nixon	1953–1961

Presidents and Vice Presidents (continued)

35. President	**John F. Kennedy**	1961–1963
Vice President	Lyndon B. Johnson	1961–1963
36. President	**Lyndon B. Johnson**	1963–1969
Vice President	Hubert H. Humphrey	1965–1969
37. President	**Richard M. Nixon**	1969–1974
Vice President	Spiro T. Agnew	1969–1973
Vice President	Gerald R. Ford	1973–1974
38. President	**Gerald R. Ford**	1974–1977
Vice President	Nelson A. Rockefeller	1974–1977
39. President	**James E. Carter**	1977–1981
Vice President	Walter F. Mondale	1977–1981

40. President	**Ronald W. Reagan**	1981–1989
Vice President	George H. W. Bush	1981–1989
41. President	**George H. W. Bush**	1989–1993
Vice President	J. Danforth Quayle	1989–1993
42. President	**William J. Clinton**	1993–2001
Vice President	Albert Gore	1993–2001
43. President	**George W. Bush**	2001–2009
Vice President	Richard Cheney	2001–2009
44. President	**Barack Obama**	2009–
Vice President	Joseph Biden	2009–

Justices of the Supreme Court

	Term of Service	Years of Service	Life Span
John Jay	1789–1795	5	1745–1829
John Rutledge	1789–1791	1	1739–1800
William Cushing	1789–1810	20	1732–1810
James Wilson	1789–1798	8	1742–1798
John Blair	1789–1796	6	1732–1800
Robert H. Harrison	1789–1790	—	1745–1790
James Iredell	1790–1799	9	1751–1799
Thomas Johnson	1791–1793	1	1732–1819
William Paterson	1793–1806	13	1745–1806
*John Rutledge**	1795	—	1739–1800
Samuel Chase	1796–1811	15	1741–1811
Oliver Ellsworth	1796–1800	4	1745–1807
Bushrod Washington	1798–1829	31	1762–1829
Alfred Moore	1799–1804	4	1755–1810
John Marshall	1801–1835	34	1755–1835
William Johnson	1804–1834	30	1771–1834
H. Brockholst Livingston	1806–1823	16	1757–1823
Thomas Todd	1807–1826	18	1765–1826
Joseph Story	1811–1845	33	1779–1845
Gabriel Duval	1811–1835	24	1752–1844
Smith Thompson	1823–1843	20	1768–1843
Robert Trimble	1826–1828	2	1777–1828
John McLean	1829–1861	32	1785–1861
Henry Baldwin	1830–1844	14	1780–1844
James M. Wayne	1835–1867	32	1790–1867
Roger B. Taney	1836–1864	28	1777–1864
Philip P. Barbour	1836–1841	4	1783–1841
John Catron	1837–1865	28	1786–1865
John McKinley	1837–1852	15	1780–1852
Peter V. Daniel	1841–1860	19	1784–1860
Samuel Nelson	1845–1872	27	1792–1873
Levi Woodbury	1845–1851	5	1789–1851
Robert C. Grier	1846–1870	23	1794–1870
Benjamin R. Curtis	1851–1857	6	1809–1874
John A. Campbell	1853–1861	8	1811–1889
Nathan Clifford	1858–1881	23	1803–1881
Noah H. Swayne	1862–1881	18	1804–1884
Samuel F. Miller	1862–1890	28	1816–1890
David Davis	1862–1877	14	1815–1886
Stephen J. Field	1863–1897	34	1816–1899
Salmon P. Chase	1864–1873	8	1808–1873
William Strong	1870–1880	10	1808–1895
Joseph P. Bradley	1870–1892	22	1813–1892
Ward Hunt	1873–1882	9	1810–1886
Morrison R. Waite	1874–1888	14	1816–1888
John M. Harlan	1877–1911	34	1833–1911
William B. Woods	1880–1887	7	1824–1887
Stanley Mathews	1881–1889	7	1824–1889
Horace Gray	1882–1902	20	1828–1902
Samuel Blatchford	1882–1893	11	1820–1893
Lucius Q. C. Lamar	1888–1893	5	1825–1893
Melville W. Fuller	1888–1910	21	1833–1910
David J. Brewer	1890–1910	20	1837–1910
Henry B. Brown	1890–1906	16	1836–1913
George Shiras Jr.	1892–1903	10	1832–1924
Howell E. Jackson	1893–1895	2	1832–1895
Edward D. White	1894–1910	16	1845–1921
Rufus W. Peckham	1895–1909	14	1838–1909
Joseph McKenna	1898–1925	26	1843–1926
Oliver W. Holmes	1902–1932	30	1841–1935
William D. Day	1903–1922	19	1849–1923
William H. Moody	1906–1910	3	1853–1917
Horace H. Lurton	1910–1914	4	1844–1914
Charles E. Hughes	1910–1916	5	1862–1948
Willis Van Devanter	1911–1937	26	1859–1941
Joseph R. Lamar	1911–1916	5	1857–1916
Edward D. White	1910–1921	11	1845–1921
Mahlon Pitney	1912–1922	10	1858–1924
James C. McReynolds	1914–1941	26	1862–1946
Louis D. Brandeis	1916–1939	22	1856–1941
John H. Clarke	1916–1922	6	1857–1945
William H. Taft	1921–1930	8	1857–1930
George Sutherland	1922–1938	15	1862–1942
Pierce Butler	1922–1939	16	1866–1939
Edward T. Sanford	1923–1930	7	1865–1930
Harlan F. Stone	1925–1941	16	1872–1946
Charles E. Hughes	1930–1941	11	1862–1948
Owen J. Roberts	1930–1945	15	1875–1955
Benjamin N. Cardozo	1932–1938	6	1870–1938

Justices of the Supreme Court (continued)

	Term of Service	Years of Service	Life Span		Term of Service	Years of Service	Life Span
Hugo L. Black	1937–1971	34	1886–1971	Arthur J. Goldberg	1962–1965	3	1908–1990
Stanley F. Reed	1938–1957	19	1884–1980	Abe Fortas	1965–1969	4	1910–1982
Felix Frankfurter	1939–1962	23	1882–1965	Thurgood Marshall	1967–1991	24	1908–1993
William O. Douglas	1939–1975	36	1898–1980	*Warren C. Burger*	1969–1986	17	1907–1995
Frank Murphy	1940–1949	9	1890–1949	Harry A. Blackmun	1970–1994	24	1908–1998
Harlan F. Stone	1941–1946	5	1872–1946	Lewis F. Powell Jr.	1972–1987	15	1907–1998
James F. Byrnes	1941–1942	1	1879–1972	*William H. Rehnquist*	1972–2005	33	1924–2005
Robert H. Jackson	1941–1954	13	1892–1954	John P. Stevens III	1975–	—	1920–
Wiley B. Rutledge	1943–1949	6	1894–1949	Sandra Day O'Connor	1981–	—	1930–
Harold H. Burton	1945–1958	13	1888–1964	Antonin Scalia	1986–	—	1936–
Fred M. Vinson	1946–1953	7	1890–1953	Anthony M. Kennedy	1988–	—	1936–
Tom C. Clark	1949–1967	18	1899–1977	David H. Souter	1990–	—	1939–
Sherman Minton	1949–1956	7	1890–1965	Clarence Thomas	1991–	—	1948–
Earl Warren	1953–1969	16	1891–1974	Ruth Bader Ginsburg	1993–	—	1933–
John Marshall Harlan	1955–1971	16	1899–1971	Stephen Breyer	1994–	—	1938–
William J. Brennan Jr.	1956–1990	34	1906–1997	John G. Roberts	2005–	—	1955–
Charles E. Whittaker	1957–1962	5	1901–1973	Samuel A. Alito, Jr.	2006–	—	1950–
Potter Stewart	1958–1981	23	1915–1985	Sonia Sotomayor	2009–	—	1954–
Byron R. White	1962–1993	31	1917–	Elena Kagan	2010–	—	1960–

Note: Chief justices are in italics.

*Appointed and served one term, but not confirmed by the Senate.

Index